Paul Kirk's

Championship

Barbecue

Paul Kirk's Championship Barbecue

Paul Kirk and Bob Lyon

BBQ YOUR WAY TO

GREATNESS WITH

575 LIP-SMACKIN'

RECIPES FROM

THE BARON OF

BARBECUE

THE HARVARD COMMON PRESS Boston, Massachusetts

The Harvard Common Press
535 Albany Street
Boston, Massachusetts 02118
www.harvardcommonpress.com

Printed in the United States

LIBRARY OF CONGRESS CATALOGING-IN-PUBLICATION DATA

Kirk, Paul

   Paul Kirk's championship barbecue : barbecue your way to greatness with 575 lip-smackin' recipes from the baron of barbecue / Paul Kirk and Bob Lyon.

       p. cm.

Includes index.

   ISBN 1-55832-241-8 (hc : alk. paper) — ISBN 1-55832-242-6 (pb : alk. paper)

   1. Barbecue cookery. I. Title: Championship barbecue. II. Lyon, Bob. III. Title.

   TX840.B3K454237 2004

   641.5'784—dc22   2003024311

Special bulk-order discounts are available on this and other Harvard Common Press books. Companies and organizations may purchase books for premiums or resale, or may arrange a custom edition, by contacting the Marketing Director at the address above.

10 9 8 7 6 5 4 3 2 1

Interior design by Richard Oriolo
Cover design by Night & Day Design

Interior photographs courtesy of *National Barbecue News* first appear on pages v, 37 (bottom), 53, 54 (bottom), 55 (all), 67, 134, 136 (top right), 137 (top middle and bottom), 161 (top), 162 (bottom), 163 (bottom), 224, 229, 231 (top right), and 272 (top right). Please visit www.barbecuenews.com.

Photographs on pages 102 (top left), 163 (top left), 272 (bottom), 301 (bottom left), and 372 (top left) courtesy of Judith M. Fertig.

All other interior photographs courtesy of Bob Lyon.

Cover photographs: flames and blue ribbon © Getty Images; chicken © Foodcollection/Stockfood America; corn © Tom DeSanto/Stockfood America; flank steak © Beatriz DaCosta/Stockfood America; ribs © Envision.

Contents

Acknowledgments

First of all, I want to thank all the barbecue greats who have gone before me and have contributed their knowledge to the art of barbecue. Then, I'd like to thank Bob Lyon, my barbecue buddy from the Pacific Northwest, who contributed a lot to this book. Third, I'd like to thank all those competition barbecuers who let me borrow their recipes, whether they knew it or not! Of course, I thank my family for helping me at barbecue contests, giving me thumbs-up or thumbs-down on my recipes, and putting up with me in general. My thanks to everyone at The Harvard Common Press for taking this concept from recipes in my head to a real book on the shelves, and to Judith Fertig for helping me with that process. And thanks also go to all those barbecuers out there who continue to practice their craft and get better and better and better. That's what good barbecue is all about.

Introduction: Meet the
BARBECUE Baron

Many years ago, and I won't tell you how many, I was born Paul Kirk. Through the years, I've tacked on my fair share of titles before and initials after my name. "Chef" Paul Kirk came first, when I started working in restaurants and discovered I had a knack for identifying and combining flavors. To this day I can make up a recipe in my head, never test it at all, and win a contest with it.

In the early 1980s, I got bitten by the barbecue bug bigtime. By barbecue, I mean the real, slow-smoked kind that requires lots of labor, attention, and skill. Soon after I won the American Royal Contest, and I was given the title Baron of Barbecue (see page 2 for the full story). Over the years, people have added more titles to me name: Barbecue Guru, Master of the Grill, Order of the Magic Mop, Ambassador of Barbecue, Certified Master Judge, and Headmaster of the School of Pitmasters (that's my own school). I've also earned my Ph.B., or doctorate in barbecue philosophy.

If you think this is boasting, you're wrong. It's confidence. Winning a contest requires the mindset of a competitive perfectionist. This attitude has helped me win big. I've won the highest, or Grand Champion, award in the American Royal, the BarbeQLossal, the Great Lenexa Barbeque Battle, and the National Lamb-B-Que Contest. My Team Kansas

City or I have won seven world barbecue championships. I've made the best barbecued brisket in Texas as judged by experts at the Terlingua contest. My Team Kansas City cohort Karen Putman and I also won the Jack Daniel's World Championship Invitational Barbecue Contest.

Now, barbecue is what I do for a living. I create barbecue rubs and sauces for different restaurants and companies, as well as sell my own at grocery stores and barbecue and grill shops. I have my own spice room at home for concocting my new blends. I teach my Pitmaster classes around the world. I write cookbooks. And I keep experimenting with barbecue, my ongoing adventure in life.

I know I'm good. And I think I can help you get really good at making great barbecue. I've taken everything I teach in my School of Pitmasters classes and enlarged upon it in this book. Many of my Pitmaster students have gone on to win barbecue championships or start their own successful restaurants. So can you, if you want.

Paul Kirk's Championship Barbecue shows you the way I create blue-ribbon championship barbecue—whether it's for a contest or for friends and family in my own back yard. I'll start by explaining the techniques of building and maintaining a fire in whatever kind of equipment you have, then I'll explain the difference between grilling hot and fast or smoking low and slow. I'll go on to how to choose a hardwood for flavoring and how to prepare meats for the grill or smoker. I'll show you how to make your own seasonings and barbecue sauces, as well as reveal the secrets of a great dry rub. There are more than 500 recipes to choose from here, so you could grill or smoke something every day for a year and never have the same thing twice! What I really want you to do, however, is practice. When I'm competing in a contest, I don't let the temperature in my rig vary more than five degrees after the first hour. The only way you can do that is to know your rig and practice, practice, practice. After a while, you'll know just how long the fire in your rig can go before you have to add more hot coals or wood or both. You'll know the hotter and cooler spots on your pit. You'll know simply by the touch of a grill fork how done your steak is. You'll know by looking at your slab of ribs how much longer they need to smoke.

So read through my book. Then put it down, use what you've learned, and create your own great barbecue. And let me know how you're doing. You can e-mail me at baronofbbq@kcbs.us if you have a quick question or a comment. I like to hear from all my students. Just get out there and barbecue!

The Secrets of a BARBECUE Champion

O f all the barbecue contests to start with, I chose the American Royal in 1981. The first American Royal was held in 1980, so this was still a new contest. I was new at competition barbecue, too. I was working as a chef at a local Kansas City restaurant, so I had to do this contest during my time off from work. But it was far from a walk in the park.

First of all, after I packed up my truck in the early hours of the morning, I noticed it had a flat tire and I didn't have a spare. I called a friend who had a van, but it wouldn't start. I got everything packed in a small Toyota—Hasty-Bake cooker and a Weber kettle grill included—but had to stop and get charcoal, which I had forgotten.

When I finally got to the Royal at 8:30 A.M., I was already way behind. When I picked up my number, it was #13. Just how my luck was going, I thought.

When the judging started at around 11:00 A.M., I had everything ready and hoped for the best. I thought my ribs got done a little too much, but then I had to rush them because I started late.

When the judging was through, I took first place in Chicken and second place in Ribs.

Any time I have a problem going to a contest now, I figure it's a good luck omen!

HOW THE BARON OF BARBECUE GOT HIS NAME

In 1983 I was very successful in barbecue competitions, having won 6 Grand Championships out of the first 10 or so contests that I competed in. One of my running buddies was Dick Mais, who was bestowed the title of King of Kansas City Barbecue by a local disc jockey named Mike Murphy (the number 1 DJ in Kansas City at the time). Dick said, "Paul, you need a title." Because "King" was already taken, he dubbed me "The Baron of Barbecue," and I've had that title ever since.

How to Get Started in Competition Barbecue

First of all, learn how to prepare and control your fire (see page 18, Setting Up Your Pit). Learn about selecting, trimming, and preparing different meats for the grill and smoker. Learn about making and using rubs, seasonings, slathers, bastes, and sauces. Take a barbecue class (from your local barbecue association or see Sources, page 451) and get some hands-on experience.

Then start cooking. Practice on your friends and family. Go to local or regional barbecue contests and see what goes on. Taste the food. Talk to the winners (after the contest—they'll be too busy beforehand).

Choosing a Contest

When you're ready to take the plunge into competition barbecue, here's what you do.

First of all, you have to know where to look for contest information. You can find contest listings in several barbecue publications, including the Kansas City Barbecue Society BullSheet (800-963-5227 or www.kcbs.us) and National Barbecue News (800-385-0002 or www.barbecuenews.com). If you become a member of a local or regional barbecue society, you'll also be put on their mailing list for upcoming cook-offs.

When you're first starting out, choose a small contest (15 to 30 competing teams) near your home. Of course, I only partly followed my own advice the first time I competed. I chose a contest near my home, but it was the American Royal, and I took home first in Poultry and second in Ribs! Maybe it was beginner's luck, but that's what got me hooked. I recommend that anyone getting serious about championship barbecue participate in three or four contests the first year.

If you're not used to hauling a lot of barbecue equipment, utensils, and food to a contest, choosing one closer to home will make this experience a little easier. Also, if you forget the charcoal, like I did, you won't have far to go back home and get it. Don't rely on the contest neighborhood to supply your needs for the cook-off. Bring everything you need from home.

Although you don't have to choose a sanctioned contest—one that is set up by a certain barbecue society's rules—a sanctioned contest will give you the best real-world experience in a barbecue cook-off. Look over the KCBS schedule in the BullSheet or another barbecue publication and try to find a smaller contest. If you choose a contest with fewer than 20 teams, such as the KCBS-sanctioned National Lamb-B-Q BBQ Cook-off held in Bonner Springs, Kansas, you'll have a greater chance of winning a ribbon the first time up. In 2000, I was the National Lamb Champion, taking first in Steaks, first in Chops, second in Leg of Lamb, and third in Miscellaneous. In 2002, only six teams (including the Baron of Barbecue, who came in third that time) competed in this all-lamb contest (Steaks, Chops, Roast, and Miscellaneous). In a small contest like this one, you'll gain more confidence and get to know your competitors better than at a bigger contest. (And here's a lamb secret: You can't go wrong with a little lemon pepper and garlic!)

You could also enter a contest just for the name. Imagine telling your friends you've entered the Best Butt in Georgia Contest, held in Moultrie, Georgia, in late February/early March and sanctioned by MIM-SCN (Memphis in May Sanctioned Contest Network).

No matter how you select your first contest, don't go expecting to win a ribbon. Go to learn and you won't be disappointed. Taste other people's barbecue. I know a guy who was 0 for 13 in contests before he won one ribbon!

The entry fee for contests can vary, but it's usually about $150 to $200 and up. Some contests provide the meat, others require you to bring it. Read the rules or call the organizer to find out.

You might also consider entering only one or two categories your first time out, especially if you are using simpler equipment, such as a kettle grill. If you don't enter all the categories, you won't be eligible for Grand or Reserve Champion, but who cares the first time? When I entered two categories at my first American Royal in 1981, there weren't nearly the number of teams that compete today in most contests. By easing your way into contest mode and just entering a few categories, you'll get valuable experience and have more fun. I recommend that you also enter a fun category such as Miscellaneous or Anything But, which is anything that is not slow smoked (grilled vegetables, for example). These categories often give a new team its best chance of a ribbon.

The word "Qualifier" placed at the end of a contest listing means that the overall Grand Champion of that contest will qualify for the American Royal Invitational and will have his or her team's name placed in the Jack Daniel's World Championship Invitational Barbecue Contest pool (both KCBS-sanctioned contests) or the Memphis in May World Championship Barbecue Cooking Contest (MIM-sanctioned contests), which is definitely a plus. Qualifying for, and thus getting invited to, these contests is a real honor.

Groups That Sanction Barbecue Contests

Three major barbecue groups, or societies, throughout the country provide the rules and regulations for most of the barbecue contests. When you read about an upcoming contest, check the fine print to see which group sanctions the contest. Then go to that group's Web site to get the rules and regulations, because they're

COMPETITION Secrets

In my barbecue classes, I am always asked the same question: "How can you teach us all your secrets and still hope to win yourself?" It's simple. I was raised with a love of good food, and I love good barbecue. I love to see my students do well in competition. I could give away every barbecue secret I have, but competition barbecue it still about the feel of it—about timing and preparation and producing the best barbecue you can at just the right moment. But here are a few of the secrets in three competition categories that have really made a difference for me.

CHICKEN: I marinate it first to give it a good flavor. I change the marinade I use in competition every year, sometimes a couple of times a year. Right before the chicken goes to the judges, I pull it off the smoker and crisp the skin for 10 to 30 seconds on each side over the hot fire of a grill. Then I glaze the chicken on the grill and serve it up for the judges. This technique has been successful every time. I won first place in Chicken at my very first competition. At the 2001 American Royal, I got the first perfect score in Chicken competing against 364 other teams.

BEEF: I prefer to use Certified Angus Beef. There is no such thing as a bad Certified Angus Beef, because this type of beef is the top 5 percent of Choice. I age it in the refrigerator for 3 weeks before competition, right in the Cryovac packaging it comes in. I may inject or marinate brisket and then use a mustard slather and maybe use a rub on the exterior of the meat. I like to use a new rub every year. I keep log sheets so I know what I've tried and how it has performed in competition.

RIBS: Barbecuers always debate about using small baby back or the larger loin back ribs. I find that the larger ribs from the loin are more forgiving, especially for first-timers.

PORK: I lightly brine pork butt for about 4 hours, then season it with a rub and slather it with mustard before cooking. I took second in the 2002 World Championship in Pork using this technique.

different for each sanctioning group. The purpose of a sanctioning group is to make sure that each barbecue contest is fair and that everyone who enters plays by the same rules. If you're a first-timer, make sure you read the rules and regulations carefully so you don't get disqualified. Ignorance is not bliss.

These sanctioning groups usually put on one really big barbecue contest a year. As part of the Memphis in May Sanctioned Contest Network (MIM-SCN), hundreds of teams compete in the Memphis in May World Championship Barbecue Cooking Contest held as part of the month-long Memphis in May festivities, which also include concerts, theater, you name it. As part of the Kansas City Barbeque Society, hundreds of teams compete in the American Royal Barbeque Contest held in Kansas City, Missouri, the first weekend in October. As part of the International Barbeque Cookers Association, nearly 100 teams compete in the Trader's Village Contest held in Grand Prairie, Texas, the second weekend in October.

The big contests have "open" and "invitational" competitions. The open is just what it says—open to any team who pays the entrance fee on time. An open contest will have lots of teams participating. The invitational is also just what it says—you have to be invited to participate. An invitational will have fewer teams participating.

If you win the Grand Champion Award at a smaller sanctioned, qualifying contest, you are invited to participate in the invitational portion of the big contest. For example, if you win the Grand Champion Award at the KCBS-sanctioned Great Lenexa Barbeque Battle, you're automatically invited to participate in the invitational contest that's part of the KCBS-sanctioned American Royal Barbeque Contest. If you're invited, it's definitely an honor. But the competition is stiff.

International Barbeque Cookers Association
www.ibcabbq.org

This sanctioning group is based in Arlington, Texas. As stated on its Web site, "The International Barbeque Cookers Association's purpose is to develop and bolster equitable competitive Barbeque cooking internationally. We give competitive cookers the peace of mind when their product is placed in the judging area." Categories are often determined by the partiticular contest's promoters.

A sampling of rules:

* **Meats must be cooked from scratch. No precooking or marinating before the contest begins.**

* **Judges can also inspect the cooking area, so it must be sanitary and as spotless as possible.**

* **One cook, one entry per category.**

* **No garnish or sauce is allowed in the presentation tray (this means the entry can be brushed or glazed with sauce but no extra sauce in a small container can be included on the tray) at turn-in for judging.**

* **IBCA requires that the secret, double number system be used. One ticket will be attached firmly to the lid of the judging tray. The matching ticket must be retained by the cook until award numbers are announced. Head cooks must sign the back of the ticket, in ink, when judging trays are issued.**

Kansas City Barbeque Society
www.kcbs.us

This sanctioning society, based in Kansas City, Missouri, also publishes a monthly newsletter, The Kansas City BullSheet, with lots of news, lists of contest winners, information about upcoming contests, recipes, and barbecuing techniques. If you contact the KCBS office, they will send you the KCBS Cook's Handbook, which contains all the rules and regulations.

The KCBS also offers barbecue judging and/or barbecue cooking classes around the country. See the schedule in the BullSheet or call the KCBS office for details.

A sampling of rules:

* Your meat must be approved by a KCBS representative before cooking. Your meats should be raw and placed on ice. They should have an internal temperature of no higher than 40 degrees F. You may use rubs and marinades before cooking.

* Entries for judging are placed in 9 x 9-inch Styrofoam containers. You may garnish your entry with green leaves of lettuce, parsley, or cilantro only.

* Your entry will be judged "double blind," using a number that is assigned to your team and written on the top of your Styrofoam entry box. This number is then swapped with a second number known only to the KCBS representative.

* Judges are KCBS trained and certified. Judges will not visit you or your cooking area as part of the overall judging process.

Memphis in May Sanctioned Contest Network
www.memphisinmay.org

The Memphis in May Sanctioned Contest Network is an organization that sanctions all-pork barbecue contests. It encourages serious competition enthusiasts by providing a uniform set of rules and regulations governing the process of selecting the contest winners. The purpose of these contests is to recognize the best barbecuers in local areas, bringing them together yearly in a single competition—Memphis in May World Championship Barbecue Cooking Contest, held in Memphis, Tennessee, in May of each year—designed to identify that year's World Champion barbecue team.

A sampling of rules:

* Each contest is required to hold a cook's meeting, conducted by the Memphis in May representative, the day before judging, during which the organizers go over the contest rules and teams can ask questions.

* Competition meat must be inspected by the appointed contest official before the preparation process begins. Competition meat must be fresh or frozen, and not precooked, sauced, injected, marinated, or cured in any way, prior to inspection. It must also be kept below an internal temperature of 40 degrees F until the cooking begins.

* Entries must be cooked on wood and/or charcoal.

* You may include two small cups of sauces, rubs, marinades, or basting sauces with your entry. No garnish of any kind is allowed, though.

* There are six judging criteria: Area and Personal Appearance, Presentation (verbal explanation of your team, cooker, etc.), Appearance of the Entry, Tenderness of the Entry, Flavor of the Entry, and Overall Impression. The first two are judged on site. The remaining categories are judged on site and blind.

* Preliminary judging is the judging of all teams and all entries in the contest. It is done one meat

category at a time, using blind and on-site judging. The purpose of the preliminary round is to identify the top three entries in each meat category and to rank the rest of the entries. The top three entries in each meat category advance to the final round, which is judged by people selected by the contest officials. They may or may not be trained or certified.

Barbecue Contest Categories

The sanctioning body (usually either IBCA, KCBS, or MIM-SCN) determines the main categories for competition, and these are judged first, usually starting around noon on Saturday of the contest. The contest organizers may add other categories, which are judged later in the afternoon, after the main categories.

An ICBA-sanctioned contest has categories determined by the contest organizers.

A KCBS-sanctioned contest usually has four main categories: Chicken, Pork Ribs (loin or spare), Pork (shoulder, picnic, butt), and Brisket (beef). There are also all-pork contests, such as the Great Pork BarbeQLossal, and all-lamb contests, including the National Lamb-B-Que contest.

An MIM-sanctioned contest has three main Pork categories: Whole Hog, Whole Pork Shoulder or Fresh Ham, and Pork Ribs.

That said, here some of the barbecue contest categories I've come across on the competition circuit:

Chicken

Whole Hog

Whole Pork Shoulder or Fresh Ham

Pork Ribs (loin or spare)

Pork Loin

Brisket (beef)

Tri-Tip (beef, popular in West Coast contests)

Lamb Steaks

Lamb Chops

Lamb Roast

Lamb Miscellaneous

Whole Animal

Sausage (must not be cured to qualify in most contests)

Salsa

Barbecue Sauce

Anything But, Cook's Choice, Miscellaneous

Beans (baked or smoked and baked)

Potato

Vegetable

Side Dish

Dessert

Anything But usually means anything but the regular slow-smoked beef, pork, and chicken that make up the main competitive categories in a barbecue contest. The Miscellaneous and Anything But categories in barbecue contests provide even more opportunities for you to learn and grow—and win. You can grill or smoke just about anything you want, as long as it tastes and looks good! When I enter something in an Anything But category, I try to think of a dish I know people will enjoy and that I like, too. I've done smoked prime rib with a side of grilled clams casino at Memphis in May. I've done grilled eggplant with garlic butter in Ireland, and a vegetarian taco with bulgur instead of meat. Foods that you like, you cook better. And that could mean a blue ribbon.

The KCBS-sanctioned American Royal BBQ Open contest offers Side Dish Overall, Beans, Potato, Vegetable, and Dessert categories. Memphis in May contests have Miscellaneous categories.

What to Bring to a Barbecue Cook-Off

Getting ready for my first contest—the American Royal in 1981—couldn't have gone worse. Since then, I've made a packing list. Some equipment I clean after a contest, then pack up again, so it's always ready to go. I've also found that it's better to have too much stuff than be missing something crucial at the eleventh hour.

You don't know what the weather is going to be like at a contest—especially in the Midwest—so be prepared for anything. A cook-off is like a campout, only you have to compete and perform, not just relax. You'll be working, sleeping, and eating outdoors for at least a day and half. You'll have a squared-off area to set up your grills, smokers, commercial-style rig, or whatever equipment you've brought. You may also want to bring a tent or awning to protect you and your cooking area from the weather, as well as bedding of some kind

so you can catch a few minutes of shut-eye here and there. Bring food and drink for you and your team, along with eating utensils, lawn or outdoor folding chairs, a folding worktable or two, aspirin, Band-Aids and other first-aid stuff, and batteries.

Have a variety of fire starters in your arsenal. If you bring only kindling and your kindling gets wet in a downpour, you're sunk. I try to avoid petro-chemicals, such as charcoal lighter fluid. I sometimes use Weber white cubes, however, which are paraffin starters. You put these in the bottom of your charcoal chimney and place 10 charcoal pieces on top. Light a match to a corner of a white cube and your fire should start.

I have a master packing list and I pack up the van the night before. I tow the cooker behind the van.

Here's what I bring for cooking:

* **Cooker(s)**
* **Charcoal chimney**
* **Newspaper**
* **Matches**
* **Weber white cubes**
* **Blowtorch (for starting a fire in really bad weather)**
* **Lump charcoal**
* **Hardwood logs, sticks, or chunks**
* **Heat-resistant gloves**
* **Leather welding gloves**
* **Long-handled fork spatula**
* **Long-handled grill spatula**
* **Pots and pans**

* Meat thermometers

* Dish mop for mopping

* Plastic spray bottles for basting

* Brushes for slathering

* My tackle box (see page 10)

* Ice (lots of it)

* 150-quart ice chest (with meats for competition wrapped in plastic and put on ice)

* Plug-in electric lights

* Spatulas, spoons, measuring cups, measuring spoons

* All the food—meats, poultry, turkey, veggies, etc.—for competition

* My flavor box filled with spices, rubs, seasonings, vinegars, sweeteners, etc.

* Lettuce, parsley, sauce, or whatever is an allowed garnish

* Large rolls of plastic wrap and aluminum foil from a restaurant supply house or discount store

* Paper towels

* Zippered-top plastic bags

* Cloth kitchen towels (place a damp one under a cutting board to keep it steady)

* 4-inch deep disposable aluminum pans (to use as water pans)

* Sauces, marinades, rubs, etc., carried in big plastic bottles or jars

* Cutting board (I use discarded countertop sink cutouts that I get from a kitchen supplier or lumberyard)

For clean-up, I bring:

* Dishwashing liquid

* Bleach (put one capful of bleach into 1 gallon of water to sanitize the cutting board and your work area)

* Water (check to see whether water is available at the site beforehand)

* 4-inch-deep disposable aluminum pans (to use as dishpans)

* Dishrags

* Paper towels

* Kitchen disinfecting wipes

* Spray cleaner

* Industrial-strength spray degreaser

* Heavy-duty trash bags

* Shovel (for taking the ashes and leftover charcoal out of the pit)

* Metal ash bucket

Controlling Your Fire

One of the most crucial things you can do to win a barbecue contest is control your fire. This may sound easy, but you're working outside in all kinds of weather. It could be hotter than hell or very cold (especially at the American Royal in Kansas City in early October). It could be pouring rain or very windy. You have to be able to maintain the temperature in your cooker no matter what.

THE BARON'S TACKLE BOX

I have a large fishing tackle box that I use to store my barbecue gadgets. I have all kinds of stuff in there, ready to go to contests or barbecue classes I'm teaching. Here's what I keep in it:

* Catfish or needlenose pliers (for pulling off the membrane from the back of rib slabs)
* Duct tape (for quick-fix repairs to equipment)
* Butcher's twine, cotton twine
* Syringes (for injecting internal marinades or brines)
* 10-inch bamboo skewers
* Extra grill and meat thermometers
* Extra Weber white cubes
* Knives: boning, paring, 14-inch slicing knives, cleavers
* Steel knife sharpener
* Sharpening stones

When I'm competing in a contest, I don't let the temperature in my rig vary more than 5 degrees F after the first hour. The only way you can maintain a consistent temperature is to know your rig and practice, practice, practice.

Developing a Grand Champion Mindset

Confidence is a big factor in producing great barbecue. Winning a contest requires the mindset of a competitive perfectionist. This attitude has helped me win big. I've won the highest or the Grand Champion award in the American Royal, the BarbeQLossal, the Great Lenexa Barbeque Battle, and the National Lamb-B-Que; between me and my team, Team Kansas City, I have won seven world barbecue championships.

When I'm at a contest, I'm there to do the best I can. I'm there to win. I always joke that I get a bad case of PMS—maybe that should be PJS, or pre-judging syndrome—an hour or so before the judging starts. As far as I'm concerned, I'm at the contest to put my expertise on the line. I'm not there for the money, per se, although the money sure is nice.

I've learned over the years to cook for myself, my team, and my family, not for the judges. You want the judges to like what you like, but if you try to second-guess what the judges will like, you could be wrong. In the mid-1980s, I entered a Memphis in May–sanctioned all-pork contest in St. Louis. The favorite barbecue sauce in St. Louis at the time was Maull's. I tried to create a new barbecue sauce that was similar, because I figured the St. Louis judges would like that. It took me two months to develop that sauce. And then on the day of the contest, the judges turned out to be from Memphis!

Sometimes you just can't win. In the mid-1980s, I also entered a contest in St. Joseph, Missouri. My pork loin was juicy and tender and had a smoke ring. But the judges were all old farmers who expected their pork to be well done and dry. I came in twelfth.

Today, I try to enter contests where the judges are certified or trained, so I know that people who know barbecue will be judging my stuff. To me, that's very important.

Championship Barbecue Standards

How do you know when your food is really, really good? If you want an honest opinion of how things taste from the pros, enter a barbecue contest and offer your food to other competitors. They'll tell you.

Here are a few hints:

APPEARANCE: People eat with their eyes first, whether they're family and friends in the back yard or barbecue contest judges. The exterior of a smoked brisket, slab of ribs, or pork butt should be a dark mahogany, not black and burnt. A smoke ring—that dark pink ring just under the surface of the meat that you see when it is sliced—is a plus. Skin on a chicken should look crisp, not rubbery. A glazed exterior is also more attractive.

TASTE: In most contests, the taste score is doubled, so this is the most important factor. Every flavor should complement and blend with every other flavor. The flavors in the dry rub or marinade used at the beginning and the sauce used at the end should complement the meat. No one flavor should overpower the others.

TENDERNESS: Texture is also important to the full experience of barbecued food. For brisket, if the piece pulls apart easily, it's tender. If it flakes apart, it's overdone and dry. If you have to work to pull it apart, it's underdone. For ribs, people fall

into two "when is it done?" categories. Some like rib meat that falls off the bone. Others, like me, like a little tug when you bite into it.

Presentation Tips for Barbecue Contests

Again, people eat with their eyes first, whether they're just regular folks or barbecue judges. When you're in the heat of battle in a barbecue contest, presentation is very important. At Memphis in May contests, the judges come to you, so everything has to look good—your cooking area, your pit, your food, what you serve your food on, and you. At blind-judged KCBS and IBCA contests, your entry has to speak for itself. Basically, you place your smoked food entry in a numbered Styrofoam box. You know your number, the contest organizers know your number, but the judges do not. At the judges' table, they open the box, look at your food, taste it, and start marking their score cards. One look could be all it takes to win—or lose.

Here's my advice on presentation.

First, presentation can get you disqualified if you do the wrong thing. Read the rules about garnish very carefully. If you don't understand the rules, ask a contest representative to explain them to you. This is important.

At a KCBS-sanctioned contest, for example, you can have only chopped, sliced, shredded, or whole leaves of fresh green lettuce or common curly parsley, flatleaf parsley, or cilantro as garnish—no kale, endive, or red-tipped lettuce. At an IBCA-sanctioned contest, you're not allowed

Grand

THE 1989 AND 1990 WORLD CHAMPIONSHIP BARBECUE CONTESTS IN LISDOONVARNA, CLARE COUNTY, IRELAND

In 1989, four Kansas City chefs who love barbecue—Ronaldo Camargo, Karen Putman, Dan Money, and I—formed Team Kansas City, with the goal of competing in the World Championship Barbecue Contest being held in Clare, Ireland, that year. The idea was to promote Kansas City barbecue, and we received funding from our local chef's association to do just that.

We knew that this was a Memphis in May–sanctioned contest, which meant it could turn into a sort of good ol' boy, who-you-know kind of thing. At Memphis in May–sanctioned contests, you have to put on a 15-minute dog and pony show, explaining your rig and how you cook, and the better everything and everybody looks, the better you do. You basically have to wine and dine the judges for part of the competition.

There were 30 teams from all over the world, representing England, Australia, Ireland, Estonia, New Zealand, and South America. People in Clare would come up to the men on our team, pat our big bellies, and say, "Gee, you're healthy!" But, basically, Team Kansas City kicked ass and took names.

Usually, Memphis in May contests are all pork, but that can also be up to the organizers of the event. Friday was the judging for Ribs, and Saturday was for Beef, Lamb, Pork, Chicken, Seafood, Sausage, and Miscellaneous categories. We won blue ribbons in almost every category and were awarded Grand Champion of the 1989 contest, despite the fact that our grass-fed Irish beef brisket still wasn't tender after smoking for 24 hours.

In 1990, we went back to defend our title. Because we had done so well the year before, the organizers changed the judging criteria (or we think that's why). The Rib category counted for one score, as it did in 1989. The other categories, however, were combined into groups, not counted separately as was done the year before. So if you won Ribs, you were halfway to winning the whole thing. "They're against us," we thought.

any garnish at all. At a Memphis in May–sanctioned contest, you can have a small cup or two of a sauce or rub to accompany your meats, but that's it. If you don't follow the garnish rules to the letter, your entry will be disqualified no matter how good it tastes.

Second, learn how to garnish attractively by taking barbecue judging classes in your area, which you can find through your local barbecue association. You'll see what entries look like in

that Styrofoam box. You'll get a good idea of what wins and what doesn't.

Third, make sure your entry looks moist and not dried out. It could be 30 minutes or so from the time you place it in the box to the time a judge opens the box. So, here's what I do.

For brisket, I don't slice it on a bevel, but straight down. I spray each slice with apple juice or roll the slices in apple juice before fanning out

Champion

The Ribs category was judged on Friday, just like the year before. But . . . the wining and dining of the judges was a little different in 1990. A team from Kentucky brought in two cases of Kentucky bourbon to help the judges wash down their ribs. You could hear the judges joining in to sing "My Old Kentucky Home" after they'd had a few. Guess who won the ribs that year?

Saturday was the day for judging every other category. I was going to be in charge of the brisket for the Beef category and pork butt for Pork. When I went to the most highly regarded butcher in Clare, the best I could buy—again—was a grass-fed brisket that was tough, tough, tough. "Oh, great," I thought. Luckily, we had also smuggled in several 21-ounce, dry-aged Porterhouse steaks. I usually don't like to grill in a barbecue contest, but there's always a first time and this was it. I also decided to enter in the Vegetarian and Miscellaneous categories and the other team members almost fell out of their seats. Why? As I explained to them, these were relatively new categories and everybody else would be doing Irish potatoes in some way.

When the judges came to our area, we offered them a salad with raspberry vinaigrette, grilled teriyaki onion mum for the vegetable, grilled eggplant (or aubergine, as they call it in Ireland) with garlic butter for the entrée, and those grilled Porterhouse steaks for the Beef category, along with the entries our other team members had prepared. Our judges were a little old Irish lady and a doctor from a nearby town. They didn't look up as they ate. They just dove into the food.

When the results were in, Team Kansas City came in third in Ribs, first in Beef, first in Pork, second in Lamb, first in Vegetarian, second in Chicken, first in Miscellaneous, and third in Seafood. Because the Kentucky team scored so high in Ribs (I wonder why?), our combined scores in the other categories were enough to beat them by only a hundredth of a point. But we successfully defended our title.

the meat, then shingle it up so the slices overlap. You should be able to see a dark pink smoke ring around the perimeter of each slice.

For sausage, I slice at an angle and arrange it in a decorative pattern.

For ribs, I glaze them with sauce every 10 minutes during the last hour of cooking. I cut the six best ribs, then arrange them individually. You don't want the ribs to look like a slab. Again,

you should be able to see the dark pink smoke ring around the perimeter and a beautiful, somewhat glossy, burnished exterior from the glaze.

For chicken breast, I brush on a glaze, crisp the skin on the grill at the end of smoking, then slice the meat and fan out the slices.

For pork butt, I usually slice the meat so you can see the "bark," or exterior, and the smoke ring.

In a typical KCBS-sanctioned contest, the judging of the four main categories (Chicken first, then Pork Ribs, Pork Shoulder or Butt, and Brisket last) takes place between noon and 1:30 or 2:00 P.M. on Saturday.

Barbecue Awards

At the end of the day—usually on Saturday—awards are given out at the contest. In each category, there is a first place (blue ribbon), second place (red ribbon), and third place (white ribbon) winner. Depending on the contest and how it is judged, points are usually awarded to each team in each category. The Grand Champion is the barbecue team that has the most points overall, probably with a blue ribbon or two in several different categories. The Reserve Grand Champion takes second place overall.

Taking Grand Champion is a great honor, and it also probably qualifies the team to be invited to other prestigious invitational contests, such as the Jack Daniel's Invitational, American Royal Invitational, and/or Memphis in May Invitational. (Most of these big invitational contests also include "open" contests, which any team can enter.) There is usually prize money for Grand and Reserve Champions, sometime several thousand dollars.

Lots of photos are taken, and representatives from the sponsoring barbecue society make sure the event is written up for the society's newspaper or newsletter. At really big contests, you get national press exposure. You could be famous by now!

Packing Up to Go Home

Now comes the not-so-fun part of the contest—cleaning and packing up everything to go home. Throw out any spices or rubs that have been contaminated by raw meat and clean every work surface with a bleach-and-water solution (one cap of bleach per gallon of water).

Cleaning Your Cooker

After a contest or a backyard barbecue, your cooker will be smoky and greasy. For smaller backyard grills and smokers, you can use a wire-bristled grill brush to clean off the debris, then a degreaser and water to clean the grill racks, the lid, and the water pan (that is, if you don't use a disposable aluminum pan).

My big pig cooker presents a different problem. Before I leave a contest, I remove as much of the grease and ash as I can. I put any hot coals in a metal ash bucket, so there is no danger of fire. When the coals have partially cooled, you can spread them out on the ground or pavement to cool further, or spray them with water, then scoop them up and throw them away.

On the way home from a contest, I either try to sneak into an automated car wash or go to a power wash station—those individual cement-block car wash "garages" where you do the washing yourself. I use a spray degreasing solution on the pig cooker, then use the power washing system to get it all clean.

Fire and the ART of Championship Barbecue

The most important ingredient in championship barbecue is confidence. When I'm at a contest, I'm there to do the best I can for the judges. I'm there to win with the best barbecue I can produce that day.

The ideal way to gain that confidence is to practice your barbecue skills. And the most important barbecue skill to acquire is preparing, maintaining, and controlling your fire. You need to be able to control your fire in any kind of weather if you want to compete in barbecue contests.

Once you have the basics down pat—and your friends and family are happily wolfing down your results—you'll be ready for the contest circuit. Here's how you get there.

Grilling versus Slow Smoking or Barbecuing

For many people, the word "barbecue" means anything cooked on a grill. But for afficionados of the real thing, "barbecue" means foods cooked slowly on a grill or in a smoker so that they tenderize and take on a real flavor of wood smoke. When I talk about barbecue, I mean slow-smoked food.

Here's the difference between grilled and smoked food:

Grilled foods cook fast over a hot fire with temperatures that can range from 400 degrees F upward to slightly char and give them a robust flavor. Because the foods cook fast, you usually grill foods that are already pretty tender, such as chicken breasts, pork chops, pork tenderloin, steaks of all kinds, fish fillets, shellfish, and vegetables.

Smoked foods cook slowly next to a low fire at temperatures between 230 and 250 degrees F in most charcoal and electric smokers; the Green Egg and other kamado-style ceramic smokers use higher temperatures, closer to 300 degrees F (see page 22). For that reason, smoked foods take on a heavier wood smoke flavor. Because the foods cook slowly and at a low temperature, you usually smoke foods that need a longer cooking time to tenderize—beef brisket, pork loin, spareribs, and pork shoulder or butt. The great thing about smoking, however, is that you can also smoke foods that you grill, such as chicken breasts, beef tenderloin, vegetables, and shellfish. These foods may take longer to cook than when grilling, but you get the bonus of wood smoke flavor. Smoked foods don't have grill marks, but rather a burnished or darkened appearance.

You can smoke or barbecue anything you can grill, but you can't always grill anything you can smoke. Grilled beef brisket or pork butt would be too tough even to contemplate eating. On the other hand, smoked tomatoes and beef tenderloin are delicious.

The smoked or barbecued recipes in this book can all be prepared using kettle grills, electric and charcoal bullet smokers, and gas grills (with two separate burners)—readily available to backyard enthusiasts and home cooks—as well as bigger competition-style smokers or cookers. The grilled recipes can all be prepared using kettle grills, gas grills, and wood pellet grills.

The direct and indirect heats mentioned in my recipes indicate that you need to prepare a certain kind of fire. I'll illustrate what this means by telling you how to prepare a direct heat fire and then an indirect heat fire in a charcoal kettle grill.

DIRECT HEAT FIRE: Start a fire in a charcoal chimney using hardwood charcoal and newspaper. Place more hardwood charcoal in the bottom of the kettle grill. When the coals are hot in the charcoal chimney, dump them on top of the charcoal in the bottom of the grill and wait for all the coals to catch fire and ash over. When they've all ashed over and turned a whitish gray, put the grill grate on. Now, you can grill over direct heat.

INDIRECT HEAT FIRE: If you want indirect heat, use a long-handled grill spatula to push the coals over to one half of the grill. One side of the grill will have hot coals, and that is direct heat. The other side will not have hot coals, and that is where you will cook with indirect heat. Carefully place a disposable aluminum pan filled with water on the indirect side, next to the hot coals, on the bottom of the grill or smoker. (Smoking is longer and slower, so you need the extra moisture from the water in the pan to keep the food from drying out.) Place aromatic hardwood chunks, sticks, chips, or pellets (for wood smoke flavoring) on top of the coals. Replace the grill grate. With an indirect fire, you can grill directly over the hot coals and smoke over the indirect side at the same time.

Sometimes, you need both types of fire for a backyard barbecue or a competition. Normally, you smoke your main entries in barbecue contests. But at the 1990 Memphis in May–sanctioned International Barbecue Championship in Lisdoonvarna, Clare County, Ireland, my original plans to smoke a brisket went out the window when I saw the tough, stringy, grass-fed beef that even the best butchers had in their shops. I ended up grilling—and winning with—dry-aged Porterhouse steaks we had smuggled into the country with our team's equipment.

In the back yard or in competition, you can smoke a chicken over the lower temperature of the indirect side, then sear or crisp the skin over the hot fire right before serving it up for your guests or the judges. In the Taster's Choice, Anything But, Miscellaneous, or similar category in competition—in which you can basically cook any food you want in any way—I sometimes use a direct fire to grill my entry, especially if I have smoked everything else in the other categories.

Preparing Food for the Grill or Smoker

Preparing food for grilling can be as simple as seasoning it with salt and pepper. This is usually true for smaller cuts of meat, fish, chicken, or pork, such as burgers, steaks, chops, or fillets. Foods for the grill can be seasoned with a dry rub or marinated beforehand. Be sure not to use a dry rub or sauce with a high sugar content, or it will burn as it grills. Also, you may want to wipe away any excess marinade, because olive or vegetable oil will flare up when it drips onto the hot coals.

Preparing food for smoking or long, slow, indirect cooking usually involves trimming the meats and poultry: marinating, brining, or injecting the food with a flavorful "inner" baste, blotting the meat dry if I'm going to use a mustard slather or, if not, applying my rub. These will usually be larger cuts of meat, fish, chicken, or pork, such as a whole brisket, shoulder, slab of ribs, or a whole chicken or fish. You can also smoke standing rib roast, chicken breasts, pork chops, and shellfish. Each recipe in this book tells you how to prepare the food for the smoker.

Preparing the Utensils, Grill, Smoker, and Other Equipment

The grill or smoker should be clean and the grill rack(s) lightly oiled (use any vegetable oil and a long-handled brush, and take care to avoid dripping oil). Have all your equipment handy, and your smoking experience will be relaxing and enjoyable in the back yard and efficient during competition.

Tools for Grilling and Smoking

Several basic tools make barbecuing and/or smoking easier. A local restaurant supply store or a barbecue and grill shop is a good source for finding the items listed, plus professional utensils are superior in quality and durability.

When you go to a barbecue contest, however, the list of utensils grows. See What to Bring to a Barbecue Cook-off on pages 8–9 for contest essentials.

* A metal charcoal chimney is necessary for starting the fire.

* A natural-bristled basting brush is useful for basting the food during smoking.

* Disposable aluminum pans, which are the easiest utensils to use on a grill or smoker, are available at grocery stores.

* Heat-resistant oven or grill mitts offer the best hand protection.

* Long-handled, spring-loaded tongs are easier to use than the scissors type. They are great for turning shrimp, scallops, sliced vegetables, and skewers.

* Candy thermometers with a 6- to 8-inch probe, available at kitchen stores, are used to gauge the temperature in your cooker through a baffle or hole in the cooker.

* Grill thermometers, available at hardware, home improvement, and barbecue and grill shops, help you monitor the temperature if you are using a charcoal kettle grill, a big smoking rig, or a gas grill.

* A metal rib rack will hold three (from Sunbeam) or four (from Weber) racks of spareribs upright on your kettle grill or smoker, freeing up space on the grill rack.

* A stiff wire brush with a scraper makes cleaning the grill or smoker a simple job (tackle this while the grill or smoker is still warm).

Setting Up Your Pit

A barbecue "pit" doesn't necessarily mean a big trench filled with wood for cooking a whole hog. A pit can be any type of equipment that maintains an indirect fire for low and slow smoking over long periods of time.

With most types of grills or smokers, and even with gas grills, you can slow smoke almost any food for delicious barbecue in your back yard. But for competition barbecue, your choice narrows to equipment that uses charcoal and wood.

To illustrate the barbecue procedure for the recipes in this book, I use a basic kettle grill. Once you've figured out how to get great barbecue from your charcoal kettle, you can try other equipment.

Charcoal Kettle Grill

The most basic kind of smoking can be done with a charcoal kettle grill, made by manufacturers such as Weber in Michigan and The Good One in Berne, Kansas, both of which are available for less than $100. I have been questioned about why I suggest a 26-inch Weber when a 22-inch model is standard for backyard cooks. The reason is because I happen to own and use a 26-inch Weber, but also because it's much harder to fit three slabs of ribs over an indirect fire on a smaller grill. I also prefer to use kettle grills with three-part baffles to regulate the air intake and the temperature.

Use hardwood charcoal to start a fire. When the coals have ashed over, use a long grill spatula to push them over to one side of the grill. Place a metal or disposable aluminum pan of water on the bottom of the grill next to the coals. Place the grill rack over the top. The side with the coals is direct heat; the side with the pan of water is indirect heat. Use grill thermometers to monitor the temperature on both sides of the grill. Ideally, smoking is done with a temperature (measured on the indirect side) between 230 and 250 degrees F.

You can grill and smoke with a charcoal kettle grill, and many teams use these in competition.

The Beaver Castors, my buddy Bob Lyon's barbecue team from the state of Washington, who all took my barbecue class, won reserve championships using kettle grills at both the American Royal and the Jack Daniel's Invitational in 1993. They still continue to kick butt in contests using Patio Classics, their kettle and grill of choice for chicken and ribs.

Charcoal "Bullet" Smoker

Many competition teams use several small Weber Smokey Mountain smokers, also known as "bullets" or WSMs, and bullet smokers manufactured by the Brinkmann Smoker Company in Fort Worth, Texas. They range in price from less than $100 for the Brinkmann to $180 for the Weber Smokey Mountain and are available at most hardware stores or barbecue and grill shops.

I recommend using real hardwood charcoal, not chemically treated and compressed charcoal. Hardwood charcoal gives a better flavor and is better for the environment. I also discourage the use of charcoal lighter fluid, as it can infuse the food with an unpleasant chemical flavor. Start your fire and charcoal in a metal charcoal chimney, available at hardware, discount, and home improvement stores. Place the coals in the bottom third of the bullet smoker. Wood chunks, wood chips, or aluminum packets of wood pellets can be placed on the coals for more smoke flavor. Fill the water pan with water and set it in the middle part of the smoker. The smoker racks take up the top third of the charcoal smoker. A charcoal "bullet" smoker provides only indirect heat. You can only smoke, not grill, with a charcoal "bullet" smoker.

You can use this type of smoker in the back yard as well as for competition. Harold Froescher, one of my barbecue students from Oregon, won a first place in Ribs at the 1994 American Royal using a Brinkmann charcoal "bullet" smoker. Judie Anderson, a barbecue student from the state of Washington, cooked first-place ribs at the Jack Daniel's Invitational in both 1993 and 1994 using a Weber Smokey Mountain.

Commercial Competition-Style Cookers or Smokers

The sky is the limit with this type of equipment, which can run into the thousands of dollars. The range of commercial cookers advertised in the pages of the Kansas City Barbeque Society's monthly BullSheet newspaper is astounding. Makers such as Ole Hickory Pits, Klingsicks, Klose Pits, Grills to Go, Belson, Southern Yankee Bar-B-Q, Southern Pride, Hasty-Bake, and Meadow Creek Welding produce cookers in every size and shape, from cast iron to stainless steel. Many are towable, which is a plus, especially if the cooker is really large. You don't want to take up all the space in the back of your vehicle with your smoker.

With a competition-style smoker, the firebox is generally a separate compartment on one side of the cooker, with hinged metal doors so you can add more charcoal or wood when necessary. Smaller models can use charcoal and wood chunks. Larger models may rely on hickory, oak, cherry, or apple logs for both heat and smoke.

The foods to be smoked are arranged on racks in the larger chamber—again, cooking on the side with indirect heat away from the direct heat of the firebox. Competition barbecuers have several different grill thermometers positioned outside on different areas of their smoking chamber to measure the exhaust temperature, so they know what is cooking at exactly what temperature, eliminating guesswork. You can also hold a candy thermometer in a hole in your cooker for a few seconds to measure the temperature quickly in that part of the cooker. (You don't want the thermometers inside because you'd have to keep opening the lid to check them, which would lower the temperature and delay the cooking time.)

I use this type of cooker for my competition barbecue. I've designed all my own cookers or smokers and had them made by Klose Pits in Houston (see Sources). My "pig cooker" is made from a 55-gallon drum (that never contained anything toxic and was well cleaned beforehand) that I cut in half vertically and hinged on the back, with a handle in front on the door. I also had a 16-gallon drum welded horizontally on one end. One drum is the firebox, the other the actual cooker, where I hang the meat for smoking. My pig cooker is painted orange with white eyes and two snouts. I prefer a more vertical cooker because I like to hang everything. In my pig cooker, I can hang 22 slabs of ribs, utilizing all the space. The ribs self-baste as they cook.

I have six grill thermometers positioned on different parts of the exterior of the smoking chamber: two on each door, two on top, and two in the middle in the back. In competition, I check the thermometers every 15 minutes and don't let the temperature vary more than 5 degrees F.

But any smoker can produce good barbecue. Any pit, cooker, or smoker that allows you to control the temperature is the best you could ever own.

Gas or Electric Grills

Follow the manufacturer's directions for starting your gas or electric grill. To prepare an indirect fire on a gas or electric grill, you need the type of grill that has two separate burners. Turn one burner on, and leave the other one off. The side with the burner on is direct heat; the side with the burner off is indirect heat. You can place a water pan in the back of the grill on the indirect side.

A gas or electric grill is very easy to use, but it does not impart the flavor that hardwood charcoal or wood pellet smoking does. To get more wood smoke flavor from your gas or electric grill, moisten the wood chips or place wood pellets in a packet made from heavy-duty aluminum foil and poke holes in the packet. Place either directly over the lava rock. The wood chips or wood pellets smolder rather than burn, giving an added wood smoke flavor. Some gas or electric grills also have a smoker box to which you can add wood chips or dry wood pellets. Do not put these directly on the lava rock, as the residue can block the holes in the burners.

You can smoke and grill some great stuff in the back yard with this type of grill. You don't use gas grills for competition, however. The best flavor for competition barbecue comes from hardwood charcoal and aromatic wood logs, sticks, or chunks.

Wood Pellet Grill

This new type of grill and smoker from Traeger Industries is idiot-proof. It uses an electric starter along with compressed wood pellets for fuel and flavor. Most wood pellet grills have controls that allow you to set the temperature. The food is already placed indirectly (away from the heat source), so even if you grill at higher temperatures, it's a milder form of grilling, as the food is at least 1 foot above the heat source. If you set the temperature between 200 and 300 degrees F and close the lid, you'll smoke the food. The wood pellets are available in many different types of wood, from alder to mesquite, so you can get the desired flavor.

The wood pellet grill is used mainly by backyard barbecue enthusiasts, not for competition—except by "Fast Eddie" Maurin (see page 21), who uses one but has to bring a generator with him to contests in case the electricity on site fails. That's too much trouble for me.

Electric "Bullet" Smoker

Like the charcoal "bullet" smoker, the electric "bullet" smoker is built in three sections. The bottom section is a bed of lava rock in which an electric coil rests. You soak wood chunks or chips in water or place an aluminum foil packet of dry wood pellets around but not touching the heating element. The next section of the smoker contains the water pan, which you fill and place on the rack. The top section contains the smoker racks, on which you place disposable aluminum pans of food. Cover the smoker, plug it in, and don't keep checking on it. The more you take the top off to check your food, the longer it will take to smoke because the temperature will keep falling. The temperature should remain at a fairly constant 200 to 250 degrees F.

Again, these smokers are mainly for backyard enthusiasts, as this type of equipment produces a good, smoky flavor in food. But for competition barbecue, you need the extra flavor of hardwood charcoal. And you don't always have a source of electricity at a contest to plug in an electric "bullet" smoker.

The Big Green Egg and Kamado Ceramic Cooker

These are very heavy, more cylindrical-shaped cookers made from a ceramic material. They cook hotter and faster, at 300 degrees F or more, so you have to adjust the cooking times I give in this book. Smaller cookers like this one cook quickly because of the greater amount of radiant heat they give off.

I have seen these on occasion at barbecue contests. As long as you use hardwood charcoal and wood in it, you'll be fine. These are smaller cookers, however, so you would be limited in what you cooked for a contest.

Fire and How to Build It

A major premise of mine is that if you have or develop the ability to control the fire or heat on your cooker, you can be a good barbecuer.

To slow smoke or barbecue, you need two elements in your fire: the fuel to burn and provide heat, and the wood to smolder and provide a smoky flavor that will then permeate the food during the hours of cooking. Backyarders have small equipment and generally use both lump charcoal and wood chunks, sticks, chips, or wood pellets. The wood is placed directly on the hot coals to smolder and provide smoke. Competition barbecuers have big enough commercial-style cookers to use larger hardwood sticks or even smaller logs placed over the hot coals to smolder and provide smoke. Barbecue restaurants or big-rig caterers use hardwoods such as hickory for both fuel and flavor in their large commercial cookers or outdoor barbecue pits.

To grill, you really only need to have the fuel. Grilling is done so quickly that you would get only a mild smoke flavor from any wood you add to the fire during the minutes of cooking. But you can grill with a Kiss of Smoke (see page 23) by throwing a chunk or two of hardwood on the coals.

For fuel, your choices are hardwood lump charcoal or charcoal briquettes and hardwoods. Of the two types of charcoal, I prefer to use hardwood lump charcoal because it has been lit on fire, left to burn, and then smothered, resulting in

Grilling with a KISS of Smoke

If you want more of a wood smoke flavor when you grill over a medium-hot fire, you can achieve it in several ways. Grilling takes a shorter amount of time, so the quantity of wood you use is less and the flavor you get is milder than if you slow smoked.

To grill with a Kiss of Smoke, you can use:

* $1/3$ cup wood pellets, dry, in a variety of woods, including alder, apple, hickory, mesquite, and sassafras. Wood pellet grills already use these for both flavor and fire. Wood pellets are available from barbecue and grill shops or by mail order (see Sources).

* 1 cup moistened wood chips, available in a variety of woods from barbecue and grill shops or by mail order (see Sources).

* 1 or 2 chunks of wood, again available in a variety of woods from barbecue and grill shops or by mail order (see Sources).

On a charcoal grill, simply place the dry pellets, moistened wood chips, or wood chunks directly on the medium-hot coals but away from where you will be placing the food. The wood will smolder and smoke, giving your food a slightly smoky flavor.

On a gas grill, make an aluminum foil pouch to enclose the dry wood pellets or moistened wood chips. (You don't want anything to fall into the gas jets.) *Do not use wood chunks.* Poke a few holes in the foil pouch to release the smoke when the wood starts to smolder. Place the foil packet on the grill grate away from where you will be placing the food.

---

carbonaceous pieces of charcoal. It comes in a variety of sizes and is all-natural. Lump charcoal also burns hotter and cleaner than briquettes. Hardwoods include hickory; oak; mesquite; fruit woods, such as apple and cherry; and nut woods, such as pecan. Charcoal briquettes are made with carbonaceous wood, anthracite coal, starch binder, and assorted other products such as glue and clay—I don't want these flavors in my barbe-cue. However, charcoal briquettes burn at a more consistent temperature.

Some barbecue afficionados like to experiment with other fuels, such as corncobs, peat, and buffalo chips, which certainly can be used, but why would you want to? "Leave corn and corncobs, peat, and buffalo chips to the survivalists," says my buddy Bob Lyon, who contributed a lot to this book.

To start your fuel, you can use a variety of products, including charcoal lighter fluid, sterno, or alcohol-based fuels (which are more environmentally friendly), fiber wax blocks, paper (newspaper), or kindling (twigs, wood shavings, or thin pieces of wood that catch fire easily). Again, I prefer the more natural approach. I don't want any chemical flavor at all lingering in my barbecue, so I use a charcoal chimney starter filled with lump charcoal and newspaper for backyard smoking, and I use kindling for competition.

Make sure that you can start a fire in any weather before you enter a contest. Practice in your back yard until you can do this in the pouring rain, cold wind, or driving hail. Sure enough, you'll encounter those conditions in a contest.

Before you start your fire, decide how big a fire you need and how long you are going to cook. For backyard or competition cooking, start your fire with about 50 pieces of lump charcoal for a large kettle grill. A piece of charcoal weighs 1 to 1.2 ounces and gives you a good, even cooking heat for about 35 to 45 minutes. That's long enough to grill something, but for longer smoking, you'll have to replenish your charcoal many times. That means several bags of lump charcoal and keeping your charcoal chimney busy!

To build a direct fire for grilling, simply arrange 40 pieces of charcoal in the bottom of a kettle grill. Place another 10 in a charcoal chimney, stuff the newspaper underneath, and light the newspaper with a match. Set the charcoal chimney on the pavement outside or on the grill rack over the grill until the coals have caught fire, burned, and ashed over, 10 to 15 minutes. Then remove the grill rack and dump the hot coals over the charcoal in the bottom of the grill to catch fire, burn, and then ash over. Replace the grill rack and you're ready to grill when all the coals are hot.

To build an indirect fire for smoking or barbecuing in a kettle grill, repeat the process for building a direct fire for grilling. When the coals have all ashed over, use a long-handled grill spatula to push them over to one half of the bottom of the grill. Place a disposable aluminum pan filled with water on the other half. Place your wood (presoaked or not) on top of the coals. Replace the grill rack and you're ready to barbecue when all the coals are hot.

In competition, if you have an indirect fire going in a kettle grill, you can smoke and grill. The water pan side is for smoking. The side directly over the coals is for grilling.

Using Hardwood Logs, Sticks, Chunks, Chips, and Pellets

Wood smoke is the main flavoring agent for slow-smoked barbecue. To get this effect, you need to use hardwoods that smolder and give off aromatic smoke. Too much wood smoke will create an acrid, bitter taste in your food. More is not better. Too much smoke is probably the number one mistake that first-timers make.

How much wood you use depends on the size of your cooker or grill, how much food you're preparing, and how long it will take to cook. For the basic kettle grill or charcoal smoker (for either backyard or competition), three chunks of hardwood (hickory, oak, mesquite, pecan, apple, etc.) on top of the coals will last about 3 to 4 hours. A handful of wood chips that have been presoaked will give you the same aroma, but will last only about 2 hours before they need to be replenished. About ⅓ cup of dry wood pellets will also give the same aroma and last about 2 hours. If you're smoking a brisket (among other things), figure on 16 hours of total cooking time. That means using about 15 chunks of wood (figure a little extra, just in case), 4 cups of wood chips, or about 3 cups of dry wood pellets.

For competition barbecue, I use "sticks" in my large, commercial-style cooker. Sticks are split logs that were originally 8 to 10 inches in diameter; they are placed in the firebox on top of the charcoal. Sticks are usually cut to fit your firebox. My firebox is about 23 inches long. The sticks I use are about 21 inches long and 4 to 5 inches in diameter, because I want a little room to spare when I put in the wood.

I start my fire with 8 to 10 pounds of lump charcoal, then use about 3 sticks—one stick each of seasoned oak, hickory, and apple—on top of the fire to smolder and provide the smoke. I add 2 sticks and maybe 3 to 4 more pounds of charcoal (some of which is started in the charcoal chimney for live coals) about every 1½ to 2 hours to smoke all the ribs, brisket, chicken, pork butt, sausage, and everything else I'm doing for a competition. I keep this process up for 12 to 16 hours, or until everything is smoked. When I'm at a cook-off, I sleep in the front seat of my van and wake up every 1½ to 2 hours to replenish the charcoal and wood and check the grill thermometers. All in all, I use about 40 pounds of lump charcoal and 17 to 20 sticks to keep the fire and smoke going for 16 hours. And that's just the smoking. If I'm also grilling, I need to bring an extra 10 pounds of lump charcoal.

Restaurants or special events that feature in-ground barbecue pits simply fill the pit with whole logs and set them alight to burn down and smolder, providing both the heat and the wood smoke flavoring for slow-smoked foods.

Types of Wood for Wood Smoke Flavoring

I prefer a mixture of seasoned oak, hickory, and apple, usually 60 percent oak, 20 percent hickory, and 20 percent apple. Other barbecuers can make good barbecue with other woods they prefer. Generally, for a heavier smoke flavor that goes well with beef, I recommend mesquite or hickory. For a medium smoke flavor that goes well with pork or fish, I like pecan, oak, maple, or alder. For a mild, sweeter flavor that goes well with chicken or shellfish, I recommend fruit woods, such as apple, cherry, and pear. But I'm always experimenting with woods and combinations of woods, and I encourage you to do the same. Any single selection or combination of woods you like is a winner.

Bags of wood chunks, wood chips, and wood pellets are readily available at barbecue and grill shops or by mail order (see Sources) for backyard equipment. For larger commercial-style cookers, you'll need sticks and logs from commercial suppliers. Having 20 split logs for an upcoming contest sent to you by freight can be expensive, so

Types of HARDWOODS and Their Flavors

Barbecuers on the contest circuit often find that it's easier to smoke with the woods available in their area, especially if they're using sticks or logs. If you're using wood chunks, chips, or pellets, these are readily available at barbecue and grill shops, at hardware stores, and by mail order.

ALDER: From the Pacific Northwest, alder has a light, aromatic flavor. Alder and salmon are a match made in heaven. Planks made from alder are used to cook salmon and other fish.

APPLE AND CHERRY: From the temperate regions of the United States, apple and cherry produce smoke that is a little sweeter and fruitier, which makes them good to use with chicken, turkey, and pork. Sometimes you can get wood directly from an orchard when the fruit trees are being pruned.

HICKORY: From Pennsylvania to Kansas, Minnesota to Arkansas, hickory is very popular in Southern-style barbecue and lends a strong, hearty wood smoke flavor to ribs, sausage, pork butt, brisket, and whole chickens.

MAPLE: From New England and the Midwest, maple smolders to a sweeter, milder smoke that pairs well with chicken, vegetables, and fish.

MESQUITE: From the Southwest, mesquite burns fast and hot, with a heavy smoke flavor. In my opinion, mesquite is better for grilling than for smoking because it's harder to control for long smoking times. Too much mesquite for too long and your food is inedible.

OAK: From the temperate regions of the United States, oak, next to hickory, is probably the second-most common wood used in barbecue because it gives a wonderful smoke aroma without being bitter. It also pairs well with other woods. I like a combination of oak, hickory, and apple for almost any food on the smoker.

PECAN: From the South and Midwest, pecan smolders to a mellow, rich aroma, which professional chefs love to use in their restaurants. It's also not overly smoky.

most big-rig barbecuers tend to use the type of hardwood that is locally or regionally available. I'm fortunate to live in Kansas City, where lots of different types of hardwoods are easy to come by.

One controversy regarding wood chunks and chips is whether or not to presoak them in water for at least 30 minutes before using. Some experts claim that soaked chunks give more smoke. Soaking the wood chunks also helps keep down the flame, which helps maintain an even temperature. Then there are other experts who ask, "Why do you need more smoke?"—myself among them. My personal opinion is not to presoak wood chunks. I don't want too much smoke. But you make the call. Either way will work.

OTHER FLAVOR ENHANCEMENTS

The predominant flavor of smoked food is just that—wood smoke. Some dedicated barbecuers also like to add herbs or other flavorings to the water pan during smoking. I've even seen people add sassafras tea, coffee, wine, beer, apple and cranberry juices, and booze to the water pan. These are fun to try, but nobody can tell the difference when you're cooking on a large scale. But if you like to jazz up your water pan, then do it.

You can also place dried herb stalks, grape vines, whole nutmegs, corncobs, or pecan shells on top of the coals instead of or along with wood chunks. The list can extend to wherever your imagination and taste buds take you. Experiment and have fun, but if you do get carried away, do it a little at a time and keep records of your results.

Reaching and Maintaining the Temperature

Reaching and maintaining a temperature is more important for longer smoking than it is for quicker grilling. When the coals are ash gray, you can judge the heat of the fire in your grill or smoker with two simple methods: the low-tech hand method or a grill or candy thermometer. For the first, hold your hand 5 inches above the heat source. If you can hold it there for only about 2 seconds, your fire is hot (about 500 degrees F or more) and perfect for grilling; 3 seconds is a medium-hot fire (about 400 degrees F), also good for grilling; 4 seconds is a medium fire (about 350 degrees F), still good for grilling or higher-heat smoking (as with a ceramic smoker); and 5 to 6 seconds is a low fire (about 230 to 250 degrees F), the ideal temperature for slow smoking. For a higher tech method, check the temperature with your exterior grill thermometer or hold the stem of a candy thermometer in the hole from which the hot exhaust escapes.

Electric smokers keep a constant temperature of between 200 and 250 degrees F, but you will need a grill thermometer or a way to judge when the indirect fire is low enough on other types of grills and smokers. The best manufactured smokers already have industrial-quality thermometers built into the lid. If you're building your own smoker or want more thermometers on your cooker, fasten them on wherever the smoky exhaust comes out to gauge the temperature of the heat within.

When you first build your fire and check the temperature (closest to where your food is), your first readings will be above 300 degrees F for about the first 15 minutes. Don't worry about that. The meat you put on the smoker is cold anyway. But if the temperature doesn't start to drop in 30 minutes, then you have some adjustments to make. Partially close the air vents on the bottom of the grill or smoker, then check again. If the temperature hasn't dropped, then continue to cover the air vents until it does. Keep watching the temperature. If it falls below 200 degrees F, open the air vents a little more.

When I'm at a contest, I check the temperature every 15 minutes in the first hour of cooking. During the night, I wake up every 1½ to 2 hours to check it again and replenish charcoal, wood, and water. I don't let the temperature vary more than 5 degrees F.

This is what I mean when I say to practice controlling your fire in the back yard first. You need to know your equipment and have a feel for when to start and then replenish the charcoal, when and how much to adjust the vents, and so on. If your temperature stays low, your food will simply take longer to smoke and may have a more pronounced smoke flavor, so you will need to adjust the amount of hardwood as well as your expected finish time. Prolonged smoking at a higher temperature (300 degrees F or more) will cause the sugar in your rub or slather to caramelize and eventually blacken. This won't really affect the taste of the food, but it will harm the appearance.

Smoking Time

Estimating smoking times is a challenge, because the time required to cook a food varies, and it is affected by the heat of the fire; the temperature outdoors; and whether the day is windy, sunny, overcast, or rainy. With smoking, it is less crucial to be exact in your timing than with grilling, as smoking is a gentler cooking process that takes longer. But you can smoke food too long, giving it a bitter, acrid flavor. Use the suggested cooking times given in each recipe, but also watch your food while it's smoking and use an internal meat or instant-read thermometer to gauge doneness. I always recommend allowing extra time—an hour, perhaps—when smoking any kind of food. You can always wrap it in plastic wrap and keep it warm and moist in a cooler if you are finished well before serving time. But you certainly don't want your backyard guests waiting to eat until late because your food is not done yet. And judges at a competition won't wait. If your food is not ready at the designated time, you're disqualified from that category. You snooze, you lose.

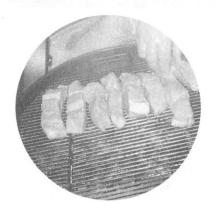

Smoking Timetable

This chart will give you an idea of how long foods take to smoke at around 230 to 250 degrees F. The better you can control your fire and thus the temperature, the more reliable these cooking times will be.

Pork ribs			
	Baby back	1½ lbs.	3 to 5 hours
	Baby back	1¾ to 2¼ lbs.	4 to 6 hours
	Spareribs	2½ to 3-plus lbs.	5 to 7 hours
Whole pork shoulder		12 to 16 lbs.	24 to 32 hours
Pork (Boston) butt		6 to 8 lbs.	8 to 12 hours
Pork loin		8 to 10 lbs.	12 to 15 hours
Pork tenderloin		1½ to 2 lbs.	2½ to 3 hours
Whole hog		up to 85 lbs.	16 to 18 hours
		85 to 135 lbs.	18 to 24 hours
Pork sausage		1½- to 2½-inch diameter	1 to 3 hours
Beef tenderloin		3 to 4 lbs.	3½ to 4 hours
Beef brisket		8 to 12 lbs. trimmed	12 to 18 hours
Lamb (leg)		7 to 9 lbs.	4 to 8 hours
Cabrito		8 to 12 lbs.	4 to 5 hours
Chicken (whole)		2½ to 3 lbs.	3 to 4 hours
		3½ to 4½ lbs.	3 to 5 hours
Chicken (breast)		5 to 8 oz.	1 to 3 hours
Turkey (whole)		10 to 12 lbs.	7 to 8 hours
Duck (whole)		4 to 5 lbs.	3½ to 4 hours
Fish (whole)		4 to 6 lbs.	3½ to 4 hours
Fish (fillets)		4 to 6 oz.	1½ to 2 hours

Doneness Chart for Smoking

Knowing at what internal temperature your smoked food is done is crucial. You want succulent, moist, tender barbecue—not dried-out jerky. Some cuts, such as beef tenderloin and leg of lamb, can be smoked to rare, medium rare, or well done. Most other meats and fish are smoked to a well-done tenderness. For ribs, the doneness test is visual—when the rib meat has pulled back about an inch from the bone. I use heat-safe meat thermometers inserted into brisket or pork butt and left in during smoking as well as instant-read thermometers quickly inserted into foods and then removed to check internal temperatures. For whole chickens, duck, and turkey, insert an instant-read thermometer into both the breast and the thigh. For cabrito, whole lamb, and whole hog, insert a fork into the hindquarter and twist to check for tenderness. Fish is done when it begins to flake when tested with a fork in the thickest part.

Pork ribs, any type	Meat pulls back from bone
Pork shoulder	195 to 205 degrees F to pull; 165 to 185 degrees F to slice
Pork (Boston) butt	195 to 205 degrees F to pull; 165 to 185 degrees F to slice
Pork tenderloin	155 to 160 degrees F
Pork loin	155 to 160 degrees F
Whole hog	185 degrees F
Pork sausage	165 degrees F
Beef brisket	185 to 195 degrees F
Beef tenderloin	130 to 140 degrees F medium rare; 150 degrees F medium;
	160 degrees F well done
Lamb (leg)	135 degrees F rare; 140 degrees F medium rare;
	150 degrees F medium; 160 degrees F well done
Cabrito	170 to 180 degrees F
Chicken	165 degrees F
Turkey	165 degrees F
Duck	165 degrees F

Grilling Timetable

When you grill, it's usually smaller, thinner cuts of meat cooking fast and hot. I prefer a medium-hot fire, around 400 degrees F, for beef and lamb; a medium fire, around 350 degrees F, for chicken, turkey, duck, and pork. When grilling food for contest judges—such as in the Anything Goes or Miscellaneous categories—remember it will continue to cook after you pull it off the grill. If you have to keep it warm for the judges, it will cook even further, so time your grilled foods accordingly. If you serve up well-done beef or pork to the judges, you might as well forget it.

Burgers	1/2 to 3/4 inch thick	7 to 9 minutes rare; 10 to 14 minutes medium; 14 to 16 minutes well done
Beef steak	1 inch thick	10 to 12 minutes rare; 12 to 14 minutes medium; 16 to 18 minutes well done
Lamb chops	1 inch thick	10 to 12 minutes rare; 12 to 14 minutes medium; 14 to 16 minutes well done
Pork loin or rib chops	1 inch thick	30 to 40 minutes medium; 40 to 50 minutes well done
Pork steak or blade	1 inch thick	30 to 40 minutes medium; 40 to 50 minutes well done
Pork tenderloin	2 inches thick	20 to 30 minutes medium; 30 to 40 minutes well done
Pork ribs	1 3/4 to 3 3/4 lbs.	2 3/4 to 4 1/2 hours
Veal chop	1 inch thick	8 to 10 minutes medium
Chicken breast	5 to 8 oz.	16 to 20 minutes
Chicken legs, thighs	5 to 8 oz.	30 minutes
Duck breast	3 to 5 oz.	6 to 10 minutes medium rare; 10 to 12 minutes medium; 12 to 14 minutes well done
Fish fillets or steaks	5 to 8 oz.	10 minutes per inch of thickness

Doneness Chart for Grilling

I recommend that if you're just starting off or you're in a contest, use an instant-read thermometer to test the doneness of most grilled foods. Just insert the thermometer in the thickest part and read the temperature. After a while, you'll be able to tell the doneness of grilled foods by touch alone. When you touch a pork tenderloin with a grill fork and it's still soft, that's rare. If the tenderloin offers some resistance, it's medium. When it's solid, it's well done.

Burgers can be made from beef, chicken, lamb, pork, or even tuna or salmon. Because they're all ground and have a similar texture and volume, they follow the same doneness guidelines. Fish doneness is best judged by appearance—fish is done when it begins to flake when tested with a fork in the thickest part, except for dense fish, such as tuna, swordfish, and monkfish, which turn opaque and the same color all the way through when well done.

Burgers	130 degrees F rare; 145 to 155 degrees F medium;
	160 degrees F well done
Beef steak and tenderloin	130 degrees F rare; 145 to 155 degrees F medium;
	160 degrees F well done
Lamb chops	135 degrees F rare
Pork loin or rib chops	145 to 150 degrees F medium
Pork steak or blade	145 to 150 degrees F medium
Pork tenderloin	145 to 150 degrees F medium
Pork ribs	Meat pulls back from the bone
Veal chops	155 to 160 degrees F medium; 160 degrees F well done
Chicken breast	165 degrees F
Chicken legs, thighs	165 degrees F
Duck breast	135 to 140 degrees F rare; 145 to 155 degrees F medium;
	165 degrees F well done
Fish fillets or steaks	Begins to flake when tested with a fork in thickest part
Shellfish	Opaque and somewhat firm to the touch

Placing Your Food in the Smoker

As you can see from the Smoking Timetable (see page 29), placing foods that need different cooking times in your smoker can be an art. For a Kansas City Barbeque Society–sanctioned cook-off, you'll be smoking two pork butts and two briskets, which take a long time, as well as 12 to 16 pieces of chicken and at least three slabs of ribs, which don't take as long. If you're at the Memphis in May invitational contest or the Great Pork BarbeQlossal in Iowa, which are both all-pork contests, you'll be doing whole pork shoulder, pork butt, pork loin/loin end, ribs, and maybe even a whole hog if you have the equipment for it. Plus, you may be entering a dish in the Miscellaneous, Side Dish, or other category that also needs to be smoked—barbecued baked beans or potato casserole, for instance.

The foods that take the longest—whole hog, pork shoulder, and brisket—start smoking the night before the contest. They should be ready in the wee hours of the morning, so you can pull them off and put on the ribs, pork butt, and whole chickens. If the pork shoulder and brisket are not quite done, then you put them in a place on your smoker where there is not as much heat and smoke and let them finish cooking. Your grill thermometers will tell you where the lower heat area is.

Generally, the foods at the top of the smoker get more smoky flavor because there's more air circulation there. If you hang your ribs and brisket, or if you have a bullet smoker with two racks, one on top of the other, you can place your ribs or brisket on the top rack and a side dish, such as a pan of barbecued baked beans, on the lower rack to catch some of the dripping juices from the barbecuing foods on the top rack.

Rotating foods in your smoker is something you learn as you go. If your ribs aren't getting done, you may have to transfer them to a hotter part of the smoker. If they're getting too done too fast, you can transfer them to a cooler part of the smoker. That's when backyard experience comes in handy. If you know what your ribs, brisket, pork butt, and whatever else you're cooking should look like and feel like every hour they're cooking, you'll know when to speed things up or slow things down at a contest. If you know the hotter and colder places on your smoker, then you'll know how to rotate your foods.

Whether in a contest or in the back yard, you'll want to make the most out of the space you have in your smoker. I hang all my food, so I have great use of space in my vertical smoker. If your smoker is more horizontal, such as a 55-gallon drum that has been cut in half or a kettle grill, you'll also want to think vertically. You can buy rib racks, which allow you to smoke your ribs vertically while sitting on the grill grate. That's also the idea behind beer-can chicken, a whole chicken that sits upright on an open beer can stuck in its cavity to slow smoke. You can fit more foods on your smoker if they're upright, rather than horizontal.

You also have to be able to keep cooked foods warm, such as your slow-smoked whole hog, pork shoulder, and brisket. For example, rules for a KCBS-sanctioned contest state that all contest food must be maintained in a covered container at an internal temperature of 140 degrees F.

If you're just doing foods in the back yard for a crowd, you always have your kitchen oven at hand to keep cooked foods warm. But if you're at a contest, you need to have one piece of equipment or an area of your smoker ready on the day of the contest to keep food warm. Some teams just use large Styrofoam coolers to keep foods warm. Others use a designated kettle grill kept going at a low temperature for this job. I have one area of my smoker that is generally low, and that's where I keep foods warm before judging.

REPLENISHING CHARCOAL, WOOD, AND WATER

When you slow smoke foods, you have to replenish the charcoal, wood, and water periodically. How often and how much depends partly on the weather and partly on the temperature you're trying to maintain. When the temperature on your grill thermometer starts to dip 5 to 10 degrees F below your ideal temperature, it's time to add more charcoal. When you see that there isn't much smoke coming out from your smoker—usually after 4 to 5 hours—it's time to add more wood. How much depends on the size of your rig. For a kettle grill or a WSM, add about 20 hot briquettes and 1 to 3 chunks of hardwood. For my pig cooker, I add 3 to 4 pounds of briquettes or 3 sticks of seasoned hardwood. The water pan generally dries out after 4 to 5 hours of smoking, so you'll need to add more water at that time.

When to Baste and Slather, Glaze, and Sauce

I like the nuances of flavor contributed by various slathers, dry rubs, and marinades applied before cooking; bastes applied during cooking; and glazes and sauces applied at the end of cooking. Slathers, dry rubs, and marinades go on the foods before they are cooked. I usually start basting and slathering my barbecue about halfway through the smoking process at 30-minute intervals. That means that if ribs are smoking for 3 hours, I start basting or slathering after 1½ hours and continue to baste or slather every 30 minutes after that, until about 30 minutes before the food is done so I can be ready to glaze.

Glazing gives your food a final, unique touch; a glaze makes certain kinds of barbecue look and taste good. You would glaze a chicken breast, a slab of ribs, or a brisket because you will see the exterior. You wouldn't glaze a pork butt that was meant to be shredded for pulled pork because you won't see the exterior among all the other shreds of meat. The final glazing is done minutes before serving. I use any number of commercial and homemade barbecue sauces and paint them on the food. Then I put the food on the smoker or over the direct heat of the grill to cook the sauce to a shiny glaze on the surface of the beef, chicken, or pork, rotating or turning it after about 15 minutes. I also pass sauce at the table in the back yard. In competition, you're not always allowed to include extra sauce with your entry.

Keeping Records

I keep records every time I barbecue for a contest or a special occasion. I have logbooks that go back to 1981. There are so many factors that determine the outcome of my barbecue, and I keep track of them all. When I win a contest, I want to know exactly what I did to get there so I can do some of the same things the next time.

I record the date and the weather—the temperature and whether the day is cloudy, sunny, rainy, windy, or calm. Because I cook outdoors, the weather is a factor that has to be accounted for. In warm, calm weather, food cooks faster. In cold, rainy, or windy weather, food cooks slower.

I also record what I've cooked and how I prepared it—which dry rub or marinade, baste or slather, sauce or glaze I used; how long it marinated or sat with the rub on; and how and when I basted, slathered, sauced, and glazed. I record how much charcoal I used, which and how much of certain kinds of woods, and what I put in the water pan (usually just water). I jot down exactly how long each type of food took to barbecue and how it looked.

Special Event Cooking Tips

Once you get to be good, people will seek you out to smoke ribs, brisket, or chicken for church festivals or school fairs. For special event cooking, I usually smoke the ribs, brisket, or whatever at least a day ahead of time. Then I wrap my smoked foods with heavy-duty plastic wrap so no more smoke will permeate. When the plastic hits the hot food, it practically shrink-wraps it. Then I place the wrapped food in the refrigerator, where it will keep for 1 to 2 weeks. I find that wrapping the meat in foil is not good because the seasoning on the meats sometimes eats through the foil, causing holes or tears that let the meat dry out.

You can keep plastic-wrapped foods warm on your smoker if the temperature is below 265 degrees F (as it should be!). At 265 degrees F, plastic begins to melt and burn. But if you are within the ideal 230 to 250 degrees F, you're fine.

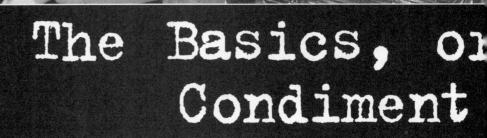

The Basics, or Condiment

The Baron's Cupboard

This chapter is for barbecue purists—and that group includes me—who want to make everything from scratch. When I compete in a barbecue contest, I use the best products available because I want to do everything I can to win. If I think a commercial product is equal to homemade, I go with convenience; otherwise, I make it from scratch.

In the big barbecue contests—Memphis in May, the American Royal, and Jack Daniel's—hundreds of teams compete. Anything you can do to give yourself that edge needed to win is a good idea. Ninety-nine percent of the time you can taste the difference between homemade and commercial, so it's worthwhile to invest the time and effort in your kitchen. I've had people write me that they made the ketchup from *Paul Kirk's Championship Barbecue Sauces* (The Harvard Common Press, 1998) and it really made a difference in their homemade barbecue sauce and their contest results.

When you make your own Hot Chile Oil (page 50) or Homemade Worcestershire Sauce (page 50) to go into marinades or sauces, you know nobody else on any of the other hundreds of teams will have anything like it. If you have homemade condiments, such as Cranberry Ketchup (page 45) or Chipotle Mango Barbecue Ketchup (page 45), you can make fantastic sandwiches with any barbecued meat, chicken, or fish. With Homemade Tomato Paste (page 39), Chili Sauce (page 42), or any of the various kinds of homemade ketchups, you can create your own signature sauce. So, on a late summer weekend when you're not signed up for a barbecue contest, go to a farmer's' market and buy a couple bushels of fresh tomatoes. Bring them home and start making paste, chili sauce, and ketchups and see whether you don't taste the difference—my bet is that you will.

Here are a few techniques that will make the process easier.

Peeling Tomatoes

To peel fresh tomatoes, place each one in boiling water for 30 seconds to 2 minutes, until you see the skin begin to crack. Remove it from the water with a slotted spoon and drain on paper towels. Let cool slightly and the peel will come off very easily by hand or with a paring knife.

Canning Tomato Pastes, Sauces, and Ketchups of All Kinds

If you're not going to use all your tomato paste or ketchup right away, then you may want to can it. This sounds harder than it actually is.

First, you need to buy glass canning jars with metal lids and rings from a hardware or grocery store. Wash the jars, lids, and rings in hot, soapy water and rinse. When you're ready to can, bring a large pot of water to a boil and place the jars, lids, and rings in the boiling water for at least 10 minutes to sterilize them. Keep them in the hot water while you're finishing up the paste or ketchup recipe.

Remove the hot jars from the water with tongs and sit them upright on a flat surface. Use a funnel or a ladle to fill the jars with the hot mixture, leaving about ⅛-inch headspace so the mixture does not touch the lid. Using kitchen towels to protect your hands, place a lid on each jar, then screw on the rings. Tighten them according to the manufacturer's directions. Set each filled canning jar back into the pot of boiling water. Usually, a large pot holds about 6 canning jars. The water should reach up to the necks of the jars.

Process in the water bath for the time the recipe states. Most ketchups need to be processed for 15 minutes. Start timing when the water begins to boil. When the time is up, remove the jars from the water bath with tongs and place them at least 1 inch apart on kitchen towels to cool. Check to make sure the seals are tight on the jars. Then store the jars in a cool, dark place for up to a year. Refrigerate any jar after you open it.

Freezing Tomato Paste, Ketchup, and Salsa

You can also freeze your homemade basics. Ladle the mixture into freezer containers, leaving ½-inch headspace. Let cool to room temperature. Label and date the containers and freeze them for up to 10 months.

Homemade Tomato Paste

Homemade tomato paste is not as dense as the commercial variety. You get a different texture that is easier to use in making barbecue sauce. MAKES 3 HALF-PINTS

> 14 to 15 pounds ripe red tomatoes, peeled and chopped
>
> ¾ cup cider vinegar

1 Put the tomatoes in an 8- to 10-quart nonreactive saucepan and bring to a boil. Reduce the heat to medium-low and simmer gently until most of the liquid has evaporated, about 1 hour. Remove from the heat.

2 Put the tomatoes through a food mill. Discard the seeds. Transfer the juice and pulp to a large nonreactive saucepan and bring to a boil. Reduce the heat to medium-low and simmer briskly until the mixture has reduced and thickened and coats the back of a spoon, 6 to 7 hours, stirring occasionally to prevent scorching and sticking.

3 Stir in the vinegar and remove from the heat.

4 Pour the hot mixture into hot, sterile canning jars, leaving ⅛-inch headspace, and seal. Can (see page 38) by processing in a water bath for 15 minutes. Or simply let cool and refrigerate. Tomato paste will keep, refrigerated, for up to 2 weeks; canned or frozen it will keep for up to 1 year.

The Baron's Basic Tomato Sauce

The flavor of homemade tomato sauce is superior to that of store-bought. My wife's aunt used to make her own tomato juice and sauce—it was so much better than what you can buy. So I've become a nut about making my own homemade tomato products for competition.

MAKES ABOUT 4 CUPS

> 6 cups peeled, seeded, and chopped ripe red tomatoes
>
> 1 cup seeded and minced green bell peppers
>
> 1 cup minced onions
>
> 1/2 cup minced celery with its leaves
>
> 1/4 cup grated carrot
>
> 1 tablespoon minced fresh parsley leaves
>
> 1 tablespoon minced fresh basil leaves
>
> 2 cloves garlic, pressed
>
> 1 teaspoon non-iodized salt
>
> 1/2 teaspoon white pepper

1 Combine all the ingredients in a large nonreactive saucepan. Bring to a boil, reduce the heat to medium-low, and simmer, uncovered, until most of the liquid has evaporated, about 45 minutes. Remove from the heat.

2 Transfer to a food processor and process until smooth. Refrigerate overnight before using to let the flavors develop. Keeps refrigerated for up to 1 week, frozen for up to 1 year.

THE BARON'S BASIC INGREDIENTS

To make the best tomato pastes and sauces, ketchups, mustards, and Worcestershire sauces, you have to use the best ingredients. For me, that means:

* Ripe, fresh vegetables, such as tomatoes, bell peppers, chiles, celery, and onions

* Granulated cane sugar (it says that on the bag), not sugar made from beets

* Fresh herbs, such as parsley and basil

* Dry mustard (I use Colman's)

* Vinegars (I use cider or white distilled, depending on the recipe)

* Fresh spices, such as cloves, allspice, cinnamon, and coriander; don't use spices that have been in your cupboard for years (if I use dry spices I buy from a spice company that sells fresh-ground spices and herbs)

* Non-iodized salt, such as kosher or sea salt (have you tasted that other stuff?)

Tomato Sauce Picante

This is a thicker tomato sauce with a more velvety texture and a little bit of a kick from the cayenne. MAKES 3 CUPS

> 1 pound ripe red tomatoes, peeled, seeded, and chopped
>
> One 6-ounce can tomato paste or 3/4 cup homemade (page 39)
>
> 1/2 cup chopped onion
>
> 1/4 cup seeded and chopped green bell pepper
>
> 1 teaspoon Worcestershire sauce, homemade (page 50) or store-bought
>
> 1 teaspoon minced fresh parsley leaves

1/4 teaspoon dried oregano leaves

1/4 teaspoon cayenne pepper

1/8 teaspoon dried basil leaves

2 tablespoons unsalted butter

2 tablespoons all-purpose flour

1 Place all the ingredients, except the butter and flour, in a food processor and process until smooth.

2 Transfer to a large nonreactive saucepan and bring to a boil. Reduce the heat to medium-low and simmer, uncovered, until the sauce starts to thicken, 45 minutes to an hour, stirring occasionally.

3 Melt the butter in a small saucepan over medium heat and blend in the flour with a wire whisk until smooth. Blend this into the tomato sauce and cook until thickened. Keeps refrigerated for up to 1 week, frozen for up to 1 year.

Onion-Garlic Tomato Sauce

A little more savory than the previous two tomato sauces, this recipe is adapted from one by my friend Kate Naug, who uses this as a base for her Bloody, Bloody Marys—a great eye-opener for early barbecue contest mornings when you've basically been up all night. I like to include celery leaves, too. They add flavor and color. MAKES ABOUT 4 CUPS

1 tablespoon olive oil

2 cups diced onions

1/2 cup diced celery with its leaves

1/4 cup seeded and diced green bell pepper

1/4 cup grated carrot

2 cloves garlic, pressed

4 cups peeled, seeded, and diced ripe red tomatoes

1 sprig fresh thyme, basil, or tarragon

2 teaspoons granulated cane sugar

1 teaspoon fine sea salt

1 teaspoon freshly ground black pepper

1 Heat the olive oil in a large nonreactive saucepan over medium-low heat. Add the onions, celery, green pepper, carrot, and garlic and cook for about 5 minutes, stirring a few times. Add the remaining ingredients and cook until thick, 45 to 50 minutes.

2 Push the sauce through a fine-mesh strainer. Keeps refrigerated for 3 or 4 days, frozen for up to 1 year.

Hot and Sweet Tomato Sauce

In competition barbecue, a touch of sweetness sometimes makes all the difference in a barbecue sauce or glaze. Not all judges have well-developed palates, but everybody can taste sweet. MAKES ABOUT 2 1/2 CUPS

1 cup diced onions

6 cloves garlic, peeled

3 tablespoons unsalted butter

2 cups peeled, seeded, and diced ripe red tomatoes

1/4 cup clover honey

1 teaspoon ground ginger

1 teaspoon ground coriander

1 teaspoon cayenne pepper

1 teaspoon fine sea salt

1 teaspoon freshly ground black pepper

1/2 teaspoon ground cinnamon

1 Place the onions and garlic in a blender or food processor and process until smooth.

2 Melt the butter over medium heat in a medium-size nonreactive saucepan; add the onion mixture and cook, stirring, until the liquid has evaporated, 7 to 10 minutes. Stir in the remaining ingredients and simmer, stirring a few times, until soft and well blended, 10 to 12 minutes. Keeps refrigerated for 3 or 4 days, frozen for up to 1 year.

Homemade Chili Sauce

A gallon of chopped tomatoes seems like a lot, but after you buy a bushel or two of tomatoes from your friendly local farmer, they'll go quickly. I love this chili sauce on smoked meatloaf or barbecued brisket sandwich. **MAKES 5 TO 6 PINTS**

> 1 gallon peeled, seeded, and chopped ripe red tomatoes
>
> 1½ cups seeded and diced red bell peppers
>
> 1½ cups seeded and diced green bell peppers
>
> 1 cup diced onions
>
> 1 clove garlic, pressed
>
> 1 teaspoon ground allspice
>
> 1 teaspoon ground cinnamon
>
> ½ teaspoon ground cloves
>
> 1 cup distilled white vinegar
>
> 1 cup cider vinegar
>
> 1 cup granulated cane sugar
>
> 2 tablespoons fine sea salt

1 Place the tomatoes, bell peppers, onions, and garlic in a large nonreactive saucepan and bring to a boil. Stir in the spices. Reduce the heat

to medium-low and simmer, covered, until the mixture is reduced by half, about 2 hours, stirring frequently.

2 Add the remaining ingredients, bring to a boil, and let boil vigorously for 5 minutes, stirring constantly. Pour the hot mixture into hot, sterile canning jars, leaving ⅛-inch headspace, and seal. Can (see page 38) by processing in a water bath for 15 minutes. Store in a cool, dark place, or in the refrigerator once opened, where it will keep for up to a year.

Spicy Sweet Chili Sauce

With crushed red pepper, pickling spice, and sugar, this chili sauce is great to use in Spicy, Hot, and Chunky Barbecue Sauce (page 145), Southern Barbecue Sauce (page 150), Jack Daniel's Barbecue Sauce (page 143), or Hot Barbecue Sauce (page 141). **MAKES 6 PINTS**

> 1 gallon peeled, seeded, and chopped ripe red tomatoes
>
> 2½ cups chopped onions
>
> 2 cups seeded and chopped red bell peppers
>
> 1 cup granulated cane sugar
>
> 3 tablespoons fine sea salt
>
> ¼ cup pickling spice
>
> 1 tablespoon crushed red pepper
>
> 1 tablespoon yellow mustard seeds
>
> 1 tablespoon celery seeds
>
> 2½ cups cider vinegar

1 Combine the tomatoes, onions, bell pepper, sugar, and salt in a nonreactive stockpot. Bring to a boil, then reduce the heat to medium-low and slowly simmer for 30 to 45 minutes.

2   Tie the pickling spice, crushed red pepper, mustard seeds, and celery seeds in a cheesecloth bag. Immerse this in the tomato mixture and cook 30 to 45 minutes longer. As the mixture thickens, stir frequently to prevent sticking.

3   Add the vinegar and cook slowly until it is as thick as you want it.

4   Pour the hot mixture into hot, sterile canning jars, leaving $\frac{1}{8}$-inch headspace, and seal. Can (see page 38) by processing in a water bath for 15 minutes. Store in a cool, dark place, or in the refrigerator once opened, where it will keep for up to 1 year.

Homemade Tomato Ketchup

For homemade ketchup, you don't have to peel the tomatoes, which saves you a step. The skins come off when you pass the cooked ketchup through a strainer or food mill. This ketchup is great used as is or as a base for your own signature barbecue sauce. MAKES 4 TO 5 PINTS

$1\frac{1}{2}$ **gallons chopped meaty, ripe red tomatoes**

2 cups chopped onions

2 cups cider vinegar

$\frac{1}{2}$ **cup seeded and chopped red bell pepper**

$\frac{1}{2}$ **cup chopped celery with its leaves**

4 cloves garlic, pressed

2 tablespoons fine sea salt

2 tablespoons coriander seeds

1 tablespoon yellow mustard seeds

1 tablespoon allspice berries

1 tablespoon black peppercorns

1 bay leaf

1 teaspoon whole cloves

$\frac{1}{4}$ **teaspoon celery seeds**

$\frac{1}{4}$ **teaspoon crushed red pepper**

$\frac{1}{2}$ **cup firmly packed light brown sugar**

$\frac{1}{4}$ **cup granulated cane sugar**

1   Place the tomatoes in a large nonreactive stockpot. Bring them to a boil, reduce the heat to medium-low, and simmer, stirring occasionally, until soft, 30 to 45 minutes.

2   Add the onions, vinegar, bell pepper, celery, garlic, and salt and return to a boil. Put all the spices and herbs in a cheesecloth bag and add to the tomato mixture. Stir in both sugars until they dissolve and simmer over medium to medium-high heat, stirring often, until it thickens, 30 to 60 minutes, depending on how ripe and juicy the tomatoes are.

3   Pour into a large sieve or china cap and strain, pressing the vegetables hard to get all the flavor and juices out of them. Press the spice bag to extract its flavor. Discard the pulp, seeds, and spice bag. Strain again through a finer sieve for smoother ketchup. If it's not thick enough, return it to a nonreactive saucepan, bring to a boil, reduce the heat to medium-low, and simmer until the ketchup clings to the back of a spoon. It will thicken more on cooling.

4   To bottle, pour into clean, hot, sterile bottles or jars, leaving $\frac{1}{2}$-inch headspace, and seal. Can (see page 38) by processing in a water bath for 10 minutes. Let the ketchup age for 2 weeks—or better yet, for a month—before using. Store in a cool, dark place, or in the refrigerator once opened, where it will keep for up to a year.

The Baron's Other Tomato Ketchup

This recipe is based on a ketchup my Great Grandma Kirk used to make. It's a favorite in our family. **MAKES 5 TO 6 PINTS**

8 pounds ripe red tomatoes, chopped

1 pound yellow onions, chopped

3 cloves garlic, pressed

2 bay leaves

1 hot red chile

1 cup firmly packed light brown sugar

2 tablespoons allspice berries

One 3-inch-long cinnamon stick

2 teaspoons kosher salt

1 teaspoon freshly ground black pepper

1 teaspoon ground cloves

2 cups cider vinegar

1 Place the tomatoes, onions, garlic, bay leaves, and chile in a large nonreactive stockpot. Bring to a boil, then simmer over medium-low heat until soft, about 45 minutes. Strain through a fine mesh sieve or put through a food mill. This should yield about 2 quarts of tomato purée.

2 Return the purée to the pot and blend in the brown sugar, stirring until dissolved. Put the allspice berries and cinnamon stick in a cheesecloth bag and add to the purée along with the salt, pepper, and cloves. Bring to a boil, reduce the heat to medium-low, and simmer briskly, stirring constantly, until reduced by half, about 15 minutes.

3 Adjust the seasonings, if needed. Remove the spice bag and stir in the vinegar. Simmer 10 to 15 minutes longer.

4 Pour into hot, sterilized bottles or jars, leaving 1/2-inch headspace, and seal. Can (see page 38) by processing in a water bath for 15 minutes. Store in a cool, dark place, or in the refrigerator once opened, where it will keep for up to a year.

French-Canadian Ketchup

This sauce makes a great base for your chunky barbecue sauce, or serve it as is with barbecue or grilled steaks and chops. Because I was born in British Columbia, I have taken several liberties with the French-Canadian version, which is more chutney-like than American ketchup. **MAKES 4 TO 6 CUPS**

4 cups peeled, seeded, and chopped red or green tomatoes

2 cups chopped white onions

1 cup chopped celery

1 cup peeled, pitted, and chopped ripe peaches

1 cup peeled, cored, and chopped pears

1 cup peeled, cored, and chopped apples

1 1/2 cups distilled white vinegar

1 1/2 cups granulated cane sugar

4 cloves garlic, pressed

2 bay leaves

1 teaspoon crushed red pepper

1 teaspoon ground allspice

1 teaspoon fine sea salt

1 teaspoon freshly ground black pepper

1 Place all the ingredients in a large, nonreactive heavy-bottomed saucepan. Cook over medium-low heat, stirring occasionally, until the ketchup is thick and has the consistency of chutney, 2 1/2 to 3 hours.

2 Ladle into hot, sterilized jars, leaving ½-inch headroom, seal, let cool, and refrigerate. Or can (see page 38) by processing in a water bath for 15 minutes. Keeps, refrigerated, for up to 1 month, canned, for up to 1 year in a cool, dark place.

Chipotle-Mango Barbecue Ketchup

Say goodbye to ho-hum ketchup. I love this on barbecue leftovers—smoked chicken, duck, turkey, or pork. I use a microplane grater to grate the ginger—sometimes I don't even peel it first because it's so easy to grate that way.
MAKES ABOUT 4 CUPS

¼ cup (½ stick) unsalted butter

2 tablespoons pressed garlic

1 cup minced red onions

4 cups tomato ketchup, homemade (page 43) or store-bought

2 cups peeled, seeded, and diced ripe mango

2 cups rice vinegar

1 cup firmly packed light brown sugar

½ cup clover honey

2 tablespoons peeled and grated fresh ginger

1 tablespoon pure ground chipotle chile

2 teaspoons ground ginger

2 teaspoons ground allspice

1 teaspoon ground cloves

1 teaspoon fine sea salt

1 teaspoon freshly ground black pepper

1 Melt the butter in a large nonreactive saucepan over medium heat, add the garlic and onions, and cook, stirring, until translucent. Add the remaining ingredients and bring to a boil. Reduce

the heat to medium-low and simmer until thickened, about 30 minutes.

2 Transfer to a food processor or blender and process until smooth. If you want a thicker ketchup, you can simmer it some more after you purée it.

3 Pour into hot, sterilized jars, leaving ½-inch headroom, seal, let cool, and refrigerate. Or can (see page 38) by processing in a water bath for 15 minutes. Keeps, refrigerated, for up to 1 month, canned, for up to 1 year in a cool, dark place.

Cranberry Ketchup

A lot of barbecuers and other cooks ask, "Why would anyone want to make, say, cranberry, beet, or—better yet—mushroom ketchup?" It's simple—just for the variety or to add to your barbecue sauce as that secret ingredient. These ketchups are all delicious on sandwiches or with smoked meats and make good bases for steak sauces and salsas. Let your imagination run wild! MAKES ABOUT 3 PINTS

3 pounds fresh cranberries, picked over for stems and rinsed

1 quart cider vinegar

3 cups granulated cane sugar

1 tablespoon ground cinnamon

2 teaspoons ground cloves

¼ teaspoon ground allspice

1 Place the cranberries in a large nonreactive stockpot and add enough of the vinegar to cover them. Bring to a boil, reduce the heat to medium-low, and simmer until the cranberries are tender, 8 to 10 minutes.

2   Work the mixture through a fine-mesh sieve or place in a food processor and process until smooth.

3   Transfer the cranberry purée to a clean large nonreactive saucepan. Blend in the sugar and spices. Heat over medium-low heat, stirring until the sugar dissolves. Simmer, stirring constantly, until the ketchup thickens, about 15 minutes.

4   Pour into hot, sterilized jars or bottles, leaving 1/2-inch headspace, seal, and let cool before refrigerating. Or can (see page 38) by processing in a water bath for 15 minutes. Keeps, refrigerated, for up to 2 weeks, canned, for up to 1 year in a cool, dark place.

Spicy Beet Ketchup

Dark purple and spicy, this ketchup is great on burgers, hot dogs, and fried potatoes. I first started making this when my son Todd was on a special diet. We ate it on everything. MAKES ABOUT 1 1/2 CUPS

> One 16-ounce can beets, with liquid
>
> 1/2 cup distilled white vinegar
>
> 1/4 cup granulated cane sugar
>
> 2 tablespoons grated onion
>
> 1/2 teaspoon non-iodized salt
>
> 1/4 teaspoon ground cinnamon
>
> 1/4 teaspoon ground ginger
>
> 1/8 teaspoon ground mace
>
> 1/8 teaspoon ground allspice

1   In a small nonreactive saucepan over medium-high heat, combine the beets, vinegar,

sugar, onion, and salt. Cook, stirring, until the sugar dissolves. Remove from the heat and let cool.

2   Transfer to a food processor, add the remaining ingredients, and process until smooth.

3   Pour into a jar with a tight-fitting lid. Keeps, refrigerated, for up to 2 weeks.

NOTE If you want this ketchup to be thicker, reduce the beet juice or blend in a flour slurry (1 tablespoon all-purpose flour shaken in a jar with 3 tablespoons water until smooth) and cook until thickened. I suggest you don't use cornstarch for the slurry.

Mushroom Ketchup

Great Grandma LeCluyse called her recipe "catsup," but it's delicious no matter how you spell it. This is great with beef, whether grilled, smoked, or roasted. MAKES 2 TO 3 CUPS

> 2 pounds mushrooms, trimmed and sliced
>
> 1 cup water
>
> 1 bay leaf
>
> 1 cup cider vinegar
>
> 1 tablespoon non-iodized salt
>
> 1 1/2 teaspoons ground cinnamon
>
> 1/2 teaspoon cayenne pepper
>
> 1/4 teaspoon ground cloves
>
> 1/4 teaspoon ground mace
>
> 1/8 teaspoon garlic powder

1   Place the mushrooms, water, and bay leaf in a large nonreactive saucepan; bring to a boil. Reduce the heat to medium-low and simmer until soft and thickened, 35 to 40 minutes. Remove the bay leaf and discard.

2 Transfer to a food processor and process until smooth or rub through a fine-mesh sieve.

3 Return to the saucepan and stir in the remaining ingredients. Cook over medium heat, stirring occasionally, until it reaches a consistency somewhere between a purée and a commercial ketchup, about 30 minutes.

4 Remove from the heat, pour into hot, sterilized bottles, leaving 1/2-inch headroom, seal, let cool, and refrigerate. Or can (see page 38) by processing in a water bath for 15 minutes. Keeps, refrigerated, for up to 2 weeks, canned, for up to 1 year in a cool, dark place.

South of the Border Ketchup

You get down to those Texas barbecue contests and you better be ready. They're serious about barbecued brisket and clod (beef shoulder), barbecued homemade sausage, and barbecued pinto bean dishes. And your ketchup better have a little kick to it, too. **MAKES 4 TO 6 PINTS**

- **2 quarts cider vinegar**
- **50 small red chiles, such as ripe jalapeño or serrano chiles, chopped**
- **4 large onions, minced**
- **2 medium-size carrots, minced**
- **1/4 cup peeled and grated fresh horseradish**
- **1 cup non-iodized salt**
- **1 cup firmly packed light brown sugar**
- **1/2 cup yellow mustard seeds**

1 Place all the ingredients in a large nonreactive stockpot and bring to a boil. Reduce the heat to medium-low and simmer until the chiles and onions are soft, 35 to 45 minutes.

2 Transfer to a fine mesh sieve and push through or put through a food mill, discarding the pulp.

3 Transfer the purée to a large nonreactive saucepan, bring to a boil, reduce the heat to medium, and simmer for 10 minutes. Let cool, then refrigerate overnight, then pour into hot, sterilized bottles. Or can (see page 38) by processing in a water bath for 15 minutes. Keeps, refrigerated, for up to 2 weeks, canned, for up to 6 months in a cool, dark place.

Roasted Red Bell Pepper Ketchup

This very gourmet ketchup is great with grilled chicken or pork. **MAKES ABOUT 4 CUPS**

- **2 tablespoons canola oil**
- **1/4 cup diced onion**
- **2 tablespoons grated carrot**
- **1 tablespoon pressed garlic**
- **2 cups roasted red peppers, homemade (page 48) or store-bought, chopped**
- **1 tablespoon seeded and minced jalapeño chile**
- **1/4 cup malt vinegar**
- **2 tablespoons clover honey**
- **2 tablespoons molasses**
- **2 tablespoons firmly packed light brown sugar**
- **1 teaspoon pure ground chipotle chile**
- **1 teaspoon ground cinnamon**
- **1/2 teaspoon ground cloves**
- **1/4 teaspoon ground nutmeg**
- **1 teaspoon fine sea salt**
- **1 teaspoon coarsely ground black pepper**

How to ROAST a Red Bell Pepper

If you want an intensified flavor, then roast your bell pepper. If you want a smoky flavor as well, smoke-roast it (see page 98).

Rub a red bell pepper all over with about 1 tablespoon of canola oil and set aside.

To roast the pepper on a grill or over a stovetop flame, prepare a hot fire in a grill or turn a gas stovetop burner on high. To roast on the grill or stovetop, use a pair of tongs to hold the pepper over the flames until it chars on all sides. Transfer the pepper to a paper bag, close the bag, and let the pepper steam for 15 minutes. Remove the skin with a paring knife, then seed and chop the pepper.

To roast the pepper in the oven, preheat the oven to 350 degrees F. Place the pepper on a baking sheet and roast for 15 minutes. Transfer the pepper to a paper bag, close the bag, and let the pepper steam for 15 minutes. Remove the skin with a paring knife, then seed and chop the pepper.

Roasted red pepper will keep, covered, in the refrigerator for up to 1 week or frozen for up to 3 months.

---

1 Heat the canola oil in a large nonreactive saucepan over medium-high heat, add the onion, carrot, and garlic, and cook, stirring, until the vegetables are soft but not browned, 5 to 7 minutes. Add the roasted red peppers and jalapeño and cook until hot, stirring, 3 to 5 minutes.

2 Transfer to a food processor or a blender and process until smooth.

3 Return the mixture to the saucepan and add the remaining ingredients. Bring to a boil, then reduce the heat to medium-low and simmer until thickened, stirring occasionally to avoid sticking, about 30 minutes.

4 Pour into hot, sterilized jars or bottles, leaving 1/2-inch headroom, seal, let cool, and refrigerate. Or can (see page 38) by processing in a water bath for 15 minutes. Keeps, refrigerated, for up to 2 weeks, canned, for up to 1 year in a cool, dark place.

Concord Grape Ketchup

Concord grapes, a true American grape, are what purple grape juice and grape jelly are made from. This ketchup is good on fish and chicken. MAKES ABOUT 5 CUPS

4 pounds Concord grapes

2 pounds granulated cane sugar

2 cups distilled white vinegar

1 teaspoon fine sea salt

2 teaspoons whole cloves

2 teaspoons allspice berries

Two 3-inch-long cinnamon sticks

1 teaspoon crushed red pepper

1 Wash and remove the stems from the grapes. Place them in a large nonreactive saucepan or skillet, cover, and steam them without water until soft. Rub the fruit through a fine-mesh sieve or put

through a food mill, discarding the skin and seeds, if any.

2 Return the purée to the saucepan and add the sugar, vinegar, and salt. Tie the cloves, allspice, cinnamon sticks, and crushed red pepper in a cheesecloth spice bag and add to the saucepan. Bring to a boil, stirring until the sugar is dissolved, then reduce the heat to medium and simmer until you have a thick purée, about 20 minutes.

3 Pour into hot, sterilized jars, leaving ½-inch headroom, seal, let cool, and refrigerate. Or can (see page 38) by processing in a water bath for 15 minutes. Keeps, refrigerated, for up to 1 month, canned, for up to 1 year in a cool, dark place.

Spicy-Hot Mustard Sauce

Caution—this sauce can become addictive. It is great to use in a mustard slather (pages 86–101) to paint on a pork butt or brisket before you sprinkle on the rub and put it all on your pit to slow smoke. I get hungry just thinking about it. MAKES ABOUT 3¼ CUPS

- 1 cup all-purpose flour
- ¾ cup granulated cane sugar
- ⅔ cup dry mustard (I use Colman's)
- 1 teaspoon ground ginger
- 1 teaspoon granulated garlic
- 1 teaspoon fine sea salt
- ½ teaspoon white pepper
- ½ teaspoon cayenne pepper or pure ground chipotle chile
- ½ cup dry white wine
- ¼ cup distilled white vinegar
- ¼ cup water

1 Combine the flour, sugar, mustard, ginger, garlic, salt, white pepper, and cayenne pepper in a sifter and sift into a medium-size nonreactive bowl.

2 Combine the wine, vinegar, and water in a large glass measuring cup. Pour the liquid mixture into the dry ingredients, blending with a wire whisk until you have a smooth paste. Cover and let rest in the refrigerator for at least 6 hours or overnight before using. Keeps, refrigerated, for up to 6 months.

Chipotle Mustard

This recipe features one of the new "flavor profiles," or new flavoring agents, that have made headway in traditional barbecue circles. Mustards—used in sauces and slathers—are becoming popular again. MAKES ABOUT ¾ CUP

- ¼ cup yellow mustard seeds
- ¼ cup cider vinegar
- ½ cup Dijon mustard
- 2 tablespoons dry mustard (I use Colman's)
- 1 tablespoon clover honey
- 2 cloves smoked garlic (page 98), mashed
- 1 teaspoon pure ground chipotle chile, or more to taste
- ½ teaspoon fine sea salt
- ½ teaspoon white pepper

Combine all the ingredients in a small nonreactive bowl until well blended. Taste and correct the salt and pepper, if necessary. Keeps, refrigerated, for up to 1 week.

Hot Chile Oil

I often use this oil in marinades for a jolt of flavor. I have also brushed it directly on chicken breasts and pork chops before grilling them. **MAKES 1 QUART**

12 fresh or dried hot chile peppers

4 large cloves garlic, halved

Two 1/4-inch-thick slices peeled fresh ginger

1 quart peanut oil

1 Place the chiles, garlic, and ginger in a sterile jar or bottle. Pour in the peanut oil to 1/2 inch from the top of the jar or bottle, seal, label, and date. Let the oil rest in the refrigerator for 10 to 14 days before using.

2 After opening, strain out the chiles and garlic, then keep the oil refrigerated. Let the oil come to room temperature before using.

Homemade Worcestershire Sauce

Making your own Worcestershire sauce can make a big difference in the taste of your food. Taste a little bit of commercial Worcestershire sauce, then taste this and you'll understand why. **MAKES ABOUT 1 CUP**

3/4 cup soy sauce

2 tablespoons blackstrap molasses

1 tablespoon firmly packed light brown sugar

1 tablespoon cider vinegar

1 hot chile pepper, such as jalapeño or serrano, split open

1/2 a whole nutmeg

6 cloves

One 1-inch-square piece lemon peel

One 1-inch piece fresh ginger, peeled and thinly sliced

1 Combine all the ingredients in a small non-reactive saucepan and heat slowly over medium-low heat. Simmer for 10 minutes, then remove from the heat, cover, and let rest, refrigerated, for 24 hours.

2 Strain and transfer to a sterilized bottle. Keeps, tightly covered in the refrigerator, for up to 3 months.

Traditional Worcestershire Sauce

Legend has it that Worcestershire sauce dates back to Roman times in England, when the Romans kept fermented barrels of fish and made a sauce called liquamen from it. This version of Worcestershire sauce is a little more involved, but it's closer to the ancient recipe, and that's good for the ancient tradition of barbecue. Tamarind pulp, which is sour tasting, is available at Asian markets. To use it, soak the pulp in hot water to cover, remove the seeds with your fingers and discard them, then use the pulp. Kidney beans are an option and are less expensive, but they are less flavorful as well. **MAKES 1 GALLON**

1 pound tamarind pulp, prepared as directed in headnote, or cooked red kidney beans, drained

3/4 cup soy sauce

4 cloves garlic, pressed

1 ounce oil-packed sardines or anchovies, rinsed with vinegar

6 quarts peeled, cored, and chopped tart apples

2 cups chopped yellow onions

3 tablespoons ground cloves

3 tablespoons ground allspice

3 tablespoons instant coffee or 3 cups strong
   brewed coffee

2 tablespoons turmeric

2 tablespoons ground mace

1 gallon cider vinegar

$1/3$ cup non-iodized salt

$1/2$ cup molasses

3 tablespoons dry mustard (I use Colman's)

2 tablespoons firmly packed light brown sugar

2 teaspoons cayenne pepper

1 Place the prepared tamarind pulp, soy sauce, garlic, and sardines in a food processor, process until smooth, and set aside.

2 Place the apples, onions, cloves, allspice, coffee, turmeric, and mace in a nonreactive 4- or 5-gallon pot. Pour in the vinegar. Bring to a boil, then reduce the heat to low and simmer, uncovered, until the apples are soft, 2 to $2^1/2$ hours, stirring frequently so the apples don't scorch. If the vinegar evaporates, replenish with half vinegar and half water, just enough so the mixture doesn't burn.

3 Remove from the heat and run the mixture through a food mill, discarding any pulp. Place 2 quarts of the apple purée in a large bowl, add the reserved tamarind mixture and the remaining ingredients, blend well, and pour into sterilized 1-gallon glass jars or jugs. Top off with cider vinegar, shake well, and let stand overnight before using. Store in a cool, dark place for up to 3 months.

Around the World Worcestershire Sauce

From the Spice Islands to the Caribbean, just about every port of call contributes some kind of flavoring to this version of Worcestershire sauce. MAKES ABOUT 3 CUPS

1 cup chopped onions

2 cloves garlic, pressed

One $1/2$-inch-thick slice fresh ginger

2 tablespoons yellow mustard seeds

1 teaspoon black peppercorns

One 3-inch-long cinnamon stick

$1/2$ teaspoon crushed red pepper

$1/2$ teaspoon whole cloves

$1/2$ teaspoon cardamom seeds

$1/4$ teaspoon ground mace

2 cups cider vinegar

$1/2$ cup blackstrap molasses

$1/2$ cup soy sauce

$1/4$ cup fresh lemon juice (about 2 lemons)

2 tablespoons fresh lime juice

$1/2$ teaspoon mild curry powder

$1/2$ cup water

$1/2$ cup clover honey

1 Combine the onions, garlic, ginger, mustard seeds, peppercorns, cinnamon, red pepper, cloves, cardamom, and mace in a medium-size bowl and set aside.

2 In a large nonreactive saucepan, bring the vinegar, molasses, soy sauce, and lemon and lime juices to a boil, whisking to combine. Reduce the heat to medium-low and simmer for 5 minutes. Add the onion mixture, cover, and simmer, stirring occasionally, until thickened, about 2 hours.

3 Mix together the curry powder and water. Add to the saucepan, reduce the heat to low, and simmer for 5 minutes, stirring a few times.

4 In a small, heavy-bottomed saucepan, bring the honey to a boil, stirring until it becomes thick and turns dark golden brown in color. Add to the other saucepan and simmer, stirring, for 5 minutes longer.

5 Remove from the heat, let cool, cover, and refrigerate until cold, about 4 hours, occasionally stirring and pressing the vegetables. Strain the mixture through a fine-mesh sieve, pressing on the vegetables and spices to extract their flavor. Pour into hot, sterilized bottles. Cover tightly and store in the refrigerator, where it will keep for up to 6 months.

Barbecue Cocktail Sauce

This sauce can be made with chili sauce, barbecue sauce, or ketchup, the choice is yours. And, of course, it is better if you use homemade rather than store-bought products. This is great to serve with grilled or smoked fish and shellfish. MAKES ABOUT 1¼ CUPS

> 1 cup chili sauce, homemade (page 42) or store-bought
>
> 1 to 2 tablespoons prepared horseradish, to your taste
>
> 1 tablespoon fresh lemon juice
>
> 1 tablespoon Worcestershire sauce, homemade (page 50) or store-bought
>
> 1 teaspoon Tabasco sauce

Combine all the ingredients in a small bowl and blend well with a wire whisk. Keeps, covered, for up to 1 week in the refrigerator.

Red Chile Hot Sauce

I use this condiment on barbecued chicken wings and grilled cheese sandwiches. MAKES ABOUT 4 CUPS

> ¼ cup bacon drippings (bacon grease)
>
> 1 cup chopped onions
>
> 3 cloves garlic, minced
>
> 3 tablespoons all-purpose flour
>
> ½ cup pickled jalapeño juice or hot pepper vinegar
>
> ½ to ¾ cup pure ground serrano chile, to your taste
>
> 1 teaspoon cumin seeds, toasted in a dry skillet over medium heat until fragrant, then ground
>
> 1 teaspoon fine sea salt
>
> 1 teaspoon freshly ground black pepper
>
> 2 to 3 cups tomato sauce of your choice, such as Tomato Sauce Picante (page 40) or Hot and Sweet Tomato Sauce (page 41)

1 Heat the bacon drippings in a medium-size nonreactive saucepan over medium heat. Add the onions and garlic and cook, stirring, until softened and golden brown, about 5 minutes. Stir in the flour and cook 4 to 5 minutes longer, stirring so the sauce doesn't scorch. Blend in the jalapeño juice, stirring until thickened.

2 Transfer to a food processor or blender and process until smooth.

3 Return the mixture to the saucepan, place over medium heat, add the ground serrano, cumin, salt, and pepper, blend well, and cook, stirring, for about 3 minutes. Add as much of the tomato sauce as you want to get the consistency

you like, blending with a wire whisk. Heat through. Pour the hot mixture into hot, sterile canning jars, leaving 1/8-inch headspace, and seal. Can (see page 38) by processing in a water bath for 15 minutes. Or simply let cool and refrigerate. Keeps, refrigerated, for up to 2 weeks, canned or frozen, for up to 1 year.

Ancho Chile Sauce

This sauce is good served with any Southwestern-style barbecue, such as Smoked Chile-Marinated Pork Tenderloin (page 197) or Ancho and Chipotle-Rubbed Pork Loin (page 201). Star anise pods are available in Asian markets.
MAKES ABOUT 2 1/2 CUPS

3 dried ancho chile peppers or 1/2 cup pure ground ancho chile

1/4 cup safflower oil

1/2 cup minced onion

4 cloves garlic, pressed

3 tablespoons seeded and minced jalapeño chiles

1 tablespoon Szechuan peppercorns, toasted in a dry skillet over medium heat until fragrant

1/2 cup dry white wine

1/2 cup white wine vinegar

4 cups chicken broth

1 tablespoon fine sea salt or kosher salt

2 teaspoons granulated cane sugar

1 to 2 star anise pods, to your taste

1 teaspoon white pepper

2 tablespoons cornstarch

3 tablespoons cold water

1 If using dried chiles, soak them in hot water to cover until soft, about 30 minutes. When soft, remove the stems and seeds, place in a food processor or blender, process until smooth, and set aside. Reserve the soaking water to add to the stock later, if desired.

2 Heat the safflower oil in a large nonreactive saucepan over medium-high heat. Add the onion and garlic, and cook, stirring, until soft and golden brown. Add the jalapeños and peppercorns and cook, stirring, for 2 to 3 minutes. Add the wine and puréed chiles, bring to a boil, and continue to boil, stirring, until the wine is almost evaporated, 5 to 7 minutes. Add the vinegar, broth, reserved soaking water (if desired), salt, sugar, anise, and white pepper and blend well. Reduce the heat to medium-low. Mix the cornstarch and water into a paste and stir into the chile mixture. Let simmer until the sauce has reduced by about half, 30 to 40 minutes.

3 Strain the sauce through a fine-mesh strainer. Serve warm as a sauce or chilled as a condiment. Keeps, refrigerated, for up to 1 month.

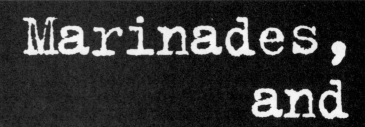

Marinades, and

Mops, Sops, Bastes

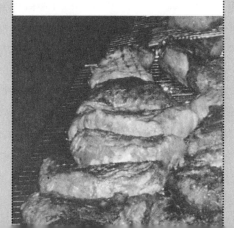

The dividing lines among marinades, mops, sops, and bastes are pretty thin. In general, marinades are used before cooking—usually grilling—and mainly for flavor. Mops, sops, and bastes are used after a rub has been applied and during the last half of cooking time, usually only when slow smoking. Mops, sops, and bastes are used mainly to provide extra moisture, but they can add some flavor as well.

A marinade can be turned into a mop, sop, or baste. If you want to use a marinade that has already touched raw meat, chicken, or fish as a mop or baste, you need to bring it to a boil, then simmer it for 5 minutes to eliminate any possibility of contamination. Alternately, make up a double batch of the marinade; use half to marinate the meat, then use the other untouched half for mopping and basting.

Marinades

Marinades are really just vinaigrettes. That's why so many people use bottled Italian salad dressing as a marinade base. A vinaigrette or salad dressing is usually two to three parts vegetable oil to one part vinegar or other acidic liquid, with or without seasonings. A marinade is usually one part oil to one part acidic liquid, with seasonings.

The trick with marinades is to know when to use them and how long to let the food marinate in them. A marinade is used to flavor meats and vegetables. It's not a tenderizer. If you keep meat, fish, or vegetables in a marinade too long, however, they will become mushy. If you marinate a large piece of meat, the marinade will penetrate only about 1/8 inch into the meat and not much more. Sometimes I will use a large syringe from a veterinary supply house to inject a large piece of meat with marinade so that the flavoring penetrates better.

Marinades are more appropriate for foods meant to be grilled rather than smoked. Basically, you marinate smaller cuts of meat, fish, chicken, or vegetables to give them extra flavor and moisture while grilling. I do like to marinate a whole chicken or turkey sometimes before slow smoking it, however. For slow smoking, I'm more of a slather-and-rub than a marinade guy. But you be the judge.

Fish and shellfish should marinate for only 30 minutes to an hour. Leave them in any longer than that and the acid in the marinade can cook the fish and you'll end up with ceviche or, worse yet, total mush, not tasty grilled or smoked fish.

Sturdy vegetables such as onions, carrots, and bell peppers can marinate for several hours. Tomatoes and mushrooms are more delicate and need only an hour or so.

Cuts of beef, pork, chicken, and lamb can marinate for 8 to 12 hours or overnight, as long as the marinade is not too acidic or intensely flavored and doesn't include ingredients, such as papayas and pineapple, that contain enzymes that break down proteins.

For the best flavor, make up a marinade right before you want to use it. Don't keep marinades around in the refrigerator because they deteriorate in flavor, and that's defeating their purpose.

INJECTING Marinades

For very thick cuts of meat or big birds, such as turkey, I might inject a marinade into the thickest part of the meat, using a large veterinary syringe that I buy at a veterinary supply house. Injecting a marinade, like injecting a brine, brings moisture and flavor to the interior part of the meat that can never be reached by simply marinating the exterior of the meat. ✱ Injecting works for dense pieces of meat, such as pork butt and whole pork shoulder; beef brisket, standing rib roast, and tri-tip; large roasting chickens; and whole turkeys. You wouldn't inject a marinade into bony ribs, flat steaks, or already flavorful beef or pork tenderloin—what's the point? ✱ Make sure the marinades you choose don't contain particles of dried herbs or spices that could clog the needle of the syringe. If necessary, let the marinade infuse with flavor, covered in the refrigerator, the day before. Then strain out any particles before injecting it. For the same no-clog reason, don't inject thick marinades with yogurt or sour cream in them. ✱ You'll need about 2 cups of strained marinade for a pork butt, whole pork shoulder, large brisket, standing rib roast, or whole tri-tip. You'll need about 1 cup for a roasting chicken (inject the breasts and thighs) and about 1½ cups for a large turkey (inject the breasts and thighs). Just keep filling the syringe, or use several filled syringes, until you've used up all the marinade. Then cover and let the meat sit, refrigerated, for at least an hour or overnight before slow smoking.

And goodness knows, they're as simple as spit to throw together at a moment's notice.

Mops, Sops, and Bastes

Mops, sops, and bastes are one and the same thing—what you call them depends on what part of the country you are from. The whole idea started with the sop. Needing to baste their 'cue with a liquid to keep it moist, barbecuers would take a clean rag, soak it in the liquid, and sop it on the meat with the rag. The mop was a step up in the evolution of the process; barbecuers would use their wives' clean dish mops to apply the basting sauce. Today, barbecuers use dish mops, pastry brushes, and spray bottles.

You mop or baste your barbecue after it has cooked long enough to set your rub. My rule of thumb is to start applying it halfway through the cooking time. I baste whenever I have the cooker open or on the half, partial, or full hour. Most bastes are used at room temperature or warm; in that case, keep them on your grill in a metal pan away from the fire.

The baste that I usually use is plain apple juice or apple cider; it does everything you want a baste to do, namely, keep the meat or whatever

Baste along with THE BARON

When you baste, you apply moisture to food during the slow-smoking or grilling process.

The art of basting is knowing which flavorings to use as a baste—often something as simple as apple juice—and when to apply it. Each of my recipes that requires basting suggests the liquid to use, but feel free to experiment and come up with your own successful bastes. Apply the baste when at least one side of the meat has developed a crust, bark, or seared side.

For smoking, I usually start basting about halfway through the cooking process. By this time, the rub should be set in a crust and won't get knocked off by the basting mixture. Generally, I baste with a dish mop or a spray bottle, whichever makes the most sense to me at the time. The bigger the cut of meat, the more likely I am to use the spray bottle. If the basting mixture has anything that could clog the sprayer, I use a dish mop instead. Simple.

For grilling, the same principle applies but in a quicker time frame. If I'm grilling a pork chop, for instance, I sear the chop on one side for a few minutes, turn it so that the seared side is up, and baste the cooked side. I baste the other side just as I take it off the grill. You can baste the uncooked side if you want, but then it will take longer to sear. It's really your choice. For grilled chicken or ribs that you may turn several times during cooking, baste each time you turn. Simple.

you are cooking moist. Some people ask why I don't use vinegar with fatty meats such as pork butt or ribs. That's simple; I don't like a strong vinegar taste in my barbecued meat. Anyway, what was vinegar before it became vinegar? If you are using cider vinegar, it was apple juice or cider.

Italian Dressing Marinade

This is where most barbecuers start when marinating. I use this for vegetables, chicken, pork, lamb, or fish destined for the grill. MAKES 1 QUART

1 cup distilled white vinegar

1/2 cup dry white wine

1/4 cup granulated cane sugar

1 tablespoon Worcestershire sauce, homemade (page 50) or store-bought

2 teaspoons kosher salt

2 teaspoons Louisiana hot sauce

1 teaspoon freshly ground black pepper

4 cloves garlic, pressed

1 1/2 teaspoons dried oregano leaves

1 teaspoon dried parsley flakes

1/2 teaspoon dried basil leaves

1/4 teaspoon dried rosemary leaves

1/4 teaspoon powdered bay leaf

3 cups safflower oil

Combine all the ingredients, except the safflower oil, in a blender. If the volume is too large to process at one time, divide all the ingredients equally and process in individual batches. Blend on high speed, then add the oil in a steady stream until thick and well combined. The blender emulsifies the dressing. If you don't want it emulsified, mix all the ingredients with a wire whisk or shake before using.

Spicy Italian Marinade

This was the marinade I used when I started competition cooking. This marinade is a great all-purpose marinade. It's good on pork, beef, chicken, and even fish and vegetables. MAKES ABOUT 3 CUPS

2 cups canola oil

1 cup distilled white vinegar

1/4 cup water

1/4 cup grated onion

1 tablespoon crushed red pepper

1 tablespoon dried basil leaves

1 tablespoon dried parsley flakes

2 teaspoons garlic paste (see box, Making Garlic Paste, page 60)

1/4 teaspoon white pepper

In a medium-size nonreactive bowl, whisk together the canola oil and vinegar until the mixture thickens. Add the remaining ingredients and mix until well blended.

Clear French Dressing and Marinade

Sometimes you don't want a pink opaque marinade for your barbecued food, but you still want the flavor of a French dressing. This marinade is good for fish, seafood, and chicken. MAKES 5 GENEROUS CUPS

1 1/4 cups granulated cane sugar

2 tablespoons onion powder

1 tablespoon kosher salt

1 tablespoon sweet Hungarian paprika

2 teaspoons dry mustard (I use Colman's)

1 teaspoon white pepper

1 teaspoon celery seeds

2 cups distilled white vinegar

1/2 cup fresh lemon juice (4 to 5 lemons)

1/4 cup white Worcestershire sauce

2 cups sunflower oil

In a large nonreactive bowl, combine the dry ingredients. In a medium-size nonreactive bowl, combine the vinegar, lemon juice, and Worcestershire sauce, then add to the dry ingredients and stir until dissolved and well blended. Add the sunflower oil and mix well with a whisk.

Making GARLIC Paste

To make a garlic paste for a marinade or slather, you can use one of two methods.

For a small quantity, press the garlic through a garlic press into a mortar or a bowl and add a sprinkling of coarse sea salt or kosher salt. Use the pestle or a fork to mash together the garlic and salt into a fine paste.

For a large quantity, buy already peeled garlic cloves from a wholesale club or food service. Place the peeled cloves in a food processor and purée.

Garlic paste will keep, tightly covered, in the refrigerator for up to 2 weeks. It will keep frozen for up to 3 months.

Chef Paul's Saffron Marinade

Sometimes I change my Baron of Barbecue hat for a Chef Paul toque when I want to prepare a more sophisticated recipe. This marinade is somewhat expensive, but your guests will thank you for making it. Saffron is delicious on chicken breasts and fish. When I make this marinade, I usually emulsify it and paint it on the meat with a pastry brush. I then wrap the pieces individually with plastic wrap and let them set for 1 to 4 hours in the refrigerator before grilling. MAKES 1½ CUPS

¼ cup orange juice

2 teaspoons saffron threads

1 cup extra virgin olive oil

¼ cup cloves garlic, ground or pressed

1 tablespoon minced orange zest

1 Combine the orange juice and saffron in a glass measuring cup and let set for at least 1 hour or overnight, stirring occasionally, to release the flavor from the saffron.

2 Add the olive oil, garlic, and orange zest and blend with a wire whisk.

THE BARON OF BARBECUE'S 10 FAVORITE MARINADES FOR CHICKEN

1 Italian Dressing Marinade *(page 58)*

2 Spicy Italian Marinade *(page 59)*

3 Fresh Herb Marinade for Chicken *(page 70)*

4 Chef Paul's Saffron Marinade *(page 60)*

5 Tarragon Herb Marinade *(page 61)*

6 Honey-Garlic Marinade *(page 61)*

7 Garlicky Caesar Marinade *(page 62)*

8 Apple-Ginger Marinade *(also great with turkey; page 63)*

9 Bourbon Turkey Marinade *(page 70)*

10 Picante Beer Marinade *(page 68)*

Tarragon Herb Marinade

This marinade pairs well with grilled chicken breast and fish. MAKES 1 CUP

1/2 cup tarragon vinegar

1 tablespoon dried summer savory leaves

1 teaspoon dried thyme leaves

1 teaspoon onion powder

1/2 teaspoon dry mustard (I use Colman's)

1/2 teaspoon kosher salt

1/2 teaspoon freshly ground black pepper

1/2 cup olive oil

Combine the vinegar, savory, thyme, onion powder, mustard, salt, and pepper in a small nonreactive bowl. Blend in the olive oil a little at a time with a wire whisk.

Honey-Garlic Marinade

Honey, where's the garlic? It's right here in this lemony marinade that's great with grilled duck breast, chicken, and pork tenderloin. MAKES 3 GENEROUS CUPS

1 cup fresh lemon juice (about 8 lemons)

1 cup canola oil

1/2 cup clover honey

1/3 cup soy sauce

1/4 cup dry sherry

2 tablespoons minced garlic

1 teaspoon kosher salt

In a medium-size nonreactive bowl, combine all the ingredients and blend well with a wire whisk.

Gingered Marinade

As you may know, Jessica is my wife. But I call ginger—fresh, dried and powdered, or candied—my girlfriend. I love this marinade on grilled pork tenderloin. Outstanding! MAKES 1 CUP

1/2 cup olive oil

1/4 cup fresh lemon juice (about 2 lemons)

1/4 cup red wine vinegar

3 tablespoons minced crystallized ginger

2 tablespoons soy sauce

1/2 teaspoon kosher salt

1/2 teaspoon freshly ground black pepper

Combine all the ingredients in a small nonreactive bowl and blend well with a wire whisk.

Balsamic Marinade

With its heartier flavor, this marinade is delicious on steak or pork chops. MAKES 2 1/2 CUPS

1/2 cup balsamic vinegar

1/2 cup cider vinegar

1/4 cup apple cider

2 tablespoons pressed garlic

2 tablespoons Dijon mustard

1 tablespoon minced fresh parsley leaves

1 cup olive oil

In a medium-size nonreactive bowl, combine the vinegars, cider, garlic, mustard, and parsley. With a wire whisk, mix in the olive oil a little at a time until well blended.

Garlicky Caesar Marinade

Caesar salad dressings and marinades can be made without anchovies and eggs, as is the case with this recipe. If you like garlic, this marinade is for you. The bold flavor is good to use on chicken and pork tenderloin destined for the grill. MAKES 2¼ CUPS

¼ cup cloves garlic, minced

1 cup olive oil

½ cup red wine vinegar

¼ cup balsamic vinegar

¼ cup fresh lemon juice (about 2 lemons)

2 tablespoons granulated cane sugar

1 teaspoon dry mustard (I use Colman's)

1 teaspoon Louisiana hot sauce

Combine all the ingredients in a blender and process until smooth.

Yogurt-Mustard Marinade

If you have never tried a marinade with yogurt, buttermilk, or sour cream, take advantage of the lactic acid in these ingredients to tenderize a little bit. But the main reason you use marinades is for flavor, and this one is tasty on game and other meats that will be grilled. MAKES ABOUT 2 CUPS

1 cup plain low-fat yogurt

2 tablespoons spicy brown mustard

4 large cloves garlic, pressed

¼ cup soy sauce

¼ cup fresh lemon juice (about 2 lemons)

¼ cup canola oil

Whisk together all the ingredients, except the oil, in a medium-size nonreactive bowl. Add the oil a little at a time, whisking vigorously after each addition.

Yogurt, Sour Cream, and Fresh Parsley Marinade

Use this on chicken and turkey for a tandoori-like effect. The marinade keeps the meat moist while grilling. MAKES ABOUT 3 CUPS

1 cup plain low-fat yogurt

¾ cup canola oil

¼ cup minced fresh parsley leaves

¼ cup red wine vinegar

¼ cup grated onion

2 tablespoons pressed garlic

1 teaspoon freshly ground black pepper

1 teaspoon non-iodized salt

½ cup sour cream

Combine all the ingredients, except the sour cream, in a food processor or blender and process until smooth. With the machine running, slowly add the sour cream, blending thoroughly.

White Wine Marinade with Peppercorns, Bay Leaf, and Juniper

This aromatic marinade is good to use with chicken, game, and beef. MAKES ABOUT 2 CUPS

1 cup dry white wine

1/4 cup canola oil

2 tablespoons granulated cane sugar

2 lemons, thinly sliced

10 black peppercorns, crushed

3 bay leaves

1 teaspoon fresh thyme leaves, chopped

1 teaspoon juniper berries, crushed

1 teaspoon non-iodized salt

1 teaspoon white pepper

Combine all the ingredients in a small nonreactive bowl and let rest for at least 1 hour or, better yet, overnight to let the flavors develop.

Apple-Ginger Marinade

This marinade smells like fall to me. Use it on turkey or pork for the grill, or on a smaller turkey to slow smoke for Thanksgiving. Marinate the turkey overnight, then sprinkle on a rub and slow smoke. MAKES 2 1/2 GENEROUS CUPS

1 cup apple cider or apple juice

2 tablespoons peeled and grated fresh ginger

1/4 cup cider vinegar

1/2 cup canola oil

1/2 cup light soy sauce

1/4 cup clover honey

2 cloves garlic, pressed

Combine all the ingredients in a medium-size nonreactive bowl and blend well.

Sweet and Tangy Marinade

The pleasantly mouth-puckering tomato flavor in this marinade is great on beef that will be either grilled or smoked. MAKES A LITTLE MORE THAN 3 CUPS

1 cup cider vinegar

1 cup ketchup, homemade (page 43) or store-bought

1/2 cup Worcestershire sauce, homemade (page 50) or store-bought

1/4 cup canola oil

1/4 cup clover honey

1/4 cup molasses

1 teaspoon ground allspice

1 teaspoon non-iodized salt

Combine all the ingredients in a medium-size nonreactive saucepan. Bring to a boil, cover, reduce the heat to medium-low, and simmer for 10 to 15 minutes. Let cool before using.

Three-Citrus Marinade with Fresh Ginger

This is stellar with shrimp and scallops—or any fish meant for the grill. MAKES 2¼ CUPS

1 cup fresh lime juice (about 16 limes)

½ cup fresh orange juice (about 2 oranges)

¼ cup fresh lemon juice (about 2 lemons)

2 tablespoons peeled and grated fresh ginger

2 tablespoons pressed garlic

¼ cup olive oil

1 teaspoon ground coriander

1 teaspoon non-iodized salt

1 teaspoon freshly ground black pepper

Combine all the ingredients in a medium-size nonreactive bowl and blend well.

Anchovy Marinade

Anchovy is one of those flavor enhancers that really works. In many Italian pasta sauces, you first cook down an anchovy with garlic as part of the flavor base. This is one of my favorite marinades for vegetables, chicken, and fish. Even if you don't like anchovy, try it. MAKES ABOUT 2 CUPS

1 cup extra virgin olive oil

½ cup sherry vinegar

¼ cup balsamic vinegar

2 tablespoons firmly packed light brown sugar

1 tablespoon whole-grain mustard

Two 2-ounce cans anchovy fillets packed in oil, drained and minced

1 teaspoon fine sea salt

1 teaspoon freshly ground black pepper

In a medium-size nonreactive bowl, whisk together all the ingredients until thoroughly combined.

Zippy Honey Marinade

For a new experience, try this marinade on country-style ribs. MAKES ABOUT 3 CUPS

1 cup red wine vinegar

1 cup water

¼ cup fresh lemon juice (about 2 lemons)

¼ cup clover honey

2 tablespoons spicy brown mustard

2 tablespoons Worcestershire sauce, homemade (page 50) or store-bought

3 large cloves garlic, pressed

1 teaspoon non-iodized salt

1 teaspoon freshly ground black pepper

¼ cup olive oil

Place all the ingredients, except the olive oil, in a blender and process until smooth. With the machine running, add the olive oil a little at a time, until the mixture is well blended and emulsified. Let rest overnight in the refrigerator to let the flavors meld before using.

Coca-Cola Marinade

Besides being a good marinade, this recipe can also be used as a baste or mop for slowsmoking brisket, ribs, or pork butt. Make sure you use regular Coca-Cola, not the diet variety; you need the sugar to get the wonderful caramelized flavor. You can also use a cherry-flavored cola.

MAKES 3½ CUPS

1 cup Coca-Cola

1 cup canola oil

1 cup beef broth

2 tablespoons prepared yellow mustard

2 tablespoons Worcestershire sauce, homemade (page 50) or store-bought

1 tablespoon ketchup

1 tablespoon soy sauce

1 tablespoon pressed garlic

1 teaspoon freshly ground black pepper

1 teaspoon non-iodized salt

½ teaspoon cayenne pepper

Combine all the ingredients in a medium-size nonreactive saucepan over medium heat, stirring and blending until everything has dissolved and is well incorporated. Let cool before using.

Jamaican Jerk Vegetable Marinade

Be sure to wear rubber gloves when working with Scotch bonnet (habanero) or any other hot pepper. And keep your hands away from your eyes! The lime and fresh thyme really give you that unmistakable Caribbean flavor. Use this marinade to create jerked chicken, pork, or beef on the grill. MAKES ABOUT 3 CUPS

1 bunch (6) green onions (green and white parts), minced

½ cup diced onion

1 to 2 Scotch bonnet peppers, to your taste, seeded and minced

1 cup light soy sauce

½ cup red wine vinegar

½ cup firmly packed light brown sugar

¼ cup canola oil

2 tablespoons fresh lime juice

2 tablespoons fresh thyme leaves, chopped and bruised

1 teaspoon ground allspice

½ teaspoon ground cloves

¼ teaspoon ground nutmeg

Combine all the ingredients in a food processor and process until smooth, 15 to 20 seconds, on high speed.

THE BARON OF BARBECUE'S 10 FAVORITE MARINADES FOR VEGETABLES

Lime-Cilantro Marinade

This gives a lively, citrusy flavor to fish, chicken, and vegetables. **MAKES 3 CUPS**

1 cup fresh lime juice (10 to 12 limes)

1/2 cup orange juice

1/2 cup extra virgin olive oil

1/2 cup fresh cilantro leaves, minced

1/4 cup minced green onions (green and white parts)

1/4 cup clover honey

1 tablespoon peeled and grated fresh ginger

1 teaspoon non-iodized salt

1 teaspoon freshly ground black pepper

Combine all the ingredients in a medium-size nonreactive bowl and blend well with a whisk.

Easy Vegetable Marinade

This marinade really brings out the flavor of vegetables on the grill or smoker. **MAKES 2 1/4 CUPS**

1 cup extra virgin olive oil

1 cup red wine vinegar

1/4 cup fresh lemon juice (about 2 lemons)

1 bunch (6) green onions (green and white parts), minced

1 tablespoon dry mustard (I use Colman's)

1 tablespoon coarsely ground black pepper

1 teaspoon fine sea salt

Place all the ingredients in a blender or medium-size nonreactive bowl and blend well.

Fajita Marinade

Use this marinade with any kind of meat or vegetables that will fit on your grill. Marinate the food for several hours, then grill on a perforated grill rack (so the food doesn't fall through to the coals). The enzymes in pineapple juice will also tenderize the meat a little bit. **MAKES ABOUT 3 CUPS**

1 cup soy sauce

1/2 cup fresh lemon juice (4 to 5 lemons)

1/2 cup pineapple juice

1/2 cup canola oil

2 tablespoons fresh lime juice

2 tablespoons granulated cane sugar

2 teaspoons cracked black peppercorns

1 teaspoon dry mustard (I use Colman's)

1 teaspoon cumin seeds, toasted in a dry skillet over medium heat until fragrant, then ground

1 teaspoon fine sea salt

1 teaspoon cayenne pepper

Combine all the ingredients in a medium-size nonreactive bowl and whisk to combine.

Spicy Shallot-Pepper Marinade

Try this marinade with fish and chicken for a nice change of pace. MAKES 2¼ CUPS

1 cup white Rhine wine, such as Liebfraumilch or Riesling

½ cup olive oil

½ cup minced shallots

2 tablespoons seeded and minced jalapeño chiles

2 tablespoons granulated cane sugar

2 cloves garlic, pressed

1 teaspoon kosher salt

1 teaspoon freshly ground black pepper

Place all the ingredients in a medium-size nonreactive bowl and whisk well to combine.

Flaming Dominican Rum Marinade

Welcome to the Dominican Republic. Use this boozy marinade on chicken or pork for a taste of the Caribbean. MAKES ABOUT 8½ CUPS

2 cups dark rum (I use Meyer's)

¾ cup soybean oil or other vegetable oil

½ cup cloves garlic, puréed

1 cup grated onions

2 cups soy sauce

2 cups fresh lime juice (about 32 limes)

¼ cup firmly packed light brown sugar

2 teaspoons fine sea salt

1 teaspoon freshly ground black pepper

1 Place the rum in a medium-size nonreactive saucepan, heat over medium heat, and, very carefully, using a long match and keeping your hair and long sleeves away from the pan, ignite the rum and allow it to burn itself out.

2 In a small skillet over medium heat, heat the oil, then add the garlic purée and onions and cook, stirring, until soft but not brown. Add to the rum (once the rum has stopped flaming), along with the remaining ingredients, and heat through, stirring, until the sugar and salt have dissolved. Let cool before using.

THE BARON OF BARBECUE'S 10 FAVORITE MARINADES FOR FISH AND SHELLFISH

1 Bloody Mary Marinade *(also great with grilled shellfish; page 71)*

2 Grill Meister's Seafood Marinade *(page 72)*

3 Tequila Lime Baste *(page 84)*

4 Clear French Dressing and Marinade *(page 59)*

5 Chef Paul's Saffron Marinade *(page 60)*

6 Tarragon Herb Marinade *(page 61)*

7 Three-Citrus Marinade with Fresh Ginger *(page 64)*

8 Lime-Cilantro Marinade *(page 66)*

9 Flaming Dominican Rum Marinade *(page 67)*

10 Lemon and Lager Marinade *(page 71)*

Toasted Sesame Asian Marinade

This is a winning flavor combination with beef, pork, poultry, fish, or vegetables. **MAKES 2 1/4 CUPS**

1/2 cup peanut oil

1/4 cup cider vinegar

1/4 cup soy sauce

2 tablespoons clover honey

2 tablespoons toasted sesame oil

4 cloves garlic, pressed

1 tablespoon peeled and grated fresh ginger

1 teaspoon dry mustard (I use Colman's)

1 teaspoon kosher salt

Combine all the ingredients in a medium-size nonreactive bowl and blend well.

Picante Beer Marinade

Pop open an extra one to enjoy while you grill beef, pork, or chicken that has taken a dip in this peppy marinade. **MAKES ABOUT 2 1/2 CUPS**

One 12-ounce can premium beer, allowed to go flat

1/2 cup canola oil

1/2 cup thinly sliced green onions (green and white parts)

1/4 cup soy sauce

2 tablespoons seeded and minced serrano chiles

2 tablespoons granulated cane sugar

4 cloves garlic, pressed

1 teaspoon kosher salt

1/2 teaspoon cayenne pepper

Combine all the ingredients in a medium-size nonreactive bowl and blend well.

Red Wine Herb Marinade

This marinade adds a hearty yet sophisticated flavor to steaks and lamb chops on the grill. **MAKES ABOUT 1 1/2 CUPS**

1/2 cup dry red wine

1/4 cup red wine vinegar

1/2 cup olive oil

2 tablespoons fresh lemon juice

2 tablespoons granulated cane sugar

1 tablespoons minced fresh basil leaves

2 cloves garlic, pressed

1 teaspoon fresh thyme leaves

1 teaspoon kosher salt

1 teaspoons freshly ground black pepper

Combine all the ingredients in a small nonreactive bowl and blend well.

Sweet Red Wine Vinegar Marinade with Cracked Pepper and Shallots

This full-flavored marinade plays well with beef, lamb, fish, and vegetables. MAKES ABOUT 2¹/₂ CUPS

1 cup red wine vinegar

1 cup granulated cane sugar

¹/₂ cup extra virgin olive oil

¹/₄ cup fresh lemon juice (about 2 lemons)

3 tablespoons minced shallots

2 tablespoons minced or pressed garlic

2 tablespoons seeded and minced red bell pepper

1 tablespoon seeded and minced green bell pepper

1 tablespoon fine sea salt

1 tablespoon cracked black peppercorns

Combine all the ingredients in a medium-size nonreactive bowl and blend well.

THE BARON OF BARBECUE'S 10 FAVORITE MARINADES FOR LAMB AND CABRITO

1 Red Wine Herb Marinade *(page 68)*

2 Sweet Red Wine Vinegar Marinade with Cracked Pepper and Shallots *(page 69)*

3 Tomato-Herb Baste *(can also be used as a marinade; page 82)*

4 Caribbean Mop Sauce *(can also be used as a marinade; page 73)*

5 Spicy Shallot-Pepper Marinade *(page 67)*

6 Balsamic Herb Marinade *(page 70)*

7 Grill Meister's Seafood Marinade *(also good on lamb; page 72)*

8 Tarragon Herb Marinade *(page 61)*

9 Italian Dressing Marinade *(page 58)*

10 White Wine Marinade with Peppercorns, Bay Leaf, and Juniper *(page 63)*

Bourbon Turkey Marinade

Try this marinade on your next Thanksgiving turkey, grilled or smoked. Use a microplane grater to grate the ginger.
MAKES ABOUT 3 CUPS

- 1 cup apple juice or cider
- 1/2 cup soy sauce
- 1/2 cup granulated cane sugar or firmly packed brown sugar
- 1/4 cup bourbon
- 1/2 cup canola oil
- 3 tablespoons minced garlic
- 2 tablespoons peeled and minced or grated fresh ginger
- 1 tablespoon crushed red pepper
- 1 teaspoon fine sea salt

Combine all the ingredients in a medium-size nonreactive bowl and blend well.

Fresh Herb Marinade for Chicken

You can't get a much fresher-tasting marinade than this. Your whole house will smell good while the chicken is marinating. MAKES 1 3/4 CUPS

- 3 tablespoons chopped fresh basil leaves
- 2 tablespoons chopped green onions (green part only)
- 2 tablespoons chopped fresh parsley leaves
- 1 tablespoon chopped yellow onion
- 1 tablespoon chopped fresh rosemary leaves
- 1 tablespoon fresh thyme leaves

- 1 tablespoon seeded and chopped red bell pepper
- 1 tablespoon minced garlic
- 2 teaspoons kosher salt
- 1 teaspoon freshly ground black pepper
- 1/4 cup fresh lemon juice (about 2 lemons)
- 1/4 cup balsamic vinegar
- 1 cup olive oil

Place the basil, green onions, parsley, yellow onion, rosemary, thyme, bell pepper, garlic, salt, and black pepper in a blender and process until smooth. Add the lemon juice and vinegar, process to combine, then add the oil and process for about 2 minutes. Don't emulsify the marinade; that will cause it to darken.

Balsamic Herb Marinade

This is great with just about anything. MAKES ABOUT 3 1/4 CUPS

- 1 cup balsamic vinegar
- 1 cup canola oil
- 1/2 cup fresh lemon juice (4 to 5 lemons)
- 1/4 cup granulated cane sugar
- 1/4 cup minced green onions (green and white parts)
- 2 tablespoons soy sauce
- 1 tablespoon pressed garlic
- 1 tablespoon minced fresh basil leaves
- 1 teaspoon minced fresh tarragon leaves
- 1 teaspoon minced fresh cilantro leaves
- 1 teaspoon dry mustard (I use Colman's)
- 1 teaspoon chicken bouillon granules or fine sea salt

1 teaspoon crushed red pepper

1 teaspoon Tabasco sauce

1 teaspoon finely ground black pepper

Combine all the ingredients in a medium-size nonreactive bowl and blend well.

Bloody Mary Marinade

This is a very good fish or shellfish marinade. Try an oyster that's been marinated in this for about 30 minutes, then grilled in its shell. Yum! MAKES ABOUT 2¼ CUPS

2 cups vegetable or tomato juice (I use V-8)

¼ cup vodka or gin

2 tablespoons Worcestershire sauce, homemade (page 50) or store-bought

1 tablespoon fresh lemon juice

1 tablespoon peeled and grated fresh horseradish

1 teaspoon Tabasco or Louisiana hot sauce

¼ cup vegetable oil (optional)

Combine all the ingredients, except the oil, in a medium-size nonreactive bowl and blend well. Pour over ice and enjoy (ha ha) or blend in the oil and use as a marinade.

Lemon and Lager Marinade

This is a good marinade for pork ribs, chicken, and fish. MAKES ABOUT 2¼ CUPS

One 12-ounce bottle beer (your choice; I prefer a dark beer), allowed to go flat

½ cup olive oil

⅓ cup fresh lemon juice (3 to 4 lemons)

1 tablespoon minced fresh chives

1 tablespoon fresh thyme leaves

2 teaspoons pressed garlic

1 teaspoon fine sea salt

1 teaspoon freshly ground black pepper

Combine all the ingredients in a medium-size nonreactive bowl and blend well.

Hot Citrus Chipotle Marinade

This marinade will spice up any meat you use it on; it's a real eye-opener. I like this marinade thick, and I paint it on ribs and chicken with a pastry brush, as I do when putting on a mustard slather. MAKES 1¼ TO 1½ CUPS

2 cups fresh orange juice (about 8 oranges)

½ cup fresh lime juice (about 8 limes)

2 teaspoons minced fresh oregano leaves

1 teaspoon cumin seeds, toasted in a dry skillet over medium heat until fragrant, then ground

One 7-ounce can chipotle chiles in adobo sauce

¼ cup red wine vinegar

4 cloves garlic, pressed

1 tablespoon grated orange zest

1 teaspoon fine sea salt

1 teaspoon freshly ground black pepper

1 Combine the orange juice, lime juice, and 1 teaspoon of the oregano in a medium-size non-reactive saucepan and bring to a boil. Reduce the heat to medium-low and simmer until reduced by half, 1 to 1¼ cups.

2 Transfer to a blender, add the remaining ingredients, and process until smooth. If the sauce is too thick, thin it down with more vinegar.

Grill Meister's Seafood Marinade

Gunner Roe, also known as the Grill Meister, is an expert on fish and shellfish. He lives in Galena, Maryland, much closer to the ocean than those of us in Kansas City. This is one of Gunner's favorite marinades for seafood. It's also great on salads as a vinaigrette. **MAKES ABOUT 1/2 CUP**

1/4 cup fresh lemon juice (about 2 lemons)

1/4 cup olive oil

1 teaspoon prepared hot mustard

1/2 teaspoon pressed garlic

5 teaspoons chopped fresh herbs of your choice (tarragon, basil, chives, parsley, cilantro, oregano)

1/2 teaspoon non-iodized salt

1/2 teaspoon freshly ground black pepper

Combine the lemon juice, olive oil, and mustard in a small nonreactive bowl and whisk vigorously. Mix in the garlic, herbs, salt, and pepper and blend well.

All-Purpose Barbecue Mop

A mop is a very flavorful liquid you apply to meat with a dish mop. Its purpose is to keep the meat moist during long, slow cooking. A mop can be as simple as brewed coffee or as delicious as this one. **MAKES NOT QUITE 2 CUPS**

1/2 cup sunflower oil

1/2 cup fresh lemon juice (4 to 5 lemons)

1/2 cup cider vinegar or red wine vinegar

1/4 cup soy sauce

2 tablespoons Worcestershire sauce, homemade (page 50) or store-bought

4 cloves garlic, pressed

2 teaspoons rubbed sage

2 teaspoons kosher salt

1 teaspoon coarsely ground black pepper

1/2 teaspoon cayenne pepper

1 Combine all the ingredients in a medium-size nonreactive saucepan and heat for 15 minutes over medium heat, stirring to blend the flavors.

2 Use warm or at room temperature. Baste or mop your barbecue after it has cooked long enough to set your rub. My rule of thumb is to start basting halfway through the cooking time. I baste whenever I have the cooker open or on the half, partial, or full hour.

VARIATIONS If you have some favorite herbs for beef, chicken, or pork, add 1/2 teaspoon of them. Also, if this mop is too acidic for your taste, use apple juice instead of vinegar.

All-Purpose Moppin', Soppin', and Bastin' Sauce

No matter what you're barbecuing, it will taste better when anointed with this sauce during cooking. **MAKES ABOUT 3 CUPS**

1 1/2 cups cider vinegar

1/2 cup fresh lemon juice (4 to 5 lemons)

1/4 cup Worcestershire sauce, homemade (page 50) or store-bought

1/4 cup chicken or beef broth or water

1/4 cup vegetable oil

3 tablespoons freshly ground black pepper

2 tablespoons sweet Hungarian paprika

1 tablespoon kosher salt

2 teaspoons cayenne pepper

1 Combine all the ingredients in a medium-size nonreactive bowl and blend well with a whisk.

2 Baste or mop your barbecue after it has cooked long enough to set your rub. My rule of thumb is to start basting halfway through the cooking time. I baste whenever I have the cooker open or on the half, partial, or full hour.

Georgia Peach Moppin' Sauce

What a great mop for pork and chicken! The combination of beef and chicken stocks gives you the flavor of home-made pork stock. Use warm so the butter stays melted. MAKES ABOUT 2 1/2 CUPS

1/2 cup beef broth

1/2 cup chicken broth

1/2 cup peach nectar

1/4 cup fresh lemon juice (about 2 lemons)

1/4 cup red wine vinegar

1/2 cup (1 stick) unsalted butter

2 tablespoons Worcestershire sauce, homemade (page 50) or store-bought

1 teaspoon granulated onion

1 teaspoon kosher salt

1 teaspoon freshly ground black pepper

1/2 teaspoon dry mustard (I use Colman's)

1 Combine all the ingredients in a medium-size nonreactive saucepan over medium heat and simmer, stirring, until the butter has melted.

2 Use warm as a baste. Baste or mop your barbecue after it has cooked long enough to set your rub. My rule of thumb is to start basting halfway through the cooking time. I baste whenever I have the cooker open or on the half, partial, or full hour.

Caribbean Mop Sauce

The rum, pineapple juice, and allspice in this sauce give a Jamaican lilt to barbecued chicken, pork, beef, or lamb. If you want the flavor of pork broth, combine 1/2 cup each of chicken and beef broth. MAKES ABOUT 3 CUPS

1 cup chicken or beef broth, or 1/2 cup chicken broth and 1/2 cup beef broth

1/2 cup water

1/2 cup pineapple juice

1/2 cup cider vinegar

1/4 cup dark rum (I use Meyer's)

1/4 cup canola oil

2 tablespoons firmly packed dark brown sugar

1 teaspoon ground allspice

1/2 teaspoon cayenne pepper

1 Combine all the ingredients in a medium-size nonreactive bowl and blend well with a whisk.

2 Baste or mop your barbecue after it has cooked long enough to set your rub. My rule of thumb is to start basting halfway through the cooking time. I baste whenever I have the cooker open or on the half, partial, or full hour.

Spicy Buttery Barbecue Mop Sauce

Here's another all-purpose mop when you want a spicier flavor but a buttery finish on beef, chicken, pork, or lamb. Keep warm so the butter stays melted. MAKES ABOUT 2 CUPS

- 1 cup beer (I use Budweiser), allowed to go flat
- 1/2 cup Worcestershire sauce, homemade (page 50) or store-bought
- 1/2 cup (1 stick) unsalted butter
- 2 tablespoons prepared yellow mustard
- 1 tablespoon chili powder, homemade (page 111) or store-bought
- 1 tablespoon Louisiana hot sauce
- 2 teaspoons sweet Hungarian paprika
- 2 teaspoons dry mustard (I use Colman's)
- 2 teaspoons fine sea salt
- 1 teaspoon granulated garlic
- 1 teaspoon finely ground black pepper
- 1 teaspoon cayenne pepper

1 Combine all the ingredients in a medium-size nonreactive saucepan over medium heat and simmer for 10 to 15 minutes, stirring so that all the ingredients are incorporated.

2 Use warm as a baste. Baste or mop your barbecue after it has cooked long enough to set your rub. My rule of thumb is to start basting halfway through the cooking time. I baste whenever I have the cooker open or on the half, partial, or full hour.

Redeye Barbecue Mop

This is a Texas beef mop, but it's great on anything you choose to barbecue. The mop gets its name from the famous redeye gravy made with black coffee that is served on country ham and biscuits. MAKES ABOUT 2 3/4 CUPS

- 1 cup brewed strong black coffee
- 1/2 cup ketchup, homemade (page 43) or store-bought
- 1/2 cup Worcestershire sauce, homemade (page 50) or store-bought
- 1/4 cup (1/2 stick) unsalted butter
- 1/4 cup soy sauce
- 1/4 cup apple cider
- 1 tablespoon finely ground black pepper
- 1 tablespoon garlic salt
- 1 teaspoon Louisiana hot sauce

1 Combine all the ingredients in a medium-size nonreactive saucepan. Heat until the butter is melted and blend well with a wire whisk.

2 Use the baste warm. Baste or mop your barbecue after it has cooked long enough to set your rub. My rule of thumb is to start basting halfway through the cooking time. I baste whenever I have the cooker open or on the half, partial, or full hour.

Buttery Moppin' Sauce

You can use this beef mop on pork and chicken also. Keep it warm so the butter stays melted. MAKES ABOUT 3 CUPS

2 cups beef broth

1/2 cup (1 stick) unsalted butter

1/4 cup canola oil

1/4 cup fresh lemon juice (about 2 lemons)

2 tablespoons balsamic vinegar

2 tablespoons Worcestershire sauce, homemade (page 50) or store-bought

1 tablespoon sweet Hungarian paprika

2 teaspoons chili powder, homemade (page 111) or store-bought

1 teaspoon freshly ground black pepper

1 teaspoon granulated garlic

1 teaspoon kosher salt

1 teaspoon Louisiana hot sauce

1 Combine all the ingredients in a medium-size nonreactive saucepan over medium heat and heat to melt the butter. Blend well with a whisk and simmer for 10 to 15 minutes.

2 Use the baste warm. Baste or mop your barbecue after it has cooked long enough to set your rub. My rule of thumb is to start basting halfway through the cooking time. I baste whenever I have the cooker open or on the half, partial, or full hour.

Southern Moppin' Sauce

If a moppin' sauce is from the South, you can bet it's for pork. Mop a whole hog with this (you'll need at least 4 cups) and you'll be in hog heaven. MAKES ABOUT 2 CUPS

1 cup canola oil

1/4 cup fresh lemon juice (about 2 lemons)

1/4 cup soy sauce

1/4 cup Worcestershire sauce, homemade (page 50) or store-bought

2 lemons, sliced

2 tablespoons seasoned salt, homemade (page 108) or store-bought

2 bay leaves

1 teaspoon freshly ground black pepper

1 Combine all the ingredients in a medium-size nonreactive saucepan over medium heat and simmer for 10 to 15 minutes. Remove the lemon slices and discard.

2 Use the baste warm. Baste or mop your barbecue after it has cooked long enough to set your rub. My rule of thumb is to start basting halfway through the cooking time. I baste whenever I have the cooker open or on the half, partial, or full hour.

Sop and Mop

Here's another baste with a smoky bacon flavor for barbecued pork. Use it warm to keep the bacon drippings melted.
MAKES ABOUT 3 1/2 CUPS

1 cup cider vinegar

1 cup fresh lemon juice (8 to 10 lemons)

1 cup bacon drippings (bacon grease)

1/4 cup Worcestershire sauce, homemade (page 50) or store-bought

2 tablespoons rub of your choice (pages 124–132)

2 tablespoons fine sea salt

2 tablespoons freshly ground black pepper

1 tablespoon sweet Hungarian paprika

1 tablespoon cayenne pepper

1 Combine all the ingredients in a medium-size nonreactive saucepan over medium heat. Simmer until the bacon drippings and spices have dis-

solved, about 10 minutes. Don't simmer too long, as it dissipates the punch of the vinegar.

2 Use the baste warm. Baste or mop your barbecue after it has cooked long enough to set your rub. My rule of thumb is to start basting halfway through the cooking time. I baste whenever I have the cooker open or on the half, partial, or full hour.

Lemon Poultry Mop

Halfway through smoking a whole chicken or turkey, mop that bird with this sauce for finger-lickin' eatin'. MAKES ABOUT 2¹/₂ CUPS

¹/₂ cup (1 stick) unsalted butter

¹/₄ cup minced onion

2 tablespoons pressed garlic

1 cup chicken broth

¹/₂ cup fresh lemon juice (4 to 5 lemons)

¹/₂ cup water

1 tablespoon prepared yellow mustard

1 tablespoon Worcestershire sauce, homemade (page 50) or store-bought

2 teaspoons Herbed Poultry Seasoning (page 119)

1 Melt the butter in a medium-size nonreactive saucepan over medium heat. Add the onion and garlic, cover, and sweat them until soft; do not let them brown. Add the remaining ingredients and simmer for 15 to 20 minutes, stirring until well blended.

2 Use the baste warm. Baste or mop your barbecue after it has cooked long enough to set your rub. My rule of thumb is to start basting halfway through the cooking time. I baste whenever I have the cooker open or on the half, partial, or full hour.

Chicken Mop and Marinade

This is a fine, fine moppin' sauce for chicken in the smoker or a fine, fine marinade for chicken headed for the grill. MAKES ABOUT 1¹/₂ CUPS

1¹/₂ cups cider vinegar

1 tablespoon chili powder, homemade (page 111) or store-bought

1 tablespoon granulated cane sugar

2 teaspoons dry mustard (I use Colman's)

1 teaspoon sweet Hungarian paprika

1 teaspoon fine sea salt

1 teaspoon cayenne pepper

¹/₂ teaspoon pure ground chipotle chile

¹/₂ teaspoon ground cumin

1 Combine all the ingredients in a medium-size nonreactive saucepan and bring to a boil, stirring to dissolve the sugar and spices.

2 Remove from the heat, cover, and set aside until it cools to warm or room temperature before using as a baste. Baste or mop your barbecue after it has cooked long enough to set your rub. My rule of thumb is to start basting halfway through the cooking time. I baste whenever I have the cooker open or on the half, partial, or full hour.

Texas Brisket Mop

This mop smells so good, you'll be tempted to slurp it down, rather than mop it on the brisket. MAKES 2¹/₄ CUPS

1 cup beer (I use Budweiser), allowed to go flat

¹/₂ cup barbecue sauce of your choice (pages 140–160)

¹/₂ cup soy sauce

¼ cup Worcestershire sauce, homemade (page 50) or store-bought

1 tablespoon granulated cane sugar

1 tablespoon finely ground black pepper

1 teaspoon non-iodized salt

1 Combine all the ingredients in a medium-size nonreactive saucepan over medium heat and simmer for 15 minutes, stirring until the ingredients are well combined.

2 Use the baste warm or at room temperature. Baste or mop your barbecue after it has cooked long enough to set your rub. My rule of thumb is to start basting halfway through the cooking time. I baste whenever I have the cooker open or on the half, partial, or full hour.

THE BARON OF BARBECUE'S 10 FAVORITE MARINADES FOR BEEF

1 **Redeye Barbecue Mop** *(can also use as a marinade; page 74)*

2 **Texas Brisket Mop** *(can also use as a marinade; page 76)*

3 **White Wine Marinade with Peppercorns, Bay Leaf, and Juniper** *(page 63)*

4 **Sweet and Tangy Marinade** *(page 63)*

5 **Coca-Cola Marinade** *(page 65)*

6 **Picante Beer Marinade** *(page 68)*

7 **Sweet Red Wine Vinegar Marinade with Cracked Pepper and Shallots** *(page 69)*

8 **All-Purpose Moppin', Soppin', and Bastin' Sauce** *(can also use as a marinade; page 72)*

9 **Caribbean Mop Sauce** *(can also use as a marinade; page 73)*

10 **Toasted Sesame Asian Marinade** *(page 68)*

Beefy Mop Sauce

Here is another great mop to use to create your own blue-ribbon brisket. MAKES ABOUT 3 CUPS

2 cups beef broth

½ cup canola oil

½ cup Worcestershire sauce, homemade (page 50) or store-bought

¼ cup fresh lemon juice (about 2 lemons)

¼ cup cider vinegar

1 tablespoon firmly packed light brown sugar

1 tablespoon kosher salt

2 teaspoons dry mustard (I use Colman's)

1 teaspoon freshly ground black pepper

1 teaspoon granulated garlic

1 teaspoon chili powder, homemade (page 111) or store-bought

1 teaspoon Louisiana hot sauce

1 Combine all the ingredients in a medium-size nonreactive saucepan over medium heat, stirring until the sugar and spices have dissolved. Let simmer for about 10 minutes.

2 Let the sauce cool to warm or room temperature before basting. Baste or mop your barbecue after it has cooked long enough to set your rub. My rule of thumb is to start basting halfway through the cooking time. I baste whenever I have the cooker open or on the half, partial, or full hour.

Barbecue Pork Mop

The reason that I combine chicken and beef stock is because most people don't make their own pork stock and this combination comes very close to it. I also like to add a tablespoon of crushed red pepper to the mixture, which gives a little bite to the mop. Keep this on your grill in a metal pan away from the fire. MAKES ABOUT 3¹/₂ CUPS

- 1 cup chicken broth
- 1 cup beef broth
- ¹/₂ cup bacon drippings (bacon grease)
- ¹/₂ cup (1 stick) unsalted butter
- ¹/₄ cup fresh lemon juice (about 2 lemons)
- 1 tablespoon Worcestershire sauce, homemade (page 50) or store-bought
- 2 teaspoons chili powder, homemade (page 111) or store-bought
- 1 teaspoon granulated garlic
- 1 teaspoon finely ground black pepper
- 1 teaspoon fine sea salt

1 Combine all the ingredients in a medium-size nonreactive saucepan and bring to a boil, stirring to dissolve the spices and blend in the melted butter and bacon grease. Reduce the heat to medium-low and simmer for about 15 minutes.

2 Use the baste warm. Baste or mop your barbecue after it has cooked long enough to set your rub. My rule of thumb is to start basting halfway through the cooking time. I baste whenever I have the cooker open or on the half, partial, or full hour.

Eastern North Carolina Lemon Mop

Y'all can use this on whole hog, pork shoulder, pork ribs, or any other cut of pork you want to barbecue. Use warm to keep the butter melted. MAKES ABOUT 2¹/₂ CUPS

- 1 cup cider vinegar
- ¹/₂ cup water
- ¹/₄ cup fresh lemon juice (about 2 lemons)
- ¹/₄ cup (¹/₂ stick) unsalted butter
- ¹/₄ cup granulated cane sugar
- 2 tablespoons Worcestershire sauce, homemade (page 50) or store-bought
- 1 tablespoon Louisiana hot sauce
- 1 lemon, thinly sliced
- 2 teaspoons kosher salt
- 1 teaspoon cayenne pepper

1 Combine all the ingredients in a medium-size nonreactive saucepan and bring to a boil. Reduce the heat to medium-low and simmer for 15 minutes. Remove the lemon slices and discard.

2 Use the baste warm. Baste or mop your barbecue after it has cooked long enough to set your rub. My rule of thumb is to start basting halfway through the cooking time. I baste whenever I have the cooker open or on the half, partial, or full hour.

THE BARON OF BARBECUE'S 10 FAVORITE MARINADES FOR PORK

1 Picante Beer Marinade *(page 68)*

2 Lemon and Lager Marinade *(page 71)*

3 Gingered Marinade *(page 61)*

4 Honey-Garlic Marinade *(page 61)*

5 Garlicky Caesar Marinade *(page 62)*

6 Balsamic Marinade *(page 61)*

7 Hot Citrus Chipotle Marinade *(page 71)*

8 Memphis Basting Sauce *(can also be used as a marinade; page 82)*

9 Eastern North Carolina Lemon Mop *(can also be used as a marinade; page 78)*

10 Zippy Honey Marinade *(page 64)*

Peppery North Carolina Mop Sauce

Use this as a peppery mop sauce on whole hog, pork butt, pork ribs, or loin. MAKES ABOUT 3¹/₂ CUPS

2 cups cider vinegar

1 cup water

3 tablespoons coarsely ground black pepper

3 tablespoons fine sea salt

2 tablespoons sweet Hungarian paprika

2 tablespoons granulated cane sugar

1 tablespoon Louisiana hot sauce or Tabasco sauce

1 tablespoon Worcestershire sauce, homemade (page 50) or store-bought

1 tablespoon chili powder, homemade (page 111) or store-bought

1 Combine all the ingredients in a medium-size nonreactive saucepan and bring to a boil, stirring to dissolve and blend the sugar and spices.

2 Remove from the heat, cover, and let set until the sauce cools to room temperature before using as a baste. Baste or mop your barbecue after it has cooked long enough to set your rub. My rule of thumb is to start basting halfway through the cooking time. I baste whenever I have the cooker open or on the half, partial, or full hour.

Sour South Carolina Mop Sauce

Cider vinegar is another variable flavor in regional styles of barbecue, like brewed coffee in Texas and apple juice in Kansas City. This one goes on barbecued pork as well as on chicken and fish. MAKES ABOUT 2 CUPS

2 cups cider vinegar

1 tablespoon granulated cane sugar

1 tablespoon cayenne pepper

1 tablespoon fine sea salt

1 tablespoon finely ground black pepper

1 to 2 tablespoons vegetable oil

1 Combine all the ingredients in a medium-size nonreactive saucepan and bring to a boil, stirring to combine and dissolve the sugar and seasonings.

2 Remove from the heat, cover, and let set for an hour to mellow and mature the flavors before using. Use at room temperature. Baste or mop

your barbecue after it has cooked long enough to set your rub. My rule of thumb is to start basting halfway through the cooking time. I baste whenever I have the cooker open or on the half, partial, or full hour.

Good Ole Boy Bourbon Mop Sauce

Good on beef or pork or anything the good ole boy (or gal) wants. MAKES ABOUT 3¹/₂ CUPS

    2 cups beef broth

    ¹/₂ cup bourbon

    ¹/₂ cup Worcestershire sauce, homemade (page 50) or store-bought

    ¹/₄ cup canola oil

    2 tablespoons Louisiana hot sauce

    1 tablespoon sweet Hungarian paprika

    2 teaspoons granulated garlic

    2 teaspoons dry mustard (I use Colman's)

    2 teaspoons non-iodized salt

    1 teaspoon chili powder, homemade (page 111) or store-bought

    1 teaspoon freshly ground black pepper

    1 teaspoon crushed red pepper

1 Combine all the ingredients in a medium-size nonreactive saucepan over medium heat and simmer for 15 minutes, stirring occasionally.

2 Use as a baste at room temperature. Baste or mop your barbecue after it has cooked long enough to set your rub. My rule of thumb is to start basting halfway through the cooking time. I baste whenever I have the cooker open or on the half, partial, or full hour.

Cuban Mojo Marinade and Mop Sauce

This can also be used as a serving sauce for grilled or smoked chicken or pork. During the winter months when blood oranges are in season, use their more sour juice to make a killer mojo. MAKES ABOUT 2³/₄ CUPS

    1³/₄ cups fresh orange juice (about 7 oranges; I prefer blood oranges)

    ¹/₄ cup fresh lime juice (about 4 limes)

    ¹/₄ cup water

    ¹/₂ cup minced onion

    4 cloves garlic, pressed

    2 chicken bouillon cubes

    1 teaspoon dried oregano leaves

    1 teaspoon cumin seeds, toasted in a dry skillet over medium heat until fragrant, then ground

    1 teaspoon fine sea salt

    1 teaspoon freshly ground black pepper

1 Combine all the ingredients in a medium-size nonreactive saucepan over medium heat and simmer until the onion is tender and the bouillon cubes have dissolved, 20 to 30 minutes.

2 Use warm or at room temperature as a baste. Baste or mop your barbecue after it has cooked long enough to set your rub. My rule of thumb is to start basting halfway through the cooking time. I baste whenever I have the cooker open or on the half, partial, or full hour.

Tennessee Moppin' Sauce

Most folks in Tennessee like their ribs served dry—that means without barbecue sauce, not dry meat. To keep slabs of ribs or whole chickens moist during slow smoking, this is a good mop to use. MAKES ABOUT 3 CUPS

1 cup cider vinegar

1 cup chicken broth, or 1/2 cup chicken broth and 1/2 cup beef broth

1/2 cup sunflower oil

1/4 cup Worcestershire sauce, homemade (page 50) or store-bought

1/4 cup (1/2 stick) unsalted butter

1 lemon, thinly sliced

4 cloves garlic, pressed

2 tablespoons peeled and grated fresh ginger

2 tablespoons prepared yellow mustard

1 Combine all the ingredients in a medium-size nonreactive saucepan over medium heat and simmer for 15 to 20 minutes, blending with a wire whisk. Strain out the lemon slices and discard.

2 Use warm or at room temperature as a baste. Baste or mop your barbecue after it has cooked long enough to set your rub. My rule of thumb is to start basting halfway through the cooking time. I baste whenever I have the cooker open or on the half, partial, or full hour.

All-Purpose Baste for Meat

This is a good hearty baste to use on brisket, ribs, pork loin, pork butt, whole hog, or beef ribs but is too strong for chicken. MAKES ABOUT 5 CUPS

4 cups bone stock (see Note below) or beef broth

1/2 cup Worcestershire sauce, homemade (page 50) or store-bought

1/2 cup beer or ale (I use Red Hook Ale), allowed to go flat

1/4 cup canola oil

1 tablespoon sweet Hungarian paprika

1 tablespoon dry mustard (I use Colman's)

1 tablespoon seasoned salt, homemade (page 108) or store-bought

2 teaspoons granulated garlic

2 teaspoons chili seasoning, homemade (page 116) or store-bought

1 teaspoon cayenne pepper

1/4 teaspoon powdered bay leaf

1 Combine all the ingredients in a medium-size nonreactive saucepan and bring to a boil. Reduce the heat to medium-low and simmer for 30 minutes.

2 Use the baste warm or at room temperature. Baste or mop your barbecue after it has cooked long enough to set your rub. My rule of thumb is to start basting halfway through the cooking time. I baste whenever I have the cooker open or on the half, partial, or full hour.

NOTE If you want to make your own bone stock, start the way you would start a soup from scratch. Buy some good beef soup bones from your butcher and roast them in the oven at 350 to 400 degrees F for 30 to 45 minutes, then place them in a large soup pot with carrots, onions, celery, bay leaves, non-iodized salt, and pepper. Cover with cold water and bring to a boil. Reduce the heat to medium-low and simmer, uncovered, for about 1 hour or so. Let cool, then refrigerate, covered, overnight. Remove the fat from the top and strain.

Memphis Basting Sauce

Barbecuers in the Memphis area proclaim that this city is the barbecue pork capital of the world. So, guess what this moppin' sauce is best on? You're right—pork: barbecued ribs, pork butt, loin, or whole hog. **MAKES ABOUT 7 CUPS**

3 cups water

1½ cups red wine vinegar

¾ cup Heinz 57 steak sauce

½ cup plus 2 tablespoons Worcestershire sauce, homemade (page 50) or store-bought

½ cup tomato ketchup, homemade (page 43) or store-bought

¼ cup prepared yellow mustard

½ cup (1 stick) unsalted butter

1 tablespoon seasoned salt, homemade (page 108) or store-bought

2 teaspoons liquid smoke flavoring (optional)

1 Combine all the ingredients in a medium-size nonreactive saucepan over medium heat and simmer for 15 minutes.

2 Use the baste warm. Baste or mop your barbecue after it has cooked long enough to set your rub. My rule of thumb is to start basting halfway through the cooking time. I baste whenever I have the cooker open or on the half, partial, or full hour.

Southwestern-Style Basting Sauce

Use this sauce warm as a baste for all types of meats and fish. **MAKES ABOUT 5 CUPS**

2 cups beef broth

1 cup distilled white vinegar

1 pound (4 sticks) unsalted butter

5 to 6 serrano chiles, to your taste, cut in half lengthwise and left unseeded

2 limes, thinly sliced

¼ cup minced onion

¼ cup minced fresh cilantro leaves

1 tablespoon pressed garlic

2 teaspoons black peppercorns, crushed

1 teaspoon fine sea salt

1 Combine all the ingredients in a medium-size nonreactive saucepan and bring to a boil. Reduce the heat to medium-low and simmer for 30 minutes.

2 Use the baste warm. Baste or mop your barbecue after it has cooked long enough to set your rub. My rule of thumb is to start basting halfway through the cooking time. I baste whenever I have the cooker open or on the half, partial, or full hour.

Tomato-Herb Baste

If you're using a slather and rub with herbs and a finishing sauce with herbs, then why not also use a baste with herbs to continue the flavor? Use this on pork, beef, lamb, or fish. **MAKES 5 CUPS**

3 cups vegetable juice (I use V-8)

1 cup red wine vinegar

1 cup olive oil

2 sprigs fresh rosemary

2 sprigs fresh basil

2 sprigs fresh oregano

1 tablespoon pressed garlic

1 teaspoon black peppercorns, crushed

1 teaspoon crushed red pepper

1 teaspoon fine sea salt

1 Combine all the ingredients in a medium-size nonreactive saucepan and bring to a boil. Reduce the heat to medium-low and simmer for 30 minutes.

2 Use the baste after it has cooled down to warm. Baste or mop your barbecue after it has cooked long enough to set your rub. My rule of thumb is to start basting halfway through the cooking time. I baste whenever I have the cooker open or on the half, partial, or full hour.

Beef Rib Basting Sauce

Use this to mop a big old slab of Dinosaur Bones (page 267). MAKES ABOUT 2³/₄ CUPS

½ cup cider vinegar

½ cup Worcestershire sauce, homemade (page 50) or store-bought

½ cup soy sauce

½ cup beef broth or water

¼ cup sweet Hungarian paprika

2 tablespoons chili powder, homemade (page 111) or store-bought

2 tablespoons firmly packed dark brown sugar

1 tablespoon granulated cane sugar

1 tablespoon cumin seeds, toasted in a dry skillet over medium heat until fragrant, then ground

1 tablespoon freshly ground black pepper

2 teaspoons dried oregano leaves

1 teaspoon cayenne pepper

1 Combine all the ingredients in a medium-size nonreactive saucepan over medium heat and simmer for 15 minutes, stirring, until the sugar and spices have dissolved.

2 Use warm or at room temperature as a baste. Baste or mop your barbecue after it has cooked long enough to set your rub. My rule of thumb is to start basting halfway through the cooking time. I baste whenever I have the cooker open or on the half, partial, or full hour.

Missouri Rib Bastin' Sauce

This lemon-flavored basting sauce is a perfect fit with slabs of tender baby backs treated with a mustard slather and a hot and spicy rub and served with a smoky tomato barbecue sauce with just a hint of celery seed and smoke. Is your mouth watering yet? MAKES A LITTLE MORE THAN 2 CUPS

1½ cups distilled white vinegar

¼ cup vegetable oil

¼ cup fresh lemon juice (about 2 lemons)

2 lemons, thinly sliced

2 tablespoons Louisiana hot sauce

2 tablespoons firmly packed dark brown sugar

1 tablespoon granulated cane sugar

2 teaspoons kosher salt

1 teaspoon freshly ground black pepper

1 Combine all the ingredients in a medium-size nonreactive saucepan and bring to a boil. Reduce the heat to medium-low and simmer for 15 minutes, stirring occasionally.

2 Use at room temperature. Baste or mop your barbecue after it has cooked long enough to set your rub. My rule of thumb is to start basting

halfway through the cooking time. I baste whenever I have the cooker open or on the half, partial, or full hour.

Tequila Lime Baste

Have a margarita and enjoy this basting sauce on grilled or smoked fish and shellfish, especially shrimp. MAKES 3¹/₂ CUPS

- 1 cup fresh lime juice (about 16 limes)
- 1 cup chicken broth
- ¹/₂ cup tequila
- 4 to 6 cloves garlic, to your taste, pressed
- 1 tablespoon Pickapeppa hot sauce
- ¹/₂ cup fresh cilantro leaves, minced
- 1 teaspoon kosher salt
- 1 teaspoon freshly ground black pepper
- 1 cup olive oil

1 Place the lime juice, broth, tequila, garlic, hot sauce, cilantro, salt, and pepper in a blender or food processor and process for about 2 minutes. With the machine running, slowly add the olive oil and process just until incorporated.

2 Baste or mop your barbecue after it has cooked long enough to set your rub. My rule of thumb is to start basting halfway through the cooking time. I baste whenever I have the cooker open or on the half, partial, or full hour.

Chipotle Vinegar Basting Sauce

If you like a hot, peppery, vinegary Carolina-style basting sauce, try this one with the heat of the Southwest on chicken, turkey, and fish. Keep warm so the lard stays melted. MAKES ABOUT 1¹/₂ CUPS

- 1¹/₄ cups cider vinegar
- ¹/₄ cup lard
- 1 tablespoon chili powder, homemade (page 111) or store-bought
- 1 tablespoon granulated cane sugar
- 1 tablespoon hot Hungarian paprika
- 2 teaspoons pure ground chipotle chile
- 1 teaspoon dry mustard (I use Colman's)
- 1 teaspoon fine sea salt
- 1 teaspoon finely ground black pepper
- ¹/₂ teaspoon cumin seeds, toasted in a dry skillet over medium heat until fragrant, then ground

1 Combine all the ingredients in a medium-size nonreactive saucepan over medium heat and simmer until the lard has melted and the spices are dissolved and incorporated, 10 to 15 minutes.

2 Use warm as a baste. Baste or mop your barbecue after it has cooked long enough to set your rub. My rule of thumb is to start basting halfway through the cooking time. I baste whenever I have the cooker open or on the half, partial, or full hour.

Gypsy Bastin' Sauce

I have no idea how this Texas mop got its name, but it works well with brisket for a hot 'n' spicy, buttery finish. Use warm so the butter stays melted. **MAKES ABOUT 5 CUPS**

  2 cups cider vinegar

  1½ cups Worcestershire sauce, homemade (page 50) or store-bought

  1 cup beef broth

  ½ cup (1 stick) unsalted butter

  ¼ cup Louisiana hot sauce

  1 tablespoon fine sea salt

  1 tablespoon freshly ground black pepper

  1 teaspoon pure ground jalapeño chile

1 Combine all the ingredients in a medium-size nonreactive saucepan over medium heat and simmer for 15 minutes, blending with a wire whisk.

2 Use warm as a baste. Baste or mop your barbecue after it has cooked long enough to set your rub. My rule of thumb is to start basting halfway through the cooking time. I baste whenever I have the cooker open or on the half, partial, or full hour.

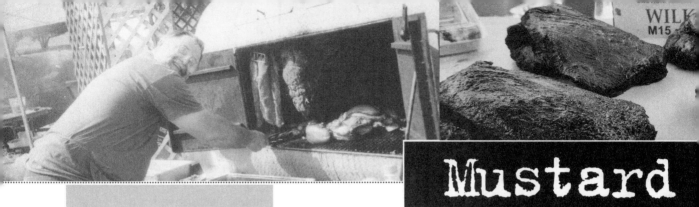

Mustard

Slathers

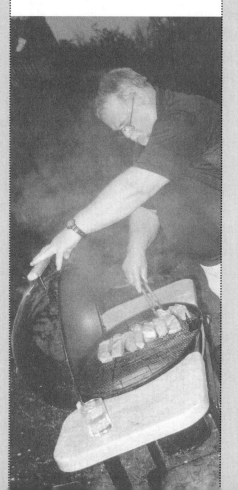

Slather: to spread on or cover thickly; to use great amounts of; to lavish.

This chapter is dedicated to—or blamed on—Kathy Richardier, a.k.a. Kathy of Calgary, and all the people who sent in their questions about mustard slathers as part of the Canadian Barbecue Smokers Association forum on the Internet.

A mustard slather is kind of an afterthought, really. Of all the procedures and processes that I perform while barbecuing, spreading mustard on the meat before I season it has always been the least copied.

It's also a procedure that I don't teach when doing Pitmaster classes around the world, unless a student requests information about it. Mustard slather is just a convenient name, although it's not very accurate, because I don't always use a great amount of mustard. I usually paint on the mustard slather with a pastry brush, sprinkle on a rub, and let the surface get tacky, usually in about 15 minutes, then put the meat on the pit. And it works, meaning it results in a flavorful bit of barbecue.

Why does this work? My theory is that the enzymes in the meat and slather ingredients work with the seasonings to form a tasty and protective crust, or bark, on the meat being barbecued. I use mustard slathers on barbecued beef, pork, and chicken, and I have also used it successfully on barbecued salmon.

As for the first time I ever saw someone using a mustard slather, I have to go back to the late '70s, when I used to go over to Brown's BBQ in northwest Wyandotte County, Kansas, just west of Kansas City, Missouri. Brown's BBQ was owned by a very kind and genteel 71-year-old black man by the name of Arthies (Art) Brown. Art's typical day would go like this: At 6 A.M., he would arrive at what he called his barbecue shack (a ramshackle old building), which had two window counters, a four-compartment homemade steam table, one deep fryer, and a heat lamp. It also contained a small walk-in cooler, washroom, restroom, and the Pit Room.

The Pit Room consisted of a homemade brick pit with heavy iron doors, workbenches with butcher-block wood tops, and a six-burner stove with an oven. After he threw a couple of logs in the firebox of the pit, he would get out the briskets. I can't ever remember Art trimming briskets. He would place them on the table fat side down and pull out a blue metal bowl with mustard sauce in it. He would stick his right hand in the mustard sauce and rub it thinly all over the lean side of the briskets. After rinsing and drying his hands, he would then season the briskets with a mixture of salt and black pepper. Then he would turn the briskets over and repeat the process, making sure the entire surface was covered. Then he would take his heavy-duty long-handled fork and strategically place each brisket in the smoker, which, by the way, had no thermometer to tell him what the temperature was. He used the same process with ribs.

Throughout the morning, he would add wood without looking at the fire or in the pit. I think he judged the heat by how it felt as he walked by the steel doors.

Art's menu consisted of barbecued brisket sandwich, barbecued ribs, homemade sausage, and fries. He cut all serving portions with a long, curved knife or big meat cleaver. I don't remember what the prices of things were, but he put every menu item on a piece of reddish butcher paper and wrapped it in newspaper that he collected from friends. The sandwiches were typical brisket rollups—brisket slices folded in slices of soft, inexpensive white bread. When all the meat for the day was gone, Art closed up.

I wish I had known then how involved I would get with barbecue, because I would have asked Art a million questions. He knew the answers and would have shared them with me. He's the one who gave me my introduction to mustard and mustard slathers. I miss him!

Art's Mustard Sauce

Arthies (Art) Brown owned Brown's BBQ on the Kansas side of Kansas City, and I used to love to go out there for good eatin' in the 1970s. This is the slather that Art kept in the blue bowl and painted on beef brisket and ribs. It's really a simple recipe, but what it does to barbecued beef and pork! **MAKES ABOUT 2³/₄ CUPS**

2 cups prepared yellow mustard

¹/₂ cup dill pickle juice

2 tablespoons Worcestershire sauce, homemade (page 50) or store-bought

1 tablespoon hot pepper sauce

Combine all the ingredients in a medium-size nonreactive bowl and blend well. Paint on your meat, then season and cook.

GOOD PAIRED WITH The Baron of Barbecue's Seasoned Salt (page 108), Barbecue Seasoning (page 114), or Barbecue Pork Rub (page 124)

Sam's Special Sauce

The original recipe for this sauce is very much like Art's Mustard Sauce. It was stolen from Crazy Sam Higgins of Texas, a barbecue character and the author of the cookbook *I'm Glad I Ate When I Did, 'Cause I'm Not Hungry Now* (self-published). Like the cover says, this book is full of Crazy Sam's redneck tales and his down-home culinary concoctions—some original, some borrowed, and some stolen (like this recipe). I met Sam at the home of Rich Davis, the creator of K. C. Masterpiece Barbecue Sauce. Rich called me and asked if I would like to have some 26-hour barbecued Texas brisket. What do you think I said? You're right—"What time is dinner served?" I am not a fan of mesquite, but that was some of the finest brisket that I have ever had the pleasure of eating!

Over my many years of barbecuing, I have used Sam's Special Sauce as my base slather—a cooking sauce, not a dipping sauce. **MAKES ABOUT 5¹/₂ CUPS**

One 12-ounce can light beer, allowed to go flat

One 32-ounce jar prepared yellow mustard

5 dashes or shakes of Tabasco sauce

1 cup firmly packed light brown sugar

Mix together all the ingredients in a large nonreactive bowl until well combined, then spread thinly over your meat before seasoning and cooking it.

GOOD PAIRED WITH The Baron's Barbecue Spice (page 115), Texas-Style Barbecue Beef Rub (page 124), or Joe D's Barbecue Rub Supreme (page 127)

The Baron's Special Sauce (a.k.a. Mustard Slather)

Any little thing you do, any extra procedure or homemade concoction, can make the difference between a blue ribbon and no ribbon in a barbecue contest. This slather just might make a big difference on your brisket, pork butt, ribs, or chicken. MAKES ABOUT 5 CUPS

> 1 generous cup firmly packed light brown sugar
>
> 1 teaspoon kosher salt
>
> 1 teaspoon white pepper
>
> One 12-ounce can beer (I use Budweiser), allowed to go flat
>
> One 32-ounce jar prepared yellow mustard
>
> 2 tablespoons Louisiana hot sauce

In a large nonreactive bowl, combine the brown sugar, salt, pepper, and beer, stirring until the sugar and salt have dissolved. Blend in the mustard and hot sauce. Paint on this slather with a pastry brush, then sprinkle on your rub before cooking.

GOOD PAIRED WITH The Baron of Barbecue's Seasoned Salt (page 108), The Baron's Barbecue Spice (page 115), or The Baron's Chili Powder (page 111)

Angel's Mustard Slather

This is a very assertive slather recipe that I got from Angel, a guy who used to compete in barbecue contests but doesn't anymore. His slather lives on, however. MAKES 2¹/₂ CUPS

> 2 tablespoons granulated garlic
>
> 1 tablespoon granulated onion
>
> 2 teaspoons finely ground black pepper
>
> 1 teaspoon white pepper
>
> 1 teaspoon cayenne pepper
>
> 1 teaspoon fine sea salt
>
> ¹/₄ cup soy sauce
>
> ¹/₄ cup Worcestershire sauce, homemade (page 50) or store-bought
>
> 2 cups Dijon mustard

Combine the garlic, onion, peppers, and salt in a medium-size nonreactive bowl. Blend in the soy sauce and Worcestershire and whisk until the spices dissolve. Stir in the mustard until well mixed. Paint thinly on your meat before seasoning and cooking it.

GOOD PAIRED WITH Mild Italian Seasoning (page 120), Scotty's Barbecue Rub (page 127), or Creole Seasoning (page 119)

Hot Bacon-Mustard Slather

You get the smoky taste of bacon with the sweetness of honey in this mustard slather, and it's good on just about anything you want to barbecue. MAKES ABOUT 2¹/₂ CUPS

1/4 cup bacon drippings (bacon grease)

2 cups honey Dijon mustard

1/2 cup firmly packed light brown sugar

3 tablespoons fresh lemon juice

3 tablespoons red wine vinegar

1 teaspoon dry mustard (I use Colman's)

1/4 cup clover honey

1/2 teaspoon cayenne pepper

Place all the ingredients in a medium-size nonreactive saucepan over medium heat and stir with a wire whisk until heated through and well blended. Use warm or at room temperature, painting it on thinly before seasoning and cooking your meat.

GOOD PAIRED WITH Barbecue Pork Rub, Texas-Style Barbecue Beef Rub, or Chuck Wagon Beef Rub (all on page 124)

Spicy Mustard Slather

With five kinds of hot—dry and prepared mustard, hot pepper sauce, ground pepper, and cayenne—this slather gives your barbecue quite a kick. **MAKES ABOUT 3 CUPS**

1/2 cup (1 stick) unsalted butter

2 cups prepared yellow mustard

1/4 cup granulated cane sugar

1/4 cup rice vinegar

2 tablespoons Worcestershire sauce, homemade (page 50) or store-bought

2 teaspoons garlic salt

1 teaspoon dry mustard (I use Colman's)

1 teaspoon hot pepper sauce

1/2 teaspoon white pepper

1/2 teaspoon cayenne pepper

Combine all the ingredients in a medium-size nonreactive saucepan. Heat over medium heat, stirring, until the butter has melted and everything is well blended. Use warm or at room temperature, painting it thinly over your meat before seasoning and cooking it.

GOOD PAIRED WITH The Baron of Barbecue's Seasoned Salt (page 108), Savory Seasoned Salt (page 109), or A Clone of Lawry's Seasoned Salt (page 110)

Soy Triple Mustard Slather

Yellow, Dijon, and spicy brown mustards team up with soy sauce to make a slather that's good on pork loin or beef brisket. **MAKES ABOUT 4 CUPS**

2 cups prepared yellow mustard

1/2 cup Dijon mustard

1/2 cup spicy brown mustard

1/3 cup soy sauce

1/4 cup soybean or canola oil

2 tablespoons Worcestershire sauce, homemade (page 50) or store-bought

2 tablespoons red wine vinegar

1 teaspoon granulated garlic

1 teaspoon finely ground black pepper

1 teaspoon fine sea salt

Combine all the ingredients in a large nonreactive bowl and blend well. Paint thinly over your meat before seasoning or cooking it.

GOOD PAIRED WITH Chinese 5-Spice Powder (for pork; page 112), Exotic Seasoned Salt (page 108), or Tellicherry Peppercorn Seasoning (page 121)

Orange Mustard Slather

With orange and rum and a hit of celery seed, this slightly sweet and aromatic slather pairs well with pork, lamb, chicken, duck, or fish. MAKES ABOUT 1 1/2 CUPS

1 cup prepared yellow mustard

1/4 cup orange juice

1/4 cup granulated cane sugar

1 tablespoon finely minced orange zest

1 tablespoon dark rum (I use Meyer's)

1 teaspoon granulated garlic

1 teaspoon white pepper

1/2 teaspoon ground celery seeds

1/2 teaspoon non-iodized salt

Combine all the ingredients in a medium-size nonreactive bowl and blend well. Paint thinly over your meat before seasoning and cooking it.

GOOD PAIRED WITH Juniper Spice Blend (page 122), Exotic Seasoned Salt (page 108), or Sodium-Free Herb Seasoning (page 114)

Tart Mustard Slather

Cider vinegar and lemon juice give this slather a bit of a sharp tang that's delicious on fattier cuts of meat, such as brisket, pork shoulder, and lamb ribs. MAKES ABOUT 3 CUPS

2 cups prepared yellow mustard

1 cup firmly packed light brown sugar

1/4 cup cider vinegar

1/4 cup fresh lemon juice (about 2 lemons)

1 1/2 tablespoons freshly ground black pepper

1 tablespoon Worcestershire sauce, homemade (page 50) or store-bought

1 teaspoon non-iodized salt

1 teaspoon Louisiana hot sauce

1/2 teaspoon cayenne pepper

Combine all the ingredients in a medium-size nonreactive bowl and blend well with a wire whisk. Paint thinly over your meat before seasoning and cooking it.

GOOD PAIRED WITH Barbecue Seasoning and Rub (page 115), Roasted Garlic and Ancho Chili Powder (page 112), or Paul Ewing's Southern-Style Rub (page 127)

Erin's Mustard Slather

Erin Kirk is my twenty-something daughter, but she is still my baby (you know how that goes). She grew up with barbecue. When I started competing in barbecue contests in the early 1980s, my wife, Jessica, and I just packed her up and took her with us, along with her older brother, Todd, and sister, Chris. Erin is a barbecue champion in her own right, starting with Kids Q and continuing on to the Missouri State Championships, where this slather helped her win first place in Ribs in 1993. She recently won fifth place in the Dessert category for the panna cotta she made for the 2002 World Championship Barbecue Contest held in Imperial Beach, California. MAKES ABOUT 4 CUPS

2 cups prepared yellow mustard

1/2 cup firmly packed light brown sugar

1/2 cup distilled white vinegar

1/4 cup tomato ketchup, homemade (page 43) or store-bought

All in THE FAMILY

When I got started in competition barbecue in 1981, I was married with three kids. My son, Todd, was five, daughter Chris was three, and daughter Erin was a little bitty baby.

My wife, Jessica, and I soon found out—by necessity—that barbecue contests could be great outings for the family. A contest is like a long weekend picnic. You can be with your family while your food is smoking, and you can invite friends to visit your cooking and sleeping area. And 95 percent of the people you meet are great. There are very few pompous asses in barbecue, so it's fun for the whole family.

A lot of people treat a barbecue contest like a campout and either sleep outside near the cooking area or in a trailer they bring. We use our van. I sleep in the front seat so I can wake up every few hours to check the fire and the food. Everybody else either sleeps in the back of the van or outside.

As they got older, the kids helped out with the cooking and even entered Kids Q contests. Chris, Todd, and Erin still help me make batches of barbecue sauce. Of the three kids, Erin is the most interested in competition barbecue, and she's done well in several contests.

My wife, Jessica, sometimes enters barbecue contests with the team name of Flaming Flamingo. She was the 1985 Kansas State Barbecue Champion, and she won with smoked catfish. She was also the Grand Champion at the Spirit Fest Barbecue Contest in Kansas City, so she's no slouch, either.

Jessica, Erin, and I were all cooking in the 2002 National Lamb-B-Que Contest held in Bonner Springs, Kansas, and we had a blast. I'm sure there are more contests to come for the Kirk family. I guess barbecue just runs in our blood.

¼ cup fresh lemon juice (about 2 lemons)

1 tablespoon olive oil

1 tablespoon granulated onion

2 teaspoons granulated garlic

1 teaspoon kosher salt

1 teaspoon freshly ground black pepper

1 teaspoon cayenne pepper

Combine all the ingredients in a large nonreactive bowl, blending with a wire whisk until well mixed. Paint thinly over your meat before seasoning and cooking it.

GOOD PAIRED WITH The Baron of Barbecue's Seasoned Salt (page 108), Barbecue Seasoning (page 114), or Barbecue Pork Rub (page 124)

Kansas State Championship Mustard Slather

I have used this slather successfully on ribs, pork butt, and brisket at the Lenexa Barbeque Battle, held every June in Lenexa, Kansas. This used to be the contest that decided the Kansas State Championship. MAKES ABOUT 5 CUPS

3 cups prepared yellow mustard

1 cup spicy brown mustard

1/2 cup firmly packed dark brown sugar

1/4 cup gin

2 tablespoons Worcestershire sauce, homemade (page 50) or store-bought

2 tablespoons fresh lemon juice

2 tablespoons balsamic vinegar

1 tablespoon lemonade powder (I use Country Time; make sure whatever you use contains sugar and not an artificial sweetener)

2 teaspoons fine sea salt

1 teaspoon white pepper

1 teaspoon granulated garlic

1 teaspoon pure ground chipotle chile

1 teaspoon ground ginger

1 teaspoon dry mustard (I use Colman's)

Combine all the ingredients in a large nonreactive 2-quart bowl. Blend well with a wire whisk until the seasonings have dissolved and are incorporated into the mixture. Paint thinly over your meat before seasoning and cooking it.

GOOD PAIRED WITH Mexican Spice Paste (page 134), Sodium-Free Herb Seasoning (page 114), or Chili Seasoning (page 116)

Sweet Green Peppercorn and Tarragon Mustard Slather

This is a more sophisticated variation on the theme of mustard slathers—green peppercorns, tarragon, clover honey, and brandy add sweetness, and three different mustards create a rich, deep flavor. This slather is great on pork loin. MAKES 2 CUPS

1 cup Dijon mustard

1/2 cup honey mustard

2 tablespoons dry mustard (I use Colman's)

2 tablespoons olive oil

2 tablespoons brandy

2 tablespoons white wine vinegar

2 tablespoons clover honey

2 teaspoons dried tarragon leaves

2 teaspoons green peppercorns, drained, smashed, and minced

1 teaspoon fine sea salt

Combine all the ingredients in a medium-size nonreactive bowl. With a wire whisk, blend until well combined. Paint thinly over your meat before seasoning and cooking it.

GOOD PAIRED WITH Creole Seasoning Mix (page 118), Sodium-Free Herb Seasoning (page 114), or Barbecue Pork Rub (page 124)

Capered French Mustard Slather

Oui, oui! Barbecue speaks an international language. Teams from all over the world compete now. Try this slather on barbecued lamb ribs. MAKES ABOUT 3 CUPS

2 cups Dijon mustard

1/4 cup fresh lemon juice (about 2 lemons)

1/4 cup sunflower oil

1/4 cup very thinly sliced green onions (green part only)

2 tablespoons capers, drained, smashed, and minced

2 cloves garlic, pressed

1 teaspoon fine sea salt

1/2 teaspoon white pepper

Place all the ingredients in a medium-size nonreactive bowl and blend well with a wire whisk. Paint thinly over your meat before seasoning and cooking it.

GOOD PAIRED WITH Exotic Seasoned Salt (page 108), My Big Fat Greek Seasoning (page 121), or Juniper Spice Blend (page 122)

Honey Mustard Slather

You'd be amazed at how many different kinds of mustard there are, and some of them are very expensive. You can just add ingredients such as herbs or honey or horseradish to regular mustards and get the same effect for less money, as in this slather, though I don't mind spending my money on horseradish mustard because I love it. Slather this on beef, chicken, or pork. MAKES ABOUT 3 CUPS

1 cup prepared yellow mustard

1/2 cup horseradish mustard

1/2 cup spicy brown mustard

1/4 cup clover honey

1/4 cup firmly packed dark brown sugar

1/4 cup distilled white vinegar

2 tablespoons prepared horseradish

1 teaspoon granulated garlic

1 teaspoon fine sea salt

1 teaspoon finely ground black pepper

1/2 teaspoon cayenne pepper

Combine all the ingredients in a medium-size nonreactive bowl and blend well with a wire whisk. Paint thinly over your meat before seasoning and cooking it.

GOOD PAIRED WITH Dale's Blue Ribbon Chicken Seasoning (page 126), Barbecue Seasoning and Rub (page 115), or MIT Barbecue Rub and Seasoning (page 131)

Horseradish Mustard Slather

Somewhat hot and spicy, this slather is great on pork. MAKES ABOUT 2 3/4 CUPS

2 cups prepared yellow mustard

1/3 cup prepared horseradish

2 tablespoons soy sauce

2 tablespoons sunflower oil

2 tablespoons clover honey

1 tablespoon sweet Hungarian paprika

1 teaspoon seasoned salt, homemade (page 108) or store-bought

1 teaspoon freshly ground black pepper

Combine all the ingredients in a medium-size nonreactive bowl and blend well with a wire whisk. Paint thinly over your meat before seasoning and cooking it.

GOOD PAIRED WITH Dale's Ribbon Chicken Seasoning (page 126), Barbecue Seasoning and Rub (page 115), or MIT Barbecue Rub and Seasoning (page 131)

1999 American Royal Mustard Slather

As you may have guessed, I used this slather in the 1999 American Royal Barbecue Contest on everything from beef brisket to ribs. Every year when I compete, I develop new rubs, slathers, and sauces. **MAKES ABOUT 5 CUPS**

- 1/2 cup (1 stick) unsalted butter
- 3 cups prepared yellow mustard
- 1 cup Dijonnaise or other Dijon-and-mayonnaise blend
- 1/4 cup firmly packed light brown sugar
- 1/4 cup rice vinegar
- 1/4 cup balsamic vinegar
- 2 tablespoons Worcestershire sauce, homemade (page 50) or store-bought
- 1 tablespoon garlic salt
- 1 tablespoon Louisiana hot sauce
- 2 teaspoons dry mustard (I use Colman's)
- 1 teaspoon white pepper
- 1 teaspoon cayenne pepper

Combine all the ingredients in a medium-size nonreactive saucepan. Heat over medium heat, stirring, until the butter has melted and everything is well blended. Use warm or at room temperature, painting it thinly over your meat before seasoning and cooking it.

GOOD PAIRED WITH IFTC Barbecue Seasoning and Rub (page 131), Eddy's Catering Kansas City Barbecue Seasoning and Rub (page 130), or The Baron's Barbecue Spice (page 115)

Minty Mustard Slather

This is another good slather to use on lamb and beef.
MAKES A GENEROUS 2 1/2 CUPS

- 1/4 cup (1/2 stick) unsalted butter
- 1/2 cup puréed shallots (about 4 large shallots)
- 4 cloves garlic, pressed
- 1/4 cup dried mint leaves
- 2 cups Dijon mustard
- 1/2 cup beef broth
- 1 tablespoon grated lemon zest
- 1 teaspoon fine sea salt
- 1 teaspoon freshly ground black pepper

Melt the butter in a medium-size nonreactive saucepan over medium heat. Add the shallots and garlic and cook, stirring, until soft, 10 to 12 minutes. Add the mint and cook, stirring, 2 to 3 minutes longer. Add the remaining ingredients, stir until well blended, and simmer 5 to 7 minutes longer. Use warm or at room temperature, painting it thinly over your meat before seasoning and cooking it.

GOOD PAIRED WITH Sodium-Free Herb Seasoning (page 114), Turkish Mixed Spices (page 122), or Creole Herb Seasoning Mix (page 118)

Mad Jack's Simple Mustard Slather

This recipe is a take-off from a recipe used by Jack Ryan's barbecue team, Mad Jack's Rib Ranchers, from Houston, Texas. Jack is also one of my students, and his team wins with this recipe, which is tasty on brisket, ribs, chicken, and even salmon. MAKES ABOUT 3 CUPS

- 4 cups prepared yellow mustard
- 1 cup firmly packed dark brown sugar
- One 12-ounce can premium beer, allowed to go flat
- 1 teaspoon ground ginger
- 1 teaspoon fine sea salt
- 1 teaspoon white pepper

Combine all the ingredients in a medium-size nonreactive saucepan, blending with a wire whisk to dissolve the spices. Simmer over medium-low heat until reduced by half, 30 to 45 minutes, stirring occasionally. Use warm or at room temperature, painting it thinly over your meat before seasoning and cooking it.

GOOD PAIRED WITH Calypso Seasoning (page 123), Jerk Seasoning (page 123), or Caribbean Chicken Rub (page 128)

Yogurt Mustard Slather

This slather is sort of like a tandoori marinade, but without the Indian spices and ginger. The yogurt helps keep the meat moist. Try it on chicken or fish. MAKES ABOUT 3 1/2 CUPS

- 2 cups spicy brown mustard
- 1 cup plain yogurt
- 2 tablespoons fresh lemon juice
- 2 tablespoons cider vinegar
- 2 tablespoons granulated cane sugar
- 1 tablespoon soy sauce
- 2 teaspoons granulated garlic
- 1 teaspoon dried basil leaves
- 1 teaspoon fine sea salt
- 1/2 teaspoon white pepper
- 1/2 teaspoon cayenne pepper

In a medium-size nonreactive bowl, combine all the ingredients, blending well with a wire whisk. Cover and refrigerate for 1 to 2 hours before using to let the flavors blend. Paint thinly over your meat before seasoning and cooking it.

GOOD PAIRED WITH Poultry Barbecue Rub (page 129), Hotsy Totsy Seafood Seasoning (page 120), or Herb Salt Seasoning Blend (page 111)

Making SMOKED VEGETABLE PASTES
for Slathers and Sauces

Here's another way to get a competitive edge in barbecue contests or the best damn barbecue you've ever had at home. Infuse vegetables with a smoky flavor, then purée them and add to the slather or sauce. You can smoke garlic, onions, tomatoes, red bell pepper, green bell pepper, fresh chiles, or almost any garden vegetable you want.

Here's how you do it:

1 Prepare the vegetables. Peel garlic cloves and thread them on wooden skewers. Peel onions and cut them in half horizontally. Stem tomatoes. Cut in half and seed bell peppers or chiles.

2 Set up your covered grill for indirect cooking. Soak mesquite or hickory wood chunks or chips in water for at least 20 minutes, then place on the hot coals.

3 Place the vegetables cut side down on the grill, positioning the onions and garlic closest to the fire, the peppers and tomatoes the farthest away. Close the lid and smoke for about 3 hours.

4 Remove the vegetables from the smoker and purée them in a food processor, then add to a slather or sauce. The purées will keep in the refrigerator for up to 1 week or in the freezer for up to 3 months.

Dijon Mustard Slather with Curry and Gin

Just a hint of curry and the juniper-berry flavor of gin make this slather good to use on barbecued beef, pork, or game.

MAKES ABOUT 2³/₄ CUPS

2 cups Dijon mustard

¹/₄ cup (¹/₂ stick) unsalted butter, melted

2 tablespoons clover honey

2 tablespoons Worcestershire sauce, homemade (page 50) or store-bought

2 tablespoons fresh lemon juice

1 tablespoon dry gin

1 teaspoon fine sea salt

¹/₂ teaspoon white pepper

¹/₂ teaspoon curry powder

Combine all the ingredients in a medium-size nonreactive bowl and blend with a wire whisk until well combined. Paint thinly over your meat before seasoning and cooking it.

GOOD PAIRED WITH Barbecue Seasoning and Rub (page 115), The Baron of Barbecue's Seasoned Salt (page 108), or Juniper Spice Blend (page 122)

Honey Wine Mustard Slather with Smoked Garlic Paste

Ground ginger, my spice "girlfriend," adds a flavor note to this slather, which is good on pork, lamb, and chicken.
MAKES ABOUT 4¹/₂ CUPS

2 cups spicy brown mustard

1 cup Dijon mustard

¹/₂ cup clover honey

¹/₂ cup dry white wine

¹/₄ cup olive oil

2 tablespoons soy sauce

1 tablespoon smoked garlic paste (page 98)

1 teaspoon ground ginger

1 teaspoon fine sea salt

¹/₂ teaspoon white pepper

Combine all the ingredients in a large nonreactive bowl and blend well with a wire whisk. Paint thinly over your meat before seasoning and cooking it.

GOOD PAIRED WITH Chuck Wagon Beef Rub (page 124), Dale's Blue Ribbon Chicken Seasoning (page 126), or Beau Monde Seasoning (page 121)

Sweet Country Mustard Slather

By sweet red wine, I mean a country wine meant for sipping, such as elderberry or even rhubarb wine, or you could use sweet red vermouth. Notice that there's just a little bit of rosemary, the "bitch" of seasonings (because a little goes a long way). Use this on ribs, pork butt, or pork loin.
MAKES ABOUT 5 CUPS

4 cups prepared yellow mustard

¹/₂ cup firmly packed light brown sugar

¹/₄ cup sweet red wine

¹/₄ cup fresh lemon juice (about 2 lemons)

1 tablespoon coarsely ground black pepper

1 tablespoon dried parsley flakes

2 teaspoons granulated garlic

1 teaspoon fine sea salt

¹/₂ teaspoon dried rosemary leaves

Combine all the ingredients in a large nonreactive bowl and blend well with a wire whisk. Paint thinly over your meat before seasoning and cooking it.

GOOD PAIRED WITH Scotty's Barbecue Rub (page 127), Creole Herb Seasoning Mix (page 118), or MIT Barbecue Rub and Seasoning (page 131)

Sweet-Sweet Mustard Slather

Two kinds of sugar make for the sweet-sweet in this slather, which also has a hit of raspberry vinegar. It's great on pork, chicken, or duck. MAKES ABOUT 3 CUPS

2 cups prepared yellow mustard

¹/₄ cup granulated cane sugar

¹/₄ cup firmly packed light brown sugar

¹/₄ cup raspberry vinegar

1 tablespoon rubbed sage

1 teaspoon granulated garlic

¹/₂ teaspoon fine sea salt

¹/₂ teaspoon white pepper

¹/₂ cup extra virgin olive oil

Combine all the ingredients, except the olive oil, in a medium-size nonreactive bowl, and blend well with a wire whisk. Slowly blend in the olive oil with the whisk. Paint thinly over your meat before seasoning and cooking it.

GOOD PAIRED WITH Exotic Seasoned Salt (page 108), Garden Blend Herb Salt (page 111), or The Baron's Cajun Seasoning (page 117)

Curry Dijon Mustard Slather

Curry powder and mustard go well together for a slightly more exotic flavor on pork, lamb, chicken, or fish. MAKES ABOUT 4¹/₃ CUPS

- 2 cups prepared yellow mustard
- 1 cup sour cream
- ¹/₂ cup Dijon mustard
- ¹/₂ cup mayonnaise
- ¹/₄ cup fresh lemon juice (about 2 lemons) or white wine
- 1 tablespoon curry powder, homemade (page 112) or store-bought
- 2 teaspoons granulated onion
- 1 teaspoon fine sea salt
- 1 teaspoon freshly ground black pepper
- ¹/₂ teaspoon ground celery seeds

Combine all the ingredients in a large nonreactive bowl, blending well with a wire whisk. Paint thinly over your meat before seasoning and cooking it.

GOOD PAIRED WITH Beau Monde Seasoning (page 121), Snail's Sprinkle (page 125), or Doug's Barbecue Seasoning (page 128)

Jersey Beef Mustard Slather

This is a good slather—with the Boss's (Bruce Springsteen's) attitude—for sirloin steak, brisket, and beef ribs. MAKES ABOUT 4 CUPS

- 3 cups prepared yellow mustard
- ¹/₄ cup Worcestershire sauce, homemade (page 50) or store-bought
- ¹/₄ cup Madeira wine
- 3 tablespoons smoked garlic paste (page 98)
- 1 tablespoon firmly packed light brown sugar
- 1 tablespoon finely ground black pepper
- 1 teaspoon fine sea salt
- ¹/₂ cup (1 stick) unsalted butter, melted

Combine all the ingredients, except the butter, in a large nonreactive bowl and blend with an electric mixer until smooth. Add the melted butter in a slow stream while blending. Paint thinly over your meat before seasoning and cooking it.

GOOD PAIRED WITH The Baron's Steak Seasoning (page 122), Lemon Pepper Steak Seasoning (page 123), or New Century Catering Barbecue Seasoning and Rub (page 132)

Fast Eddie's Miracle Mustard Slather

This mustard slather is dedicated to Fast Eddie Maurin, a firefighter who also makes wood pellet grills. Several barbecuers have asked Eddie whether he uses mustard in his slather and he says no, Miracle Whip is his secret ingredient. That inspired me to come up with this slather, which is good on beef brisket and pork. **MAKES ABOUT 6¼ CUPS**

3 cups prepared yellow mustard

2 cups Miracle Whip salad dressing

1 cup dill pickle juice

¼ cup firmly packed brown sugar

2 tablespoons granulated garlic

Combine all the ingredients in a large nonreactive bowl until well blended. Paint thinly over your meat before seasoning and cooking it.

GOOD PAIRED WITH The Baron's Barbecue Spice (page 115), Texas-Style Barbecue Beef Rub (page 124), or Doug's Barbecue Seasoning (page 128)

Championship Seasonings

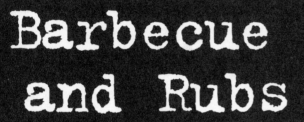

Barbecue and Rubs

Sugar and spice . . . and everything nice!"

That's my standard answer when someone asks me what's in my competition or private barbecue rub. It may sound like a joke, but I'm serious when I say it. I will tell people what's in my recipes if they ask me. If they identify an ingredient, I will confirm their guess. The main thing that I don't do is give the quantities. I put a lot of work into creating special seasonings and rubs every year to use in competition. I don't use the same rub or seasoning year after year.

Although I won't tell you what's in the seasonings and rubs I am creating for competition this year, I am happy to give you the recipes for seasoning blends I've used successfully in the past. They're all in this chapter. And I'll also tell you how to develop your own successful blends for prize-winning barbecued foods.

Why? The most important aspect of any recipe, especially in barbecuing, is the seasoning. The art of seasoning is paramount! To me, it is the essence of all cooking.

When using any spice or herb, a good rule of thumb is: A little goes a long way. Whatever you do, don't smother your food with spices. The more you learn and know about seasoning, the better cook you will be.

How do you perfect or develop your seasoning ability? I suggest that you start with your olfactory skills—what do you smell? If you smell a flavor, find out what it is, taste it, touch it, look at it, smell it again, and, most important, remember it. In short, do whatever it takes to experience and remember that flavor. One easy example is coffee that has been left on the warmer too long. Another is garlic being sautéed. If it's a spice, pick it up and smell it, then crush or rub it between your fingers, smell it again, identify it, and remember it. Next, find a recipe that uses it, make the dish, and see whether you can identify what the spice does for or to the recipe.

We basically taste and smell food at the same time, but they are two separate senses. However, it's difficult or almost impossible to accomplish one without the other occurring. Your taste buds are most sensitive when food is between 85 and 105 degrees F, the temperature at which most slow-smoked foods are served. Foods served cold, such as salads and side dishes, need to have heightened flavors because coldness mutes seasoning; you season the food after it has chilled to make sure it has enough flavor.

There are four major tastes: sour, bitter, sweet, and salty. I'll add a fifth one: spicy. The areas of the tongue that distinguish taste are the tip for sweet and the back sides for sour and salty; bitter shows up on the middle top of the tongue. "Spicy" can connote such a variety of things. It can be one spice's flavor or a combination of spices. In most cases, spicy means "hot"! Various sources report that cayenne pepper affects the tip of the tongue, crushed red pepper affects the back of the tongue, and the habanero, or Scotch bonnet (one of the hottest chiles known to man), affects the entire tongue. All of this sounds impressive, but there is no scientific evidence to back it up. I suggest that you experiment on your own.

Because I am writing this in my spice room, and I just couldn't resist: I dipped my finger into a

5-pound canister of 50,000 Scoville heat units of cayenne pepper and touched it to the tip of my tongue. I could feel the effects on the tip, sides, and back of my tongue, but the effects lasted the longest at the tip of my tongue.

This is what I mean by experimenting and learning about spices, but you may want to start with something that has a little less fire.

Seasonings versus Rubs

A seasoning can be a special herb-and-salt blend that you sprinkle over grilled vegetables or a spice blend as simple as equal parts of ground cumin and coriander that you sprinkle on a pork tenderloin before grilling. But a rub is something different.

A dry rub is a dry mixture of spices, herbs, and sugar that is applied to the surface of the meat, chicken, or fish you want to grill or smoke both to flavor the meat and to create an attractive crust. A rub is one component of the total flavor of a dish, along with the flavor derived from grilling or smoking and from the sauce or glaze at the end. They all have to work together.

To me, the term "dry rub" is a misnomer. I think calling it barbecue seasoning is more accurate, because when I barbecue, I season the meat; I don't rub it in. I feel that rubbing just smothers the meat, sort of clogging its pores. When I season, I apply the rub like heavy salt and pepper, letting the meat "breathe" and interact with the heat and smoke of the cooker.

Salt and sugar are the carriers for other spices that you want the meat to absorb. The salt and sugar in a rub or barbecue seasoning are drawn up into the meat and bring the other spices with them. Also, the sugar helps mask the salty flavor.

Over the years, I've developed hundreds of rub recipes, and I know what I think works best. For example, I prefer cane sugar to that made from sugar beets. I think cane sugar has a better flavor and texture than that of beet sugar, which tends to clump. When you buy sugar, the term "cane sugar" is usually on the front of the bag. I don't usually use brown sugar for rubs because it's too moist. If I do use brown sugar, I dry it out first (see page 115), then run it through a sieve to remove any lumps.

I like all the ingredients in a rub to have the same dry, granular consistency so there is no clumping and so the rub stays in suspension after you store it. If the ingredients are all different granular sizes, you have to shake and reblend a rub each time you want to use it.

I have yet to find a spice or an herb that I wouldn't use in a rub, although I don't want a lot of certain flavors, such as dried rosemary, because a little of that goes a long way.

A rub also affects the final appearance of barbecued food, helping to form a dark crust on the exterior of the meat. The redder the rub, the better it looks on beef, pork, or lamb. To get that color, you use chili powder and sweet Hungarian paprika.

My best advice: Start simple and basic, then work from there. Keep notes about ingredients and proportions, and make up 18 to 20 ounces of rub (about 3 cups) at a time, so you don't run out.

Rub DO'S AND Don'ts

Do's

1 Do use cane sugar for better flavor and texture.

2 Do balance the amounts of sugar (cane) and salts (sseasoned [like Lawry's], onion, garlic, and celery).

3 Do use between 2 tablespoons and ¼ cup of chili powder and black pepper.

4 Do add sweet Hungarian paprika for color.

5 Do add three different spices or herbs that you like or you think will enhance the meat that you intend to cook.

Don'ts

1 Don't use brown sugar, as it tends to clump.

2 Don't use too many powders with different granular sizes, or the rub won't stay in suspension and you'll have to shake it every time you use it.

3 Don't overpower your rub with one dominant flavor, which can easily happen if you use too much nutmeg, mace, clove, oregano, or rosemary.

4 Don't put fresh product in a dry rub. For example, you don't want minced fresh garlic or chopped fresh parsley in a dry rub because fresh ingredients will cause the rub to clump. A rub is supposed to be a seasoning blend that can be stored in a jar at room temperature. If you add fresh products, you can't do that.

5 Don't use meat tenderizer in a rub. If you're not careful, it will make the meat mushy.

6 Don't keep a rub for longer than a year, as the flavor will diminish over time.

That's about the amount you'll need for a barbecue contest.

The Spice Is Right

Spices should be approached with care and respect. Yes, respect! You need to care for them as if they were very delicate, because they are. The better care you take of spices and herbs, the better they will help you show off your cooking skills. The fresher the spice, the truer the flavor, so doesn't it make sense to store them in the best way possible? The true chile-heads do it right; they store their spices in the freezer. In my recipes for rubs and seasonings, I suggest storing them in an airtight container in a cool, dark place. Air, light, and heat cause the strength of spices to deteriorate at an accelerated rate. Your spice rack may be pretty, but it doesn't help keep your spices fresh. They would be far better off in airtight containers in a spice cabinet with doors to keep out light and heat. Oh, and do me a favor—don't store your spices over or next to your stove.

I buy my dried herbs and spices in bulk at good spice emporiums. I always smell the dried herbs and spices before I buy them to make sure they have a good aroma, which means they're fresh.

Try different spice blends, such as chili and curry powders. You may no realize it, but there are many different chili and curry powder blends. Each spice company seems to make a slightly different version. Find one you like and use it in your rubs and seasonings. Or make your own!

Sometimes I use whole spices and toast them. For some recipes, such as Szechuan Peppercorn Salt (page 110), I toast whole spices, including Szechuan peppercorns, salt, and five-spice powder, in a skillet over medium-high heat for several minutes to bring out maximum flavor. Then I discard the peppercorns (they've flavored the other ingredients enough) and blend the remaining seasonings with the other ingredients in my recipe. Sometimes I grind the spices I've toasted, such as cumin seeds, in a clean coffee grinder

RECIPES ARE GUIDELINES

At home, I use my kitchen as well as my outdoor grill and smokers as laboratories for the many new recipes I am always dreaming up. When I have an idea for a recipe, I put the flavors together in my head. I have a very good flavor memory that stays filed away until I need it, but I do write them down in case my memory fails me.

I tell my barbecue students that a recipe is a guideline. You can always change the proportions to get the flavor and texture that you like.

used expressly for grinding spices. But I basically use already ground herbs and spices for convenience and because I use them in large quantities. A small electric coffee grinder isn't up to the job of grinding 3 cups of a spice when you need a lot for a contest.

Because I make and market my own barbecue seasonings and sauces, cater barbecues, enter barbecue cook-offs, and write cookbooks, I have a small spice room in my house where I keep all my seasonings and blend new ones with the help of a large spice grinder. I also have a flavor box filled with spices, rubs, seasonings, vinegars, and sweeteners that I take with me to contests.

So I hope you see how important rubs and seasonings are—they're a basic building block of not only good barbecue but also good cooking.

The Baron of Barbecue's Seasoned Salt

This seasoning blend fires on all the burners—salty, spicy, slightly sweet, hot, and bitter. It's a great all-purpose seasoning for everything from grilled burgers to baked potatoes. MAKES ABOUT 1³/4 CUPS

1 cup non-iodized salt

¹/4 cup sweet Hungarian paprika

2 tablespoons dry mustard (I use Colman's)

2 teaspoons dried thyme leaves

2 teaspoons dried marjoram leaves

2 teaspoons garlic powder

2 teaspoons mild curry powder

2 teaspoons ground celery seeds

2 teaspoons onion powder

1 teaspoon dillweed

1 Combine all the ingredients in a small bowl and blend well, then pour through a fine-mesh sieve to mix even more completely.

2 Store in an airtight container in a cool, dark place for up to 1 year.

Exotic Seasoned Salt

Containing cumin, turmeric, cardamom, and fenugreek, this blend is great on lamb, pork, turkey, or grilled vegetables. MAKES ABOUT 2 CUPS

1 cup non-iodized salt

¹/2 cup sweet Hungarian paprika

¹/4 cup granulated cane sugar

1 tablespoon finely ground black pepper

1 tablespoon rubbed sage

1 tablespoon garlic powder

2 teaspoons ground celery seeds

1 teaspoon ground cumin

1 teaspoon turmeric

¹/2 teaspoon ground cardamom

¹/2 teaspoon ground fenugreek seeds

¹/2 teaspoon dried thyme leaves

¹/2 teaspoon cayenne pepper

1 Combine all the ingredients in a small bowl and blend well, then pour through a fine-mesh sieve to mix even more completely.

2 Store in an airtight container in a cool, dark place for up to 1 year.

Mason Steinberg's Seasoned Salt

Mason Steinberg is a Barbecue Guru from Omaha, Nebraska. He owned Old Mill Barbecue and Jason Foods and now does consulting and recipe development. Sprinkle Mason's classic seasoned salt on fried potatoes, pork chops, or anything else you want. MAKES ABOUT 1¹/2 CUPS

1 cup non-iodized salt

¹/4 cup sweet Hungarian paprika

1 tablespoon dry mustard (I use Colman's)

2 teaspoons garlic powder or granulated garlic

1¹/2 teaspoons dried oregano leaves

1 teaspoon onion powder or granulated onion

1 Combine all the ingredients in a small bowl and blend well.

2 Store in an airtight container in a cool, dry, dark place for up to 1 year.

Making a SEASONED Salt

Salt is one of the carriers that will help take ground spices or dried herbs into the meat, chicken, fish, or vegetables that you cook. A seasoned salt can be as simple as salt and pepper—the seasonings that my parents used on the ribs and chicken they barbecued in our backyard barbecue pit. Or it can be a complex blend of salt, spices, and herbs. But it is essentially a dry mixture.

I've already suggested that you taste different herbs and spices. Now I'm going to tell you to taste salt. Yeah, salt. You may think that all salt tastes the same, but you will find out the truth once you try a few different kinds.

Line up small dishes with that familiar iodized salt, some fine non-iodized kosher salt, and some non-iodized sea salt. Now, lick the tip of your finger and dip it into one of the salts and taste. Take a sip of water and repeat the process with another type of salt. And so on.

You'll find that iodized salt has a very harsh taste. Do you really want that in your seasoning blends? I don't.

I use either kosher salt or sea salt, depending on what I have on hand. These salts have a truer salt flavor.

When you're concocting your own seasoned salt, start simple. Start with 1 cup of salt in a bowl, then add 1/4 cup of sweet Hungarian paprika for a little color. For a little sweetness, try 1 or 2 teaspoons of ground celery seeds or basil leaves. For a little heat, stir in 1 or 2 teaspoons of ground black or cayenne pepper. For a savory punch, use 1 or 2 teaspoons of garlic and onion powders. Sift everything through a fine-mesh sieve into another bowl to make sure all the ingredients are well blended.

Now, you've got a very basic seasoned salt that you can sprinkle on everything from a baked potato to a grilled pork chop.

Savory Seasoned Salt

With turmeric and paprika for color, and white pepper and nutmeg for a deep, savory flavor hit, this blend is great with pork, beef, or chicken. MAKES 1/3 CUP

3 tablespoons fine sea salt

1 tablespoon sweet Hungarian paprika

1 tablespoon celery salt

2 teaspoons garlic powder or granulated garlic

1 teaspoon granulated cane sugar

1 teaspoon onion powder or granulated onion

1/2 teaspoon turmeric

1/2 teaspoon cayenne pepper

1/4 teaspoon white pepper

1/8 teaspoon ground nutmeg

1 Combine all the ingredients in a small bowl and blend well.

2 Store in an airtight container in a cool, dark place for up to 1 year.

A Clone of Lawry's Seasoned Salt

A work in progress! I'm still getting all the kinks out of this one, but here is the recipe to date. Lawry's seasoned salt is, of course, the most recognizable brand of seasoned salt on grocery store shelves. Now you can make something very close to it. MAKES ABOUT 1/4 CUP

2 tablespoons fine sea salt

1 tablespoon granulated cane sugar

2 teaspoons sweet Hungarian paprika

1 teaspoon ground coriander

1 teaspoon onion powder

1 teaspoon turmeric

1/2 teaspoon finely ground black pepper

1/2 teaspoon garlic powder

1/2 teaspoon cornstarch

1/4 teaspoon ground celery seeds

1/4 cup ground cumin

1 Combine all the ingredients in a small bowl and blend well, then pour through a fine-mesh sieve to mix even more completely.

2 Store in an airtight container in a cool, dark place for up to 1 year.

Easy, Quick, and Good Seasoned Salt

The title says it all. Use this blend as an all-purpose seasoning for savory foods. MAKES ABOUT 1 1/2 CUPS

1 cup fine sea salt

1/4 cup sweet Hungarian paprika

2 tablespoons dry mustard (I use Colman's)

2 teaspoons poultry seasoning

1 teaspoon garlic powder

1 teaspoon onion powder

1 Combine all the ingredients in a small bowl and blend well, then pour through a fine-mesh sieve to mix even more completely.

2 Store in an airtight container in a cool, dark place for up to 1 year.

Szechuan Peppercorn Salt

This is an outstanding choice for my favorite food—duck, grilled or smoked. It also works deliciously well with chicken and steak. MAKES ABOUT 1/4 CUP

1/4 cup coarse kosher salt or sea salt

1 tablespoon Szechuan peppercorns

2 teaspoons Chinese 5-spice powder, homemade (page 112) or store-bought

1 Heat a small, heavy dry skillet over medium heat until it is hot. Add the salt, peppercorns, and 5-spice powder and dry-roast the mixture, stirring and shaking constantly, until the mixture turns very dark—but don't let it burn!

2 Pour the mixture into a small bowl to keep it from darkening even more in the still-hot pan. Remove and discard the peppercorns.

3 Store the seasoned salt in an airtight container in a cool, dark place for up to 1 year.

Garlic Salt

This is a method I like to use, but according to Ann Wilder, the owner and CEO of Vanns Spices Ltd., in Baltimore, Maryland, "When you blend salt like this in a blender, it tends to get bitter." I have not experienced any bitterness when I have made different salts, but because Ann is so knowledgeable in the world of spices, I thought I should mention it. **MAKES 1 1/2 CUPS**

> 1 cup fine sea salt
>
> 1/2 cup dehydrated garlic or granulated garlic

1 Combine the ingredients in a small bowl and blend well. Transfer to a blender and process to the desired degree of fineness.

2 Store in an airtight container in a cool, dark place for up to 1 year.

CELERY SALT

Substitute 1/2 cup celery seeds or dehydrated celeriac (celery root) for the garlic.

Herb Salt Seasoning Blend

This is a good seasoning for the salad you serve with your barbecue. **MAKES ABOUT 3 1/2 TABLESPOONS**

> 1 tablespoon fine sea salt
>
> 1 tablespoon dried cilantro leaves
>
> 2 teaspoons granulated onion
>
> 1 teaspoon granulated garlic
>
> 1 teaspoon dried basil leaves
>
> 1/2 teaspoon dried thyme leaves
>
> 1/4 teaspoon cayenne pepper

1 Combine all the ingredients in a small bowl and blend well.

2 Store in an airtight container in a cool, dark place for up to 1 year.

Garden Blend Herb Salt

This is a good salt to sprinkle on vegetables, seafood, and meat. **MAKES ABOUT 3/4 CUP**

> 1/4 cup fine sea salt
>
> 2 teaspoons granulated garlic
>
> 2 teaspoons finely ground black pepper
>
> 2 teaspoons rubbed sage
>
> 1 teaspoon sugar
>
> 1 teaspoon dried parsley flakes
>
> 1/2 teaspoon dried basil leaves
>
> 1/2 teaspoon dried thyme leaves
>
> 1/4 teaspoon ground nutmeg

1 Combine all the ingredients in a small bowl and blend well.

2 Store in an airtight container in a cool, dry place for up to 1 year.

The Baron's Chili Powder

A good ground chile for this recipe is the very popular California Fancy Chile Powder. Use Mexican oregano, available from spice companies such as Penzeys (www.Penzeys.com), as it has a more vibrant flavor than the Italian kind. **MAKES ABOUT 2 1/2 TABLESPOONS**

1 tablespoon pure ground mild red chile

1 1/2 teaspoons ground cumin

1 teaspoon non-iodized salt

1/2 teaspoon garlic powder

1/2 teaspoon ground coriander

1/4 teaspoon dried Mexican oregano leaves

1/8 teaspoon ground cloves

1/8 teaspoon ground allspice

1 Combine all the ingredients in a small bowl and blend well.

2 Store in an airtight container in a cool, dark place for up to 1 year.

Roasted Garlic and Ancho Chili Powder

This one is also better than most chili powders you can get commercially. The granulated roasted garlic and Mexican oregano, available from spice companies such as Penzeys (www.Penzeys.com), add great savory notes. MAKES ABOUT 1/2 CUP

1/4 cup pure ground ancho chile

2 tablespoons granulated roasted garlic

1 tablespoon granulated cane sugar

2 teaspoons cumin seeds, toasted in a dry skillet over medium heat until fragrant, then ground

1 1/2 teaspoons dried Mexican oregano leaves

1 teaspoon non-iodized salt

1 teaspoon finely ground black pepper

1/4 teaspoon ground cloves

1 Combine all the ingredients in a small bowl and blend well.

2 Store in an airtight container in a cool, dark place for up to 1 year.

Chinese 5-Spice Powder

Chinese 5-spice powder works very nicely as a barbecue seasoning, but use it with a light hand. You can find star anise and Szechuan peppercorns at Asian markets. MAKES A SCANT 1/2 CUP

2 tablespoons star anise

2 tablespoons whole cloves

2 tablespoons Szechuan peppercorns

2 tablespoons fennel seeds

1/2 ounce cinnamon sticks, broken into pieces

1 Grind each spice in a spice or coffee grinder. Combine in a small bowl.

2 Store in an airtight container in a cool, dark place for up to 1 year.

NOTE

To get the very best tasting results, you should first toast the whole spices to intensify their flavors. Place the whole spices in a cast-iron skillet and heat over medium-high heat until they become fragrant, 2 to 3 minutes. Let cool, then grind. You can also make this recipe using already ground spices.

The Baron's Curry Powder

There are so many spices that can go into a curry powder that you can experiment with them and find the blend and level of fire you like. Spices that are commonly used in

SHOPPING with the Baron

If you become a competition barbecuer, you will shop in some places you never thought you would. But necessity is the mother of invention. Here are some of the places where I shop to get ready for a competition.

BULK HERB AND SPICE EMPORIUM: I buy my herbs and spices in bulk for my dry rubs and sauces. I think they're fresher, and they're definitely cheaper.

JUNKYARD: I look here for 55-gallon drums, old grates, braces, and parts that I can adapt for my smoker. When I was a kid and we built our own barbecue pit, my Dad and I would go to the junkyard to get big metal grates to use for grill racks over the barbecue pit. I made my own pig cooker with parts from the junkyard.

VETERINARY SUPPLY HOUSE: This is where I get boxes of syringes to use for injecting marinades into chicken and pork. You need a bigger syringe and needle than those used for humans.

CABINET SHOPS, HARDWARE EMPORIUMS, LUMBERYARDS, HOME IMPROVEMENT STORES: I buy Formica sink cutouts—what's left over after kitchen installers cut the countertop from around the sink in new kitchens—for around $2 to $3 each. These make great cutting boards for cook-offs.

RESTAURANT SUPPLY OR PROFESSIONAL CUTLERY STORES: For me, cutlery is second only to the cooker in the importance of barbecue equipment. I buy used knives, which you can get for as little as $50 for a whole set or $3 to $8 apiece. I like to try them out first to see whether I like the feel of the knife before I spend a lot of money on a new one.

---

curries are ginger, coriander, cayenne, cumin, cardamom, chiles, cinnamon, fennel, mace, black pepper, mustard, and turmeric, which gives curry its golden color. MAKES 6 1/2 TABLESPOONS

1 tablespoon ground coriander

1 tablespoon freshly ground black pepper

1 tablespoon ground cumin

1 tablespoon pure ground chile (see Note)

1 tablespoon turmeric

1 tablespoon ground cardamom

1 teaspoon ground ginger

1/2 teaspoon cayenne pepper

1 Combine all the ingredients in a small bowl and blend well.

2 Store in an airtight container in a cool, dark place for up to 1 year.

NOTE I mean pure chile (with an E) powder, not a chili powder blend. New Mexico Hot and Tres Ochos are two good suggestions.

Sodium-Free Herb Seasoning

This is a very good seasoning for fish and seafood. You can add it to a flavor carrier, such as sugar, and use it as a rub rather than just a seasoning. I also like to add some ground chipotle or cayenne to spice it up. MAKES ABOUT 3/4 CUP

- 2 tablespoons dried basil leaves
- 1 tablespoon dillweed
- 1 tablespoon dried mint leaves
- 1 tablespoon dried tarragon leaves
- 2 teaspoons dried thyme leaves
- 1 teaspoon coriander seeds, toasted in a dry skillet over medium heat until fragrant, then ground
- 1/2 teaspoon freshly ground white pepper

1 Combine all the ingredients in a small bowl and blend well.

2 Store in an airtight container in a cool, dark place for up to 1 year.

No-Salt Seasoning

This is a great salt substitute for people on a low-sodium diet or those trying to limit their salt intake. MAKES ABOUT 1/3 CUP

- 2 tablespoons granulated onion
- 1 tablespoon granulated garlic
- 1 tablespoon sweet Hungarian paprika
- 1 tablespoon dry mustard (I use Colman's)
- 1 teaspoon ground coriander
- 1/2 teaspoon dried thyme leaves
- 1/2 teaspoon freshly ground white pepper
- 1/2 teaspoon ground celery seeds

1 Combine all the ingredients in a small bowl and blend well.

2 Store in an airtight container in a cool, dark place for up to 1 year.

Barbecue Seasoning

This seasoning may look like it has a few exotic ingredients, but most are in your grocery store if you know where to look. Packaged chili seasoning is found right by the taco seasoning mixes in the supermarket—or make your own (page 116) for a much better flavor. Or use chili powder. Powdered citric acid is in the canning section (it's used to keep fruits from darkening). Worcestershire powder, however, you have to order from a spice company, such as Zach's Spice Company (www.zachsspice.com). Use this on anything you want to slow smoke. MAKES ABOUT 2 1/4 CUPS

- 1 cup granulated cane sugar
- 1/2 cup chili seasoning, homemade (page 116) or store-bought
- 1/4 cup sweet Hungarian paprika
- 1/4 cup seasoned salt, homemade (page 108) or store-bought
- 2 tablespoons ground coriander
- 1 tablespoon ground celery seeds
- 2 teaspoons ground cumin
- 1 teaspoon cayenne pepper
- 1 teaspoon Worcestershire powder
- 1 teaspoon citric acid powder

1 Combine all the ingredients in a medium-size bowl and blend well. Pour through a fine-mesh strainer to mix even more completely.

2 Store in an airtight container in a cool, dry place for up to 1 year.

Drying BROWN Sugar

Whenever I use more than about $1/4$ cup of brown sugar in a rub recipe, I always try to dry it first. Brown sugar has a lot of moisture and tends to clump. I dry it so it will get powdery and stay in suspension with the other ingredients in the rub. You don't have to dry brown sugar, but it saves you time later on when you don't have to crumble the rub between your fingers before you use it. Plus, you don't want a judge to get a clump of brown sugar on his or her piece of your barbecue, which would distort the flavor.

The careful reader may notice, however, that The Baron's Barbecue Spice calls for just 1 tablespoon of dried brown sugar. That's because I cut down the recipe for this book. At home, I make this recipe in a larger quantity because I use it all the time.

To dry brown sugar, sprinkle it over an ungreased cookie sheet and spread out. Let air-dry for 2 hours. Sift out the lumps and use.

The Baron's Barbecue Spice

This medium-hot blend is good on barbecued ribs, brisket, or pork butt. Dry the brown sugar first so it won't clump and will stay in suspension with the other ingredients.
MAKES ABOUT $1/4$ CUP

2 tablespoons sweet Hungarian paprika

1 tablespoon dry mustard (I use Colman's)

1 tablespoon firmly packed light brown sugar, dried (see Drying Brown Sugar, above)

1 teaspoon freshly ground black pepper

1 teaspoon ground celery seeds

$1/2$ teaspoon non-iodized salt

$1/2$ teaspoon cayenne pepper

$1/4$ teaspoon dried thyme leaves

$1/4$ teaspoon dried marjoram leaves

1 Combine all the ingredients in a small bowl and blend well.

2 Store in an airtight container in a cool, dark place for up to 1 year.

Barbecue Seasoning and Rub

This rub is complex and worth a try. Your next pork butt or slab of ribs will be a winner. With this rub, you get an extra smoky hit from the hickory salt, which is available, along with the horseradish powder, from better spice companies, such as McCormick's. MAKES ABOUT 3 CUPS

½ cup granulated cane sugar

½ cup firmly packed dark brown sugar, dried (see page 115)

½ cup hickory salt

½ cup sweet Hungarian paprika

¼ cup celery salt

¼ cup garlic salt

2 tablespoons freshly ground black pepper

2 tablespoons chili seasoning, homemade (page 116) or store-bought

1 tablespoon dry mustard (I use Colman's)

2 teaspoons rubbed sage

2 teaspoons dried basil leaves

2 teaspoons dried parsley flakes

1 teaspoon horseradish powder or wasabi powder

1 teaspoon dried thyme leaves

½ teaspoon curry powder

1 Combine all the ingredients in a medium-size bowl and blend well.

2 Store in an airtight container in a cool, dark place for up to 1 year.

Chili Seasoning

This seasoning may be as good as any you can buy commercially. Remember, chili seasoning is one thing, chili powder another. Chili powder is made from different dried chiles ground together with oregano, cumin, and unsweetened cocoa powder; every spice company makes its version a little differently. This chili seasoning has chiles, oregano, and cumin, as well as coriander, allspice, and cloves for a headier mix. MAKES ABOUT ¼ CUP

2 large dried pasilla chiles, preferably leathery, not brittle

1 dried ancho chile, preferably leathery, not brittle

1 tablespoon fine sea salt

1 tablespoon granulated garlic

1 tablespoon dried oregano leaves

1 tablespoon ground cumin

½ teaspoon ground coriander

½ teaspoon ground allspice

¼ teaspoon ground cloves

1 Remove the stems and seeds from the chiles. You should have about 1 ounce of flesh. Tear the chiles into small pieces and place them in a small dry skillet over low heat, stirring, until you can smell them and they crackle, about 2 minutes. Remove from the heat and let cool completely.

2 Once the chiles are cool, transfer them to a small spice grinder, add the salt, and grind until fine. Combine in a small bowl with the remaining ingredients and blend well.

3 Store in an airtight container in a cool, dark place for up to 1 year.

Spicy Hamburger Seasoning

This seasoning is also good on steaks and pork chops or stirred into a cream sauce served over pasta. MAKES ABOUT ⅓ CUP

1 tablespoon Barbecue Seasoning (page 114)

1 tablespoon seasoned salt, homemade (page 108) or store-bought

2 teaspoons sweet Hungarian paprika

2 teaspoons granulated cane sugar

2 teaspoons dried thyme leaves

1 teaspoon granulated garlic

1 teaspoon granulated onion

1 teaspoon cayenne pepper

$^1/_2$ teaspoon white pepper

1 Combine all the ingredients in a small bowl and blend well.

2 Store in an airtight container in a cool, dark place for up to 1 year.

The Baron's Cajun Seasoning

Really, you're not seeing things—that is $^1/_4$ cup of cayenne. You may not believe me, but this blend is not hot to my taste buds—but you be the judge. Use this to give a Cajun flavor to barbecued brisket, ribs, or pork butt. MAKES ABOUT $^3/_4$ CUP

$^1/_4$ cup cayenne pepper

$^1/_4$ cup sweet Hungarian paprika

2 tablespoons chili seasoning, homemade (page 116) or store-bought

2 teaspoons freshly ground black pepper

1 teaspoon white pepper

1 teaspoon dry mustard (I use Colman's)

1 teaspoon ground thyme

1 teaspoon garlic powder

1 teaspoon onion powder

$^1/_2$ teaspoon rubbed sage

1 Combine all the ingredients in a small bowl and blend well.

2 Store in an airtight container in a cool, dark place for up to 1 year.

Cajun Seasoning, Part Deux

This is a fun recipe to play with, and I've suggested some variations below. The taste buds of both Chef Pauls—myself and the better known Paul Prudhomme—really appreciate a ragin' Cajun seasoning. MAKES ABOUT 1 $^1/_3$ CUPS

3 tablespoons sweet Hungarian paprika

2 tablespoons seasoned salt, homemade (page 108) or store-bought

2 tablespoons granulated garlic

1 tablespoon cayenne pepper

1 tablespoon granulated onion

2 teaspoons dried thyme leaves

2 teaspoons freshly ground black pepper

1 teaspoon white pepper

1 teaspoon dried oregano leaves

1 Combine all the ingredients in a small bowl and blend well.

2 Store in an airtight container in a cool, dark place for up to 1 year.

VARIATIONS

Trying adding 1 teaspoon dried marjoram leaves, or 1 to 2 teaspoons lemon pepper seasoning, or 1 teaspoon crushed or ground fennel seeds with a dash or two of ground nutmeg.

Cajun Pork Seasoning

This flavors pulled pork beautifully! MAKES ABOUT ³/₄ CUP

- ¹/₂ cup sweet Hungarian paprika
- 2 tablespoons granulated garlic
- 1 tablespoon cayenne pepper
- 1 teaspoon dry mustard (I use Colman's)
- 2 teaspoons dried oregano leaves, crushed
- 2 teaspoons seasoned salt, homemade (page 108) or store-bought
- 1 teaspoon finely ground black pepper
- 1 teaspoon cumin seeds, toasted in a dry skillet over medium heat until fragrant, then ground
- 1 teaspoon freshly ground white pepper
- ¹/₂ teaspoon ground nutmeg

1 Sift all the ingredients through a fine-mesh strainer into a small bowl and blend well.

2 Store in an airtight container in a cool, dark place for up to 1 year.

Creole Seasoning

The difference between a Cajun and a Creole seasoning is in the degree of heat. Cajun is definitely hotter, Creole more refined. Use this blend to flavor cream sauces, mayonnaise, salad dressings, grilled fish and shellfish, and veal. MAKES A LITTLE MORE THAN 1 CUP

- ¹/₄ cup non-iodized salt
- ¹/₄ cup cayenne pepper
- ¹/₄ cup sweet Hungarian paprika
- 2 tablespoons freshly ground black pepper
- 2 tablespoons garlic powder

- 2 tablespoons onion powder
- 1 tablespoon ground thyme

1 Combine all the ingredients in a small bowl and blend well.

2 Store in an airtight container in a cool, dark place for up to 1 year.

Creole Herb Seasoning Mix

In this blend, I use whole dried herb leaves rather than crushed. It's amazing how the flavors change from fresh to dried, as well as from whole dried leaves to crushed to rubbed or powdered herb leaves. This seasoning is great on chicken and fish and can be used to make Creole-style sausage. MAKES ABOUT ¹/₂ CUP

- 2 tablespoons dried parsley flakes
- 1 tablespoon dried thyme leaves
- 1 tablespoon dried marjoram leaves
- 2 teaspoons rubbed sage
- 1 teaspoon cayenne pepper
- 1 teaspoon crushed red pepper
- 1 teaspoon dried oregano leaves
- 1 teaspoon dried rosemary leaves
- 1 teaspoon dried tarragon leaves
- 1 teaspoon cumin seeds, toasted in a dry skillet over medium heat until fragrant, then ground
- ¹/₂ teaspoon powdered bay leaf

1 Combine all the ingredients in a small bowl and blend well.

2 Store in an airtight container in a cool, dark place for up to 1 year.

Creole Seafood Seasoning

Hot or not? You make the call. This seasoning is great on crayfish, shrimp, or redfish. MAKES 1 3/4 CUPS

- 1/3 cup fine sea salt
- 1/3 cup sweet Hungarian paprika
- 1/3 cup cayenne pepper
- 1/4 cup freshly ground black pepper
- 1/4 cup granulated garlic
- 3 tablespoons granulated onion
- 1 tablespoon ground thyme
- 1 teaspoon white pepper
- 1 teaspoon dried oregano leaves

1 Combine all the ingredients in a small bowl and blend well.

2 Store in an airtight container in cool, dark place for up to 1 year.

Old Bay-Style Seasoning

This is reputed to be a copy of the original Old Bay seasoning. It can be used on almost any fish or seafood that you want to smoke or grill. It's also good on chicken. MAKES ABOUT 1/2 CUP

- 2 tablespoons powdered bay leaf
- 2 tablespoons celery salt
- 1 tablespoon dry mustard (I use Colman's)
- 2 teaspoons finely ground black pepper
- 1 teaspoon white pepper
- 1 teaspoon ground nutmeg
- 1 teaspoon ground ginger

- 1 teaspoon sweet Hungarian paprika
- 1 teaspoon cayenne pepper
- 3/4 teaspoon ground cloves
- 1/2 teaspoon ground cardamom

1 Combine all the ingredients in a small bowl and blend well.

2 Store in an airtight container in a cool, dark place for up to 1 year.

Herbed Poultry Seasoning

You can find a lot of different poultry seasonings in the grocery store, but you will have a hard time beating this one. Who knows how long those seasonings have been on the grocery store shelf? If you make it yourself, it will be fresh, and that makes all the difference in flavor. MAKES ABOUT 2 TABLESPOONS

- 1 tablespoon dried marjoram leaves
- 1 tablespoon ground parsley (see Note)
- 1 tablespoon dried summer savory leaves
- 1 tablespoon ground sage
- 1 teaspoon ground thyme

1 Combine all the ingredients in a small bowl and blend well.

2 Store in an airtight container in a cool, dark place for up to 1 year.

NOTE It is very hard to find ground parsley, so you will probably have to grind up dried parsley flakes yourself in a small spice grinder.

That's Italian Herb Seasoning

This is a robust seasoning for chicken and fish as well as for pork and beef. It can provide a flavor punch when used in simple vinegar-based barbecue sauces and oil-and-vinegar marinades. You can also use it to season vegetables, bread, and compound butters. **MAKES ABOUT ²/₃ CUP**

- 2 tablespoons dried oregano leaves
- 2 tablespoons dried marjoram leaves
- 2 tablespoons dried basil leaves
- 2 tablespoons dried summer savory leaves
- 1 tablespoon dried rosemary leaves
- 2 teaspoons dried thyme leaves
- 2 teaspoons rubbed sage

1 Combine the oregano, marjoram, basil, savory, rosemary, and thyme in a small bowl and crumble the leaves with your fingers. Add the sage and blend as well as possible.

2 Store in an airtight container in a cool, dark place for up to 1 year.

Mild Italian Seasoning

This blend contains basically the same ingredients as those in That's Italian Herb Seasoning, but in different quantities. If you like a milder Italian seasoning, then this one is for you. It makes a great sprinkle for pasta. Or try it over fresh tomatoes, then drizzle with olive oil and red wine vinegar. **MAKES ABOUT 3 TABLESPOONS**

- 1 tablespoon dried marjoram leaves
- 2 teaspoons rubbed sage

- 1 teaspoon dried thyme leaves
- 1 teaspoon dried rosemary leaves
- 1 teaspoon dried basil leaves
- 1 teaspoon dried summer savory leaves
- ¹/₂ teaspoon dried oregano leaves

1 In a small bowl, combine all the ingredients and crumble them together with your fingers, blending them as well as you can.

2 Store in an airtight container in a cool, dark place for up to 1 year.

Italian Seafood Seasoning

Fennel gives a sweet Italian kick, and lemon pepper and coriander add a citrus twist—both flavors are great with grilled or smoked fish. **MAKES ABOUT 3 TABLESPOONS**

- 2 tablespoons fennel seeds, finely crushed
- 1 teaspoon lemon pepper seasoning
- 1 teaspoon granulated garlic
- 1 teaspoon ground coriander
- ¹/₂ teaspoon dried thyme leaves
- ¹/₄ teaspoon cayenne pepper

1 Combine all the ingredients in a small bowl and blend well.

2 Store in an airtight container in a cool, dark place for up to 1 year.

Hotsy Totsy Seafood Seasoning

Bob Lyon, my barbecue buddy from the Pacific Northwest, thinks that the amount of cayenne in this recipe dominates the seasoning. If you agree, then by all means, cut down on it. I think the balance is just fine. MAKES ABOUT ²/₃ CUP

    2 tablespoons fine sea salt

    2 tablespoons sweet Hungarian paprika

    1½ tablespoons cayenne pepper

    1 tablespoon dried parsley flakes

    1 tablespoon granulated garlic

    1 tablespoon granulated onion

    1 tablespoon white pepper

    2 teaspoons freshly ground black pepper

    2 teaspoons dried basil leaves

    1 teaspoon dried oregano leaves

    1 teaspoon dried thyme leaves

1 Combine all the ingredients in a small bowl and blend well.

2 Store in an airtight container in a cool, dark place for up to 1 year.

My Big Fat Greek Seasoning

This is a good seasoning for lamb and fish, as well as for Greek salads made with feta, cucumber, and black olives. MAKES ABOUT 2 TABLESPOONS

    2 teaspoons dried oregano leaves

    1 teaspoon fine sea salt

    1 teaspoon granulated garlic

    1 teaspoon dried thyme leaves, minced or crushed

    1 teaspoon dried rosemary leaves, minced or crushed

    1 teaspoon finely ground black pepper

1 Combine all the ingredients in a small bowl and blend well.

2 Store in an airtight container in a cool, dark place for up to 1 year.

Tellicherry Peppercorn Seasoning

Once you use Tellicherry peppercorns, you may never use any other kind. These black peppercorns from Tellicherry, India, are larger, darker, and more pungent than other varieties from Indonesia. You can get these peppercorns at better kitchen shops or from a spice emporium. Add this to salad dressing or sprinkle it on fish to be grilled. MAKES ABOUT 3 TABLESPOONS

    2 teaspoons dried basil leaves

    1 teaspoon dried oregano leaves

    1 teaspoon granulated garlic

    1 teaspoon Tellicherry black peppercorns, coarsely ground

    1 teaspoon kosher salt

    1 teaspoon sesame seeds, toasted in a dry skillet over medium heat until fragrant

    1 teaspoon dried lemon zest

    ½ teaspoon fennel seeds, crushed

1 Combine all the ingredients in a small bowl and blend well.

2 Store in an airtight container in a cool, dark place for up to 1 year.

Beau Monde Seasoning

Roughly translated, *beau monde* means "beautiful world" in French. Maybe everything looks better after you've tasted something seasoned with this. I certainly like it on pork tenderloin and chops. Sometimes I use it in place of celery salt for more flavor. MAKES ABOUT ¼ CUP

2 tablespoons fine sea salt

1 tablespoon granulated cane sugar

1 tablespoon ground celery seeds

1 teaspoon onion powder

¼ teaspoon freshly ground white pepper

1 Combine all the ingredients in a small bowl and blend well.

2 Store in an airtight container in a cool, dark place for up to 1 year.

Turkish Mixed Spice Seasoning

This spice blend is for the adventurous. Try it with game, seafood, or pork. The flavors of mint and cinnamon really suggest the Middle East. MAKES ABOUT 2 TABLESPOONS

1 tablespoon mixed pickling spices

1½ teaspoons dried summer savory leaves

1 teaspoon freshly ground black pepper

1 teaspoon dried mint leaves

½ teaspoon ground cinnamon

½ teaspoon ground cumin

¼ teaspoon ground nutmeg

1 Grind the pickling spices in a spice or coffee grinder until coarse. Add the remaining ingredients and grind until the spices are the consistency of granulated garlic.

2 Store in an airtight container in a cool, dark place for up to 1 year.

Juniper Spice Blend

German and Austrian cooks use juniper berries in game casseroles and sauerkraut.

Try this seasoning on steaks, lamb, fish, and game. Whole juniper berries are available at better grocery stores and from spice companies. You can grind them yourself in a spice or coffee grinder. MAKES ABOUT 3 TABLESPOONS

2 tablespoons juniper berries, ground

1 teaspoon freshly ground black pepper

1 teaspoon fine sea salt

½ teaspoon ground allspice

¼ teaspoon ground cloves

⅛ teaspoon powdered bay leaf

1 Combine all the ingredients in a small bowl and blend well.

2 Store in an airtight container in a cool, dark place for up to 1 year.

VARIATION

You can also prepare this starting with whole spices and coarse kosher salt, grinding everything together to an even, granular size.

The Baron's Steak Seasoning

My wife, Jessica, is a special education teacher, and I always tease her that I'm her prize pupil. When I want to make a special dinner for the two of us (or when I want to get out of the proverbial doghouse), that sometimes means a great grilled steak. This is the seasoning I use. MAKES ABOUT ¾ CUP

¼ cup gourmet 4-peppercorn blend

2 tablespoons coarse kosher salt

2 tablespoons granulated garlic

1 tablespoon raw cane sugar

1 teaspoon cumin seeds, toasted in a dry skillet over medium heat until fragrant, then coarsely ground

1 teaspoon dry mustard (I use Colman's)

1 Run the peppercorns through a pepper mill set for a coarse grind.

2 Combine the ground peppercorns with the remaining ingredients in a small bowl and blend well.

3 Store in an airtight container in a cool, dark place for up to 1 year.

Lemon Pepper Steak Seasoning

This is a good steak seasoning, but if you don't have a tolerance for heat, use it sparingly. MAKES ABOUT ½ CUP

⅓ cup finely ground black pepper

1 tablespoon granulated garlic

1 tablespoon freshly ground white pepper

2 teaspoons cayenne pepper

2 teaspoons seasoned salt, homemade (page 108) or store-bought

1 teaspoon light brown sugar

1 teaspoon ground coriander

1 teaspoon pure ground chipotle chile

1 teaspoon dried lemon zest

1 Combine all the ingredients in a small bowl and blend well.

2 Store in an airtight container in a cool, dark place for up to 1 year.

Calypso Seasoning

With a taste of the Caribbean, this seasoning is good on pork, chicken, and fish, not to mention squid. The habanero, or Scotch bonnet, peppers give a sustained heat. MAKES A GENEROUS ¼ CUP

1 tablespoon black peppercorns

2 teaspoons cumin seeds

1 teaspoon yellow mustard seeds

1 teaspoon coriander seeds

½ teaspoon allspice berries

½ teaspoon whole cloves

2 teaspoons firmly packed light brown sugar

2 teaspoons fine sea salt

1 teaspoon ground ginger

½ teaspoon ground cinnamon

½ teaspoon pure ground habanero chile

1 Place the peppercorns, cumin, mustard seeds, coriander, allspice, and cloves in a dry skillet over medium heat and toast until fragrant and just smoking, about 2 minutes. Transfer to a coffee or spice grinder and grind into a fine powder.

2 Transfer to a small bowl and combine with the remaining ingredients, blending well.

3 Store in an airtight container in a cool, dark place for up to 1 year.

Jerk Seasoning

If you like the flavor of Scotch bonnet peppers (also known as habaneros) but not all the heat, use 1 teaspoon of Scotch bonnet pepper and 1 teaspoon of cayenne; this blend will still have a good bite, but it won't be as pungent. On the other hand, if you like more fire, go for the 2 full teaspoons of Scotch bonnet pepper. Use this for jerk pork or chicken grilled over a hot fire. **MAKES ABOUT 1/3 CUP**

- 2 tablespoons non-iodized salt
- 1 tablespoon granulated cane sugar
- 2 teaspoons pure ground Scotch bonnet chile
- 2 teaspoons granulated onion
- 1 teaspoon granulated garlic
- 1 teaspoon ground allspice
- 1 teaspoon ground ginger
- 1 teaspoon finely ground black pepper
- 1/2 teaspoon ground cinnamon
- 1/4 teaspoon ground cloves
- 1/4 teaspoon ground nutmeg

1 Combine all the ingredients in a small bowl and blend well.

2 Store in an airtight container in a cool, dark place for up to 1 year.

Barbecue Pork Rub

This is delicious on slow-smoked ribs, pork butt, pork loin, or even grilled pork chops. The celery salt, dry mustard, and paprika provide a sweet and hot combination that is hard to beat. **MAKES ABOUT 1 1/2 CUPS**

- 1 generous cup firmly packed light brown sugar, dried (see page 115)
- 2 tablespoons sweet Hungarian paprika
- 1 tablespoon dry mustard (I use Colman's)
- 1 tablespoon onion salt
- 1 tablespoon celery salt
- 1 tablespoon chili seasoning, homemade (page 116) or store-bought

- 1 tablespoon seasoned salt, homemade (page 108) or store-bought
- 1 tablespoon freshly ground black pepper

1 Combine all the ingredients in a small bowl and blend well. Pour through a fine-mesh sieve to blend even more completely.

2 Store in an airtight container in a cool, dark place for up to 1 year.

Texas-Style Barbecue Beef Rub

This is a simple but good rub for that Texas brisket or for barbecued beef ribs. **MAKES 1 CUP**

- 1/2 cup sweet Hungarian paprika
- 1/4 cup non-iodized salt
- 1/4 cup freshly ground black pepper
- 1 teaspoon cayenne pepper

1 Combine all the ingredients in a small bowl and blend well.

2 Store in an airtight container in a cool, dark place for up to 1 year.

Chuck Wagon Beef Rub

Use this on chuck roast or beef ribs. The beef base powder, available in a tub in the dried soup section of the grocery store, adds a rich beefy flavor. **MAKES 1 GENEROUS CUP**

- 1/4 cup firmly packed light brown sugar
- 2 tablespoons sweet Hungarian paprika
- 2 tablespoons seasoned salt, homemade (page 108) or store-bought

2 tablespoons onion salt

2 tablespoons fine sea salt

1 tablespoon chili powder, homemade (page 111) or store-bought

1 tablespoon freshly ground black pepper

1 tablespoon lemon pepper seasoning

1 tablespoon beef base powder

1 tablespoon white pepper

1 tablespoon dried rosemary leaves

1 tablespoon cayenne pepper

2 teaspoons ground thyme

1 Combine all the ingredients in a small bowl and blend well. Pour through a fine-mesh sieve and mix well. Because the brown sugar is moist, you it may need to rub it through the mesh screen.

2 Store in an airtight container in a cool, dark place for up to 1 year.

Mary Beth's Barbecue Rub

Mary Beth is my big sister, and she is a very good cook. According to one of my brothers-in-law, I'm the third or fourth best cook in my family, behind my mother and sisters. They're also great cooks as well as barbecuers. Here is one of Mary Beth's rubs, which she uses on chicken and turkey. MAKES ABOUT 2 3/4 CUPS

1 cup granulated cane sugar

1/2 cup garlic salt

1/4 cup onion salt

1/4 cup celery salt

1/2 cup sweet Hungarian paprika

2 tablespoons medium-grind black pepper

1 tablespoon chili powder, homemade (page 111) or store-bought

2 teaspoons lemon pepper seasoning

1/4 teaspoon cayenne pepper

1 Sift all the ingredients through a fine-mesh sieve into a 3- or 4-quart bowl. Blend together.

2 Store in an airtight container and store in a cool, dark place for up to 1 year.

Snail's Sprinkle

Snail is one of my barbecue students who does quite well. One of his passions has been to build a smoker that's easy to use, maintains an even heat, and gives off a little smoke and the right amount of moisture to keep everything juicy and tender. On the barbecue circuit, his barbecue team is called Snail's Slow Smoke-In. Keep your eyes open—if you're out on the highway and see a big pin-striped Peter-Bilt (18 wheeler) truckin' your way, that's Snail—he's known all over the United States for his artwork. Use this blend on brisket, ribs, and pork butt. MAKES A LITTLE MORE THAN 3 CUPS

1 cup granulated cane sugar

1/2 cup seasoned salt, homemade (page 108) or store-bought

1/2 cup garlic salt

1/2 cup sweet Hungarian paprika

2 tablespoons chili seasoning, homemade (page 116) or store-bought

2 tablespoons freshly ground black pepper

2 teaspoons garlic powder

2 teaspoons onion powder

2 teaspoons rubbed sage

2 teaspoons dry mustard (I use Colman's)

1 teaspoon ground celery seeds

1/2 teaspoon ground cumin

1/2 teaspoon MSG (optional)

1/4 teaspoon ground cloves

1/4 teaspoon cayenne pepper

1 Sift all the ingredients through a fine-mesh sieve into a medium-size bowl and blend well.

2 Store in an airtight container in a cool, dark place for up to 1 year.

Dale's Blue Ribbon Chicken Rub

Dale is one of those barbecuers who is at a lot of barbecue contests and whose name is never called out until it comes to his or her category—chicken is Dale's. He is usually at the Blue Ribbon level when the judging results come in. This is one of his prized rub "formulas," as he refers to them. Horseradish powder is available from spice companies, or you could use wasabi powder instead. MAKES ABOUT 2³/₄ CUPS

1 cup granulated cane sugar

1 cup coarse kosher salt, pulverized in a food processor

¹/₂ cup sweet Hungarian paprika

2 tablespoons dry mustard (I use Colman's)

1 tablespoon white pepper

1 teaspoon garlic powder

1 teaspoon dried oregano leaves

1 teaspoon dried parsley flakes

1 teaspoon horseradish powder

¹/₂ teaspoon ground cloves

1 Combine all the ingredients in a medium-size bowl and blend well. Sift through a fine-mesh sieve to mix even more thoroughly. There will be residue of salt and parsley in the sieve; dump it into the rub and blend well again.

2 Store in an airtight container in a cool, dark place for up to 1 year.

Sweet Brown Sugar Rub

Sweet Georgia Brown, this is a down home rub! The old saying "brown sugar rubbed and hickory smoked" fits right in here. There are several MSG blends on the market; I usually use Accent. I add a little MSG to bring up the flavors in the rub. Use this rub on pork, chicken, or chuck.
MAKES ABOUT 3¹/₂ CUPS

³/₄ cup seasoned salt, homemade (page 108) or store-bought

³/₄ cup firmly packed light brown sugar, dried (see page 115)

¹/₂ cup granulated cane sugar

¹/₂ cup sweet Hungarian paprika

¹/₄ cup chili seasoning, homemade (page 116) or store-bought

¹/₄ cup freshly ground black pepper

2 tablespoons garlic salt

1 tablespoon onion salt

1 tablespoon celery salt

1 tablespoon dry mustard (I use Colman's)

1 tablespoon lemon pepper seasoning

1 tablespoon Barbecue Spice (page 115) or Barbecue Seasoning (page 114)

2 teaspoons white pepper

1 teaspoon garlic powder

1 teaspoon MSG (optional)

¹/₂ teaspoon ground cumin

¹/₂ teaspoon dried oregano leaves

¹/₂ teaspoon cayenne pepper

1 Combine all the ingredients in a medium-size bowl and blend well. Pour through a fine-mesh sieve and blend well again.

2 Store in an airtight container in a cool, dark place for up to 1 year.

Paul Ewing's Southern-Style Rub

Paul is not J. R. or Bobby Ewing's long-lost brother from Dallas. Paul S. Ewing proudly hails from Nashville, Tennessee. He claims to be the world's best barbecuer on his block. You know what? He is! Just ask him. The best thing about this great recipe is that Paul doesn't know I have it! He carelessly left it lying where I could see it one afternoon. Thanks, Paul! I hope everyone enjoys this recipe as much as I did getting it. Citric acid is available in the canning section of the grocery store. Worcestershire powder is available from better spice companies, such as Zach's Spice Company (www.zachsspice.com). This rub is good on ribs, pork butt, pork loin, brisket, and chicken. **MAKES ABOUT 3 CUPS**

> 1 cup granulated cane sugar
>
> 3/4 cup non-iodized salt
>
> 1/3 cup sweet Hungarian paprika
>
> 1/4 cup onion salt
>
> 2 tablespoons freshly ground black pepper
>
> 2 tablespoons lemon pepper seasoning
>
> 1 tablespoon Worcestershire powder
>
> 1 tablespoon citric acid
>
> 1 tablespoon chili seasoning, homemade (page 116) or store-bought
>
> 1 1/2 teaspoons ground ginger
>
> 1/2 teaspoon garlic powder
>
> 1/2 teaspoon MSG (optional)
>
> 1/2 teaspoon ground coriander
>
> 1/2 teaspoon ground cloves

1 Sift all the ingredients through a fine-mesh sieve into a medium-size bowl and blend well.

2 Store in an airtight container in a cool, dark place for up to 1 year.

Joe D's Barbecue Rub Supreme

Joe D. is a long-lost barbecue guru, who, for some reason or other, just dropped out of competition barbecue. Maybe he's a big hit in his neighborhood now. I'm jealous of those folks who get to enjoy Joe D's barbecued brisket made with this rub. **MAKES ABOUT 2 3/4 CUPS**

> 1 cup granulated cane sugar
>
> 1/2 cup fine sea salt
>
> 1/3 cup sweet Hungarian paprika
>
> 3 tablespoons garlic salt
>
> 3 tablespoons onion salt
>
> 2 tablespoons celery salt
>
> 2 tablespoons freshly ground black pepper
>
> 2 tablespoons chili seasoning, homemade (page 116) or store-bought
>
> 1 teaspoon dried basil leaves
>
> 1 teaspoon dried marjoram leaves
>
> 1 teaspoon rubbed sage

1 Combine all the ingredients in a medium-size bowl and blend well.

2 Store in an airtight container in a cool, dark place for up to 1 year.

Scotty's Barbecue Rub

This recipe is from one of the few barbecuers who took his hobby and transformed it into a successful business—or should I say two successful businesses? It's Scott O'Meara (and a word to the wise, don't call him "Scotty") of Board Room Barbecue and The BBQ Sauce of the Month Club (9600 Antioch, Overland Park, KS 66212). If you're ever in Kansas City, stop by his restaurant and have a great taste treat. Try some of his hot wings; they come in a variety of heats, from mild to nuclear. Scott uses this all-purpose rub on his brisket, chicken wings, ribs—you name it! MAKES ABOUT 2 3/4 CUPS

    1 cup granulated cane sugar

    1/2 cup seasoned salt, homemade (page 108) or store-bought

    1/2 cup onion salt

    1/3 cup sweet Hungarian paprika

    2 tablespoons chili seasoning, homemade (page 116) or store-bought

    2 tablespoons lemon pepper seasoning

    1 tablespoon freshly ground black pepper

    1 tablespoon garlic salt

    1 teaspoon cayenne pepper

    1/2 teaspoon dried rosemary leaves

1 Combine all the ingredients in a medium-size bowl and blend well.

2 Store in an airtight container in a cool, dark place for up to 1 year.

Doug's Barbecue Rub

Here is another example of a hobby-to-successful-barbecue-joint. That would be Doug Brobeck of Stillwell Smoke House (19300 Metcalf, Stillwell, KS 66085), just south of Overland Park, Kansas. It's good, or, as their sign says, it's "the Best Little Smoke House in Kansas." Doug uses this all-purpose rub on brisket, chicken, and pork. MAKES ABOUT 3 CUPS

    1/2 cup granulated cane sugar

    1/2 cup corn sugar (see Note)

    1/2 cup sweet Hungarian paprika

    1/3 cup garlic salt

    1/3 cup seasoned salt, homemade (page 108) or store-bought

    1/3 cup celery salt

    2 tablespoons freshly ground black pepper

    2 tablespoons chili seasoning, homemade (page 116) or store-bought

    1 tablespoon lemon pepper seasoning

    1 tablespoon ground coriander

    1 tablespoon ground ginger

    1 teaspoon rubbed sage

    1 teaspoon garlic powder

    1 teaspoon granulated onion

    1 teaspoon ground celery seeds

    1/2 teaspoon cayenne pepper

    1/4 teaspoon MSG (optional)

1 Sift all the ingredients through a fine-mesh sieve into a medium-size bowl and blend well.

2 Store in an airtight container in a cool, dark place for up to 1 year.

NOTE Corn sugar is light brown, has medium-size granules, and is not as sweet as cane sugar. It's usually used to make beer. You can find it at a beer-brewer's supply store.

Caribbean Chicken Rub

This seasoning actually works on any island—or inland—grilled chicken. MAKES ABOUT 1 CUP

    1/4 cup granulated cane sugar

    3 tablespoons fine sea salt

    2 tablespoons freshly ground black pepper

    2 tablespoons ground coriander

    2 tablespoons granulated garlic

2 tablespoons granulated onion

1 tablespoon ground ginger

1 tablespoon ground allspice

1 Combine all the ingredients in a small bowl and blend well.

2 Store in an airtight container in a cool, dark place for up to 1 year.

Poultry Barbecue Rub

This recipe is a backyard special for grilling or smoking.
MAKES ABOUT 1 CUP

1/3 cup sweet Hungarian paprika

1/4 cup granulated cane sugar

2 tablespoons seasoned salt, homemade (page 108) or store-bought

2 tablespoons celery salt

2 tablespoons finely ground black pepper

1 tablespoon granulated garlic

1 tablespoon dry mustard (I use Colman's)

2 teaspoons dried basil leaves

2 teaspoons dried lemon zest

1 teaspoon cayenne pepper

1 In a small bowl, combine all the ingredients and blend well.

2 Store in an airtight container in a cool, dark place for up to 1 year.

Chinese Barbecue Seasoning and Rub

My twin loves of Oriental-style cooking and barbecue come together in this recipe. Try it on Chinese-Style Barbecued Baby Back Ribs (page 215). MAKES ABOUT 3/4 CUP

1/4 cup granulated cane sugar

2 tablespoons sweet Hungarian paprika

1 tablespoon firmly packed dark brown sugar

1 tablespoon garlic salt

1 tablespoon seasoned salt, homemade (page 108) or store-bought

1 tablespoon celery salt

1 tablespoon onion salt

1 tablespoon finely ground black pepper

1 tablespoon dry mustard (I use Colman's)

2 teaspoons ground ginger

1 teaspoon Chinese 5-spice powder, homemade (page 112) or store-bought

1 teaspoon cayenne pepper

1 Combine all the ingredients in a fine-mesh sieve and sift into a small bowl, then blend well.

2 Store in an airtight container in a cool, dark place for up to 1 year.

Catering QUANTITY for Eddy's Catering Kansas City Barbecue SEASONING and Rub

When you're barbecuing for a crowd, you'll need this quantity for lots of barbecued ribs, whole chickens, pork butts, briskets—whatever your guests have a hankering for. **MAKES ABOUT 13 CUPS**

2 cups granulated cane sugar

2 cups firmly packed dark brown sugar, dried (see page 115)

2 cups seasoned salt, homemade (page 108) or store-bought

1 cup The Baron's Barbecue Spice (page 115)

1 cup garlic salt

1/2 cup celery salt

1/2 cup onion salt

2 cups sweet Hungarian paprika

1 cup chili seasoning, homemade (page 116) or store-bought

1 cup freshly ground black pepper

2 tablespoons rubbed sage

1 tablespoon ground allspice

1 tablespoon cayenne pepper

Eddy's Catering Kansas City Barbecue Seasoning and Rub

I have worked for a lot of different catering companies. Most of them have asked me to develop rubs and barbecue sauces for them, rather than buy them from a supplier. It's much cheaper to make them and, in some cases, much better. I'll let you decide! When I was at Eddy's Catering, we prepared meals for special guests at the Kansas City Chiefs' football games and the Kansas City Royals' baseball games. The quantities here are for a small backyard barbecue. See the sidebar above for the larger catering quantity if you're barbecuing for a crowd. **MAKES ABOUT 3 1/4 CUPS**

1/2 cup granulated cane sugar

1/2 cup firmly packed dark brown sugar, dried (see page 115)

1/2 cup seasoned salt, homemade (page 108) or store-bought

1/4 cup The Baron's Barbecue Spice (page 115)

1/4 cup garlic salt

2 tablespoons celery salt

2 tablespoons onion salt

1/2 cup sweet Hungarian paprika

1/4 cup chili seasoning, homemade (page 116) or store-bought

1/4 cup freshly ground black pepper

1½ teaspoons rubbed sage

1 teaspoon ground allspice

1 teaspoon cayenne pepper

1 Combine all the ingredients in a fine-mesh sieve over a large bowl and sift, then blend well.

2 Store in an airtight container in a cool, dark place for up to 1 year.

IFTC Barbecue Seasoning and Rub

Bean counters, insurance guys, bankers, and even loan sharks can come together over a plate of barbecued ribs or brisket. When I slow-smoked for Investor's Fiduciary Trust Company using this rub, everybody belonged to the clean plate club. McCormick's makes hickory salt or you can buy it through mail order (see Sources). **MAKES ABOUT 6 CUPS**

1 cup granulated cane sugar

½ cup sweet Hungarian paprika

¼ cup chili powder, homemade (page 111) or store-bought

¼ cup finely ground black pepper

¼ cup seasoned salt, homemade (page 108) or store-bought

¼ cup celery salt

¼ cup garlic salt

2 tablespoons onion salt

2 tablespoons hickory salt

1½ tablespoons poultry seasoning

1½ tablespoons rubbed sage

1½ tablespoons dry mustard (I use Colman's)

1½ tablespoons ground ginger

½ teaspoon ground allspice

¼ teaspoon ground cloves

1 Combine all the ingredients in a fine-mesh sieve and sift into a large bowl, then blend well.

2 Store in an airtight container in a cool, dark place for up to 1 year.

MIT Barbecue Rub and Seasoning

I developed this recipe for MIT (Massachusetts Institute of Technology) in Boston, where the techies were having a party and planning to barbecue half a steer. They needed a rub, and I supplied it. Will using this make you feel as smart as those MIT guys? Sure. **MAKES ABOUT 3 CUPS**

½ cup firmly packed light brown sugar, dried (see page 115)

½ cup granulated cane sugar

½ cup sweet Hungarian paprika

¼ cup seasoned salt, homemade (page 108) or store-bought

¼ cup garlic salt

2 tablespoons celery salt

2 tablespoons onion salt

2 tablespoons chili powder, homemade (page 111) or store-bought

1 tablespoon freshly ground black pepper

1 tablespoon lemon pepper seasoning

1 tablespoon lemonade powder (I use Country Time; make sure whatever you use contains sugar, not artificial sweetener)

1½ teaspoons ground ginger

1½ teaspoons ground cumin

1½ teaspoons cayenne pepper

1½ teaspoons horseradish powder or wasabi powder

½ teaspoon dried rosemary leaves

1 Combine all the ingredients in a medium-size bowl and blend well.

2 Store in an airtight container in a cool, dark place for up to 1 year.

New Century Catering Barbecue Seasoning and Rub

When I worked at New Century Catering and developed this recipe, my associate chef, Gary Hild, used this for everything he smoked or grilled; it's especially good on salmon.
MAKES ABOUT 3¹/₄ CUPS

> ¹/₂ cup firmly packed light brown sugar, dried (see page 115)
>
> ¹/₂ cup granulated cane sugar
>
> ¹/₂ cup fine sea salt
>
> ¹/₂ cup granulated garlic
>
> ¹/₄ cup lemon pepper seasoning
>
> ¹/₄ cup lemonade powder (I use Country Time; make sure whatever you use contains sugar, not artificial sweetener)
>
> 2 tablespoons The Baron's Barbecue Spice (page 115)
>
> 2 tablespoons ground ginger

1 Combine all the ingredients in a large bowl and blend well.

2 Store in an airtight container in a cool, dark place for up to 1 year.

Fresh Garlic and Sea Salt Paste

Okay, we've been through the dry seasonings—seasoned salts and dry rubs. Now we're into the moister seasoning blends. This recipe is truly a garlic-lover's idea of heaven and, to my mind, it's good on anything. MAKES ABOUT 1¹/₂ CUPS

> 4 ounces cloves garlic, peeled
>
> ³/₄ cup coarse sea salt

1 Place the garlic in a blender or food processor and process until smooth. Add the salt a little at a time, processing until the mixture is blended into a paste.

2 Store in an airtight container in the refrigerator for up to 1 month. This paste can also be frozen for up to 6 months.

3 To use, spread the paste all over the food, cover with plastic wrap, and refrigerate for 2 to 4 hours to marinate before cooking. Leave the paste on when grilling or smoking.

Fresh Garlic and Olive Oil Paste

This paste is great to slather over steaks, chicken, lamb, pork, or even fresh fish before grilling. The garlic gives flavor and the olive oil keeps the food moist over high heat.
MAKES ABOUT 2 CUPS

> 1 pound garlic, peeled (about 8 heads)
>
> 1 teaspoon coarse kosher or sea salt
>
> 1 cup extra virgin olive oil

1 Place the garlic and salt in a blender or food

Catering Quantity for MIT BARBECUE Rub and Seasoning

When you really do need to barbecue half a steer, this is your rub. **MAKES ABOUT 11 CUPS**

2 cups firmly packed light brown sugar, dried (see page 115)

2 cups granulated cane sugar

2 cups sweet Hungarian paprika

1 cup seasoned salt, homemade (page 108) or store-bought

1 cup garlic salt

$1/2$ cup celery salt

$1/2$ cup onion salt

$1/2$ cup chili powder, homemade (page 111) or store-bought

$1/4$ cup freshly ground black pepper

$1/4$ cup lemon pepper seasoning

$1/4$ cup lemonade powder (I use Country Time; make sure whatever you use contains sugar, not artificial sweetener)

2 tablespoons ground ginger

1 tablespoon ground cumin

1 tablespoon cayenne pepper

1 tablespoon horseradish powder or wasabi powder

2 teaspoons dried rosemary leaves

processor and process until smooth. With the machine running, add the olive oil in a slow stream through the feed tube until well combined.

2   Store in an airtight container in the refrigerator for up to 1 month or freeze for up to 6 months.

3   To use, spread the paste all over the food, cover with plastic wrap, and refrigerate for 2 to 4 hours to marinate before cooking. Leave the paste on when grilling or smoking.

North African Spice Paste

This paste is an intriguingly different approach worth trying on chicken. **MAKES ABOUT 3 CUPS**

$2^{1}/2$ cups chopped onions

10 cloves garlic, chopped

3 tablespoons caraway seeds, crushed

3 tablespoons ground coriander

$2^{1}/2$ teaspoons cayenne pepper

1 teaspoon fine sea salt

1 teaspoon freshly ground black pepper

1 Combine all the ingredients in a blender or food processor and process until the garlic and onions are finely chopped enough to form a paste.

2 Store, tightly covered, for up to 2 weeks in the refrigerator.

3 To use, spread the paste all over the food, cover with plastic wrap, and refrigerate for 2 to 4 hours to marinate before cooking. Leave the paste on when grilling or smoking.

Mexican Spice Paste

This paste is very good on country-style pork ribs or St. Louis–style pork steak. Like curry or chili powder, adobo seasoning has many different variations. Adobo seasoning is basically a blend of ground chipotle chiles, oregano, garlic, and cumin and is used to marinate pork dishes in the Spanish-speaking world. It is available in powdered form or as a paste in Hispanic markets and better grocery stores. You can use either form in this recipe. MAKES ABOUT 1 CUP

2 tablespoons pure ground chipotle chile

2 tablespoons adobo seasoning

2 tablespoons tomato paste

1/4 cup pressed or minced garlic

1/4 cup red wine vinegar

2 teaspoons fine sea salt

1 teaspoon freshly ground black pepper

1 Combine all the ingredients in a small bowl and blend well, using a fork.

2 Store in an airtight container in the refrigerator for up to 2 weeks.

3 To use, spread the paste all over the food, cover with plastic wrap, and refrigerate for 2 to 4 hours to marinate before cooking. Leave the paste on when grilling or smoking.

Barbecue Sauces, and Dipping

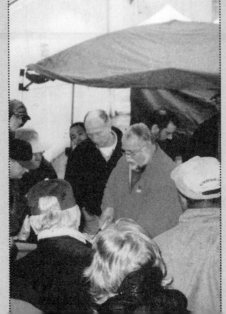

BURNING DESIRES
Fireside Shoppe
• GAS LOGS   • GRILLS
• WOOD STOVES   • AWNINGS
574-9276

Salsas, Relishes, Sauces

BARBECUE

Some folks feel that barbecue ain't barbecue without sauce, it's just smoked meat if there's no sauce to go with it. I like barbecue either way—wet or dry, as they say in Memphis—but I do admit that a really good sauce can take grilled or smoked foods into another dimension. A good sauce can add a beautiful sheen to barbecue at a competition. A burnished glaze of barbecue sauce on perfectly smoked ribs adds to both the appearance and the taste of the finished product.

The real secrets of making a successful barbecue sauce are to balance the flavors in it and to pair the sauce with the correct smoked food. It used to be that sauces were pretty regional. You'd find vinegar- and mustard-based sauces in the Carolinas; mayonnaise-based sauce in the Carolinas, Alabama, Georgia, and Florida; spicy tomato-based sauce in Memphis; deep, rich tomato-based sauce in Texas; a thinner Texas-style sauce in Oklahoma; sweeter and smokier tomato-based sauces in Kansas City; and anything, sauce-wise, in California.

Now, people move around so much that they take their favorite sauces with them. At a contest, you may see many kinds of sauces served with meats.

Anatomy of a Barbecue Sauce

To make a good barbecue sauce, you start with a base, add sweetness or sourness, stir in some liquids, then add seasoning. That's the proto recipe for the thousands of barbecue sauces that are on the market and in barbecuers' refrigerators.

Base: Start with a quart of either ketchup, vinegar, mustard, mayonnaise, or even a thick fruit purée.

Sweetener: Add brown sugar, molasses, clover honey, light or dark corn syrup, or granulated cane sugar to taste.

Sour Note: If you wish, stir in distilled white or cider vinegar, lemon or lime juice, beer, wine, or tamarind pulp to bring out a touch of sourness.

Liquids: For a more pourable consistency and for flavor, add orange juice, liquid smoke flavoring, Worcestershire sauce, soy sauce, or fruit jelly or jam.

Seasoning: Spice up the sauce with salt and pepper, chili powder, and your choice of three of the following: the dried herb of your choice, ground allspice, ground celery seeds, granulated garlic, granulated onion, ground cumin, or ground ginger.

Besides anointing slow-smoked foods at the end of cooking, barbecue sauce has many more uses. You can marinate with it, add it to your own unique version of baked or barbecued beans, and even combine it half and half with bottled Italian dressing to make barbecue vinaigrette.

Dedicated barbecuers like to develop their own unique sauces to get that extra edge in competition. They may enter a special sauce in the barbecue sauce category in a regional contest before taking it to a big contest such as the American Royal or Jack Daniel's Invitational. If you have a really good prize-winning sauce, you could successfully bottle, market, and sell it—like I do!

The ART OF Glazing

I don't glaze meats for my catering jobs or for family dinners at home. I just glaze for competition. That's because glazing is an extra step you take to make your food more visually appealing to the judges at a barbecue competition. I glaze about 30 minutes before my entry is due in to the judges. It takes 10 to 15 minutes for the glaze to set. That leaves me 15 minutes to cut up the meat, arrange the presentation in the Styrofoam box, and take it to the drop-off table. From there, it's only about 5 more minutes before my box of barbecue goes to the judges' table. Glazing is not meant for food that will sit.

And it's not meant for meat that will not benefit from a shiny appearance—such as pulled pork butt (where you want to see evidence of the shaggy exterior or bark amongst the shreds) or even brisket (where you're more concerned with it being tender and moist).

To glaze, I transfer the meat from indirect to direct heat, either on the pit or on an additional grill. I brush a barbecue sauce or homemade glaze—a mixture that generally contains some sugars—on one side of a slab of ribs, a chicken breast, a pork loin, a pork steak, or any other cut that will benefit from a shiny exterior. Then I cover and cook for about 3 to 5 minutes on medium heat to set the glaze on the surface of the meat. Then I turn the meat and repeat the process on the other side. I glaze each surface only once. And that should do it.

In this book, I give glazing instructions for all the meats that need it for competition. Of course, you don't have to glaze at all. And you don't have to win a blue ribbon, either, to enjoy your barbecue.

Kept in the refrigerator, barbecue sauces will last indefinitely.

Glazing with Barbecue Sauce

If you want to give a glazed appearance with barbecue sauce to your ribs, pork butt, brisket, chicken breasts, or other food, there are two different techniques, depending on whether you're smoking or grilling.

If you're smoking or barbecuing at a lower temperature, start glazing about 30 to 60 minutes before you're ready to pull the meat off the pit.

Use a pastry brush to brush the barbecue sauce on the surface of the meat and let it cook for 15 to 30 minutes, then turn the meat, brush the sauce on again, and cook. When the surface of the meat has a dull glow, the glaze has set. In competition, I glaze my ribs several times, but chicken only once—front and back.

If you're grilling (at a higher temperature than smoking, of course), then there's an increased chance that the sugars in the barbecue sauce can caramelize and even blacken. I'm sure we've all had the odd chicken breast or two that got a little blacker than we wanted. The trick is to start no earlier than about 20 to 30 minutes before the meat is done. Apply the barbecue sauce with a pastry brush all over the meat, then try to place it away from the hottest part of the grill. Turn and glaze every 10 minutes if the fire is still pretty hot, every 15 minutes if it's medium hot or lower. When the surface of the meat has a dull glow with some caramelized patches, the glaze has set.

Barbecue Sauces, Salsas, Relishes, and Dipping Sauces

Any barbecue sauce that is thick and chunky I call a salsa. And salsas can be just as varied in flavor as sauces, from Watermelon Fire and Ice Salsa (page 156) to Jamaican Red Bean and Mango Salsa (page 155). A good salsa works on the same principles that a good sauce does—a base plus sweetener, sour note, liquid (not as much as for a sauce), and seasoning. It should make your taste buds happy and go well with grilled or smoked foods.

A chutney made to go with barbecue needs to be both sweet and hot, usually based on a fruit. I love the Peach and Jalapeño Chutney (page 158) I developed. It goes especially well with grilled pork tenderloin or smoked pork loin for a little more elegant fare.

To me, a barbecue relish is chunkier and fresher than a salsa. Try my Red Pepper and Fresh Mint Relish (page 159) on grilled or smoked lamb and you'll never go back to plain old mint jelly.

Salsas, chutneys, and relishes, which contain more fresh ingredients than barbecue sauces, last up to only about 2 weeks in the refrigerator.

For finger food barbecue, such as ribs and satay, dipping sauces also add another dimension of flavor.

Bare Bones Barbecue Sauce

This sauce recipe can be used by anyone as a base from which to develop his or her own signature barbecue sauce.
MAKES ABOUT 2 CUPS

- 1 cup tomato ketchup, homemade (page 43) or store-bought
- 1/2 cup firmly packed light brown sugar
- 3 tablespoons distilled white vinegar
- 2 tablespoons water
- 1 tablespoon Worcestershire sauce, homemade (page 50) or store-bought
- 1 teaspoon non-iodized salt
- 1/2 teaspoon garlic powder
- 1/4 teaspoon onion powder

1 Combine all the ingredients in a medium-size nonreactive saucepan and blend well. Bring to boil, reduce the heat to medium-low, and simmer for 30 minutes to let the flavors blend, stirring occasionally.

2 Now add 1/4 to 1/2 teaspoon of your favorite spice, maybe some chili powder; start experimenting to develop your own championship barbecue sauce.

Hot Barbecue Sauce

This is just a little on the spicy side. Three doses of capsicums give this sauce a big jolt of flavor. Serve with lip-smackin' barbecued ribs, brisket, or pork butt. MAKES ABOUT 3 CUPS

    2 tablespoons unsalted butter

    1 cup minced onions

    ¹/₂ cup water

    2 tablespoons soy sauce

    1 tablespoon Worcestershire sauce, homemade (page 50) or store-bought

    ¹/₄ cup fresh lemon juice

    2 tablespoons firmly packed light brown sugar

    1 cup chili sauce, homemade (page 42) or store-bought

    ¹/₂ teaspoon non-iodized salt

    ¹/₂ teaspoon crushed red pepper

    1 teaspoon cayenne pepper

    1 teaspoon sweet Hungarian paprika

    1 teaspoon prepared yellow mustard

    2 teaspoons chili seasoning, homemade (page 116) or store-bought

In a medium-size nonreactive saucepan over medium heat, melt the butter, then add the onions and cook, stirring, until soft. Add the remaining ingredients, bring to a boil, reduce the heat to medium-low, and simmer for 20 to 30 minutes to let the flavors blend, stirring occasionally.

Barbecue Sauce for Chicken

This sauce is a good one for the backyard chef to start with. Try it on grilled or smoked chicken wings. MAKES ABOUT 3¹/₃ CUPS

    ¹/₃ cup bacon drippings (bacon grease)

    1 medium-size onion, minced

    1 cup tomato ketchup, homemade (page 43) or store-bought

    ¹/₂ cup water

    ¹/₃ cup fresh lemon juice (3 to 4 lemons)

    ¹/₄ cup firmly packed light brown sugar

    2 tablespoons Worcestershire sauce, homemade (page 50) or store-bought

    1 tablespoon sweet Hungarian paprika

    1 teaspoon fine sea salt

    1 teaspoon freshly ground black pepper

Heat the bacon drippings in a medium-size non-reactive saucepan over medium heat, then add the onion and cook, stirring, until soft but not browned. Add the remaining ingredients and blend well. Bring to a boil, then reduce the heat to medium-low and simmer for 30 minutes to let the flavors blend.

Molly's "I Hate Ketchup" Barbecue Sauce

Molly, one of my students, doesn't like ketchup. She came up with this recipe for a non-ketchup barbecue sauce that still tastes of tomato, and it's good! Serve it just like you would regular barbecue sauce. MAKES ABOUT 3 CUPS

2 cups tomato sauce, homemade (page 40) or
   store-bought

1/2 cup firmly packed light brown sugar

1/2 cup distilled white vinegar

2 tablespoons chili seasoning, homemade (page
   116) or store-bought

1 tablespoon freshly ground black pepper

1 teaspoon liquid smoke flavoring

1 teaspoon dry mustard (I use Colman's)

1/2 teaspoon rubbed sage

1/2 teaspoon granulated onion

1/2 teaspoon granulated garlic

1/2 teaspoon fine sea salt

1/4 teaspoon cayenne pepper

Combine all the ingredients in a medium-size nonreactive saucepan over medium-high heat and blend well. Bring to a boil, stirring. Reduce the heat to medium-low and simmer, stirring occasionally, for 20 minutes to let the flavors blend.

Carolina Vinegar Barbecue Sauce

This sauce, traditional in the Carolinas, is great served on the side with chopped or pulled barbecue pork. MAKES ABOUT 1 CUP

1 cup cider vinegar

2 tablespoons granulated cane sugar

1 tablespoon dry mustard (I use Colman's)

1 teaspoon crushed red pepper

1 teaspoon fine sea salt

1 teaspoon freshly ground black pepper

1/2 teaspoon celery salt

Combine all the ingredients in a small nonreactive saucepan and bring to a boil. Reduce the heat to medium-low and simmer for 15 minutes.

No-Cook Blender Barbecue Sauce

This sauce is quick, easy, and good, and it requires no cooking. If I need a barbecue sauce in a hurry, I use this one as my base. MAKES ABOUT 2 CUPS

1 cup tomato sauce, homemade (page 40) or
   store-bought

1/2 cup vegetable oil

2 cloves garlic, pressed

1/4 cup chopped onion

1/4 cup fresh lemon juice

1 teaspoon fine sea salt

1/2 teaspoon freshly ground black pepper

1 teaspoon Worcestershire sauce, homemade
   (page 50) or store-bought

1/2 teaspoon Louisiana hot sauce

Combine all the ingredients in a blender and process until smooth, 3 to 6 minutes.

Sugar-Free Barbecue Sauce

During the eight years that I was chef at a hospital in Kansas City, I used this recipe for my diabetic patients when I served barbecue. The only patients who didn't get barbecue were those on a liquid diet. So you see, barbecue is good for your health! MAKES 3 CUPS

1/2 cup red wine vinegar

1/2 cup vegetable oil

1 cup dry red wine

3 cloves garlic, pressed

1/2 teaspoon dried rosemary leaves

1/2 teaspoon liquid sugar substitute

1/2 teaspoon fine sea salt

1/2 teaspoon freshly ground black pepper

1/4 teaspoon ground cloves

1/4 teaspoon powdered bay leaf

1/2 cup chopped onions

1 teaspoon minced fresh parsley leaves

1 tablespoon soy sauce

Combine all the ingredients in a medium-size nonreactive bowl and stir until well blended.

VARIATIONS

Try adding 1 cup of tomato paste to this sauce. Also, if you want to heat it, combine everything except the liquid sweetener in a medium-size nonreactive saucepan over medium-low heat and simmer for 20 to 30 minutes. Remove from the heat, let cool, then stir in 1 teaspoon of liquid sweetener. You need more because liquid sweetener breaks down when hot. Another way to sweeten up this sauce is to replace the wine, or part of it, with a naturally sweet fruit juice, such as apple juice, apricot nectar, or pineapple juice.

This sauce is best used as a marinade or baste. Place the meat in a glass or other nonreactive baking dish or zippered-top plastic bag, pour the sauce over the meat, and let marinate for 3 to 12 hours in the refrigerator. Drain the meat and reserve the sauce; transfer the remaining marinade to a saucepan and bring to a boil over medium-high heat. Cook for 5 minutes, set aside to cool, then refrigerate if not using right away. Use it to baste the meat frequently during the cooking process. **MAKES ABOUT 2 CUPS**

Jack Daniel's Barbecue Sauce

This was the sauce I formulated for the Sauce category at the Jack Daniel's Invitational World Championship Barbecue Contest. MAKES 6 TO 7 CUPS

1/4 cup (1/2 stick) unsalted butter

2 cups minced onions

1 cup seeded and minced green bell peppers

4 cloves garlic, minced

2 cups chili sauce, homemade (page 42) or store-bought

1 cup firmly packed dark brown sugar

1/4 cup Worcestershire sauce, homemade (page 50) or store-bought

1/4 cup distilled white vinegar

1/4 cup Red Hook Ale or other good beer

1/4 cup Jack Daniel's Sour Mash Whiskey

2 tablespoons dry mustard (I use Colman's)

2 tablespoons honey

2 tablespoons chili seasoning, homemade (page 116) or store-bought

1 tablespoon liquid smoke flavoring (optional)

2 teaspoons fine sea salt

1 teaspoon freshly ground black pepper

1 teaspoon ground coriander

1 teaspoon cayenne pepper

In a medium-size nonreactive saucepan over medium-high heat, melt the butter. Add the onions, green peppers, and garlic and cook until the vegetables are soft, stirring frequently. Add the rest of the ingredients and blend well. Bring to a boil, reduce the heat to medium-low, and simmer for 30 to 45 minutes to let the flavors blend, stirring occasionally.

Jack Daniel's Apricot Barbecue Sauce

This is another of my entries into the Jack Daniel's Barbecue Sauce competition. You don't have to add Jack Daniel's whiskey to a sauce you enter in that contest, but if you don't, it doesn't have a chance of winning! Surprisingly, apricot really complements barbecue, a nice sweet flavor to blend with the smokiness of brisket, pork butt, ribs, or chicken. MAKES ABOUT 6 CUPS

1 pound fresh apricots, peeled, pitted, and cut into chunks, or canned apricots, drained and cut into chunks

1/4 cup minced shallots

1/4 cup cider vinegar

2 tablespoons Jack Daniel's Sour Mash Whiskey

2 tablespoons fresh lemon juice

2 large cloves garlic, pressed

1 tablespoon Worcestershire sauce, homemade (page 50) or store-bought

1 tablespoon liquid smoke flavoring

1 tablespoon peeled and minced fresh ginger

2 teaspoons chili seasoning, homemade (page 116) or store-bought

2 teaspoons fine sea salt

1/2 teaspoon white pepper

2 cups water or fruit juice of your choice

2 cups tomato paste, homemade (page 39) or store-bought

1 cup firmly packed light brown sugar

1/2 teaspoon ground allspice

1 Place the apricots, shallots, vinegar, whiskey, lemon juice, garlic, and Worcestershire sauce in a food processor and process until smooth.

2 Transfer to a medium-size nonreactive saucepan, add the remaining ingredients, blend well, bring to a boil, reduce the heat to medium-low, and simmer for 30 minutes to let the flavors blend, stirring occasionally.

Apricot-Plum Sauce

Thicker basting sauces like this one can also be used as a finishing barbecue sauce. Sweet and flavorful, this sauce is great with grilled or smoked pork, chicken, and game birds. MAKES ABOUT 5 CUPS

1 cup diced onion

6 cloves garlic, pressed

1/4 cup peeled and minced fresh ginger

2 limes, thinly sliced and minced

1 pound fresh apricots, peeled, pitted, and diced

1 cup cider vinegar

1/2 cup Tawny Port wine

2 cups firmly packed light brown sugar

2 teaspoons crushed red pepper

1 teaspoon ground cinnamon

1 teaspoon ground allspice

1 teaspoon kosher salt

1/4 cup minced fresh cilantro leaves

1 In a medium-size nonreactive saucepan, combine all the ingredients except the cilantro. Bring to a boil over medium-high heat, reduce the heat to medium-low, and simmer until the sauce thickens, about 1 hour. Stir frequently to avoid scorching.

2 Remove from the heat and let cool. Stir in the cilantro. You can store, tightly covered, in the refrigerator for up to 2 weeks. Serve or use warm or at room temperature.

Honey-Orange Barbecue Sauce

This is a good finishing sauce for fish, pork, or chicken.
MAKES ABOUT 1 QUART

- ¼ cup olive oil
- 4 cloves garlic, pressed
- ¼ cup minced shallots
- 3 cups fresh orange juice (about 12 oranges)
- 1 cup fresh lime juice (about 16 limes)
- ¼ cup clover honey
- 2 tablespoons peeled and finely minced fresh ginger
- 1 tablespoon finely minced orange zest
- 1 tablespoon finely minced lime zest
- 1 teaspoon fine sea salt
- 2 tablespoons cornstarch
- 3 tablespoons cold water
- 2 to 3 teaspoons hot chile oil, homemade (page 50) or store-bought, to your taste

1 Heat the olive oil in a medium-size nonreactive saucepan over medium heat, add the garlic and shallots, and cook, stirring, for 1 to 3 minutes. Add the orange juice, lime juice, honey, ginger, orange and lime zests, and salt, stirring to combine, and bring to a light boil.

2 In a small bowl, blend together the cornstarch and cold water with a wire whisk. Whisk the cornstarch mixture into the hot sauce, stirring until the sauce thickens. Remove the sauce from the heat. Stir in the hot chile oil to taste.

Spicy, Hot, and Chunky Barbecue Sauce

This recipe is more like you combined a sauce and a salsa, but it's good. If you don't want the sauce as hot as it is, reduce the amount of cayenne or omit it. Serve this with chicken wings or ribs. MAKES ABOUT 7 CUPS

- 3 cups tomato ketchup, homemade (page 43) or store-bought
- 1 cup chili sauce, homemade (page 42) or store-bought
- 1 cup firmly packed brown sugar
- 1 cup red wine vinegar
- 1 cup roasted (page 48), peeled, seeded, and diced red bell peppers
- ½ cup diced onion
- 8 large cloves garlic, minced
- 2 tablespoons chili powder, homemade (page 111) or store-bought
- 1 tablespoon freshly ground black pepper
- 1 tablespoon crushed red pepper
- 1 teaspoon cayenne pepper (optional)
- 1 teaspoon cumin seeds, toasted in a dry skillet over medium heat until fragrant, then ground
- 1 teaspoon dry mustard (I use Colman's)
- 1 teaspoon fine sea salt
- ½ teaspoon ground allspice

Combine all the ingredients in a large nonreactive saucepan and bring to a boil. Reduce the heat to medium-low and simmer for 30 minutes to let the flavors develop, stirring several times to make sure all the spices are dissolved.

Sweet Indonesian-Style Barbecue Sauce

This sauce has a sweet flavor, but it can be overpowering, so use it when you really want an exotic flavor on chicken, beef, or pork satay. MAKES ABOUT 6 CUPS

> 4 cups tomato ketchup, homemade (page 43) or store-bought
>
> 1/2 cup molasses
>
> 1/2 cup firmly packed light brown sugar
>
> 1/2 cup red wine vinegar
>
> 1/4 cup soy sauce
>
> 2 tablespoons freshly ground black pepper
>
> 2 tablespoons chili powder, homemade (page 111) or store-bought
>
> 1 teaspoon ground ginger
>
> 1 teaspoon fine sea salt

Combine all the ingredients in a large nonreactive saucepan and bring to a boil. Reduce the heat to medium-low and simmer, stirring occasionally, for 30 minutes to let the flavors develop.

Sweet and Mild Barbecue Sauce

This is a good beginning barbecue sauce to use on barbecued ribs and brisket or grilled hot dogs. MAKES ABOUT 3 CUPS

> 2 cups tomato ketchup, homemade (page 43) or store-bought
>
> 1/4 cup firmly packed dark brown sugar
>
> 1/4 cup apple juice
>
> 1/4 cup cider vinegar

> Juice of 1 lemon
>
> 1 teaspoon grated lemon zest
>
> 1/2 teaspoon fine sea salt
>
> 1/2 teaspoon freshly ground black pepper

Combine all the ingredients in a medium-size nonreactive saucepan, bring to a boil, reduce the heat to medium-low, and simmer until heated through, 15 to 20 minutes.

Smoked Chile Barbecue Sauce

This is smoky, hot, and good with barbecued game and pork. MAKES 6 CUPS

> 1/2 cup red wine vinegar
>
> 2 teaspoons juniper berries, crushed
>
> 1 teaspoon ground cinnamon
>
> 1/2 teaspoon ground cloves
>
> 1/4 cup canola oil
>
> 1 cup diced onion
>
> 6 cloves garlic, pressed
>
> 1/2 cup firmly packed light brown sugar
>
> 6 smoked dried chiles, pasilla or chipotle, rehydrated in hot water to cover, drained, and diced
>
> Two 6-ounce cans tomato paste
>
> 2 cups apple juice
>
> 1/4 cup Worcestershire sauce, homemade (page 50) or store-bought
>
> 1 teaspoon kosher salt
>
> 1 teaspoon freshly ground black pepper

1 Place the vinegar, juniper berries, cinnamon, and cloves in a small nonreactive saucepan, bring to a boil, let boil for 3 minutes, and set aside.

2   Heat the oil in a large nonreactive saucepan over medium heat, add the onion and garlic, and cook, stirring, until soft. Add the brown sugar, bring to a boil, and let boil for 3 minutes. Stir in the vinegar and spice mixture, then add the chiles, tomato paste, apple juice, Worcestershire sauce, salt, and pepper. Return to a boil, reduce the heat to medium-low, and simmer for 30 minutes to let the flavors develop.

3   Remove from the heat, let cool to room temperature, and serve.

Zippy Barbecue Sauce

This barbecue sauce is for all the barbecuers out there who tell me that they really don't want to make their own barbecue sauce. This is based on a commercial barbecue sauce and is a good basting and dipping sauce for chicken and pulled pork. MAKES ABOUT 3¹/₂ CUPS

> 2 cups store-bought barbecue sauce of your choice
>
> 1 cup cider vinegar
>
> ¹/₄ cup canola oil
>
> 1 tablespoon crushed red pepper
>
> 2 teaspoons freshly ground black pepper
>
> 1 teaspoon fine sea salt
>
> ¹/₂ teaspoon cayenne pepper

Combine all the ingredients in a medium-size nonreactive saucepan and bring to a boil. Reduce the heat to medium-low and simmer for 15 to 20 minutes to let the flavors develop, stirring occasionally.

Smoky Barbecue Sauce

This is a good basting, finishing, and dipping sauce for barbecued pork ribs, pork loin, and pulled pork. Add the liquid smoke until the sauce is to your taste. If you live in the Pacific Northwest, you'll probably add ¹/₄ cup! MAKES ABOUT 4 CUPS

> 2 cups tomato ketchup, homemade (page 43) or store-bought
>
> 1 cup cider vinegar
>
> ¹/₂ cup (1 stick) unsalted butter
>
> ¹/₄ cup Worcestershire sauce, homemade (page 50) or store-bought
>
> 1 to 2 tablespoons liquid smoke flavoring, to your taste
>
> 2 teaspoons granulated onion
>
> 2 teaspoons Louisiana hot sauce
>
> 1 teaspoon fine sea salt
>
> 1 teaspoon freshly ground black pepper
>
> ¹/₂ teaspoon granulated garlic
>
> ¹/₄ teaspoon cayenne pepper

In a medium-size nonreactive saucepan, combine all the ingredients and bring to a boil. Reduce the heat to medium-low and simmer, stirring occasionally, for 20 minutes.

Tangy Maple Barbecue Sauce

Stu Carpenter is one of my barbecue students, and he created this great sauce. Pair this with grilled steak or pork chops. MAKES ABOUT 3¹/₂ CUPS

2 cups tomato ketchup, homemade (page 43) or store-bought

$1/2$ cup pure maple syrup

$1/4$ cup firmly packed light brown sugar

2 tablespoons Worcestershire sauce, homemade (page 50) or store-bought

2 tablespoons Heinz 57 steak sauce

2 tablespoons prepared yellow mustard

2 tablespoons distilled white vinegar

2 tablespoons canola oil

1 tablespoon fresh lemon juice

1 teaspoon fine sea salt

1 teaspoon lemon pepper seasoning

$1/2$ teaspoon ground cloves

Combine all the ingredients in a medium-size nonreactive saucepan and bring to a boil. Reduce the heat to medium-low and simmer for 20 minutes, stirring occasionally.

Bourbon Barbecue Sauce

Always remember when putting booze or wine in a sauce to make sure it's the best you can buy. That means that it's sippin' whiskey or wine. You add the alcohol at the end of cooking so the flavors don't cook off. Serve with Southern-style pulled pork, ribs, or pork loin. MAKES ABOUT 4 CUPS

$1/4$ cup ($1/2$ stick) unsalted butter

$1/2$ cup minced onion

4 cloves garlic, minced

Two 8-ounce cans tomato sauce or 2 cups homemade (page 40)

$1/4$ cup firmly packed light brown sugar

$1/4$ cup Worcestershire sauce, homemade (page 50) or store-bought

$1/4$ cup fresh orange juice

2 tablespoons bourbon

2 tablespoons distilled white vinegar

2 tablespoons fresh lemon juice

1 tablespoon chili powder, homemade (page 111) or store-bought

2 teaspoons freshly ground black pepper

1 teaspoon grated orange zest

1 teaspoon fine sea salt

$1/2$ teaspoon ground allspice

$1/2$ teaspoon cayenne pepper

Melt the butter over medium heat in a medium-size nonreactive saucepan, add the onion and garlic, and cook, stirring, until softened. Add the remaining ingredients and bring to a boil. Reduce the heat to medium-low and simmer for 30 minutes to let the flavors develop, stirring occasionally.

Blackberry Barbecue Sauce

This barbecue sauce was developed for Chef Black Berry Dan, in memory of our world championship in Ireland. It's delicious served with Cornish game hens or duck. MAKES 6 CUPS

3 cups fresh blackberries

1 cup Merlot

$1/4$ cup clover honey

$1/4$ cup granulated cane sugar

2 tablespoons soy sauce

2 tablespoons orange juice

1 teaspoon grated orange zest

1 sprig fresh basil

1 teaspoon fine sea salt

$1/2$ teaspoon freshly ground black pepper

4 cups your favorite barbecue sauce

1 Place the blackberries in a food processor or blender and process to a smooth purée. Strain the purée through a fine-mesh sieve to remove the seeds.

2 Place the puréed berries and Merlot in a large nonreactive saucepan and bring to a boil over medium-high heat. Reduce the heat to medium-low and simmer until the volume has reduced by half, about 20 minutes.

3 Stir in the honey, sugar, soy sauce, orange juice and zest, basil, salt, and pepper and simmer for 10 to 15 minutes. Remove the basil and discard. Stir in the barbecue sauce and simmer 15 minutes longer.

Memphis-Style Smoky Barbecue Sauce

This is a sauce with that Southern barbecue vinegar twang, straight from Beale Street with some rhythm and blues. In Memphis, you order your ribs "wet" or "dry." Wet means with sauce, dry means with just the dry rub and the sauce on the side. In addition to ribs, serve this sauce with pulled pork, pork loin, or chicken. MAKES ABOUT 5 CUPS

    3 cups tomato ketchup, homemade (page 43) or
        store-bought
    1/2 cup firmly packed light brown sugar
    1/2 cup molasses
    1/4 cup prepared yellow mustard
    2 tablespoons fresh lemon juice
    2 tablespoons Worcestershire sauce,
        homemade (page 50) or store-bought
    2 tablespoons liquid smoke flavoring
    2 teaspoons granulated onion

    1 teaspoon granulated garlic
    1 teaspoon fine sea salt
    1 teaspoon freshly ground black pepper
    1/2 teaspoon cayenne pepper

Combine all the ingredients in a large nonreactive saucepan over medium heat and simmer for 20 minutes, stirring occasionally.

Mustard Barbecue Sauce

This sauce will bring you closer to the Carolinas. Serve it over barbecued pork of all kinds. MAKES ABOUT 3 CUPS

    2 cups prepared yellow mustard
    1/2 cup white balsamic vinegar
    1/3 cup firmly packed light brown sugar
    2 tablespoons (1/4 stick) unsalted butter
    2 tablespoons dark corn syrup
    2 tablespoons fresh lemon juice
    1 tablespoon Worcestershire sauce, homemade
        (page 50) or store-bought
    1 teaspoon cayenne pepper

Combine all the ingredients in a medium-size nonreactive saucepan. Heat over medium heat, stirring until the butter has melted and is incorporated into the sauce, about 15 minutes.

Golden Gourmet Mustard Barbecue Sauce

This barbecue sauce fits the bill if you like mustard-based sauces, as it contains prepared yellow and Dijon mustards and dry mustard. The difference between this sauce and a mustard slather (pages 86–101) is that slathers are applied early on in the cooking process, so they can't have too high a sugar content or the slather may blacken on the meat during cooking. Finishing barbecue sauces like this one can have a higher sugar content because they're either applied as a glaze at the end of cooking or served on the side. Serve this with all kinds of slow-cooked pork.

MAKES A LITTLE OVER 5 CUPS

2 cups prepared yellow mustard

1 cup Dijon mustard

1 cup firmly packed light brown sugar

1/2 cup orange juice

1/2 cup ginger ale

3 tablespoons canola oil

2 tablespoons white wine vinegar

1 tablespoon dry mustard (I use Colman's)

1 tablespoon crushed red pepper

1 teaspoon ground ginger

1 teaspoon fine sea salt

1/2 teaspoon ground cloves

Combine all the ingredients in a large nonreactive bowl. Blend well with a wire whisk.

Southern Barbecue Sauce

This sauce is very close to being a Memphis-style sauce, but with my own Kansas City twist—celery seeds and a little more tomato and sugar. I love this on brisket, burgers —you name it. MAKES ABOUT 5 CUPS

2 tablespoons (1/4 stick) unsalted butter

1 tablespoon minced garlic

2 cups tomato ketchup, homemade (page 43) or store-bought

1 cup chili sauce, homemade (page 42) or store-bought

1 cup firmly packed light brown sugar

1/2 cup apple juice

1/4 cup prepared yellow mustard

1/4 cup Worcestershire sauce, homemade (page 50) or store-bought

2 teaspoons celery seeds

1 teaspoon Louisiana hot sauce

1 teaspoon fine sea salt

1 teaspoon freshly ground black pepper

Melt the butter in a large nonreactive saucepan over medium heat, add the garlic, and cook, stirring, until soft but not browned. Add the remaining ingredients and bring to a boil. Reduce the heat to medium-low and simmer for 20 minutes.

Quick Barbecue Sauce

The title says it all. This sauce is not what you would call a sweet sauce; if it's too tart for your taste, add a little sugar or honey. Experiment with your own creative additions and have some fun. Enjoy it on ribs, chicken, and brisket. MAKES ABOUT 3 1/2 CUPS

3 tablespoons unsalted butter

1/4 cup minced onion

2 cloves garlic, pressed

2 cups tomato ketchup, homemade (page 43) or store-bought

1/3 cup fresh lemon juice (3 to 4 lemons)

1/4 cup firmly packed dark brown sugar

1/2 cup tomato juice

2 tablespoons Worcestershire sauce, homemade (page 50) or store-bought

1 tablespoon dry mustard (I use Colman's)

1 teaspoon freshly ground black pepper

1 teaspoon kosher salt

Melt the butter in a medium-size nonreactive saucepan over medium-low heat, add the onion and garlic, and cook, stirring, until soft but not browned. Add the remaining ingredients, cover, and simmer for about 15 minutes.

Peppery Barbecue Sauce

With both capsicum and black pepper, this sauce is good served with fish and shellfish. I love it as a cocktail sauce with grilled oysters. **MAKES ABOUT 2 CUPS**

1 tablespoon canola oil

1 large onion, minced

1 ancho chile, seeded and minced

1 tablespoon pure ground chile of your choice

$1/2$ teaspoon pure ground chipotle chile

$1/4$ teaspoon cayenne pepper

1 tablespoon canola oil

1 cup orange juice

$1/2$ cup fresh lime juice (about 8 limes)

$1/4$ cup granulated cane sugar

2 tablespoons fresh lemon juice

1 tablespoon minced fresh cilantro leaves

1 teaspoon kosher salt

1 teaspoon freshly ground black pepper

1 In a medium-size nonreactive saucepan, heat the canola oil. Add the onion, ancho, and ground chile powders and cook, stirring frequently, until the onion is tender, 5 to 7 minutes.

2 Stir in the remaining ingredients and bring to a boil. Reduce the heat to medium-low and simmer, uncovered, for about 10 minutes, stirring occasionally.

Beefy Honey Barbecue Sauce

With the flavor of beef from consommé or beef stock, the sweetness of honey, and a little garlic, this sauce is great served with grilled onions or other grilled vegetables. Make sure you use clover honey or another mild honey so as not to overpower the flavor of the sauce. This is not a thick sauce; if you want a thicker sauce, you can simmer it down to the thickness you want or add one 6-ounce can of tomato paste with the other ingredients and simmer for a total of 30 minutes. **MAKES ABOUT 3 $1/3$ CUPS**

1 tablespoon unsalted butter

6 cloves garlic, minced or pressed

One 10.5-ounce can beef consomme or 2 cups homemade beef stock (page 81)

1 cup tomato ketchup, homemade (page 43) or store-bought

$1/2$ cup clover honey

$1/4$ cup soy sauce

$1/4$ cup Worcestershire sauce, homemade (page 50) or store-bought

1 teaspoon kosher salt

1 teaspoon finely ground black pepper

Melt the butter in a medium-size nonreactive saucepan over medium heat and cook the garlic, stirring, until soft; be careful not to brown. Add the remaining ingredients and bring to a boil. Reduce the heat to medium-low and simmer for 15 minutes, stirring occasionally.

Spicy Honey Mustard Barbecue Sauce

Sweet with a kick! This sauce is great with barbecued or grilled pork. MAKES ABOUT 4¹/₂ CUPS

- 2 cups spicy brown mustard
- 1 cup light clover honey
- 1 cup firmly packed light brown sugar
- ¹/₃ cup prepared horseradish
- ¹/₄ cup dry vermouth
- 2 tablespoons Worcestershire sauce, homemade (page 50) or store-bought
- 1 tablespoon pressed garlic
- 1 tablespoon freshly ground black pepper
- 2 teaspoons cayenne pepper
- 1 teaspoon cumin seeds, toasted in a dry skillet over medium heat until fragrant, then ground
- 1 teaspoon fine sea salt

In a medium-size nonreactive bowl, combine all the ingredients and blend well with a wire whisk.

Raspberry Chipotle Barbecue Sauce

When I was catering, we served this sauce with smoked beef tenderloin as an appetizer. MAKES 6 TO 7 CUPS

- ¹/₄ cup (¹/₂ stick) unsalted butter
- ¹/₄ cup minced shallots
- 2 cloves garlic, pressed
- ¹/₂ cup granulated cane sugar
- ¹/₂ cup frozen orange juice concentrate, thawed
- 1 tablespoon peeled and grated fresh ginger
- 1 teaspoon fine sea salt
- 1 teaspoon freshly ground black pepper
- ¹/₂ teaspoon ground cinnamon
- ¹/₄ teaspoon ground cloves
- One 7-ounce can chipotle chiles in adobo sauce, puréed with the sauce
- 1 cup seedless raspberry jam
- 4 cups tomato ketchup, homemade (page 43) or store-bought
- ¹/₄ cup Grand Marnier or other orange-flavored liqueur (optional)

1 Melt the butter in a large nonreactive saucepan over medium-high heat, add the shallots and garlic, and cook until soft, stirring, about 5 minutes. Add the sugar, orange juice concentrate, ginger, salt, pepper, cinnamon, and cloves, blending with a wire whisk, and cook until the sugar has dissolved. Blend in the chipotle purée, jam, and ketchup, stirring until well blended. Bring to a boil, reduce the heat to medium-low, and simmer for 30 minutes.

2 If you are using the Grand Marnier, add it during the last 5 minutes of cooking.

Raspberry Ginger Barbecue Sauce

This is a good steak sauce, and it is also delicious with grilled duck. Melba sauce is available at better grocery stores, or simply thaw frozen raspberries in syrup, purée in a food processor or blender, then strain out the seeds. MAKES ABOUT 5 CUPS

Ed Levesque's End-of-the-Year BARBECUE Sauce

Ed Levesque, owner of Lakewood Auto Wrecking in Tacoma, Washington, serves barbecue at least twice a month to customers and friends at his place of business. Ed is also a guy with an eye on the financial bottom line. After his barbecue soirées, he saves leftover sauces in the refrigerator and then combines them with whatever sauces he buys for the next time. The end-of-the-year sauce is usually an improvement on what one gets on any specific visit to a Lakewood Auto Wrecking barbecue lunch.

If you want to recreate something similar, here's what you do:

At the end of barbecue contest season in the fall, combine at least five of the leftover barbecue sauces in your refrigerator. Warm them in a stainless-steel saucepan. Add ¼ cup of Jack Daniel's Sour Mash Whisky, and you'll have a unique sauce that is truly one of a kind.

---

2 cups tomato ketchup, homemade (page 43) or store-bought

3 tablespoons peeled and grated fresh ginger

4 cloves garlic, pressed

1½ cups prepared Melba sauce or sweetened raspberry purée

¼ cup firmly packed light brown sugar

¼ cup clover honey

¼ cup fresh orange juice (about 1 orange)

2 tablespoons Grand Marnier or other orange-flavored liqueur

2 tablespoons Worcestershire sauce, homemade (page 50) or store-bought

2 tablespoons soy sauce

2 tablespoons cider vinegar

1 tablespoon grated orange zest

2 green onions (white and green parts), chopped

2 teaspoons pure ground chipotle chile

1 teaspoon ground allspice

1 teaspoon fine sea salt

1 Combine all the ingredients in a medium-size nonreactive saucepan and bring to a boil, stirring constantly. Reduce the heat to medium-low and simmer, stirring occasionally, for 30 minutes to let the flavors develop.

2 Strain through a fine-mesh strainer and remove the green onions before using.

Carolina Pig Pickin' Sauce

Many variations on this vinegar sauce theme can be found throughout the Carolinas. In South Carolina you'll probably find a little mustard in the sauce; in the western regions of the Carolinas, ketchup starts to creep in. South Carolinians also use a slightly sweet, vinegar-based sauce like this one to sprinkle over pulled pork when it is piled on the buns.

MAKES ABOUT 1 CUP

1 cup cider vinegar

1 tablespoon firmly packed light brown sugar

1 teaspoon non-iodized salt, or to taste

$\frac{1}{2}$ teaspoon cayenne pepper

$\frac{1}{2}$ teaspoon freshly ground black pepper

Combine all the ingredients in a small storage container, cover, and refrigerate overnight to let the flavors develop. Will keep almost forever. Serve at room temperature.

Orange Chile Salsa

This piquant salsa is good with both fish and pork. The Rainbow Gourmet peppercorn blend—white, black, green, and pink—gives you a smorgasbord of flavor and color.

MAKES ABOUT 4 CUPS

1 ancho chile, seeded and diced

1 tablespoon clover honey

4 cups quartered orange sections (about 6 oranges)

$\frac{1}{4}$ cup fresh lime juice (about 4 limes)

1 tablespoon minced fresh cilantro leaves

1 tablespoon Rainbow Gourmet peppercorns

1 teaspoon fine sea salt

Grated zest of 1 lime

1 Place the ancho chile in a small saucepan, add a little water to soften, and simmer over medium-low heat until the water has evaporated, about 15 minutes. Stir in the honey and remove from the heat. Set aside to cool.

2 In a medium-size nonreactive bowl, combine the oranges, lime juice, cilantro, peppercorns, salt, and lime zest. Gently toss with the ancho honey until well coated. Serve at room temperature.

Grilled and Smoked Tomato Salsa

This salsa is easy and fun. It gives the cook some new techniques and shows just how versatile a barbecue pit can be. Serve this with grilled steak, fish, or chicken.

MAKES ABOUT 6 GENEROUS CUPS

4 large cloves garlic, skewered

3 medium-size onions, cut in half

1 large red bell pepper, cut in half and seeded

2 Anaheim chiles

8 large, ripe tomatoes

2 tablespoons fresh lime juice

1 tablespoon canola oil

2 tablespoons minced fresh parsley leave

1 tablespoon minced fresh cilantro leaves

$\frac{1}{2}$ teaspoon cayenne pepper

$\frac{1}{2}$ teaspoon fine sea salt, or to taste

$\frac{1}{2}$ teaspoon freshly ground black pepper, or to taste

1 Set up your covered grill for indirect cooking. Soak mesquite or hickory wood chunks or chips in water for at least 20 minutes, then place on the hot coals. Place the vegetables cut side down on the grill, placing the onions and garlic closest to the fire, the peppers and the tomatoes the farthest away. Close the lid and smoke for about 3 hours.

2 Remove everything from the smoker, peel the tomatoes, bell pepper, and chiles, and coarsely chop everything.

3 In a large nonreactive bowl, combine the vegetables with the remaining ingredients and toss gently to combine. Serve at room temperature.

Brazilian Barbecue Sauce

Known as *molho campanha*, or country sauce, in Brazil, this sauce is the perfect accompaniment for grilled steaks and chicken and a good example of how sauces differ around the country and around the world. To many, this would be considered a salsa. Its vinegary taste just seems to bring out the best flavor in grilled foods. Make only a small batch at a time; this is a sauce that is not going to improve with age, as the vegetables tend to wilt. MAKES ABOUT 4¹/₂ CUPS

2 cups peeled, seeded, and coarsely chopped ripe red tomatoes

1 cup minced onions

¹/₂ cup seeded and minced green bell pepper

1 cup red wine vinegar

1 tablespoon minced fresh cilantro leaves

Place all the ingredients in a medium-size glass or other nonreactive bowl and stir to blend well. Cover with plastic wrap and store at room temperature for 1 hour so that the flavors can develop. Serve at room temperature.

Tomato–Orange Caper Salsa

I like to serve this salsa, instead of tartar sauce, with grilled fish. It also pairs well with grilled turkey or chicken. MAKES ABOUT 6 CUPS

3 cups peeled, seeded, and diced ripe red tomatoes

1¹/₂ cups orange segments, cut in half (about 3 oranges)

1¹/₄ cups diced red onions

¹/₄ cup minced fresh parsley leaves

¹/₄ cup fresh orange juice (about 1 orange)

¹/₄ cup capers, drained

1 tablespoon minced fresh cilantro leaves

1 tablespoon granulated cane sugar

1 teaspoon kosher salt

1 teaspoon freshly ground black pepper

In a large nonreactive bowl, combine all the ingredients and toss gently to combine. Serve at room temperature or chilled.

Jamaican Red Bean and Mango Salsa

This salsa is great with grilled pork, chicken, and fish, or it can be served with corn chips for scooping. MAKES 5 GENEROUS CUPS

1¹/₂ cups cooked or one 15.5-ounce can red beans, drained and rinsed

1 cup peeled, seeded, and diced ripe mango

¹/₂ cup diced red onion

¹/₂ cup balsamic vinegar

¹/₄ cup seeded and diced red bell pepper

¹/₄ cup seeded and diced green bell pepper

¹/₄ cup seeded and diced yellow bell pepper

¹/₄ cup extra virgin olive oil

2 tablespoons dark rum (I use Meyer's)

2 tablespoons minced garlic

1 tablespoon peeled and minced fresh ginger

1 teaspoon seeded and finely minced habanero (Scotch bonnet) chile

2 teaspoons kosher salt

1 teaspoon freshly ground black pepper

¹/₄ cup chopped fresh cilantro leaves

1 In a medium-size nonreactive saucepan, combine all the ingredients, except for the cilantro, and bring to a boil. Reduce the heat to medium-low and simmer for 15 minutes.

2 Stir in the cilantro just before serving. Serve hot, at room temperature, or chilled.

Peach Chipotle Salsa

In 1997, this recipe won first place in the Midwest Division of the Chilean Fresh Fruit Summer-in-Winter Contest. Serve it with grilled fish or chicken. MAKES 3¹/₂ CUPS

- 2 cups peeled, pitted, and diced ripe peaches
- ¹/₂ cup fresh lemon juice (4 to 5 lemons)
- ¹/₂ cup diced red onion
- ¹/₂ cup seeded and diced red bell pepper
- ¹/₄ cup canned chipotle chiles in adobo sauce, rinsed, seeded, and minced
- 1¹/₂ teaspoons pressed garlic
- 1¹/₂ teaspoons cumin seeds, toasted in a dry skillet over medium heat until fragrant, then crushed
- 1 teaspoon minced fresh oregano leaves
- 1 teaspoon kosher salt
- 1 teaspoon freshly ground black pepper

Combine all the ingredients in a medium-size nonreactive bowl. Toss lightly to combine the flavors. Serve at room temperature.

Sweet Apple Salsa

A fresh-tasting salsa, this is good with grilled pork tenderloin or smoked turkey. MAKES A LITTLE MORE THAN 4 CUPS

- 2 cups cored and chopped Golden Delicious apples
- 1 cup cored and chopped Red Delicious apples
- 1 cup diced red onions
- ¹/₂ cup seeded and diced green bell pepper
- ¹/₄ cup fresh orange juice
- 2 tablespoons soy sauce
- 1 tablespoon peeled and grated fresh ginger
- 1 tablespoon pressed garlic
- 1 tablespoon cider vinegar
- 1 tablespoon olive oil
- 1 teaspoon fine sea salt
- 1 teaspoon freshly ground black pepper
- 2 tablespoons minced fresh cilantro leaves

1 Combine the apples, onions, and bell pepper in a large nonreactive bowl.

2 In a small bowl, combine the remaining ingredients, except the cilantro, stirring and blending well. Pour over the apple mixture and gently toss, coating well. Add the cilantro and toss again. Serve chilled or at room temperature.

Watermelon Fire and Ice Salsa

This salsa makes a great accompaniment to grilled chicken breast, fish, or pork chops. A good addition to this salsa is 1 tablespoon of peeled and grated fresh ginger. The biggest problem for me is dicing all the watermelon without eating it! MAKES ABOUT 4¹/₄ CUPS

- 3 cups seeded and diced watermelon
- ¹/₂ cup seeded and diced yellow bell pepper
- ¹/₄ cup thinly sliced green onions (green and white parts)
- 3 tablespoons fresh lime juice (about 3 limes)

2 tablespoons seeded and minced jalapeño chiles

1 tablespoon granulated cane sugar

1 tablespoon rinsed and minced canned chipotle chiles in adobo sauce

1 tablespoon minced fresh cilantro leaves

1 tablespoon minced fresh parsley leaves

1 teaspoon garlic salt

1 teaspoon freshly ground black pepper

Combine all the ingredients in a medium-size nonreactive bowl. Blend the salsa gently but thoroughly. Cover and chill for at least 1 hour before serving to let the flavors blend.

Barbecue Salsa

This recipe is based on one of my barbecue salsas that I use with pork in competition. Serve this with burgers, grilled chicken, or slow-smoked brisket. MAKES ABOUT 9 CUPS

6 cups peeled, seeded, and diced ripe plum tomatoes

2 cups barbecue sauce of your choice

1 cup diced red onions

1/2 cup minced fresh parsley leaves

1/4 to 1/2 cup minced fresh cilantro leaves, to your taste

2 tablespoons olive oil

1 tablespoon granulated cane sugar

4 cloves garlic, pressed

1 serrano chile, seeded and minced

Juice and grated zest of 1 lime

1 teaspoon fine sea salt

1 teaspoon freshly ground black pepper

Combine all the ingredients in a large nonreactive bowl and toss gently to blend. Cover and set aside for at least 2 hours to let the flavors to meld. Serve at room temperature.

VARIATIONS

There are a couple of good variations of this salsa. Try first roasting the tomatoes, onion, and chile on a baking sheet in a preheated oven at 350 or 400 degrees F for 30 to 40 minutes, being careful not to overcook the vegetables, as they will get mushy. You can also smoke the vegetables; see Grilled and Smoked Tomato Salsa (page 154) for directions.

Roasted Jalapeño Salsa

You can make this salsa using canned roasted chiles, but it won't be as good. Shortcuts are not for competition barbecuers! This is great with tortilla chips or spooned over cream cheese as a snack. MAKES ABOUT 5 1/2 CUPS

Four 1/2-inch-thick slices red onion

6 cloves garlic, left unpeeled

1/2 cup olive oil

16 jalapeño chiles, cut in half and seeded

4 Anaheim chiles, cut in half and seeded

2 teaspoons dried oregano leaves

Juice of 2 limes

4 cups peeled, seeded, and diced ripe plum tomatoes

1 teaspoon fine sea salt

1 teaspoon freshly ground black pepper

1 In a large cast-iron skillet over high heat, char the onion slices on both sides, then remove and

set aside. Add the garlic to the skillet and toast until just browned, remove from the pan, and peel when cool enough to handle.

2 Add 2 to 3 tablespoons of the olive oil to the skillet and sear all the chiles until charred on all sides. Add the remaining olive oil, the oregano, and the lime juice and cook for 1 minute.

3 Transfer all the ingredients to a food processor and process until the mixture is roughly chopped.

4 Place the tomatoes in a large nonreactive bowl and pour the chile mixture over them. Season with the salt and pepper and toss gently to combine. Cover and let rest for at least 2 hours for the flavors to develop, or leave overnight in the refrigerator. Serve cold or at room temperature.

Peach Jalapeño Chutney

I love this chutney with grilled or smoked pork, chicken, and fish. It's even good on crackers or spread over a warm wheel of Brie. MAKES 5 TO 6 CUPS

- 2 cups peeled, pitted, and diced ripe peaches
- 2 to 3 fresh red jalapeño chiles, to your taste, thinly sliced (about 1/4 cup if you want to feel some burn)
- 1 cup diced onions
- 1 cup fresh or frozen cranberries, thawed if necessary, picked over for stems, and diced
- 1/2 cup seeded and diced red bell pepper
- 1/2 cup golden raisins
- 1/2 cup cider vinegar
- 1/2 cup clover honey

- 1/4 cup firmly packed light brown sugar
- 1/4 cup fresh lemon juice
- 2 tablespoons chopped fresh cilantro leaves
- 1 tablespoon grated lemon zest
- 1 tablespoon peeled and grated fresh ginger
- 1 teaspoon kosher salt

Combine all the ingredients in a large nonreactive saucepan with a tight-fitting lid and bring to a boil. Stir the mixture, reduce the heat to medium-low, cover, and simmer for 10 to 15 minutes. The peaches should not be mushy. Remove from the heat. Serve hot, at room temperature, or cold.

Smoked Sun-Dried Tomato Relish

With this relish, you'll be stepping up to the gourmet side of barbecue. You can toss this relish with hot pasta or serve it with grilled fajitas. The sun-dried tomatoes plump up in the hot water to catch more smoke, then begin to dry out again in the smoker. The sour-smoky note of the sun-dried tomatoes with the fresh vegetables is fabulous. MAKES 8 TO 10 CUPS

- 16 ounces sun-dried tomatoes
- 1/2 cup olive oil
- 4 cups peeled, seeded, and diced fresh tomatoes
- 2 cups diced celery
- 1 cup minced green onions (green and white parts)
- 1/2 cup fresh lime juice (about 8 limes)
- 1/2 cup minced fresh parsley leaves
- 1/3 cup minced fresh cilantro leaves
- Salt and freshly ground black pepper to taste

1 Prepare an indirect fire. Soak apple wood chunks or chips in water for at least 20 minutes, then place on the hot coals.

2 Place the sun-dried tomatoes in a pie tin and cover with hot water. Place in the smoker, cover, and cook for about 3 hours, stirring about every 45 minutes.

3 Remove the sun-dried tomatoes from the smoker, drain, place in a large bowl, and reconstitute the semi-dried, smoked tomatoes with the olive oil. Chop coarsely.

4 In a large nonreactive bowl, combine the fresh tomatoes, celery, green onions, lime juice, and smoked tomatoes and toss until well combined. Stir in the parsley and cilantro and season with salt and pepper. Serve at room temperature.

Red Pepper and Fresh Mint Relish

A spin on traditional mint sauce, this relish is great with grilled lamb and cabrito. **MAKES ABOUT 2¹/₂ CUPS**

   1 cup seeded and diced red bell peppers

   1 cup packed fresh mint leaves, minced

   ¹/₂ cup diced white onion

   1 serrano chile, seeded and minced

   ¹/₂ cup cider vinegar

   ¹/₄ cup granulated cane sugar

   2 teaspoons peeled and grated fresh ginger

   1 teaspoon yellow mustard seeds

   1 teaspoon fine sea salt

1 Combine the bell peppers, mint, onions, and chile in a medium-size nonreactive bowl.

2 In a small nonreactive saucepan, combine the vinegar, sugar, ginger, mustard seeds, and salt and bring to a boil, stirring to dissolve the sugar and salt. Reduce the heat to medium-low and simmer for 15 minutes.

3 Remove from the heat and let cool to about room temperature. Pour over the bell pepper mixture, stirring gently to blend. Cover and let set for at least 30 minutes for the flavors to further develop. Serve at room temperature.

Balsamic Vinegar Sauce

This is a thin sauce but very tasty, either as a dipping or as a basting sauce for hot wings or grilled chicken breasts.
MAKES ABOUT 2 CUPS

   ¹/₂ cup dry red wine

   ¹/₂ cup chicken broth

   ¹/₄ cup balsamic vinegar

   ¹/₂ cup firmly packed light brown sugar

   2 tablespoons tomato paste

   2 teaspoons crushed red pepper

   1 teaspoon fine sea salt

   1 teaspoon freshly ground black pepper

   ¹/₂ teaspoon dried tarragon leaves

Combine all the ingredients in a medium-size nonreactive saucepan over medium heat. Slowly heat and stir the ingredients until well blended, about 15 minutes. Don't let the mixture boil. Use or serve warm.

Spicy Peanut Sauce

Although this sauce is generally associated with satay and Thai cooking and grilling, it is also good served as a dipping sauce with chicken, pork, fish, or seafood. MAKES ABOUT 2 CUPS

3/4 cup creamy or chunky peanut butter

1/2 cup fresh lemon juice (4 to 5 lemons)

1/2 cup water

1/4 cup soy sauce

2 teaspoons crushed red pepper

2 teaspoons granulated cane sugar

2 teaspoons ground ginger

1 teaspoon granulated garlic

1 teaspoon fine sea salt

Combine all the ingredients in a medium-size nonreactive saucepan over low to medium heat. Heat, stirring, until the peanut butter has melted. This sauce is best served warm.

Chile Peanut Sauce

This sauce is good enough to dip with bread or chicken and pork. Unfiltered apple juice, which is more natural tasting and less sweet than supermarket varieties, is available at health food stores. MAKES ABOUT 2 CUPS

3/4 cup unfiltered apple juice

1/2 cup chunky peanut butter

1/4 cup rice vinegar

2 tablespoons soy sauce

2 tablespoons firmly packed dark brown sugar

2 teaspoons crushed red pepper

2 teaspoons dried basil leaves

1 teaspoon ground ginger

1 teaspoon granulated garlic

1 teaspoon fine sea salt

1/4 cup water, if needed

Combine all the ingredients, except the water, in a medium-size nonreactive saucepan over medium-low heat. Stir with a wire whisk until well blended. If you want to thin the sauce, add the water. Serve warm.

Capered Tartar Sauce

Chef Jim Snyder of Chestertown, Maryland, says, "Once you try this, you won't go back to traditional tartar sauce," and I would have to agree. It makes an excellent accompaniment to any grilled or smoked seafood dish. MAKES ABOUT 2 CUPS

One 3-ounce jar capers, drained

1/2 cup full-fat sour cream

1/2 cup full-fat mayonnaise

1/2 cup peeled, seeded, and diced fresh tomato

1/4 cup sweet pickle relish, drained

Juice of 1/2 lemon

1/4 teaspoon fine sea salt

1/4 teaspoon freshly ground black pepper

In a medium-size bowl, blend all the ingredients together well. Cover with plastic wrap and chill before serving.

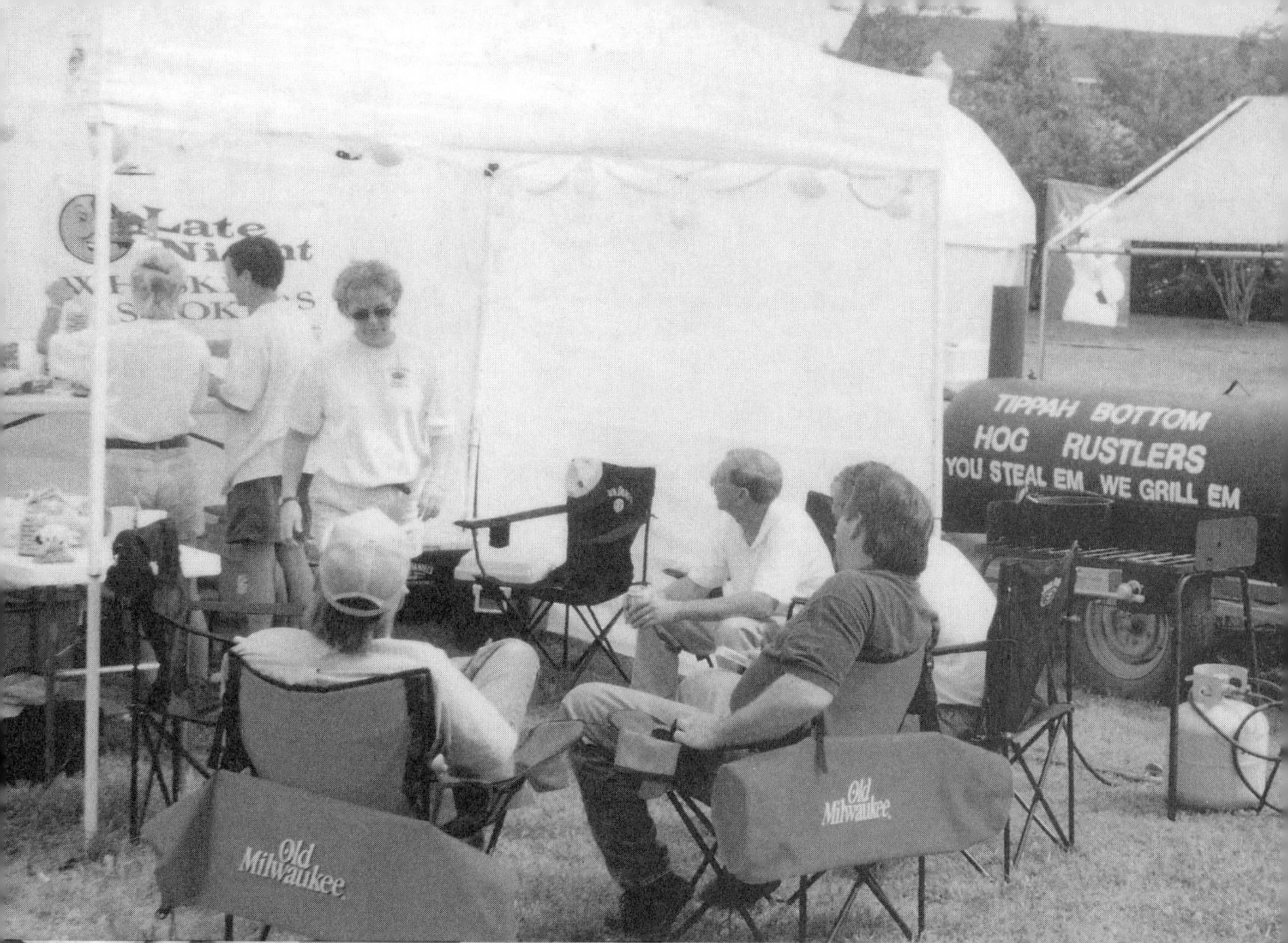

Late
Night
TIPPAH BOTTOM
HOG RUSTLERS
YOU STEAL EM WE GRILL EM
Old Milwaukee
Old Milwaukee

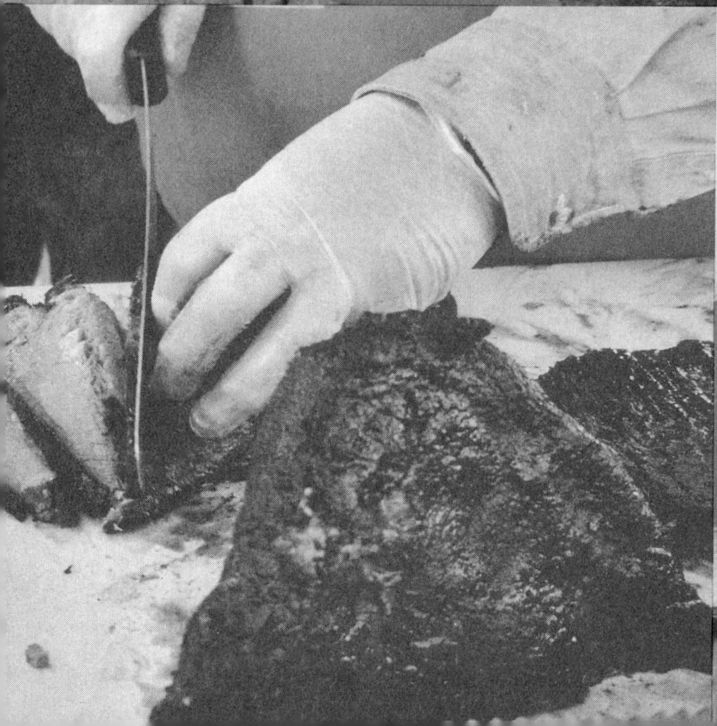

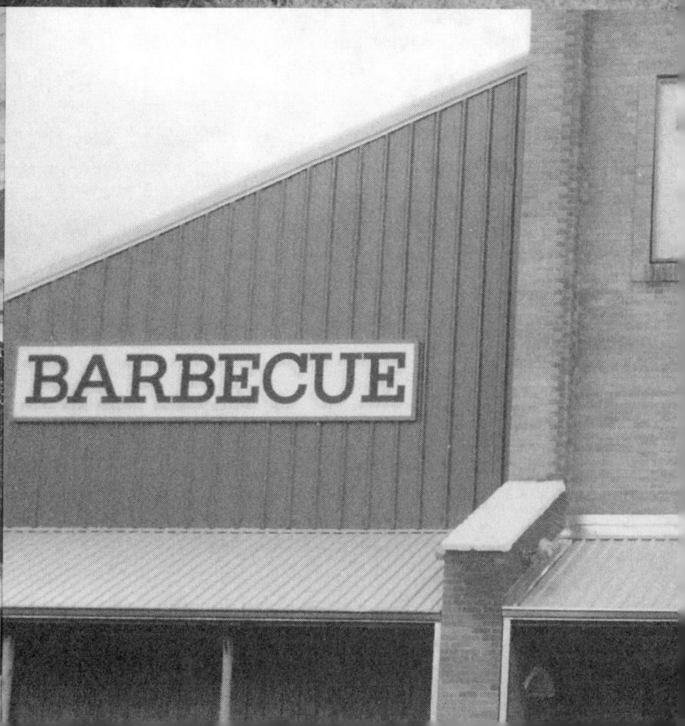

BARBECUE

Rudy Mikeska's
BAR-B-Q
CAFETERIA

Rudy Mikeska's Bar-B-Q, inc.

CATERING SPECIALISTS

Heaven

Every year at the Memphis in May World Championship Barbecue Cooking Contest and the BarbeQLossal Contest in Des Moines, Iowa, in June, competition barbecuers put the pig through its paces. Although I'm known especially for my barbecued beef brisket, I do love slow-smoked pork in all its forms—ribs, shoulder or butt, loin, and whole hog. I also love pork on the grill—chops, steaks, tenderloin, or a rotisseried pork roast. With its marbling of fat, pork is an ideal meat for barbecuing or grilling. As the meat cooks, it bastes itself.

At its best, slow-smoked pork is tender and moist with a hint of wood smoke. Slow-smoked ribs will have just a little bit of give, not falling-off-the-bone tender. (God forbid they have been boiled first, a sure sign of fake barbecue.) Pork butt will be so tender you can pull it apart into shreds with two forks. Pork loin slices will have that dark pink smoke ring and be tender enough to cut with a fork.

Grilled pork is best when it's still a little juicy, cooked to a medium doneness, with a little char on the exterior.

All kinds of flavors—carried in rubs and seasonings, marinades, slathers, and sauces—can be paired with pork for a marriage made in heaven.

The Anatomy of a Porker

A 250-pound hog will yield about 125 pounds of meat and, of that 125 pounds, only a few cuts are not commonly grilled or slow smoked. Ham from the leg and bacon from the belly section are traditionally cured with a mixture of salt, sugar, herbs, spices, and compounds such as saltpeter to draw out extra moisture from the meat. After curing for a period of time, the ham or bacon is then cold smoked (at a temperature under 200 degrees F), most often with hickory. Farms used to have smokehouses, where hams and bacon hung in the rafters and a slow smoldering fire on the floor filled the structures with smoke. Pig's feet are pickled in brine or cured and smoked as ham hocks. The meat from the head goes into a gelatinous lunchmeat called, appropriately, head cheese. Old-time farmers joke that they used every part of the pig except the squeal.

People who like to grill or smoke use several other cuts of pork. I'm going to focus most on those cuts—ribs and pork butt—that are judged at barbecue contests and the preparation techniques associated with them.

Pork Cuts for Grilling

The already tender, thinner cuts of pork, such as chops, steaks, tenderloin, and a loin roast, are great for grilling. Chops, steaks, and loin have some fat that help keep the meat moist during high-heat cooking, but pork tenderloin, which has very little fat, tastes best when treated with a slather or marinade first.

You can also grill spareribs or baby backs, but over a medium fire; you'll have to turn them every 15 to 20 minutes and baste them with apple juice or another liquid, or they will most assuredly dry out. Prolonged cooking at temperatures over 300

It's BRINE Time

When I was growing up, a brine meant a super-salty water that was heavy enough to float an egg. Some old-fashioned cooks would soak chuck roast or whole chickens in a brine solution to remove any blood, then rinse them several times and proceed with cooking.

The first time I tried a heavily brined turkey in the 1970s, it hadn't been rinsed enough and was too salty, so I discounted it. In the mid-1990s, I started looking at brining again because people were raving about how moist and delicious foods were that had been brined ahead of time. So I've experimented with brining and I now recommend it for pork butt, pork loin, and pork tenderloin, as well as chicken and turkey.

I use a light brine, which means about a $1/2$ cup of non-iodized salt (kosher, sea, or canning salt) dissolved in 1 gallon of water. You can also add other ingredients such as brown sugar or crab boil seasoning. If you think a seasoning goes well with that kind of meat, put it in the brine.

Brining can be done in one of two ways: soaking the meat or fowl in brine or injecting it with brine. I just soak pork tenderloin, whole chicken, or turkey in a light brine about 2 hours before I'm ready to cook. With a light brine, there's not enough salt to have to rinse out. You just get a pleasant flavor and more moistness in the end product.

Because pork butt and pork loin are so dense, if you just soak them in the brine, you won't be reaching the inner part. So I use big syringes I get from a veterinary supply house and inject the pork butt or pork loin with brine about 4 hours before I'm ready to barbecue it. If you're going to inject the brine into the meat with syringes, then make sure the brine doesn't include particles that could clog the needle. I use about 2 cups of brine for a pork butt or pork loin—that's about four full veterinary syringes.

degrees F will cause the rub nearest the charcoal to caramelize and blacken. For competition barbecue—and the best flavor, to my mind—slow smoking ribs is the only way to go.

Pork Chops

Pork rib chops, similar in shape and texture to beef ribeye, and center-cut pork chops from the loin should have a pink color, but not too dark. A deep, dark pink means that the meat is from an older animal and will not be as tender as that with a lighter pink color. I like my pork chops cut to about a 3/4-inch thickness if I'm going to grill them. At that thickness, they'll get done but not dry out during the shorter but hotter grilling time. I also prefer to marinate or sprinkle the chops with a seasoning blend before grilling.

Pork Tenderloin

Pork tenderloin is a 2- to 3-inch-wide and 6- to 9-inch-long cylinder of meat that sits along the backbone of the hog. A pork tenderloin generally weighs about 1½ to 2 pounds. I like it grilled over a hot or medium fire until tender and juicy, about 145 degrees F on a meat thermometer. You can also smoke pork tenderloin; if you do, it will have a dark pink smoke ring, a slightly drier texture, and a smokier flavor.

To prepare pork tenderloin for grilling or smoking, use a paring knife to trim away any membrane or silverskin from the meat. Grilled or smoked pork tenderloin can be rubbed, seasoned, brined, marinated, slathered, or sauced any way you want it, which makes it a great entry in the Anything Goes or Miscellaneous category in barbecue cook-offs.

Pork Loin

A whole pork loin from the upper back portion of the hog will weigh anywhere from 5 to 8 pounds. You can also buy smaller loins from 3 to 5 pounds. Most of the time, pork loin has already been boned when you buy it at the grocery store. If not, ask your butcher to bone the meat. Loin is the cut your mother braised for pork roast, but it's also delicious rotisseried on the grill over a medium fire. You can buy rotisserie kits for almost any kind of grill at hardware or barbecue and grill stores. Basically, a rotisserie turns the pork loin for you so that it cooks evenly. You can also slow smoke a pork loin.

Pork Steaks and Burgers

Pork steaks, cut from the shoulder, can be tough, so I marinate them at least several hours before grilling. You can also smoke them, in which case I like to apply a mustard slather first, then season them before smoking. I also enjoy pork burgers. They can take on lots of flavorings and they stay moist and juicy if you don't overcook them.

Pork Cuts for Smoking

Slow smoking pork is an ancient art. In this country, slow-smoked pork—usually whole hog—is a technique that traveled from the South to all the other regions. Whole hog cooking is still featured at some barbecue contests and community festivals. The most common cut to smoke these days, however, is ribs. Pork butt or shoulder is now coming a close second. In St. Louis, pork steak is the preferred cut for the smoker. You can also smoke a pork tenderloin, but basically, traditional pork cuts for smoking are those you would cook lower and slower in your oven—pork roasts, ribs, and pork butt. Pork is a natural for both the grill and the smoker because it bastes itself and stays moist.

Pork Loin and Pork Steak

Barbecue cook-offs are more likely to include ribs and pork butt than loin or steak, but you never know.

Pork loin is the big piece of meat on a pork chop. If it were a big piece of beef, it would be called a strip loin. If it were a big piece of venison, it would be called the back strap. It's more tender than butt, ribs, or steaks, but not as tender as pork tenderloin. A pork steak is cut from a pork butt and is sometimes called a Boston butt steak, butt steak, or blade steak. Barbecued pork steaks are especially popular in St. Louis.

How to Barbecue Pork Loin and Pork Steaks
I slather and season pork loin and pork steak the same way as I do ribs, then baste them during cooking and sometimes finish them with a glaze—also the same way I do ribs. Then I smoke them over an indirect fire with a temperature between 230 and 250 degrees F for about 3 hours, until the loin has an internal temperature of 145 to 165 degrees F. Thinner pork steaks are done when they seem tender to the touch of a grill fork but are slightly chewy when you take a bite, 2 to 3 hours.

Pork Ribs
The pork ribs you barbecue on your backyard kettle can be better than any you've had in any restaurant anywhere. The only ribs that will be better are those prepared by the best teams in America for competition. The information I provide here will allow you to make championship ribs any time you want.

Let's start with rib selection. You'll be using either spareribs, which are attached to the breastbone of the hog, or loin back ribs (commonly referred to as baby back or back ribs), which separate the loin section of the hog from the tenderloin section but do not contain any of the backbone. Although slabs of spareribs weighing 2.8 pounds or less can be purchased from meat companies in commercial pork centers such as Kansas City and Memphis, the kind you can buy at good supermarket meat counters weigh 3.8 pounds or less and are commonly referred to as $3\frac{1}{2}$ and down or 3.8 and down. (I suggest that you avoid slabs of ribs 4 pounds and up unless

you want to cook them a couple hours longer and gamble on whether they'll ever get tender.) Slabs of loin back or baby back ribs usually weigh $1\frac{1}{2}$ to $2\frac{1}{4}$ pounds and cost at least a dollar a pound more, but, after all, you're getting loin and tenderloin meat on them and no heavy bone to trim, so the extra cost is understandable.

When picking out ribs, no matter which type, choose slabs with meat showing over the entire slab, with no bones or ribs in which the meat has been cut away down to the bone (called shiners). With spareribs, there's usually some fat cover on the first three ribs, which can be easily trimmed. Avoid spareribs with lots of big fat pockets or that are half covered by fat. Checking for shiners on back ribs is especially important.

You're going to be tempted by grocery store specials on very cheap ribs with ads such as "Previously frozen to ensure quality." Quality at 99 cents a pound? Okay, try them once. They probably aren't going to be more than barely edible, with lots of fat and little meat. You can also buy wholesale frozen cases of ribs that may be just great when you're going to cook up a bunch of ribs. However, you can also end up with a lot of freezer burn and shiners. Finally, you'll sometimes spot several slabs of ribs packaged individually with especially large bones, weighing just less than $3\frac{1}{2}$ pounds. When you get them home, you'll discover that the breastbone has been removed, there are only 10 bones in the slab, and it still weighs 3.47 pounds. There will probably be lots of meat, but you'd better allow 8 hours of cooking time after scraping lots of fat off the bone side.

Get to KNOW Your Local BUTCHER

In my classes, I pass along a tip that my students always find helpful. And that is to develop a relationship with your local butcher.

Call ahead and ask for the head butcher by name. Then go in the day he or she is there (usually on Sunday, I have found). Tell the butcher you're getting started in competition barbecue. Ask him or her to pick out the three best slabs of ribs for you. Ask why he or she chose those slabs and see whether you can notice the same things.

Barbecue the ribs at home, then take the butcher a sample, maybe 1 or 2 ribs, to try.

Now the butcher knows you're serious.

I got a call one Sunday from one of my students, and he said, "Paul, it works! It works!"

This barbecue student befriended the butcher, using my technique, and the butcher offered to sell him meat at cost for the rest of the competition season.

If you develop this kind of relationship, make sure you find out the butcher's ordering timetable so you don't try to order 20 slabs of ribs two days before you need them and run the risk of not being able to get that quantity.

I also avoid meat that is injected with sodium phosphate, a preservative. It should be listed on the meat package, or ask your butcher.

Establish a relationship with your friendly head butcher, and ask him or her whether you can look over a case of fresh ribs and pick out the four best slabs, or ask the butcher to do it for you. You'll get much better results this way.

Preparing Ribs for Barbecuing For rib preparation, you'll need a cutting board, sharp boning and paring knives, paper or cloth towels, and perhaps a kitchen teaspoon. Place the slab of spareribs on the cutting board bone side down. Trim off the excess fat from the first three ribs. Don't cut away all the fat—some is needed to render out during the cooking process and acts as a baste. Turn over the slab so you can take off the thick membrane that covers the ribs. Why? Because it keeps seasoning and smoke from penetrating the meat and is both tough and inedible. Make an incision just below the length of the breastbone. Start to work your fingers underneath the membrane until you have 2 or 3 square inches cleared. You can now grasp the membrane with a towel and pull it away from about two-thirds of the slab, and then all the way off. Why the towel? It keeps the membrane from slipping through your fingers. Don't worry about the membrane underneath the skirt—the flap of meat that runs from the bottom of the breastbone to the bottom of the last three ribs on the bone side of the rib slab. You can trim it off or leave it on. I leave it on, but I trim any of the thick membrane from the edges. I want as much rib meat as possible to be directly exposed to both seasoning and smoke.

Kansas City–style ribs are spareribs that have the breastbone and skirt removed.

For loin back or baby back ribs, work your fingers under the membrane at whichever end seems the more likely to have easy access and proceed to the towel-aided pull when enough membrane area has been loosened to get a firm grip. Another method is to start in the middle of the membrane and pull it off. With either type of ribs, pulling off the membrane will expose loose fat that needs removing. A paring knife works very well in scraping fat from the meat. So does an ordinary kitchen spoon, with less danger of penetrating the meat or scraping it from the bone. Remember to leave a little fat for self-basting.

St. Louis–Style Ribs: For backyard kettles (but not for larger smokers or cookers), you'll have to make a St. Louis–style cut with the spareribs—basically, cutting them in half lengthwise. Why the St. Louis cut? In most cases, your kettle lid won't be tall enough for a full slab of spareribs to stand vertically in a rib rack. (Baby or loin back ribs are smaller, so you can skip the St. Louis cut.)

Performing the St. Louis cut means using your boning knife to separate the ribs from the breastbone but not using a curved cut as the ribs get shorter. Rather, pick the longest bone next to the breastbone and make a horizontal cut the length of the slab. Yep, you're going to have to apply some pressure, but you'll have two slabs of ribs that look almost the same as the loin backs—5 to 6 inches in length—except there isn't the significant curve to the bones. The shorter ribs will have a meat flap extension rather than being trimmed down to about a 3-inch length.

Next, it's time to prepare one to four slabs of ribs (if you have room, cook as many slabs as your cooker will handle, because they freeze well and, as long as you're cooking, you may as well get the most out of the experience). I will assume that you have trimmed the excess fat from the ribs and removed the thick membrane from the bone sides and, in the case of spareribs, cut them down to make St. Louis–style ribs. Put the ribs meat side down on your cutting board and lightly apply a mustard slather with a pastry brush on the bone sides. Then shake on the rub of your choice, lightly covering the entire surface. Turn the ribs over and repeat the process with the meat side up, and it's time to put the ribs on the pit.

How to Barbecue Ribs Start the charcoal 30 minutes before you want to put your ribs on the pit, then begin the slather and rub process. After you've arranged the hot charcoal to one side for indirect cooking and added a couple of wood chunks, drop the top grill into place and place the rib rack with the rib slots slanting away from the charcoal so that the first slot has at least 1 inch of clearance from the charcoal. Now, gingerly place each slab in a slot with the meat side facing the

If You Don't Have a RIB RACK

If you don't have a rib rack to put the ribs on, try this technique. After the mustard slather–rub anointing, roll up the slabs in loose jelly-roll style; secure them with an aluminum guttering nail, a wooden or metal skewer, or string; and place the rolled-up ribs on the grill with the bones pointing up. Barbecue them on the same timetable up until 30 minutes before the end of the cooking time, then unroll them so they are as flat as possible on the grill.

Don't be alarmed at the splotchiness of the meat. The ribs will look underdone wherever they touched each other, but that's okay. If you're glazing, glaze the bone side, turn them over, glaze the meat side, and cook for 10 to 15 minutes, then glaze the meat side again and cook 10 to 15 minutes longer. Remove the ribs from the grill or smoker and let them rest for 10 to 15 minutes. Cut as desired and let the good times roll!

heat. Yes, it's a messy business and the ends with the shortest ribs will curl around a bit. Either wipe your hands with one of the paper towels or lick your fingers, if nobody's looking, before you put the lid of the kettle on. Otherwise, the handle will be a mess, as will everything else you touch. With the lid on, you should get the great smell of hardwood smoke passing across barbecuing meat for the next hour. If the smoke dies away, drop in two more wood chunks at the first "hot" fuel addition.

You've already read in Setting Up Your Pit (pages 18–22) about replenishing charcoal and using a thermometer to check the heat. The air vents on the bottom of the kettle grill are the sources of air intake. Your first temperature readings will undoubtedly be above 300 degrees F for at least 15 minutes. That's not too bad for a start, as all the meat is cold. If the temperature doesn't start to drop at that point, then it's time to cut the

air intake in half or even more until it does. You're aiming for 230 to 250 degrees F. Prolonged cooking at heat over 300 degrees F will cause the rub nearest the charcoal to caramelize and become black. That won't hurt the flavor much, but it's not the prettiest appearance. Some cooks even make the front slab a sacrificial one in competition, putting their best three slabs in the back slots.

It takes a minimum of 4 hours for loin backs or baby backs and 5 for spareribs to be done, although an hour longer for each is more likely, depending on air temperature, wind, and altitude. Check the charcoal every 45 minutes to an hour if you're using chunk charcoal. If you need to ignite briquettes, start them 20 minutes before you need to add fuel.

When the rub has set, about halfway through the cooking time, begin to baste the ribs every 30 minutes or so with plain apple juice or a sauce such as Memphis Basting Sauce (page 82). Apply the baste with a spray bottle, mop it on with a dish mop, or sop it on with a clean cloth dipped into the baste.

At the second addition of fuel, it's time to shift the positions of the ribs, moving the front slab to the third slot and that slab to the front. The second and forth slabs could also change slots. If the meat on the bones at the top of the ribs has started to pull away, the slabs should be inverted, because the temperature at the top of the ribs is hotter than it is at grill level. If the meat hasn't started to pull away, this change of position can wait until the third fuel addition. With all this shifting, be sure to keep the meat side facing the heat.

A medium dark brown color, bones exposed top and bottom, and enough cooking time all signal the doneness of the ribs. Pull the slab you think is the most done and put it on a clean cutting board. Cut the first two ribs from where you cut off the breastbone and taste the meat. If the meat doesn't yet pull away cleanly from those bones, the ribs aren't done and require another 30 minutes to an hour of cooking time, but with no increase in heat. Return the slab to its slot.

When you finally pull the ribs, let them rest (set) for at least 10 minutes. Rib meat will shred if you cut the ribs too soon after they've come off the pit. Cut them meat side down with a sharp boning knife; wipe it off with a paper towel and touch it up with a steel between slabs. Have room temperature barbecue sauce on the side for those who need it, but don't destroy the taste of your handiwork by smothering it in sauce, as if you had something to hide.

SUGGESTED WOODS FOR PORK

I almost always use a mixture of seasoned oak, hickory, and apple when I'm at a contest. At home in my back yard, however, I like to experiment a little bit. For a medium smoke flavor that goes well with pork, I like pecan, oak, maple, or alder.

HOW TO GLAZE RIBS: If you want to glaze your ribs with barbecue sauce, at the almost-done stage (30 minutes before they should be coming off the pit), pull one slab from its slot and put it on the cutting board, meat side down. Brush your favorite barbecue sauce over it lightly. Turn it over and repeat the process on the meat side. Return it to its slot in the rib rack (another messy procedure requiring finger wiping or licking). When the time comes to taste the ribs, you can decide, when your guests have tested samples both ways, whether you want to repeat the process in the future. Many cooks do it in competition only. Feel ambitious? Try different barbecue sauces on two slabs of ribs.

Pork Butt

I have yet to get a legitimate or believable answer as to why this piece of meat—from the shoulder of a hog—is called a butt. I have been told that it is the butt end of the pork loin, which makes no sense whatsoever. The pork butt is the top half of the pork shoulder with part of the shoulder blade bone in it. It is also known as Boston butt. The bottom half of the shoulder is called a picnic ham. Also cut from the butt are country-style ribs,

Barbecuing a FEW SNACKS for the Cook

What about that extra space on the grill or smoker? If you're doing spareribs, there's no problem. You have those leftover breastbone pieces, meat flaps, and a few extra knuckles. After cutting them into usable sections, give them the mustard and rub treatment and put them on the grill both in front of and behind the rib racks. You can do this simultaneously with the start of the ribs or at the first fuel addition. I favor the former, moving the rib rack back 2 inches and putting some in front of the ribs and the rest behind. Thus I reward myself with tasty rib snacks from the second fueling on as I check on just how the cooking process is going. If you've ever enjoyed those tiny sweet-and-sour spareribs in Chinese restaurants, you'll like these little rib snacks, too.

For loin backs or baby back ribs, I can always pitch on chicken wings or thighs for snacks. An even better choice is a half-dozen country-style ribs, usually three or four to the pound. These come from the blade end of the pork loin or from the pork butt. The latter usually come bone-in. Requiring only some trimming of fat, country-style spareribs are also prepared with a mustard slather and rub, although there are four sides to worry about. There should be room for at least six in your pit. Start with two in front and the rest in the rear of the rack. They take 3 to 4 hours to cook, providing snacks at the second and third fuel additions, if you start them at the same time as your loin backs. You can cook a dozen or more in 3 or 4 hours if you don't want to spend all your time on prepping and barbecuing spareribs and loin backs, but would still like that pork rib taste. Watch for store specials and pick out the leanest ones.

which are actually 1-inch-wide strips of pork butt, some with bone and some boneless.

For barbecue contests, you can either do boned or bone-in pork butt. Boned butt advocates think they get more flavor because they have more surface area to apply barbecue rub to. Bone-in supporters think that the bone itself creates a tastier product. Whatever your decision, at home or in competition, the results will be delicious.

I always tell my students that the pork butt is the worst piece of meat on the hog. Its redeeming quality is that it is also the tastiest piece of meat on the hog. It's the worst because, in Kansas City,

we try to slice it and it's hard to get a good-looking slice in competition because the meat is very fatty and the muscles go in six or seven different directions. Southerners have the right idea—they pull or chop the pork butt and don't worry about slices.

If I'm slicing the butt, I cook it to an internal temperature of 165 to 185 degrees F. I let it rest for 10 to 15 minutes, then remove the bone and slice it. If I'm pulling and chopping the butt, I cook it to an internal temperature of 190 to 205 degrees F. The bone should just pull out cleanly. I let it rest for 10 to 15 minutes, then put it on a

Whole PORK SHOULDER versus Pork Butt

The whole pork shoulder is used in Memphis in May–sanctioned contests. A whole pork shoulder weighs anywhere from 12 to 16 pounds, which can take 12 to 18 hours to slow smoke. In KCBS-sanctioned contests, the pork butt or upper half is the meat of choice, although the entire shoulder, lower half, or picnic may also be used. A pork butt weighs anywhere from 3^1/$_2$ to 9 pounds or more and contains about 20 percent or more fat, often twice as much as the picnic. A pork butt takes anywhere from 8 to 16 hours to slow smoke.

Because of the time involved and because I compete mainly in KCBS-sanctioned contests, the recipes I give in this book are for pork butt, not whole pork shoulder. However, my pork butt recipes will also work with a whole pork shoulder. Simply double the rub, slather, or sauce ingredients and adjust the cooking times, figuring on 2 hours per pound for whole pork shoulder. A picnic takes about the same amount of time to slow smoke as a pork butt, but a picnic has to be basted because it contains less fat than a pork butt.

cutting board and cut or chop it into the desired pieces. You can also take two forks and shred the pork if you want. Recently, I've tried lightly brining pork butt for about 4 hours (see page 165), then applying a mustard slather and a barbecue rub before slow smoking it. With this technique, I won third place in the California Barbecue Contest and second place in the World Championship Contest, both held in Imperial Beach, California, in 2002, in part because the brining kept the pork butt moister.

Preparing Pork Butt for Barbecuing To prepare pork butt for barbecuing, I trim almost all the fat away from the exterior on the top side or fat side, all the way down to a layer of lean pork or the false cap, because right below it is another layer of fat! I trim away the false cap and the layer of fat

beneath it. Then I turn the butt over and trim the fat from the other side.

I normally leave the bone in. If you want to remove the bone, use a sharp boning knife and follow the contour of the shoulder blade bone. The bone is about the size of your hand with your fingers closed, flat on one side with a knuckle raised on the other side. Keep working with your knife around the contours until you can pull the bone out.

To season pork butt, I apply mustard slather and season it all over with my favorite rub.

How to Barbecue Pork Butt I cook pork butt in much the same way I do ribs (pages 169–171), over an indirect fire with a temperature between 230 and 250 degrees F for 8 to 16 hours, depending on how big the butt is and whether it is bone-in or boneless. A boned pork butt slow smokes to tender doneness in about 1½ hours per pound. The timing for a bone-in pork butt is 2 hours per pound.

Turn and rotate the butt at 4 hours or half of the projected cooking time. When the rub has set, about halfway through cooking, begin to baste every 30 minutes or so with plain apple juice or a sauce such as Memphis Basting Sauce (page 82). Apply the baste with a spray bottle, mop it on with a dish mop, or sop it on with a clean cloth dipped into the baste.

Turn and rotate the butt again at 6 hours, or 2 more hours, then again at 7 hours, then finish cooking. Baste with apple juice when you turn the meat the first time, then baste every hour or when you replenish your fire.

PULLED PORK FOR A CROWD

For parties and group feeding, pulled pork is the way to go. The pork can be reheated in a 200 degree F oven in aluminum catering pans with a little apple juice added and cling wrap stretched over the top to keep it from drying out. To serve pulled pork, I put the pieces in a bowl or on a plate, mix 1 cup of barbecue sauce with ¼ to ½ cup of distilled white or cider vinegar and maybe a little bit of my favorite rub, and pour this mixture over the pork. Then I toss it to blend and serve. Anywhere from 3 to 4 ounces of pork, slaw, and either hot sauce or barbecue sauce make a marvelous sandwich, with plenty left for seconds.

WHAT TO DO WITH PORK BUTT LEFTOVERS

Pork butts and picnics, both raw and cooked, have many other uses for barbecues. Ground raw pork is the base for lots of sausages, both fresh and cured. Individual raw muscles trimmed of fat and cubed are much cheaper than pork tenderloin for kabobs or satay. Leftover unsliced cooked pork butt makes for a tasty hash. Burnt ends and trimmings give marvelous flavor to pots of pinto and red beans.

Whole Hog

A trimmed whole hog can weigh up to 150 pounds, but I prefer to use a smaller hog around 75 to 85 pounds. Bigger doesn't always mean better. Make sure you alert your butcher anywhere from 2 weeks to a month before you need your hog so he or she can get it in.

It's quite a project to lift that pig onto the pit and then to turn it later on. You need equipment big enough to handle a whole hog—a cooker at least 4 feet long and 18 inches wide—and you'll need some hefty help. I usually have Steve Holbrook, the best hog man I know, help me out at contests. To lift and turn the hog, we use a pig rack (see page 175) and heavy-duty rubber gloves. You need about 10 cups of your favorite rub, lots of mustard slather, and a whole lot of patience. A whole hog can take between 16 and 18 hours to slow smoke. The trick is to get the hams and shoulders done at the same time as the loin. To do this, you have to cook to your fire. By the thermometers you have stationed around your

Pig Turnin', or WHY YOU NEED to Build a Pig Rack

When you know you're going to be barbecuing a whole hog, you have some serious thinking to do. How are you going to turn the hog on the pit? You sure can't use a grill fork or a spatula, or even twenty grill forks or twenty spatulas.

You have to make your own pig rack.

If you've ever baked a layer cake and had to flip the cake out of the pan using two wire racks (one on top of the cake in the pan, one on the bottom), then you get the general idea of how you need to turn the hog on the pit. You need two layers of metal mesh that will enclose the hog so you can turn it with the help of a partner or two (or three).

Large dressed pigs are about 5 feet long, and smaller ones about 4 feet long, so you'll need to buy two of the appropriate lengths of heavy-gauge wire mesh from the hardware store. The mesh should extend about 6 inches beyond the pig on all sides. The mesh should be sturdy enough so that a 75- to 85-pound pig won't bulge through. Old-timers used bedsprings.

You'll also need two somewhat flexible metal rods to weave through the mesh at the head and foot of the hog. Or you can use bailing wire and wire cutters to tie the mesh together at the head and foot of the hog.

When you're ready to put the hog on the pit, lay a length of mesh on the pit first. Then place the hog on the mesh and place the second length of mesh on top of the hog. Secure the head and foot ends of the mesh with the metal rods or the bailing wire. Cover and cook.

When it's time to turn the hog, everyone needs to put on heat-resistant gloves that reach up their arms, then grasp a corner or end of the mesh and turn the hog.

When the hog has cooked, remove the metal rods or the bailing wire from the mesh, remove the top length of mesh, transfer the hog to a cutting surface, then remove the other length of mesh.

cooker, you should know which spots are hotter and cooler and move your hog accordingly.

Preparing a Whole Hog Some barbecuers have the butcher gut, skin, and remove about ¼ inch of fat from the hog beforehand. I have my butcher only gut the hog; the rest I do myself. I think that

leaving the skin and fat on for the first 5 hours of cooking gives a moister result.

Before you put your hog on the pig rack and then the pit, remove the membrane from the inside of the ribs. Basically, your hog is butterflied, or open, from the belly side like a book. You remove the membrane just like you do for ribs (see pages

168–169); it's just a little more difficult than when you have a slab of ribs on a cutting board. Season the hog inside and out with about 3 cups of rub.

For appearance's sake, cover the snout, ears, and tail with foil before cooking so that these parts don't burn. If you want to show your barbecued whole hog with an apple in its mouth, insert an empty can into the mouth before you start to smoke. That will keep the mouth open so you can place the fresh apple in there right before presentation.

How to Barbecue a Whole Hog Place the hog on the pit, right side up so that the hams are in the hottest part of the cooker, usually the part that's nearest the fire. Slow smoke at 230 to 250 degrees F for 5 hours.

After 5 hours, remove the hog from the cooker, peel away the softened skin with a knife, and trim away all but about 1/4 inch of the exterior fat. This is much easier to do after the hog has cooked a bit. Then slather it all over with your favorite mustard slather and sprinkle on the rest of the rub, inside and out. Reach inside the hog and find the tenderloins on either side of the backbone up to the middle of the hog. Cover the tenderloin area with aluminum foil, and secure the foil with toothpicks or wooden skewers.

Place your hog back on the pit, this time with the shoulders closer to the hottest part. When the rub has set, about halfway through the cooking time, begin to baste every 30 minutes or so with plain apple juice or a sauce such as Memphis Basting Sauce (page 82). Apply the baste with a spray bottle, mop it on with a dish mop, or sop it on with a clean cloth dipped into the baste.

Cook for another 5 hours, then turn again. With an instant-read meat thermometer, check the temperature in different parts of the hog so you'll know what parts are cooking faster or slower than others.

Cook for 5 hours more. With the thermometer, check the temperature in different parts of the hog periodically. The whole hog is done when every part registers 165 degrees F.

SERVING A WHOLE HOG

Some real Southern barbecuers think it's a crime to carve a whole hog. Instead, wearing clean heavy-duty gloves, they tear it apart into chunks. But I'm not Southern, so if you want to carve it, that's fine by me. Just cut it up right on the pit, slicing everything in sight. A sprinkling or two of Carolina Vinegar Barbecue Sauce (page 142) or Mustard Barbecue Sauce (page 149) on the tender meat makes for pretty good eatin'.

Fiesta Pork Burgers

When someone suggests having burgers out on the grill, they're usually thinking beef burgers. If you like hamburgers, you'll really like pork burgers. *Aye caramba!* Why have the same old, plain old when you could have a fiesta? SERVES 6

FIESTA FILLING

1/4 cup minced onion

1/4 cup peeled, seeded, and minced fresh tomato

Grand Champion

THE 1999 GREAT PORK BARBEQLOSSAL CONTEST

Since 1987, this contest, held every June in Des Moines, Iowa, has been putting pork through its paces. The contest has a special sanction from the KCBS because there are only four categories, and they're all pork, unlike a regular KCBS-sanctioned contest, which has Chicken, Pork Ribs, Pork Butt, and Beef Brisket categories.

I enjoy this contest, which is part of a weekend event that salutes Iowa's claim to fame—pork. The weather is generally pretty good, the drive's not bad, and our entire family usually goes up for it. When our daughter Erin was 11 or 12, she won the hog-calling contest that's part of this event. (You yell "soooo-eeee" or something like that to get the hogs back to the yard.) There aren't any hogs in our suburb of Kansas City, but I guess she just watched other people and listened and learned how to do it. You never know what life skills you'll pick up at a contest.

The four pork categories at the Great Pork BarbeQlossal are Whole Hog, Pork Shoulder, Pork Ribs, and Pork Loin. As far as I know, this is the only contest that offers Pork Loin as a category. I do a lot of pork loin for our family, but I don't get much chance to cook it competitively, so I get excited about this.

For the 1991 competition, I put a mustard slather on everything, sprinkled on the rub for that year, and smoked everything at 230 to 250 degrees F until it was tender.

Barbecuing a whole hog is not the easiest thing in the world. You have to be really careful making sure the hams and the shoulders get done at the same time as the loin.

I took the blue ribbon in Pork Loin and won the Grand Championship overall. I don't call hogs. I just cook 'em.

1/4 cup drained and minced canned green chiles

AVOCADO TOPPING

1 large ripe avocado, peeled, pitted, and chopped

1/4 cup sour cream

2 teaspoons fresh lemon juice

1/2 teaspoon Louisiana hot sauce

BURGERS

1 1/2 pounds lean ground pork

1/4 cup dry bread crumbs

2 tablespoons water

1 tablespoon Worcestershire sauce, homemade (page 50) or store-bought

1/2 teaspoon non-iodized salt

1/2 teaspoon freshly ground black pepper

1 large egg

6 hamburger buns, toasted or grilled

1 To make the filling, in a small bowl, combine the filling ingredients and set aside.

2 To make the topping, in a medium-size bowl, combine the topping ingredients and set aside.

3 To make the burgers, in a large bowl, combine the burger ingredients with your hands until well blended. Shape the mixture into 12 equal-size patties, each about 4 inches in diameter. Spread 6 of the patties with 2 tablespoons of the filling mix to within ½ inch of the edges, top with the remaining 6 burgers, and seal the edges firmly together. (Sometimes, when I'm in a hurry, I blend the filling directly into the burger mixture; both ways work well.)

4 Prepare a medium-hot fire in your grill.

5 Place the burgers directly over the coals, cover, and cook until no longer pink in the middle, 6 to 7 minutes per side.

6 When done, place the burgers on the buns and garnish with the avocado topping.

Pig Burgers

This one is for Porky and Miss Piggy. When you add fresh green apple wood to the fire, you also get a smoky finish to the burgers. SERVES 6

- 1½ pounds ground lean pork
- ½ cup fresh bread crumbs
- ½ cup minced green onions (white and green parts)
- ¼ cup barbecue sauce of your choice (pages 136–161)
- 1 tablespoon prepared horseradish
- 1 teaspoon non-iodized salt
- 1 teaspoon freshly ground black pepper

- 1 large egg
- 6 hamburger buns, toasted or grilled
- 2 cups vinegar-based cole slaw of your choice (pages 437–438; optional)

1 Prepare a medium-hot fire in your grill.

2 Meanwhile, in a large bowl, combine the pork, bread crumbs, green onions, barbecue sauce, horseradish, salt, pepper, and egg and blend well with your hands. Form into 6 equal-size patties, each 4 to 5 inches in diameter.

3 Before you grill the burgers, add several chunks of green apple wood to the coals. Place the burgers directly over the coals, cover, and cook until no longer pink in the middle, 5 to 7 minutes per side.

4 Place the burgers on the buns, top with the cole slaw, if desired, and serve immediately.

Sour Cream Pork Burgers

Serve this with home-fried potatoes or French fries and some kind of salad. SERVES 6

- 1½ pounds lean ground pork
- 1 teaspoon non-iodized salt
- 1 teaspoon freshly ground black pepper
- 1 teaspoon onion powder
- ½ teaspoon ground nutmeg
- 12 slices French bread or 6 hard rolls
- 6 to 12 thin ripe tomato slices
- ½ cup Sour Cream Sauce (recipe follows), refrigerated

1 Prepare a medium-hot fire in your grill.

2 Combine the pork, salt, pepper, onion powder, and nutmeg in a large bowl and blend well with your hands. Shape into 6 equal-size patties 4 to 5 inches in diameter.

3 Place the burgers directly over the coals, cover, and cook until no longer pink in the middle, 5 to 7 minutes per side.

4 Place the burgers on the French bread, top with the tomato slices and a dollop of Sour Cream Sauce, and serve immediately.

Sour Cream Sauce

If you like traditional cream gravy, you'll love this. It's also good on fried pork chops, chicken, and breakfast sausage.
MAKES 1¹/₄ CUPS

- ¹/₂ cup full-fat sour cream
- ¹/₂ teaspoon rubbed sage
- ¹/₄ teaspoon non-iodized salt

Combine all the ingredients and blend well.

Cajun Burgers

This recipe comes directly from Chef Paul's kitchen, meaning my kitchen. I'm sure the other Chef Paul—Paul Prudhomme, that is—would like these, too. SERVES 8

- 2 pounds lean ground pork
- 1 small onion, minced
- 1 medium-size green bell pepper, seeded and minced
- 1 bunch (6) green onions (white and green parts), minced
- 6 cloves garlic, pressed
- 1 large egg, slightly beaten
- 2 tablespoons Worcestershire sauce, homemade (page 50) or store-bought
- 2 tablespoons dry bread crumbs
- 1 teaspoon Louisiana hot sauce
- ¹/₄ teaspoon seasoned salt, homemade (page 108) or store-bought
- ¹/₄ teaspoon non-iodized salt
- ¹/₄ teaspoon freshly ground black pepper
- ¹/₄ teaspoon dried thyme leaves
- ¹/₄ teaspoon dried marjoram leaves
- ¹/₄ teaspoon dry mustard (I use Colman's)
- 8 hamburger buns, split

1 Prepare a medium fire in your grill.

2 In a large bowl, combine all the ingredients, except the buns, and blend well with your hands. Shape into 8 equal-size patties 4 to 5 inches in diameter.

3 Place the burgers directly over the coals, cover, and cook until no longer pink in the middle, 12 to 15 minutes per side.

4 Place the burgers on the hamburger buns and serve immediately.

Chop House Burgers with Pancho Sauce

This burger isn't as famous as the one from the Chop House in Chicago, but I think it's better. The blue and mozzarella cheeses and the Pancho Sauce make a perfect taste marriage with this burger. SERVES 8

2 tablespoons canola oil

1 small onion, minced

4 cloves garlic, pressed

2 pounds lean ground pork

1 large egg, lightly beaten

1 tablespoon minced fresh parsley leaves

1 teaspoon kosher salt

1 teaspoon freshly ground black pepper

2 tablespoons crumbled blue cheese

2 tablespoons shredded mozzarella cheese

2 tablespoons (¼ stick) unsalted butter, at room temperature

8 hamburger buns

1 recipe Pancho Sauce (recipe follows)

1 Heat the oil in a small skillet over medium-high heat. Add the onion and cook, stirring, until translucent. Add the garlic and cook, stirring, just until it begins to brown. Transfer to a large bowl and blend in the pork, egg, parsley, salt, and pepper with your hands. Shape into 16 patties 4 to 5 inches in diameter.

2 Prepare a medium-hot fire in your grill.

3 Meanwhile, combine the cheeses and butter in a small bowl, blending well. Place an equal amount of the cheese mixture on top of 8 of the patties, then top those with the remaining patties. Seal the edges of the burgers with your fingertips.

4 Place the burgers directly over the coals, cover, and cook until no longer pink in the middle, 8 to 10 minutes per side.

5 Serve the burgers on the buns topped with some of the Pancho Sauce.

Pancho Sauce

This sauce is very easy to make. It's sweet with a little heat and is also good with grilled chicken. MAKES ABOUT 1³/₄ CUPS

1 cup barbecue sauce of your choice (pages 136–161)

6 tablespoons mayonnaise

2 tablespoons chili sauce, homemade (page 42) or store-bought

2 tablespoons pineapple juice

1 tablespoon red wine vinegar

1 tablespoon prepared yellow mustard

2 teaspoons peeled and grated fresh horseradish

1 teaspoon peeled and minced fresh ginger

½ teaspoon Louisiana hot sauce

Combine all the ingredients in a medium-size bowl and blend well. Serve at room temperature.

Teriyaki Pork Kabobs

These kabobs, served over a rice pilaf, are great for a party or dinner. You can use any cut of pork for kebabs; the loin or tenderloin are traditional, but I like to use shoulder cuts—the pork butt—because I feel they are more flavorful. If you're using wooden skewers, be sure to soak them in water first for 30 minutes so they don't burn on the grill. SERVES 6

12 large mushroom caps

1 large onion, cut into 1-inch squares

1½ pounds boneless Boston pork butt, trimmed of fat and cut into 1-inch cubes

1 large green bell pepper, seeded and cut into 1-inch squares

1 large red bell pepper, seeded and cut into 1-inch squares

TERIYAKI MARINADE

1 cup pineapple juice

½ cup soy sauce

¼ cup clover honey

1 tablespoon toasted sesame oil

1 teaspoon peeled and grated fresh ginger

2 cloves garlic, pressed

1 Thread each skewer as follows: mushroom cap, onion, pork, onion, green pepper, onion, pork, red pepper, onion, pork, onion, green pepper, red pepper, and mushroom cap. Repeat this process 5 more times. Place the skewers in a nonreactive baking dish.

2 To make the marinade, combine the marinade ingredients in a medium-size nonreactive bowl and pour over the kabobs, turning to coat everything well. Let marinate at room temperature while you prepare a medium-hot fire in your grill.

3 Place the skewers directly over the coals, cover, and cook for 5 to 7 minutes. Turn the skewers a quarter turn and cook for 5 to 7 minutes; repeat two more times or until the pork is cooked through. Serve immediately.

Naked Skewered Pork with Sweet Soy Marinade

If nothing else, the title of these tasty little morsels should get your attention. I call them "naked" because you can see right through the marinade to the pork. Again, I prefer to use pork butt, but you could use pork loin or tenderloin if you prefer. Remember, if you're using wooden skewers, soak them in water first to keep them from scorching. For the best flavor and tenderness, let the pork marinate overnight in the refrigerator. SERVES 6 TO 8

SWEET SOY MARINADE

2 cloves garlic, pressed

1 tablespoon ground coriander

1 tablespoon chili seasoning, homemade (page 116) or store-bought

1 teaspoon kosher salt

¼ cup canola oil

1 medium-size onion, minced

¼ cup fresh lemon juice (about 2 lemons)

¼ cup dry sherry

¼ cup soy sauce

2 tablespoons firmly packed light brown sugar

1 teaspoon freshly ground black pepper

4 pounds boneless lean pork, trimmed of fat and cut into 1-inch cubes

1 To make the marinade, in a medium-size nonreactive bowl, combine the garlic, coriander, chili seasoning, salt, and canola oil and blend well. Add the remaining marinade ingredients. Place the cubed pork in a zippered-top plastic bag, pour the marinade over the pork, seal, and let marinate overnight in the refrigerator.

2   When you're ready to cook, prepare a hot fire in your grill.

3   Drain the pork. Transfer the remaining marinade to a saucepan and bring to a boil over medium-high heat; let simmer for 5 minutes, then set aside.

4   Push the pork onto the skewers, leaving a bit of room between each piece. Grill directly over the coals, covered, for 6 to 7 minutes for each quarter turn of the skewer, basting each cooked side with the marinade, until the pork is just cooked through. Serve immediately.

Japanese-Style Pork Kabobs with Sesame-Ginger Marinade

Here is another side of the Oriental barbecue spectrum most people don't think about, Japanese. You may not think to use shiitake mushrooms on a kabob, but they're great. For the best flavor and tenderness, let the pork kabobs marinate for at least 2 to 3 hours or overnight in the refrigerator. SERVES 8

SESAME-GINGER MARINADE

1/2 cup soy sauce

1/4 cup canola oil

1/4 cup rice vinegar

2 tablespoons toasted sesame oil

1 tablespoon peeled and grated fresh ginger

1 tablespoon minced garlic

1 teaspoon kosher salt

1/2 teaspoon freshly ground white pepper

4 pounds boneless Boston pork butt, trimmed of fat and cut into 1-inch cubes

1/2 pound fresh shiitake mushrooms, stems removed

1 large onion, cut into 1-inch chunks

1 to 2 green bell peppers, seeded and cut into 1-inch squares

1 to 2 red bell peppers, seeded and cut into 1-inch squares

1   To make the marinade, combine the marinade ingredients in a medium-size nonreactive bowl and blend well with a wire whisk.

2   Assemble the kabobs on 8 skewers, alternating the pork and vegetables as you like. Place the skewers in a large nonreactive baking dish and pour the marinade over them, turning the kabobs to coat them well. Cover with plastic wrap and let marinate for at least 2 to 3 hours or overnight in the refrigerator, turning them several times.

3   When ready to cook, prepare a medium-hot fire in your grill.

4   Remove the kabobs from the marinade. Transfer the remaining marinade to a nonreactive saucepan and bring to a boil over medium-high heat; let simmer for 5 minutes, then set aside.

5   Place the kabobs directly over the coals, cover, and cook for 6 to 8 minutes per quarter turn of the kabobs, basting the cooked sides of the kabobs with the reserved marinade, until the pork is just cooked through. Serve hot over rice.

Curried Pork Kabobs

These kabobs are hot and tasty! Again, I prefer pork butt for these kabobs, but you can also use pork loin or tenderloin. Marinate the pork for at least 2 to 3 hours or overnight in the refrigerator. SERVES 6 TO 8

CURRY YOGURT MARINADE

1 cup plain yogurt

3 tablespoons mild curry powder

1 tablespoon fresh lemon juice

1 small onion, minced

1 jalapeño or serrano chile, seeded and minced

2 cloves garlic, pressed

1 teaspoon peeled and grated fresh ginger or minced crystallized ginger

1 teaspoon ground cardamom

1 teaspoon kosher salt

3 to 4 pounds boneless lean pork, trimmed of fat and cut into 1-inch cubes

1 To make the marinade, combine half of each of the marinade ingredients in a medium-size nonreactive bowl and blend well with a wire whisk. Place the pork in a zippered-top plastic bag and pour the marinade over it. Seal the bag, shake to coat the meat with the marinade, and let marinate for at least 2 to 3 hours or overnight in the refrigerator.

2 When ready to cook, prepare a medium-hot fire in your grill.

3 Remove the pork from the marinade and discard the marinade. Combine the remaining half of each of the marinade ingredients in a small bowl and blend well with a wire whisk. Push the pork onto 6 to 8 skewers, leaving a bit of space between the pieces. Place the skewers directly over the coals, cover, and cook for 6 to 8 minutes per quarter turn, basting the cooked sides of the kabobs with the new marinade as you go, until the pork is just cooked through. Serve immediately.

Zesty Pork Kabobs

This is a hearty meal on a stick, great to serve in summer when you don't feel like cooking indoors. For the best flavor, marinate the pork kabobs for at least 2 hours or overnight in the refrigerator. SERVES 4 TO 6

HOT BARBECUE MARINADE

1 cup canola oil

1 cup minced or grated onions

1 cup red wine

1 cup barbecue sauce of your choice (pages 136–161)

1/2 cup minced fresh parsley leaves

2 teaspoons crushed red pepper

1 teaspoon kosher salt

1 teaspoon freshly ground black pepper

2 pounds boneless lean pork, trimmed of fat and cut into 1-inch cubes

3 medium-size green bell peppers, seeded and cut into 1-inch squares

12 small white onions, peeled, parboiled for 7 to 8 minutes, and drained

8 to 10 large mushroom caps

8 to 10 tomato wedges or cherry tomatoes

Eight to ten 1-inch chunks summer squash

1 To make the marinade, heat the oil in a medium-size nonreactive saucepan over medium

heat. Add the onions and cook, stirring, until soft, but not browned. Add the remaining marinade ingredients and mix well. Bring to a boil over medium heat. Reduce the heat to low and simmer gently for about 10 minutes to blend the flavors, stirring occasionally.

2 Assemble the kabobs on the skewers, alternating the pork and vegetables. Place the kabobs in a large nonreactive baking dish, pour the marinade over them, turn to coat well, cover with plastic wrap, and let marinate for at least 2 hours or overnight in the refrigerator.

3 When ready to cook, prepare a medium-hot fire in your grill.

4 Remove the kabobs from the marinade. Transfer the remaining marinade to a saucepan and bring to a boil over medium-high heat; let simmer for 5 minutes, then set aside. Grill the kabobs directly over the coals, covered, 5 to 7 minutes per quarter turn, basting the cooked sides with the reserved marinade as you go, until the pork is just cooked through. Serve immediately.

Italian Garden Pork Kabobs

These kabobs are even more fun and entertaining than the other recipes because you can use whatever comes out of the garden. I know that parboiling is not the done thing in real slow-smoked barbecue, but this is grilling, not smoking. For the best flavor, marinate the pork kabobs for at least 2 to 3 hours or overnight in the refrigerator.
SERVES 8

- 3 pounds boneless lean pork, trimmed of fat and cut into 1-inch cubes
- 3 to 4 ears of corn, cut into 1-inch-thick slices
- 1 pound baby red potatoes, parboiled for 10 minutes and drained
- 1 pound small white onions, peeled, parboiled for 7 to 8 minutes, and drained
- 2 small zucchini, cut into 1-inch chunks
- 1 small basket cherry tomatoes
- 8 jalapeño chiles
- 3 cups Italian Salad Dressing Marinade (page 58)

1 Divide the pork, corn, potatoes, onions, zucchini, and cherry tomatoes into 8 groups. Thread on to 8 skewers and end each with a jalapeño. Place in a large nonreactive baking dish and cover with the marinade, turning them to coat. Cover with plastic wrap and let marinate for at least 2 to 3 hours or overnight in the refrigerator, turning the skewers several times.

2 When ready to cook, prepare a medium-hot fire in your grill.

3 Remove the kabobs from the marinade. Transfer the remaining marinade to a saucepan

and bring to a boil over medium-high heat; let simmer for 5 minutes, then set aside.

4 Place the kabobs directly over the coals, cover, and cook for 8 to 10 minutes per quarter turn, basting the cooked sides with the reserved marinade as you go, until the pork is just cooked through. Serve immediately.

Grilled Chinese Pork (Char Siu)

Char siu, also known as Chinese sweet roasted pork or Chinese barbecued pork, is the pork that you get in Chinese egg rolls and eat with sweet-and-sour sauce, sesame seeds, and hot mustard. The pork needs to marinate for at least 4 to 6 hours or overnight in the refrigerator. **SERVES 10 TO 12**

    One 4- to 6-pound boneless Boston pork butt, trimmed of excess fat (see page 173)

    1 cup soy sauce

    ½ cup firmly packed light brown sugar

    ¼ cup clover honey

    ¼ cup hoisin sauce

    2 tablespoons gin or rum

    1 tablespoon kosher salt

    2 cloves garlic, pressed

    ½ teaspoon Chinese 5-spice powder, homemade (page 112) or store-bought

    ½ teaspoon red food coloring paste

    1 recipe dipping sauce, such as Apricot Plum Sauce (page 144)

1 Butterfly or cut the butt in half and cut into strips 1½ inches wide and about 10 inches long. Trim the excess fat as you go along and place the pork in a 1- or 2-gallon zippered-top plastic bag. Combine the remaining ingredients in a medium-size nonreactive bowl and blend well. Pour the marinade evenly over the pork strips, seal the bag, shake to coat the strips, and let marinate for at least 4 to 6 hours or overnight in the refrigerator.

2 When you are ready to cook, prepare a medium-hot fire in your grill.

3 Remove the pork from the marinade. Transfer the remaining marinade to a saucepan and bring to a boil over medium-high heat; let simmer for 5 minutes, then set aside.

4 Place the pork strips directly over the coals, cover, and grill for 30 minutes. Turn the strips, baste with the reserved marinade, cover, and grill 30 minutes longer. Baste, turn, and cook 30 minutes longer, until just cooked through and still moist.

5 Slice and serve, hot or cold, with the dipping sauce.

Grilled Pork Fajitas

This is barbecue Tex-Mex at its finest, served with some re-fried beans or Spanish rice on the side. Your guests will be amazed to find that pork fajitas are more tender than beef. Accompany these with bowls of sour cream, guacamole, shredded cheddar cheese, and salsa or, better yet, Grilled and Smoked Tomato Salsa (page 154). **SERVES 4 TO 6**

2 pounds boneless pork loin, trimmed of excess fat

2 tablespoons soybean oil

2 tablespoons orange juice

2 tablespoons distilled white vinegar

4 cloves garlic, pressed

1 teaspoon ground cumin

1/2 teaspoon seasoned salt, homemade (page 108) or store-bought

1/2 teaspoon dried oregano leaves

1/2 teaspoon cayenne pepper

1 medium-size onion, cut in half and thinly sliced into half moons

1 red bell pepper, cut in half, seeded, and thinly sliced

1 green bell pepper, cut in half, seeded, and thinly sliced

Twelve 6-inch flour tortillas, wrapped in aluminum foil and warmed on the grill

1 Slice the pork loin across the grain into 1/4-inch-thick slices. In a large nonreactive bowl, combine the oil, orange juice, vinegar, garlic, cumin, seasoned salt, oregano, and cayenne and blend well. Add the pork, stir to coat the slices well with the marinade, and let marinate at room temperature for 15 minutes.

2 Prepare a medium-hot fire in your grill. Set your grill up with a grill-top wok or cover the grill rack with a perforated grill rack.

3 Drain the pork and grill the pork, onion, and bell peppers together directly over the coals until the pork is no longer pink, 3 to 5 minutes.

4 Serve the pork, onion, and peppers with the flour tortillas.

Spicy Thai Pork Fajitas

This recipe has outstanding flavor for those who dare. Many large supermarkets now carry fresh lemongrass. To use it, remove the large, tough outer layers and use the tender inside core. You'll need a perforated metal grill wok (these usually come in a hexagonal shape) or a perforated grill rack so the pork and vegetables don't fall into the coals. Use grill tongs or wooden utensils for stir-grilling.

SERVES 4 TO 6

1 1/2 to 2 pounds boneless pork loin or tenderloin, trimmed of excess fat and silverskin

THAI MARINADE

1/4 cup canola oil

1/4 cup soy sauce

1/4 cup creamy peanut butter

2 tablespoons minced lemongrass

2 tablespoons fresh lemon juice

6 green onions (white and green parts), minced

3 stalks celery, minced

2 teaspoons peeled and grated fresh ginger

1 teaspoon curry powder

1 teaspoon freshly ground black pepper

1 teaspoon crushed red pepper

1/2 teaspoon cayenne pepper

1 pound snow peas, strings trimmed

2 medium-size red bell peppers, seeded and cut into thin strips

Twelve 6-inch flour tortillas, wrapped in aluminum foil and warmed on the grill

6 green onions (white and green parts), chopped

1 Slice the pork thinly across the grain.

2 To make the marinade, in a large nonreactive bowl, combine the marinade ingredients and

blend well. Add the pork to the bowl and mix well to coat. Cover with plastic wrap and let marinate at room temperature for 20 to 30 minutes.

3 Prepare a medium-hot fire in your grill. Set your grill up with a grill-top wok or cover the grill rack with a perforated grill rack.

4 Remove the pork from the marinade and drain. Place the pork in the wok and stir-grill with grill tongs until it is no longer pink, 3 to 5 minutes. Add the snow peas and bell peppers and stir-grill 2 minutes longer.

5 Remove from the grill and serve in tortillas topped with the green onions.

Grilled Honey-Mustard Pork Chops

This is what I'm having for dinner tonight. And I'm also going to have grilled corn on the cob and a salad. SERVES 6

HONEY-MUSTARD GLAZE

1/2 cup clover honey

2 tablespoons Dijon mustard

2 tablespoons fresh orange juice

1 tablespoon cider vinegar

1 tablespoon dark rum (I use Meyer's)

1 tablespoon minced fresh basil leaves

1 teaspoon Worcestershire sauce, homemade (page 50) or store-bought

1/2 teaspoon onion powder or granulated onion

6 center-cut boneless pork chops, 1 inch thick

1 Prepare a medium-hot fire in your grill.

2 Meanwhile, to make the glaze, combine the glaze ingredients in a small nonreactive saucepan over medium heat, stirring until the honey and mustard are well blended.

3 Place the pork chops directly over the coals, cover, and cook for 15 to 20 minutes total, turning them three or four times during cooking and brushing the cooked sides with the glaze each time.

Grilled Cuban Garlic and Lime Pork Chops with Citrus Salsa

If you haven't tried Cuban barbecue, which is marinated in spiced citrus juice, you are in for a real treat. Serve this dish with black beans and rice. For the best flavor, marinate the pork chops for at least 4 to 6 hours or overnight in the refrigerator. SERVES 6

CUBAN GARLIC AND LIME MARINADE

1/4 cup olive oil

3 tablespoons fresh lime juice

2 tablespoons fresh orange juice

1 tablespoon minced garlic

1 teaspoon non-iodized salt

1/2 teaspoon freshly ground black pepper

1/2 teaspoon crushed red pepper

6 boneless center-cut pork chops, 1 inch thick

CITRUS SALSA

2 oranges, peeled, seeded, and chopped

1 lime, peeled and chopped

1 medium-size cucumber, peeled, seeded, and chopped

1 small red onion, diced

2 tablespoons granulated cane sugar

2 tablespoons minced fresh cilantro leaves

2 tablespoons minced fresh parsley leaves

1 teaspoon non-iodized salt

1 teaspoon freshly ground black pepper

1 To make the marinade, combine the marinade ingredients in a small nonreactive bowl and blend well with a wire whisk. Place the pork chops in a large nonreactive baking dish or a zippered-top plastic bag and pour the marinade over the chops, making sure all surfaces are coated. Cover with plastic wrap or seal and let marinate for at least 4 to 6 hours or overnight in the refrigerator.

2 To make the salsa, remove all of the white pith from the oranges and limes, because it can make your salsa bitter. Combine all the salsa ingredients in a medium-size nonreactive bowl, gently tossing them. Cover with plastic wrap and refrigerate for at least 1 hour—overnight is better —to blend the flavors.

3 When ready to cook, prepare a medium-hot fire in your grill.

4 Remove the chops from the marinade. Place directly over the hot coals, cover, and cook for 8 to 10 minutes per side or to your preferred degree of doneness. Serve immediately with the salsa.

Grilled Breakfast Pork Chops

We're not at Burger King, Dorothy! Serve these with home fries or grilled potatoes and eggs. This is a meal fit for a king or, better yet, a baron! SERVES 6 TO 8

2 tablespoons celery salt

1 tablespoon sweet Hungarian paprika

1 tablespoon freshly ground black pepper

1 teaspoon poultry seasoning

1 teaspoon dry mustard (I use Colman's)

12 to 14 boneless pork chops, 1/2 inch thick

1 Prepare a medium-hot fire in your grill.

2 Combine the seasonings in a small bowl and blend well. Season the pork chops to taste on both sides with the mixture.

3 Place the chops directly over the coals, cover, and cook until no longer pink in the middle, 4 to 6 minutes per side, turning as needed and being careful not to burn the chops. Serve immediately.

Grilled Iowa Chops with Spicy Red Chile Sauce

This recipe will spice up your day. Remember to wear rubber gloves when handling chiles. SERVES 6

SPICY RED CHILE SAUCE

4 dried small red chiles, about 2 inches long

1/2 cup boiling water

4 cloves garlic, pressed

1 teaspoon minced fresh oregano leaves

1 teaspoon ground cumin

1 cup chicken broth

1 tablespoon olive oil

1 cup tomato juice

1 cup tomato sauce

1 teaspoon kosher salt

6 Iowa chops (boneless or bone-in center-cut chops, cut 1½ to 2 inches thick)

¼ cup olive oil

2 tablespoons garlic salt

2 teaspoons freshly ground black pepper

1 To make the chile sauce, in a medium-size bowl, cover the chiles with the boiling water and let soak for 30 minutes. Drain the chiles, then, wearing rubber gloves, remove and discard the stems and seeds and dice the chiles. Place the chiles, garlic, oregano, cumin, and broth in a blender and process until smooth.

2 Heat the olive oil in a medium-size nonreactive saucepan over medium heat. Carefully strain the chile mixture through a fine-mesh strainer into the hot oil. Stir in the tomato juice and tomato sauce and cook, stirring occasionally, until the mixture is reduced by about half, about 30 minutes. Season with the salt and keep warm.

3 Prepare a medium-hot fire in your grill.

4 Rub the chops all over with the olive oil, then season evenly with the garlic salt and pepper.

5 Place the chops directly over the coals, cover, and cook for 12 to 15 minutes. Turn, glaze with the chile sauce, and cook until no longer pink in the middle, about 15 minutes longer. Glaze again and cook 1 or 2 minutes longer. Serve immediately with the rest of the sauce on the side.

Cheesy Smoked Iowa Chops with Honey-Ginger Marinade

You don't have to be from Iowa to enjoy these fabulous chops. Iowa chops are center-cut boneless or bone-in pork chops, cut 1½ to 2 inches thick. For the best flavor, marinate them for at least 2 to 3 hours or overnight in the refrigerator. Smoking ensures these chops will be succulent. SERVES 6

HONEY-GINGER MARINADE

½ cup soy sauce

½ cup apple juice

¼ cup fresh lemon juice

¼ cup canola oil

¼ cup clover honey

2 teaspoons peeled and grated fresh ginger

4 cloves garlic, pressed

6 Iowa chops

2 teaspoons peeled and grated fresh ginger

6 slices Monterey Jack cheese

6 slices sharp cheddar cheese

1 To make the marinade, combine the marinade ingredients in a medium-size nonreactive bowl and blend well. Place the chops in a large nonreactive baking dish or zippered-top plastic bag. Pour the marinade over the chops, turning to coat all sides, cover with plastic wrap or seal, and let marinate for at least 2 to 3 hours or overnight in the refrigerator.

2 When ready to cook, prepare an indirect fire.

3 Remove the chops from the marinade. Transfer the remaining marinade to a saucepan and

bring to a boil over medium-high heat; let simmer for 5 minutes, then set aside.

4 Place the chops on the pit, cover, and smoke at 230 to 250 degrees F for 30 to 45 minutes, brushing frequently with the reserved marinade. Turn and smoke, brushing with the marinade, until no longer pink in the middle, about 30 minutes longer.

5 When the chops are done, sprinkle them with the ginger and place a slice of Monterey Jack, then a slice of cheddar cheese, on top of each. Cover and smoke until the cheese has melted, about 2 minutes, and serve immediately.

Smoked Double Pork Chops au Poivre with Creamy Sauce Robert

This recipe is for you gourmet types, especially the ones who don't think that barbecue can be elegant, oh ye of little faith! Smoke these chops at about 250 degrees F so they stay succulent. SERVES 2

- 2 tablespoons coarsely ground black pepper
- 2 center-cut double pork chops (³/₄ pound each), 2 ribs per chop
- 1 tablespoon kosher salt
- 2 tablespoons heavy cream
- 1 tablespoon unsalted butter, at room temperature
- 1 tablespoon firmly packed light brown sugar
- 1 tablespoon fresh lemon juice
- ¹/₂ cup Sauce Robert (recipe follows), warm

1 Prepare an indirect fire.

2 Rub the pepper into the chops, patting it firmly into the meat. Sprinkle the chops evenly with the salt. Place the chops on the pit, cover, and smoke at 230 to 250 degrees F for 30 to 40 minutes. Turn and smoke until no longer pink in the middle, 30 to 40 minutes longer.

3 Meanwhile, stir the cream, butter, brown sugar, and lemon juice into the warm Sauce Robert until the butter has melted and the brown sugar has dissolved.

4 When the chops are done, serve immediately with the sauce on the side.

Sauce Robert

This is my take on the classic French Sauce Robert. Maybe I should call mine Bob's Sauce, instead. It's also great with grilled chicken and fish. MAKES ABOUT 1 CUP

- 1 tablespoon unsalted butter
- 2 shallots, minced
- 2 tablespoons white wine vinegar
- 1 tablespoon cornstarch
- 1 cup beef broth
- 1 tablespoon Dijon mustard
- 1 teaspoon granulated cane sugar
- 1 tablespoon minced gherkins
- 1 tablespoon capers, drained and minced

1 Melt the butter in a medium-size nonreactive saucepan over medium heat. Add the shallots and cook, stirring, until light brown. Add the vinegar, bring to a boil, and continue to boil until the vinegar is reduced down to a few drops, 2 to 3 minutes.

2 In a small bowl, combine the cornstarch and ½ cup of the beef broth and blend together. Pour it into the saucepan along with the remaining ½ cup broth, the mustard, and the sugar, and simmer for 5 minutes. Stir in the gherkins and capers and keep warm.

Grilled Garlicky Herb-Marinated Pork Steaks

Pork steaks—sliced pork butt—are overlooked in most barbecue circles, but they are easy to prepare and very tasty. You can buy them bone-in or boneless. Pork steaks are the chuck steak of pork and very popular in St. Louis. For the best flavor, marinate them for at least 2 to 3 hours or overnight in the refrigerator. SERVES 6

GARLICKY FRESH HERB MARINADE

½ cup olive oil

2 tablespoons fresh lemon juice

2 tablespoons minced fresh basil leaves

1 tablespoon minced fresh oregano leaves

3 cloves garlic, pressed

1 teaspoon freshly ground black pepper

½ teaspoon kosher salt

6 pork chuck steaks, ½ inch thick

1 To make the marinade, combine all the marinade ingredients in a small bowl and blend well. Place the pork steaks in a zippered-top plastic bag and pour in the marinade, covering the steaks. Seal the bag and let marinate for at least 2 to 3 hours or overnight in the refrigerator.

2 When ready to cook, prepare a medium-hot fire in your grill.

3 Remove the pork steaks from the marinade. Place directly over the coals, cover, and cook for 15 to 20 minutes. Turn, cover, and cook until no longer pink in the middle, about 15 minutes longer. Serve immediately.

Grilled St. Louis-Style Pork Steaks

I used to make fun of John Lillich, who was from St. Louis and used to grill these in barbecue competition, when they were legal. SERVES 4 TO 6

6 pork shoulder steaks, about ½ inch thick

1 tablespoon garlic salt

2 teaspoons freshly ground black pepper

2 cups barbecue sauce of your choice (pages 136–161)

1 Prepare a hot fire in your grill.

2 Season the pork steaks evenly on both sides with the garlic salt and pepper. Place directly over the coals, cover, and cook for 10 to 15 minutes. Turn, cover, and grill until just a little pink in the middle, 10 to 15 minutes longer.

3 With a pastry brush, coat the steaks with the barbecue sauce on one side, turn, glaze the other side, cover, and cook for 2 to 3 minutes. Glaze, turn, glaze, cover, and cook 2 to 3 minutes longer. Turn and glaze about two more times, letting the sauce set on the steaks, but not letting them caramelize or burn. Serve immediately.

Pork Tenderloin Vindaloo

The spicy marinade in this recipe is based on an Indian stew. If you like curry, you'll like this dish. Tamarind pulp is sour. To use it, soak the pulp in hot water to cover, then remove the seeds with your fingers. For the best flavor, let the pork marinate for at least 4 to 6 hours or overnight in the refrigerator. Serve with your favorite barbecue sauce on the side. SERVES 4 TO 6

Two 1½-pound pork tenderloins

1 cup distilled white vinegar

½ cup tamarind pulp (see Note)

½ cup peanut oil

1 medium-size onion, minced

6 cloves garlic, pressed

1 tablespoon peeled and grated fresh ginger

1 tablespoon minced fresh cilantro leaves

2 teaspoons seeded and minced green chiles or
   1 teaspoon cayenne pepper

1 teaspoon curry powder

1 teaspoon ground cumin

1 teaspoon finely ground black pepper

½ teaspoon dry mustard (I use Colman's)

1 Trim the tenderloins of fat and silverskin.

2 Combine the remaining ingredients in a medium-size nonreactive bowl and blend well.

3 Place the tenderloins in a zippered-top plastic bag and pour the marinade over them. Seal the bags, shake to coat everything, and let marinate for at least 4 to 6 hours or overnight in the refrigerator.

4 When ready to cook, prepare a medium-hot fire in your grill.

5 Remove the tenderloins from the marinade and pat dry with paper towels. Discard the marinade. Place on the grill directly over the coals, cover, and cook for 10 to 15 minutes. Turn, cover, and cook 10 to 15 minutes longer. Turn, cover, and cook until an instant-read meat thermometer inserted into the center registers at least 145 degrees F; if you like your pork more done, then aim for 155 to 165 degrees F.

6 Let the tenderloins rest for 10 minutes before slicing.

NOTE Tamarind pulp can be purchased at Indian grocery stores or health food stores.

Jerk Pork Tenderloin

I've enjoyed jerk pork from a roadside vendor on the island of St. Thomas, and it was delicious. Sambal is a hot Indonesian chile paste made with a variety of chopped peppers mixed with vinegar and salt. It's available at Asian markets and better grocery stores. Use fresh, hot chiles of your choice—either habaneros (also known as Scotch bonnets) or serranos. I can't stress enough that, when working with capsicums, you must wear rubber gloves. The soy sauce may sound odd in a jerk recipe, but it works. For the best flavor, let the pork marinate overnight in the refrigerator. Serve with your favorite barbecue sauce on the side. SERVES 6 TO 8

Three 12- to 16-ounce pork tenderloins

JERK MARINADE

4 fresh hot chiles, seeded and diced

1 large onion, diced

1 large piece fresh ginger, peeled and grated

¼ cup hot chile paste (sambal oelek)

¼ cup peanut oil

¼ cup soy sauce

1 teaspoon ground allspice

1 teaspoon garlic salt

½ teaspoon powdered bay leaf

½ cup water

1 Trim the tenderloins of fat and silverskin.

2 To make the marinade, in a food processor, process the chiles, onion, and ginger into a smooth purée. Add the chile paste, peanut oil, soy sauce, allspice, garlic salt, and bay leaf and process to blend well. Divide the marinade in half and, wearing rubber gloves, rub half the marinade over the pork. Cover the tenderloins with plastic wrap and let marinate overnight in the refrigerator. Reserve the remaining marinade.

3 When ready to cook, prepare a hot fire in your grill.

4 Remove the pork from the marinade and pat dry with paper towels. Place directly over the coals, cover, and cook, turning every 10 minutes, until an instant-read meat thermometer inserted into the center registers at least 145 degrees F, about 30 minutes. Cover between turns. If you like your pork more done, then aim for 155 to 165 degrees F.

5 While the pork is cooking, combine the reserved marinade in a small saucepan with the water and simmer gently over low heat for 10 to 15 minutes, stirring to prevent scorching or burning.

6 Remove the pork from the grill and let it rest for 10 minutes before slicing. Serve with the heated marinade and barbecue sauce on the side.

Spicy-Hot Caribbean Pork Tenderloin

Lime, allspice, peppers, and nutmeg are common ingredients in the Caribbean and make for a great marinade. If you don't like too much fire, cut down on the amount of jalapeño you use. For the best flavor, let the tenderloins marinate for at least 2 hours or overnight in the refrigerator. Serve with your favorite barbecue sauce on the side.
SERVES 6 TO 10

Four 12- to 16-ounce pork tenderloins

2 jalapeño chiles, seeded and chopped

⅓ cup fresh lime juice (about 6 limes)

¼ cup clover honey

2 tablespoons canola oil

1 tablespoon fresh thyme leaves

1 teaspoon kosher salt

¼ teaspoon ground allspice

¼ teaspoon ground nutmeg

1 Trim the tenderloins of fat and silverskin.

2 Place the remaining ingredients in a food processor and process until smooth, about 30 seconds.

3 Place the tenderloins in a zippered-top plastic bag and pour the marinade over them. Seal the bag, shake it to coat the tenderloins, and let marinate for at least 2 hours or overnight in the refrigerator.

4 When ready to cook, prepare a medium fire in your grill.

5 Remove the tenderloins from the marinade. Transfer the remaining marinade to a saucepan

and bring to a boil over medium-high heat; let simmer for 5 minutes, set aside to cool, and refrigerate.

6 Pat the tenderloins dry with paper towels, place directly over the coals, cover, and cook for 12 to 15 minutes. Turn, baste with the reserved marinade, cover, and cook, turning and basting every 12 to 15 minutes, until an instant-read meat thermometer inserted into the center registers at least 145 degrees F. If you like your pork more done, then aim for 155 to 165 degrees F.

7 Let the tenderloins rest for 10 minutes before slicing.

Grilled Pork Tenderloin with Mustard Caper Sauce

I am considered a traditional barbecue-type person but, I have to say, I prefer cooking pork tenderloin hot and fast on the grill. I think it's much tastier, and it comes out juicier.
SERVES 6 TO 8

Three 12- to 16-ounce pork tenderloins

2 tablespoons garlic salt

1 tablespoon finely ground black pepper

2 teaspoons onion salt

3 tablespoons olive oil

1 recipe Mustard Caper Sauce (recipe follows)

1 Prepare a hot fire in your grill.

2 Trim the tenderloins of fat and silverskin.

3 Combine the garlic salt, pepper, and onion salt in a small bowl and blend well. Rub the tenderloins with the olive oil and season evenly with the spice mixture.

4 Place the tenderloins directly over the coals, cover, and cook for 8 to 10 minutes. Turn, cover, and cook until an instant-read meat thermometer inserted into the center registers at least 145 degrees F, 8 to 10 minutes longer, covered. If you like your pork more done, then aim for 155 to 165 degrees F.

5 Let the tenderloins rest for 10 minutes before slicing. The tenderloins may be served hot or cold as an appetizer or as an entrée. Slice thinly and top with the Mustard Caper Sauce down the center. Pass the remainder of the sauce separately.

Mustard Caper Sauce

This sauce also tastes great with grilled or smoked beef and fish. Because this sauce contains raw eggs, make sure you buy them fresh from a reliable source to avoid any possibility of salmonella. MAKES ABOUT 2 CUPS

3 tablespoons whole-grain Dijon mustard

2 very fresh large egg yolks

2 green onions (white and green parts), minced

1/4 teaspoon minced fresh marjoram leaves

2 tablespoons fresh lemon juice

3/4 cup olive oil

1/4 cup canola oil

1/2 cup heavy cream, lightly whipped to soft peaks

2 tablespoons capers, well drained

1 Combine the mustard, egg yolks, green onions, marjoram, and lemon juice in a food

processor and process until pale and creamy. With the machine running, gradually add the oils in a thin, steady stream through the feed tube until thickened.

2 Transfer to a large bowl and fold in the whipped cream and capers. Refrigerate until ready to serve.

Mesquite-Grilled Pork Tenderloin with Plum Sauce

West Texas never had a pork tenderloin this good. The sweet plum sauce offsets the bitterness that you get from grilling with mesquite. SERVES 4

    2 cups chicken broth
    1 cup Riesling or other fruity white wine
    1½ pounds red plums, pitted and chopped
    2 tablespoons granulated cane sugar
    1 teaspoon fresh lemon juice
    1 teaspoon kosher salt
    ½ teaspoon freshly ground black pepper
    Two 1-pound pork tenderloins
    4 red plums, pitted and sliced into thin wedges

1 Bring the chicken broth and wine to a boil in a large nonreactive saucepan; continue to boil until reduced to ½ cup, 20 to 30 minutes. Stir in the chopped plums, sugar, lemon juice, salt, and pepper. Return to a boil, then reduce the heat to medium-low and simmer, stirring, for 6 to 7 minutes longer. Remove from the heat. Taste for seasoning and adjust the sugar and lemon juice, if necessary. Pour the mixture into a food processor

and process until smooth. Pass through a food mill or strainer. If the sauce is not thick enough to hold its shape, return it to the saucepan and cook it down a little longer. Set aside.

2 Prepare a hot fire in your grill.

3 Remove the fat and silverskin from the tenderloins. Add 2 to 4 chunks of mesquite to the hot coals, place the tenderloins directly over the coals, cover, and cook for 10 minutes. Turn, cover, and cook 10 minutes longer. Turn, cover, and cook until an instant-read meat thermometer inserted into the center registers at least 145 degrees F; if you like your pork more done, then aim for 155 to 165 degrees F.

4 Remove the tenderloins from the grill and let rest on a warm platter for 10 to 15 minutes.

5 Meanwhile, stir 3 of the sliced plums into the reserved sauce and heat gently. Cut the tenderloins into ¼-inch-thick slices. Spoon about ½ tablespoon of the sauce on each warmed dinner plate and arrange the pork slices on top of the sauce. Garnish with the remaining plum slices. Serve hot.

Spice Island Pork Tenderloin with Mango-Peach Glaze

Oh yeah, this is good! Serve with rice pilaf or grilled zucchini and yellow summer squash. Serve with your favorite barbecue sauce on the side. SERVES 6 TO 8

SPICE ISLAND RUB

1/4 cup firmly packed light brown sugar, dried (see page 115)

1/4 cup granulated cane sugar

2 tablespoons seasoned salt, homemade (page 108) or store-bought

2 tablespoons garlic salt

2 tablespoons celery salt

2 tablespoons chili powder

2 tablespoons finely ground black pepper

1 teaspoon ground allspice

1 teaspoon ground ginger

1/2 teaspoon dry mustard (I use Colman's)

1/2 teaspoon cayenne pepper

1/4 teaspoon ground cloves

1/8 teaspoon ground mace

MANGO-PEACH GLAZE

1 cup mango purée or 1 1/2 cups fresh or canned mango slices puréed in a food processor or blender to make 1 cup

1 cup peach preserves

1/4 cup clover honey

1/4 cup fresh orange juice

2 tablespoons soy sauce

2 tablespoons fresh lime juice

1 tablespoon peeled and grated fresh ginger

1 teaspoon fine sea salt

1/2 teaspoon ground allspice

1/2 teaspoon freshly ground white pepper

1 tablespoon Triple Sec or other orange liqueur

Four 12- to 16-ounce pork tenderloins

1 To make the rub, combine the rub ingredients in a medium-size bowl and blend well. Set aside.

2 To make the glaze, place the mango purée, peach preserves, honey, and orange juice in a food processor or blender and process until smooth.

Pour the mixture into a medium-size nonreactive saucepan, add the soy sauce, lime juice, ginger, salt, allspice, and white pepper, and cook, stirring with a wire whisk, over medium heat until well blended. Let simmer over medium-low heat for about 10 minutes, until the sauce is well incorporated. Add the liqueur and simmer, stirring, for 3 minutes longer.

3 Prepare a medium hot fire in your grill.

4 Trim the tenderloins of fat and silverskin, then season them evenly all over with the reserved rub. Place directly over the coals, cover, and cook for 40 to 45 minutes. Fifteen minutes before they're done, brush the tenderloins all over with the glaze, using a pastry brush, cover, and cook until an instant-read meat thermometer inserted into the center registers at least 145 degrees F; if you like your pork more done, then aim for 155 to 165 degrees F.

5 Let the pork tenderloins rest for 10 minutes before slicing.

Apple-Smoked Apple-Basted Pork Tenderloin

Trim off all the silverskin, a shiny membrane, from the tenderloin with a sharp paring or boning knife. If you've only had grilled pork tenderloin, experiment with this recipe. Apple wood–smoked pork tenderloin is wonderful. Add the apple wood chunks to the coals when you start cooking and when you add more hot coals. Serve with your favorite barbecue sauce on the side. SERVES 4 TO 6

Three 1½-pound pork tenderloins

2 cups apple juice

¼ cup firmly packed light brown sugar

2 tablespoons garlic salt

1 tablespoon sweet Hungarian paprika

2 teaspoons onion salt

1 teaspoon celery salt

1 teaspoon dry mustard (I use Colman's)

1 teaspoon freshly ground black pepper

1 Trim the fat and silverskin from the tenderloins, place them in a zippered-top plastic bag, add the apple juice, and let marinate in the refrigerator for 2 hours.

2 Combine the remaining ingredients in a small bowl and blend well.

3 When ready to cook, prepare an indirect fire and throw 3 chunks of apple wood on the coals.

4 Remove the tenderloins from the marinade. Transfer the remaining marinade to a saucepan and bring to a boil over medium-high heat; let simmer for 5 minutes, then set aside. Sprinkle the tenderloins evenly with the sugar-and-spice mixture.

5 Set the tenderloins on the pit, cover, and smoke at 230 to 250 degrees F for 1½ to 2 hours, basting with the cooked reserved marinade after 1 hour of cooking. Baste and turn the tenderloins every 30 minutes. Tenderloins are done when an instant-read meat thermometer inserted into the center registers at least 145 degrees F; if you like your pork more done, then aim for 155 to 165 degrees F.

6 Let the pork tenderloins rest for 10 minutes before slicing.

Smoked Chile-Marinated Pork Tenderloin

With great flavor and a little bite, this recipe is delicious. You can get the pasilla chile powder from a good spice company. For the best flavor, let the tenderloins marinate for at least 2 to 3 hours or overnight in the refrigerator. Serve with your favorite barbecue sauce on the side.
SERVES 4 TO 6

3 tablespoons pure ground pasilla chile

1 tablespoon fine sea salt

1 teaspoon cumin seeds, toasted in a dry skillet over medium heat until fragrant, then ground

1 teaspoon freshly ground black pepper

2 tablespoons canola oil

1 tablespoon fresh lime juice

4 cloves garlic, minced

2 pounds pork tenderloins

1 Combine the ground chile, salt, toasted cumin seeds, and black pepper in a small bowl. Stir in the oil and lime juice with a wire whisk and blend into a paste. Add the garlic and blend well.

2 Trim the fat and silverskin from the tenderloins. With rubber gloves, rub the tenderloins all over with the chile paste. Set on a plate, cover with plastic wrap, and let marinate in the refrigerator for at least 2 to 3 hours or overnight.

3 When ready to cook, prepare an indirect fire.

4 Place the tenderloins on the pit, cover, and smoke at 230 to 250 degrees F for 1½ to 2 hours. The tenderloins are done when an instant-read meat thermometer inserted into the center registers

at least 145 degrees F; if you like your pork more done, then aim for 155 to 165 degrees F.

5 Let the pork tenderloins rest for 10 minutes before slicing.

Grilled Garlic Butter-Basted Pork Loin

This recipe requires some planning to do it right. You need to let the beer go flat and let the loin marinate for 2 hours, but I promise that it will be well worth it. The baste is better with flat beer because it doesn't foam up, making it easier to work with. Serve with your favorite barbecue sauce on the side. SERVES 6 TO 8

GARLIC BUTTER BASTE

1 cup (2 sticks) unsalted butter

$1/4$ cup clover honey

6 cloves garlic, pressed

$1/4$ cup grated onion

1 cup flat beer

1 tablespoon minced fresh parsley leaves

1 teaspoon coarsely ground black pepper

One 3- to 5-pound boneless pork loin, trimmed of excess fat (but don't remove all of it)

1 To make the baste, melt the butter in a medium-size nonreactive saucepan over medium heat, then add the honey, garlic, and onion and cook, stirring occasionally, until the onion is soft, but not browned. Add the beer and bring to a boil, stirring. Remove from the heat and stir in the parsley and pepper.

2 Place the pork loin in a zippered-top gallon-size plastic bag, pour the baste over the loin, and seal. Shake the bag to coat the loin, then let marinate for at least 2 hours or overnight in the refrigerator.

3 When ready to cook, prepare a medium-hot fire in your grill.

4 Remove the pork from the marinade and pat dry with paper towels. Transfer the remaining marinade to a saucepan and bring to a boil over medium-high heat; let simmer for 5 minutes, then set aside to cool.

5 Place the loin directly over the coals fat side up, cover, and grill for 15 to 20 minutes, then turn, baste with the reserved marinade, and cover again. Turn and baste every 15 to 20 minutes for about $1 1/2$ hours, until an instant-read meat thermometer inserted into the center registers 145 degrees F. If you like your pork more done, then aim for 155 to 165 degrees F.

6 Let the pork loin rest for 10 minutes before slicing.

Grill-Smoked Pork Loin with Cherry Almond Glaze

In this recipe, you smoke the loin over higher heat than usual. Build an indirect fire in a grill so that the temperature is 300 to 350 degrees F, not the usual 230 to 250 degrees F. Cook the pork loin on the indirect side, so that it's not directly over the coals. With this technique, you get a smokier flavor than if you grilled it, and your pork loin is

done faster than if you slow smoked it. The Cherry Almond Glaze can also be used for ham or chicken. Serve this with green beans and spaetzle or wild rice pilaf. Have a homemade Black Forest cake for dessert. SERVES 6 TO 8

One 3- to 5-pound boneless pork loin, trimmed of excess fat

2 tablespoons kosher salt

2 teaspoons coarsely ground black pepper

1 teaspoon granulated garlic

CHERRY ALMOND GLAZE

One 10-ounce jar cherry preserves

1/4 cup red wine

1/4 cup light corn syrup

1/4 teaspoon ground cinnamon

1/4 teaspoon ground cloves

1/4 teaspoon ground mace

1/4 cup silvered almonds, toasted (see page 322)

1 Build an indirect fire (see headnote).

2 Season the pork loin evenly all over with the salt, pepper, and garlic.

3 Place the pork on the pit, cover, and smoke at 300 to 350 degrees F for 1 1/2 hours. Turn, cover, and cook for 1 hour longer.

4 To make the glaze, in a medium-size non-reactive saucepan, combine the glaze ingredients, except the almonds, and bring to a boil, stirring constantly with a wire whisk. Reduce the heat to medium-low and simmer for 5 minutes. Stir in the almonds.

5 Turn the pork loin, brushing it all over with the glaze. Cover and continue to turn and brush the loin with the glaze every 30 minutes until an instant-read meat thermometer inserted into the center registers 145 degrees F. If you like your pork more done, then aim for 155 to 165 degrees F.

6 Let the pork loin rest for 10 minutes before slicing. Serve the remaining glaze on the side.

Sweet Smoked Pork Loin

This pork seasoning is not a traditional barbecue rub, but it really brings out the flavor of pork. This sort of German meal isn't traditional either, because the typical German pork loin is cured and cold smoked, then heated up before serving—not hot smoked like this version. Serve this pork loin with German potato salad and another twist on tradition—grilled red cabbage. To grill red cabbage, cut the cabbage into quarters, brush with oil, season with salt and pepper, and grill until wilted and tender. SERVES 4 TO 6

PORK SEASONING

2 tablespoons granulated cane sugar

2 tablespoons firmly packed light brown sugar

1 tablespoon garlic salt

1 tablespoon celery salt

1 tablespoon onion salt

1 tablespoon seasoned salt, homemade (page 108) or store-bought

1 tablespoon dry mustard (I use Colman's)

1 tablespoon freshly ground black pepper

1 tablespoon chili powder, homemade (page 111) or store-bought

1/4 teaspoon cayenne pepper

One 3- to 5-pound boneless pork loin, trimmed of excess fat

1/4 cup olive oil

1/2 cup thinly sliced onion rings

1 Prepare an indirect fire.

2 To make the seasoning, combine all the seasoning ingredients in a small bowl and blend well. Rub the pork loin all over with the olive oil. Sprinkle liberally with the seasoning.

3 Place the loin on the pit, then arrange the onion slices down the center of the loin. Cover and smoke at 230 to 250 degrees F for 1½ hours. Remove the onions, rotate the loin, rearrange the onions down the center of the loin, cover, and cook 1 hour longer. Then remove the onions, rotate the loin, rearrange the onions down the center of the loin, and continue to cook until an instant-read meat thermometer inserted into the center registers 145 degrees F, about 30 minutes longer. If you like your pork more done, then aim for 155 to 165 degrees F.

4 Let the loin rest for 10 minutes before slicing. Garnish each slice with the smoked onion rings.

Smoked Calypso Pork Loin

Serve this island pork with some fried plantains and candied yams. The Calypso Rub has ingredients common to the Caribbean for a truly authentic flavor. Serve with your favorite barbecue sauce on the side. SERVES 8

CALYPSO RUB

1 tablespoon firmly packed light brown sugar

1 tablespoon garlic salt

1 tablespoon lemon pepper seasoning

1 teaspoon ground ginger

1 teaspoon cayenne pepper

½ teaspoon ground allspice

½ teaspoon ground cloves

¼ teaspoon ground nutmeg

¼ teaspoon powdered bay leaf

One 5- to 6-pound boneless pork loin, trimmed of excess fat

CALYPSO MOP AND GLAZE

2 cups chicken broth

1 cup dark rum

½ cup firmly packed dark brown sugar

¼ cup fresh lime juice (about 4 limes)

1 teaspoon ground allspice

1 teaspoon non-iodized salt

1 teaspoon freshly ground black pepper

2 teaspoons cornstarch

1 tablespoon cold water

1 Prepare an indirect fire.

2 To make the rub, combine the rub ingredients in a small bowl and blend well.

3 Score the fat side of the pork loin, creating a diamond pattern. Season the loin all over with the rub, rubbing the mixture into the scored surface.

4 Place the loin on the pit, cover, and smoke at 230 to 250 degrees F until an instant-read meat thermometer inserted into the center registers 145 degrees F, about 3 hours; if you like your pork more done, then aim for 155 to 165 degrees F.

5 While the pork is cooking, make the mop. Place 1 cup of the broth, ½ cup of the rum, ¼ cup of the brown sugar, 2 tablespoons of the lime juice, and ½ teaspoon of the allspice in a medium-size nonreactive saucepan and heat over medium heat until the sugar has dissolved and the mixture is well blended. Baste every 15 minutes

with this mixture after the pork loin has cooked for about 1½ hours.

6   During the last 30 minutes of cooking time, add the remaining 1 cup broth, ½ cup rum, ¼ cup brown sugar, 2 tablespoons lime juice, ½ teaspoon allspice, the salt, and the pepper to the leftover baste in the saucepan and bring to a boil. Reduce the heat to medium-low and simmer for 10 minutes. In a small bowl, make a paste with the cornstarch and cold water. Add this to the simmering mixture, stirring with a wire whisk, and cook until thickened. Fifteen minutes before the pork is done, brush with the glaze all over, using a pastry brush; cover, and cook until the glaze sets.

7   Let the pork loin rest for 10 minutes before slicing.

Ancho and Chipotle-Rubbed Smoked Pork Loin

This pork loin is not for the faint of heart. The chiles add mucho gusto and liven up those taste buds. For the best flavor, let the pork loin marinate for at least 6 to 8 hours or overnight in the refrigerator. SERVES 8 TO 12

   3 dried chipotle chiles

   2 dried ancho chiles

   Boiling water, as needed

   ¼ cup grated onion

   1 tablespoon minced garlic

   2 tablespoons lard (vegetable oil may be
      substituted, but I don't recommend it)

1 tablespoon cumin seeds, toasted in a dry
   skillet over medium heat until fragrant,
   then ground

2 teaspoons fine sea salt

1 teaspoon freshly ground black pepper

½ teaspoon ground cloves

One 5- to 6-pound boneless pork loin, trimmed
   of excess fat

1 recipe Barbecue Salsa (page 157) or Peach
   Chipotle Salsa (page 156)

1   Place both dried chiles in a preheated 200 degree F oven for 3 to 4 minutes. Remove the chiles, let cool, and, wearing rubber gloves, open them up. Remove the stems and seeds. Place the chiles in a heat-resistant bowl and cover them with boiling water. When they are soft, about 15 minutes, drain and place in a blender or food processor fitted with a steel blade. Add the onion, garlic, lard, toasted cumin seeds, salt, black pepper, and cloves and pulse on and off until you have a rough paste. Wearing rubber gloves, rub the paste all over the pork loin. Place in a non-reactive baking dish or large zippered-top plastic bag, cover with plastic wrap or seal, and let marinate in the refrigerator for at least 6 to 8 hours or overnight.

2   When ready to cook, prepare an indirect fire.

3   Place the pork on the pit, cover, and smoke at 230 to 250 degrees F. Turn and rotate the loin after about 1½ hours. Continue to smoke until an instant-read meat thermometer inserted into the center registers 145 degrees F, 3 to 4 hours total; if you like your pork more done, then aim for 155 to 165 degrees F.

4   Let the pork loin rest for 10 minutes before slicing. Serve sliced with the salsa of your choice.

Barbecued Pork Loin with Garlic and Five Peppers

This recipe features the great flavor of garlic, which blends perfectly with the spice and aroma of the peppercorns. Serve with potatoes and a green salad. SERVES 6 TO 8

One 5- to 6-pound boneless pork loin, trimmed of excess fat

1/4 cup olive oil

1/2 cup cracked 5-peppercorn blend (black, white, green, red, and Jamaican)

1/4 cup minced garlic

2 tablespoons kosher salt

1 tablespoon granulated cane sugar

1 Prepare an indirect fire.

2 Rub the pork all over with the olive oil. Cover completely with the peppercorns and garlic. Sprinkle the loin evenly with the salt and sugar.

3 Place the pork on the pit, cover, and smoke at 230 to 250 degrees F. Turn and rotate the loin after about 1 1/2 hours. Continue to smoke until an instant-read meat thermometer inserted into the center registers 145 degrees F, 3 to 4 hours total; if you like your pork more done, then aim for 155 to 165 degrees F.

4 Let the pork loin rest for 10 minutes before slicing.

Smoked Sweet and Hot Crown of Pork

Crown of pork is a great cut of meat for a party meal; it's delicious, makes a wonderful show, and is not hard to cook. A crown roast—basically a string of loin chops that are tied together in a circle to form a crown—must be ordered in advance from a butcher. Make sure the butcher ties it securely. Apple wood is great to use on the pit for this recipe. SERVES 8 TO 12

SWEET AND HOT SPICE RUB

2 tablespoons granulated cane sugar

2 tablespoons firmly packed dark brown sugar

2 tablespoons sweet Hungarian paprika

2 tablespoons garlic salt

1 tablespoon onion salt

1 tablespoon chili powder

1 tablespoon freshly ground black pepper

2 teaspoons seasoned salt, homemade (page 108) or store-bought

1 teaspoon celery salt

1 teaspoon ground ginger

1/2 teaspoon ground allspice

1/4 teaspoon ground cloves

1/4 teaspoon dried rosemary leaves

One 9- to 12-rib pork loin crown roast
Apple juice as needed

1 Prepare an indirect fire.

2 To make the rub, combine all the rub ingredients in a medium-size bowl and blend well. Sprinkle the roast evenly all over with the rub. Cover the pork bones with aluminum foil to keep them from browning.

3   Place the roast on the pit, cover, and smoke at 230 to 250 degrees F for about 2 hours, basting with apple juice after the first hour of cooking. Rotate the roast 180 degrees, baste, and cook for 2 hours longer, basting every hour. Rotate another 180 degrees, baste, and cook until an instant-read meat thermometer inserted into the center away from any bone registers 145 degrees F, about 1 hour longer. If you like your pork more done, then aim for 155 to 165 degrees F.

4   Untie the roast and remove the foil. Let the pork rest for 10 minutes before slicing.

Basic Barbecued Ribs

This is the way my parents taught me to prepare barbecued ribs when I was a mere lad of nine; those ribs were blue-ribbon quality—the best! If you prefer to use another style of rib, that's fine. It is quite all right to substitute other rib styles in any of these recipes. I grew up with spareribs and prefer them to loin back ribs. SERVES 6 TO 8

    3 slabs 3.8 and down spareribs

    3 tablespoons salt, or to taste

    2 tablespoons freshly ground black pepper, or to taste

    3 cups barbecue sauce of your choice (pages 136–161)

1   Prepare an indirect fire.

2   Prepare the ribs by removing the membrane and trimming them of large pieces of fat (see pages 168–169). Season on all sides with the salt and rub it in. Season with the pepper and rub it in. Don't forget to season under the skirt.

3   Place the ribs on the pit, cover, and cook according to the directions on pages 169–171.

4   Half an hour before the end of cooking, glaze the bone side of the slabs lightly with the barbecue sauce, turn, glaze the meat side, and cook 10 to 15 minutes longer. Lightly glaze the meat side again, turn, and cook 10 to 15 minutes longer.

5   Remove from the grill and let rest for 10 minutes before cutting into individual ribs. These are best served hot but still taste dandy served cold.

Garlicky Barbecued Ribs

This rib recipe is another good place to start. Give me garlic, and I'm on my way to heaven. SERVES 6 TO 8

    3 slabs 3.8 and down spareribs

    2 tablespoons garlic salt

    1 tablespoon sweet Hungarian paprika

    1 tablespoon freshly ground black pepper

    3 cups barbecue sauce of your choice (pages 136–161)

1   Prepare an indirect fire.

2   Prepare the ribs by removing the membrane and any large pieces of fat (see pages 168–169). Season the ribs evenly on both sides with the salt, paprika, and pepper, rubbing each of them in; don't forget to season under the skirt.

3   Place the ribs on the pit, cover, and cook according to the directions on pages 169–171.

4   Half an hour before the end of the cooking time, glaze the bone side of the slabs lightly with the barbecue sauce, turn, glaze the meat side, and

cook for 10 to 15 minutes. Lightly glaze the meat side again, turn, and cook for 10 to 15 minutes more.

5 Remove from the grill and let rest for 10 minutes before cutting into individual ribs. Serve hot or cold.

Lemon Barbecued Ribs

This recipe involves a light brining procedure, which makes it easier to keep the ribs moist during cooking. Don't extend the marinating or brining time; if you do, the ribs may come out salty. I don't usually glaze these ribs, but you can, using your favorite barbecue sauce, if you want. SERVES 6 TO 8

    3 slabs 3.8 and down spareribs
    1 quart brine solution ($\frac{1}{4}$ cup kosher salt to 1
        quart water)
    $\frac{1}{4}$ cup salt-free lemon pepper seasoning
    3 cups barbecue sauce of your choice (pages
        136–161; optional)

1 Prepare an indirect fire.

2 Prepare the ribs by removing the membrane and trimming away any large pieces of fat (see pages 168–169). Place the ribs in a plastic pan large enough to hold them and pour the brine solution over them, making sure they are covered. Let set, covered with plastic wrap, at room temperature for 30 minutes.

3 Remove the ribs from the brine and pat dry. Season on all sides with the lemon pepper, rubbing it in; don't forget to season under the skirt.

4 Place the ribs on the pit, cover, and cook according to the directions on pages 169–171.

5 Remove from the grill and let rest for 10 minutes before cutting into individual ribs. Serve hot, with barbecue sauce on the side if desired.

Bombay Spareribs

These ribs are for the more adventurous, but they are certainly worth the journey. Sandra Lyon, the wife of my good barbecue buddy Bob, loves Bombay gin. When I was visiting them at their home in the Pacific Northwest, I started with Sandra's gin and matched other flavors to it to create this recipe. SERVES 6 TO 8

    3 slabs 3.8 and down spareribs
    2 tablespoons plus 1 teaspoon kosher salt
    1 tablespoon freshly ground black pepper
    One 12-ounce can ginger ale
    1$\frac{1}{2}$ ounces Bombay gin
    $\frac{1}{4}$ cup ($\frac{1}{2}$ stick) unsalted butter or vegetable oil
    1 cup minced onion
    2 teaspoons curry powder, or to taste
    Three 4-ounce jars strained applesauce (baby
        food)
    2 tablespoons fresh lemon juice

1 Prepare an indirect fire.

2 Prepare the ribs by removing the membrane and trimming away any large pieces of fat (see pages 168–169). Lightly sprinkle both sides of the ribs with 2 tablespoons of the salt and the pepper; don't forget to season under the.skirt. Combine the ginger ale and gin in a medium-size bowl.

3 Place the ribs on the pit, cover, and cook according to the directions on pages 169–171,

basting with the ginger ale–and-gin mixture every 30 to 45 minutes.

4   While the ribs are cooking, heat the butter in a medium-size saucepan on the grill, if possible, or on the stovetop over medium heat, add the onion, and cook, stirring until softened. Add the curry powder, cook, stirring, for about 2 minutes, then stir in the applesauce, lemon juice, and the remaining 1 teaspoon of salt. Heat until bubbly. Remove from the heat.

5   Half an hour before the end of the cooking time, brush both sides of the ribs generously with the curry sauce and cook, turning gently and brushing often on the meat side with the remaining curry sauce, until the ribs are tender and browned.

6   Remove from the grill and let rest for 10 minutes before cutting into individual ribs. Serve hot.

Sweet and Hot Spareribs with Apricot-Plum Sauce

I get hungry just thinking about these sticky little morsels. They're finger-lickin' good. As with any rib recipe, you can also use baby backs instead of spareribs. SERVES 6 TO 8

    3 slabs 3.8 and down spareribs
    2 tablespoons kosher salt
    1 tablespoon coarsely ground black pepper

    1 cup apple juice or cider
    1 cup Apricot-Plum Sauce (page 144)

1   Prepare an indirect fire.

2   Prepare the ribs by removing the membrane and trimming away large pieces of fat (see pages 168–169). Season on both sides with the salt and pepper, rubbing them in; don't forget to season under the skirt.

3   Place the ribs on the pit, cover, and cook according to the directions on pages 169–171.

4   While the ribs are cooking, combine the apple juice and plum sauce in a medium-size nonreactive saucepan over medium heat until hot.

5   Thirty minutes before the end of the cooking time, brush the ribs on both sides with the sauce and turn frequently to keep the sauce from burning or caramelizing.

6   Remove from the grill and let rest for 10 minutes before cutting into individual ribs. Serve hot with any extra sauce on the side.

Sweet Hoisin Spareribs

For this recipe, I usually start with Kansas City-style ribs— spareribs with the breastbone and skirt removed—then cut them into narrow St. Louis–style ribs (see page 169), but you can use any style or size ribs you like. These ribs make a great appetizer or entrée for a Chinese feast and New Year's celebration. Allow at least 4 to 6 hours, or preferably overnight, for these ribs to marinate in the Asian seasonings before smoking. SERVES 4 TO 6

BARBECUE Lingo

If you're gonna walk the walk, you gotta talk the talk.

BARBECUE: Slow-smoked food, with or without barbecue sauce.

BROWNIES: Smoked pieces of beef, chicken, or pork that fall off during slicing. Brownies are great blended into a baked or smoked bean dish.

BURNT ENDS: The narrow end of a beef brisket that is slow smoked once, then chopped into pieces and smoked again. You can get a plate of burnt ends or a burnt-end sandwich at barbecue restaurants.

COLD SMOKING: Smoking foods at a temperature below 200 degrees F. Cold-smoked foods are usually cured or brined first to draw out extra moisture.

DIRECT HEAT: The heat source is directly under the food being cooked.

HOT SMOKING: Smoking foods at a temperature of at least 230 degrees F for slow smoking, 300 degrees F and greater for faster smoking. To me, real barbecue is slower smoked at 230 to 250 degrees F.

INDIRECT HEAT: The heat source is away from the food being cooked.

SHINERS: Slabs of ribs that have been cut so that the meat has been sliced away from the bone. This is a bad thing.

SMOKE RING: The dark pink ring that forms around the exterior of slow-smoked meat. You can see this ring when you slice through a brisket, pork butt, or pork rib. It's a sign of real barbecue.

3¹/₂ AND DOWNS: A slab of spareribs that weighs 3¹/₂ pounds or less. This is the preferred size for competition cooking.

WET OR DRY RIBS: In Memphis barbecue circles, "wet" ribs have been sauced, while "dry" ribs just have dry rub seasoning on them, with the sauce served on the side.

¹/₂ cup soy sauce

¹/₄ cup chicken broth

¹/₄ cup firmly packed light brown sugar

¹/₄ cup hoisin sauce

1 tablespoon dry sherry

4 cloves garlic, pressed

1 teaspoon red food coloring (optional)

¹/₂ teaspoon Chinese 5-spice powder, homemade (page 112) or store-bought

2 slabs 3.8 and down spareribs, cut in half lengthwise in the St. Louis style (ask your butcher to do this)

1 Combine the soy sauce, broth, brown sugar, hoisin sauce, sherry, garlic, food coloring, if using, and 5-spice powder in a medium-size nonreactive bowl and blend well.

2 Prepare the ribs by removing the membrane and cutting away any large pieces of fat (see pages 168–169). Place them in a nonreactive baking dish or a large zippered-top plastic bag. Pour the marinade over the ribs, coating them on all sides. Cover with plastic wrap or seal and let marinate for at least 4 to 6 hours or overnight in the refrigerator.

3 When ready to cook, prepare an indirect fire.

4 Remove the ribs from the marinade and pat dry. Place the ribs on the pit, cover, and cook according to the directions on pages 169–171.

5 Remove the ribs from the grill and let rest for 10 minutes before cutting into individual ribs. Serve hot or cold.

Taiwan Spareribs

Bob Lyon, my barbecue buddy, and I both like Oriental flavors, maybe because both of us have spent time in the Pacific Northwest where Pacific Rim cuisine is popular. Fresh ginger makes these ribs really aromatic. SERVES 4 TO 6

- ¼ cup canola oil
- ¼ cup soy sauce
- 6 green onions (white and green parts), minced
- 4 cloves garlic, pressed
- 3 slices fresh ginger, peeled and smashed
- 2 tablespoons granulated cane sugar
- 2 tablespoons toasted sesame oil
- 2 tablespoons white wine vinegar
- 1 teaspoon non-iodized salt
- 2 slabs 3.8 and down spareribs

1 Combine the canola oil, soy sauce, green onions, garlic, ginger, sugar, sesame oil, vinegar, and salt in a small bowl and blend well.

2 Prepare the ribs by removing the membrane and trimming away any large pieces of fat (see pages 168–169). Place the ribs in a nonreactive baking dish or a zippered-top plastic bag. Pour the marinade over the ribs, making sure they're all coated. Cover with plastic wrap or seal and let marinate for at least 5 to 6 hours or overnight in the refrigerator.

3 When ready to cook, prepare an indirect fire.

4 Remove the ribs from the marinade and shake off the excess marinade. Place the ribs on the pit, cover, and cook according to the directions on pages 169–171.

5 Remove the ribs from the grill and let rest for 10 minutes before cutting into individual ribs. Serve hot.

Mustard Barbecued Spareribs

The mustard helps bring out the flavor of these ribs but doesn't result in a mustardy taste. So, slather on the mustard for a crisp, brown finish. SERVES 6 TO 8

3 slabs 3.8 and down spareribs

9 cloves garlic, smashed

2 tablespoons non-iodized salt

1 tablespoon freshly ground black pepper

2 cups apple juice

1 cup firmly packed light brown sugar

1/2 cup Dusseldorf or other grainy mustard

1/4 cup cider vinegar

1/4 cup molasses

2 tablespoons dry mustard (I use Colman's)

1 tablespoon dark rum

1 Prepare an indirect fire.

2 Prepare the ribs by removing the membrane and trimming away any large pieces of fat (see pages 168–169). Rub the garlic into both sides of the ribs and season with the salt and pepper, rubbing it in; don't forget to season under the skirt.

3 Place the ribs on the pit, cover, and cook according to the directions on pages 169–171, turning and basting with the apple juice every 30 minutes.

4 While the ribs are cooking, combine the remaining ingredients in a medium-size nonreactive saucepan on the grill, if there is room, or over medium heat on the stovetop, stirring to dissolve the sugar. Simmer for 10 to 15 minutes, then let the glaze cool slightly.

5 When the ribs are done, brush them on both sides with the glaze and cook until the glaze is brown and crispy.

6 Remove the ribs from the grill and let rest for 10 minutes before cutting into individual ribs. Serve hot.

Smokehouse Spareribs

This title is just a play on words, because any and all of your barbecue pits can be called or considered your smokehouse. If you follow this recipe to the letter, you'll end up with some great smokehouse-style ribs. "Mop" means to use a dish mop to anoint the ribs with the flavored butter mixture. SERVES 4 TO 6

2 slabs 3.8 and down spareribs

1/2 cup Worcestershire sauce, homemade (page 50) or store-bought

1 cup (2 sticks) unsalted butter

1/2 cup cider vinegar

1 tablespoon garlic salt

1 teaspoon freshly ground black pepper

1 Prepare the ribs by removing the membrane and trimming away any large pieces of fat (see pages 168–169).

2 Combine the remaining ingredients in a medium-size nonreactive saucepan over medium heat. Simmer until the butter has melted and the garlic salt has dissolved. Set aside to cool. Transfer half the mop to a bowl and set aside. Mop the ribs on both sides with half the mop mixture, cover with plastic wrap, and marinate for 1 hour in the refrigerator.

3 When ready to cook, prepare an indirect fire.

4 Remove the ribs from the marinade and discard the marinade. Place the ribs on the pit, cover, and cook according to the directions on pages 169–171, turning and basting with the reserved marinade every 20 to 30 minutes.

5 Remove the ribs from the grill and let rest for 10 minutes before cutting into individual ribs. Serve hot.

Spritzer Spareribs

These ribs are for you yuppies out there, but almost everyone will enjoy them. You'll get more of a sweet lime flavor in this rib recipe. SERVES 4 TO 6

> 1 cup dry white wine
>
> ¼ cup club soda
>
> ¼ cup lemon-lime soda
>
> 2 tablespoons fresh lemon juice
>
> 2 tablespoons clover honey
>
> 2 cloves garlic, pressed
>
> 2 slabs 3.8 and down spareribs

1 Combine the wine, club soda, lemon-lime soda, lemon juice, honey, and garlic in a medium-size nonreactive bowl and blend well.

2 Prepare the ribs by removing the membrane and trimming away any large pieces of fat (see pages 168–169). Place them in a nonreactive baking dish or zippered-top plastic bag and pour the spritzer marinade over them, making sure to coat all the ribs, cover with plastic wrap or seal, and let marinate in the refrigerator for at least 4 to 5 hours or overnight. Turn them several times.

3 When ready to cook, prepare an indirect fire.

4 Remove the ribs from the marinade and shake off any excess marinade. Place the ribs on the pit, cover, and cook according to the directions on pages 169–171.

5 Remove the ribs from the grill and let rest for 10 minutes before cutting into individual ribs. Serve hot.

Ginger Honey-Glazed Barbecued Spareribs

If you like your barbecue sweet, this will do you dandy. I use clover honey because it's mild and complements rather than distracts from the overall flavor of the ribs. SERVES 4 TO 6

> PINEAPPLE-HONEY MARINADE
>
> 2 cups chicken broth
>
> 1 cup soy sauce
>
> 1 cup tomato ketchup, homemade (page 43) or store-bought
>
> ½ cup pineapple juice
>
> ½ cup clover honey
>
> ¼ cup cream sherry
>
> 2 tablespoons firmly packed light brown sugar
>
> 1 teaspoon peeled and grated fresh ginger
>
> 2 cloves garlic, pressed
>
> 1 teaspoon freshly ground black pepper
>
> 1 teaspoon non-iodized salt
>
> 2 slabs 3.8 and down spareribs
>
> GINGER-HONEY GLAZE
>
> 1 cup clover honey
>
> 2 tablespoons soy sauce
>
> 2 teaspoons peeled and grated fresh ginger
>
> ½ teaspoon freshly ground black pepper

1 To make the marinade, combine the marinade ingredients in a medium-size nonreactive sauce-

pan and bring to a boil. Reduce the heat to medium-low and simmer for 15 minutes, stirring to blend. Remove from the heat and let cool.

2 Prepare the ribs by removing the membrane and trimming away any large pieces of fat (see pages 168–169). Place the ribs in a nonreactive baking dish or zippered-top plastic bag and pour the marinade over them. Cover with plastic wrap or seal and let marinate for at least 4 to 6 hours or overnight in the refrigerator.

3 When ready to cook, prepare an indirect fire.

4 Remove the ribs from the marinade, shaking off any excess marinade. Reserve enough of the marinade to use as a baste and transfer to a saucepan. Bring to a boil over medium-high heat; let simmer for 5 minutes, then set aside.

5 Place the ribs on the pit, cover, and cook according to the directions on pages 169–171. Halfway through the cooking time, begin basting the ribs every 30 minutes with the cooked marinade.

6 While the ribs are cooking, make the glaze. Combine the glaze ingredients in a medium-size nonreactive saucepan and simmer over medium-low heat for 10 minutes, stirring. Let cool.

7 Thirty minutes before the end of the cooking time, paint the glaze all over the ribs, two or three times, turning to keep the glaze from burning or caramelizing.

8 Remove the ribs from the grill and let rest for 10 minutes before cutting into individual ribs. Serve hot.

Texas–Thai Barbecued Ribs

To me, the combination of mint and citrus gives these Texas-style ribs a Thai twist. If you like your ribs hot and spicy, you're going to like this. You can buy lemon powder from a spice company, or simply substitute a sugar-based (not one containing artificial sweetener) powdered lemonade drink mix such as Country Time. Powdered chicken or beef base can be found in tubs in the soup section of the grocery store. SERVES 4 TO 6

- ¼ cup granulated cane sugar
- 2 tablespoons lemon powder
- 2 tablespoons powdered chicken or beef base
- 1 tablespoon garlic salt
- 1 tablespoon onion salt
- 1 tablespoon chili powder, homemade (page 111) or store-bought
- 1 tablespoon freshly ground black pepper
- 1 tablespoon dried mint leaves, pulverized
- 2 teaspoons pure ground jalapeño chile
- 1 teaspoon cayenne pepper
- 2 slabs 3.8 and down spareribs

1 Prepare an indirect fire.

2 Combine all the ingredients, except the ribs, in a small bowl and blend well.

3 Prepare the ribs by removing the membrane and trimming away any large pieces of fat (see pages 168–169). Season the ribs on both sides with the seasoning mixture; don't forget to season under the skirt.

4 Place the ribs on the pit, cover, and cook according to the directions on pages 169–171.

5 Remove the ribs from the grill and let rest for 10 minutes before cutting into individual ribs. Serve hot.

Spicy Asian Spareribs

I like this recipe a little spicier, so I use 1$^{1}/_{2}$ to 2 teaspoons of cayenne pepper for a really peppy rib. Make a sweet, mild cole slaw to accompany these ribs. Serve with a fruit barbecue sauce, such as Jack Daniel's Apricot Barbecue Sauce (page 144) or Apricot-Plum Sauce (page 144), on the side for dipping. **SERVES 4 TO 6**

2 slabs 3.8 and down spareribs

3 tablespoons soy sauce

2 tablespoons toasted sesame oil

2 tablespoons garlic salt

2 tablespoons firmly packed dark brown sugar

2 teaspoons freshly ground black pepper

$^{1}/_{2}$ to 1 teaspoon cayenne pepper, to your taste

$^{1}/_{2}$ teaspoon Chinese 5-spice powder, homemade (page 112) or store-bought

1 Prepare an indirect fire.

2 Prepare the ribs by removing the membrane and trimming away any large pieces of fat (see pages 168–169).

3 Combine the soy sauce and sesame oil in a small bowl, blending with a wire whisk. Combine the garlic salt, brown sugar, black pepper, cayenne pepper, and 5-spice powder in another small bowl, blending well.

4 Brush the ribs with the soy sauce mixture, coating on all sides. Season all over with the spice mixture; don't forget to season under the skirt.

5 Place the ribs on the pit, cover, and cook according to the directions on pages 169–171.

6 Remove the ribs from the grill and let rest for 10 minutes before cutting into individual ribs. Serve hot.

Jazzi Barbecued Ribs

This recipe salutes the Kansas City Jazz Museum at 18th Street and Vine, not 12th Street and Vine, as the song suggests. I even developed a special Jazzi Rub and Jazzi Barbecue Sauce to go with these ribs. Kansas City–style ribs mean spareribs with the breastbone and skirt removed. **SERVES 4 TO 6**

2 slabs 3.8 and down Kansas City–style spareribs

JAZZI RUB

$^{1}/_{4}$ cup firmly packed light brown sugar

2 tablespoons onion salt

1 tablespoon seasoned salt, homemade (page 108) or store-bought

1 tablespoon freshly ground black pepper

1 tablespoon chili powder, homemade (page 111) or store-bought

1 teaspoon cayenne pepper

1 teaspoon dried lemon zest

$^{1}/_{2}$ teaspoon ground thyme

JAZZI BARBECUE SAUCE

2 tablespoons canola oil

1 medium-size onion, minced

$^{1}/_{2}$ cup seeded and minced green pepper

1 tablespoon seeded and minced jalapeño chile

One 24-ounce bottle ketchup

$^{1}/_{2}$ cup firmly packed light brown sugar

$^{1}/_{2}$ cup clover honey

$^{1}/_{4}$ cup Worcestershire sauce, homemade (page 50) or store-bought

3 tablespoons prepared yellow mustard

3 tablespoons fresh lemon juice

1 teaspoon ground ginger

1 teaspoon cayenne pepper

$^{1}/_{2}$ cup water

1 Prepare an indirect fire.

2 Prepare the ribs by removing the membrane and trimming away any large pieces of fat (see pages 168–169).

3 To make the rub, combine the rub ingredients in a small bowl and blend well. Season the ribs on both sides with the rub.

4 Place the ribs on the pit, cover, and cook according to the directions on pages 169–171.

5 While the ribs are cooking, make the barbecue sauce. Heat the oil in a large nonreactive saucepan over medium-high heat, add the onion, green pepper, and jalapeño and cook, stirring, until softened but not browned. Add the ketchup, brown sugar, honey, Worcestershire sauce, mustard, lemon juice, ginger, and cayenne pepper, stir well to combine, and bring to a boil. Stir in the water, reduce the heat to medium-low, and simmer for 30 minutes, stirring occasionally.

6 Thirty minutes before the end of the cooking time, brush the ribs once on both sides with the sauce and turn to keep the sauce from burning or caramelizing.

7 Remove the ribs from the grill and let rest for 10 minutes before cutting into individual ribs. Serve hot, passing the remaining barbecue sauce at the table.

Silky's Memphis-Style Barbecued Ribs

If you are ever in Memphis, you need to look up Silky Sullivan. He owns a pub called Silky O'Sullivan's and he will entertain you with stories about his Legendary BBQ in the good old Irish tradition. There's more Memphis than Irish in these ribs, though, so don't let him fool you. SERVES 6 TO 8

3 slabs 3.8 and down loin back ribs

2 tablespoons seasoned salt, homemade (page 108) or store-bought

1 tablespoon coarsely ground black pepper

2 cups apple juice

1 cup red wine vinegar

2 cups chopped onions

2 cloves garlic, chopped

1/4 cup prepared yellow mustard

1/2 cup firmly packed light brown sugar

1/2 teaspoon Louisiana hot sauce

2 cups tomato ketchup, homemade (page 43) or store-bought

2 lemons, thinly sliced

1 Prepare an indirect fire.

2 Prepare the ribs by removing the membrane and trimming away any large pieces of fat (see pages 168–169). Sprinkle evenly with the seasoned salt and pepper on both sides, rubbing each of them in.

3 Place the ribs on the pit, cover, and cook according to the directions on pages 169–171. Baste the ribs with the apple juice every 15 to 20 minutes.

4 While the ribs are cooking, combine the vinegar, onions, garlic, mustard, brown sugar, and hot

sauce in a blender and process until smooth. Transfer to a medium-size nonreactive saucepan, stir in the ketchup, bring almost to a boil, then reduce the heat to medium-low and simmer for 15 to 20 minutes after bubbles first appear. Add the lemon slices and, stirring occasionally to prevent sticking, simmer for about 10 minutes.

5   Halfway through the rib cooking time, begin basting with the sauce every 15 minutes, being careful not to let the sauce burn on the ribs.

6   Remove the ribs from the grill and let rest for 10 minutes before cutting into individual ribs. Serve hot with the remaining sauce on the side.

Soy Sauce-Basted Sweet-and-Sour Ribs

This is a recipe I learned in Hawaii, and it is more in the Asian style. We enjoyed these ribs at several luaus.
SERVES 6 TO 8

- 2 tablespoons garlic salt
- 1 tablespoon freshly ground black pepper
- 1 teaspoon ground ginger
- 3 slabs 3.8 and down loin back ribs
- 1 cup soy sauce
- 3 tablespoons cornstarch
- 1½ cups pineapple juice
- 1 cup tomato ketchup, homemade (page 43) or store-bought
- ½ cup firmly packed light brown sugar
- ¼ cup distilled white or cider vinegar
- 1 teaspoon ground celery seeds
- 1 teaspoon chili seasoning, homemade (page 116) or store-bought
- 1 teaspoon kosher salt

1   Prepare an indirect fire.

2   Combine the garlic salt, pepper, and ginger in a small bowl and blend well.

3   Prepare the ribs by removing the membrane and trimming away any large pieces of fat (see pages 168–169). Season lightly on both sides with the seasoning mixture.

4   Pour the soy sauce into a medium-size nonreactive saucepan and bring to a boil. In a small bowl, combine the cornstarch and ½ cup of the pineapple juice, blending until dissolved. Add this to the boiling soy sauce, whisking constantly. Return to a boil and simmer until the baste is slightly thickened.

5   Place the ribs on the pit, cover, and cook according to the directions on pages 169–171. Turn them halfway through the cooking time, then baste every hour for 4 hours. Turn the remaining baste into a sauce by adding the remaining 1 cup of the pineapple juice and the ketchup, brown sugar, vinegar, celery seed, chili seasoning, and salt, blending well. Cook the sauce over medium heat for 20 minutes, reduce the heat to low, and simmer for 10 minutes longer.

6   Thirty minutes before the end of the cooking time, brush the ribs on both sides with the sauce, turning so that the glaze doesn't burn or caramelize.

7   Remove the ribs from the grill and let rest for 10 minutes before cutting into individual ribs. Serve hot with the remaining sauce on the side.

Memphis in May WORLD CHAMPIONSHIP Barbecue Cooking Contest

Okay, I'll admit it. I don't really like competing in the big annual Memphis in May World Championship Barbecue Cooking Contest. This contest is a major event in the month-long Memphis in May Festival. The contest was first held in 1977 in a vacant lot. But because Memphis calls itself "the pork barbecue cooking capital of the world," the contest didn't stay small for long. Today, Memphis-area teams—with names such as Pepto Porkers, Boss Hawg, Super Swine Sizzlers, Paddlewheel Porkers, Hogaholics, Boss Pit, Pork Forkers, and Pig Diamonds—compete with teams from everywhere else.

Although Memphis in May is not my favorite contest, that doesn't mean that I don't encourage my students to enter it or that I haven't competed in it myself. I have. And I have a twelfth-place ribbon in Ribs to show for it.

I started getting invited to the Memphis in May Contest in the mid-1980s. For me, it was cooking out of my realm. My biggest problem was handling the judges. You have to know how to play the game.

As part of the judging, you have to be a salesman. The judges come to your booth. You have to show the judges your cooker, tell them how you cooked the meat, tell them how great you are without telling them how great you are. Schmooze. You wine and dine them and their groupies.

I'm a barbecue cook and a teacher, but a salesman I'm not. Schmoozing is just not my thing.

But some teams are really good at it and really go all out. Some teams bring out the silver candelabra and the fine linens, right next to their smoky, greasy cookers (which have been cleaned up as much as possible before the judges come over). You'll see high-rise booths with a stove, refrigerator, a big ventilation hood, toilets, the works. One year, the rumor was that a high-rise booth we nicknamed Motel Barbecue had cost $30,000!

But Memphis in May is also the Mardi Gras of barbecue, and you can have a really good time. It's a party atmosphere. And there's definitely good barbecue there.

Luau Ribs

These ribs were very popular where my wife, Jessica, and I lived in Hawaii, out in the country in Milie on the island of Oahu. We ate these ribs with one-, two-, and three-fingered poi, starchy taro root that is cooked and mashed to varying thicknesses (judged by your fingers). Luaus are actually potluck occasions with Japanese, Portuguese, and American dishes all on the same table. SERVES 6 TO 8

3 slabs 3.8 and down loin back ribs

2 tablespoons garlic salt

1 tablespoon lemon pepper seasoning

One 6-ounce can frozen pineapple concentrate, thawed

One 9-ounce can crushed pineapple, with its juice

$1/4$ cup clover honey

1 teaspoon aromatic bitters (look in the mixers section of the supermarket)

1 Prepare an indirect fire.

2 Prepare the ribs by removing the membrane and trimming away any large pieces of fat (see pages 168–169). Season both sides with the garlic salt and lemon pepper, rubbing in each one; don't forget to season under the skirt.

3 Place the ribs on the pit, cover, and cook according to the directions on pages 169–171.

4 While the ribs are cooking, combine the remaining ingredients in a medium-size nonreactive saucepan and simmer for 15 minutes, stirring occasionally, on the grill, if there is room, or over medium-low heat on the stovetop.

5 Thirty minutes before the end of the cooking time, brush both sides of the ribs with the glaze and turn the ribs about every 10 minutes until they are richly glazed, being careful not to burn or caramelize the glaze.

6 Remove the ribs from the grill and let cool for 10 minutes before cutting into individual ribs. Serve hot.

Spicy Barbecued Baby Back Ribs

This recipe will impress your guests and be the highlight of your party. These ribs are good hot, cold, or in between. SERVES 6 TO 8

3 slabs baby back ribs

3 tablespoons granulated cane sugar

2 tablespoons firmly packed light brown sugar

2 tablespoons sweet Hungarian paprika

1 tablespoon garlic salt

1 tablespoon onion salt

1 tablespoon celery salt

1 tablespoon dry mustard (I use Colman's)

1 tablespoon freshly ground black pepper

1 Prepare an indirect fire.

2 Prepare the ribs by removing the membrane and trimming away any large pieces of fat (see pages 168–169). Combine the remaining ingredients in a small bowl and blend well. Sprinkle evenly over both sides of the ribs and rub in well.

3 Place the ribs on the pit, cover, and cook according to the directions on page 169–171.

4 Remove the ribs from the grill and let rest for 10 minutes before cutting into individual ribs.

Chinese-Style Barbecued Baby Back Ribs

It's much more fun and enjoyable to cook these ribs than to buy them from a Chinese restaurant. They taste better, too, with a kiss of smoke. SERVES 6 TO 8

3 slabs baby back ribs

9 cloves garlic, smashed

2 tablespoons non-iodized salt

1 tablespoon freshly ground black pepper

1/4 cup canned crushed pineapple

2 tablespoons dry sherry

2 tablespoons firmly packed light brown sugar

2 tablespoons clover honey

2 tablespoons soy sauce

1 clove garlic, pressed

1/2 teaspoon Chinese 5-spice powder, homemade (page 112) or store-bought

1 Prepare an indirect fire.

2 Prepare the ribs by removing the membrane and trimming away any large pieces of fat (see pages 168–169). Rub the ribs on both sides with the smashed garlic, then season all over with the salt and pepper.

3 Place the ribs on the pit, cover, and cook according to the directions on pages 169–171.

4 While the ribs are cooking, combine the remaining ingredients in a medium-size nonreactive saucepan and simmer on the stovetop for 10 to 15 minutes over medium heat or on the grill, if there is room. Start basting the ribs with the glaze after the first time you turn them, turning them often enough to keep the glaze from burning or caramelizing.

5 Remove the ribs from the grill and let rest for 10 minutes before cutting into individual ribs. Serve hot.

Polynesian Baby Back Ribs

These ribs seem very similar to the Chinese-style ribs (page 112), but there is quite a difference. These have a sweeter, fruitier flavor, more like a teriyaki rib. Marinate the ribs in the refrigerator for at least 4 to 6 hours or overnight before smoking. You could almost barbecue ribs every day of the year and have a different flavor each time. SERVES 4 TO 6

½ cup pineapple juice

¼ cup soy sauce

2 tablespoons firmly packed light brown sugar

2 tablespoons clover honey

2 tablespoons cream sherry

3 cloves garlic, pressed

2 slabs baby back ribs

1 In a medium-size nonreactive bowl, combine the pineapple juice, soy sauce, brown sugar, honey, sherry, and garlic.

2 Prepare the ribs by removing the membrane and trimming away any large pieces of fat (see pages 168–169). Place the ribs in a nonreactive baking dish or zippered-top plastic bag. Pour the marinade over the ribs, making sure to coat them on all sides, cover with plastic wrap or seal, and let marinate for at least 4 to 6 hours or overnight in the refrigerator.

3 When ready to cook, prepare an indirect fire.

4 Remove the ribs from the marinade, shaking off any excess marinade. Transfer the remaining marinade to a saucepan and bring to a boil over medium-high heat; let simmer for 5 minutes, set aside to cool, and refrigerate.

5 Place the ribs on the pit, cover, and cook according to the directions on pages 169–171, basting with the cooked marinade during the last hour of cooking, turning the ribs as often as needed so the baste doesn't burn or caramelize.

6 Remove the ribs from the grill and let rest for 10 minutes before cutting into individual ribs.

Tex-Mex Barbecued Baby Back Ribs

These ribs are from south of the Red River, not south of the border. The cumin and chili powder really bring out the Tex-Mex flavor. SERVES 4 TO 6

TEX-MEX RUB

1 tablespoon firmly packed dark brown sugar

1 tablespoon granulated cane sugar

1 tablespoon chili powder, homemade (page 111) or store-bought

1 tablespoon sweet Hungarian paprika

1 tablespoon garlic salt

2 teaspoons ground cumin

2 teaspoons seasoned salt, homemade (page 108) or store-bought

1 teaspoon freshly ground black pepper

1/2 teaspoon dried oregano leaves

2 slabs baby back ribs

FINISHING AND DIPPING SAUCE

1 cup tomato ketchup, homemade (page 43) or store-bought

1/2 cup firmly packed dark brown sugar

1/4 cup cider vinegar

2 tablespoons Worcestershire sauce, homemade (page 50) or store-bought

2 teaspoons dry mustard (I use Colman's)

1 teaspoon crushed red pepper

1/4 teaspoon cayenne pepper

1 To make the rub, in a small bowl, combine the rub ingredients and blend well.

2 Prepare the ribs by removing the membrane and trimming away any large pieces of fat (see pages 168–169). Season the ribs on both sides with the rub.

3 Prepare an indirect fire.

4 Place the ribs on the pit, cover, and cook according to the directions on pages 169–171.

5 While the ribs are cooking, make the sauce. Combine the sauce ingredients in a medium-size nonreactive saucepan. Bring to a boil, cover, reduce the heat to medium-low heat, and simmer for 15 minutes.

6 Thirty minutes before the end of the cooking time, brush the ribs on both sides with the sauce. Continue to glaze and turn to keep the sauce from burning or caramelizing.

7 Remove the ribs from the grill and let rest for 10 minutes before cutting into individual ribs. Serve hot with the remaining sauce on the side.

Kansas City–Style Baby Back Ribs

You can get these ribs only from somebody's backyard barbecue or at a barbecue contest because they don't make ribs this good at most barbecue restaurants. The seasoning, with its emphasis on celery salt, and the tomato-based barbecue sauce are what make this a Kansas City–style rib recipe. SERVES 4 TO 6

2 tablespoons garlic salt

1 tablespoon freshly ground black pepper

2 teaspoons celery salt

1 teaspoon onion salt

2 slabs baby back ribs

KANSAS CITY BARBECUE SAUCE

¹/₄ cup canola oil

1 medium-size onion, minced

2 cloves garlic, minced

Two 6-ounce cans tomato paste

¹/₄ cup distilled white vinegar

¹/₄ cup Worcestershire sauce, homemade (page 50) or store-bought

¹/₄ cup clover honey

¹/₄ cup firmly packed light brown sugar

2 tablespoons prepared yellow mustard

1 tablespoon freshly ground black pepper

2 teaspoons rubbed sage

2 teaspoons liquid smoke flavoring (optional)

1 teaspoon dried basil leaves

1 teaspoon non-iodized salt

¹/₂ teaspoon cayenne pepper

1 Prepare an indirect fire.

2 Combine the garlic salt, pepper, celery salt, and onion salt in a small bowl and blend well.

3 Prepare the ribs by removing the membrane and trimming away any large pieces of fat (see pages 168–169). Season the ribs on both sides with the seasoning mix.

4 Place the ribs on the pit, cover, and cook according to the directions on pages 169–171.

5 While the ribs are cooking, prepare the barbecue sauce. Heat the oil over medium-high heat in a medium-size nonreactive saucepan. Add the onion and garlic and cook, stirring, for about 2 minutes; don't let the onion brown. Stir in the tomato paste and vinegar, then blend in the remaining ingredients. Bring to a simmer, reduce the heat to medium-low, and continue to simmer for 15 minutes, stirring occasionally.

6 Thirty minutes before the end of the cooking time, brush the ribs on both sides with the sauce and continue to glaze and turn to keep the sauce from burning or caramelizing.

7 Remove the ribs from the grill and let rest for 10 minutes before cutting into individual ribs. Serve hot with the remaining barbecue sauce on the side.

Honey Mustard-Coated Baby Back Ribs with Brown Sugar Rub

For those of you who think all you will taste is mustard, you've got to try these wonderful ribs. The slather and rub give you a one-two punch of flavor. SERVES 4 TO 6

HONEY MUSTARD SLATHER

¹/₄ cup spicy brown mustard

¹/₄ cup firmly packed dark brown sugar

2 tablespoons clover honey

2 tablespoons white wine vinegar

BROWN SUGAR RIB RUB

¹/₂ cup firmly packed dark brown sugar, dried (see page 115)

2 tablespoons garlic salt

2 tablespoons seasoned salt, homemade (page 108) or store-bought

1 tablespoon onion salt

1 tablespoon celery salt

1 tablespoon medium-grind black pepper

1 tablespoon rubbed sage

1 teaspoon dried rosemary leaves

$^1\!/_2$ teaspoon dried thyme leaves

2 slabs baby back ribs

1 To make the slather, combine the slather ingredients in a medium-size nonreactive bowl and blend well with a wire whisk. Cover and set aside.

2 To make the rub, combine the rub ingredients in a small bowl and blend well.

3 Prepare an indirect fire.

4 Prepare the ribs by removing the membrane from the back of the ribs and trimming away any large pieces of fat (see pages 168–169). Using a pastry brush, coat the bone side of the ribs thinly with the mustard slather, then lightly and evenly season the ribs on the slathered side. Turn the ribs over, slather them thinly on the meat side, and season with the rub.

5 Place the ribs on the pit, cover, and cook according to the directions on pages 169–171.

6 Remove the ribs from the grill and let rest for 10 minutes before cutting into individual ribs. Serve hot.

Southern Barbecued Ribs

These ribs come from the West Memphis, Arkansas, kitchen of one of my cooks, Cora Mae Spilding, who got the recipe from her grandpa, and it's good. SERVES 6 TO 8

3 slabs your favorite style ribs

2 tablespoons non-iodized salt

1 tablespoon freshly ground black pepper

1 lemon, thinly sliced

1 medium-size onion, thinly sliced

2 cups water or chicken, pork, or vegetable broth

$^1\!/_3$ cup Worcestershire sauce, homemade (page 50) or store-bought

$^1\!/_4$ cup fresh lemon juice

1 teaspoon chili powder, homemade (page 111) or store-bought

1 teaspoon Louisiana hot sauce

1 cup ketchup, homemade (page 43) or store-bought

$^1\!/_4$ cup firmly packed light brown sugar

1 Prepare an indirect fire.

2 Prepare the ribs by removing the membrane and trimming away any large pieces of fat (see pages 168–169). Season with the salt and pepper on both sides, rubbing each of them in; don't forget to season under the skirt.

3 In a medium-size nonreactive saucepan, combine the lemon slices, onion, water, Worcestershire sauce, lemon juice, chili powder, and hot sauce and bring to a boil. Reduce the heat to medium-low and simmer until the onion and lemon are limp. Remove from the heat.

4 Place the ribs on the pit, cover, and cook according to the directions on pages 169–171. Baste with the lemon baste every hour after you turn them, starting halfway through the cooking time.

5 When ribs are done, add the ketchup and brown sugar to the remaining lemon baste, blend in, and simmer over your fire for about 15 minutes. Use it as your finishing sauce, glazing both sides of the ribs and cooking for 10 minutes longer.

6 Remove the ribs from the grill and let rest for 10 minutes before cutting into individual ribs. Serve hot.

Ribs à l'Orange

This is the French connection to barbecue. Orange really brings out the great flavor of ribs. SERVES 6 TO 10

- 3 slabs your favorite style ribs
- One 12-ounce can ginger ale
- 1 cup orange juice
- 1 cup barbecue sauce of your choice (pages 136–161)
- $1/3$ cup fresh lemon juice (about 3 lemons)
- $1/2$ cup firmly packed light brown sugar
- 2 tablespoons minced onion
- 2 tablespoons soy sauce
- 1 tablespoon minced orange zest
- 1 teaspoon kosher salt

1 Prepare an indirect fire.

2 Prepare the ribs by removing the membrane and trimming away any large pieces of fat (see pages 168–169).

3 Place the ribs on the pit, cover, and cook according to the directions on pages 169–171, basting with the ginger ale every 30 minutes, until the ribs are tender.

4 While the ribs are cooking, in a medium-size saucepan combine the remaining ingredients and simmer for 30 minutes on the grill, if there is space, or over medium-low heat on the stovetop.

5 Thirty minutes before the end of the cooking time, brush both sides of the ribs with the sauce and turn the ribs about every 10 minutes, until

they are richly glazed. Be careful not to burn or caramelize the glaze.

6 Remove the ribs from the grill and let cool for 10 minutes before cutting into individual ribs. Serve hot or cold.

Barbecued Ribs with Garlic and Herbs

All the garlic makes this recipe one of my favorites, and the butter baste doesn't hurt, either. Butter is one of the best flavor enhancers God has created. You can use it by itself or combine it with other seasonings. It brings out the flavor and the moistness of ribs, as it does with chicken. Keep the butter at room temperature, even though you may think a baste means a liquid. The hot ribs will melt the room-temperature butter soon enough, but at a slow rate. Serve with your favorite barbecue sauce for a dipping sauce. SERVES 6 TO 8

- 3 slabs your favorite style ribs
- 9 cloves garlic, pressed
- 1 tablespoon fresh rosemary leaves, minced
- 2 teaspoons fresh thyme leaves, minced
- 2 teaspoons freshly ground black pepper
- 2 teaspoons non-iodized salt, or to taste
- 1 cup (2 sticks) unsalted butter, at room temperature

1 Prepare an indirect fire.

2 Prepare the ribs by removing the membrane and trimming away any large pieces of fat (see pages 168–169). Combine the garlic, rosemary, thyme, pepper, and salt in a small bowl and mash

into a paste. Rub the garlic paste all over the ribs; don't forget to season under the skirt, if appropriate.

3 Place the ribs on the pit, cover, and cook according to the directions on pages 169–171.

4 About halfway through the cooking time, baste with the butter (rub it over the ribs) and continue to baste about every hour for the remainder of the cooking time.

5 Remove the ribs from the grill and let rest for 10 minutes before cutting into individual ribs. Serve hot.

Spicy Country-Style Ribs

This spicy country-style rub is way out of character for me, because of the granular size of the salt and sugar, but it works really well because the salt and sugar granules are the same size. Country-style ribs come from the tougher blade end of the pork loin or pork butt, which is cut into individual 1-inch-wide strips to look like ribs, so they require a long, slow smoking time of 3 to 4 hours. SERVES 6 TO 8

SPICY COUNTRY RUB

1/4 cup raw or turbinado sugar

2 tablespoons coarse kosher salt

1 tablespoon garlic salt

1 tablespoon seasoned salt, homemade (page 108) or store-bought

1/4 cup sweet Hungarian paprika

2 tablespoons chili powder, homemade (page 111) or store-bought

2 tablespoons coarsely ground black pepper

1 tablespoon cayenne pepper

1 teaspoon ground ginger

1 teaspoon ground allspice

1/2 teaspoon ground cloves

5 pounds country-style ribs, trimmed of excess fat

2 cups apple juice

1 To make the rub, combine the rub ingredients in a medium-size bowl and blend well. Sprinkle the rub evenly all over the ribs.

2 Prepare an indirect fire.

3 Place the ribs on the pit, cover, and cook according to the directions on pages 169–171. About halfway through the cooking time, 1 1/2 to 2 hours, start basting the ribs every 30 minutes with the apple juice. Serve hot.

Rosemary-Garlic Barbecued Country-Style Ribs

This recipe is one of the culinary experiments that Bob Lyon and I conducted before going on a radio talk show in Seattle. We had to cook the results of our experiment—these ribs—for the host and give the recipe to his listeners. Blush wine is light and more on the sweet side, so it works well with ribs. Allow enough time for these ribs to marinate—at least 4 hours or overnight in the refrigerator. SERVES 6 TO 8

2 tablespoons (1/4 stick) unsalted butter

1 tablespoon fresh rosemary leaves, minced

2 cloves garlic, pressed

1/2 cup blush wine

1 teaspoon non-iodized salt

1/2 teaspoon freshly ground black pepper

3 pounds country-style ribs, trimmed of excess fat

1 Melt the butter in a small saucepan over medium-high heat. Add the rosemary and garlic and cook, stirring, until fragrant, 5 to 7 minutes. Remove from the heat and blend in the wine, salt, and pepper. Let cool.

2 Put the ribs in a zippered-top plastic bag and pour the cooled marinade over the ribs, turning to coat each one. Seal and let marinate for at least 4 hours or overnight in the refrigerator, turning occasionally.

3 When ready to cook, prepare an indirect fire.

4 Remove the ribs from the marinade; transfer the remaining marinade to a saucepan and bring to a boil over medium-high heat; let simmer for 5 minutes, set aside to cool, and refrigerate.

5 Place the ribs on the pit, cover, and cook according to the directions on pages 169–171, basting with the cooked marinade during the last hour of cooking and turning the ribs as often as needed so the baste doesn't burn or caramelize.

6 Remove the ribs from the grill and let rest for 10 minutes before serving.

Smoky Glazed Country-Style Ribs

Although country-style ribs are not allowed in most barbecue contests, they are all winners in the backyard contest. Country-style ribs are meatier, more forgiving of mistakes, and just as tasty as spareribs or baby backs.
SERVES 8 TO 10

> 1 tablespoon non-iodized salt
> 1 teaspoon granulated garlic
> 1 teaspoon granulated onion

$1/2$ teaspoon ground celery seeds

$4^1/_2$ to 5 pounds country-style ribs, trimmed of excess fat

SMOKY BARBECUE SAUCE

$3/4$ cup tomato ketchup, homemade (page 43) or store-bought

2 tablespoons Worcestershire sauce, homemade (page 50) or store-bought

2 tablespoons firmly packed light brown sugar

1 teaspoon dry mustard (I use Colman's)

1 teaspoon chili seasoning, homemade (page 116) or store-bought

1 teaspoon liquid smoke flavoring

$1/4$ teaspoon cayenne pepper

1 Prepare an indirect fire.

2 Combine the salt, garlic, onion, and celery seeds in a small bowl and mix well. Sprinkle evenly over the ribs.

3 Place the ribs on the pit, cover, and cook according to the directions on pages 169–171.

4 While the ribs are cooking, make the sauce. Combine the sauce ingredients in a small nonreactive saucepan over medium heat. Bring to a boil, then reduce the heat to medium-low and simmer, stirring, for 20 minutes.

5 Remove the ribs from the grill and let rest for 10 minutes before serving with the sauce on the side hot or at room temperature.

Maple Leaf Country-Style Ribs

I got this recipe from my good friend Tim Gainor of Calgary, Canada. The flavor is much better using the maple sugar,

which is a change of pace for me. Barbecuers in Calgary also like to use local maple and birch woods for smoking. SERVES 4 TO 6

- 1 tablespoon maple sugar or firmly packed dark brown sugar
- 1 tablespoon garlic salt
- 2 teaspoons freshly ground black pepper
- 1 teaspoon ground ginger
- 3 pounds country-style ribs, trimmed of excess fat

MAPLE LEAF BARBECUE SAUCE

- 1 cup pure maple syrup
- 1/2 cup tomato ketchup, homemade (page 43) or store-bought
- 1/4 cup unsweetened applesauce
- 3 tablespoons fresh lemon juice
- 1/2 teaspoon granulated garlic
- 1/2 teaspoon finely ground black pepper
- 1/2 teaspoon non-iodized salt
- 1/4 teaspoon ground cinnamon

1 Prepare an indirect fire.

2 Combine the maple sugar, garlic salt, pepper, and ginger in a small bowl and mix well. Sprinkle evenly all over the ribs.

3 Place the ribs on the pit, cover, and cook according to the directions on pages 169–171.

4 While the ribs are cooking, make the sauce. Combine the sauce ingredients in a medium-size nonreactive saucepan and bring to a boil. Reduce the heat to medium-low and simmer, stirring, for 15 minutes.

5 After cooking the ribs for 2 hours, brush them with the glaze and turn, then brush them with the glaze and turn again in 20 minutes. Brush the ribs with the glaze and turn them every 10 to 15 minutes until the ribs are done and sticky sweet.

6 Remove the ribs from the heat and let rest for 10 minutes before serving.

Gingery Brown Sugar Country-Style Ribs

These ribs go great with some hot-and-sour soup and a spring roll. SERVES 4 TO 6

- 4 to 5 pounds country-style ribs, trimmed of excess fat
- 1/2 cup Barbecue Seasoning (page 114) or your favorite rub

GINGERY BROWN SUGAR BARBECUE SAUCE

- 3/4 cup firmly packed light brown sugar
- 1/2 cup soy sauce
- 1/4 cup clover honey
- 2 tablespoons distilled white vinegar
- 1 tablespoon peeled and grated fresh ginger
- 4 large cloves garlic, pressed
- 1 teaspoon kosher salt
- 1 teaspoon freshly ground black pepper
- 1/2 to 1 teaspoon crushed red pepper, to your taste

1 Prepare an indirect fire.

2 Sprinkle the ribs all over with the seasoning, place on the pit, cover, and cook according to the directions on pages 169–171.

3 While the ribs are cooking, make the sauce. Combine the sauce ingredients in a small nonreactive saucepan and bring to a boil. Reduce the

heat to medium-low and simmer, stirring, for 15 minutes.

4 After cooking the ribs for 2 hours, brush them on all sides with the sauce, turn, cover, and cook 30 minutes longer, then brush them again all over and turn. Glaze and turn again every 30 minutes until the ribs are done and coated with a thick, gooey glaze.

5 Remove from the grill and let rest for 10 minutes before serving.

Grilled Green Chile Country-Style Ribs

These are good ribs to cook for your outlaws, I mean in-laws, when they're over for Saturday's backyard cookout. Serve these with barbecued beans, grilled potatoes, and a green salad. These ribs need to marinate for at least 4 to 6 hours or overnight in the refrigerator. SERVES 4 TO 6

3 to 4 pounds country-style ribs, trimmed of
    excess fat

GREEN CHILE MARINADE

One 4-ounce can chopped green chiles, left
    undrained

$1/4$ cup canola oil

$1/3$ cup red wine vinegar

1 tablespoon hot mustard

2 teaspoons dried Italian seasoning

2 cloves garlic, pressed

1 cup barbecue sauce of your choice (pages
    136–161)

3 tablespoons clover honey

1 Place the ribs in a zippered-top plastic bag or a large nonreactive baking dish.

2 To make the marinade, combine all the marinade ingredients in a medium-size nonreactive bowl and blend well. Pour over the ribs, turning to coat them well, and cover with plastic wrap or seal. Let marinate for at least 4 to 6 hours or overnight in the refrigerator, turning occasionally.

3 When you are ready to cook, prepare an indirect fire.

4 Remove the ribs from the marinade, reserving $1/4$ cup of the marinade.

5 Place the ribs on the pit, cover, and cook according to the directions on pages 169–171.

6 While the ribs are cooking, place the reserved marinade in a small saucepan, bring to a boil, reduce the heat to medium-low, and simmer for 3 minutes. Add the barbecue sauce and honey and simmer 15 minutes longer.

7 Fifteen minutes before the ribs are done, brush them on all sides with the sauce, turn them, cover, and cook until the ribs are done and coated with the glaze.

8 Remove the ribs from the pit and let rest for 10 minutes before serving.

Barbecued Pork Butt with Sweet Barbecue Rub

Pork butt is the hardest piece of meat to cook on a hog. It can be tough and stringy if you don't cook it low and slow, as in this recipe. The redeeming quality of pork butt, though, is that it's also the best-tasting piece of meat on the hog. SERVES 6 TO 8

SWEET BARBECUE RUB

2 tablespoons firmly packed light brown sugar

2 tablespoons granulated cane sugar

2 tablespoons onion salt

1 tablespoon celery salt

1 tablespoon seasoned salt, homemade (page 108) or store-bought

2 tablespoons sweet Hungarian paprika

1 tablespoon chili powder, homemade (page 111) or store-bought

1 tablespoon lemon pepper seasoning

$1/2$ teaspoon cayenne pepper

$1/2$ teaspoon ground allspice

$1/4$ teaspoon ground cloves

$1/4$ cup olive oil

One 5- to 6-pound bone-in Boston pork butt, trimmed (see page 173)

4 cups apple juice as needed

1 Prepare an indirect fire.

2 To make the rub, in a small bowl, combine the rub ingredients and blend well.

3 Brush the olive oil all over the pork butt. Sprinkle the rub evenly over the pork butt.

4 Place the pork on the pit, cover, and cook according to the directions on pages 173–174. Baste with the apple juice when you turn the meat the first time, then baste every hour or when you replenish your fire.

5 If you want to slice the butt, cook it until an instant-read meat thermometer inserted into the center registers 165 to 185 degrees F. Let it rest for 10 to 15 minutes, then remove the bone and slice it. If you want to pull and chop the butt, cook it to an internal temperature of 190 to 205 degrees F. The bone should just pull out cleanly. Let it rest for 10 to 15 minutes, then put it on a cutting board and cut or chop into the desired pieces. You can also use two forks to shred the pork if you want.

To serve pork butt, you can slice it, dice it, or shred it. I put the pieces in a bowl or on a plate, mix 1 cup of barbecue sauce with $1/4$ to $1/2$ cup of distilled white or cider vinegar and maybe a little bit of rub, and pour this mixture over the pork. Then I toss it to blend and serve.

Apple-Smoked Pork Butt with Sweet Garlic Rub

Pork smoked with apple wood is a great flavor combination you will enjoy. Apple wood gives a lighter smoke and is less harsh than hickory or mesquite over a long smoking time. I've adapted this recipe from one by my barbecue buddy Bob Lyon. He likes to wrap his pork butt in aluminum foil, and that's his prerogative. I don't wrap my barbecue in foil, but I've given his technique here in case you want to try it. Add the apple wood chunks to the coals when you start cooking and when you add more hot coals. SERVES 8 TO 10

SWEET GARLIC RUB

1/4 cup granulated cane sugar

2 tablespoons garlic salt

2 tablespoons seasoned salt, homemade (page 108) or store-bought

2 tablespoons sweet Hungarian paprika

1 tablespoon chili powder, homemade (page 111) or store-bought

1 tablespoon freshly ground black pepper

1 teaspoon dry mustard (I use Colman's)

1/2 teaspoon cayenne pepper

1/2 teaspoon ground ginger

1/4 cup prepared yellow mustard

One 5-pound bone-in Boston pork butt, trimmed (see page 173)

4 cups apple juice as needed

1 Prepare an indirect fire.

2 To make the rub, combine the rub ingredients in a small bowl and blend well.

3 Brush the prepared mustard lightly over the entire pork butt. Sprinkle the rub evenly all over the pork butt.

4 Place the pork on the pit, cover, and cook according to the directions on pages 173–174, adding apple wood chunks (see page 26). Baste with the apple juice when you turn the meat the first time, then baste every hour or when you replenish your fire.

5 If you want to slice the butt, cook it until an instant-read meat thermometer inserted into the center registers 165 to 185 degrees F. Let it rest for 10 to 15 minutes, then remove the bone and slice it. If you want to pull and chop the butt, cook it to an internal temperature of 190 to 205 degrees F. The bone should just pull out cleanly.

Let it rest for 10 to 15 minutes, then put it on a cutting board and cut or chop into the desired pieces. You can also use two forks to shred the pork if you want.

To serve pork butt, you can slice it, dice it, or shred it. I put the pieces in a bowl or on a plate, mix 1 cup barbecue sauce with 1/4 to 1/2 cup distilled white or cider vinegar and maybe a little bit of rub, and pour this mixture over the pork. Then I toss it to blend and serve.

Championship Barbecued Whole Hog

This recipe is traditional Southern barbecue at its best. At Memphis in May and the Great Pork BarbeQlossal Contest in Iowa in June, teams compete in the Whole Hog category, but it requires brains, brawn, and a lot of patience. A whole hog can take anywhere from 16 to 18 hours to slow smoke at 230 to 250 degrees F. At Memphis in May–sanctioned contests, the judges come to you and see the whole hog in your pit, so the prettier it looks (with a fresh apple in its mouth), the better. To serve, pull it apart or carve it, accompanied by a Carolina-style vinegar or mustard barbecue sauce—or any sauce you like. Slice or pull the most tender and best-looking portions to serve the judges. A hog this size will give you about 25 pounds of succulent barbecued pork, enough for 50 people. Serve with your favorite barbecue sauce. SERVES 50

One 75- to 85-pound whole hog, dressed (see page 175)

10 cups Eddie's Catering Barbecue Rub (page 130) or your favorite rub

3 to 4 cups mustard slather of your choice (pages 86–101)

6 cups apple juice, 1 recipe Memphis Basting Sauce (page 82), or mop or baste of your choice

1 Prepare an indirect fire.

2 Prepare the hog by removing the membrane from the inside of the ribs and covering the snout, tail, and ears with aluminum foil. Season the hog inside and out evenly with 3 cups of the rub.

3 Place the hog in the pig rack (see page 175). Place the hog right side up on your pit so that the hams are in the hottest part of the cooker, usually the part that's nearest the fire. Cook according to the directions on pages 175–176 for 5 hours.

4 Remove the hog from the pig rack and the pit, skin it, and remove all but about 1/4 inch of the exterior fat. Paint it all over with the mustard slather and sprinkle on the remaining 7 cups of rub, inside and out. Cover the tenderloin area with foil.

5 Place the hog in the pig rack and set your hog back on the pit, this time with the shoulders closer to the hottest part. When the rub has set, about halfway through the cooking time, begin to baste every 30 minutes or so with the apple juice. Cook 5 hours longer, then turn the hog again. With an instant-read meat thermometer, check the temperature in different parts of the hog so you'll know which parts are cooking faster or slower than others. When the hams reach 110 to 120 degrees F, remove the foil from the ears, snout, and tail so they can brown.

6 Turn the hog again, positioning it so the parts that have the lowest internal temperature are closest to the hottest part of the pit. Cook 3 to 5 hours longer. With a meat thermometer, check the temperature in different parts of the hog periodically.

The whole hog is done when every part registers 165 degrees F.

7 Remove the hog to a large cutting board. Slice or pull into portions and serve.

Oooh and Aaaah Barbecued Suckling Pig

Suckling pig is not a real barbecue contest category, although you could do it for Anything But or Miscellaneous. Most people, however, like to barbecue a suckling pig for a special event. And it's good practice before you tackle a barbecued whole hog. Suckling pig takes about 4 to 8 hours to slow smoke, depending on its size. Prepare the pig the same way you would a whole hog (see page 175) and serve with your favorite barbecue sauce on the side. The final verdict? It's delicious! SERVES 6 TO 8

One 20- to 25-pound suckling pig, dressed (see page 175)

1 cup barbecue rub of your choice (pages 115–132)

1 cup mustard slather of your choice (pages 86–101)

1 apple (optional)

1 Prepare an indirect fire.

2 Prepare the pig by covering the snout, tail, and ears with aluminum foil. Place a ball of aluminum foil in the mouth if you're planning to serve it with an apple in its mouth. Season inside and out with 1/2 cup of the rub.

3 Place the pig right side up on your pit so that the hams are in the hottest part of the cooker, usually the part that's nearest the fire. Cover and cook at 230 to 250 degrees F for 2 hours.

Spit-Roasting or OUTDOOR Rotisserie Cooking

Suckling pig, pork loin roast, whole turkey, whole chicken, and boneless beef ribeye roast are all delicious spit-roasted or rotisseried on your pit. Unless electricity is available in your cooking area at a barbecue contest, which is unlikely, this is more of a backyard technique.

The earliest colonists in New England spit-roasted huge cuts of meat on the hearth in front of the fire. A servant or family member was in charge of rotating the spit so that the meat basted itself during cooking. If only they had had the electric rotisserie and barbecue seasonings and sauces that we do today!

When you buy an electric rotisserie for your grill or pit, make sure the motor has adequate power to turn the size and weight of the meat you want to cook. The manufacturer's directions should make this clear. For a suckling pig, that's about 25 pounds; for a whole turkey, 10 to 12 pounds; for a boneless prime rib roast, 9 to 14 pounds; for a whole pork loin roast, 5 to 6 pounds; for a whole chicken, 4 to 5 pounds.

To spit-roast or rotisserie, first set up your rotisserie on the grill or pit, then prepare a medium fire.

Remove the excess fat from the meat, then brush it with mustard slather and season with your favorite rub. Place the meat on the spit so that it will not spin loose. The meat should be balanced on the spit so it can turn easily. Tie any loose bits to the body of the meat with kitchen string.

Insert a meat thermometer into the thickest part of the meat, away from bone. Make sure the thermometer is positioned so you can read it and so it will turn freely as the meat turns.

Place the spit on the rotisserie. Place a drip pan (you can use a disposable aluminum pan for this) under the meat on the spit. If you want, you can fill the pan with water, apple juice, or whatever, just like you would fill a water pan when smoking.

Start the rotisserie. Cover and cook, checking the meat, the fire, and the drip pan at least every hour. The cooking times are about the same as for barbecuing or slow smoking. Keep checking the meat thermometer and you'll know when your meat is done. During the last hour of cooking, apply any finishing sauce or glaze once every 30 minutes.

Remove the meat from the spit and let rest at least 15 minutes before slicing or carving.

4   Remove the pig from the grill and lightly paint the pig all over with the mustard slather. Sprinkle on the remaining ½ cup rub, inside and out, and cover the tenderloin area along both sides of the backbone with foil.

5   Place the pig back on the pit, this time with the shoulders closer to the hottest part. Cover and cook for 2 hours longer, then turn again. With an instant-read meat thermometer, check the temperature in different parts of the pig so you'll know which parts are cooking faster or slower than others. Position the pig so the parts that have the lowest internal temperature are closest to the hottest part of the pit. The pig is done when every part registers 165 degrees F.

6   Remove the pig to a large platter. Remove the ball of foil and insert a fresh apple, if desired. To serve, slice or pull into portions.

Steer

Crazy

hen someone asks about barbecued beef, I have tunnel vision—I automatically think of brisket. For many years, I have had barbecued brisket on the brain. After the 1989 World Championship in Ireland, when I had to use grass-fed Irish brisket that still wasn't tender after smoking it for 24 hours, I went on a brisket binge. I was determined to do the best barbecued brisket I could. In the next 10 or 12 contests, I took top honors for it. I have won the World Brisket Championship in Terlingua, Texas; the Best Brisket at Jack Daniel's in Lynchburg, Tennessee; and the Best Brisket at the American Royal in Kansas City, Missouri. To me, brisket is the perfect cut of beef to barbecue. What happens to sinewy beef brisket when you slather it with mustard, rub it with barbecue seasoning, and then slow smoke it over my favorite combination of apple, hickory, and oak woods defines the word "miracle" in my book.

But the thing is, there's a whole lot more to beef than brisket.

Because I know I'll go on and on and on about brisket, let me talk about the other cuts of beef first.

First of all, start with the best meat you can find. I use suppliers I have known for years, and they get me the very best beef possible. I always use Certified Angus Beef. There is no such thing as a bad Certified Angus cut of beef, because this type of beef is the top 5 percent of Choice. If you're grilling a steak for an important occasion, or if you want to have a terrific standing rib roast, then find a butcher who can get you prime grade beef, which has more fat marbling through the middle than choice does. I'll stick with Certified Angus, though.

Beef Cuts for Grilling and Slow Smoking

Whether choice or prime, the cut of beef you select for grilling or slow smoking should be well marbled, meaning that small veins of fat should run through the beef muscle. The fat should be white, not off-white. White fat indicates a grain-fed steer, which means more tender meat. Grass-fed beef has off-white fat and is much tougher. There are people who think grass-fed beef is healthier beef, but not me.

Starting from the shoulder, you have the shoulder clod and chuck area, which runs into the rib section of the steer; this whole piece is known as the front quarter or forequarter of beef. Texas barbecue joints just love to slow smoke beef clod, but you don't find it in too many other areas.

Out of the front quarter you also get ribeye steaks for grilling and standing rib roast or prime rib (really a beef grade, not a cut of meat) for slow smoking or roasting. To my mind, ribeye steak has the finest flavor because ribeyes are marbled better than other steaks.

The hindquarter is where you get your steaks for grilling—porterhouse, T-bone, strip steak, tenderloin, sirloin, skirt, hangar, and flank steak—and cuts such as the steamship round (also called a baron of beef) for slow smoking and roasting; off the round, you have an inside and an outside

Great STEAKS

A beef or veal steak is a relatively thin, tender cut of meat that tastes great cooked on the grill. Normally, you don't slow smoke a steak; the reason you barbecue or slow smoke is to end up with tenderness and flavor in a tough cut of meat. Steaks are already tender and flavorful, so why cook something for hours when minutes will do? The exception is for large cuts, such as tri-tip.

Because veal is younger and less well marbled than beef, only a few cuts are usually grilled. Marinate them first, then grill quickly to medium-rare doneness so the meat doesn't dry out.

Generally, the more tender the steak—filet mignon, for example—the milder the flavor. Chewier steaks such as flank, skirt, and hangar have great natural flavor, but they must be sliced thinly across the grain. For steaks with added flavor, marinate them for several hours or overnight in the refrigerator. Or add a rub or seasoning before cooking and a sauce afterward.

The thicker the steak is cut, the longer it will take to grill. A filet mignon or a 2- to 3-inch-thick double sirloin takes longer to grill than does a 1-inch-thick ribeye, even if the steaks are the same weight. A 2- to 3-inch-thick steak takes 20 to 30 minutes to grill to medium rare; a 1-inch-thick steak takes about 10 minutes. A large tri-tip, which weighs about 3 pounds and is also thick, takes 30 to 40 minutes to grill to medium rare.

round and the eye of round, also for roasting. One of the current favorites on the competitive barbecue circuit—especially on the West Coast—is tri-tip. This is basically the sirloin butt. It's called a tri-tip because it's shaped like a rounded triangle. You can barbecue or slow smoke the whole tri-tip, which can weigh about 20 pounds, or you can cut it into steaks of any size you want and grill them. The traditional wood for Santa Maria–style tri-tip is red oak.

I also like to grill, rotisserie, or slow smoke sirloin tip, which is a triangular piece of meat that comes from where the torso of the steer joins the leg on the underside. You can grill this as a steak if you marinate it first to tenderize it a little. But I prefer to marinate a 3- to 4-pound roast and cook it on a spit or indirectly on the pit for maximum flavor and tenderness.

Short ribs are created when about 4 inches of ribs on a rib roast is trimmed off. They are meaty and without a lot of fat, so they take well to marinating ahead of time, then grilling over a medium fire for about 30 to 45 minutes. While the ribs are grilling, you need to baste them so they don't dry out and get even chewier. You can also slow smoke short ribs, coated first with a mustard slather and then sprinkled with a rub, for about 2 to 3 hours.

Beef

FILET MIGNON: These thick (2- to 3-inch), very tender steaks are cut from the long, cylindrical beef tenderloin. Thin (1/2-inch) slices of filet mignon are known as medallions. Whether thick or thin, season or marinate and grill.

PORTERHOUSE: This bone-in tender steak includes part of the beef tenderloin on one side of the bone and sirloin on the other. Season or marinate and grill.

T-BONE: This bone-in tender steak (the bone creates a T) is similar to but not as large as the Porterhouse cut and contains less of the tenderloin. Season or marinate and grill .

STRIP: This boneless steak is also known as Kansas City strip, New York strip, boneless club steak, or shell steak. It has great flavor but is slightly chewy. Season or marinate and grill.

CLUB: This is a strip steak with the bone in. Like strip steak, it has great flavor but is slightly chewy. Season or marinate and grill.

RIBEYE: Cut from a standing rib roast or prime rib, ribeye is boneless, mildly flavorful, and tender. Season or marinate and grill.

BONE-IN SIRLOIN: Usually 1-inch thick cuts of sirloin, this steak is best marinated first, then grilled, as it is moderately chewy but very flavorful. Cut into thin slices to serve.

DOUBLE SIRLOIN: This steak is usually 2 to 3 inches thick, one large steak serves a crowd. Season or marinate and grill.

SIRLOIN BUTT: This boneless top sirloin is called rump steak in England. It is moderately chewy and very flavorful. Season or marinate and grill.

TRI-TIP: This large steak from the bottom cap of the sirloin butt is moderately chewy and very flavorful. Like double sirloin, tri-tip is generally sliced for serving. It can be grilled or slow smoked like brisket.

CHUCK: Also known as patio steak, this is a thin, chewier slice of beef chuck (beef arm or shoulder) that is best marinated and then grilled to medium rare. Chuck is usually a thick cut of beef slowly braised for pot roast.

FLANK: A large, thin, flat steak that is flavorful and chewy, flank steak is great marinated, then quickly grilled and sliced across the grain.

HANGAR: This is another large, thin, flat steak that is great marinated and is flavorful and chewy. Slice it thinly across the grain to serve.

SKIRT: This cut, from the diaphragm muscle, is most often used in fajitas. It is nicely marbled with fat and very flavorful, though chewy. Marinate, then grill to medium rare or medium. Slice it thinly across the grain to serve.

Veal

LOIN CHOPS: Available bone-in or boneless, these tender chops should be seasoned or marinated and grilled.

RIB CHOPS: Available bone-in or boneless, treat these tender chops like loin chops.

T-BONES: This tender bone-in steak (the bone creates a T) is similar to but not as large as the

Porterhouse cut, with less of the tenderloin. Season or marinate and grill.

How to Prepare Beef or Veal for Grilling

I like to marinate tougher cuts of beef, such as flank steak or tri-tip, for several hours or overnight. Marinating can help tenderize the meat, especially if you use pineapple juice or papaya, which contain enzymes that break down proteins. If you want to marinate ribeye or tenderloin, you can for the flavor. I'm always trying new mixtures, and I really like the Mojo Marinade on Miami Cuban-Style Steak with Mojo (page 248). Or try Grilled Lemon Tri-Tip with Fresh Basil Marinade (page 263), cooked in the California Santa Maria style over a red oak fire. We're really talking Planet Barbecue here.

Veal, or baby beef, does not have as much marbling and can dry out during grilling. I usually marinate it first or brush it with a glaze during cooking.

I also like to use rubs or seasonings on beef that will be grilled. The seasoning can be as simple as salt and pepper or lemon pepper or a blend such as Savory Steak Seasoning (page 250), which I use on grilled Savory Kansas City Strip Steaks (page 250). Sprinkle on the seasoning; don't rub or press it in. Seasonings also go into the ground beef mixture for grilled Spicy Texas Ranch Burgers (page 243) and Erin's Barbecue Beef Burgers (page 243).

Sometimes I like to finish a great grilled steak or burger with a sauce. Once you've tasted the elegant Apple-Smoked Filet of Beef (page 259) with two colorful and delicious sauces—Chipotle–Roasted Red Pepper Sauce and Mustard Chive Sauce—you'll want to make that recipe a summertime staple. But like a barbecue sauce, any kind of sauce is an accompaniment, not the main event.

How to Grill a Great Steak, Burger, or Veal Chop

At barbecue contests, you very rarely grill beef unless it's for an Anything Goes or Miscellaneous category. Beef is usually slow smoked at contests. But Team Kansas City won the 1982 World Championship in Ireland in part by dazzling the Irish judges with grilled porterhouse steaks. Besides, a great grilled steak or burger is one of the best pleasures in life, so here is my advice on how to do it.

Prepare a medium-hot direct fire (about 400 degrees F) in your grill, using hardwood charcoal. Although sometimes it's more convenient to use a gas grill, a charcoal grill gives you the best flavor for burgers and steaks. Grill steaks over the coals for 8 minutes per side for rare to medium rare, turning once. Grill burgers for 5 to 7 minutes per side for medium rare, turning once. A veal chop, depending on how thick it is, takes 7 to 8 minutes per side.

When Is MY BEEF Done?

Whether it's grilled quickly over a hot fire or smoked slowly with low indirect heat, beef reaches the same temperatures to signal degrees of doneness. It's more important to know these internal temperatures for grilled burgers and steaks and slow-smoked roasts such as ribeye and standing rib because they're tender enough to eat rare, medium, or well done. A brisket, which is a tougher cut of meat, is not edible cooked rare or even medium; you have to cook brisket s-l-o-w-l-y to a well done temperature of 160 degrees F or it won't be tender. It's even better if cooked to an internal temperature of 180 degrees F—it takes time and heat to break down the connective tissue of a brisket.

For a burger or steak, use an instant-read meat thermometer inserted into the thickest part to check the temperature. For a roast, use a meat thermometer inserted before cooking.

For brisket, when it's tender, it's done. To test for doneness, pierce the brisket against the grain with a fork; if it goes in easily and pulls out with resistance, the brisket is done.

Remember that your food will continue to cook for a little while after you take it off the grill. You can always finish cooking a steak that's a little too rare by putting it back on the grill or in the microwave. If it's too well done, there's nothing you can do.

Very rare	approximately 130 degrees F
Rare	140 degrees F
Medium rare	145 degrees F
Medium	160 degrees F
Medium well	165 degrees F
Well done	170 degrees F
Very well done	180 degrees F

—from the 1995 American Meat Science Association and *The Meat Buyers Guide* by the North American Meat Processors Association

How to Barbecue a Beef Tenderloin or Beef Roast

If you've never had a slow-smoked beef tenderloin, boneless ribeye roast, or standing rib roast, then you should get cracking. Basically, you prepare these cuts just like you would for roasting—by patting on a flavorful herb or garlic paste or by simply sprinkling with salt, pepper, and herbs.

Set up your pit (see pages 18–22), using whatever wood you prefer. I like apple wood with beef.

Season the beef, then place it on a baking sheet or in a disposable aluminum pan. Place the roast in your pit, cover, and smoke. You don't have to baste or glaze because there's enough fat in ribeye and standing rib roast to do it for you. An 8- to 12-pound rib roast takes anywhere from 4 to 6 hours of slow smoking (230 to 250 degrees F) to reach 135 degrees F for rare on a meat thermometer. For a 4- to 5-pound beef tenderloin, smoke for 1½ to 2 hours to reach 135 degrees F for rare.

SUGGESTED WOODS FOR BEEF

I prefer a mixture of seasoned oak, hickory, and apple for almost everything I slow smoke. Other barbecuers can make good barbecue with other woods they prefer. Generally, for a heavier smoke flavor that goes well with beef, I recommend mesquite, hickory, or pecan.

Championship Brisket

The brisket, which is located at the front of the steer, comes from the breast of the animal, in front of the shoulder. What do I look for when I'm picking out world championship brisket? First, I want a thick blade end—that's the flat part of the brisket, which is what we call the money piece. The reason for the name is because this piece gives you the best slices—lean and flavorful. Also, because brisket is a rather fatty cut, I choose a leaner piece. You get a meat yield of only 50 to 65 percent from a whole brisket. I'd rather not pay for all that extra fat I'll just trim off anyway or that will melt off during cooking.

I look for beef brisket that has a layer of hard white fat on the top. That tells me the steer ate grain. If the fat's got an off-white color, it probably ate grass or orange peels and was finished off with grain. I want a brisket from a one-hundred-percent grain-fed steer.

I age my Certified Black Angus brisket in the refrigerator for 3 weeks before competition, right in the Cryovac packaging it comes in.

If you're just starting out barbecuing brisket for the backyard or competition, here's my advice. Go to your local supermarket or meat shop and ask for the head cutter. Introduce yourself as a serious barbecue nut, and tell him or her that you need help. If you're entering a contest or getting ready for an important party, say so.

Insist on fresh-cut meat. Don't just pick something out of the display case. When the party comes off well, or when you take home that blue ribbon, go back to the butcher and show off your prize. Give him or her a taste of what you cooked up. The good cutters are happy to see you succeed and should rightly feel that they had a hand in it. You'll make a good friend and a loyal supplier, and that's what it's all about.

When you get your brisket home, trim it yourself. Never buy a trimmed brisket or just the point cut or flat cut. A whole brisket weighs between 8 and 10 pounds total, maybe more.

Trimming a Brisket

Brisket has two parts: the point, also called the deckle or fat end, and the flat. These two pieces of meat are connected by a layer of fat. There is a layer of fat on the outside, which I will call the bottom; the inside, which I will call the top, is relatively lean.

With the fat side (bottom) down, the fat seam will be larger on one side of the brisket. Trim this fat even with the contour of the brisket. Turn the brisket over and trim the covering fat to ¼ to ⅛ inch thick. Cut out the fat seam on this side by cutting into the seam about 1 inch. A lot of people do not believe in trimming away any of the fat. The reason I do is because smoke and seasoning do not penetrate an inch of fat. The ¼ inch of fat I leave on the outside is enough to provide the moisture the long cooking process needs to keep the brisket juicy.

Marking the Brisket

The last thing I do to prepare my brisket for the pit is to track the grain of the meat in the thick part of the brisket, then cut the corners of the brisket so they are perpendicular to the grain. This is called marking the brisket, and it may need to be done at an angle, depending on how the grain runs through the brisket. You have to do this when the meat is still raw and you can easily see the grain. Once it's been smoking and has a bark or darkened crust, you won't be able to see the grain. I mark the brisket to ensure that, when it is done, I can cut my slices across the grain. Across-the-grain slices are the most tender.

Preparing the Brisket for the Pit

Over the years, I have tried lots of different ways to season a brisket. Here are the main contenders:

Inject a marinade or paint on a slather: I sometimes use a large veterinary syringe to inject the meat with a mop/marinade/basting sauce, such as Gypsy Bastin' Sauce (page 85). But more often, I thinly paint on a mustard slather, such as 1999 American Royal Mustard Slather (page 96). The injected marinade helps flavor the meat and keeps it moist during the long cooking time. The slather coats the meat and helps set the rub to make the darkened coating known as the bark. The slather also adds flavor.

Sprinkle on a rub: The word "rub" is a misnomer. Do you smear salt and pepper over your food when you eat it? Of course not. You season your meat with your favorite blend by shaking the mixture onto all sides, but you don't pack spices into every crevice. At least I don't.

Sprinkling on a rub, not packing it into the meat, is my secret to getting a beautiful smoke ring that never fails to impress the judges. Every year I develop and use a new competition rub. Brisket rubs I've used successfully in competition include The Baron's Barbecue Spice (page 115), Texas-Style Barbecue Beef Rub (page 124), and Joe D's Barbecue Rub Supreme (page 127).

How to Barbecue a Brisket

Let's move on to the cooker. Build an indirect fire (see Setting Up Your Pit, pages 18–22). I usually use a combination of apple, hickory, and oak woods for brisket, but you can use what you like and what is available in your area.

It's really important to learn how to control the heat. I can cook a great brisket on just about

Grand Champion

THE 1989 JACK DANIEL'S WORLD CHAMPIONSHIP INVITATIONAL BARBECUE CONTEST

After we won our first international barbecue contest in Ireland in 1989, Team Kansas City was invited to participate in the First Jack Daniel's World Championship Invitational Barbecue Contest in Lynchburg, Tennessee, at the end of October. Now, this is a big deal.

Ronaldo Camargo and Dan Money couldn't go, but Karen Putman and I did. The Jack Daniel's folks really know how to treat you right down there. Even the ribbons are a better quality than the ribbons you win in other contests. On Friday night before the contest, the organizers put on a big feed and it's delicious food.

Well, I was on a mission at that contest, and it was a beef brisket mission. We had just done the competition in Ireland and had to use grass-fed Irish beef for the brisket. We slow smoked that brisket for 24 hours and it was still tough. I was disgusted with it, even though we still placed.

I wanted to make sure we did the best beef brisket we could at Jack Daniel's to make up for it. But I overcooked it. I was so upset with my brisket that I didn't even want to serve it. I didn't even want to serve leftovers to the public.

I had to slice it $1/2$ inch thick so it wouldn't fall apart. It had a decent-enough flavor, I thought, but I was ashamed. We turned it in to the judges.

Well, it won. And we beat all the other 29 teams by 29 points, and that's a lot. We think the judges must have been from Texas, where they like thicker-sliced, fall-apart tender brisket.

That just goes to show you that regardless of what you think of your product, turn it in to the judges.

anything, because I take the time to figure out how to get an even, steady fire. Once you've mastered that, you're in. Be precise. Observe and take notes. Control your fire by controlling your airflow, not your smoke flow. In other words, regulate the amount of air coming in at the base, don't just shut it down at the chimney end of things. When adding more coals to a Weber, get them going first in a charcoal chimney, then add them to maintain the temperature.

A whole brisket takes from 10 to 12 hours on a Weber-type smoker at a temperature between 230 and 250 degrees F. It's smart to make a cut or notch in the flat part, perpendicular to the grain, before you start cooking so that it's easier to orient yourself to the meat once it's done. A well-cooked brisket doesn't bear much resemblance to what you started with.

Cook it fat side up for the first half of the time, then fat side down for the next quarter of time, and finally fat side up again for the last quarter. About halfway through the cooking time, turn the brisket over and start basting every 30 minutes with Gypsy Bastin' Sauce (page 85), Coca-Cola Marinade (page 65), or plain old apple juice. Don't take a lot of time to peek at it, or the temperature in your smoker will take a nosedive. There's no need to keep checking if you keep your fire going right. Good things take time.

How to Know When It's Done

A brisket is not edible cooked rare or even medium; you have to cook brisket s-l-o-w-l-y to a well-done temperature of 160 degrees F or it won't be tender. For brisket, when it's tender, it's done. To test for doneness, pierce the brisket against the grain with a fork; if it goes in easily and pulls out without resistance, the brisket is done.

Slicing the Brisket

Let the meat rest for 5 to 10 minutes after taking it out of the cooker. Cut your slices while keeping your knife parallel to the notch you cut before cooking. You want to slice thinly across the grain, because it shows and eats better that way. The blade or flat-cut portion is lean, with just a layer of fat in the middle. The point-cut portion is more heavily marbled. It's very tender and tasty.

Trim off the ends that are too narrow to slice, chop them up, then put them back on the smoker in an aluminum pan. In another hour or so, you'll have a tasty plate of burnt ends to serve with or without barbecue sauce.

Finally, serve some sauce on the side. Sauce is an accompaniment, not the main event when it comes to good barbecue.

Pecan-Crusted Beef Burgers

This recipe is pure Southern. The pecans and beef work wonders on your taste buds. For an extra treat, use a different type of nut, such as black walnut or macadamia. Another taste treat is to coat the burger patties, hot off the grill, with softened butter or a compound butter before you put them on the Italian bread. SERVES 4 TO 6

> 1 pound ground chuck
> 1/2 cup pecans, finely chopped
> 1/2 cup shredded baby Swiss cheese
> 1/3 cup minced green onions (white and green parts)
> 1 tablespoon minced fresh parsley leaves
> 1 large egg
> Non-iodized salt and freshly ground black pepper to taste
> Italian bread
> Barbecue sauce of your choice

1 Prepare a medium-hot fire in your grill.

2 Combine the beef, pecans, Swiss cheese, green onions, parsley, egg, salt, and pepper in a large bowl, mixing well with your hands. Shape into 4 to 6 patties 1/2 to 3/4 inch thick.

3 Place the burgers directly over the coals, cover, and grill to your preferred degree of doneness, 5 to 7 minutes per side for medium rare. Be careful of flare-ups.

4 Serve on fresh Italian bread slathered with your favorite barbecue sauce.

BUILDING A BETTER BEEF BURGER

I love a good, juicy burger just off the grill. For just a plain burger, I usually go for regular ground beef, which is 70 percent meat to 30 percent fat. I always have a spray bottle of water near the grill to douse any flare-ups from dripping fat. If I'm going to do something a little fancier with the burger, maybe add a sauce or combine other ingredients with the burger, I go for lower fat ground chuck, about 80 percent meat to 20 percent fat. I don't use ground round or other lean ground beef, which can be 90 to 93 percent meat to 10 to 7 percent fat, because there is a greater chance of ending up with a dry, uninteresting burger.

Tex-Mex Burgers

They're better than tacos, honest! SERVES 6

    1 pound ground chuck

    1/3 cup BBQ Salsa (page 157)

    1 tablespoon chopped pickled jalapeño chile

    1 teaspoon cumin seeds, toasted in a dry skillet
        over medium heat until fragrant, then
        ground

    1 teaspoon kosher salt

    1 teaspoon freshly ground black pepper

    1 teaspoon crushed red pepper

    6 ripe red tomato slices

    6 hamburger buns or warm soft corn tortillas

    1 recipe Guacamole (recipe follows)

1 Prepare a medium-hot fire in your grill.

2 Combine the beef, salsa, jalapeño, cumin seeds, salt, black pepper, and red pepper in a large bowl, mixing well with your hands. Shape into 6 patties 1/2 to 3/4 inch thick.

3 Place the burgers directly over the coals, cover, and grill to your desired degree of doneness, 5 to 7 minutes per side for medium rare.

4 To serve, place a tomato slice on top of the bottom bun, then the burger, then a dollop of guacamole and the top bun.

Guacamole

This is a chunky, fresh-tasting version of the classic.
MAKES ABOUT 2 CUPS

    2 large, ripe avocados, peeled, pitted, and diced

    1/2 cup minced onion

    2 tablespoons minced fresh cilantro leaves

    1 tablespoon minced fresh parsley leaves

    1 tablespoon fresh lemon juice

    1 teaspoon Worcestershire sauce, homemade
        (page 50) or store-bought

    1 teaspoon Louisiana hot sauce

    1 teaspoon kosher salt

    1 teaspoon granulated cane sugar

Combine all the ingredients in a medium-size bowl, blending and stirring gently. Try not to mash the avocados. Serve immediately.

Caesar Salad Burger

Caesar's not just a salad anymore. One night, we had Caesar salad and grilled burgers and I had a moment of inspiration. Serve these when you're tired of the same old, same old grilled burger. SERVES 6 TO 8

- 2 pounds ground chuck
- 4 cloves garlic, pressed
- 1 teaspoon anchovy paste
- 1 teaspoon freshly ground black pepper
- 1 large egg
- 1/4 cup fine dry Italian-seasoned bread crumbs
- 1 loaf Italian bread, cut at an angle into 3/4-inch-thick slices
- 1/2 cup olive oil
- 4 to 6 large cloves garlic, to your taste, cut in half
- 6 to 8 leaves Romaine lettuce
- 1/4 cup shredded Parmesan cheese

1 Prepare a medium-hot fire in your grill.

2 Combine the beef, pressed garlic, anchovy paste, pepper, egg, and bread crumbs in a large bowl and blend well, working the meat with your hands until it is sticky. Shape into 6 to 8 oval patties that will fit on the Italian bread.

3 Place the burgers directly over the coals, cover, and grill to your desired degree of doneness, 5 to 7 minutes per side for medium rare.

4 Drizzle or paint with a pastry brush one side of each slice of bread with the olive oil and grill until well toasted. Rub the toasted side with the garlic halves. Place a Romaine leaf on top, then the burger, then top with some Parmesan cheese and another slice of bread.

Blue Ribbon Barbecue Burger

What did you expect? It's down home cookin'. All the flavor of a blue ribbon barbecue sauce is in the burger itself. SERVES 6 TO 8

- 2 pounds ground chuck
- 2 tablespoons barbecue sauce of your choice (pages 136–161), plus more for serving
- 2 tablespoons minced onion
- 1 tablespoon Heinz 57 steak sauce
- 1 tablespoon spicy brown mustard
- 1 tablespoon Worcestershire sauce, homemade (page 50) or store-bought
- 1 tablespoon granulated cane sugar
- 1 teaspoon Louisiana hot sauce
- 1 teaspoon kosher salt
- 1 teaspoon freshly ground black pepper
- 6 to 8 hamburger buns, toasted or grilled
- Sliced ripe red tomatoes
- Sliced onions

1 Prepare a medium-hot fire in your grill.

2 Combine the beef, barbecue sauce, onion, steak sauce, mustard, Worcestershire sauce, sugar, hot sauce, salt, and pepper in a large bowl and blend well with your hands. Form into 6 to 8 patties 1/2 to 3/4 inch thick.

3 Place the burgers directly over the coals, cover, and grill to your preferred degree of doneness, 5 to 7 minutes per side for medium rare.

4 Serve on toasted or lightly grilled buns with sliced tomatoes and onions, slathered with barbecue sauce.

Erin's Barbecue Burgers

This recipe comes from my daughter, who grew up going to barbecue contests. She now competes on her own and does pretty darn well. She's a much prettier chip off the old block. When she participated in Kids Q contests, she entered this recipe. Our family still makes it. SERVES 6

1½ pounds ground chuck

½ cup fine dry bread crumbs

¼ cup barbecue sauce of your choice (pages 136–161, plus more for serving)

1 tablespoon firmly packed dark brown sugar

1 tablespoon fresh lemon juice

1 tablespoon prepared yellow mustard

1 teaspoon seasoned salt, homemade (pages 108–111) or store-bought

1 teaspoon freshly ground black pepper

6 hamburger buns, grilled or toasted

1 Prepare a medium-hot fire in your grill.

2 Mix the beef, bread crumbs, barbecue sauce, brown sugar, lemon juice, mustard, salt, and pepper together in a large bowl, blending well with your hands. Form into 6 patties ½ to ¾ inch thick.

3 Place the burgers directly over the coals, cover, and grill to your desired degree of doneness, 5 to 7 minutes per side for medium rare.

4 Serve on grilled buns with more barbecue sauce and any other condiments you desire.

Spicy Texas Ranch Burgers

Wherever your back yard may be, whether on a Texas ranch or not, this recipe is a winner. SERVES 4 TEXANS OR 6 TO 8 REGULAR PEOPLE

1 pound ground chuck

1 medium-size onion, minced

2 tablespoons Spicy Hamburger Seasoning (page 116)

4 large leaves romaine

4 extra-large buns (Texas size)

1 cup bottled ranch salad dressing

8 to 12 slices ripe red tomatoes

One 3.5-ounce can French's canned fried onions or homemade

1 Prepare a medium-hot fire in your grill.

2 Combine the beef, onion, and hamburger seasoning in a large bowl, blending well with your hands. Form into four ¾-inch-thick patties.

3 Place the burgers directly over the coals, cover, and grill to your desired degree of doneness, 8 to 10 minutes for medium rare.

4 To serve, place a lettuce leaf on the bottom bun, add the burger, spoon ranch dressing over the burger, top with sliced tomatoes, and sprinkle with the fried onions. Cover with the top of the bun, eat, and be a Texan.

Colonel Bob Roberts's Spicy Burgers

This recipe is from one of the Fathers of Barbecue, Bob Roberts, unofficial Barbecue Advisor to the Governor of Texas. Bob was also one of the originators of the Taylor Texas BBQ Contest. I still treasure a special birthday present Bob gave me—an American flag that flew over the state capitol in Austin.   **SERVES 6**

BURGERS

1½ pounds ground chuck

One 4-ounce can chopped green chiles, drained

2 teaspoons granulated garlic

1 teaspoon ground cumin

1 teaspoon seasoned salt, homemade (page 108) or store-bought

1 teaspoon finely ground black pepper

½ teaspoon fine sea salt

COLONEL BOB'S SALSA

1 cup Grilled and Smoked Tomato Salsa or Spicy Honey Mustard Barbecue Sauce (page 154 or 152)

¼ cup thinly sliced green onions (green and white parts)

1 tablespoon minced fresh cilantro leaves

1 tablespoon minced fresh parsley leaves

1 tablespoon bottled ranch salad dressing

1 teaspoon crushed red pepper

1 teaspoon fine sea salt

1 teaspoon freshly ground black pepper

6 hamburger buns, grilled or toasted

Lettuce leaves

Sliced ripe red tomatoes

Thinly sliced sweet Texas onions

1 Prepare a medium-hot fire in your grill.

2 To make the burgers, combine the meat, chiles, garlic, cumin, seasoned salt, black pepper, and sea salt in a large bowl, mixing well with your hands. Form into 6 patties ½ to ¾ inch thick, cover, and set aside.

3 To make the salsa, in another bowl, combine the salsa ingredients and blend well. Cover and set aside.

4 Place the burgers directly over the coals, cover, and grill to your desired degree of doneness, 5 to 7 minutes per side for medium rare.

5 Place the burgers on the bottom halves of the buns and top with lettuce, tomato, onions, and lots of Colonel Bob's salsa.

Vince's Famous Burgers with Vince's Hamburger Mayonnaise Relish

They say copying is the sincerest form of flattery. I enjoyed these burgers as they were first prepared for me by Rick Vincent, one of my barbecue students, who, in real life, is a very good baker. And since he wouldn't give me his recipe, here is my rendition and, of course, it's better.   **SERVES 6 TO 8**

VINCE'S HAMBURGER MAYONNAISE RELISH

¼ cup mayonnaise

1 tablespoon French dressing

1 tablespoon sweet pickle relish

2 teaspoons granulated cane sugar

1 teaspoon white wine vinegar

1 teaspoon fresh lemon juice

1 teaspoon sweet Hungarian paprika

BURGERS

2 pounds ground sirloin

6 to 8 cloves garlic, to your taste, pressed

3 tablespoons grated onion

1 tablespoon Worcestershire sauce, homemade (page 50) or store-bought

1 tablespoon Dijon mustard

2 teaspoons Louisiana hot sauce

1 teaspoon fine sea salt

1 teaspoon freshly ground black pepper

6 to 8 hamburger buns, grilled or toasted

Chopped lettuce

Sliced ripe red tomatoes

Pickles, thinly sliced onions, and sliced American cheese

1 Prepare a medium-hot fire in your grill.

2 To make the relish, in a small bowl, combine the relish ingredients. Refrigerate until needed.

3 To make the burgers, combine the sirloin, garlic, onion, Worcestershire sauce, mustard, hot sauce, salt, and pepper in a large bowl, mixing well with your hands. Shape into 6 to 8 patties $1/2$ to $3/4$ inch thick.

4 Place the burgers directly over the coals, cover, and grill to your desired degree of doneness, 5 to 7 minutes per side for medium rare.

5 To build one of Vince's famous burgers, on the bottom bun, place about $1/3$ cup chopped lettuce, a slice of tomato, pickles, onions, a burger, and a slice of cheese. Slather about 1 tablespoon of the mayonnaise relish on the top bun, cover, serve, and enjoy.

Bacon and Onion Burgers

I came across this burger while catering for Farmland Foods. They were promoting two new burgers, one with onions and sun-dried tomatoes in it, the other with fried bacon and onions. I liked both of them, but Farmland decided not to mass-produce them for consumer enjoyment. Here's my copy of the one I liked best. SERVES 6

$1^{1}/2$ pounds ground chuck

$1/2$ cup minced bacon, fried until crisp and drained on paper towels

$1/2$ cup barbecue sauce of your choice (pages 136–161)

$1/4$ cup minced onion

1 teaspoon fine sea salt

1 teaspoon freshly ground black pepper

6 hamburger buns, grilled or toasted

6 slices Swiss cheese

Lettuce, sliced tomatoes, thinly sliced sweet onions, and pickle of your choice

1 Prepare a medium-hot fire in your grill.

2 Combine the beef, bacon, barbecue sauce, onion, salt, and pepper in a large bowl, blending well with your hands. Form into 6 patties $1/2$ to $3/4$ inch thick.

3 Place the burgers directly over the coals, cover, and grill to your desired degree of doneness, 5 to 7 minutes for medium rare.

4 Place the burgers on the buns and top with lettuce, tomato, onion, pickles, and barbecue sauce.

Thai-Style Burgers

I like to add a teaspoon of cayenne to this recipe to get more of a Thai effect and taste. Either way, if you like Asian flavors, you will enjoy this burger. SERVES 6

1½ pounds ground chuck

½ cup creamy or crunchy peanut butter

2 tablespoons sour cream

2 tablespoons soy sauce

1 tablespoon fresh lime juice

1 tablespoon minced fresh cilantro leaves

2 teaspoons peeled and grated fresh ginger

2 teaspoons light brown sugar

1 teaspoon crushed red pepper

½ teaspoon fine sea salt

½ teaspoon finely ground black pepper

6 hamburger buns, grilled or toasted

Lettuce, sliced tomatoes, and sliced onions

Barbecue sauce of your choice (pages 136–161)

1 Prepare a medium-hot fire in your grill.

2 Combine the beef, peanut butter, sour cream, soy sauce, lime juice, cilantro, ginger, brown sugar, red pepper, salt, and black pepper in a large bowl, blending well with your hands. Shape into 6 patties ½ to ¾ inch thick.

3 Place the burgers directly over the coals, cover, and grill to your desired degree of doneness, 5 to 7 minutes for medium rare.

4 Place the burgers on the buns and top with lettuce, tomato, onion, and barbecue sauce.

Asian Beef Skewers

Few people know that Chinese and other Asian cuisine are some of my favorite foods, especially grilled or barbecued. Serve these as an appetizer. SERVES 8

ASIAN MARINADE

1 cup soy sauce

¼ cup toasted sesame oil

¼ cup chopped lemongrass (soft, inner part of the stalk only)

¾ cup granulated cane sugar

¾ cup garlic cloves, minced

¾ cup minced onion

1 teaspoon crushed red pepper

1 teaspoon non-iodized salt

1 teaspoon freshly ground black pepper

1 pound sirloin steak, trimmed of fat and cut into thin strips

16 bamboo skewers, soaked in water for 30 minutes and drained

1 To make the marinade, place all the marinade ingredients in a blender or food processor and process until well combined.

2 Place the steak in a shallow nonreactive baking dish or a zippered-top plastic bag, pour the marinade over the meat, cover with plastic wrap or seal, and let marinate in the refrigerator for 2 to 4 hours.

3 Prepare a medium-hot fire in your grill.

4 Remove the strips from the marinade and thread onto the skewers. Discard the marinade. Place the skewers directly over the coals, cover, and grill 3 to 4 minutes per side, being careful not to overcook and dry out the meat. Serve on the skewers.

Ginger-Lime Marinated Beef Kabobs

These kabobs can be made in any size and served as an appetizer or as an entrée. The marinade is also good with grilled fish or chicken. SERVES 6 AS A MAIN COURSE, 12 AS AN APPETIZER

GINGER-LIME MARINADE

1 cup fresh lime juice (about 16 limes)

1/2 cup light soy sauce

1/3 cup peanut oil

1 teaspoon peeled and grated fresh ginger

1 teaspoon pressed garlic

1 teaspoon non-iodized salt

1 teaspoon freshly ground black pepper

1 1/2 pounds lean beef sirloin, trimmed of any fat and cut into 1- to 1 1/2-inch cubes

3/4 pound red onions, cut into 1-inch squares

3/4 pound red bell peppers, seeded and cut into 1-inch squares

3/4 pound green bell peppers, seeded and cut into 1-inch squares

Twelve 6- to 8-inch bamboo skewers, soaked in water for at least 30 minutes and drained

1 To make the marinade, combine the marinade ingredients in a medium-size nonreactive bowl and blend well.

2 Place the beef cubes in a shallow nonreactive baking dish or a zippered-top plastic bag and pour the marinade over them, making sure all the cubes are covered. Cover with plastic wrap or seal and let marinate for at least 2 to 4 hours or overnight in the refrigerator.

3 Prepare a medium-hot fire in your grill.

4 Thread the onions and both peppers, alternating with the beef, onto the skewers. Place directly over the coals, cover, and grill about 3 minutes per side, on each of the four sides, for medium rare or to your desired degree of doneness.

Terrific T-Bone with Redeye Marinade

This steak is for big eaters and, as the title says, it's terrific! The marinade is based on the idea of redeye gravy, that thin black-coffee gravy Southerners eat with country ham. SERVES 2 TO 4

REDEYE MARINADE

1 cup brewed strong black coffee

1/2 cup Kahlua liqueur

1 tablespoon firmly packed brown sugar

1 tablespoon fresh lemon juice

1 tablespoon garlic salt

1 tablespoon crushed red pepper

1 teaspoon coarsely ground black pepper

One 1 1/2-pound T-bone or porterhouse steak

1 To make the marinade, combine the marinade ingredients in a small bowl.

2 Place the steak in a nonreactive baking dish or zippered-top plastic bag. Pour the marinade over the steak, making sure it is covered, cover with plastic wrap or seal, and marinate in the refrigerator for at least 6 to 8 hours or overnight, turning occasionally.

3 Prepare a medium-hot fire in your grill.

4 Remove the steak from the marinade and shake off any excess marinade. Discard the marinade. Place the steak directly over the coals, cover, and grill to your desired degree of doneness, about 8 minutes per side for rare to medium rare. Serve immediately.

Steak Diane

The classic steak dish escapes from the kitchen sauté pan to the backyard grill—and is better for it, if you ask me.
SERVES 4 TO 6

> One 2- to 3-pound sirloin steak
>
> 2 to 3 tablespoons tricolored peppercorns (a mix of black, white, and pink), to your taste
>
> 1 tablespoon dry mustard (I use Colman's)
>
> 1/4 pound (1 stick) unsalted butter, softened
>
> 1/4 cup sliced mushrooms
>
> 1/4 cup thinly sliced green onions (green and white parts)
>
> 2 tablespoons fresh lemon juice
>
> 1 tablespoon Worcestershire sauce, homemade (page 50) or store-bought

1 Prepare a medium-hot fire in your grill.

2 Coarsely grind the peppercorns, then sprinkle half of them evenly over one side of the steak and press them in. Sprinkle half the mustard on and do the same. Repeat on the other side with the remaining peppercorns and mustard. Spread the butter on each side of the steak, reserving 2 tablespoons. Set the steak aside.

3 Melt the remaining 2 tablespoons of butter in a medium-size cast-iron skillet over the coals. Add the mushrooms and green onions and cook,

stirring, until softened. Add the lemon juice and Worcestershire sauce and heat through. Remove from the grill and set aside.

4 Place the steak directly over the coals, cover, and grill to your desired degree of doneness, about 8 minutes per side for rare to medium rare.

5 Place the steak on a serving platter, top with the mushroom sauce, and serve hot.

Miami Cuban-Style Steak with Mojo

Cuban-style cuisine is new to me but what recipes I have done, this one included, I like a lot. Blood oranges, darker orange and slightly more sour than navel or Valencia oranges, are often available during the winter months. I usually grill my steaks and burgers over medium-hot coals, but this one tastes better slightly charred over hot coals. **SERVES 6 TO 8**

> **MOJO SAUCE AND MARINADE**
>
> 1 cup fresh orange juice (about 4 oranges; blood orange juice, which is more sour, is best, if you can obtain it)
>
> 1/2 cup fresh lime juice (about 8 limes)
>
> 1/4 cup water
>
> 2 teaspoons fine sea salt
>
> 1 teaspoon dried oregano leaves
>
> 1 teaspoon freshly ground black pepper
>
> 1/2 cup olive oil
>
> 12 large cloves garlic, thinly sliced crosswise
>
> 1 teaspoon ground cumin
>
> Six to eight 8-ounce sirloin steaks
>
> 3 tablespoons chopped fresh cilantro leaves
>
> 1 sweet onion, sliced 1/4 inch thick
>
> Vegetable oil

1 To make the marinade, combine the orange juice, lime juice, water, salt, oregano, and pepper in a medium-size nonreactive bowl and blend well. Set aside.

2 Heat the olive oil in a medium-size nonreactive saucepan over medium heat. Add the garlic and cumin and cook, stirring, until the garlic is fragrant and golden, 2 to 3 minutes. Very carefully (it's going to spatter when it hits the hot oil) add the juice mixture and bring to a boil. Remove from the heat and let the mojo cool to room temperature.

3 Arrange the steaks in a nonreactive baking dish or zippered-top plastic bag. Stir the cilantro into the cooled mojo and pour half the mixture over the steaks, making sure all the steaks are covered with marinade. Reserve the remaining mojo. Cover with plastic wrap or seal and let marinate for at least 1 to 3 hours or overnight in the refrigerator, turning the steaks a few times.

4 Prepare a hot fire in your grill. Lightly brush the grate with the vegetable oil.

5 Remove the steaks from the marinade, discarding it, and pat the steaks dry with paper towels. Brush the onion slices with the reserved mojo and grill over the cooler part of the grill until they are lightly charred and tender, 8 to 10 minutes. Remove from the grill and set aside.

6 Place the steaks directly over the hot coals, cover, and grill to your desired degree of doneness, 5 to 7 minutes per side for medium rare.

7 Transfer the steaks to a serving platter and top with the onions and the remaining mojo sauce.

Spicy Sirloin Steak with Citrus Salsa

The bite is just right with this recipe. Only the timid will think it's hot. Peel and then section the lemon and lime just like you would an orange. SERVES 6 TO 8

RED PEPPER SOY MARINADE

1/2 cup soy sauce

1/4 cup canola oil

1/4 cup minced green onions (green and white parts)

2 tablespoons fresh lime juice

2 tablespoons firmly packed light brown sugar

1 teaspoon crushed red pepper

2 cloves garlic, pressed

1 1/2 pounds sirloin steaks, 1 inch thick

CITRUS SALSA

2 navel oranges, peeled (with white pith removed), sectioned, and chopped

1/4 cup minced green onions (green and white parts)

1/4 cup fresh orange juice

1/4 cup red wine vinegar

1 lemon, peeled, sectioned, and chopped

1 lime, peeled, sectioned, and chopped

2 tablespoons granulated cane sugar

2 tablespoons minced fresh parsley leaves

1 tablespoon minced fresh cilantro leaves

1 teaspoon seeded and finely minced jalapeño chile

1 teaspoon minced lemon zest

1 teaspoon minced lime zest

1 teaspoon kosher salt

1   To make the marinade, combine the marinade ingredients in a small nonreactive bowl and blend well. Place the steaks in a nonreactive baking dish or zippered-top plastic bag, pour the marinade over the steaks, cover with plastic wrap or seal, and let marinate in the refrigerator for at least 2 hours or overnight, turning occasionally.

2   To make the salsa, combine the salsa ingredients in a large serving bowl. Set aside.

3   Prepare a medium-hot fire in your grill.

4   Drain the steaks and discard the marinade. Place the steaks directly over the coals, cover, and grill to your desired degree of doneness, about 7 minutes per side for rare to medium rare.

5   Let rest for 5 minutes, then cut the steaks into thin slices and serve with the salsa.

Savory Kansas City Strip Steaks

This is the steak that Easterners call a New York strip steak. No matter what the name, it's a fine cut of meat, part of a meal fit for a king—or queen. The Savory Steak Seasoning is also good on grilled burgers. **SERVES 8 VERY WELL**

SAVORY STEAK SEASONING

1 tablespoon kosher salt
2 teaspoons granulated garlic
2 teaspoons coarsely ground black pepper
1 teaspoon dried marjoram leaves
1 teaspoon dried rosemary leaves
1 teaspoon dried thyme leaves
1 teaspoon granulated cane sugar
1/2 teaspoon dried oregano leaves

Eight 1-pound Kansas City strip steaks
1 cup olive oil

1   Prepare a medium-hot fire in your grill.

2   To make the seasoning, combine the seasoning ingredients in a small bowl and blend well.

3   Rub the steaks with the olive oil and sprinkle evenly on both sides with the seasoning, making sure you don't coat them too heavily. Place the steaks directly over the coals, cover, and grill to your desired degree of doneness, 15 to 18 minutes per side for rare to medium rare, but turning them every 8 minutes or so; otherwise, they'll get too charred.

Grilled Steak au Poivre

Steaks with a bite! Serve this dish with grilled or steamed asparagus and lemon butter. **SERVES 6**

1/4 cup rainbow peppercorns (green, pink, black, two kinds of white, and some Szechuan peppercorns)
Six 12-ounce Kansas City strip steaks
1 cup (2 sticks) unsalted butter, softened

1   Prepare a hot fire in your grill.

2   Grind or crush the peppercorns, using a spice grinder or a mortar and pestle. If you don't have either, place the peppercorns in a tea towel and smash them with a hammer. Don't crush them too much; they should be coarse. Season the steaks evenly on both sides with the pepper, pressing it in. Smear the softened butter evenly on both sides of the steaks.

3   Place the steaks directly over the coals, cover, and grill to your desired degree of doneness, 7 to 9 minutes per side for medium rare.

Lemon Herb Ribeye Steaks

Ribeye steak is about the best-tasting steak there is, in my humble opinion, and this seasoning really brings out its full flavor. SERVES 6

LEMON HERB RUB

2 tablespoons granulated garlic

2 tablespoons lemon pepper seasoning

1 tablespoon non-iodized salt

1 tablespoon granulated onion

1 tablespoon dried parsley flakes

1 teaspoon dried marjoram leaves

6 ribeye steaks, 1 to 1^1/$_2$ inches thick

^{1}/$_2$ cup olive oil

1   Prepare a hot fire in your grill.

2   To make the rub, combine the rub ingredients in a small bowl and blend well. Rub both sides of the steaks with the olive oil. Sprinkle the rub as desired, but not too heavily, on both sides of the steaks.

3   Place the steaks directly over the coals, cover, and grill to your desired degree of doneness, 7 to 8 minutes per side for medium rare.

Ribeye Steaks with Caramelized Onion-Mushroom Sauce

This sauce complements any steak you choose, though you could put caramelized onions on an old sock and the sock would taste good to me. This is much better! SERVES 4

4 ribeye steaks, ^{3}/$_4$ to 1 inch thick

^{1}/$_4$ cup Jersey Beef Mustard Slather (page 100)

1 tablespoon kosher salt

1 tablespoon freshly ground black pepper

CARAMELIZED ONION-MUSHROOM SAUCE

^{1}/$_4$ cup (^{1}/$_2$ stick) unsalted butter

2 tablespoons olive oil

1 large onion, diced

^{1}/$_2$ pound button mushrooms, sliced

2 cups beef broth

^{1}/$_4$ cup red wine vinegar

1 clove garlic, pressed

1 tablespoon granulated cane sugar

1 teaspoon non-iodized salt

1 teaspoon freshly ground black pepper

1   Cover both sides of the steaks evenly with the mustard slather, season with the salt and pepper, and set aside to rest, covered, at room temperature for 30 minutes.

2   Prepare a medium-hot fire in your grill.

3   Meanwhile, make the sauce. In a skillet, heat the butter and olive oil together over medium-high heat until the butter melts. Add the onion and cook, stirring, until soft and browned. Add the mushrooms, cook, stirring, for 3 minutes, then add

the broth, vinegar, garlic, sugar, salt, and pepper. Bring the mixture to a simmer, reduce heat to medium, and cook, stirring occasionally, until it has reduced by half, about 15 minutes. Set aside.

4   Place the steaks directly over the coals, cover, and grill to your desired degree of doneness, 7 to 10 minutes per side for medium rare.

5   Remove the steaks to serving plates, top with the reserved sauce, and serve immediately.

Red Wine-Marinated Ribeye Steaks

With its great flavor and supple tenderness, ribeye really is the king of steaks. The wine marinade gives this steak an unforgettable flavor. SERVES 4

BEEFY RED WINE MARINADE

- ½ cup beef broth, or 2 beef bouillon cubes dissolved in ½ cup water
- ¼ cup red wine vinegar
- 3 tablespoons minced onion
- 2 tablespoons olive oil
- 2 tablespoons soy sauce
- 1 clove garlic, pressed
- 1 teaspoon sweet paprika
- 1 teaspoon freshly ground black pepper

Four 12-ounce ribeye steaks, about 1 inch thick

1   To make the marinade, in a small nonreactive bowl, combine the marinade ingredients.

2   Place the steaks in a nonreactive baking dish or zippered-top plastic bag and pour ½ cup of the marinade over them. Cover with plastic wrap or seal and let marinate in the refrigerator for at

least 8 hours or overnight. Reserve the remaining marinade.

3   Prepare a medium-hot fire in your grill.

4   Remove the steaks from the marinade, discarding the used marinade. Place the steaks directly over the coals, cover, and grill to your desired degree of doneness, 5 to 8 minutes per side for medium rare.

5   Meanwhile, heat up the reserved marinade and serve spooned over the steaks.

Smoky Cumin Spice-Rubbed Ribeye Steaks

This recipe is my adaptation of the winning recipe for the National Accent BBQ Challenge Recipe Contest. You can get smoked paprika from Penzeys (see Sources) or another major spice company. It really adds an unmistakable and unusual flavor punch. SERVES 4

SMOKY CUMIN SPICE PASTE

- 2 tablespoons cumin seeds, toasted in a dry skillet over medium heat until fragrant, then ground
- 1 tablespoon smoked paprika
- 1 teaspoon ground coriander
- 2 teaspoons Accent seasoning (optional)
- ½ teaspoon freshly ground black pepper
- ½ teaspoon Louisiana hot sauce
- 2 tablespoons olive oil

4 ribeye steaks, 1 inch thick

Lemon wedges and chopped fresh Italian parsley leaves for garnish

1 To make the spice paste, combine the toasted ground cumin, paprika, coriander, Accent (if using), and pepper in a small bowl and blend well. Add the hot sauce and olive oil and blend to form a paste. Rub the paste all over the steaks, then place them in a nonreactive baking dish or zippered-top plastic bag, cover with plastic wrap or seal, and let marinate in the refrigerator for at least 2 to 6 hours or overnight.

2 Prepare a medium-hot fire in your grill.

3 Place the steaks directly over the coals, cover, and grill to your desired degree of doneness, 5 to 7 minutes per side for medium rare. To serve, garnish with the lemon wedges and parsley.

1 To make the rub, combine the paprika, ancho, guajillo, salt, sugar, and pepper in a medium-size bowl and blend well. Blend in the olive oil until the mixture forms a paste. Rub the paste evenly over both sides of the steaks, pressing the seasoning in. Place the steaks on a plate or in a zippered-top plastic bag, cover with plastic wrap or seal, and let marinate in the refrigerator for at least 8 to 10 hours or overnight.

2 Prepare a medium-hot fire in your grill.

3 Place the steaks directly over the coals, cover, and grill to your desired degree of doneness, 12 to 15 minutes per side for medium rare, turning after 8 minutes to prevent charring.

Three Chile-Rubbed Club Steaks

A club steak is a ribeye steak with the bone. This recipe is spicy, spicy, and spicy, but, man, the flavor is good. Ground chiles such as ancho and guajillo are available from spice companies, including Penzeys (see Sources). **SERVES 4**

THREE-CHILE RUB

¼ cup sweet Hungarian paprika

2 tablespoons pure ground ancho chile

2 tablespoons pure ground guajillo chile

2 tablespoons kosher salt

1 tablespoon turbinado sugar

1 tablespoon coarsely ground black pepper

½ cup olive oil

Four 1-pound club steaks, 1½ inches thick

California Sirloin Steak with Merlot Marinade

Select your favorite California Merlot to flavor this mild marinade that really complements beef. A whole sirloin butt is about an 18-pound piece of meat. I buy a whole sirloin butt from Sam's Club and cut my own steaks. For this steak, I use a 2- to 3-pound cut of sirloin—it actually looks more like a sirloin roast. You can request this from a butcher. A larger cut of beef like this is meant to be grilled, then sliced and served like you would a flank steak. **SERVES 6 TO 8**

MERLOT MARINADE

1 cup Merlot or other red wine

1 clove garlic, pressed

$1/2$ cup minced onion

$1/4$ cup ($1/2$ stick) unsalted butter

1 tablespoon prepared horseradish

1 tablespoon prepared yellow mustard

1 tablespoon thinly sliced green onions (white and green parts)

1 tablespoon Worcestershire sauce, homemade (page 50) or store-bought

1 tablespoon minced fresh parsley leaves

1 tablespoon clover honey

1 teaspoon non-iodized salt

1 teaspoon freshly ground black pepper

One 2- to 3-pound sirloin steak roast

1 To make the marinade, combine all the marinade ingredients in a medium-size nonreactive saucepan and heat, stirring a few times, over medium heat until the butter has melted. Let cool to room temperature.

2 Place the steak in a shallow nonreactive baking dish or a zippered-top plastic bag, pour in the marinade, cover with plastic wrap or seal, and let marinate in the refrigerator for at least 4 to 6 hours or overnight, turning occasionally.

3 Prepare a medium fire in your grill.

4 Remove the steak from the marinade and place it directly over the coals. Discard the marinade. Cover and grill to your desired degree of doneness, 10 to 15 minutes per side for rare to medium rare. If your fire is hotter, turn it at 5- to 7-minute intervals 4 to 6 times, so the steak doesn't get overcooked on one or both sides.

Orange-Ginger-Horseradish Black Angus Medallions with Red Pepper and Fresh Mint Relish

This recipe makes my mouth water—it is simply delicious. Try making this with sirloin or flank steak, but increase the marination time to 8 hours or overnight. SERVES 4 TO 6

ORANGE-GINGER-HORSERADISH MARINADE

4 cups beef broth

$1/2$ cup olive oil

2 tablespoons peeled and grated fresh horseradish

2 tablespoons Worcestershire sauce, homemade (page 50) or store-bought

2 tablespoons sweet vermouth

2 tablespoons fresh orange juice

2 tablespoons peeled and grated fresh ginger

1 teaspoon minced orange zest

1 teaspoon crushed red pepper

16 to 24 Black Angus beef tenderloin medallions, $3/8$ inch thick

1 recipe Red Pepper and Fresh Mint Relish (page 159)

1 To make the marinade, place the marinade ingredients in a large nonreactive bowl and blend well. Add the beef medallions to the bowl or place them in a zippered-top plastic bag and pour in the marinade. Cover with plastic wrap or seal and let marinate in the refrigerator for 2 to 4 hours.

2 Prepare a hot fire in your grill.

3 Drain the medallions and discard the marinade. Place the medallions directly over the coals, cover, and grill to your desired degree of doneness. Because the medallions are thin, they will cook very quickly, about 1 minute per side for medium rare.

4 Place 3 to 4 medallions on each serving plate and serve with about ¼ cup of the relish, on top or on the side.

Filet Mignon au Poivre with Cognac Cream Sauce

And the bite goes on and on! Tableside preparations at fancy restaurants pale in flavor comparison to this backyard version. SERVES 4

Four 8- to 10-ounce filet mignons
1 tablespoon garlic salt
¼ cup cracked black peppercorns
¼ cup (½ stick) unsalted butter, softened
1 tablespoon Cognac
½ cup whipping cream

1 Bring the filets to room temperature.

2 Prepare a medium-hot fire in your grill.

3 Pat the filets dry with a paper towel, then season them lightly all over with the garlic salt. Spread the peppercorns out on a plate and coat the filets evenly on both sides with the cracked pepper, pressing it in with the heel of your hand.

Spread the butter evenly over both sides of the filets, being careful not to knock off the pepper.

4 Place the filets directly over the coals, cover, and grill to your desired degree of doneness, 10 to 15 minutes per side for medium rare. Remove the filets from the grill, place in a large skillet, and set aside.

5 In a small skillet, heat the Cognac to the boiling point, then pour over the filets. Very carefully, keeping long hair and hanging sleeves away from the flame, light the cognac with a long kitchen match. It will flare up momentarily. Gently shake the skillet over the coals until the flames die down. Transfer the filets to serving plates and keep warm. Add the cream to the skillet and bring to a boil over the coals, scraping any browned bits from the bottom of the pan. Reduce the cream until it coats the back of a spoon, whisking all the time, about 7 minutes. Pour the sauce over the steaks and serve immediately.

Filet Mignon with Garlicky Herb Butter

This recipe belongs in the Gilroy Hall of Fame, as in the California town famous for its garlic festivals. The flavor is not too strong, just right in my opinion, but you have to remember that I'm a garlic fanatic. SERVES 4 VERY WELL

GARLICKY HERB BUTTER

6 cloves garlic, pressed

$1/4$ cup ($1/2$ stick) unsalted butter, softened

1 tablespoon olive oil

2 tablespoons minced green onions (green and white parts)

1 tablespoon minced fresh parsley leaves

1 tablespoon minced fresh thyme leaves

1 teaspoon cognac

1 teaspoon fine sea salt

1 teaspoon freshly ground black pepper

Four 8-ounce filet mignons

1 To make the herb butter, in a small bowl, combine the flavored butter ingredients until well blended. Rub half the butter mixture all over the filets, cover with plastic wrap, and let rest at room temperature for 30 minutes to 1 hour. Reserve the remaining butter mixture.

2 Prepare a medium-hot fire in your grill.

3 Place the filets directly over the coals, cover, and grill to your desired degree of doneness, 8 to 10 minutes per side for medium rare.

4 Serve the filets topped with a dollop of the reserved butter mixture.

The Flank Steak King's Grilled Flank Steak

This recipe is for Matt Hoy, the undisputed Flank Steak King at the Kansas State Championship (The Great Lenexa Barbeque Battle) held at the end of June in Lenexa, Kansas.

Be sure to slice your flank steak on the bias for the most tender result. **SERVES 6 TO 8**

HONEY-SOY MARINADE

1 cup vegetable oil of your choice

$1/2$ cup soy sauce

$1/4$ cup clover honey

$1/4$ cup thinly sliced or minced green onions (white and green parts)

1 tablespoon red wine vinegar

1 teaspoon garlic powder

1 teaspoon ground ginger

$1/2$ teaspoon non-iodized salt

One $1^1/2$- to 2-pound flank steak, trimmed of any fat

1 To make the marinade, combine the marinade ingredients in a medium-size nonreactive bowl and blend well. Add the steak or place it in a zippered-top plastic bag and pour the marinade over it. Cover with plastic wrap or seal and let marinate in the refrigerator for at least 6 to 8 hours or overnight.

2 Prepare a hot fire in your grill.

3 Remove the steak from the marinade, discarding the marinade. Place the steak directly over the coals, cover, and grill to your desired degree of doneness, 6 to 8 minutes per side for medium rare.

4 Let rest for 5 minutes. To serve, slice thinly across the grain on a 60-degree bias.

Bloody Mary Flank Steak

This is a drinkin' and eatin' recipe, so let's have a party! If you really want to go all out, make a batch of Bloody Marys using my friend Kate Naug's Onion Garlic Tomato Sauce (page 41) to drink with this. **SERVES 6 TO 8**

BLOODY MARY MARINADE

2 cups tomato or V-8 juice

$1/4$ cup Worcestershire sauce, homemade (page 50) or store-bought

2 tablespoons prepared horseradish

2 tablespoons vodka, gin, or rum

1 tablespoon celery salt

1 teaspoon granulated garlic

1 teaspoon freshly ground black pepper

$1/2$ teaspoon cayenne pepper

Two 1$1/2$-pound flank steaks, trimmed of any fat

1 To make the marinade, combine the marinade ingredients in a medium-size nonreactive bowl, blending well. Place the steaks in a shallow nonreactive baking dish or a zippered-top plastic bag. Pour the marinade over the steaks, making sure it covers all the steak. Cover with plastic wrap or seal and let marinate in the refrigerator for at least 4 hours or overnight.

2 Prepare a medium-hot fire in your grill.

3 Remove the steaks from the marinade, discarding the marinade. Place the steak directly over the coals, cover, and grill to your desired degree of doneness, 6 to 8 minutes per side for medium rare.

4 Let rest for 5 minutes. To serve, slice thinly across the grain on a 60-degree bias.

Garlic-Mustard Marinated Flank Steak

Simply delicious. **SERVES 6 TO 8**

GARLIC-MUSTARD MARINADE

$1/2$ cup soy sauce

$1/4$ cup red wine vinegar

$1/4$ cup olive oil

2 tablespoons granulated cane sugar

2 tablespoons Worcestershire sauce, homemade (page 50) or store-bought

2 tablespoons minced green onions (white and green parts)

4 cloves garlic, pressed

2 teaspoons dry mustard (I use Colman's)

1 teaspoon freshly ground black pepper

1 teaspoon minced fresh parsley leaves

Two 1$1/2$-pound flank steaks, trimmed of any fat

1 To make the marinade, combine the marinade ingredients in a medium-size nonreactive bowl until well blended. Place the flank steaks in a shallow nonreactive baking dish or a zippered-top plastic bag. Pour the marinade over the meat, making sure they're covered. Cover with plastic wrap or seal and let marinate in the refrigerator for at least 4 to 6 hours or overnight.

2 Prepare a medium-hot fire in your grill.

3 Remove the steaks from the marinade, discarding the marinade. Place the steaks directly over the coals, cover, and grill to your desired degree of doneness, 6 to 8 minutes per side for medium rare.

4 Let rest for 5 minutes. To serve, slice thinly across the grain on a 60-degree bias.

Smoked Beef Tenderloin with Tomato-Horseradish Sauce

This recipe is an elegant dinner party in the making. Try adding apple wood chunks to the fire; they'll bring out the great flavor of the beef. SERVES 8 TO 10

- One 3- to 4-pound beef tenderloin, trimmed of any fat and silverskin
- 1 tablespoon extra virgin olive oil
- 1 tablespoon garlic salt
- 1 tablespoon freshly ground black pepper
- 1 recipe Tomato-Horseradish Sauce (recipe follows)

1 Prepare an indirect fire.

2 Rub the tenderloin all over with the olive oil, then sprinkle evenly with the garlic salt and pepper.

3 Place the tenderloin on the pit, cover, and smoke at 230 to 250 degrees F until an instant-read meat thermometer is inserted into the thickest part registers between 130 and 135 degrees F for medium rare, about 3½ hours, or to your desired degree of doneness.

4 Remove from the pit and let cool to room temperature. To serve, slice the tenderloin thinly. Arrange on a large serving platter and serve with the sauce on the side.

Tomato Horseradish Sauce

This is a colorful sauce that's great with smoked tenderloin or smoked shellfish. MAKES 2 CUPS

- ½ cup tomato purée
- ½ cup peeled, seeded, and minced cucumber
- ¼ cup seeded and minced green bell pepper
- ¼ cup seeded and minced red bell pepper
- ¼ cup minced red onion
- 2 tablespoons thinly sliced green onions (green and white parts)
- 1 tablespoon grated carrot
- 1 tablespoon granulated cane sugar
- 1 teaspoon minced mixed fresh basil, tarragon, and thyme leaves
- 1 teaspoon peeled and grated fresh horseradish
- 2 cloves garlic, pressed
- 1 teaspoon non-iodized salt
- ½ teaspoon white pepper
- ½ teaspoon cayenne pepper

Combine all the ingredients in a medium-size bowl and blend well. Cover with plastic wrap and refrigerate for at least 8 hours or, better yet, overnight to allow the flavors to blend. Serve cold or at room temperature.

Apple-Smoked Filet of Beef with Chipotle-Roasted Red Pepper Sauce and Mustard Chive Sauce

At elegant parties that I have catered, this dish can be either an appetizer served chilled or an entrée served warm. For an appetizer, I chill the smoked tenderloin, slice it thin, then serve it on crackers or French bread. For an entrée, I like to serve it warm with each slice in a pool of Chipotle-Roasted Red Pepper Sauce, then finished with a dollop of Mustard Chive Sauce on top. Using apple wood to smoke the beef gives you a smoky, slightly sweet flavor.

SERVES 16 TO 20 AS AN APPETIZER, 8 TO 10 AS A MAIN COURSE

One 4- to 5-pound beef tenderloin, trimmed of any fat and silverskin

2 tablespoons Worcestershire sauce, home-made (page 50) or store-bought

2 tablespoons olive oil

2 tablespoons Lemon Pepper Steak Seasoning (page 123)

CHIPOTLE-ROASTED RED PEPPER SAUCE

3 cups roasted red peppers, chopped

1/4 cup olive oil

One 7-ounce can chipotle chiles in adobo sauce, chopped

1 tablespoon Worcestershire sauce, homemade (page 50) or store-bought

1 teaspoon fine sea salt

1 teaspoon freshly ground black pepper

MUSTARD CHIVE SAUCE

2 cups sour cream

1/2 cup Dijon mustard

2 tablespoons minced fresh chives

1 tablespoon brandy

1 shallot, minced

1/2 teaspoon minced fresh thyme leaves

1/2 teaspoon fine sea salt

1/4 teaspoon freshly ground black pepper

Bread rounds, toasted, or crackers (for appetizer)

1 Using a pastry brush, coat the tenderloin with the Worcestershire sauce and oil and sprinkle all over with the lemon pepper seasoning.

2 Prepare an indirect fire and throw on 3 chunks of apple wood.

3 Place the tenderloin on the pit, cover, and cook at 230 to 250 degrees F until an instant-read meat thermometer inserted into the thickest part registers between 130 and 135 F degrees for medium rare, 1 1/2 to 2 hours, or to your desired degree of doneness. Let cool, then chill at least 2 hours to serve as an appetizer or keep warm to serve as an entrée.

4 To make the Chipotle-Roasted Red Pepper Sauce, combine all the ingredients in a medium-size bowl, blend well, and chill. To make the Mustard Chive Sauce, combine all the ingredients in a medium-size bowl, blend well, and chill.

5 To serve as an appetizer, slice the beef thin and place on the toasted bread rounds with the sauces on the side. For an entrée, slice the beef thinly and serve warm with the sauces on the side.

Barbecued Lip-On Ribeye with Horseradish Paste

A lip-on ribeye is a boneless prime rib or standing rib roast. These boneless roasts weigh between 9 and 14 pounds, as compared to a prime rib roast, with the rib bones in, which weighs 18 to 22 pounds. This recipe is great to do for a Super Bowl party. **SERVES 12 TO 16**

HORSERADISH PASTE

1 cup peeled and grated fresh horseradish

$1/2$ cup olive oil

$1/4$ cup garlic cloves, pressed or minced

$1/4$ cup kosher salt

$1/4$ cup cracked black peppercorns

2 tablespoons firmly packed dark brown sugar

2 tablespoons cumin seeds, toasted in a dry skillet over medium heat until fragrant, then ground

1 tablespoon spicy brown mustard

One 12-pound lip-on ribeye roast, trimmed of excess fat

1 Prepare an indirect fire.

2 To make the paste, combine the paste ingredients in a medium-size bowl and blend well with a wire whisk.

3 Place the roast on a baking sheet and rub the paste all over the roast.

4 Place the roast on the pit, cover, and cook at 230 to 250 degrees F until an instant-read meat thermometer inserted into the thickest part registers between 130 and 135 degrees F for medium rare, 4 to 6 hours, or to your desired degree of doneness.

5 Let rest for 15 minutes before slicing.

The Baron's Barbecued Rosemary Prime Rib Roast

Call me when it's done. Let's eat! This barbecuing technique is a little bit different than the one I use in the Barbecued Lip-On Ribeye, which is slow smoked the traditional way. With this recipe, you build a hotter (medium) indirect fire and place the roast over the coals, not on the indirect side. You have to turn the roast frequently to keep it from charring and add coals often to keep the heat up. If the roast looks like it's browning too much, move it to the indirect side for a while. If you don't want to check on the roast every 35 minutes, you can also barbecue it using the technique for the Barbecued Lip-On Ribeye (left); it will take about 1 to 2 hours longer to cook. **SERVES 6 TO 8**

2 tablespoons garlic salt

One 6- to 8-pound rib roast

2 tablespoons fresh rosemary leaves, minced

2 tablespoons freshly ground black pepper

1 Prepare a medium indirect fire.

2 Sprinkle the garlic salt evenly over the entire roast; repeat the process with the rosemary and pepper. Place the roast directly over the coals, bone side down, and cover. Every 35 to 45 minutes or when the temperature begins to fall from 350 degrees F, turn the roast and replenish the fire with hot coals. Repeat this process until

an instant-read meat thermometer inserted into the thickest part registers 140 degrees F, 3 to 4 hours for medium rare, or to your desired degree of doneness.

3 Let rest for 15 minutes before slicing.

Barbecued Sirloin Tip Sandwiches

While I was working for a restaurant chain, I suggested that we smoke our sirloin tip and serve it as a sandwich. Sales increased 200 percent and, no, I didn't get a bonus. I got more work, but it was worth it. The roast is basted with softened butter, which is applied with a pastry brush; once applied, it will melt and run down the roast. I prefer this technique to using already melted butter. SERVES 6 TO 8

One 3- to 4-pound sirloin tip roast

1 tablespoon garlic salt

1 tablespoon lemon pepper seasoning

1 cup (2 sticks) unsalted butter, softened

2 medium-size red onions, thinly sliced

6 to 8 Kaiser rolls, split

Sliced ripe tomato

Barbecue sauce of your choice (pages 136–161), warm or room temperature

1 Build an indirect fire.

2 Season the roast evenly all over with garlic salt and lemon pepper.

3 Place the roast in the pit, cover, and smoke at 230 to 250 degrees F until an instant-read meat thermometer inserted into the thickest part registers 145 degrees F for medium rare, 2 to 2 1/2 hours, or to your desired degree of doneness. Or grill to your desired degree of doneness. If smoking, start

basting with the softened butter after 1 hour, and baste until the butter is gone. If smoking, baste every 15 minutes.

4 While the roast is cooking, dip or coat the onions with some of the butter and grill until soft and tender; to do this, it's best to use a perforated grill rack. Set aside until you're ready to fix the sandwiches.

5 When the roast is ready, remove it from the pit and let it rest for 15 to 20 minutes. Slice it thinly and serve on the Kaiser rolls with tomato slices, the grilled onion, and barbecue sauce on the side.

Sirloin Tip on the Rotisserie

You can also rotisserie this cut to make my famous Barbe-cued Sirloin Tip Sandwiches (left). Try marinating the roast overnight, then season it and cook it on a spit, basted with softened butter applied with a pastry brush; once applied, the butter will melt and run down the roast. If you want a Kiss of Smoke (see page 23) for this rotisseried beef, use apple wood. SERVES 6 TO 8

One 3- to 4-pound sirloin tip roast

1 recipe Sweet and Tangy Marinade (page 63) or Picante Beer Marinade (page 68)

1 tablespoon garlic salt

1 tablespoon lemon pepper seasoning

1/2 pound (2 sticks) unsalted butter, softened

1 Place the sirloin in a zippered-top plastic bag, pour the marinade over it, and seal. Refrigerate and let marinate for 2 to 4 hours or, preferably, overnight.

How to Cook BEEF AND VEAL on an Outdoor Rotisserie

Instead of that same old, same old roasted prime rib, why not try something with a little more smoke and sizzle? Beef and veal roasts are delicious spit-roasted or rotisseried in your back yard.

When you buy an electric rotisserie, make sure the motor has adequate power to turn the size and weight of the meat you want to cook—for a sirloin roast, from 3 to 20 pounds; for boneless rib roast, from 8 to 12 pounds; for boneless lip-on ribeye, from 9 to 14 pounds; for prime rib roast with bones, from 18 to 22 pounds. The manufacturer's directions should make clear the capacity of its particular product.

Because the rotisserie is positioned away from the coals, this is considered indirect cooking or barbecuing.

To spit-roast or rotisserie, first set up your rotisserie on the grill and prepare a medium fire. You can cook with a Kiss of Smoke (see page 23) by throwing a chunk or two of wood on the coals during cooking.

For tougher cuts, such as tri-tip and sirloin roast, marinate the meat for at least 4 hours or overnight in the refrigerator. For tender roasts, including boneless ribeye and standing rib roast, just pat on a flavorful herb or garlic paste or sprinkle with salt, pepper, and herbs.

Place the meat on the spit so that it will not spin loose. The meat should be balanced on the spit so it can turn easily. Tie any loose bits with kitchen string.

Insert a meat thermometer into the thickest part of the meat, away from the bone. Make sure the thermometer is positioned so that you can read it and it can turn freely as the meat turns.

Place the spit on the rotisserie. Set a drip pan (you can use a disposable aluminum pan for this) under the spit. If you want, you can fill the pan with water, apple juice, or whatever, just as you would fill a water pan when smoking.

Start the rotisserie. Cover and cook, checking the meat, the fire, and the drip pan at least every hour. Tender cuts don't need to be basted; their exterior fat will do the job. Tougher cuts such as sirloin and tri-tip will benefit from basting. After the rub has set (about 1 hour for tougher cuts), start basting every 30 minutes with apple juice, melted butter, or whatever you like.

The cooking times are about the same as for barbecuing or slow smoking—an 8- to 12-pound rib roast takes 3 to 5 hours, a whole 5- to 8-pound tri-tip takes 5 to 8 hours, to reach 135 degrees F for rare on a meat thermometer. Remove from the spit and let rest at least 15 minutes before carving.

2 Set up your rotisserie on the grill, then prepare a hot fire.

3 Remove the beef from the marinade, discard the marinade, and season it all over with the garlic salt and lemon pepper. Place the beef on the spit so that it will not spin loose. The beef should be balanced on the spit so it can turn easily. Tie any loose bits with kitchen string. Insert a meat thermometer into the thickest part. Make sure the thermometer is positioned so that you can read it and it can turn freely as the spit turns.

4 Place the spit on the rotisserie. Place a drip pan (you can use a disposable aluminum pan for this) under the spit. If you want, you can fill the pan with water or apple juice. Start the rotisserie. Cover and cook, checking the beef, the fire, and the drip pan at least every hour. After the first hour, start brushing every 20 minutes with the softened butter. Cook until the internal temperature is 135 degrees F for medium rare, 1½ to 2 hours more, or to your desired degree of doneness. Let the meat rest 15 to 20 minutes before carving.

Grilled Lemon Tri-Tip with Fresh Basil Marinade

Tri-tip is the bottom sirloin butt and the current darling of California barbecuers. It is more readily available on the West Coast, but you can order it from your butcher. The first time that I had tri-tip, it was cooked Santa Maria style (grilled over red oak), and it was outstanding. SERVES 6 TO 8

FRESH BASIL MARINADE
1 cup beef broth or water

2 tablespoons balsamic vinegar

2 tablespoons canola oil

2 tablespoons minced fresh basil leaves

1 tablespoon Dijon mustard

2 cloves garlic, pressed

1 teaspoon fine sea salt

1 teaspoon finely ground black pepper

One 2- to 3-pound tri-tip roast, trimmed of excess fat

1 tablespoon minced lemon zest

1½ teaspoons ground cumin

1 teaspoon fine sea salt

1 teaspoon finely ground black pepper

1 To make the marinade, combine the marinade ingredients in a medium-size nonreactive bowl and mix with a wire whisk until well blended.

2 Place the tri-tip in a nonreactive baking dish or zippered-top plastic bag and pour the marinade over it. Cover with plastic wrap or seal and let marinate in the refrigerator for at least 4 to 8 hours or overnight.

3 Prepare a medium-hot fire in your grill.

4 Remove the roast from the marinade, discard the marinade, and pat dry with paper towels. Sprinkle evenly with the lemon zest and rub it in on both sides of the tri-tip. Combine the cumin, salt, and pepper, blending well. Sprinkle evenly over the tri-tip.

5 Place the tri-tip directly over the coals, cover, and grill to your desired degree of doneness, 15 to 20 minutes per side for medium rare (or when an instant-read meat thermometer inserted into the thickest part registers 135 degrees F). Cook longer if desired, turning every 10 minutes. Let it rest for 15 minutes before slicing.

The Baron and BARBECUED Beef Brisket

After Team Kansas City won the World Championship in Ireland in 1989, despite a grass-fed Irish beef brisket that was still tough after cooking for 24 hours, I was on a barbecued beef brisket mission.

I wasn't happy, either, with the brisket that Karen Putman and I did to win the Jack Daniel's Invitational that year, so my compulsion got worse.

I entered—and won—in the Beef Brisket category in the next ten barbecue contests, including the World Brisket Championship in Welfare, Texas. That streak really established my reputation for brisket madness.

Other barbecue friends made fun of me because I was so focused on brisket, and one of them got a little artistic.

I still have a cartoon that I clipped from a barbecue newsletter, and it makes me chuckle every time I look at it. It's a picture of the Pearly Gates with St. Peter standing in a cloud of smoke. The caption says: "That's God practicing. He wants to beat Paul Kirk in brisket."

The Baron's Famous Barbecued Brisket

Barbecued brisket takes patience and steady, smoky heat. I've barbecued thousands of briskets and, believe me, it's worth the work and the wait! Be prepared to smoke this for 12 to 16 hours, or until you can easily push a meat thermometer into the meat against the grain and pull it out again easily. Then you know the brisket is truly tender.

SERVES 12 TO 24

One 7- to 12-pound brisket

1/2 cup Worcestershire sauce, homemade (page 50) or store-bought

1/4 cup firmly packed dark brown sugar

1 tablespoon garlic salt

1 tablespoon coarsely ground black pepper

1 tablespoon sweet Hungarian paprika

1 tablespoon chili powder, homemade (page 111) or store-bought

1 teaspoon celery salt

1/4 teaspoon ground allspice

1/4 teaspoon ground thyme

1 Prepare an indirect fire, using a combination of apple, hickory, and oak woods (like I do), or use your favorite wood.

2 Trim the brisket (see pages 237–238). Pour the Worcestershire sauce over the brisket and rub it in.

3 Combine the remaining ingredients in a small bowl and mix well. Season the brisket with the mixture as you would if you were seasoning heavily with salt and pepper.

4 Place the brisket on the pit, fat side down. Cover and cook at 230 to 250 degrees F for 45 minutes to 1 hour per pound, turning it halfway through, then turning it again three quarters of the

way through (if you're cooking for 12 hours, then halftime would be 6 hours and three quarters would be 8 hours). To test for doneness, pierce the brisket against the grain with a fork; if it goes in easily and pulls out without resistance, the brisket is done.

5 Let it rest for 5 minutes, then slice across the grain.

Best Barbecued Beef Brisket with Salad Dressing Barbecue Sauce

Don't laugh, it's good! Again, barbecued brisket is a labor of love. This smaller brisket is slow smoked for 8 to 10 hours. SERVES 6 TO 8

SPECIAL BRISKET RUB

1 tablespoon granulated cane sugar

2 tablespoons firmly packed light brown sugar

2 tablespoons celery salt

2 tablespoons garlic salt

1 tablespoon onion salt

1 tablespoon freshly ground black pepper

1 teaspoon cayenne pepper

SALAD DRESSING BARBECUE SAUCE

1 cup French or Russian salad dressing

1 cup Smoky Barbecue Sauce (page 147)

$1/4$ cup clover honey

$1/4$ cup firmly packed light brown sugar

1 tablespoon Italian Seasoning (page 120)

1 teaspoon fine sea salt

1 teaspoon freshly ground black pepper

One 4- to 5-pound brisket, trimmed (see pages 237–238)

$1/4$ cup Worcestershire sauce, homemade (page 50) or store-bought

1 Prepare an indirect fire using a combination of apple, hickory, and oak woods (like I do), or use your favorite wood.

2 Meanwhile, make the rub. Combine the rub ingredients in small bowl and mix well.

3 To make the sauce, combine the barbecue sauce ingredients in a medium-size nonreactive saucepan over low heat and cook, stirring, until well blended and the sugar has dissolved and everything is heated, 15 to 20 minutes. Divide the sauce in half.

4 Rub the brisket all over with the Worcestershire sauce, then season evenly all over with the rub. Place the brisket on the pit, fat side down. Cover and cook for 8 to 10 hours at 230 to 250 degrees F, turning it at 4 to 5 hours, again at 6 to $6^{1}/_{2}$ hours, and finally at 7 to $7^{1}/_{2}$ hours. During the last 45 minutes of cooking time, paint half the barbecue sauce over all sides of the brisket with a pastry brush. Let cook for 10 to 15 minutes and repeat the process 2 more times. To test for doneness, pierce the brisket against the grain with a fork; if it goes in easily and pulls out without resistance, the brisket is done.

5 Let it rest for 5 minutes, then slice across the grain. Serve with the remaining barbecue sauce on the side.

Building a BETTER Barbecued Brisket

By now, the astute reader who started this chapter and has read all the way through to this point will realize something. After yammering on about how much I love brisket and providing lots of in-depth information on how to barbecue it, I've given you only two barbecued brisket recipes.

Am I keeping all the prize-winning ones to myself? Am I afraid of the competition?

The answer to both these questions is NO.

Getting really good at barbecued brisket is a hands-on thing. It's more about technique—managing and maintaining the temperature and smoke levels—than about recipes. I want to encourage you to get into brisket like I did—by doing, not reading.

So, read this and then get busy.

On a weekend, or when you have 12 to 16 hours to dedicate to this project, prepare an indirect fire in your pit, using any wood you prefer. Trim your brisket. Select one of the mustard slathers (pages 86–101) or make up your own and paint it all over the meat. Sprinkle on one of the rubs (pages 115–132) or one you've made up. Place your brisket on the pit, fat side up.

Cover and cook for 8 to 10 hours at 230 to 250 degrees F. Check your fire, your wood, your water pan, and your temperature every hour or find out what your pit needs are. About halfway through the cooking time, turn the brisket over and start basting with Gypsy Bastin' Sauce (page 85), Coca-Cola Marinade (page 65), apple juice, or your own concoction.

Take notes as you're cooking. How long did it take for the temperature in the pit to go from more than 300 degrees F to less than 250 degrees F? What is the weather like? What does the brisket look like after 2, 4, 6, and 8 hours? How tender is it after 8 hours? How much wood have you used?

And, finally, does your brisket have a dark pink smoke ring? How does it slice? How tender is it? How does it taste? What sauce would best complement it?

Now you're smoking.

Grilled Beef Short Ribs

For some reason, most people think short ribs are difficult to barbecue, but they are really quite easy, as this recipe shows. SERVES 6 TO 8

3 to 4 pounds beef short ribs, trimmed of excess fat

1 cup water

1/2 cup Worcestershire sauce, homemade (page 50) or store-bought

1/4 cup fresh lemon juice (about 2 lemons)

1/4 cup salad oil of your choice

1 tablespoon garlic salt

1 teaspoon Louisiana hot sauce

1/2 teaspoon freshly ground black pepper

1   Place the ribs in a large nonreactive bowl or a zippered-top plastic bag. Combine the remaining ingredients and pour over the ribs. Cover with plastic wrap or seal and let marinate overnight in the refrigerator, turning several times.

2   Remove from the refrigerator and let rest at room temperature for about 1 hour.

3   Prepare a medium fire in your grill.

4   Drain the ribs, reserving the marinade. Transfer the marinade to a small saucepan, bring to a boil, and let simmer for 5 minutes.

5   Place the ribs directly over the coals, cover, and grill. Once they're browned on both sides, baste frequently with the reserved marinade until brown, crisp, and tender, 30 to 45 minutes.

Smoked Dinosaur Bones

These huge beef ribs, the equivalent of spareribs on a hog, are delicious and fun. One rib can be a meal, though. A slab of pork spareribs weighs 3 to 4 pounds. A slab of beef ribs weighs 7 to 8 pounds, so you can see that these Dinosaur Bones are gigantic compared to what most people expect. The trick with beef ribs is to get them tender, so low and slow is the way to go. SERVES 4 TO 6

    Two 7- to 8-pound slabs beef back ribs
    3 cups Beefy Mop Sauce (page 77)
    1/2 cup Jersey Beef Mustard Slather (page 100)
    1 cup Texas-Style Barbecue Beef Rub (page 124)
        or Sweet Brown Sugar Rub (page 126)

1   Peel off the membrane from the back of the ribs and trim away any fat clinging to the bones. A long, thin knife is best for this job. Then take a sharp pointed knife, such as a paring knife, and outline the bones with the point of the knife, cutting into the meat about 1/16 to 1/8 inch.

2   Place the ribs in a shallow nonreactive baking dish or zippered-top plastic bags, if they will fit. Pour the mop sauce over the ribs, coating them, cover with plastic wrap or seal, and let marinate for at least 3 to 4 hours or overnight in the refrigerator.

3   Prepare an indirect fire.

4   Remove the ribs from the mop, reserving the excess. Pat the ribs dry with a paper towel. Transfer the mop to a small saucepan, bring to a boil, and let simmer for 5 minutes. Set aside.

5   Coat the rib bones with the mustard slather and sprinkle evenly with the rub. Turn the ribs over and repeat the process. Place the ribs on the pit, cover, and cook until tender, 4 to 6 hours. Baste with the reserved mop sauce frequently after the ribs have cooked for 1 1/2 hours. The ribs are done when they seem tender when pierced with a knife.

Grilled Veal Loin Chops with Roasted Garlic Mustard Glaze

Veal is considered very elegant, but it is also good barbecued or grilled. I prefer to grill these chops to a medium-rare doneness, as they're more tender and juicy that way. SERVES 4

Beef Ribs VERSUS Pork Ribs

Beef ribs are becoming more available in markets across the country. If you've only grilled or slow smoked pork ribs, there is a difference in how you handle beef ribs. The main difference is that pork ribs have less weight and more fat and, because of that, practically baste themselves during cooking. Beef ribs can be chewier, benefit from marination, and need to be basted during cooking. Beef ribs just need more attention.

At Jack's Stack barbecue restaurant in Kansas City, you can spend the big bucks for their special cut known as beef crown ribs, which have a big hunk of prime rib meat attached at the end of each rib. Slow smoked, they are absolutely delicious. If you want this cut, however, you have to make very good friends with your butcher—or the folks at Jack's Stack.

Like pork ribs, which can come from the shoulder (country-style), back (baby backs), or sides (spareribs) of the pig, beef ribs also have distinct styles.

Short ribs are created when about 4 inches of the ribs on a rib roast are trimmed off. They are meaty and without a lot of fat, so they take well to marination; grill them over a medium fire for 30 to 45 minutes. While the ribs are grilling, you'll need to baste them so they don't dry out and get even chewier. You can also slow smoke short ribs, coated first with a mustard slather and then sprinkled with a rub, for about 2 to 3 hours.

Large beef ribs, also known as dinosaur bones, are the equivalent of baby back ribs on a hog. Beef ribs are created when the butcher bones out a rib roast. A slab of beef ribs can weigh 7 to 8 pounds, compared to pork spareribs, which weigh 3 to 4 pounds. The trick is to get beef ribs tender, so marinate them overnight, then use a mustard slather and sprinkle on a rub. Cook them low and slow for 4 to 6 hours, or until they seem tender when pricked with a knife.

ROASTED GARLIC MUSTARD GLAZE

8 to 10 cloves smoked garlic (page 98), squeezed from the skins

1/4 cup spicy brown mustard

2 tablespoons firmly packed light brown sugar

2 tablespoons dark corn syrup

1 tablespoon cider vinegar

2 teaspoons Worcestershire sauce, homemade (page 50) or store-bought

1 teaspoon fine sea salt

1/2 teaspoon freshly ground black pepper

1/4 teaspoon cayenne pepper

Four 12-ounce veal loin chops

1 teaspoon fine sea salt

1 teaspoon freshly ground black pepper

1 cup (2 sticks) unsalted butter, softened

1 Prepare a medium-hot fire in your grill, adding apple wood (see Kiss of Smoke, page 23).

2   To make the glaze, place the glaze ingredients in a blender or food processor and process until smooth and well blended, about 2 minutes.

3   Season the chops all over with salt and pepper, smear with the butter on all sides, place directly over the coals, cover, and grill for 4 to 5 minutes. Turn the chops, brush with the glaze, and cover. Cook for 2 to 3 minutes longer. Turn and brush the other side with the remaining glaze and cook 2 minutes longer.

Veal Rib Chops with Lemon Sage Marinade and Mango Coulis

Veal chops become exotic when combined with mango. The marinade brings out the flavor of the veal without over-powering it. I prefer medium-rare doneness for veal so it stays tender and juicy. SERVES 4

MANGO COULIS
2 cups peeled, seeded, and diced ripe mango

1/2 cup diced red onion

2 tablespoons minced fresh mint leaves

1 tablespoon minced fresh basil leaves

1 tablespoon balsamic vinegar

1 teaspoon fine sea salt

1/2 teaspoon freshly ground black pepper

1/4 teaspoon fresh thyme leaves

LEMON SAGE MARINADE
1/2 cup canola oil

1/4 cup fresh lemon juice (about 2 lemons)

1 tablespoon rubbed sage

2 cloves garlic, pressed

2 teaspoons peeled and grated fresh ginger

1 teaspoon minced lemon zest

1 teaspoon fine sea salt

1/2 teaspoon white pepper

4 veal rib chops (2 pounds), 1 inch thick

1   To make the coulis, place the coulis ingredients in a food processor and process until smooth. Pour the purée into a medium-size nonreactive saucepan and simmer over medium heat for about 5 minutes. Pour into a container, cover, and refrigerate until needed.

2   To make the marinade, combine the marinade ingredients in a medium-size nonreactive bowl and blend well with a wire whisk.

3   Place the chops in a shallow nonreactive baking dish or a zippered-top plastic bag and pour the marinade over them. Cover with plastic wrap or seal and let marinate in the refrigerator for 6 to 8 hours.

4   Prepare a medium-hot fire in your grill, adding apple wood (see A Kiss of Smoke, page 23).

5   Remove the chops from the marinade. Transfer the marinade to a small saucepan, bring to a boil, and let simmer for 5 minutes.

6   Place the chops directly over the coals, cover, and grill for 4 to 5 minutes. Turn the chops and grill 4 to 5 minutes longer for medium rare or to your desired degree of doneness, basting with the reserved marinade.

7   Serve each chop in a pool of the reserved coulis, dolloped with the coulis, or with the coulis on the side.

Grilled Sweetbreads with Balsamic Beurre Blanc

If you like sweetbreads, this is an outstanding way to fix them. The beurre blanc is luscious, and it really brings out the Chef Paul rather than the Baron of Barbecue in me. I serve this dish with steamed asparagus. Admittedly, sweetbreads are a little time-consuming, preparation-wise. You'll need to soak them in cold water, changing the water several times, for 2 hours, then blanch them, cool them, and weight them down overnight in the refrigerator before grilling the next day. But this dish is well worth all the effort. SERVES 6 TO 8

3 pounds veal or beef sweetbreads

BALSAMIC BEURRE BLANC

10 tablespoons (1¼ sticks) chilled unsalted butter, cut into 10 pieces

½ cup minced shallots

½ cup dry white wine

¼ cup balsamic vinegar

½ teaspoon dried tarragon leaves

¼ teaspoon dried thyme leaves

2 tablespoons whipping cream

½ teaspoon non-iodized salt

½ teaspoon freshly ground black pepper

2 teaspoons garlic salt

1 teaspoon freshly ground black pepper

½ cup olive oil

1 Soak the sweetbreads in cold water, changing the water several times, for 2 hours. Drain and immerse in a pan of boiling water for 2 minutes. Drain and plunge into ice water to stop the cook-ing. Let cool until they can be handled, discard the membranes, and separate into 2 lobes. Place in a nonreactive baking dish in a single layer, cover with plastic wrap, and weight down with a 5-pound weight overnight in the refrigerator.

2 To make the beurre blanc, melt 2 tablespoons of the butter in a medium-size nonreactive saucepan over medium-low heat, add the shallots, and cook until softened, stirring often. Add the wine, vinegar, tarragon, and thyme, bring to a boil, reduce the heat to low, and simmer until most of the liquid has evaporated, about 15 minutes. Add the cream, return to a boil, and let boil, stirring, for about 30 seconds. Reduce the heat to low and whisk in the remaining 8 tablespoons butter 1 piece at a time, lifting the pan from the heat to cool the mixture and adding a new piece of butter as the previous piece is incorporated into the sauce. This sauce should not get hot enough to liquefy. Strain the sauce through a fine-mesh strainer and season with the salt and pepper. Keep warm.

3 Prepare a medium-hot fire in your grill.

4 Cut the sweetbreads in half crosswise. Season with the garlic salt and pepper, brush with the olive oil, place directly over the coals, and grill for 4 to 6 minutes per side. Transfer to a cutting board and cut in half horizontally. Brush the cut side with olive oil, return to the grill, cut side down, and grill about 5 minutes longer.

5 Using tongs, dip each piece of grilled sweetbread into the sauce to coat, place on a serving platter, and serve hot. Serve the remaining sauce on the side.

BURNING DESIRES
Fireside Shoppe
GAS LOGS • GRILLS
WOOD STOVES • AWNINGS
574-9276

Lamb and
on the

Cabrito Baa-becue

SMOKIN JOES

Lamb, as a category in competition cooking, is almost nonexistent in the Midwest. One of the original categories in the American Royal Barbecue Contest, as well as in the American Royal Invitational, lamb was dropped because many of the cooks didn't know what to do with the frozen leg of lamb given to them. Sometimes the lamb did not thaw until midnight, and then it had to be prepped.

Also, many judges didn't want to judge it. Barbecued lamb is hard to find in restaurants, so many people have never tasted it. In Kansas City, Gates' BBQ offers barbecued breast of lamb, while at Jack's Stack you can get barbecued Denver lamb ribs, but they are the exception and not the rule. It's hard to judge a food you are not familiar with.

My first experience with lamb in competition was at the Great Lenexa Barbeque Battle, the original Kansas State championship. (My wife, Jessica, won the first Kansas State Barbecue Championship.) I was boning a leg of lamb and the usual crowd was gathered around, asking questions. When I explained what I was doing and why, one spectator replied that he hated lamb. When I asked his reasons, he replied that he was stationed in Australia and New Zealand during World War II and he could smell the mutton boats coming 30 miles off the coast. I tried to explain that there was a big difference between lamb and mutton. A lamb is less than a year old and mutton is its smelly older brother. Because of its tender age, lamb doesn't have the strong taste that mutton does. The spectator didn't buy anything I was saying and went back to his team area.

The next day after the judging, when everybody was coming by for samples, I slipped a couple of lamb slices in his direction. He remarked that the meat was really good and asked what it was. I delighted in telling him that it was lamb.

Lamb, as a barbecue category, needs someone to get behind it again. Bob Lyon and the Pacific Northwest Barbecue Association (PNWBA) have the right idea. Because lamb was an original American Royal category, they got Superior Farms in the state of Washington to be a sponsor and make lamb a category in at least seven PNWBA competitions a year. PNWBA teams have done well in the category at the American Royal, and one even took the blue ribbon twice in the Invitational.

The PNWBA teams do well in lamb because they're a talented bunch of barbecuers, and also because they've educated themselves about it. Superior Farms has asked Jim Erickson, the head cook of Bob's barbecue team the Beaver Castors, to cook lamb for them at several promotional events. They've also rounded up Merle Ellis, a.k.a. "The Butcher," who has performed his half-lamb dissection twice during PNWBA July grilling lessons and has demonstrated cooking lamb sirloins for attendees. Merle has also judged lamb in PNWBA contests.

If you don't like lamb because you don't know how to cook it, then learn, just as the PNWBA teams have done. Lamb is making a comeback in barbecue. I know this because there is a relatively new all-lamb contest—the National Lamb-B-Q

Grand Champion
2000 NATIONAL LAMB-B-Q BBQ COOK-OFF

One of my favorite contests is the National Lamb-B-Q BBQ Cook-Off held every September in Bonner Springs, Kansas, at the Agricultural Hall of Fame. This contest is sanctioned by the KCBS.

I love lamb. Slow-smoked lamb ribs are out of this world. Lamb is great barbecued or grilled, so to have a contest devoted just to lamb is fantastic. But either not too many people know about cooking lamb or other people don't share my love of this meat.

The contest is usually small—fewer than 20 teams—so it's low-key and everybody really gets to know each other. The weather is generally good, if maybe a little hot. The contest has only four categories: Steak, Chops, Whole Leg of Lamb, and Miscellaneous.

In 2000, I won the Lamb Grand Championship, taking first in Steaks and Chops, second in Whole Leg of Lamb, and third in Miscellaneous (I did Denver-style lamb ribs and my own lamb sausage).

Lamb is a little different to cook on the smoker, so you can learn a lot by participating in this contest. Lamb ribs can be fattier than baby back or spareribs, but that makes them succulent, I think. If a whole leg of lamb is overdone, it has a stronger flavor, which is not to everyone's taste, so you have to be careful.

Here's a secret with lamb: You can never go wrong with a little lemon pepper.

Today, lamb is grain fed, which gives it a better flavor and texture. Naturally tender, lamb should have a deep pinkish red to a dull brick red color and the fat should be hard, white, and waxy. For grilling and barbecuing, lamb graded "Choice" is fine to use. I encourage you to buy fresh lamb, not frozen, as it has a better flavor. A whole dressed lamb can weigh anywhere between 40 and 75 pounds.

Because lamb is naturally tender, most cuts can be either grilled or smoked. The main sections of a dressed lamb, starting from the front, are the shoulder and breast, the ribs, the loin, and the leg.

BBQ Cook-off. In 2000 the National Lamb Championship was held in Bonner Springs, Kansas, and The Baron of Barbecue was the Grand Champion!

Cuts of Lamb for Grilling

With very little marbling, lamb needs to be handled carefully so it doesn't dry out. Usually, it's marinated first before grilling. Lamb chops, cut from the rib area or the loin, are great on the grill. Individual steaks cut from the leg—like veal cutlets from the veal leg—are also delicious marinated and then grilled. A boneless whole leg of lamb, marinated first, is tasty over charcoal. Loin of lamb, or basically rack of lamb with the bones removed, can be grilled over hot coals for 15 minutes per side for medium rare and with just the barest of seasonings—garlic, salt, and pepper. You'll probably have to ask your butcher for this cut, but it's worth trying in Grilled Lamb Loins with Peppered Plum Sauce (page 288). Ground lamb mixed with spices and seasonings can be formed into patties and grilled or turned into delicious sausage (see pages 320–323).

Just don't cook lamb to well done! I prefer grilled lamb that is rare or medium rare, with an internal temperature of 135 to 145 degrees F. If lamb reaches 170 degrees F, or well done, it's dry and not as flavorful.

Cuts of Lamb for Slow Smoking

Larger or bone-in cuts of lamb are mainly slow smoked for flavor, not to achieve tenderness, as in the case of beef brisket or pork butt. A full rack of lamb with 8 ribs reaches succulent perfection in just hours on the smoker. Denver ribs are a special cut comprising the middle 6 ribs, usually about 3 inches wide and 6 inches long and trimmed of surface fat. Denver lamb ribs need long, slow cooking to cook out the fat, but that's also what makes them good, in my opinion. A full lamb breast with ribs and breast meat attached is also good slow smoked; order these cuts from your butcher, as they're not readily available on barbecue restaurant menus or in the grocery store. Lamb roasts with the bone in, cut from the shoulder, breast, or loin, are also good slow smoked. Lamb sausage is delicious barbecued. Slow-smoked lamb stays moist during cooking if

you've slathered it, sprinkled on a rub, then mopped or basted it during cooking.

SUGGESTED WOODS FOR LAMB AND CABRITO

To me, nothing beats the combination of seasoned oak, hickory, and apple to smoke lamb at a contest. A medium to light smoke flavor accentuates the flavor of lamb, so in the back yard I choose oak, hickory, maple, or pecan.

Preparing Lamb for Grilling or Barbecuing

If you don't want to go to the trouble to bone a leg of lamb or French the bones on a rack of lamb, you can get your butcher to do it, but it will cost you more. Why not learn how to do it yourself?

To bone a leg of lamb, you need a sharp, thin-bladed boning knife. Follow the hip bone around the edges to the joint and remove. Then cut around the leg bone joint and down the leg bone to the shank. Remove the shank and leg bone. You can now turn the leg inside out; this will enable you to get to the fat pockets, which have glands in some of them; remove these pockets. Doing so will help get rid of any strong lamb taste, which some people object to.

To butterfly a leg of lamb for stuffing and then grilling or slow smoking, cut it in half lengthwise, without cutting all the way through, and remove the bone. Cut again down the center of the boned lamb leg and halfway through the meat, until the lamb leg opens like a book. Place the lamb leg between two sheets of parchment paper and pound with the side of a heavy meat mallet or a rolling pin until the meat is uniformly thick.

To prepare ribs for smoking, trim away as much of the surface fat as possible. To French the bones, take a sharp boning or paring knife and trim the meat back from the bones about 1 inch down the rib. This is one case in which a "shiner," a bone with no meat on it, is desirable! Usually, you put a frilly paper "hat" on each bone. You can also French the bone on a leg of lamb by trimming the meat 2 to 3 inches from the end of the bone.

Getting Your Goat

Cabrito, or baby goat, is a 30- to 40-day-old kid that weighs between 12 and 18 pounds. Depending on where you live, you'll have to get one from a farmer or maybe a halal, or Muslim, butcher. Cabrito is tender enough to be grilled or barbecued and is popular in Texas, Mexico, and the Caribbean.

After goats are weaned and start eating grass, their flavor changes and they get tougher. This type of goat is better slow smoked. In the Caribbean, you can get barbecued goat with a jerk seasoning that's really delicious. Try my Caribbean Jerked Leg of Goat (page 300) for a taste sensation.

You prepare goat much as you do lamb, mainly by trimming off excess fat.

Greek Gyro Burger

This is a good backyard party burger. SERVES 6 TO 8

1 tablespoon granulated garlic
2 teaspoons fine sea salt
1 teaspoon freshly ground black pepper
1 teaspoon dried oregano leaves
1 teaspoon granulated onion
1/2 teaspoon ground cumin
2 pounds lean ground lamb
6 to 8 hamburger buns or pita bread
Lettuce and sliced tomato
1 recipe Tzatziki Sauce (recipe follows)

1 Prepare a medium-hot fire in your grill.

2 Combine the garlic, salt, pepper, oregano, onion, and cumin in a small bowl and blend well.

3 Place the ground meat in a large bowl, sprinkle one-third of the seasoning over the meat, and blend in with your hands. Repeat the process two more times, or until all the seasoning is blended in. Form into 6 to 8 patties.

4 Place the burgers directly over the coals, cover, and cook, turning once, 4 to 6 minutes per side for medium rare or to your desired degree of doneness.

5 Serve on the hamburger buns with lettuce and tomato and topped with the sauce.

Tzatziki Sauce

This traditional cooling Greek sauce goes well with grilled lamb, chicken, or fish. Don't freeze it because it will separate when thawed, as I found out the hard way. MAKES ABOUT 1 1/2 CUPS

1 cup sour cream or low-fat plain yogurt

1/2 cup peeled, seeded, and finely shredded or minced cucumber

2 green onions (white and green parts), minced

3 cloves garlic, pressed

1/2 teaspoon fine sea salt

Combine all the ingredients in a medium-size bowl and blend well. Cover with plastic wrap and refrigerate until ready to use. Keeps for 2 days.

2 In a large bowl, combine all the ingredients, except the buns, blending well with your hands. Form into 6 patties.

3 Place the burgers directly over the coals, cover, and cook, turning just once, 4 to 6 minutes per side for medium rare or to your desired degree of doneness.

4 Serve on the hamburger buns.

Pakistani-Style Lamb Burgers

This burger is packed with flavors that will expand your culinary horizons. This is great served with the barbecue sauce of your choice (pages 136–161) or Tzatziki Sauce (page 277). SERVES 6

1 1/2 pounds lean ground lamb

1/2 cup minced onion

1/4 cup dry bread crumbs

3 tablespoons milk

1 large egg

2 large cloves garlic, pressed

1 teaspoon fine sea salt

1 teaspoon peeled and grated fresh ginger

3/4 teaspoon ground cumin

1/2 teaspoon cayenne pepper

1/4 teaspoon ground cardamom

1/4 teaspoon ground cinnamon

1/4 teaspoon ground cloves

6 hamburger buns, split and grilled

1 Prepare a medium-hot fire in your grill.

Lebanese Lamb Burgers with Pine Nuts

Your friends who like lamb will ask for this one again and again. The pine nuts add a great texture and richness to the burgers. SERVES 6

1 1/2 pounds lean ground lamb

1/2 cup minced onion

1/4 cup pine nuts, toasted (see page 322)

1 tablespoon dried parsley flakes

1 tablespoon dried mint leaves

1 teaspoon granulated cane sugar

1 teaspoon fine sea salt

1 teaspoon freshly ground black pepper

1/2 teaspoon granulated garlic

1/2 teaspoon ground cinnamon

1/4 teaspoon ground nutmeg

6 hamburger buns, split and toasted

Lettuce, sliced tomatoes, sliced onions, and sliced Swiss cheese

1 recipe Tzatziki Sauce (page 277)

1 Prepare a medium-hot fire in your grill.

2 Combine the lamb, onion, pine nuts, parsley, mint, sugar, salt, pepper, garlic, cinnamon, and nutmeg in a large bowl and blend well with your hands. Form into 6 patties.

3 Place the burgers directly over the coals, cover, and cook, turning once, 5 to 7 minutes for medium rare or to your desired degree of doneness.

4 Serve on the hamburger buns, topped with lettuce, tomato, onion, a slice of Swiss, and a dollop of sauce.

Bacon-Wrapped Lamb Burgers

I first tasted this burger while helping with the 2001 Accent Barbecue Recipe contest, but this is my version. The bacon helps keep the burgers moist while grilling. SERVES 6

- 1 tablespoon granulated garlic
- 1 teaspoon freshly ground black pepper
- 1 teaspoon seasoned salt, homemade (page 108) or store-bought
- $1/2$ teaspoon ground rosemary
- $1^1/2$ pounds lean ground lamb
- $1/4$ cup milk
- 6 slices lean bacon
- Toothpicks
- 6 hamburger buns, split and grilled

1 Prepare a medium-hot fire in your grill.

2 Combine the garlic, pepper, seasoned salt, and rosemary in a small bowl. Place the lamb in a large bowl and add the seasonings one-third at a time, along with one-third of the milk, blending and mixing in each addition thoroughly with your hands. Form into 6 equal-size patties and wrap a strip of bacon around each patty, securing it with a toothpick.

3 Place the burgers directly over the coals, cover, and cook, turning once, 8 to 10 minutes per side for medium rare or to your desired degree of doneness.

4 Remove the toothpicks and place on the hamburger buns to serve.

Spicy Lamb Kabobs

If you like curry, you will like these kabobs, especially when served with Israeli couscous and a fresh fruit relish. SERVES 6 TO 8

CHILE-CURRY MARINADE
- $1/4$ cup fresh lemon juice
- $1/4$ cup olive oil
- 2 tablespoons grated onion
- 2 tablespoons pure ground serrano chile
- 1 tablespoon fine sea salt
- 1 to 2 teaspoons curry powder, to your taste, homemade (page 112) or store-bought
- 1 teaspoon ground coriander
- 1 teaspoon ground ginger
- 4 cloves garlic, pressed

- 2 pounds lamb shoulder, trimmed of fat and cut into $1^1/2$- to 2-inch cubes
- Bamboo skewers, soaked in water for 30 minutes and drained
- Vegetables of your choice, such as green, yellow, and/or red bell peppers cut into 1-inch squares; mushroom caps; corn on the cob cut into 1-inch pieces; cherry tomatoes; or onions, zucchini, or fruit cut into large chunks

1 To make the marinade, combine the marinade ingredients in a large nonreactive bowl, add the meat, stirring to coat, cover with plastic wrap, and let marinate in the refrigerator for at least 2 hours or overnight.

2 Prepare a medium-hot fire in your grill. Thread the meat cubes onto the prepared skewers, alternating with different vegetables. Transfer the remaining marinade to a saucepan and bring to a boil over medium-high heat; let simmer for 5 minutes, then set aside.

3 Place the skewers directly over the coals, cover, and grill, turning and basting the cooked sides with the reserved marinade every 15 minutes, until cooked to your desired degree of doneness, about 30 minutes for medium rare.

Teriyaki Lamb Shish Kabobs

I've enjoyed lamb like this in Korean, Chinese, and Japanese restaurants, but it's even better grilled at home.
SERVES 6 TO 8

TERIYAKI MARINADE

1/2 cup soy sauce

1/2 cup tomato ketchup, homemade (page 43) or store-bought

1/2 cup granulated cane sugar

1 teaspoon ground ginger

1 teaspoon granulated garlic or garlic powder

2 pounds lamb sirloin or round, trimmed of fat and cut into 1 1/2-inch cubes

1 1/2 cups fresh or canned, drained pineapple cut into 1-inch chunks

1/2 pound mushrooms, stems discarded

1 large yellow onion, cut into 1-inch pieces

1 large red or green bell pepper, seeded and cut into 1-inch squares

Bamboo skewers, soaked in water to cover for 30 minutes and drained

1 To make the marinade, combine the marinade ingredients in a large nonreactive bowl and blend well. Add the lamb, stirring to coat, cover with plastic wrap, and let marinate in the refrigerator overnight.

2 Prepare a medium-hot fire in your grill. Drain the lamb, reserving the marinade. Transfer the remaining marinade to a saucepan and bring to a boil over medium-high heat; let simmer for 5 minutes, then keep warm. Thread the lamb, alternating with the pineapple and vegetables, onto the prepared skewers.

3 Place the skewers directly over the coals, cover, and grill for 4 to 5 minutes per side for medium rare or to your desired degree of doneness.

4 Serve with the reserved marinade on the side.

Japanese Skewered Lamb

This recipe is not only low in calories, but it's also delicious. This makes a great appetizer your guests can cook themselves. Put a hibachi in the middle of the table with all the ingredients in bowls and let people do their thing.
SERVES 4 TO 6

1 pound lean boneless lamb, trimmed of any fat

1/4 cup light soy sauce

2 tablespoons clover honey

2 tablespoons rice vinegar

2 cloves garlic, pressed

$^1/_2$ teaspoon peeled and grated fresh ginger

1 cup chicken broth

Bamboo skewers, soaked in water to cover for 30 minutes and drained

1 Cut the lamb across the grain into thin strips $^1/_8$ inch thick x $^1/_2$ inch wide x 3 inches long.

2 Combine the soy sauce, honey, vinegar, garlic, ginger, and chicken broth in a small nonreactive saucepan over medium heat. Heat the mixture, stirring until the honey has dissolved. Remove from the heat and let cool.

3 Place the meat in a nonreactive baking dish or zippered-top plastic bag, pour the cooled marinade over the meat, turning to coat, cover with plastic wrap or seal, and let marinate for at least 1 to 2 hours or overnight in the refrigerator, turning the meat a few times.

4 Prepare a medium-hot fire in your grill.

5 Drain the lamb, discard the marinade, and weave the slices of meat onto the prepared skewers. Place directly over the coals and grill for about 2 minutes per side for medium rare or to your desired degree of doneness.

Curry-Spiced Lemon Shish Kabobs

This recipe is worth the work of threading these kabobs.
SERVES 4 TO 6

CURRY-SPICED LEMON MARINADE

Juice of 2 lemons

$^1/_4$ cup olive oil

2 tablespoons grated onion

1 tablespoon chili powder, homemade (page 111) or store-bought

1 tablespoon kosher salt

2 teaspoons granulated garlic

1 teaspoon curry powder, homemade (page 112) or store-bought

1 teaspoon ground coriander

1 teaspoon ground ginger

2 pounds lean lamb, trimmed of fat and cut into 1$^1/_2$-inch cubes

6 plum tomatoes, cut in half lengthwise

1 large yellow onion, cut into 2-inch chunks

2 red bell peppers, seeded and cut into 2-inch squares

12 large mushrooms, stems removed

Bamboo skewers, soaked in water to cover for 30 minutes and drained

1 To make the marinade, combine the marinade ingredients in a large nonreactive bowl and blend well with a wire whisk. Place the lamb cubes in a nonreactive baking dish or a zippered-top plastic bag, pour the marinade over the meat, turning to coat, cover with plastic wrap or seal, and let marinate in the refrigerator for at least 2 to 3 hours or overnight.

2 Prepare a medium-hot fire in your grill.

3 Drain the lamb, discarding the marinade. Thread the marinated meat, alternating it with the vegetables as desired, onto the prepared skewers. Place the skewers directly over the coals, cover, and grill for 3 to 4 minutes per side for medium rare or to your desired degree of doneness.

Caribbean-Style Lamb Kabobs

You can make this dish as hot as you wish. It's even good mild! I prefer these kabobs grilled to medium rare.
SERVES 4 TO 6

- 2 pounds lean lamb, trimmed of fat and cut into 1½-inch cubes
- ¼ cup Jerk Seasoning (page 123)
- 2 to 3 red bell peppers, seeded and cut into 1½-inch squares
- 2 to 3 yellow bell peppers, seeded and cut into 1½-inch squares
- 2 to 3 red onions, cut into 1½-inch squares
- Bamboo skewers, soaked in water to cover for 30 minutes and drained

1 Prepare a medium-hot fire in your grill.

2 Season the lamb all over with the jerk seasoning. Thread the vegetables and lamb onto the prepared skewers.

3 Place the skewers directly over the coals, cover, and grill for 7 to 8 minutes per side for medium rare or to your desired degree of doneness.

Lamb Fajitas in Sizzling Citrus Marinade

Yes, Dorothy, there are recipes for lamb fajitas, even in Kansas. Serve this dish with traditional fajita accompaniments, such as pico de gallo, sour cream, guacamole, cheese, and shredded lettuce. SERVES 4 TO 6

SIZZLING CITRUS MARINADE

- ½ cup canola oil
- ¼ cup fresh lemon juice
- ¼ cup fresh lime juice (about 4 limes)
- ¼ cup red wine vinegar
- 2 teaspoons ground cumin
- 1 teaspoon granulated garlic
- 1 teaspoon chili powder, homemade (page 111) or store-bought
- 1 teaspoon dried oregano leaves
- 1 teaspoon fine sea salt
- 1 teaspoon freshly ground black pepper
- ½ teaspoon dried thyme leaves

- 2 pounds boneless lamb shoulder, trimmed of fat and cut into strips ½ inch x ½ inch x 3 inches long
- 1 large red onion, cut into matchsticks
- 1 to 2 red bell peppers, seeded and cut into matchsticks
- 1 green bell pepper, seeded and cut into matchsticks
- 2 jalapeño chiles, seeded and cut into matchsticks
- Warm flour tortillas
- 1 recipe Barbecue Salsa (page 157)
- Sour cream
- 1 recipe Guacamole (page 241)
- Shredded cheddar cheese
- Shredded lettuce

1 To make the marinade, combine the marinade ingredients in a large nonreactive bowl and blend well. Add the lamb and vegetables, stir to coat, cover with plastic wrap, and let marinate for at least 2 hours or overnight in the refrigerator.

2 Prepare a medium-hot fire in your grill.

3   Drain the meat and vegetables, discarding the marinade. If your grill has a wide or large grate, use a perforated grill rack, grill wok, or cast-iron plate to cook the fajitas. Grill the meat and vegetables directly over the coals, stirring and tossing continually, to your desired degree of doneness.

4   Serve in a large bowl, accompanied by the tortillas, pico de gallo or salsa, sour cream, guacamole, cheese, and lettuce for diners to construct their own fajitas.

Simple Grilled Lemon Lamb Chops

Simple, simple, simple, easy, easy, easy—do I need to say more? SERVES 4 TO 8

8 loin lamb chops, 1¹/₂ inches thick

Minced zest and juice of 1 lemon

2 tablespoons garlic salt

2 teaspoons freshly ground black pepper

1   Cut pockets in the fat of each chop. Stuff the lemon zest in the pockets. Season the chops all over with the garlic salt and pepper.

2   Prepare a medium-hot fire in your grill.

3   Place the chops directly over the coals, cover, and grill for 7 to 10 minutes per side for medium rare or to your desired degree of doneness.

4   Serve piping hot with a bit of lemon juice drizzled over each chop.

Grilled Basil-Garlic Lamb Chops

You don't need any mint jelly for this one. The basil and garlic give these lamb chops an irresistible flavor. SERVES 4 TO 8

4 cloves garlic, pressed

¹/₄ cup chopped fresh basil leaves

2 tablespoons fresh lemon juice

2 tablespoons freshly grated Parmesan cheese

1 teaspoon fine sea salt

¹/₂ teaspoon freshly ground black pepper

¹/₄ cup olive oil

8 center-cut lamb chops, 1 inch thick

1   In a food processor, combine the garlic, basil, lemon juice, cheese, salt, and pepper and pulse until well blended. Add the olive oil and process until incorporated, but don't emulsify or over-blend it.

2   Place the chops in a zippered-top plastic bag, pour the marinade over them, turning to coat, seal, and let marinate for at least 4 to 6 hours or overnight in the refrigerator, turning a few times.

3   When ready to cook, prepare a medium-hot fire in your grill.

4   Place the chops directly over the coals, cover, and grill for 5 to 6 minutes per side for medium rare or to your desired degree of doneness.

Chile-Rubbed Lamb Chops with Hot Pepper and Mint Jelly

Some people say this is spicy, but it really isn't if you like heat. SERVES 8

- 1 tablespoons medium-hot chile powder (see Note)
- 1 tablespoon ground cumin
- 1 tablespoon granulated cane sugar
- 1 teaspoon fine sea salt
- 1 teaspoon freshly ground black pepper
- 1/2 teaspoon ground allspice
- 16 rib lamb chops, 1 to 1 1/2 inches thick, trimmed of fat
- 1/2 cup Hot Pepper and Mint Jelly (recipe follows; make at least the day before to let the flavors develop)

1 In a small bowl, combine the ground chile, cumin, sugar, salt, black pepper, and allspice and blend well. Sprinkle the spice mixture evenly over both sides of the chops, cover with plastic wrap, and let marinate in the refrigerator for at least 4 hours or overnight.

2 Prepare a medium-hot fire in your grill.

3 Place the chops directly over the coals, cover, and grill for 5 to 7 minutes per side for medium rare or to your desired degree of doneness. Serve with the jelly on the side.

NOTE Chile powder is one or two types of ground dried capsicums blended, while chili seasoning is capsicums blended with cumin, garlic, oregano, and other spices.

Hot Pepper and Mint Jelly

If you like Southern-style red pepper jelly, you'll love this green version with a hint of mint. When removing the stems, seeds, and membranes from the hot peppers, wear rubber gloves and don't touch any sensitive parts of your body, such as your eyes. MAKES ABOUT 7 HALF-PINTS

- 3 large green bell peppers, seeded and membranes removed
- 4 to 6 jalapeño chiles, to your taste, seeded and membranes removed
- 1 cup fresh mint leaves
- 1 1/2 cups distilled white vinegar
- 7 cups granulated cane sugar
- 9 fluid ounces fruit pectin (available in canning section of grocery store)

1 Place the bell peppers, jalapeños, mint, and vinegar in a blender and process until smooth. Transfer to a large nonreactive saucepan and combine with the sugar. Bring to a boil, reduce the heat to medium-low, and simmer for 20 minutes.

2 Remove from the heat and strain through cheesecloth into another nonreactive saucepan. Add the pectin and bring to a full rolling boil, stirring constantly. Boil for 1 minute, remove from the heat, ladle into sterile jars, and seal tightly. Keeps refrigerated indefinitely.

Lemon-Ginger Lamb Chops

Talk about international. I got this recipe from a Japanese lady in a Chinese cooking class in Hawaii. SERVES 4 TO 8

- 1/2 cup pineapple juice
- 1/4 cup firmly packed light brown sugar

¼ **cup granulated cane sugar**

2 teaspoons peeled and minced fresh ginger

2 teaspoons grated lemon peel

1 teaspoon fine sea salt

½ **teaspoon freshly ground black pepper**

2 tablespoons cold water

1 tablespoon cornstarch

8 center-cut lamb chops, 1 inch thick

1 Combine the pineapple juice, brown and white sugars, ginger, lemon peel, salt, and pepper in a small nonreactive saucepan and bring to a boil, stirring to dissolve the sugar. Reduce the heat to medium-low and simmer for 10 minutes. In a small bowl, combine the water and cornstarch to make a paste. Stir into the pineapple mixture and cook until thickened. Remove from the heat and let cool.

2 Place the lamb chops in a nonreactive baking dish or a zippered-top plastic bag, pour the cooled marinade over the lamb chops, turning to coat, and let marinate for 2 to 3 hours or overnight in the refrigerator, turning several times.

3 Prepare a medium-hot fire in your grill. Remove the chops from the marinade, shaking off any excess and reserving the marinade. Transfer the remaining marinade to a saucepan and bring to a boil over medium-high heat; simmer for 5 minutes, then set aside.

4 Place the chops directly over the coals, cover, and grill for 5 to 7 minutes per side for medium rare or to your desired degree of doneness. While grilling, baste the cooked sides with the reserved marinade.

Balsamic-Marinated Lamb Chops with Roasted Red Pepper Butter

This marinade brings out the flavor in both lamb and beef. The Roasted Red Pepper Butter can also be tossed with hot pasta or served over vegetables. SERVES 6

BALSAMIC MARINADE

½ **cup balsamic vinegar**

¼ **cup olive oil**

¼ **cup minced shallots**

4 large cloves garlic, pressed

1 teaspoon dried thyme leaves

1 teaspoon fine sea salt

1 teaspoon lemon pepper seasoning

6 loin lamb chops, 1½ inches thick, trimmed of fat

ROASTED RED PEPPER BUTTER

½ **cup (1 stick) unsalted butter, softened**

¼ **cup roasted red bell peppers, minced**

1 tablespoon granulated cane sugar

1 teaspoon lemon pepper seasoning

1 clove garlic, pressed

½ **teaspoon fine sea salt**

½ **teaspoon white pepper**

1 To make the marinade, combine the marinade ingredients in a small nonreactive bowl and blend with a wire whisk.

2 Place the chops in a nonreactive baking dish or zippered-top plastic bag and pour the marinade over them, turning to coat, then cover with plastic wrap or seal and let marinate for at least 2 to 4 hours or overnight in the refrigerator.

3 To make the flavored butter, combine the red pepper butter ingredients with a wire whisk or electric mixer in a medium-size bowl until blended well. Set aside.

4 Prepare a medium-hot fire in your grill.

5 Remove the chops from the marinade, shaking off any excess, and discard the marinade. Place the chops directly over the coals, cover, and grill for 7 to 10 minutes per side for medium rare or to your desired degree of doneness.

6 Served topped with a dollop of the red pepper butter.

Chili-Garlic Sirloin Lamb Steaks

When I prepare steaks in the National Lamb Contest, I like to use sirloin lamb steaks or chops. Lamb sirloin is a tender, tasty piece of meat and you don't see it that often in contests. Anything you can do to distinguish your food is the makings of championship barbecue. SERVES 6

CHILI-GARLIC MARINADE

$1/2$ cup red wine vinegar

$1/4$ cup olive oil

$1/4$ cup thinly sliced onion

2 tablespoons fresh lemon juice

3 cloves garlic, pressed

1 teaspoon chili powder, homemade (page 111) or store-bought

1 teaspoon freshly ground black pepper

1 teaspoon dried basil leaves

1 teaspoon seasoned salt, homemade (page 108) or store-bought

1 teaspoon crushed red pepper

$1/2$ teaspoon dried oregano leaves

6 sirloin lamb steaks (chops), 6 to 8 ounces each

1 To make the marinade, combine the marinade ingredients in a medium-size nonreactive bowl and mix well with a wire whisk.

2 Place the lamb in a zippered-top plastic bag and pour the marinade over them, turning to coat, then seal and let marinate for at least 4 to 6 hours or overnight in the refrigerator.

3 Prepare a medium-hot fire in your grill.

4 Remove the steaks from the marinade, shaking off any excess marinade, and discard the marinade. Place the steaks directly over the coals, cover, and grill for 4 to 5 minutes per side for medium rare or to your desired degree of doneness.

Sirloin Lamb Steaks with Garlic and Rosemary

The marinade in this recipe is mild and the garlic and rosemary combination brings out the flavor of the lamb. SERVES 8

2 tablespoons minced garlic

2 tablespoons fresh rosemary leaves

1 teaspoon fine sea salt

1 teaspoon freshly ground black pepper

Eight 10-ounce sirloin lamb steaks, trimmed of fat

1/2 cup Merlot or other red wine

1/2 cup olive oil

1 Chop the garlic and rosemary together and combine with the salt and pepper to form a paste. Rub the steaks with the paste and place in a non-reactive baking dish. Pour the wine and olive oil over the steaks, cover with plastic wrap, and let marinate for at least 2 hours or overnight in the refrigerator.

2 Prepare a medium-hot fire in your grill.

3 Remove the steaks from the marinade, shaking off any excess marinade, and discard the marinade. Place the steaks directly over the coals, cover, and grill for 5 to 8 minutes per side for medium rare or to your desired degree of doneness.

Lamb Sirloin Santa Fe with New Mexico Avocado Salsa

This dish is a pleasant change from traditional lamb recipes, and the avocado salsa makes a colorful addition to the plate and enhances the overall flavor. SERVES 8

SEASONING MIXTURE

2 tablespoons chili powder, homemade (page 111) or store-bought

2 teaspoons garlic powder

2 teaspoons dried cilantro leaves

1 teaspoon ground cumin

1 teaspoon dried oregano leaves

1 teaspoon freshly ground black pepper

1 teaspoon fine sea salt

Eight 6- to 8-ounce lamb sirloin steaks, 1 inch thick

1/2 cup olive oil

1 recipe New Mexico Avocado Salsa (recipe follows)

1 To make the seasoning mixture, combine the seasoning mixture ingredients in a small bowl and blend well. Season both sides of each steak with the seasoning. Let the steaks rest for 30 to 45 minutes at room temperature, covered with plastic wrap.

2 Prepare a medium-hot fire with a Kiss of Smoke (see page 23).

3 Dip each steak into the olive oil, place directly over the coals, cover, and grill for 5 to 7 minutes per side for medium rare or to your desired degree of doneness. Serve with the salsa on the side.

New Mexico Avocado Salsa

The citrus zest really adds a punch of flavor to this salsa, which is also delicious as a dip for tortilla chips. MAKES 2 TO 3 CUPS

2 to 3 ripe avocados, peeled, pitted, and cubed

4 green onions (green and white parts), thinly sliced

1 jalapeño chile, seeded, deveined, and minced

2 tablespoons minced fresh cilantro leaves

2 cloves garlic, pressed

2 tablespoons fresh lemon juice

2 tablespoons fresh lime juice

1 teaspoon grated lemon zest

1 teaspoon grated lime zest

1 teaspoon fine sea salt

Combine all the ingredients in a medium-size nonreactive bowl and blend gently. Cover with plastic wrap and refrigerate for at least 2 hours to let the flavors develop before serving.

Lamb Loins with Peppered Plum Sauce

This recipe is so simple you will love it. Lamb loins are boned racks of lamb. Ask your butcher for them. Slice the loins into medallions and nap with the sauce. **SERVES 6 TO 8**

> 3 tablespoons garlic salt
>
> 1 tablespoon freshly ground black pepper
>
> 2 teaspoons dried rosemary leaves, minced
>
> 1/4 cup olive oil
>
> Four 1-pound boneless lamb loins, trimmed of fat
>
> 1/2 cup Peppered Plum Sauce (recipe follows)

1 Prepare a medium-hot fire in your grill.

2 Combine the garlic salt, pepper, and rosemary in small bowl and blend well. Rub the olive oil over the loins and season evenly with the spice mixture.

3 Place the loins directly over the coals, cover, and grill for 10 to 15 minutes per side for medium rare or to your desired degree of doneness. During the last 10 minutes of cooking time, glaze both sides of the loins with the plum sauce. If your fire is too hot and the glaze is darkening too quickly, pull the loins to the cool side of your grill and cook, covered, off the coals.

4 Let rest for several minutes, then slice and serve with the remaining sauce.

Peppered Plum Sauce

Sweet, sour, and savory all at the same time, this sauce is also good with dim sum. **MAKES ABOUT 2 CUPS**

> 2 tablespoons unsalted butter
>
> 1/2 cup minced onion
>
> 1/4 cup granulated cane sugar
>
> 1 1/2 pounds canned red plums, drained (juice reserved) and pitted
>
> 2 tablespoons red wine vinegar
>
> 1 tablespoon bottled green peppercorns, drained
>
> 1 teaspoon fine sea salt

1 Melt the butter over medium heat in a medium-size nonreactive saucepan. Add the onion and cook, stirring, until softened but not browned. Add the sugar, plums, 1/2 cup of the reserved plum juice, vinegar, peppercorns, and salt, bring to a boil, reduce the heat to medium-low, and simmer for 15 minutes. Remove from the heat and let cool.

2 Transfer to a blender and process until smooth. Return to the saucepan and reheat; if you want the sauce thicker, simmer 5 minutes longer. Use warm as a baste or pass separately at the table.

Grilled Luau Lamb Ribs with Pineapple-Soy Marinade

These ribs make great little appetizers or an entire meal. Denver ribs are slabs of lamb ribs that have been squared off at the small end and usually contain 7 or 8 ribs. A full slab is usually called a lamb breast, and both cuts are delicious. SERVES 4 TO 6

PINEAPPLE-SOY MARINADE

$1/2$ cup soy sauce

$1/2$ cup pineapple juice

$1/4$ cup hoisin sauce

$1/4$ cup rice vinegar

2 tablespoons clover honey

2 tablespoons sugar

2 tablespoons peanut oil

4 cloves garlic, pressed

2 teaspoons crushed red pepper

1 teaspoon fine sea salt

1 teaspoon freshly ground black pepper

1 teaspoon red food coloring (optional)

3 slabs Denver lamb ribs (see page 276), trimmed of fat

1 To make the marinade, combine the marinade ingredients in a medium-size nonreactive bowl and blend with a wire whisk.

2 Place the ribs in a nonreactive baking dish or a zippered-top plastic bag. Pour the marinade over them, turning to coat, then cover with plastic wrap or seal and let marinate for at least 4 to 6 hours or overnight in the refrigerator.

3 Prepare a medium-hot fire in your grill.

4 Remove the ribs from the marinade, shaking off any excess marinade, and discard the marinade. Place the slabs directly over the coals, cover, and grill, turning every 15 minutes, until an instant-read meat thermometer inserted into the thickest part registers 135 to 140 degrees F for medium rare, 45 minutes to 1 hour, or to your desired degree of doneness.

5 Transfer the ribs to a cutting board and let rest for 10 minutes before cutting into chops.

BARBECUED LUAU LAMB RIBS WITH PINEAPPLE-SOY MARINADE

To barbecue a rack of lamb, prepare an indirect fire. Place the rack on your pit, cover, and cook at 230 to 350 degrees F until an instant-read thermometer inserted into the thickest part registers 135 to 140 degrees F for medium rare, 2 to 3 hours, or to your desired degree of doneness. Let rest for 15 minutes before slicing and serving. SERVES 6 TO 8

Grilled Herbed Mustard Rack of Lamb

This dish is better than anything you could order in a restaurant. SERVES 4 TO 6

HERBED MUSTARD MARINADE

1/4 cup Dijon mustard

2 tablespoons olive oil

8 cloves garlic, pressed

2 teaspoons dried rosemary leaves

1 teaspoon dried thyme leaves

1 teaspoon fine sea salt

1 teaspoon freshly ground black pepper

4 racks of lamb, about 1 1/2 pounds each,
   trimmed of fat and Frenched (see page 277)

1 To make the marinade, combine the marinade ingredients in a small bowl and mix well.

2 Rub the marinade all over the lamb, cover with plastic wrap, and let marinate overnight in the refrigerator. Bring the lamb to room temperature 1 hour before cooking.

3 Prepare a medium-hot fire in your grill.

4 Place the lamb directly over the coals, cover, and grill, turning every 15 minutes, until an instant-read meat thermometer inserted into the thickest part registers 135 to 140 degrees F for medium rare, 45 minutes to 1 hour, or to your desired degree of doneness.

5 Transfer the lamb to a cutting board and let rest for 10 minutes before cutting into the chops.

BARBECUED HERBED MUSTARD RACK OF LAMB

To barbecue a rack of lamb, prepare an indirect fire. Place the rack on your pit, cover, and cook at 230 to 350 degrees F until an instant-read thermometer inserted into the thickest part registers 135 to 140 degrees F for medium rare, 2 to 3 hours, or to your desired degree of doneness. Let rest for 15 minutes before slicing and serving.

Barbecued Rack of Lamb with Red Currant Glaze

Chef Ronaldo Camargo of Disney University in Florida, a co-captain of Team Kansas City, worked with me on this recipe. We used to call Ronaldo "commandante" because he tried to be the boss when we competed in Ireland. SERVES 4

1/4 cup Orange Mustard Slather (page 92)

2 racks of lamb, 7 to 9 chops each, trimmed of
   fat and Frenched (see page 277)

2 tablespoons garlic salt

1 tablespoon freshly ground black pepper

1 recipe Red Currant Glaze (recipe follows)

1 Prepare an indirect fire.

2 Spread the mustard slather all over the lamb racks and season with the garlic salt and pepper.

3 Place the lamb on the pit, cover, and cook for 2 1/2 hours at 230 to 250 degrees F, then begin to brush with the glaze and turn the rack every 15 minutes. Keep checking the internal temperature with an instant-read meat thermometer inserted

into the thickest part of the rack. It should reach 135 to 140 degrees F for medium rare in about 3 hours, or cook it to your desired degree of doneness.

4 Transfer the rack to a cutting board and let rest for 10 minutes before cutting into the chops.

Red Currant Glaze

This glaze is also good with grilled or smoked wild game. I usually have to order fresh red currants from a produce supplier. You can also use the same amount of red currant jelly if you can't get fresh red currants. MAKES ABOUT 2 1/4 CUPS

> 1 cup fresh red currants, picked over for stems
>
> 1/2 cup red wine vinegar
>
> 1/2 cup chicken broth
>
> 2 tablespoons granulated cane sugar
>
> 2 tablespoons frozen orange juice concentrate
>
> 2 tablespoons frozen mango juice concentrate (available at health food stores)
>
> 1 tablespoon Triple Sec liqueur
>
> 1 teaspoon fine sea salt
>
> 1/4 teaspoon ground cloves

1 Place all the ingredients in a medium-size nonreactive saucepan, bring to a boil, reduce the heat to medium-low, and simmer for 15 minutes, stirring occasionally.

2 Press the sauce through a sieve or process in a food processor until smooth. Return to the saucepan and simmer for 10 minutes longer, reducing the mixture until slightly thickened. Use hot as a glaze.

Herb-Crusted Barbecued Rack of Lamb with Roasted Garlic Sauce

This dish is what you order at the fancy restaurants for $22.95 per person. I've prepared this in restaurants and at barbecue competitions. SERVES 4 TO 8

> 1/4 cup olive oil
>
> 1 teaspoon crushed red pepper
>
> 4 cloves garlic, pressed
>
> 2 teaspoons dried thyme leaves
>
> 1/2 cup fresh bread crumbs
>
> Salt and freshly ground black pepper to taste
>
> 1/4 cup minced fresh parsley leaves
>
> 1/4 cup Dijon mustard
>
> 2 tablespoons mayonnaise
>
> 2 racks of lamb, 7 or 8 ribs each, trimmed of fat and Frenched (see page 277)
>
> 1 recipe Roasted Garlic Sauce (recipe follows)

1 Prepare an indirect fire.

2 In a small skillet over medium heat, heat the olive oil until hot, but not smoking. Add the red pepper and garlic and cook, stirring, for about 30 seconds. Add the thyme and stir for about 15 seconds. Stir in the bread crumbs and season with salt and pepper to taste. Remove the skillet from the heat and stir in the parsley.

3 Combine the mustard and mayonnaise in a small bowl and blend well. Spread a thin layer of the mustard mixture all over the meat of the racks and pat evenly with the herbed crumbs, but not too heavily.

4   Place the racks on the pit, cover, and cook at 230 to 250 degrees F until an instant-read meat thermometer inserted into the thickest part registers 130 to 135 degrees F for medium rare, 2 to 3 hours, or to your desired degree of doneness.

5   Transfer the racks to a cutting board and let rest for 10 minutes before cutting into the chops. Serve with the garlic sauce on the side.

Roasted Garlic Sauce

To me, this sauce goes with anything—hot dogs, potato chips, mussels, hamburgers, vegetables, you name it.
MAKES 1 TO 1¹/₂ CUPS

> 2 tablespoons olive oil
>
> 1 head garlic, top cut off to expose the
>   individual cloves
>
> 2 tablespoons unsalted butter
>
> ¹/₂ cup chopped shallots
>
> 1 cup Cabernet Sauvignon
>
> 1 cup beef broth
>
> ³/₄ cup chicken broth
>
> ¹/₂ teaspoon kosher salt
>
> ¹/₂ teaspoon freshly ground black pepper

1   Preheat the oven to 350 degrees F.

2   Rub 1 tablespoon of the olive oil all over the head of garlic, place in a small baking dish, and roast in the oven until quite soft, 35 to 45 minutes. Remove from the oven and let cool. Squeeze the softened garlic from the skins and set aside.

3   Heat the remaining 1 tablespoon of olive oil and 1 tablespoon of the butter in a medium-size skillet over medium heat until the butter melts. Add the shallots and cook, stirring, until golden brown, about 10 minutes. Add the wine and simmer until reduced by half. Add both broths and simmer until reduced to ³/₄ to 1 cup, about 10 minutes.

4   Transfer to a blender, add the softened garlic, and process until smooth. Return the sauce to the skillet and heat to simmering. Remove from the heat, whisk in the remaining 1 tablespoon of butter, stir in the salt and pepper, and keep warm until ready to serve.

Barbecued Lemon-Garlic Marinated Breast of Lamb

Breast of lamb is the same as a side of spareribs on a hog, but smaller and more delicate in flavor. Very few restaurants serve breast of lamb, so this is a real treat to make at home. Serve with your favorite barbecue sauce (pages 136–161) on the side. SERVES 2

LEMON-GARLIC MARINADE

> 1 cup fresh lemon juice (about 8 lemons)
>
> ¹/₃ cup olive oil
>
> 3 cloves garlic, pressed
>
> 2 tablespoons grated onion
>
> 1 teaspoon minced fresh rosemary leaves
>
> 1 teaspoon non-iodized salt
>
> ¹/₂ teaspoon freshly ground black pepper

One 2-pound breast of lamb

1   To make the marinade, combine the marinade ingredients in a medium-size nonreactive bowl and blend well.

2   Place the lamb in a nonreactive baking dish or zippered-top plastic bag, pour the marinade over the lamb, turning to coat, then cover with plastic wrap or seal and let marinate for at least 1 hour or overnight in the refrigerator.

3   Prepare an indirect fire.

4   Remove the lamb from the marinade, shaking off any excess marinade, and discard the marinade. Place the lamb on the pit, cover, and cook at 230 to 250 degrees F for 1½ to 2½ hours, turning every 45 minutes, until an instant-read meat thermometer inserted into the thickest part registers 130 to 135 degrees F for medium rare or to your desired degree of doneness.

5   Let rest for about 15 minutes before slicing and serving.

Grilled Tomato-Marinated Lamb Shanks

The extra work that lamb shanks take is well worth the effort. For tender results, keep basting and turning.
SERVES 6 TO 8

TOMATO MARINADE

1 cup tomato juice

½ cup dill pickle juice

¼ cup fresh lemon juice

¼ cup minced onion

¼ cup seeded and minced green bell peppers

2 cloves garlic, pressed

2 teaspoons cracked black peppercorns

1 teaspoon ground cumin

1 teaspoon dried marjoram leaves

1 teaspoon fine sea salt

6 to 8 lamb shanks

1   To make the marinade, combine the marinade ingredients in a medium-size nonreactive bowl and blend well with a wire whisk.

2   Place the lamb in a nonreactive baking dish or in a zippered-top plastic bag, pour the marinade over them, turning to coat, cover with plastic wrap or seal, and let marinate for at least 4 to 6 hours or overnight in the refrigerator.

3   Prepare a medium-hot fire in your grill.

4   Remove the shanks from the marinade, reserving the marinade. Transfer the marinade to a medium-size nonreactive saucepan and bring to a boil over medium-high heat; let simmer for 5 minutes, then set aside.

5   Place the shanks directly over the coals, cover, and grill, basting the cooked sides with the reserved marinade and turning about every 15 minutes until tender, about 1 hour.

Grilled Red Wine-Marinated Leg of Lamb

This is a good recipe for lamb beginners. You can also cook a boneless rolled lamb breast this way. Serve with garlic mashed potatoes and grilled asparagus. **SERVES 6 TO 10**

RED WINE MARINADE

1 cup dry red wine

1/2 cup chicken broth

1/4 cup olive oil

4 cloves garlic, pressed

2 tablespoons minced pimentos

2 teaspoons non-iodized salt

1 teaspoon sweet Hungarian paprika

1 teaspoon freshly ground black pepper

One 4- to 9-pound leg of lamb, boned (see page 276) and trimmed of fat

1 To make the marinade, combine the marinade ingredients in a medium-size nonreactive bowl and blend well with a wire whisk.

2 Place the lamb in a nonreactive baking dish or in a zipper-topped plastic bag, pour the marinade over it, cover with plastic wrap or seal, and let marinate for at least 4 to 6 hours or overnight in the refrigerator, turning several times.

3 Prepare a medium-hot fire in your grill.

4 Remove the lamb from the marinade, shaking off any excess marinade. Transfer the remaining marinade to a saucepan and bring to a boil over medium-high heat; let simmer for 5 minutes, then set aside.

5 Place the lamb directly over the coals, cover, and grill, turning every 15 minutes and basting the cooked sides with the reserved marinade until an instant-read meat thermometer inserted into the thickest part of the leg registers 135 to 140 degrees F for medium rare, 1 to 1 1/2 hours, or to your desired degree of doneness.

6 Let rest for 15 minutes before slicing.

BARBECUED RED WINE–MARINATED LEG OF LAMB
Prepare an indirect fire. Place the lamb on the pit, cover, and smoke for 2 hours at 230 to 250 degrees F. Then begin to baste with the reserved marinade every 30 minutes. Keep checking the internal temperature in the thickest part of the leg. At 135 to 140 degrees F, it should be medium rare, 3 to 4 hours total, or cook to your desired degree of doneness. Let rest for 15 minutes before slicing.

Beginner's Barbecued Leg of Lamb

This is what I consider a basic recipe; if you have never barbecued lamb, start with this one. **SERVES 6 TO 8**

VINEGAR MARINADE

1 cup red wine vinegar

1/2 cup canola oil

2 cloves garlic, pressed

1/4 cup grated carrot

1/4 cup grated onion

1 teaspoon fine sea salt

1 teaspoon freshly ground black pepper

1/2 teaspoon dried oregano leaves

1/4 teaspoon ground cloves

One 4- to 5-pound boneless leg of lamb, trimmed of fat

1 To make the marinade, combine the marinade ingredients in a medium-size nonreactive bowl and blend well.

2 Place the lamb in a nonreactive baking dish or a zippered-top plastic bag, pour the marinade over the lamb, coat well, cover with plastic wrap or seal, and let marinate for at least 6 to 8 hours or overnight in the refrigerator, turning several times.

3 Prepare an indirect fire.

4 Remove the lamb from the marinade, shaking off any excess. Transfer the remaining marinade to a medium-size nonreactive saucepan and bring to a boil over medium-high heat. Simmer for 5 minutes, set aside to cool, then refrigerate until ready to use.

5 Place the lamb on the pit, cover, and smoke for 2 hours at 230 to 250 degrees F. Then start basting the lamb every 45 minutes with the reserved marinade. Keep checking the internal temperature in the thickest part of the leg with an instant-read meat thermometer. At 135 to 140 degrees F, it should be medium rare, 3 to 4 hours total, or cook to your desired degree of doneness.

6 Let rest for 15 minutes before slicing.

JoEllyn's Championship Barbecued Leg of Lamb

I received this recipe in Lisdoonvarna, County Clare, Ireland, from JoEllyn Sullivan. JoEllyn won the blue ribbon in the Lamb category at the World Cup Barbecue Championship, and my team took second. JoEllyn and I were talking about what we did with our lamb at the competition, as we both have a reputation for doing well with it. She is married to Silky Sullivan, owner of Silky O'Sullivan's pub in Memphis, Tennessee. (Silky is a great barbecuer himself.) Her recipe is very simple, but it works. SERVES 6 TO 8

1 leg of lamb (any size), bone-in or boneless, trimmed of fat

1/4 cup olive oil

1 tablespoon granulated garlic

3 tablespoons lemon pepper seasoning

1 Prepare an indirect fire.

2 Rub the leg of lamb all over with the olive oil. Sprinkle with the granulated garlic, then season with the lemon pepper.

3 Place the lamb on the pit, cover, and cook at 230 to 250 degrees F, checking the internal temperature in the thickest part of the leg with an instant-read meat thermometer. It should reach 135 to 140 degrees F, medium rare, in 3 to 4 hours.

4 Let the meat rest for 15 minutes before slicing.

Garlicky Barbecued Leg of Lamb

This is the way we prepared lamb when I was the chef at The Kerry Patch Restaurant in Kansas City. We ran it as a special and it was always popular. SERVES 6 TO 8

> One 5- to 7-pound boneless leg of lamb, trimmed of fat
>
> 8 to 10 cloves garlic, to your taste, sliced in half
>
> 1 tablespoon Kitchen Bouquet
>
> 2 tablespoons kosher salt
>
> 1 tablespoon cracked black peppercorns
>
> 1/2 cup olive oil
>
> 1/2 cup sweet vermouth

1 Prepare an indirect fire.

2 Cut small slits all over the leg and stuff the garlic slivers into the slits. Rub the Kitchen Bouquet over the lamb and season with the salt and cracked pepper. Combine the olive oil and vermouth and blend well.

3 Place the lamb on the pit, cover, and smoke for 2 hours at 230 to 250 degrees F. Then start basting the lamb every 45 minutes with the vermouth mixture. Keep checking the internal temperature in the thickest part of the leg with an instant-read meat thermometer. It should reach 135 to 140 degrees F, medium rare, in 3 1/2 to 4 1/2 hours total cooking time.

4 Let rest for 15 minutes before slicing.

Barbecued Rosemary Leg of Lamb

When I teach my Pitmaster classes, I always say that ginger is my girlfriend, but rosemary is a bitch. Rosemary can easily overpower any dish, but it tastes great in this recipe. Leg of lamb is also great to spit-roast or rotisserie (see page 297). Serve with mint jelly, a mint sauce, or your favorite barbecue sauce. SERVES 8 TO 10

> One 7- to 9-pound leg of lamb, boned (see page 276) and trimmed of fat
>
> 1/4 cup olive oil
>
> 1 tablespoon garlic salt
>
> 1 tablespoon freshly ground black pepper
>
> 1 tablespoon dried rosemary leaves

1 Prepare an indirect fire.

2 Rub the leg of lamb all over with the olive oil, then season evenly with the garlic salt, pepper, and rosemary.

3 Place the lamb on the pit, cover, and smoke at 230 to 250 degrees F for 2 hours. Turn and cook, covered, for 2 hours longer. Keep checking the internal temperature in the thickest part of the leg with an instant-read meat thermometer. It should reach 135 to 140 degrees F, medium rare, in 3 to 4 hours total cooking time.

4 Let the meat rest for 5 to 10 minutes before slicing.

How to Cook LAMB AND CABRITO on an Outdoor Rotisserie

Whole baby lambs or goats and leg of lamb are all delicious spit-roasted or rotisseried in your back yard. When everyone else is doing burgers and hot dogs, you'll be the talk of your neighborhood. Whole lamb and goat may not be your traditional Midwestern barbecue entrées, but they're favorites in Caribbean, Mexican, and Greek cuisines and well worth a try.

When you buy an electric rotisserie, make sure the motor has adequate power to turn the size and weight of the meat you want to cook—for a whole baby goat or lamb, 10 to 12 pounds, for a boned leg of lamb, 4 to 9 pounds. The manufacturer's directions should make clear the capacity of their particular product.

Because the rotisserie is positioned away from the coals, it is considered indirect cooking or barbecuing.

To spit-roast or rotisserie, first set up your rotisserie on the grill and prepare a medium fire. You can cook with a Kiss of Smoke (see page 23) by throwing a chunk or two of wood on the coals during cooking.

Marinate the meat for at least 4 hours or overnight in the refrigerator, or simply rub it with olive oil and sprinkle on a rub or seasoning right before you're ready to cook. Place the meat on the spit so that it will not spin loose. The meat should be balanced on the spit so it can turn easily. Tie any loose bits to the body with kitchen string. Insert a meat thermometer into the thickest part of the meat, away from the bone. Make sure the thermometer is positioned so you can read it and it can turn freely as the meat turns.

Place the spit on the rotisserie. Place a drip pan (you can use a disposable aluminum pan for this) under the spit. If you want, you can fill the pan with water, apple juice, or whatever you like, just as you would fill a water pan when smoking.

Start the rotisserie. Cover and cook, checking the meat, the fire, and the drip pan, at least every hour. When the rub has set after about 1 hour, start basting every 30 minutes with apple juice, melted butter, or whatever you like.

The cooking times are about the same as for barbecuing or slow smoking—3 to 4 hours for a boneless leg of lamb, 4 to 6 hours for a 10- to 12-pound whole lamb or goat. Cover and cook for 1 hour. Then start mopping every 20 minutes until the meat is fork tender. For a whole lamb or goat, I usually stick a fork in the hindquarter and twist it to check tenderness; the internal temperature should be 150 to 160 degrees F for well done. For a leg of lamb, I prefer it medium rare, at an internal temperature of 140 degrees F. Remove the meat from the spit and let rest at least 15 minutes before cutting into pieces or carving.

Greek-Style Rotisseried Lamb

In traditional households, this is the dish to serve on Greek Orthodox Easter. But to me, this dish is good any time! Serve it with a Greek salad of greens, cucumber, Kalamata olives, and feta cheese. You may also do roast potatoes drizzled with olive oil and sprinkled with a little of My Big Fat Greek Seasoning. Invite me over when you do. SERVES 8 TO 10

1 baby lamb (about 12 pounds), trimmed of fat

1 cup olive oil

My Big Fat Greek Seasoning (page 121) as needed

GREEK LAMB MOP

2 cups dry white wine

1/2 cup olive oil

1/4 cup fresh lemon juice

1/4 cup Worcestershire sauce, homemade (page 50) or store-bought

2 tablespoons granulated cane sugar

2 tablespoons granulated onion

2 tablespoons dried parsley flakes

1 tablespoon granulated garlic

1 tablespoon My Big Fat Greek Seasoning (page 121)

1 teaspoon kosher salt

1 teaspoon freshly ground black pepper

1 Rinse the lamb with cold water, inside and out, and pat dry with paper towels. Rub the lamb all over with the olive oil, then sprinkle all over with the seasoning.

2 To make the mop, combine the mop ingredients in a medium-size nonreactive bowl and set aside.

3 Set up your rotisserie on the grill. Prepare a hot fire in your grill.

4 Place the lamb on the spit so that it will not spin loose. The lamb should be balanced on the spit so it can turn easily. Tie any loose bits to the body with kitchen string. Insert a meat thermometer into the thigh, away from bone. Make sure the thermometer is positioned so you can read it and it can turn freely as the lamb turns. Place the spit on the rotisserie. Place a drip pan (you can use a disposable aluminum pan for this) under the spit. If you want, you can fill the pan with water or apple juice. Start the rotisserie. Cover and cook, checking the lamb, the fire, and the drip pan at least every hour. After the first hour, start mopping every 20 minutes with the Greek Lamb Mop. Cook, covered, for 3 to 4 hours more, until you can stick a fork in the hindquarter, twist it, and the meat falls apart; the internal temperature should be 150 to 160 degrees F for well done.

Picnic Cabrito

The first time I had cabrito was at a picnic with a group of people I used to make beer with. They had a kid about 14 pounds cooking 2 feet away from a hot fire. Someone got up and mopped and turned the goat every 20 minutes for about 3 hours. Man, that was good eatin'. Goat dries out easily, so make sure you mop regularly. Cabrito is also great to spit-roast or rotisserie (see page 297). SERVES 15 TO 20

GOAT RUB

1/4 cup firmly packed light brown sugar

2 tablespoons seasoned salt, homemade (page 108) or store-bought

2 tablespoons garlic salt

1 teaspoon granulated onion

1 teaspoon dried oregano leaves

1 teaspoon ground cumin

1 teaspoon finely ground black pepper

GOAT MOP

2 cups dry white wine

1/2 cup (1 stick) unsalted butter

1/4 cup fresh lemon juice (about 2 lemons)

1/4 cup Worcestershire sauce, homemade (page 50) or store-bought

2 tablespoons granulated cane sugar

2 tablespoons granulated onion

2 tablespoons dried parsley flakes

1 tablespoon granulated garlic

1 tablespoon Italian Seasoning (page 120)

1 teaspoon kosher salt

1 teaspoon freshly ground black pepper

1 kid goat (8 to 12 pounds), trimmed of fat

1 cup olive oil

1 Prepare an indirect fire.

2 To make the rub, combine the rub ingredients in a small bowl. Set aside.

3 To make the mop, combine the mop ingredients in a medium-size nonreactive saucepan over medium heat, stirring, and cook until the butter melts and the salt dissolves. Keep warm.

4 Rub the goat down with the olive oil and season it all over with the reserved rub.

5 Place on the kid on the pit, cover, and smoke at 230 to 250 degrees F for 1 hour. Then start mopping with the reserved mop and turning every 20 minutes until the meat is fork-tender, 3 to 4 hours. I usually stick a fork in the hindquarter and twist it to check tenderness; the internal tem-

perature should register 150 to 160 degrees F on an instant-read meat thermometer.

6 Let the meat rest for 15 minutes, then cut into pieces and serve.

Barbecued Cabrito

Even if you don't have a big cooker, you can still make this dish, which is very popular at Texas barbecues. If goat is your thing, then make sure you go to the World Championship Barbecue Goat Cook-off held every Labor Day weekend in Brady, Texas. SERVES 6 TO 8

BASTING SAUCE

2 cups water

One 8-ounce can tomato sauce

2 tablespoons (1/4 stick) unsalted butter

2 tablespoons cider vinegar

1 tablespoon coarsely ground black pepper

1 tablespoon firmly packed light brown sugar

1 large carrot, grated

2 cloves garlic, minced

6 cloves

1 teaspoon non-iodized salt

1 teaspoon ground cumin

1/2 teaspoon dried oregano leaves

1 kid goat (8 to 12 pounds), trimmed of fat

3 tablespoons garlic salt

1 tablespoon finely ground black pepper

1 To make the sauce, combine the basting sauce ingredients in a medium-size nonreactive saucepan and bring to a boil. Reduce the heat to low and let simmer for 30 minutes. Keep warm.

2 Prepare an indirect fire.

3 Cut the young goat into serving pieces or have your butcher do it. Rinse and pat dry with paper towels. Season evenly with the garlic salt and pepper.

4 Place the goat on the pit, cover, and smoke at 230 to 250 degrees F for 1 hour. Then start basting and turning every 20 minutes until an instant-read meat thermometer inserted into the thickest part of the goat registers 150 to 160 degrees F, 3 to 4 hours total cooking time.

Caribbean Jerked Leg of Goat

On our trip to St. Thomas, we saw lots of roadside stands serving this delicacy. You can make this one mild or authentically hot and spicy. Either way, it's delicious. Leg of goat is also great to spit-roast or rotisserie (see page 297).

SERVES 6 TO 8

JERK SEASONING

1 cup chopped onions

¹/₄ cup soy sauce

6 cloves garlic, minced

1 tablespoon fresh thyme leaves

1 tablespoon ground allspice

1 tablespoon fine sea salt

2 teaspoons freshly ground black pepper

1 teaspoon ground cinnamon

¹/₂ teaspoon ground nutmeg

1 habanero or jalapeño chile, chopped (if you want this to have extra chile power, don't remove the seeds)

1 leg of goat, trimmed of fat

BEER MOP

One 12-ounce can beer

¹/₄ cup fresh lemon juice

1 To make the seasoning, combine all the jerk seasoning ingredients in a food processor and process until smooth.

2 Pierce the goat leg all over with a sharp knife. Wearing rubber or plastic gloves, rub the seasoning all over the goat leg. Place on a large piece of plastic wrap and wrap it up, sealing the jerk rub in. Let marinate overnight in the refrigerator.

3 Prepare an indirect fire. Remove the leg from the plastic wrap.

4 To make the mop, combine the mop ingredients in a medium-size nonreactive bowl.

5 Place the leg on the pit, cover, and smoke at 230 to 250 degrees F for 1 hour. Start mopping every 20 minutes until an instant-read meat thermometer inserted into the thickest part of the leg registers 150 to 160 degrees F, 2 to 3 hours total cooking time.

6 Let rest for 15 minutes before slicing.

Putting on

the Dog

Sausage, I believe, is one of the most misunderstood forms of food preparation. When I teach my Pitmaster classes, I ask the class how many of them have ever made sausage. Most say that they haven't, and I, in turn, tell them they are all liars! As they sit there in shock, I then ask how many have made meatballs or meat loaf. Of course, most of them have. Okay, then they have made sausage. Sausage is nothing more than seasoned chopped meat, vegetables, or seafood. It's that simple. Don't complicate it!

Selecting Meats for Sausage Making

Most sausages use ground pork or mixtures of pork, beef, lamb, and veal. Usually, tougher cuts, such as pork butt, beef chuck, and lamb shoulder, are used to make sausage. Because there is usually such a small quantity of ground veal used in sausage—usually about 1 pound—I buy that at the grocery store already ground, but the rest of the meat I grind myself.

For a tender, moist sausage, you want a total fat content of 20 to 30 percent. Most of the time, the fat comes from the pork, so trim off some but not all of the fat from the pork butt you use to make sausage.

Grinding Meat for Sausage

If you plan on grinding your own meat, you should cut it into 1- to 2-inch cubes, then lightly freeze the meat for about an hour, until the meat is very firm but not frozen solid. This firming up allows the meat to be ground and extruded much more cleanly, which helps the fat stay in suspension and gives you a better sausage. It also saves you some money to grind the meat yourself, rather than buying it already ground at the grocery store.

You can't go wrong with an old-fashioned hand-cranked meat grinder, which you can buy at hardware stores. Basically, you attach the metal grinder to a table or countertop with a vise, then you place the meat in the opening on the top and turn the metal crank. The meat gets chopped and then extruded through the holes on the grinding plate into a bowl or through a stuffing tube directly into the casings.

If you really get into making sausage, I advise you to invest in an electric grinder, such as the Hamilton Beach model 226 grinder/stuffer. KitchenAid also makes an electric stand mixer with a grinding/stuffing attachment that works well. Make sure the grinder you use has both fine and coarse grinding plates. Don't use a food processor, as these machines cut the meat but don't grind and extrude it to make sausage.

For most sausages, I like a coarse grind from a $3/16$- or $1/4$-inch grinding plate; I feel that it gives a more flavorful product. If you like the meat ground finer, such as on a $1/8$-inch hamburger plate, by all means try it; it's your taste buds that you want to please, not mine.

The meat coming out of the grinder should look like small, firm, solid tubes. If it doesn't, then either your meat isn't cold enough or the grinder needs to be adjusted.

Sausage Seasonings

There are some classic seasoning combinations for different types of sausage, such as ground white pepper, mace or nutmeg, and granulated onion for bratwurst; fennel seeds, crushed red pepper, granulated or fresh garlic, and oregano for sweet Italian sausage; and rubbed sage, crushed red pepper, cayenne pepper, and nutmeg for breakfast sausage.

For barbecue competitions that have a Sausage category, or if I'm developing a sausage to use in a Miscellaneous or Anything Goes category, I'm a little more adventurous with the seasonings. I might add ground coriander or ginger or maybe powdered bay leaf or chipotle powder—anything to give my sausage a delicious edge in competition.

Several sausage recipes in this chapter call for powdered milk; *make sure the milk you buy is powdered and not granulated.* The meat mixture usually has enough moisture to absorb and distribute the powdered milk throughout the sausage. Granulated milk, on the other hand, does not dissolve as readily. If you need moisture in your mixture, you can use whole milk, water, stock, wine, or eggs, as you do with a meat loaf.

Combine the ground meat with your seasonings in a large bowl or a plastic tub. The sausage mixture should be made a day or two in advance and refrigerated so the flavors have a chance to mature before is the sausages are shaped.

Forming Sausages

I have had many people tell me that the reason they don't make sausage is because they don't have a stuffer. Well, I don't either, but that doesn't stop me. Here are several ways around that problem. One, you can make patties. My favorite way to do this is to place a glob of meat mixture in the middle of a large piece of plastic wrap. Then I roll it up and pull it to the size that I want with my thumb and index finger, forming a cylindrical log. The size can range from the diameter of a dime to a quarter or even to the size of a large meatloaf. You can roll the formed sausage right out of the plastic wrap and onto the grill. I cut patties from a cylindrical roll so that each patty weighs about 4 ounces and is 4 to 5 inches in diameter, the perfect size to fit on a hamburger bun.

I also make sausage sticks. Sticks are sausages formed by patting the sausage mixture around a foot-long $1/2$-inch-diameter wooden dowel—kind of like a corn dog without the cornbread coating.

Sometimes I refrigerate the sausage so that it firms up before grilling or smoking, especially on a hot day. If I'm at a barbecue contest, the sausage is already chilled in a cooler over ice, as there are rules about keeping all meats cold before cooking.

If the sausage meat is too lean and won't hold together to form a log or stick, you can place the sausage in plastic wrap over indirect heat (230 to 250 degrees F), close the grill, and cook the sausage for about 30 minutes. You can then roll the sausage out of the plastic; the meat should have firmed up and you can continue cooking until it's done. Don't worry about the plastic wrap melting. At 265 degrees F, plastic wrap gets brittle and cracks; it will melt only if it touches a hot piece of metal, such as the grill grate over hot coals.

The Case for Casings

Now, don't get grossed out, but most sausages are stuffed into natural casings, which are the cleaned intestines of hogs or sheep that have been packed in brine. You can get casings from your local butcher or meat market in 1-pound containers or through mail-order sources (see Sources). If you have any leftover casings after making sausage, repack them in salt or a heavy brine solution. Store them in the refrigerator, but do not freeze them, as this breaks down the tissues and makes them burst when cooking.

Different types of sausages take different sizes of casings, which are measured in millimeters (mm). Most bratwurst, chorizo, breakfast, Cajun, and Italian sausages are stuffed into casings with a diameter of 28 to 32mm, or about 1¼ inches, and can be up to 20 feet long (but that would be a little difficult to fit on your pit!). Most of the time, these sausages are then twisted or tied into 4- to 6-inch-long links. Polish sausages are usually stuffed into a slightly larger casing of 38 to 42mm, or slightly over 1½ inches in diameter. Polish-type sausages are tied into 10- to 12-inch-long ropes.

To prepare the casings for stuffing, rinse them, soak them in cold water to cover and store overnight in the refrigerator. You can also add some lemon juice or pineapple juice to the soaking water to eliminate any possibility of "off" flavors.

Making Sausage Links or Ropes

To stuff your sausage mixture into casings, grind the meat, then mix it with the seasonings and other ingredients in a large bowl or a plastic tub. You'll need to use a stuffer horn, which looks like a funnel. Knot the end of a piece of casing, then attach the open end to the horn of the stuffer. Accordion the casing onto the horn so that the stuffing mixture doesn't have to go so far to reach the end of the casing. Or use shorter lengths of casing.

To use a stuffer to form your sausage into links or ropes, add a little ice water to the meat; this helps the meat slide through the stuffer more easily. If you want to stuff the mixture into a casing and don't have a stuffer, you can use a funnel that has an opening of the desired size. You will also need a plunger, usually an 8- to 12-inch-long dowel stick a little smaller in diameter than the diameter of the stuffer horn or funnel opening; this is to push the meat mixture down into the casings. Then just start spooning and pressing the sausage mixture into the opening of the stuffer horn or funnel and push it down into the casing. Stuff the casings until they are firm but not bulging.

If you're using the stuffer attachment on a stand mixer, it will feed automatically, but you may want a helper when doing this; one person feeds in the sausage mixture, the other person manages the links as they fill.

To make links or ropes, twist the casing around several times to tie off the sausage at 4- or 6-inch intervals or however long you want the links or ropes to be. Some people knot kitchen string to tie off each link or rope. Do whatever works for you.

Homemade sausage will last up to 1 week in the refrigerator and can be wrapped well and frozen for up to 6 months. Defrost in the refrigerator overnight before cooking.

Cooking Sausage

The techniques for cooking most sausages—whether patties, loaves, links, or ropes—are the same, whether you're grilling over direct heat or smoking over indirect heat.

Sausage patties are usually grilled over direct heat. Cook them over medium-hot coals, with the lid of the grill closed, for about 10 minutes per side for a 4-ounce patty 4 to 5 inches in diameter. That should give you nice, juicy sausage "burgers." They should be cooked until they are no longer pink in the middle but are still moist. You can also slow smoke sausage patties over indirect heat; they take about 1½ to 2 hours to cook completely.

Stuffed or linked sausage can be grilled or smoked. If you're grilling, do so over medium coals with the lid down, turning every 10 minutes

so the casings don't burst. If fat pockets form bubbles on the sausage, move the sausages away from the coals and poke a small hole in the side of the bubble to drain the fat away from the hot coals, so there are no flare-ups. Then move the sausage back to the direct heat. A linked sausage about 1¼ inches in diameter should take 10 to 20 minutes to grill.

To slow smoke or barbecue linked sausage or sausage loaves of any size, simply place the sausage on the indirect side of the grill or on your pit. After the sausage has cooked for about 1 hour, turn and baste if you want. Linked sausage and loaves take 2½ to 3 hours to smoke. Sausage sticks take a little less time, 1½ to 2½ hours.

Cook sausage to an internal temperature of 165 degrees F, being careful not to dry it out. Cooking sausage too hot can toughen the casings. Cooking with moisture (such as a water pan) usually helps, as does pricking the casings before cooking, which allows the sausage to be basted by its own fat. If you prick the casings first, be sure to place the sausage in a disposable aluminum pan to grill, so you don't have flare-ups.

Beginner's Chili Sausage

This is a very good sausage for barbecue competition, especially for first-time sausage makers. I use ground oregano and powdered bay leaf because they both blend into invisibility, leaving the flavor but no color. If I plan ahead or I'm using the sausage in competition, I let the mixture set overnight to let the flavors blend before stuffing the casings. But even without the wait, this sausage will still be good even if you make it and cook it the right way. MAKES 2 POUNDS

- 2 pounds boneless Boston pork butt, trimmed of excess fat, cubed, then chilled for about 1 hour to firm up
- 1 tablespoon chili seasoning, homemade (page 116) or store-bought
- 2 teaspoons sweet Hungarian paprika
- 1 teaspoon granulated onion
- 1 teaspoon seasoned salt, homemade (page 108) or store-bought
- 1/2 teaspoon pure ground chipotle chile
- 1/2 teaspoon granulated garlic
- 1/2 teaspoon finely ground black pepper
- 1/2 teaspoon ground cumin
- 1/4 teaspoon ground thyme
- 1/4 teaspoon ground allspice
- 1/4 teaspoon dried oregano leaves, crushed, then ground into a powder in a spice grinder
- 1/4 teaspoon cayenne pepper
- 1/8 teaspoon powdered bay leaf
- About 5 feet (38 to 42mm-diameter) hog casings (optional), prepared for stuffing (see page 306)

1 Grind the chilled pork butt cubes through a 1/4-inch grinder plate into a large bowl.

2 Combine the spices and herbs in a small bowl and blend well. Add one-third of the seasoning

mixture to the pork and blend well. Add another third of the seasoning mixture and blend. Add the rest of the seasoning mixture and blend well. Knead the mixture until it is blended well. For the best flavor, cover with plastic wrap and refrigerate overnight.

3 Form the mixture into patties or stuff into the casings, if using (see page 306), and cook as desired (see page 307).

Fresh Kielbasa

When you make your own sausage, such as this fresh kielbasa, it just naturally tastes better because there are no fillers or extenders—just pure pleasure and flavor. If you want smoked kielbasa, prepare an indirect fire with hickory wood and smoke the sausage for 2 1/2 to 3 hours. MAKES ABOUT 5 POUNDS

- 5 pounds boneless Boston pork butt, trimmed of excess fat, cubed, then chilled until firm
- 3 tablespoons minced garlic
- 1 tablespoon dried marjoram leaves
- 1 tablespoon coarsely ground black pepper
- 1 tablespoon kosher salt
- 2 teaspoons dry mustard (I use Colman's)
- 1 teaspoon ground coriander
- 1/2 cup ice water, as needed
- About 5 feet (38 to 42mm-diameter) hog casings (optional), prepared for stuffing (see page 306)

1 Grind the pork butt through a 1/4-inch grinder plate into a large bowl.

2 Combine the garlic, marjoram, pepper, salt, dry mustard, and coriander in a small bowl and blend well. Add the seasoning mixture to the pork

one-third at a time, mixing well after each addition. Knead the mixture until it is blended well. The mixture should be sticky so that it binds together; if it is too dry, add as much of the ice water as necessary to get the right consistency. For the best flavor, cover with plastic wrap and refrigerate overnight.

3 Form the mixture into patties or stuff into the casings, if using (see page 306). Refrigerated, the sausage mixture will keep for up to 3 days, in the freezer, up to 6 months. Cook as desired (see page 307).

Garlic Kielbasa

This is my favorite Polish sausage; I love it grilled and served with potato salad and baked beans. MAKES 5 POUNDS

- 5 pounds boneless Boston pork butt, trimmed of excess fat, cubed, then chilled until firm
- 3 tablespoons sweet Hungarian paprika
- 2 tablespoons granulated garlic
- 1 tablespoon freshly ground black pepper
- 1 tablespoon seasoned salt, homemade (page 108) or store-bought
- 2 teaspoons dried marjoram leaves
- 1 teaspoon ground coriander
- 1 teaspoon dried savory leaves
- 1 cup ice water, as needed
- About 5 feet (38 to 42mm-diameter) hog casings (optional), prepared for stuffing (see page 306)

1 Grind the pork through a 5/16-inch plate into a large bowl.

2 Combine the paprika, garlic, pepper, salt, marjoram, coriander, and savory in a small bowl and blend well.

3 Add one-third of the seasoning mixture to the ground pork and knead well to blend. Repeat the process two more times until all the seasonings are well blended into the meat. The mixture should be sticky so that it binds together; if it is too dry, add as much of the ice water as necessary to get the right consistency. (If you are going to stuff the sausage into casings, it will be easier if it has more moisture.) For the best flavor, cover with plastic wrap and refrigerate overnight.

4 Form the mixture into patties, logs, loaves, or sticks or stuff into the casings, if using (see page 306). It will keep for up to 3 days in the refrigerator and up to 6 months in the freezer. Cook as desired (see page 307).

Spicy Polish Smoked Sausage

This recipe is very close to Cajun andouille, which has more garlic in it. Polish sausage ranks second behind Italian sausage as the favorite of competition barbecue teams. Morton's Tender Quick is a curing mixture available in the spice section of the grocery store. Serve this sausage with red beans and rice. MAKES 5 POUNDS

5 pounds boneless Boston pork butt, trimmed of excess fat, cubed, then chilled until firm

1 cup powdered milk (not granulated milk)

3 tablespoons fine sea salt

1 tablespoon yellow mustard seeds

1 tablespoon rubbed sage

1 tablespoon crushed red pepper

1 tablespoon firmly packed light brown sugar

1 tablespoon finely ground black pepper

1 teaspoon Morton's Tender Quick

2 teaspoons granulated garlic

1 teaspoon dried marjoram leaves

1 teaspoon cayenne pepper

1/2 teaspoon ground mace

1 cup ice water

1 tablespoon liquid smoke flavoring (optional)

About 5 feet (38 to 42mm-diameter) hog casings (optional), prepared for stuffing (see page 306)

1 Grind the pork butt through a 1/4-inch grinder plate into a large bowl.

2 Combine the powdered milk, salt, mustard seeds, sage, red pepper, brown sugar, black pepper, Tender Quick, garlic, marjoram, cayenne, and mace in a small bowl and blend well. In another small bowl, combine the water and liquid smoke.

3 Add one-third of the seasoning mixture and half of the smoky water mixture to the ground pork and blend well. Add another third of the seasoning mixture and knead well to blend in, then add the remaining seasoning mixture and knead well to blend. The mixture should be sticky so that it binds together; if it is too dry, add more of the smoky water as necessary to get the right consistency. For the best flavor, cover with plastic wrap and refrigerate overnight.

4 Form the mixture into patties or stuff into the casings, if using (see page 306). The mixture will keep for up to 3 days in the refrigerator, up to 6 months in the freezer. Cook as desired (see page 307).

Portuguese Chourico

This sausage is similar to linguica, a Portuguese chorizo that can be either dry-cured like salami or cooked fresh. Chourico has a different spice mixture and a bit of cayenne to give it more heat. It also has a higher ratio of fat to lean, so you add some fatback and use all the fat from the pork butt itself. **MAKES ABOUT 3 1/2 POUNDS**

3 tablespoons sweet Hungarian paprika

4 teaspoons kosher salt

1 tablespoon minced garlic

1 teaspoon freshly ground black pepper

1 teaspoon cayenne pepper

1 teaspoon ground cumin

1/2 teaspoon dried marjoram leaves

1/2 teaspoon ground coriander

3 tablespoons red wine vinegar

3 pounds boneless Boston pork butt

1/2 pound pork fatback

About 4 feet (38 to 42mm-diameter) hog casings, prepared for stuffing (see page 306)

1 Combine the paprika, salt, garlic, black pepper, cayenne, cumin, marjoram, coriander, and vinegar in a small bowl to create a paste.

2 Trim all the external fat from the pork and refrigerate the fat along with the fatback. Meanwhile, cut the lean meat into strips 3 inches long

by 1 inch wide and liberally coat them with the seasoning paste. Reserve any extra paste. Pack the meat into a plastic tub or nonreactive bowl, cover tightly, and refrigerate overnight to let the flavors develop.

3 The next day, grind the lean pork through a very coarse (3/8- or 1/2-inch) plate, then grind the fat through a 1/4-inch plate into a large bowl. Mix together the lean meat and fat along with any remaining seasoning paste. Knead and squeeze the mixture until all the ingredients are thoroughly blended. Stuff into the hog casings and tie into 10-inch links (see page 306). The mixture will keep for up to 3 days in the refrigerator and up to 6 months in the freezer. Cook as desired (see page 307).

CHORIZO

Chorizo is the Spanish word referring to sausage in general, so it can be a bit confusing when you find the word referring to different types of sausages made in Spain, Mexico, South America, and (with slightly different spellings) in Portugal (chourico) and Louisiana (chaurico).

Linguica

Linguica is one of a family of smoked sausages that are coarse in texture and usually fairly spicy. This sausage traditionally is not hot smoked as barbecue, but it's still mighty good. MAKES ABOUT 3 1/2 POUNDS

3 tablespoons sweet Hungarian paprika

4 teaspoons kosher salt

1 tablespoon freshly ground black pepper

1 tablespoon minced garlic

1/2 teaspoon dried marjoram leaves

1/2 teaspoon dried oregano leaves

Pinch of ground coriander

3 tablespoons red wine vinegar

3 pounds boneless Boston pork butt

1/2 pound pork fatback

About 4 feet (38 to 42mm-diameter) hog casings, prepared for stuffing (see page 306)

1 Combine the paprika, salt, pepper, garlic, marjoram, oregano, coriander, and vinegar in a small bowl.

2 Trim all the external fat from the pork and refrigerate the fat along with the fatback. Cut the lean meat into strips 3 inches long by 1 inch wide and liberally coat them with the seasoning paste. Reserve any remaining paste. Pack the meat into a plastic tub or nonreactive bowl, cover tightly, and refrigerate overnight to let the flavors develop.

3 The next day, grind the lean pork through a very coarse (3/8- or 1/2-inch) plate, then grind the fat through a 1/4-inch plate into a large bowl. Mix together the lean meat and the fat along with any remaining seasoning paste. Knead and squeeze the mixture until all the ingredients are thoroughly blended. Stuff into the casings and tie into 10-inch links (see page 306). The mixture will keep for up to 3 days in the refrigerator and up to 6 months in the freezer. Cook as desired (see page 307).

Spanish Hot Mama Sausage

This sausage will wake you up! **MAKES ABOUT 2 POUNDS**

- 2 pounds lean pork, such as tenderloin or loin, cubed and chilled until firm
- 1/4 cup distilled white vinegar
- 2 tablespoons chili powder, homemade (page 111) or store-bought
- 1 to 2 tablespoons crushed red pepper, to your taste
- 2 teaspoons fine sea salt
- 1 teaspoon dried oregano leaves
- 1 teaspoon freshly ground black pepper
- 1/4 teaspoon ground cumin
- About 5 feet (38 to 42mm-diameter) hog casings, prepared for stuffing (see page 306)

1 Grind the pork through a 3/8-inch plate into a large bowl. Add the remaining ingredients, except the casings, and knead thoroughly to blend well. For the best flavor, cover with plastic wrap and refrigerate overnight.

2 Stuff the meat mixture into the prepared casings and tie into 10-inch links (see page 306). The mixture will keep for up to 3 days in the refrigerator and up to 6 months in the freezer. Cook as desired (see page 307).

The Baron's Breakfast Sausage

This is an excellent sausage to make sausage gravy with, either from the raw state or smoked first. I have also made this sausage using turkey and chicken meat. The biggest problem with using chicken or turkey is that the meat is so lean that it can get rubbery, especially if it's overcooked. But it still tastes good. **MAKES ABOUT 5 POUNDS**

- 2 tablespoons fine sea salt or seasoned salt, homemade (page 108) or store-bought
- 2 tablespoons rubbed sage
- 1 1/2 teaspoons crushed red pepper (optional)
- 1 teaspoon ground coriander
- 1/2 teaspoon ground ginger
- 1/2 teaspoon ground thyme
- 1/2 teaspoon cayenne pepper
- 1/4 teaspoon ground nutmeg
- 5 pounds boneless Boston pork butt, trimmed of excess fat, cubed, then chilled until firm
- 1/2 to 1 cup ice water, as needed
- About 5 feet (38 to 42mm-diameter) sheep casings (optional), prepared for stuffing (see page 306)

1 Combine the seasonings in a small bowl and blend well.

2 Grind the pork through a 3/16-inch grinder plate into a large bowl. Add the seasoning mixture one-third at a time, kneading after each addition, until everything is blended well. The mixture should be sticky so that it binds together; if it is too dry, add as much of the ice water as necessary to get the right consistency. For the best flavor, cover with plastic wrap and refrigerate overnight.

3 Form the mixture into patties, sticks, or logs or stuff into the casings, if using (see page 306). The mixture will keep for up to 3 days in the refrigerator and up to 6 months in the freezer. Cook as desired (see page 307).

Creole Pork Sausage

Directly from Chef Paul K's Kitchen (my own, when I put on my chef's and not my barbecue hat), this sausage has a light bite. MAKES ABOUT 5 POUNDS

- 2 tablespoons dried parsley flakes
- 2 tablespoons seasoned salt, homemade (page 108) or store-bought
- 1 tablespoon granulated garlic
- 1 tablespoon granulated onion
- 1 tablespoon freshly ground black pepper
- 1 teaspoon crushed red pepper
- 1 teaspoon sweet Hungarian paprika
- 1/2 teaspoon cayenne pepper
- 1/2 teaspoon ground allspice
- 1/4 teaspoon powdered bay leaf
- 5 pounds boneless Boston pork butt, trimmed of excess fat, cubed, then chilled until firm
- 1/2 cup ice water, as needed (optional)
- 9 to 12 feet (28 to 32mm-diameter) hog casings (optional), prepared for stuffing (see page 306)

1 Combine all the seasonings in a small bowl.

2 Grind the pork through a 3/8-inch grinder plate into a large bowl. Add the seasoning mixture one-third at a time, kneading after each addition to combine everything thoroughly. The mixture should be sticky so that it binds together; if it is too dry, add as much of the ice water as necessary to get the right consistency. For the best flavor, cover with plastic wrap and refrigerate overnight.

3 Form the mixture into patties, logs, sticks, or loaves or stuff into the casings, if using (see page 306). The mixture will keep for up to 3 days in the refrigerator and up to 6 months in the freezer. Cook as desired (see page 307).

Andouille

You will enjoy this prized Louisiana sausage, which flavors all kinds of gumbos, red beans and rice, and étouffées. MAKES 5 POUNDS

- 1/4 cup cracked black peppercorns
- 2 tablespoons cayenne pepper
- 2 tablespoons sweet Hungarian paprika
- 1 tablespoon ground thyme
- 1 tablespoon kosher salt
- 2 teaspoons rubbed sage
- 1 teaspoon ground allspice
- 1/2 teaspoon powdered bay leaf
- 5 pounds boneless Boston pork butt, trimmed of excess fat, cubed, then chilled until firm
- 1/2 cup minced garlic
- About 5 feet (38 to 42mm-diameter) hog casings (optional), prepared for stuffing (see page 306)

1 Combine all the seasonings in a medium-size bowl.

2 Grind the pork through a 3/8-inch grinder plate into a large bowl.

Add the garlic, kneading to combine well. Add the seasoning mixture one-third at a time, kneading well after each addition, until fully combined. For the best flavor, cover with plastic wrap and refrigerate overnight.

3 Form the mixture into patties, loaves, logs, or sticks or stuff into the casings, if using (see page 306). The mixture will keep for up to 3 days in the refrigerator and up to 6 months in the freezer. Cook as desired (see page 307).

Acadian Andouille

This recipe is also a good representative of Louisiana; it has less garlic flavor than the regular andouille (page 313).

MAKES 5 POUNDS

- ¼ cup granulated garlic
- ¼ cup coarsely ground black pepper
- 2 tablespoons cayenne pepper
- 2 tablespoons seasoned salt, homemade (page 108) or store-bought
- 1 tablespoon dried thyme leaves
- 4½ pounds boneless Boston pork butt, trimmed of excess fat, cubed, then chilled until firm
- ½ pound pork fatback, chilled
- About 5 feet (38 to 42mm-diameter) hog casings (optional), prepared for stuffing (see page 306)

1 Combine the seasonings in a small bowl.

2 Grind the pork through a ³/₈-inch grinder plate, then grind the fatback through a ¼-inch plate into a large bowl. Knead together thoroughly until the fat is evenly distributed throughout the mixture. Add the seasoning mixture one-third at a time, kneading well after each addition. For the best flavor, cover with plastic wrap and refrigerate overnight.

3 Form the mixture into patties, sticks, logs, or loaves or stuff into the casings, if using (see page 306). The mixture will keep for up to 3 days in the refrigerator and up to 6 months in the freezer. Cook as desired (see page 307).

The Baron's Sweet Italian Sausage

I have used this recipe in competition many times. Won some, lost some, but I still love it. The "sweet" in this sausage comes from fennel seeds. MAKES 5 POUNDS

- 2 tablespoons seasoned salt, homemade (page 108) or store-bought
- 2 tablespoons dried parsley flakes
- 1 tablespoon granulated garlic
- 1 tablespoon freshly ground black pepper
- 1 tablespoon granulated cane sugar
- 2 teaspoons fennel seeds
- 1 teaspoon dried oregano leaves
- 5 pounds boneless Boston pork butt, trimmed of excess fat, cubed, then chilled until firm
- About 5 feet (38 to 42mm-diameter) hog casings (optional), prepared for stuffing (see page 306)

1 Combine the seasonings in a small bowl and blend well.

2 Grind the pork through a ³/₈-inch grinder plate into a large bowl. Add the seasoning mixture one-third at a time, kneading well after each addition, until the meat is sticky and holds together. For the best flavor, cover with plastic wrap and refrigerate overnight.

3 Form the mixture into patties, logs, loaves, or sticks or stuff into the casings, if using (see page 306). The mixture will keep for up to 3 days in the refrigerator and up to 6 months in the freezer. Cook as desired (see page 307).

School of Pitmasters Italian Pepper Sausage

I usually prepare this sausage for my Pitmasters class. Add only 1 tablespoon of crushed red pepper if you don't want to overwhelm delicate taste buds; either way, it's good.
MAKES 5 POUNDS

- 2 tablespoons seasoned salt, homemade (page 108) or store-bought
- 1 to 2 tablespoons crushed red pepper, to your taste
- 1 tablespoon granulated garlic
- 1 tablespoon granulated onion
- 1 tablespoon freshly ground black pepper
- 1 tablespoon sweet Hungarian paprika
- 2 teaspoons fennel seeds
- $1/2$ teaspoon powdered bay leaf
- $1/4$ teaspoon ground thyme
- $1/4$ teaspoon ground coriander
- 5 pounds boneless Boston pork butt, trimmed of excess fat, cubed, then chilled until firm
- $1/2$ cup red wine or ice water, as needed
- 9 to 12 feet (28 to 32mm-diameter) hog casings (optional), prepared for stuffing (see page 306)

1 Combine the seasonings in a small bowl.

2 Grind the pork through a $5/16$-inch grinder plate into a large bowl. Mix in the seasoning mixture one-third at a time, kneading after each addition, until the mixture is sticky and holds together. If it is too dry, add as much wine as needed to get the right consistency. For the best flavor, cover with plastic wrap and refrigerate overnight.

3 Form the mixture into patties, logs, sticks, or loaves or stuff into the casings, if using (see page 306). The mixture will keep for up to 3 days in the refrigerator and up to 6 months in the freezer. Cook as desired (see page 307).

Italian Garlic Sausage

Barbecue this sausage and serve it over pasta with a mixture of 1 cup barbecue sauce and 1 cup tomato sauce. Have lots of garlic bread on hand to mop up the sauce. **MAKES 5 POUNDS**

- 2 tablespoons fine kosher or sea salt
- 1 tablespoon freshly ground black pepper
- 1 tablespoon granulated cane sugar
- 1 tablespoon crushed red pepper
- 2 teaspoons fennel seeds
- 1 teaspoon dried oregano leaves
- 1 teaspoon rubbed sage
- $1/2$ teaspoon ground thyme
- 5 pounds boneless Boston pork butt, trimmed of excess fat, cubed, then chilled until firm
- $1/4$ cup minced or pressed garlic
- $1/2$ cup ice water, as needed
- About 5 feet (38 to 42mm-diameter) hog casings (optional), prepared for stuffing (see page 306)

1 Combine the seasonings in a small bowl and blend well.

2 Grind the pork through a $3/8$-inch grinder plate into a large bowl.

3 Add the garlic to the ground pork and knead until evenly distributed through the meat. Add the seasoning mixture one-third at a time, blending

well until the mixture is sticky and holds together. If it is too dry, add as much of the ice water as necessary to get the right consistency. For the best flavor, cover with plastic wrap and refrigerate overnight.

4 Form the mixture into patties, logs, sticks, or loaves or stuff into the casings, if using (see page 306). The mixture will keep for up to 3 days in the refrigerator and up to 6 months in the freezer. Cook as desired (see page 307).

Spicy Good-Enough-for-a-Barbecue-Contest Sausage

This recipe is a multiple blue-ribbon winner! MAKES 5 POUNDS

- 2½ pounds boneless Boston pork butt, trimmed of excess fat, cubed, then chilled until firm
- 2½ pounds beef chuck, cubed and chilled until firm
- 1 cup powdered milk (not granulated milk)
- 2 tablespoons Barbecue Spice (page 115)
- 1 tablespoon granulated garlic
- 1 tablespoon seasoned salt, homemade (page 108) or store-bought
- 1 tablespoon chili powder, homemade (page 111) or store-bought
- 1 tablespoon granulated cane sugar
- 1 tablespoon freshly ground black pepper
- 1 tablespoon rubbed sage
- 2 teaspoons ground cumin
- 2 teaspoons crushed red pepper
- 1 heaping teaspoon ground marjoram

- 1 teaspoon cayenne pepper
- 1 cup ice water, as needed
- 2 large eggs, if needed
- 5 feet (38 to 42mm-diameter) hog casings (optional), prepared for stuffing (see page 306)

1 Grind the pork and beef through a 5/16-inch grinder plate into a large bowl. Combine the meats with your hands until thoroughly mixed, cover with plastic wrap, and set aside.

2 In a medium-size bowl, combine the powdered milk, Barbecue Spice, garlic, seasoned salt, chili powder, black pepper, sage, cumin, red pepper, marjoram, and cayenne, blending well. Add seasoning mixture one-third at a time to the meat mixture, kneading after each addition until well combined. The mixture should be sticky so that it binds together; if it is too dry, add as much of the ice water as necessary to get the right consistency. If it still does not bind together, add the eggs. For the best flavor, cover with plastic wrap and refrigerate overnight.

3 Form the mixture into patties, logs, loaves, or sticks or stuff into the casings, if using (see page 306). The mixture will keep for up to 3 days in the refrigerator and up to 6 months in the freezer. Cook as desired (see page 307).

Texas Hill Country Hot-Gut Sausage

Don't let the title scare you. This traditional spicy Texas sausage is a good one. If you go to butcher shops throughout Texas, you'll find lots of versions of hot gut, which is hot sausage packed in hog gut. MAKES 5 POUNDS

2 tablespoons granulated onion

2 tablespoons crushed red pepper

1 tablespoon granulated garlic

1 tablespoon rubbed sage

1 tablespoon seasoned salt, homemade (page 108) or store-bought

1 tablespoon coarsely ground black pepper

1 teaspoon cayenne pepper

3 pounds boneless Boston pork butt, trimmed of excess fat, cubed, then chilled until firm

2 pounds beef chuck, cubed and chilled until firm

1/2 cup ice water, as needed

About 5 feet (38 to 42mm-diameter) hog casings (optional), prepared for stuffing (see page 306)

1 Combine the seasonings in a small bowl and blend well.

2 Grind the pork and beef through a 5/16-inch grinder plate into a large bowl. Mix them together with your hands until thoroughly combined. Add the seasoning mixture one-third at a time, kneading after each addition. The mixture should be sticky so that it binds together; if it is too dry, add as much of the ice water as necessary to get the right consistency. For the best flavor, cover with plastic wrap and refrigerate overnight.

3 Form the mixture into patties, sticks, logs, or loaves or stuff into the casings, if using (see page 306). The mixture will keep for up to 3 days in the refrigerator and up to 6 months in the freezer. Cook as desired (see page 307).

Texas Smoky Spiced Links

This is a very good sausage. I ought to know—I stole it from Glenn Chandler, the owner of Krause's Cafe in New Braunfels, a town that could be called the Sausage Capital of Texas. If you are ever in the area, stop in and say hey! Besides great barbecue, Glenn has some of the best German food around. You'll have to rib him for leaving this recipe lying around where I could get my hands on it, especially because it took an Honorable Mention at the American Royal Barbecue Contest in the Sausage category.

MAKES 5 POUNDS

1 tablespoon ground coriander

1 tablespoon ground cumin

1 tablespoon granulated garlic

1 tablespoon seasoned salt, homemade (page 108) or store-bought

1 tablespoon freshly ground black pepper

2 teaspoons crushed red pepper

1 teaspoon ground allspice

1/2 teaspoon ground cloves

3 pounds boneless Boston pork butt, trimmed of excess fat, cubed, then chilled until firm

2 pounds beef chuck, cubed and chilled until firm

1/2 cup ice water, as needed

About 5 feet (38 to 42mm-diameter) hog casings (optional), prepared for stuffing (see page 306)

1 Combine the seasonings in a small bowl and blend well.

2 Grind the pork through a 3/8-inch grinder plate into a bowl. Grind the beef through a 3/16-inch grinder plate into a bowl.

3 Transfer both meats to a very large bowl and mix together with your hands until thoroughly

combined. Add the seasoning mixture one-third at a time, kneading after each addition. The mixture should be sticky so that it binds together; if it is too dry, add as much of the ice water as necessary to get the right consistency. For the best flavor, cover with plastic wrap and refrigerate overnight.

4 Form the mixture into patties, sticks, logs, or loaves or stuff into the casings, if using (see page 306). The mixture will keep for up to 3 days in the refrigerator and up to 6 months in the freezer. Cook as desired (see page 307).

Spicy Green Onion Sausage

I came across this sausage while conducting a Pitmasters class in Slidell, Louisiana, for the Slidell Lions Club. I really enjoyed it, so I went home and replicated the flavor and texture in this recipe. This sausage is really, really good barbecued over your choice of wood. MAKES 5 POUNDS

- 2 tablespoons seasoned salt, homemade (page 108) or store-bought
- 1 tablespoon granulated garlic
- 1 tablespoon medium-grind black pepper
- 1 tablespoon sweet Hungarian paprika
- 2 teaspoons crushed red pepper
- 2 teaspoons sugar
- 1 teaspoon cayenne pepper or or pure ground chipotle chile
- 1 teaspoon chili powder, homemade (page 111) or store-bought
- 1 teaspoon ground cumin
- 3 pounds boneless Boston pork butt, trimmed of excess fat, cubed, then chilled until firm
- 2 pounds beef chuck, cubed and chilled until firm

- 1 cup thinly sliced green onions (green and white parts) or 1/3 cup dried chives
- 1/2 cup buttermilk
- About 5 feet (38 to 42mm-diameter) hog casings (optional), prepared for stuffing (see page 306)

1 Combine the seasonings in a small bowl and blend well.

2 Grind the pork through a 3/8-inch grinder plate into a bowl. Grind the beef through a 3/16-inch grinder plate into a bowl.

3 Transfer the pork and beef to a very large bowl, add the green onions, and mix together with your hands until thoroughly combined. Pour 1/4 cup of the buttermilk over the meat mixture along with one-third of the seasoning mixture and mix well. Pour the remaining 1/4 cup of buttermilk over the meat and another third of the seasoning mixture and mix well. Add the remaining seasoning mixture and blend well. Cover with plastic wrap and refrigerate for 2 to 4 hours to let the flavors develop.

4 Form the mixture into patties, loaves, sticks, or logs or stuff into the casings, if using (see page 306). The mixture will keep for up to 3 days in the refrigerator and up to 6 months in the freezer. Cook as desired (see page 307).

The Baron's Bratwurst

I like to simmer this sausage in beer for 5 to 10 minutes, then grill it and enjoy it with spicy brown mustard and some barbecue sauce. MAKES 5 POUNDS

1 cup powdered milk (not granulated milk)

¼ cup fine dry bread crumbs

1 tablespoon fine sea salt

1½ teaspoons freshly ground white pepper

1 teaspoon granulated onion

½ teaspoon ground mace

¼ teaspoon ground cloves

4 pounds boneless Boston pork butt, trimmed of excess fat, cubed, then chilled until firm

1 pound boneless veal or white chicken or turkey meat, cubed and chilled until firm

½ cup ice water or chicken broth, or more as needed

About 5 feet (38 to 42 mm-diameter) hog casings (optional), prepared for stuffing (page 306)

1 Combine the powdered milk, bread crumbs, and seasonings in a medium-size bowl and blend well.

2 Grind the pork through a $^4/_{16}$-inch grinder plate into a bowl. Grind the veal through a $^3/_{16}$-inch grinder plate into a bowl.

3 Transfer the pork and veal to a large bowl and mix with your hands until thoroughly combined. Add one-third of the seasoning mixture , kneading until well blended. Blend in one-third of the seasoning mixture, then add ¼ cup of the water and knead thoroughly. Add the remaining seasoning mixture and water, kneading. The mixture should be sticky so that it binds together; if it is too dry, add more ice water as necessary to get the right consistency. For the best flavor, cover with plastic wrap and refrigerate overnight.

4 Form the mixture into patties, loaves, logs, or sticks or stuff into the casings, if using (see page 306). The mixture will keep for up to 3 days in the refrigerator and up to 6 months in the freezer. Cook as desired (see page 307).

Onion Bratwurst

This is a new sausage that I was introduced to while running the Red, Hot, and Wild barbecue contest in Topeka, Kansas. One of my students, Mark Born, a.k.a. Grandpa Cheese, made it for the Sausage category. He offered me a taste, and I was hooked; the bratwurst flavor has a slight hint of onion. MAKES 5 POUNDS

4 pounds boneless Boston pork butt, trimmed of excess fat, cubed, then chilled until firm

1 pound boneless veal or white chicken or turkey meat, cubed and chilled until firm

1 cup powdered milk (not granulated milk)

¼ cup fine dry bread crumbs

2 tablespoons fine sea salt

2 tablespoons granulated onion

2 teaspoons freshly ground white pepper

1 teaspoon rubbed sage

½ teaspoon ground mace

½ teaspoon ground ginger

½ teaspoon finely ground black pepper

¼ teaspoon ground cloves

1 large egg

½ cup ice water or chicken broth, or more as needed

About 5 feet (38 to 42mm-diameter) hog casings (optional), prepared for stuffing (see page 306)

1 Grind the pork through a $^3/_8$-inch grinder plate into a bowl. Grind the veal through a $^3/_{16}$-inch grinder plate into a bowl.

2 Combine the powdered milk, bread crumbs, salt, onion, white pepper, sage, mace, ginger, black

pepper, and cloves in a medium-size bowl and blend well.

3 Transfer the pork and veal to a large bowl, add the egg, and blend until thoroughly combined. Add one-third of the seasoning mixture, kneading well. Add one-third of the seasoning mixture, blend well, then add ¼ cup of the water and knead thoroughly. Add the remaining seasoning mixture and the remaining ¼ cup of water and knead. The mixture should be sticky so that it binds together; if it is too dry, add more ice water as necessary to get the right consistency. For the best flavor, cover with plastic wrap and refrigerate overnight.

4 Form the mixture into patties, logs, loaves, or sticks or stuff into the casings, if using (see page 306). The mixture will keep for up to 3 days in the refrigerator and up to 6 months in the freezer. Cook as desired (see page 307).

Lamb and Pork Sausage with Cilantro and Juniper

Lamb sausage is very difficult to find in the Kansas City area, even though we have several very good sausage makers in town, so I make my own. When I enter the annual National Lamb-B-Que Cook-off held over Labor Day weekend in Bonner Springs, Kansas, I usually make a lamb sausage like this one or Garlic-Mint Lamb Sausage (page 321). MAKES 5 POUNDS

2 tablespoons granulated garlic

2 tablespoons seasoned salt, homemade (page 108) or store-bought

2 tablespoons dried cilantro leaves

1 tablespoon freshly ground black pepper

1 tablespoon granulated cane sugar

1 teaspoon ground cumin

1 teaspoon granulated onion

½ teaspoon ground juniper berries

½ teaspoon ground nutmeg

3 pounds boneless lamb shoulder, cubed and chilled until firm

2 pounds boneless Boston pork butt, trimmed of excess fat, cubed, then chilled until firm

½ cup red wine or ice water, as needed

About 5 feet (38 to 42mm-diameter) hog casings (optional), prepared for stuffing (see page 306)

1 Combine the seasonings in a small bowl and blend well.

2 Grind the lamb and pork through a ⅜-inch grinder plate into a large bowl. Add the seasoning mixture one-third at a time, kneading after each addition. The mixture should be sticky so that it binds together; if it is too dry, add as much of the wine as necessary to get the right consistency. For the best flavor, cover with plastic wrap and refrigerate overnight.

3 Form the mixture into patties, logs, loaves, or sticks or stuff into the casings, if using (see page 306). The mixture will keep for up to 3 days in the refrigerator and up to 6 months in the freezer. Cook as desired (see page 307).

Garlic-Mint Lamb and Pork Sausage

This is my favorite lamb sausage, which helped me take a third-place white ribbon at the 2002 National Lamb-B-Que Cook-off. **MAKES 5 POUNDS**

    2 tablespoons dried mint leaves

    1 tablespoon granulated garlic

    1 tablespoon seasoned salt, homemade (page 108) or store-bought

    2 teaspoons finely ground black pepper

    2 teaspoons granulated onion

    1 teaspoon dried summer savory leaves

    1/2 teaspoon ground mace

    3 pounds boneless lamb shoulder, cubed and chilled until firm

    2 pounds boneless Boston pork butt, trimmed of excess fat, cubed, then chilled until firm

    1/2 cup ice water, as needed

    About 5 feet (38 to 42mm-diameter) hog casings (optional), prepared for stuffing (see page 306)

1 Combine the seasonings in a small bowl and blend well.

2 Grind the lamb through a 5/16-inch grinder plate into a bowl. Grind the pork through a 3/16-inch grinder plate into a bowl.

3 Transfer the lamb and pork to a large bowl and mix together with your hands until thoroughly combined. Add the seasoning mixture one-third at a time, kneading after each addition. The mixture should be sticky so that it binds together; if it is too dry, add as much of the ice water as necessary to get the right consistency. For the best flavor, cover with plastic wrap and refrigerate overnight.

4 Form the mixture into patties, logs, loaves, or sticks or stuff into the casings, if using (see page 306). The mixture will keep for up to 3 days in the refrigerator and up to 6 months in the freezer. Cook as desired (see page 307).

Rosemary-Mustard Lamb and Beef Sausage

Here are all the seasonings you love on a roasted rack of lamb, only in a different composition. Grill and serve this with a béarnaise sauce for a touch of haute smoke! **MAKES 5 POUNDS**

    1 tablespoon granulated garlic

    2 teaspoons dried rosemary leaves

    1 teaspoon ground ginger

    1 teaspoon kosher salt

    1/2 teaspoon cayenne pepper

    1/4 teaspoon ground nutmeg

    3 pounds boneless lamb shoulder, cubed and chilled until firm

    2 pounds beef chuck, cubed and chilled until firm

    2 tablespoons coarse-grain mustard

    2 tablespoons fruity olive oil

    1 tablespoon soy sauce

    1/2 cup ice water, as needed

    About 5 feet (38 to 42mm-diameter) hog casings (optional), prepared for stuffing (see page 306)

1 Combine the garlic, rosemary, ginger, salt, cayenne, and nutmeg in a small bowl and blend well.

Toasting WHOLE SPICES, Nuts, and Noodles

To get the maximum flavor from whole spices, nuts, and noodles, I toast them first. This step releases the oils and the aroma in the dry ingredients so that they flavor the dish before cooking or right before serving.

Toasting nuts and noodles is also an extra step I take if I want to make a really good side dish, such as Toasted Sesame Oriental Cabbage Slaw (page 438). In that recipe, I toast the sesame seeds, the almonds, and the dry ramen noodles.

I only toast and then grind whole spices, such as black and Szechuan peppercorns, allspice, cumin, coriander, and sesame seeds. Cloves are too difficult to grind, so I buy that spice already ground. I have found that 1 heaping teaspoon of a whole spice gives you pretty close to 1 teaspoon of ground spice.

To toast spices—in Indian cuisine, this is called "dry frying"—you need a cast-iron skillet. Place it over medium heat and, when the skillet is hot, add the whole spices or noodles and shake the skillet gently so the spices toast on all sides. When you can smell the wonderful aroma—after a few minutes— the spices are toasted. Remove from the heat, pour into a bowl to keep them from toasting further in the still-hot pan, and let cool. Then grind the spices in a spice grinder or a clean coffee grinder and use in your sausage recipe.

To toast nuts and noodles, place them on a cookie sheet, put in a preheated 350-degree-F oven, and toast until golden brown, 10 to 15 minutes.

2 Grind the lamb and beef through a 3/8-inch grinder plate into a large bowl. Add the mustard, olive oil, and soy sauce and mix together with your hands until thoroughly combined. Add the seasoning mixture one-third at a time, kneading well after each addition. The mixture should be sticky so that it binds together; if it is too dry, add as much ice water as necessary to get the right consistency. For the best flavor, cover with plastic wrap and refrigerate overnight.

3 Form the mixture into patties, logs, loaves, or sticks or stuff into the casings, if using (see page 306). The mixture will keep up to 3 days in the refrigerator and up to 6 months in the freezer. Cook as desired (see page 307).

Spicy Green Onion Lamb Sausage

This is a takeoff on Spicy Green Onion Sausage (page 318) made with pork. I made this up fresh and then barbecued it for the 2000 National Lamb-B-Que Cook-off, and it helped me win the Grand Championship. Granulated roasted garlic is available from better spice companies.
MAKES 5 POUNDS

- 2 tablespoons seasoned salt, homemade (page 108) or store-bought
- 1 tablespoon granulated roasted garlic
- 1 tablespoon medium-grind black pepper
- 1 tablespoon sweet Hungarian paprika
- 2 teaspoons crushed red pepper
- 2 teaspoons granulated cane sugar
- 1 teaspoon cayenne pepper or pure ground chipotle chile
- 1 teaspoon chili powder, homemade (page 111) or store-bought
- 1 teaspoon cumin seeds, toasted in a dry skillet over medium heat until fragrant, then ground
- 3 pounds lean lamb, such as loin, cubed and chilled until firm
- 1 pound boneless Boston pork butt, trimmed of excess fat, cubed, then chilled until firm
- 1 pound beef chuck, cubed and chilled until firm
- 1 cup thinly sliced green onions (white and green parts) or 1/3 cup dried chives
- 1/2 cup buttermilk
- 1/2 cup ice water, as needed
- About 5 feet (38 to 42mm-diameter) hog casings (optional), prepared for stuffing (see page 306)

1 Combine the seasonings in a small bowl and blend well.

2 Grind the lamb, pork, and beef through a 3/8-inch grinder plate into a large bowl. Add the green onions and mix together with your hands until thoroughly combined. Pour 1/4 cup of the buttermilk over the meat mixture, sprinkle one-third of the seasoning mixture over the top, and mix well. Pour the remaining 1/4 cup buttermilk over the meat and another third of the seasoning mixture and mix well. Add the remaining seasoning mixture and knead well. The mixture should be sticky so that it binds together; if it is too dry, add as much of the ice water as necessary to get the right consistency. Cover with plastic wrap and refrigerate for 2 to 4 hours to let the flavors develop.

3 Form the mixture into patties, loaves, sticks, or logs or stuff into the casings, if using (see page 306). The mixture will keep for up to 3 days in the refrigerator and up to 6 months in the freezer. Cook as desired (see page 307).

Gyro Sausage

This sausage is usually shaped into a big cone or loaf, loaded onto a skewer or metal rod, and cooked on an Autodon or a vertical broiler. Cooked strips are sliced off as the spit turns, placed in grilled pita bread, and topped with onions, tomatoes, lettuce, and tzatziki sauce, a garlicky yogurt sauce. The original recipe did not have pork in it; I added it for the flavor and moistness it gives the sausage. The original recipe called for 3 pounds of lamb and 2 pounds of beef. MAKES 5 POUNDS

2½ pounds boneless lamb shoulder, cubed and chilled until firm

1½ pounds boneless Boston pork butt, trimmed of excess fat, cubed, then chilled until firm

1 pound beef chuck, cubed and chilled until firm

4 large cloves garlic, minced

3 tablespoons minced fresh oregano leaves

2 teaspoons fine sea salt

2 teaspoons coarsely ground black pepper

1 teaspoon ground coriander

Juice of 1 lemon

About 5 feet (38 to 42mm-diameter) hog casings (optional), prepared for stuffing (see page 306)

1 Grind the lamb, pork, and beef through a ⁵⁄₁₆-inch grinder plate into a large bowl. Mix them together with your hands until thoroughly combined. Combine the garlic and oregano in a small bowl; combine the salt, pepper, and coriander in another bowl. Add one-third of both seasoning mixtures to the meat mixture and knead well; repeat the process two more times, or until all of the seasonings are incorporated into the sausage. Add the lemon juice and blend well. For the best flavor, cover with plastic wrap and refrigerate overnight.

2 Form the mixture into patties, logs, loaves, or sticks or stuff into the casings, if using (see page 306). The mixture will keep for up to 3 days in the refrigerator and up to 6 months in the freezer. Cook as desired (see page 307).

Garlic Chicken Sausage

Even though this sausage is made with chicken, I don't consider it low-fat, but it is leaner than other sausages. Chicken sausages usually have a finer texture than pork sausages. MAKES ABOUT 3 POUNDS

2½ pounds boneless chicken legs and thighs (do not remove the skin or fat), cubed and chilled until firm

½ pound pork fatback, cut into large chunks and chilled until firm

3 cloves garlic, minced

2 teaspoons seasoned salt, homemade (page 108) or store-bought

1 teaspoon dried parsley flakes or 1 tablespoon minced fresh parsley leaves

½ teaspoon dried basil leaves

½ teaspoon white pepper

½ teaspoon ground cinnamon

¼ teaspoon dry mustard (I use Colman's)

¼ teaspoon ground allspice

¼ cup white wine

1 tablespoon balsamic vinegar

About 5 feet (38 to 42mm-diameter) hog casings (optional), prepared for stuffing (see page 306)

1 Grind the chicken and fatback through a ³⁄₁₆-inch grinder plate into a large bowl. Combine the garlic, salt, parsley, basil, white pepper, cinnamon, dry mustard, and allspice in a small bowl and blend well. Combine the wine and vinegar in another small bowl. Add one-third of both seasoning mixtures and the wine mixture to the meat mixture and blend well. Add the rest of the seasoning mixture in two more batches, kneading after each addition. The mixture should be sticky

and hold together; if it is too dry, add as much of the remaining wine mixture as necessary to get the right consistency. For the best flavor, cover with plastic wrap and refrigerate overnight.

2 Form the mixture into patties, logs, sticks, or loaves or stuff into the casings if using (see page 306). The mixture will keep for up to 3 days in the refrigerator and up to 6 months in the freezer. Cook as desired (see page 307).

Chicken and Apple Sausage

This sausage rivals Aidells'. I love it grilled and served on a bun with a barbecue relish or a fruit salsa, such as Sweet Apple Salsa (page 156). MAKES 5 POUNDS

1½ cups apple cider

1 tablespoon fine sea salt

1 tablespoon rubbed sage

2 teaspoons finely ground black pepper

1 teaspoon ground allspice

½ teaspoon ground ginger

¼ teaspoon ground cinnamon

⅛ teaspoon ground nutmeg

5 pounds boneless chicken thighs (don't trim away the fat or skin), cubed and chilled until firm

4 ounces dried apples, diced

1 chicken bouillon cube dissolved in 2 tablespoons boiling water, cooled

About 5 feet (38 to 42mm-diameter) hog casings (optional), prepared for stuffing (see page 306)

1 Pour the cider into a small nonreactive saucepan over medium-high heat and reduce it to ¼ cup, until it's almost like apple syrup, about 15 minutes. Remove from the heat, let cool, and set aside.

2 Combine the seasonings in a small bowl and blend well.

3 Grind the chicken through a ³⁄₈-inch grinder plate into a large bowl. Add the apples and chicken broth and blend well. Add the seasoning mixture one-third at a time, kneading after each addition. Knead the mixture until it is sticky and holds together. For the best flavor, cover with plastic wrap and refrigerate overnight.

4 Form the mixture into patties, loaves, logs, or sticks or stuff into the casings, if using (see page 306). The mixture will keep for up to 3 days in the refrigerator and up to 6 months in the freezer. Cook as desired (see page 307).

Smoky Turkey Sausage

This is probably the healthiest recipe in this chapter, but don't hold that against me! Liquid smoke flavoring provides a smoky taste—until you barbecue it, that is. MAKES 5 POUNDS

- 1 tablespoon sweet Hungarian paprika
- 2 teaspoons granulated garlic
- 2 teaspoons rubbed sage
- 1½ teaspoons cayenne pepper
- 1 teaspoon ground thyme
- 1 teaspoon ground coriander
- 1 teaspoon fine sea salt
- 1 teaspoon white pepper
- ½ teaspoon ground nutmeg
- 3 pounds boneless turkey thighs (don't trim away the skin or fat), cubed and chilled until firm
- 2 pounds boneless turkey breast (don't trim away the skin or fat), cubed and chilled until firm
- 1 cup fine dry bread crumbs
- 1 tablespoon brandy (optional)
- 2 teaspoons liquid smoke flavoring (optional)
- About 5 feet (38 to 42mm-diameter) hog casings (optional), prepared for stuffing (see page 306)

1 Combine the seasonings in a small bowl and blend well.

2 Grind the turkey thighs through a ³/16-inch grinder plate into a bowl. Grind the turkey breast through a ⁵/16-inch grinder plate into a bowl.

3 Transfer the meats to a large bowl, sprinkle with the bread crumbs, and knead until the crumbs are evenly distributed and the white and dark meats are thoroughly mixed together. Sprinkle the brandy and liquid smoke, if using, over the meat and work them in. Add the seasoning mixture one-third at a time, kneading after each addition, until the mixture is sticky and holds together. For the best flavor, cover with plastic wrap and refrigerate overnight.

4 Form the mixture into patties, logs, sticks, loaves or stuff into the casings, if using (see page 306). The mixture will keep for up to 3 days in the refrigerator and up to 6 months in the freezer. Cook as desired (see page 307).

Rabbit and Apple Breakfast Sausage

This sausage is meant to be very lean. If you don't want it that way, use 3 pounds of rabbit to 2 pounds of pork butt. Either way, it's a good sausage and great on the grill. MAKES ABOUT 5 POUNDS

- 2 tablespoons fresh lemon juice
- 1³/4 cups water
- 1 cup peeled, cored, and minced tart apples (I use Granny Smith)
- 5 pounds rabbit, boned and diced
- 1 tablespoon rubbed sage
- 2 teaspoons fine sea salt
- 2 teaspoons white pepper
- 1 teaspoon ground cinnamon
- ³/4 teaspoon ground nutmeg
- 2 tablespoons canola oil
- About 6 feet (28 to 32mm-diameter) hog casings (optional), prepared for stuffing (see page 306)

1 Combine the lemon juice and water in a medium-size bowl, add the apples, cover with plastic wrap, and place in the refrigerator.

2 In a large bowl, combine the rabbit, sage, salt, pepper, cinnamon, nutmeg, and canola oil and blend well. Cover with plastic wrap and refrigerate overnight.

3 The next day, grind the rabbit mixture through a $3/8$-inch grinder plate or in small batches in a food processor until coarsely ground.

4 Drain the apples, then stir them into the rabbit mixture until well combined. Form the mixture into loaves, logs, sticks, or patties or stuff into the casings, if using (see page 306). The mixture will keep for up to 3 days in the refrigerator and up to 6 months in the freezer. Cook as desired (see page 307).

Venison Breakfast Sausage

This recipe gives you one more way to show off your hunting trophy deer—and get breakfast on the table. MAKES 5 POUNDS

> 3 pounds venison, cubed and chilled until firm
>
> 2 pounds boneless Boston pork butt, trimmed of excess fat, cubed, then chilled until firm

> 2 tablespoons rubbed sage
>
> 1 tablespoon freshly ground black pepper
>
> 1 tablespoon granulated cane sugar
>
> 2 teaspoons fine kosher salt
>
> 1 teaspoon ground thyme
>
> 1 teaspoon dried summer savory leaves
>
> $1/2$ teaspoon cayenne pepper
>
> $1/2$ cup ice water, as needed
>
> About 6 feet (28 to 32mm-diameter) hog casings (optional), prepared for stuffing (see page 306)

1 Grind the venison and pork butt through a $3/16$-inch grinder plate into a large bowl.

Mix them together with your hands until thoroughly combined. Combine the sage, black pepper, sugar, salt, thyme, savory, and cayenne pepper in a small bowl and blend well. Add the seasoning mixture one-third at a time to the meat mixture, kneading after each addition. The mixture should be sticky so that it binds together; if it is too dry, add as much of the ice water as necessary to get the right consistency. For the best flavor, cover with plastic wrap and refrigerate overnight.

2 Form the mixture into patties, logs, loaves, or sticks or stuff into the casings, if using (see page 306). The mixture will keep for up to 3 days in the refrigerator and up to 6 months in the freezer. Cook as desired (see page 307).

Plentiful

Poultry

Most backyard barbecuers have cooked chicken more or less successfully. The more successful efforts come from grilling smaller pieces with almost constant attention, frequent turning, and some use of a baste or mop applied periodically. The less successful undertakings are usually the result of lack of constant attention, leading to chicken that is burned on the outside and raw on the inside, a state of affairs that is disguised with a liberal application of barbecue sauce.

Converting your grill to a barbecue pit, with its greater temperature control and a longer cooking time over indirect heat, will guarantee scrumptious chicken, Cornish hen, turkey, or duck every time. And the cook doesn't have to turn the pieces even once.

For Best Results, Try Barbecuing—Not Grilling—Poultry

Instead of having company looking, commenting, kibitzing, and telling stories about how marvelous somebody else's chicken or turkey or duck is, you can lift the lid to add charcoal, enlisting the help of a guest, and show off the golden brown meat with its accompanying delicious smell.

Then it's time to check the temperature and serve a few sacrificial wing joints that have been pulled off the pit earlier or at the time of the charcoal addition. An unhurried pace for cocktails and hors d'oeuvres, with chicken served right off the pit, is most impressive, especially given the apparent ease with which everything is accomplished. Of course, establishing the serving time and working backward from it guarantees such results.

The slow smoking time required is approximately 8 to 12 hours for a whole turkey, 5 to 6 hours for a turkey breast, $4^1/2$ hours for chicken halves or Cornish hens, $3^1/2$ to 4 hours for whole duck or chicken, 3 hours for chicken thighs and drumsticks, 2 to 3 hours for chicken breasts, and 2 hours for chicken wings. You can also slow smoke whole duck, duck breast and legs, quail, and pheasant, which take about the same time to smoke as their chicken counterparts.

Selecting Poultry

For chicken, I usually buy whole broiler-fryers and cut them up myself. You save a little money buying a whole chicken, and you can use the neck, back, and wing tips to make broth. But chicken that's already cut up is very convenient, so go ahead and buy your favorite parts for the grill. Chicken legs, quarters, thighs, and wings often show up as weekly specials at the supermarket and may be as cheap to buy as whole chickens. Leg quarters are usually cheaper when bought in 10-pound packages. Chicken breasts and breast quarters usually cost more and require more attention during cooking.

Cornish hens, turkey, and duck must be special ordered if you want them fresh; however, you can easily find them frozen at most grocery stores. Just allow an extra day for them to thaw out in the refrigerator. Baby turkey must be ordered in ad-

Bone-In versus BONELESS Chicken Breasts

There really shouldn't be any controversy about bone-in versus boneless chicken breasts when you slow smoke or grill. One is great for slow smoking, the other is perfect for quick grilling.

FOR SLOW SMOKING During the long, slow-smoking process, you need a chicken breast with its skin on to help it stay moist. And a chicken breast with the bone in it means more flavor, another plus at a contest. You will want to slow smoke several bone-in, skin-on chicken breasts at a contest to make sure when you slice them up for the judges that you get the best-looking slices—at most contests, you need at least 6 slices. And that will probably be from several smoked chicken breasts. At home, you don't have to worry about perfect slices, but you'll get the benefit of full, delicious flavor anyway.

You can grill bone-in, skin-on chicken breasts over a medium fire, but they take longer to cook than their leaner boneless, skinless counterparts.

FOR QUICK GRILLING Boneless, skinless chicken breasts were made for life in the fast lane and the backyard griller. They're quick to sauté, quick to steam, quick to broil, and quick to grill over a medium-hot to hot fire. I usually marinate them before grilling because there is no protection from the skin against the high heat of the grill and no extra flavor from the bone.

Boneless, skinless chicken breasts don't really benefit from long, slow smoking—they're done so fast that they don't take on the smoky flavor that bone-in chicken does.

For the dinner-in-under-30-minutes crowd, boneless, skinless chicken breasts are the way to go.

---

vance from a specialty supplier. For wild turkey or pheasant, you'll have to befriend a hunter or find a mail-order game supplier that carries it. Wild turkey and pheasant are stronger in flavor and less fatty than domestic birds, so they take well to long, slow smoking.

Preparing Poultry for Grilling or Smoking

Whole birds are quite simple to halve. Cut them through the back first, alongside the backbone, then open the chicken and split the breast. The easier way is to ask your butcher to do the job with a meat saw, which will cost you about 7 to 12 cents extra per pound.

All poultry requires a bit of trimming of loose skin and pulling away or cutting out pockets of fat. Wings should be cut from the halves; their outer third joint, or tip, may be trimmed and discarded, if desired.

When grilling or smoking a whole bird, secure the wings with wooden skewers or kitchen string so the bird sits evenly on the grill grate.

Try the Mustard Slather and Rub Process

For the sake of learning, try this experiment: Pat half the poultry portions with paper towels and use the mustard slather and rub process. Leave the other half moist from washing the chicken in cold water and use rub only. Both processes will give great taste, and your fellow eaters will let you know which they think is better.

To perform the mustard slather and rub process, place the chicken pieces on a cutting board, meat side up, for a light anointing with mustard or a mustard slather (pages 86–101) applied with a pastry brush, then lightly sprinkle on one of the rubs (pages 115–132). A grocery store pork or chicken seasoning will also work.

While the rub and mustard combination are working together and becoming tacky, you need to head outside, set up the pit, and start the charcoal—about half a chimney full. Then it's back to the cutting board; turn over the chicken so the skin side is up and repeat the mustard slather and rub process.

What about marinades? No problem. There are several dandies included in this chapter; check out the marinade chapter (pages 54–71) for others. One rule of thumb for any meat, including chicken, is not to leave it in the marinade too long. I indicate in the recipes the length of time that the poultry should marinate for the best results.

How to Barbecue Poultry

When the charcoal is ready, follow the procedure described in Setting up the Pit (see pages 18–22). Put one thumb-size chunk of hardwood of your choice on the hot coals for smoke flavor. Why such a small piece of wood? Sixty to 90 minutes of smoke are sufficient for chicken. Add a second chunk if the first is used up at the first fuel addition. And if you're still not convinced that's enough smoke, check out the aroma in your refrigerator the next morning and taste one small bite of any leftover smoked chicken, turkey, Cornish hen, or duck.

Place the chicken portions everywhere around the pit except over the charcoal. If chicken wings are included, put two quite close to the heat. You'll need to check on things periodically and even a slightly scorched wing is a delicious snack after the first 2 hours of barbecuing. You may have to shift the position of the portions closest to the charcoal if they show signs of browning faster than those in the middle of the pit. At first, you won't believe that the fire is hot enough to cook the chicken and you'll wonder if anything is happening at all. But just give it time. You're aiming for the same slow-smoking temperature of 230 to 250 degrees F.

I baste the chicken at least once with apple juice, but you don't have to do that. Want to apply a glaze? Try one of the recipes on pages 72–85. Brush it on the poultry with a pastry brush about 45 minutes before it will come off the pit.

When using a marinade or mustard slather and rub first, then slow smoking and applying a glaze, you're getting close to competition-quality barbecue.

How to Grill Poultry Without Burning It

To grill chicken, Cornish hens, turkey, or duck without burning it, there are two secrets: Keep the heat low and brush on the sauce at the last minute.

The combination of fatty skin, sweet barbecue sauce, and high heat results in what often looks like chunks of poultry cinder. You can try scraping off that bitter, black coating, but its flavor and aroma—what I call "eau d'ashtray"—will continue to flavor the meat. The secret to great grilled poultry—a bird with moist, tender meat and sticky, pleasantly smoky skin—is to lower the heat of the fire and apply the sauce only during the last few minutes.

Prepare a medium or medium-hot fire and place the chicken pieces over the coals. You'll have to be vigilant and keep turning the chicken pieces every few minutes so they don't begin to char. Wait until the chicken is cooked through before basting with the sauce. The sauce needs only 5 minutes to adhere nicely to the chicken. Because the fire isn't really hot, the chicken won't get that charred look, just a nice shine. But this is the time to be even more attentive; if the fire has gotten hot, the sauce will burn in a heartbeat. Be armed with tongs to remove the chicken at the first sign of charring.

To grill domestic duck breast, which has more fat than a chicken breast, a medium fire is essential. You will get more flare-ups than with chicken because the duck fat drips onto the hot coals, so keep a spray bottle of water handy. Douse any flare-ups with water. Duck breasts usually take 3 to 5 minutes per side to grill to medium rare, but turn them more often if you get a lot of flare-ups.

You can substitute duck breasts for chicken breasts in recipes such as Gingered Apricot Chicken Breasts (page 343), Honey-Raspberry Chicken Breasts (page 343), and Blue Ribbon Grilled Cornish Hens with Hot Onion Rub (page 354). Tart and fruity flavors, as well as Asian flavors, go well with duck. Just make sure you grill duck over a medium fire and have that spray bottle handy.

WHEN IS MY BIRD DONE?

There are two ways to tell when your bird is cooked through. You can prick or slice it in the thickest part (the joint between the leg and the thigh is a good place to check if you're barbecuing a whole bird); if the juice runs clear, it's done. You can also insert an instant-read thermometer into the thickest part; when the internal temperature registers 165 degrees F, it's done.

Chicken and Turkey Burgers

If using frozen ground chicken or turkey, you should be aware that it may exude excess moisture after it thaws. If your poultry burger is too moist, either you can place it in a fine-mesh strainer over a bowl and press out the moisture or you can cover it with plastic wrap, put on a plate in the refrigerator, and let it drain overnight. You can also add some bread crumbs to absorb the moisture. When making chicken or turkey burgers, I prefer to use only white meat. Being lean, white meat has a tendency to stick to the grill grate. To keep that from happening, coat the burgers with nonstick cooking spray or rub them lightly with olive or vegetable oil before putting them on the grill.

Smoking Chicken, Duck, and Turkey

Barbecuing or slow smoking chicken, duck, and turkey is the way to go, in my opinion. You can slow smoke a whole bird or parts and end up with a deliciously moist, aromatic, tender result. I prefer doing whole birds or lots of parts when I set up my pit. Why go to all the time and trouble for only four chicken breasts? When you barbecue poultry, think leftovers for sandwiches or casseroles, and add more poultry to the pit.

You may not want to slow smoke poultry for leftovers, however. In that case, you can adapt any of my slow smoke recipes in this chapter for a smaller turkey breast or turkey legs instead of a whole turkey. The slow smoking time is approximately 8 to 12 hours for a whole turkey, $4\frac{1}{2}$ hours for a turkey breast, $3\frac{1}{2}$ to 4 hours for a whole duck or chicken or turkey legs, 3 hours for chicken thighs or duck legs, and 2 hours for chicken wings.

Set up your pit by preparing an indirect fire the same way you do for beef, pork, or lamb. I insert a meat thermometer into the thigh or the thickest part of the bird. I usually baste at least once with apple juice or another mixture. If I'm slow smoking a whole bird, I usually start it breast side down, then turn it once during the smoking process. If I'm slow smoking turkey legs or chicken breasts or wings, I don't turn them at all unless they look a little more burnished than usual. Then I move them to a cooler part of the pit. When the internal temperature reaches 165 degrees F, the bird is done.

As a final touch at a contest, I brush the poultry with a special glaze, then crisp the skin of a smoked chicken breast or Cornish hen over a hot fire on the grill, but I usually don't do that at home.

SUGGESTED WOODS FOR POULTRY

When I'm a competitor in a barbecue contest, everything I smoke gets the same wood smoke flavoring—a combination of seasoned oak, hickory, and apple. But for other occasions—when I'm cooking for friends and family—I try other woods. For a mild, sweeter flavor that goes well with chicken, I recommend fruit woods, such as apple, cherry, and pear.

Grilling and Smoking Game Birds

I am fortunate that I have friends who hunt and will share their game birds with me for several reasons. One, they already have a freezer full and need to empty it before the new hunting season approaches. Two, they're looking for new recipes and ways to fix their game birds.

Game birds such as quail, pheasant, duck, and wild turkey are naturally less fatty, and this is good for the griller and the barbecuer. You don't get the flare-ups you do with domestic birds, which have more fat. And you can control the amount of melted butter or oil you use to baste the birds, just as you do for other foods.

Because game birds are less fatty and more muscular than domestic birds, you usually grill or smoke the boneless breasts or the whole bird. The wings, legs, and thighs are too tough to grill, but they tenderize slightly during long, slow smoking.

If you don't have a friendly neighborhood hunter, you can often find quail, pheasant, and duck in the frozen food section of better grocery stores. You can also order fresh game birds from specialty companies.

When you grill or smoke game birds, you mainly have to make sure they don't dry out. You can prevent this in two ways. First, marinate or baste the game birds with a mixture that has melted butter or vegetable oil in it. Basting can be as simple as brushing melted butter on before grilling. Secondly, don't cook the birds too long. For grilling, I aim for medium rare to medium at the most. If you cook game birds to well done, they'll probably be dry. And no amount of sauce can hide that.

At one time, the Jack Daniel's contest had a game category, but too many people were unfamiliar with it and so it became hard to judge. Today, you can enter a game entrée in the Anything But or Miscellaneous categories in a barbecue contest or enjoy game birds in your back yard.

Santa Fe Chicken Burgers

This is a taco burger with all of the trimmings. Kids love them. SERVES 2 TO 4

    1 pound ground chicken or turkey

    1/2 cup shredded Monterey Jack cheese

    1/4 cup salsa of your choice or Barbecue Salsa
        (page 157)

    1/4 cup crushed tortilla chips

    1/4 cup thinly sliced green onions (green and
        white parts)

    1 teaspoon ground cumin

    1 teaspoon garlic salt

    1/2 teaspoon freshly ground black pepper

    Nonstick cooking spray

    4 hamburger buns

    Sliced ripe tomatoes, lettuce leaves, and sliced
        onions (optional)

1 Prepare a medium-hot fire in your grill.

2 In a medium-size bowl, combine the chicken, cheese, salsa, tortilla chips, green onions, cumin, garlic salt, and pepper and mix lightly with your

hands. Form into 4 patties ½ to ¾ inch thick. Coat with nonstick spray.

3 Place the burgers directly over the coals, cover, and grill for 5 to 7 minutes per side, until cooked through.

4 Place the burgers on the buns, top with tomato, lettuce, and onion, if desired, and serve immediately.

Fresh Basil Chicken Burgers

This recipe is good with ranch dressing or garlic mayonnaise. **SERVES 4 TO 8**

    2 pounds ground chicken

    1 small onion, minced

    2 tablespoons minced fresh basil leaves

    2 cloves garlic, pressed

    1 teaspoon non-iodized salt

    1 teaspoon freshly ground black pepper

    ½ teaspoon cayenne pepper (optional)

    Nonstick cooking spray

    8 hamburger buns, split and grilled

1 Prepare a medium-hot fire in your grill.

2 In a medium-size bowl, combine the chicken, onion, basil, garlic, salt, black pepper, and cayenne, if using, and blend well with your hands. Form into 8 patties ½ to ¾ inch thick. Coat with nonstick spray.

3 Place the burgers directly over the coals, cover, and grill for 5 to 7 minutes per side, until cooked through. Serve on the grilled buns.

Curried Chicken Almond Burgers

When I mention this burger, some people say, "Ugh, not curry." I try to tell them what they are missing, oh ye of little faith. I suggest that if you are in this group, start with 1 teaspoon of curry powder or less. A somewhat fruity barbecue sauce goes well with the curry flavor. **SERVES 2 TO 4**

    1 pound ground chicken

    ½ cup mayonnaise

    ½ cup shredded Monterey Jack cheese

    ⅓ cup ground almonds

    ¼ cup minced fresh parsley leaves

    2 teaspoons fresh lemon juice

    2 large shallots, minced

    2 teaspoons curry powder

    1 teaspoon non-iodized salt

    1 teaspoon freshly ground black pepper

    ½ teaspoon cayenne pepper

    Nonstick cooking spray

    4 hamburger buns

    Barbecue sauce of your choice, homemade
        (pages 136–161) or store-bought

1 Prepare a medium-hot fire in your grill.

2 In a medium-size bowl, combine the chicken, mayonnaise, cheese, almonds, parsley, lemon juice, shallots, curry, salt, black pepper, and cayenne, blending well with your hands. Form into 4 patties ½ to ¾ inch thick. Coat with nonstick spray.

3 Place the burgers directly over the coals, cover, and grill for 5 to 7 minutes per side, until cooked through.

4   Toast the buns on the grill. Place the burgers on the buns, top with a dollop of barbecue sauce, and serve immediately.

Chinese Chicken Burgers

I used to make a version of these burgers for a friend who had a bar and restaurant. We served them in pita bread with a sweet-and-sour sauce. SERVES 2 TO 4

  1 pound ground chicken
  1/4 cup minced water chestnuts
  2 tablespoons light soy sauce
  1 tablespoon clover honey
  1 tablespoon cider vinegar
  1 teaspoon peeled and grated fresh ginger
  1 teaspoon fine sea salt
  1 teaspoon freshly ground black pepper
  1/2 teaspoon minced garlic
  Nonstick cooking spray

1   In a medium-size bowl, combine all the ingredients, except the cooking spray, blending well with your hands. Cover with plastic wrap and place in the refrigerator for at least 2 to 3 hours or overnight to let the flavors develop. If, after the meat has marinated, there is any liquid in the bowl, drain it away.

2   Form the mixture into 4 patties 1/2 to 3/4 inch thick. Coat with nonstick spray.

3   Prepare a medium-hot fire in your grill.

4   Place the burgers directly over the coals, cover, and grill for 5 to 7 minutes per side, until cooked through.

Grilled Fire and Smoke Chicken Wings

These wings are kissed with fire and blessed with smoke! Chicken wings never tasted so good. SERVES 6 TO 8

  HOT TEQUILA MARINADE
  1/2 cup soy sauce
  1/4 cup tequila
  1/4 cup sunflower oil
  2 tablespoons clover honey
  1 tablespoon Dijon mustard
  1 tablespoon Louisiana hot sauce
  2 cloves garlic, pressed
  1 teaspoon crushed red pepper
  1/2 teaspoon cayenne pepper

  4 pounds chicken wings (about 20)

1   To make the marinade, combine all the marinade ingredients in a medium-size nonreactive bowl and mix well. Place the chicken wings in a zippered-top plastic bag, pour in the marinade, turning to coat, seal, and let marinate for at least 2 to 3 hours or overnight in the refrigerator.

2   Prepare a medium-hot fire in your grill.

3   Remove the wings from the marinade, discard the marinade, place directly over the coals, cover, and grill for about 15 minutes, then turn, cover, and grill 25 to 20 minutes longer, until cooked through.

BARBECUED FIRE AND SMOKE CHICKEN WINGS

Prepare an indirect fire. Place the chicken on the pit, cover, and cook at 230 to 250 degrees F, turning the wings every 40 to 45 minutes and basting once with apple juice, if desired, until cooked through, about 2 hours.

Kicked-Up Horseradish Grilled Chicken Wings

If you like a little kick, these are the wings for you.
SERVES 6 TO 8

KICKED-UP HORSERADISH BARBECUE SAUCE

2 tablespoons garlic salt

¼ cup (½ stick) unsalted butter

¼ cup prepared horseradish

¼ cup tomato ketchup, homemade (page 43) or store-bought

2 tablespoons cider vinegar

2 tablespoons Worcestershire sauce, homemade (page 50) or store-bought

1 tablespoon fresh lemon juice

1 tablespoon Louisiana hot sauce

2 teaspoons crushed black peppercorns

2 tablespoons garlic salt

4 pounds chicken wings (about 20), disjointed (reserve tips for other uses)

1 To make the sauce, combine the barbecue sauce ingredients in a medium-size nonreactive saucepan and bring to a boil, stirring occasionally. Remove from the heat and set aside.

2 Prepare a medium-hot fire in your grill.

3 Sprinkle the garlic salt evenly over the chicken wings. Place directly over the coals, cover, and grill for about 15 minutes, then turn and start basting with the sauce every 10 minutes until you have a good glaze on the wings. Grill 15 to 20 minutes longer, or until done.

KICKED-UP HORSERADISH SMOKED CHICKEN WINGS

Prepare an indirect fire. Place the chicken on the pit, cover, and cook at 230 to 250 degrees F, turning the wings every 40 to 45 minutes and basting once with the barbecue sauce, until cooked through, about 2 hours.

Sweet and Hot Barbecued Chicken Wings

My favorite parts of the chicken are the wings, and these have a little sweet and a little fire! When cooking chicken wings, depending on the distance between the rungs of your grill rack, you may have to cover it with a perforated grill rack. For bigger rigs, you can use a piece of expanded metal mesh, which you can get at most good hardware stores. **SERVES 6 TO 8**

SWEET AND HOT RUB

½ cup granulated cane sugar

2 tablespoons garlic salt

2 tablespoons seasoned salt, homemade (page 108) or store-bought

2 tablespoons sweet Hungarian paprika

1 tablespoon chili seasoning, homemade (page 116) or store-bought

1 tablespoon freshly ground black pepper

1 teaspoon ground ginger

$1/2$ teaspoon ground allspice

$1/4$ teaspoon ground mace

4 pounds chicken wings (about 20)

1 cup apple juice (optional)

1 Prepare an indirect fire.

2 To make the rub, combine the rub ingredients in a small bowl and blend well.

3 Rinse the chicken wings under cold running water and pat dry with paper towels. Season evenly with the rub. Place the chicken on the pit, cover, and cook at 230 to 250 degrees F, turning every 40 to 45 minutes and basting once with apple juice, if desired, until cooked through, about 2 hours.

Curried Honey-Mustard Chicken Thighs

Add a little vinegar, sugar, and apple juice to this recipe and you have a salad dressing or another marinade.
SERVES 8

CURRIED HONEY-MUSTARD MARINADE

$1/4$ cup ($1/2$ stick) unsalted butter

$1/2$ cup clover honey

4 cup prepared yellow mustard

1 teaspoon kosher salt

1 teaspoon mild curry powder

$1/2$ teaspoon white pepper

8 boneless, skinless chicken thighs

1 To make the marinade, melt the butter in a shallow saucepan over low heat. Add the honey, mustard, salt, curry powder, and pepper and blend together until you have a smooth liquid. Remove from the heat and let cool.

2 Place the chicken in a zippered-top plastic bag, pour the marinade over the thighs, turning to coat, and seal. Let marinate for 3 to 4 hours or overnight in the refrigerator.

3 Prepare a medium-hot fire in your grill.

4 Remove the chicken from the marinade, reserving the marinade. Transfer the marinade to a small nonreactive saucepan and bring to a boil over medium-high heat; let simmer for 5 minutes, then set aside.

5 Place the chicken directly over the coals, cover, and grill, turning frequently, until cooked through, 8 to 10 minutes per side. During the last 5 minutes of cooking, glaze with the reserved marinade.

Hickory-Grilled Jerk Chicken Breasts

This recipe has flavor and fire all in one. If you want to tone down the heat (why would you want to do that?), reduce the amount of habanero pepper or use cayenne pepper instead. But what are you, a wimp or a fire eater? Remember when working with hot peppers such as habaneros to wear rubber gloves and never to touch your eyes with your fingers. SERVES 8

WET JERK PASTE

2 cups chopped green onions (green and white parts)

2 tablespoons chopped fresh thyme leaves

2 tablespoons peeled and minced fresh ginger

6 cloves garlic, peeled and smashed

$1/2$ cup chopped habanero chiles or more, if you can take it

1 tablespoon fresh lime juice

1 tablespoon vegetable oil

1 teaspoon freshly ground black pepper

1 teaspoon ground coriander

1 teaspoon ground allspice

1 teaspoon fine sea salt

$1/2$ teaspoon ground cinnamon

$1/4$ teaspoon ground nutmeg

$1/8$ teaspoon powdered bay leaf

8 boneless, skinless chicken breast halves

1 To make the paste, place all the paste ingredients in a food processor and process until smooth, scraping down the sides if necessary.

2 Apply the paste to the chicken breasts, rubbing all over, place on a plate, cover with plastic wrap, and let marinate in the refrigerator for at least 3 to 4 hours or overnight.

3 Prepare a medium-hot fire in your grill, adding hickory chips or chunks for flavor (see A Kiss of Smoke, page 23).

4 Place the chicken directly over the coals, cover, and grill, turning frequently, until cooked through, 8 to 10 minutes per side.

HICKORY-BARBECUED JERK CHICKEN BREASTS

Prepare an indirect fire, adding hickory chips or chunks for flavor (see A Kiss of Smoke, page 23).

Place the chicken on the pit, cover, and cook at 230 to 250 degrees F for $3 1/2$ to 4 hours, basting once with apple juice, if desired, until cooked through.

Aromatic Herb-Grilled Chicken Breasts

This recipe will impress your guests. SERVES 8

AROMATIC SPICE RUB

$1/4$ cup onion salt

2 tablespoons granulated cane sugar

1 teaspoon granulated garlic

1 teaspoon ground ginger

1 teaspoon ground coriander

1 teaspoon dried cilantro leaves

1 teaspoon ground dried lemon peel

$1/2$ teaspoon ground cardamom

$1/2$ teaspoon ground cumin

$1/4$ teaspoon turmeric

$1/4$ teaspoon cayenne pepper

$1/8$ teaspoon ground cloves

$1/8$ teaspoon ground cinnamon

8 boneless, skinless chicken breast halves
Nonstick cooking spray

1 To make the rub, combine all the rub ingredients in a small bowl and blend well. Coat the chicken breasts on one side with nonstick spray and season as desired with the rub. Repeat on the other side. Cover with plastic wrap and let rest at room temperature for about 30 minutes.

2 Prepare a medium-hot fire in your grill.

3 Place the chicken directly over the coals, cover, and grill, turning frequently, until cooked through, 8 to 10 minutes per side.

AROMATIC HERB-SMOKED CHICKEN BREASTS

Prepare an indirect fire. Place the chicken on the pit, cover, and cook at 230 to 250 degrees F for 3 1/2 to 4 hours, basting once with apple juice, if desired, until cooked through.

MAKING DRAWN BUTTER AND ROASTED GARLIC DRAWN BUTTER

Most people recognize drawn or clarified butter as the clear butter you dip cooked crab claws or lobster into at fancy restaurants. But chefs and home cooks like to use it for frying or making sauces because it is less likely to burn. When you clarify butter, you remove the milk solids and other impurities that burn over high heat.

Clarifying butter is easy to do. Just melt it in a skillet over low heat and skim off with a spoon or a spatula the foam and milk solids that appear on the surface. Carefully pour off the clear yellow butter, leaving the milky residue in the bottom of the pan.

To make Roasted Garlic Drawn Butter, whisk in roasted or smoke-roasted garlic (see page 98) to taste.

Grilled Beau Monde Breast of Chicken with Mushroom Sour Cream Sauce

This chicken is good, but the sauce makes it outstanding!
SERVES 8

2 tablespoons Beau Monde Seasoning (page 121)

2 teaspoons granulated cane sugar

1 teaspoon freshly ground black pepper

8 boneless, skinless chicken breast halves

1/4 cup drawn butter (see bottom left)

MUSHROOM SOUR CREAM SAUCE

3 tablespoons unsalted butter

1/2 pound fresh mushrooms, sliced

1/2 cup minced green onions (green and white parts)

1 teaspoon dried tarragon leaves

1/2 cup dry white wine

1/2 cup sour cream

1 Combine the seasoning, sugar, and pepper in a small bowl and blend well. Dip the chicken breasts into the drawn butter and season lightly and evenly with the seasoning mixture. Place on a plate, cover with plastic wrap, and set aside while you prepare the fire and make the sauce.

2 Prepare a medium-hot direct fire in your grill.

3 To make the sauce, melt the butter in large skillet over medium heat. Add the mushrooms and cook, stirring, until softened, about 8 minutes. Add the green onions and tarragon and cook, stirring, until softened, 3 to 4 minutes. Add the

wine and simmer until reduced by one-third, about 10 minutes. Blend in the sour cream and heat through. Do not bring to a boil. Remove from the heat and set aside, keeping warm.

4 Place the chicken directly over the coals, cover, and grill, turning frequently, until cooked through, 8 to 10 minutes per side.

5 To serve, place each chicken breast on a hot serving plate and top with the mushroom sauce. Serve immediately.

BARBECUED BEAU MONDE BREAST OF CHICKEN

Prepare an indirect fire. Place the chicken on the pit, cover, and cook at 230 to 250 degrees F for 3 $1/2$ to 4 hours, basting once with apple juice, if desired, until cooked through.

Grilled Chicken Breasts with Pineapple Mint Chutney Sauce

Easy, low in fat, and flavorful, this recipe is for the backyard gourmet. SERVES 8

2 tablespoons garlic salt

1 tablespoon freshly ground black pepper

1 teaspoon cayenne pepper

8 boneless, skinless chicken breast halves

PINEAPPLE-MINT CHUTNEY SAUCE

1 ripe pineapple, peeled, cored, and diced

1 cup pineapple juice

1 cup golden raisins

1 cup firmly packed light brown sugar

Two 3-inch-long cinnamon sticks

$1/2$ teaspoon ground cloves

1 teaspoon kosher salt

1 cup packed fresh mint leaves, minced

1 Combine the garlic salt, black pepper, and cayenne in a small bowl and blend well. Season the chicken breasts evenly with the spice mixture and set aside at room temperature.

2 To make the sauce, combine the pineapple, pineapple juice, raisins, brown sugar, cinnamon sticks, cloves, and salt in a medium-size nonreactive saucepan and bring to a boil. Reduce the heat to medium-low and simmer for 30 minutes. Remove from the heat and strain through a fine-mesh strainer, reserving the liquid and solids. Place the pineapple and raisins in a medium-size nonreactive bowl and stir in the mint leaves; discard the cinnamon sticks. Return the liquid to the pan, bring to a boil over high heat, and continue to boil until the liquid reduces to a sticky glaze, 5 to 10 minutes. Combine the liquid mixture with the pineapple and raisin mixture and blend well. Let cool.

3 Prepare a medium-hot fire in your grill.

4 Place the chicken directly over the coals, cover, and grill, turning frequently, until cooked through, 8 to 10 minutes per side. Serve with the chutney sauce warm or at room temperature over the chicken or on the side.

Gingered Apricot Chicken Breasts

Rice pilaf would go well with this chicken. SERVES 8

8 boneless, skinless chicken breast halves

GINGERED APRICOT MARINADE

1/2 cup apricot preserves

2 tablespoons fresh lemon juice

1 tablespoon peeled and minced fresh ginger

1/2 teaspoon kosher salt

1/2 teaspoon freshly ground black pepper

1/4 cup walnut oil

1 Place the chicken in a large zippered-top plastic bag.

2 To make the marinade, place the marinade ingredients, except the walnut oil, in a blender or food processor and process for about 30 seconds. Scrape down the sides. Blend in the oil a little at a time. Pour the marinade over the chicken breasts and seal the bag. Let marinate in the refrigerator for 1 to 3 hours.

3 Prepare a medium-hot fire in your grill.

4 Remove the chicken from the marinade, discarding the marinade; place directly over the coals, cover, and grill, turning frequently, until cooked through, 7 to 10 minutes per side.

Honey-Raspberry Chicken Breasts

If raspberry seeds bother you, strain them out before you cool the marinade. SERVES 8

A HONEY OF A RASPBERRY MARINADE

One 12-ounce package individually frozen raspberries, thawed

1/4 cup distilled white vinegar

1/4 cup clover honey

2 tablespoons olive oil

1/2 teaspoon dried thyme leaves

1/4 teaspoon powdered bay leaf

1/2 teaspoon kosher salt

1/2 teaspoon freshly ground black pepper

8 boneless, skinless, chicken breast halves

1 To make the marinade, place the marinade ingredients in a medium-size nonreactive saucepan. Bring to a boil, stirring and mashing the berries, and let boil for 2 minutes. Remove from the heat and let cool to room temperature.

2 Place the chicken in a shallow nonreactive baking dish or a zippered-top plastic bag. Pour the cooled marinade over the chicken, turn to coat, seal, and let marinate in the refrigerator for 2 to 4 hours.

3 Prepare a medium-hot fire in your grill.

4 Remove the chicken from the marinade, discarding the marinade; place directly over the coals, cover, and grill, turning frequently, until cooked through, 7 to 10 minutes per side. Serve hot.

Cantonese Chicken Salad with Plum Glaze

This dish makes a tasty light lunch or dinner for summer entertaining. SERVES 8

PLUM GLAZE

4 cups unpeeled, pitted, and coarsely chopped ripe plums

1 cup chopped yellow onions

Grated zest from 1 orange

1¹/₂ cups water

1 cup granulated cane sugar

¹/₃ cup rice vinegar

3 tablespoons canola oil

2 tablespoons oyster sauce (optional)

2 tablespoons fresh lemon juice

1 tablespoon soy sauce

1 tablespoon toasted sesame oil (optional)

1 teaspoon kosher salt

1 teaspoon ground cinnamon

¹/₄ teaspoon ground allspice

2 tablespoons garlic salt

1 teaspoon ground ginger

¹/₂ teaspoon Chinese 5-spice powder, homemade (page 112) or store-bought

¹/₄ cup ground allspice

8 boneless, skinless, chicken breast halves

Nonstick cooking spray

1 gallon mixed greens (1 to 3 ounces per person)

¹/₂ to ³/₄ pound rice noodles or angel hair pasta, cooked according to package instructions and drained

8 ripe plums, pitted and sliced

1 tablespoon sesame seeds, toasted in a dry skillet over medium heat until fragrant

1 To make the glaze, combine the chopped plums, onions, orange zest, and water in a large nonreactive saucepan and bring to a boil. Reduce the heat to medium-low and simmer, covered, for 4 to 5 minutes. Remove from the heat and let sit for 30 minutes. Transfer to a food processor and process on high until smooth. Return to the saucepan. Stir in the remaining glaze ingredients and bring to a boil. Reduce the heat to medium-low and simmer slowly, uncovered, until reduced to about 3 cups, about 5 minutes, stirring occasionally. Let cool, then refrigerate.

2 Prepare a medium-hot fire in your grill.

3 Combine the garlic salt, ginger, 5-spice powder, and allspice in a small bowl, blending well. Sprinkle evenly all over the chicken. Spray the chicken with nonstick spray. Place the chicken directly over the coals, cover, and grill, turning frequently, until cooked through, 8 to 10 minutes per side. Glaze on both sides with the plum sauce, turning once, during the last half of the cooking time. Reserve the remaining marinade. Remove the chicken from the grill and let cool or keep warm, according to your preference.

4 To serve, arrange 2 cups of the salad greens on 8 individual plates and top with ¹/₂ cup of the rice noodles, one sliced plum, and a sliced chicken breast half. Drizzle with some of the remaining plum glaze, sprinkle with the sesame seeds, and serve.

Slathered and Rubbed Barbecued Chicken Breasts

This Dijon and Italian seasoning makes for a tasty cross-cultural twist. SERVES 6

- 3 whole bone-in chicken breasts, halved
- 1 cup Dijon mustard
- 2 to 3 tablespoons Italian Seasoning (page 120), to your taste
- 2 tablespoons garlic salt
- 1 tablespoon freshly ground black pepper
- 1 cup apple juice (optional)

1 Rinse the chicken and pat dry with paper towels. Using a pastry brush, paint the mustard all over the chicken breasts. Season evenly with the Italian seasoning, garlic salt, and pepper. Cover with plastic wrap and let rest for 30 minutes at room temperature or up to 4 hours in the refrigerator.

2 Prepare an indirect fire.

3 Place the chicken on the pit, cover, and cook at 230 to 250 degrees F for 1½ hours. Turn and baste once with the apple juice, if desired. Continue to cook for 1½ to 3 more hours, until cooked through.

Barbecue Contest Tandoori Chicken Breasts

One of the most winning recipes on the barbecue circuit is tandoori chicken. Here is our competition version, which is slow smoked. SERVES 4 TO 8

TANDOORI MARINADE

- One 8-ounce container (1 cup) plain yogurt
- ¼ cup fresh lemon juice (about 2 lemons)
- 2 teaspoons peeled and grated fresh ginger
- 2 cloves garlic, pressed
- 1 teaspoon ground coriander
- ½ teaspoon crushed red pepper
- ¼ teaspoon ground cumin
- ¼ teaspoon turmeric
- ¼ teaspoon cayenne pepper

- 4 whole bone-in chicken breasts, trimmed of fat

1 To make the marinade, combine all the marinade ingredients in a medium-size nonreactive bowl and blend well with a whisk. Divide the marinade in half.

2 Place the chicken in a zippered-top plastic bag. Pour in half the marinade, turning to coat, seal, and let marinate for at least 3 hours or overnight in the refrigerator. Refrigerate the remaining marinade until ready to use.

3 Prepare an indirect fire.

4 Remove the chicken from the marinade, place on the pit rib side down, cover, and cook at 230 to 250 degrees F, turning every hour for 3 hours. Baste with the reserved marinade about every 10 minutes during the last 30 minutes of cooking time.

The CASE FOR Chicken Skin

Chicken skin can be a problem when you grill or slow smoke because it can get rubbery and look unappetizing. And some people, namely barbecue judges and the very health conscious, just don't like it at all.

If you've marinated your chicken before grilling, then you don't really need the skin, as the oil in the marinade should keep the chicken moist if you turn it often enough. Remove the skin before grilling.

If you haven't used a marinade, then keep the skin on because the little bit of fat underneath the skin acts as a baste during the barbecuing process and keeps the rest of the meat moist. If you're using a mustard slather and a dry rub, the skin helps the paste adhere to the chicken. You can remove the skin after grilling, but I prefer not to. After all, you'll lose the mustard slather and rub flavor.

Here's what I do to crisp up chicken skin after low, slow smoking. Right before the chicken goes to the judges or my guests, I pull it off the smoker and crisp the skin for 10 to 30 seconds on each side directly over the hot fire of a grill. Then I glaze the chicken and serve it up.

Grilled Lemon-Sage Chicken

I got this recipe from my grandmother, who used to make a great lemon-sage fried chicken. I took the liberty of omitting the flour and the frying and came up with this tasty version. **SERVES 4 TO 8**

>Two 3- to 4-pound chickens, split in half along the backbone
>
>1/4 cup lemon pepper seasoning
>
>2 tablespoons lemonade powder (I use Country Time; make sure whatever you use contains sugar, not artificial sweetener)
>
>2 tablespoons rubbed sage
>
>1 tablespoon garlic salt
>
>1/4 cup olive oil

1 Prepare a medium fire in your grill.

2 Rinse the chickens under cold running water and pat dry with paper towels. Combine the lemon pepper, lemonade powder, sage, and garlic salt in a small bowl, blending well. Moisten the chicken all over with the olive oil. Season on all sides with the lemon-sage seasoning.

3 Place the chicken directly over the coals, cover, and grill, turning frequently, until cooked through, about 30 minutes.

BARBECUED LEMON-SAGE CHICKEN

Prepare an indirect fire. Place the chicken on the pit, cover, and cook at 230 to 250 degrees F for 3 1/2 to 4 hours, basting once with apple juice, if desired, until cooked through.

Double Lemon Soy Chicken

Light, simple, and delicious—this recipe has it all.
SERVES 4 TO 8

Two 3- to 4-pound chickens, split in half along the backbone

DOUBLE LEMON SOY MARINADE

$1/2$ cup fresh lemon juice (4 to 5 lemons)

$1/4$ cup soy sauce or light soy sauce

$1/4$ cup water

$1/4$ cup sunflower oil

2 tablespoons minced lemon zest

3 cloves garlic, pressed

1 teaspoon kosher salt

1 teaspoon freshly ground black pepper

1 Rinse the chicken halves under cold running water and pat dry with paper towels.

2 To make the marinade, combine the marinade ingredients in a medium-size nonreactive bowl and blend well. Place each chicken half in a zippered-top plastic bag and divide the marinade among the bags. Turn to coat, seal, and let marinate for at least 3 to 5 hours or overnight in the refrigerator.

3 Prepare a medium-hot fire in your grill.

4 Remove the chicken from the marinade, place directly over the coals, cover, and grill, turning frequently, until an instant-read meat thermometer inserted into a thigh, away from the bone, registers 165 degrees F, about 30 minutes total.

BARBECUED DOUBLE LEMON SOY CHICKEN

Prepare an indirect fire. Place the chicken on the pit, cover, and cook at 230 to 250 degrees F for $3 1/2$ to 4 hours, basting once with apple juice, if desired, until cooked through.

Honey Smoked Chicken

This is momma's favorite. **SERVES 4 TO 8**

Two 4- to 5-pound chickens, split in half along the backbone

2 cups Spicy Italian Marinade (page 59)

2 cups barbecue sauce of your choice (pages 136–161)

$1/2$ cup clover honey

$1/4$ cup soy sauce

$1/4$ cup Jack Daniel's Sour Mash Whiskey

2 teaspoons rubbed sage

1 cup apple juice (optional)

1 Rinse the chicken under cold running water and pat dry with paper towels. Place each chicken in a zippered-top plastic bag and pour 1 cup of the Italian marinade into each bag. Turn to coat, seal, and let marinate in the refrigerator for at least 4 hours or overnight.

2 Combine the barbecue sauce, honey, soy sauce, whiskey, and sage in a medium-size nonreactive saucepan over medium heat and simmer until well blended, about 15 minutes. Set aside.

3 Prepare an indirect fire.

4 Remove the chicken from the marinade, place rib side down on the pit, cover, and cook at 230 to 250 degrees F for $3 1/2$ to 4 hours, basting once with the apple juice, if desired, until an

instant-read meat thermometer inserted into a thigh, away from the bone, registers 165 degrees F. During the last 30 minutes of cooking, increase the heat of the fire to about 350 degrees F and glaze with the reserved barbecue sauce, turning every 10 minutes, until well glazed. Be careful not to caramelize (that means incinerate) the sauce.

Barbecued Polynesian Chicken

This dish is a good start for a luau. SERVES 4 TO 8

POLYNESIAN MARINADE

1 cup pineapple juice

¹/₂ cup soy sauce

¹/₄ cup sweet sherry

¹/₄ cup fresh lemon juice

¹/₄ cup granulated cane sugar or firmly packed brown sugar

1 tablespoon toasted sesame oil

2 teaspoons dry mustard (I use Colman's)

¹/₂ teaspoon cayenne pepper

2 tablespoons cornstarch

¹/₃ cup cold water

Two 4- to 5-pound broiling chickens, split in half along the backbone or quartered

1 cup apple juice (optional)

1 To make the marinade, combine the pineapple juice, soy sauce, sherry, lemon juice, sugar, sesame oil, mustard, and cayenne in a medium-size nonreactive saucepan and bring to a boil, stirring to dissolve the spices and sugar. Reduce the heat to medium-low. Combine the cornstarch and cold water in a small bowl and blend well. Bring the mixture back to a boil, blend in the cornstarch mixture with a wire whisk, and stir until smooth and glossy. Remove from the heat and let cool.

2 Rinse the chickens under cold running water and pat dry with paper towels. Place each chicken in a zippered-top plastic bag and divide the marinade evenly between them. Turn to coat, seal, and let marinate for at least 4 to 5 hours or overnight in the refrigerator.

3 Prepare an indirect fire.

4 Remove the chicken from the marinade, reserving the marinade. Transfer the remaining marinade to a medium-size nonreactive saucepan and bring to a boil over medium-high heat. Let simmer for 5 minutes, then set aside to cool.

5 Place the chicken on the pit, cover, and cook at 230 to 250 degrees F, basting once with the apple juice, if desired, until an instant-read meat thermometer inserted into a thigh, away from the bone, registers 165 degrees F, 4 to 5 hours. Turn and baste the chicken with the reserved marinade twice during the last 45 minutes of cooking time.

Jim Erickson's 36-35-11 Sandbagged Chicken

Jim Erickson competed on the barbecue contest circuit. This was his entry in the first American Royal Invitational Barbecue Contest and it did not score well because one

judge sandbagged it with a score of 11. If the third judge had given Jim another score of 35 or 36, he would have won the contest. (A composite score of 36 is tops in some barbecue contests.) SERVES 8

- 1 tablespoon grated lemon zest (I also like to add orange zest)
- 2 cloves garlic, crushed into a paste
- 2 tablespoons chopped fresh mint leaves
- 1 tablespoon chopped fresh tarragon leaves
- 1 tablespoon Sweet Brown Sugar Rub (page 126) or firmly packed light brown sugar
- 1/4 cup corn oil or safflower oil
- Two 3- to 4-pound chickens, split in half along the backbone
- 1 cup Dijon mustard or mustard slather of your choice (pages 86–101)
- 2 cups rub of your choice (pages 115–132)
- 1 cup apple juice (optional)

1 Combine the lemon zest, garlic, mint, tarragon, and sweet rub in a small bowl. With a wire whisk, slowly beat in the oil, until well blended.

2 Rinse the chicken under cold running water and pat dry with paper towels. Place each chicken in a zippered-top plastic bag and divide the lemon zest mixture evenly between them. Turn to coat, seal, and let marinate in the refrigerator for at least 9 hours or overnight.

3 Prepare an indirect fire.

4 Remove the chicken from the marinade and pat dry. Lightly slather on the mustard, then lightly and evenly sprinkle on the rub. Place the chickens on the pit, rib side down, cover, and cook at 230 to 250 degrees F, basting once with the apple juice, if desired, until an instant-read meat thermometer inserted into a thigh, away from the bone, registers 165 degrees F, 3 1/2 to 4 hours.

Barbecued Garlic Chicken with Pineapple-Honey Glaze

Forget tomato-based barbecue sauce! Slow smoked with the flavors of pineapple, garlic, and honey, this barbecued chicken will become your favorite. SERVES 4 TO 6

- One 3- to 4-pound chicken
- 1 cup boiling water
- 20 cloves garlic
- 2 tablespoons olive oil
- 2 tablespoons (1/4 stick) unsalted butter, at room temperature
- 2 teaspoons dried rosemary leaves
- 1 teaspoon onion salt
- 1/2 teaspoon white pepper

PINEAPPLE-HONEY GLAZE

- 1 cup clover honey
- 1/2 cup pineapple juice
- 1/4 cup white wine
- 2 teaspoons curry powder
- 1 teaspoon kosher salt

- 1 cup apple juice (optional)

1 Rinse the chicken under cold running water, inside and out, and pat dry with paper towels.

2 In a medium-size heat-resistant bowl, pour the boiling water over the garlic cloves and set aside.

3 Meanwhile, cut 20 slits all over the chicken for the garlic. Drain the garlic and peel. Insert a garlic clove into each slit.

4 Combine the olive oil and butter in a small bowl with a wire whisk and rub all over the chicken.

5 Combine the rosemary, onion salt, and pepper in another small bowl and blend well. Sprinkle evenly over the chicken inside and out. Let the chicken rest at room temperature for 30 minutes.

6 Prepare an indirect fire.

7 To make the glaze, combine the glaze ingredients in a medium-size nonreactive saucepan over low heat and whisk together until you have a smooth liquid. Keep warm.

8 Place the chicken on the pit, cover, and cook at 230 to 250 degrees F, basting once with apple juice, if desired, until an instant-read meat thermometer inserted into a thigh, away from the bone, registers 165 degrees F, 4 to 5 hours. During the last 45 minutes of cooking time, turn and baste the chicken all over with the honey glaze about every 15 minutes.

Rotisseried Chicken with Honey-Garlic Marinade

Slightly sweet and lip-smackin' good, this rotisserie chicken puts all others to shame. While you're at it, rotisserie several birds at once, if your equipment can handle the weight, and use the leftovers for delicious chicken salads or sandwiches. See page 351 for more information on cooking poultry on an outdoor rotisserie. SERVES 6 TO 8

> One 3- to 4-pound chicken
> 2 cups Honey-Garlic Marinade (page 61)
> ¼ cup turbinado or raw sugar

¼ cup fine sea salt
1 tablespoon granulated garlic
1 tablespoon cracked black peppercorns
2 teaspoons dried basil leaves
1 teaspoon dried tarragon leaves
1 teaspoon dried parsley leaves
4 cups apple juice (optional)

1 Rinse the chicken under cold running water inside and out and pat dry with paper towels. Place the chicken in a zippered-top plastic bag, pour the marinade over it, turn to coat, and seal. Refrigerate and let marinate for 2 to 4 hours.

2 Meanwhile, combine the sugar, salt, garlic, peppercorns, basil, tarragon, and parsley in a small bowl and set aside.

3 Set up your rotisserie on the grill. Prepare a hot fire in your grill.

4 Season the chicken all over with the spice mixture. Place the chicken on the spit so that it will not spin loose. The chicken should be balanced on the spit so it can turn easily. Tie the wings, legs, and any loose bits to the body of the bird with kitchen string. Insert an instant-read meat thermometer into the thigh, away from the bone. Make sure the thermometer is positioned so you can read it and it can turn freely as the bird turns.

5 Place the spit on the rotisserie. Set a drip pan (you can use a disposable aluminum pan for this) under the bird on the spit. If you want, you can fill the pan with water or apple juice. Start the rotisserie. Cover and cook, checking the chicken, the fire, and the drip pan at least every hour, until the thermometer registers 165 degrees F, about 1½ hours.

How to COOK POULTRY on an Outdoor Rotisserie

Whole turkeys, chickens, and ducks are all delicious spit-roasted or rotisseried in your back yard. You only spit-roast larger birds, not quail or Cornish hens, because larger birds benefit from the longer, slower, rotating style of rotisserie cooking.

When you buy an electric rotisserie, make sure the motor has adequate power to turn the size and weight of the bird you want to cook—for a whole turkey, 10 to 12 pounds; for a whole chicken, 4 to 5 pounds; or for two chickens cooking at the same time, 10 pounds. The manufacturer's directions should make clear the capacity of their particular product.

Because the rotisserie is positioned away from the coals, this is considered indirect cooking or barbecuing.

To spit-roast or rotisserie, first set up your rotisserie on the grill and prepare a medium fire. You can cook with a Kiss of Smoke (see page 23) by throwing a chunk or two of wood on the coals during cooking.

Marinate the poultry for at least 4 hours or overnight in the refrigerator. When you're ready to cook, remove the bird from the marinade and season all over with a rub or seasoning. Place the bird on the spit—using the natural cavities of the neck and rear—so that it will not spin loose. The bird should be balanced on the spit so it can turn easily. Tie the wings, legs, and any loose bits to the body of the bird with kitchen string.

Insert a meat thermometer into the thickest part of the thigh, away from the bone. Make sure the thermometer is positioned so you can read it and it can turn freely as the bird turns.

Place the spit on the rotisserie. Set a drip pan (you can use a disposable aluminum pan for this) under the bird on the spit. If you want, you can fill the pan with water, apple juice, or whatever, just as you would fill a water pan when smoking.

Start the rotisserie. Cover and cook, checking the bird, the fire, and the drip pan at least every hour. After the rub has set, about halfway through the cooking time, start basting every 30 minutes with apple juice, melted butter, or whatever you like.

Rotisserie cooking times are about the same as for barbecuing or slow smoking—about $1^1/2$ to 2 hours for a whole chicken, $2^1/2$ to 3 hours for a whole duck (you'll want it done, not medium rare), and 6 to 8 hours for a 12-pound turkey. Keep checking the meat thermometer and you'll know your bird is done when it reaches an internal temperature of 165 degrees F. During the last hour of cooking, apply any finishing sauce or glaze once every 30 minutes.

Remove the bird from the spit and let it rest for at least 15 minutes before carving.

Sandra's Smoked Chicken Fajitas

If you ever happen to have any leftover smoked chicken, this is a great way to use it up. My barbecue buddy Bob Lyon, a force in the Pacific Northwest Barbecue Association (PNWBA) and on the competition barbecue circuit, is a hero to his neighbors, relatives, sponsors, and travel agent. Four chicken halves, six quarters, or a dozen thighs (Bob's favorite) get distributed to willing tasters every time he fires up his Patio Classic and practices for competition. This is how Bob's wife, Sandra, copes with the leftovers.
SERVES 8

> 2 cups smoked chicken pulled apart into small strips
>
> 1 cup plain yogurt or sour cream (nonfat works well)
>
> 1 cup salsa of your choice, homemade (pages 154–157) or store-bought
>
> 1 cup guacamole (page 241)
>
> 1/2 head iceberg lettuce, coarsely chopped
>
> 1/2 cup finely shredded sharp cheddar or pepper jack cheese
>
> 1 bunch (6) green onions, chopped
>
> 1/2 cup peeled, seeded, and diced ripe tomatoes
>
> Sixteen 10- or 12-inch flour tortillas

1 Place the pulled meat in a heatproof baking dish. Cover, and heat at 225 degrees F for 30 to 40 minutes, or until warm.

2 Place each of the ingredients, except the tortillas, in its own small bowl.

3 Warm the tortillas in a preheated 350 degree F oven, keeping them covered in aluminum foil or that special warmer you bring out to impress guests.

4 To assemble the fajitas, arrange 1 to 1½ ounces of chicken plus the additional ingredients of your choice about one third of the way across the tortilla. Then roll it up in soft taco fashion. Want things hotter? Serve two salsas, one mild, one hot. Have your favorite hot sauce on hand for a few drops to clear nasal passages and make the top of your head start to sweat.

Sandra's Smoked Chicken Quesadillas

These quesadillas are great for a party or a Super Bowl snack. Give your guests the choice of putting the condiments on top of the quesadilla and cutting off bites with a knife and fork or peeling back one side a bit, putting the condiments inside, and eating it like a sandwich. Both ways work well. **SERVES 8**

> Sixteen 10- to 12-inch flour tortillas
>
> 2 cups smoked chicken pulled apart into small strips

FILLINGS

> 1 to 1½ cups finely shredded sharp cheddar or pepper jack cheese
>
> 1 cup cooked black beans, mashed, or refried beans (optional)
>
> 1 cup peeled, seeded, and diced fresh tomatoes
>
> 1 bunch (6) green onions, chopped

CONDIMENTS

> 1 cup guacamole (page 241)
>
> 1 cup salsa of your choice, homemade (pages 154–157) or store-bought

1 In a preheated 350 degree F oven, warm the tortillas, wrapped in aluminum foil, so they'll fold easily.

2 Dot half of each tortilla with the chicken and your choice of fillings, making sure none of them comes within 1½ inches of the edge. Fold the plain tortilla half over the filling half and, cooking a few at a time, brown both sides in a large non-stick skillet over medium heat on the stovetop or on the grill. Keep the finished ones warm until all are browned and the cheese has melted.

3 Serve with the guacamole and salsa on the side.

Cornish Hens with Peppered Port Wine Sauce

Remember that the marinade in this recipe is for the birds, not for your drinking pleasure. SERVES 4 TO 8

PEPPERED PORT WINE SAUCE

½ cup minced onion

2 cloves garlic, pressed

2 teaspoons peeled and minced fresh ginger

2 teaspoons rainbow peppercorns, freshly ground

¼ cup orange juice

¼ cup chicken broth

2 tablespoons Port wine

1 tablespoon cider vinegar

2 to 4 tablespoons black raspberry jam, to your taste

¼ teaspoon cayenne pepper

Four 18- to 24-ounce Cornish hens, split in half along the backbone

1 To make the sauce, in a medium-size nonreactive saucepan, combine the sauce ingredients and cook over medium heat, stirring, until the mixture blends together. Remove from the heat and let cool.

2 Remove the giblets from the hens, rinse the hens inside and out under cold running water, and pat dry with paper towels. Place them in a shallow nonreactive baking dish or two zippered-top plastic bags and pour the cooled sauce over them. Cover with plastic wrap or seal and let marinate for 2 to 4 hours in the refrigerator.

3 Prepare a medium-hot fire in your grill.

4 Remove the hens from the sauce, reserving the sauce. Transfer the remaining sauce to a medium-size nonreactive saucepan and bring to a boil over medium-high heat; let simmer for 5 minutes, then set aside.

5 Place the hens breast side up directly over the coals, cover, and grill, turning frequently and basting with the sauce every 15 minutes, until an instant-read meat thermometer inserted into the breast and thigh, away from the bone, registers 165 degrees F, about 1 hour total. Serve hot.

Blue Ribbon Grilled Cornish Hens with Hot Onion Rub

This recipe took a first-place ribbon at the Lenexa Barbecue Contest in the Miscellaneous category, before it was legal to use Cornish hens in the Chicken category. SERVES 4 TO 8

Four 18- to 24-ounce Cornish hens, split in half along the backbone

HOT ONION RUB

2 tablespoons onion salt

2 teaspoons hot Hungarian paprika

½ teaspoon garlic powder

½ teaspoon freshly ground black pepper

SWEET SOY BASTE

½ cup tomato ketchup, homemade (page 43) or store-bought

3 tablespoons firmly packed dark brown sugar

1 tablespoon soy sauce

1 tablespoon prepared yellow or Dijon mustard

1 Rinse the hens inside and out under cold running water and pat dry with paper towels.

2 To make the rub, combine the rub ingredients in a small bowl and blend well. Sprinkle the hens evenly all over, inside and out, with the rub and set aside.

3 To make the baste, in a small nonreactive saucepan over medium heat, combine the baste ingredients, stirring to blend. Let simmer for about 15 minutes, until all the ingredients are incorporated. Set aside.

4 Prepare a medium-hot fire in your grill.

5 Place the hens directly over the coals breast side up, cover, and grill for 10 minutes. Turn the hens over, cover, and grill 10 minutes longer. Turn the hens again and baste with the sauce. Cover, cook for 30 minutes, turn, and baste one more time. The total cooking time is 30 to 45 minutes per pound or when an instant-read meat thermometer inserted into the breast and thigh, away from the bone, registers 165 degrees F.

Cornish Hens with Raspberry Barbecue Sauce

These birds are great for any dinner party, indoors or out. SERVES 4

Four 22-ounce Cornish hens, split in half along the backbone

2 tablespoons kosher salt

1 tablespoon coarsely ground black pepper

¼ cup Dijon mustard

1 cup Raspberry Chipotle Barbecue Sauce or Raspberry Ginger Barbecue Sauce (both page 152)

1 Prepare a medium-hot fire in your grill.

2 Remove the giblets from the hens, rinse the hens inside and out under cold running water, and pat dry with paper towels. Combine the salt and pepper and blend well. Rub each Cornish hen half with 1 tablespoon of the mustard and season evenly with the salt-and-pepper mixture.

3 Place the hens directly over the coals, cover, and grill for 10 to 15 minutes. Turn the hens,

cover, and grill 10 to 15 minutes longer. Twenty minutes before the end of the cooking time, baste with the barbecue sauce, cover, cook 10 minutes longer, turn, baste again, and cook 10 minutes longer. Turn and grill until an instant-read meat thermometer inserted into the breast and thigh, away from the bone, registers 165 degrees F, 50 to 60 minutes total. Serve with the remaining sauce on the side.

Smoked Garlic-Herb Cornish Hens in Orange and Ale Baste

These birds are a little tastier than chicken, even though they are in the same family. **SERVES 4**

Four 18- to 24-ounce Cornish hens

GARLIC-HERB RUB

1 tablespoon garlic salt

1 teaspoon dried oregano leaves

1 teaspoon dried basil leaves

1 teaspoon freshly ground black pepper

ORANGE AND ALE BASTE

1/2 cup (1 stick) unsalted butter

One 12-ounce bottle premium beer (I use Redhook Ale), allowed to go flat

1 cup orange juice

1 Prepare an indirect fire.

2 Reserve the giblets from the hens, rinse the hens inside and out under cold running water, and pat dry with paper towels. Reserve the giblets for

another use or season them with the rub, cook them with the hens, and snack on them when they are done.

3 To make the rub, in a small bowl, combine the rub ingredients and mix well. Season the hens evenly inside and out with it.

4 To make the baste, combine the baste ingredients in a medium-size nonreactive saucepan over medium heat, stirring, until the butter has melted. Remove from the heat.

5 Place the hens on the pit breast side up, cover, and cook at 230 to 250 degrees F for 1 hour. Turn, baste the hens, close the lid, and continue to baste and turn every 30 minutes. The total cooking time is 30 to 45 minutes per pound or until an instant-read meat thermometer inserted into the thigh and breast, away from the bone, registers 165 degrees F.

Smoked Cornish Hens with Peachy Marmalade Glaze

You can split this glaze or make the double batch that is in this recipe and serve the hens with biscuits and extra glaze on the side. **SERVES 8**

Eight 18- to 24-ounce Cornish hens

2 tablespoons granulated cane sugar

1 tablespoon onion salt

1 teaspoon finely ground black pepper

1/2 teaspoon poultry seasoning

1/4 teaspoon cayenne pepper

1/4 cup Kitchen Bouquet

PEACHY MARMALADE GLAZE

1 cup orange marmalade

1/2 cup (1 stick) unsalted butter

2 tablespoons peach schnapps

1 Remove the giblets from the hens, rinse the hens inside and out under cold running water, and pat dry with paper towels. Combine the sugar, onion salt, black pepper, poultry seasoning, and cayenne in a small bowl and blend well. Rub the hens with the Kitchen Bouquet, then sprinkle evenly with the seasoning mixture inside and out.

2 To make the glaze, combine the glaze ingredients in a medium-size nonreactive saucepan over medium heat and whisk together until the butter has melted and the ingredients are well blended. Remove from the heat.

3 Prepare an indirect fire.

4 Place the hens on the pit breast side up, cover, and cook at 230 to 250 degrees F for 1 hour. Turn, glaze the hens, cover, and continue to glaze and turn every 30 minutes. The total cooking time is 30 to 45 minutes per pound or until an instant-read meat thermometer inserted into the thigh and breast, away from the bone, registers 165 degrees F.

Mexican Turkey Burgers

The kids will really like this recipe, but go easy on the jalapeños. SERVES 6

1 1/2 pounds ground turkey

1/2 cup dry bread crumbs

2 tablespoons minced roasted red peppers

2 tablespoons minced green onions (green and white parts)

1 small jalapeño chile, seeded and minced

1 tablespoon minced fresh cilantro leaves

2 teaspoons olive oil

1 teaspoon chili powder, homemade (page 111) or store-bought

1 teaspoon ground cumin

1 teaspoon fine sea salt

1 teaspoon finely ground black pepper

Nonstick cooking spray

6 hamburger buns, grilled or toasted

6 slices Monterey Jack cheese

Lettuce leaves, sliced ripe tomatoes, sliced onions, and salsa or barbecue sauce of your choice

1 Prepare a medium-hot fire in your grill.

2 In a medium-size bowl, combine the turkey, bread crumbs, red pepper, green onion, jalapeño, cilantro, olive oil, chili powder, cumin, salt, and pepper and blend well with your hands. Form into 6 patties 1/2 to 3/4 inch thick. Coat with the nonstick spray.

3 Place the burgers directly over the coals, cover, and grill for 5 to 7 minutes per side, until cooked through.

4 To assemble the burgers, place a hot burger on the bottom half of each grilled bun, top with a slice of cheese, then add lettuce, tomatoes, sliced onions, and salsa or barbecue sauce to your taste.

Turkey Burgers with Fresh Pineapple Salsa

These burgers are easy, delicious, and low in fat. Ground turkey can give off a lot of moisture, so make sure you drain or pat it somewhat dry with paper towels before mixing in the other ingredients. Fresh ground turkey is usually drier than frozen, thawed ground turkey. **SERVES 8**

FRESH PINEAPPLE SALSA

2 cups peeled, cored, and minced fresh pineapple

$1/4$ cup minced green onions (white and green parts)

$1/4$ cup clover honey

2 tablespoons peeled and grated fresh ginger

$1/2$ teaspoon crushed red pepper

$1/2$ teaspoon kosher salt

BURGERS

2 pounds fresh ground turkey

$1/2$ cup dry bread crumbs

$1/4$ cup minced or sliced green onions (white and green parts)

$1/4$ cup mayonnaise

2 cloves garlic, pressed

1 teaspoon kosher salt

$1/2$ teaspoon freshly ground black pepper

$1/4$ cup olive oil or nonstick cooking spray

8 hamburger buns

1 To make the salsa, combine the salsa ingredients in a medium-size nonreactive bowl and blend thoroughly. Set aside for at least 30 minutes to let the flavors develop. (It's actually best fixed the day before.)

2 To make the burgers, combine the turkey, bread crumbs, green onion, mayonnaise, garlic, salt, and black pepper in a large bowl and blend with your hands until the mixture binds together. Form into 8 patties $1/2$ to $3/4$ inch thick.

3 Prepare a medium-hot fire in your grill.

4 Dip each burger into the olive oil or coat with the cooking spray. Place directly over the coals, cover, and grill, turning frequently, until cooked through, 6 to 7 minutes per side. Serve on hamburger buns topped with the salsa.

Tuscan Turkey Burgers

These burgers are good topped with a cool ranch dressing, tomatoes, and onion. The seasonings are what give this burger its Tuscan flavor. **SERVES 2 TO 4**

1 pound ground turkey thigh meat

$1/4$ cup freshly grated Parmesan cheese

2 tablespoons olive oil

1 tablespoon dry vermouth

1 teaspoon crushed dried rosemary leaves

$1/2$ teaspoon rubbed sage

Salt and freshly ground black pepper to taste

Nonstick cooking spray

4 Italian hard rolls, cut in half

1 Prepare a medium-hot fire in your grill.

2 In a medium-size bowl, combine the turkey, cheese, olive oil, vermouth, rosemary, and sage, season with the salt and pepper, and blend well with your hands. Form into 4 patties $1/2$ to $3/4$ inch thick. Coat with the nonstick spray.

3 Place the burgers directly over the coals, cover, and grill for 5 to 7 minutes per side, until cooked through. Serve on the hard rolls.

Grilled Sweet-and-Sour Turkey Steaks

This recipe is quick, easy, and good. Cut the turkey steaks, about 1/2 inch thick, out of turkey breast or turkey tenderloins. Place them between two sheets of wax paper or plastic wrap and tenderize or pound with a meat mallet. SERVES 8

8 turkey steaks, tenderized

SWEET-AND-SOUR MARINADE

1 cup red wine vinegar

1/2 cup minced onion

1/4 cup granulated cane sugar

1/4 cup olive oil

2 cloves garlic, pressed

1/2 teaspoon dried tarragon leaves

1/2 teaspoon kosher salt

1/2 teaspoon freshly ground black pepper

1 Place the steaks in a shallow nonreactive baking dish or zippered-top plastic bag.

2 To make the marinade, combine the marinade ingredients in a medium-size nonreactive bowl and pour over the steaks, coating them. Cover with plastic wrap or seal and let marinate in the refrigerator for up to 2 hours.

3 Prepare a hot fire in your grill.

4 Remove the turkey from the marinade. Transfer the remaining marinade to a medium-size non-

reactive saucepan and bring to a boil over medium-high heat; let simmer for 5 minutes, then set aside.

5 Place the turkey directly over the coals, cover, and grill, turning frequently and basting the cooked sides with the reserved marinade, until cooked through, 4 to 6 minutes more per side.

Turkey Tenderloins in Bahamian Rum Marinade

You can have this tasty treat without the expense of that big boat ride and all the seasickness. Serve with rice and your favorite barbecue sauce (pages 136–161). SERVES 8

BAHAMIAN RUM MARINADE

1/4 cup fresh lime juice (about 4 limes)

1/4 cup clover honey

1/4 cup soy sauce

1/4 cup canola oil

2 tablespoons light rum

1 teaspoon kosher salt

1 teaspoon freshly ground black pepper

1/2 teaspoon ground allspice

1/2 teaspoon dried tarragon leaves

4 pounds turkey tenderloins

1 To make the marinade, combine the marinade ingredients in a small nonreactive bowl or large measuring cup and mix well.

2 Place the tenderloins in a shallow nonreactive baking dish or a zippered-top plastic bag and pour the marinade over them, turning to coat. Cover with plastic wrap or seal and let marinate for at least 3 to 4 hours or overnight in the refrigerator.

3 Prepare a medium-hot fire in your grill.

4 Remove the turkey from the marinade. Transfer the remaining marinade to a medium-size non-reactive saucepan and bring to a boil over medium-high heat; let simmer for 5 minutes, then set aside.

5 Place the turkey directly over the coals, cover, and grill, turning and basting the cooked sides with the reserved marinade frequently, until cooked through, 5 to 7 minutes per side. To serve, slice at an angle.

Grilled Baby Turkey with Sweet Garlic Rub and Chili Apple Baste

The most difficult part of this recipe is finding the baby turkey. I usually have to order mine from a poultry supplier, who makes me buy the whole case, 4 to 6 of them, at a time. SERVES 6 TO 8

One 6-pound young turkey, split in half along the backbone

SWEET GARLIC RUB

2 tablespoons garlic salt

1 tablespoon celery salt

1 tablespoon freshly ground black pepper

1 tablespoon granulated cane sugar

CHILI APPLE BASTE

1/2 cup apple juice

1/2 cup chili sauce, homemade (page 42) or store-bought

1/4 cup cider vinegar

2 tablespoons canola oil

2 tablespoons Worcestershire sauce, homemade (page 50) or store-bought

1 tablespoon soy sauce

1 teaspoon Louisiana hot sauce

1/2 teaspoon ground coriander

1 Remove the giblets and neck from the turkey and reserve for another use. Rinse the turkey inside and out under cold running water and pat dry with paper towels. Bend the wings so they fit under the back.

2 To make the rub, combine the rub ingredients in a small bowl and blend well. Season the turkey all over with the mixture. Cover with plastic wrap and set aside.

3 To make the basting sauce, combine the ingredients in a medium-size nonreactive saucepan and bring to a boil. Reduce the heat to medium-low and simmer for 15 minutes, stirring occasionally. Let cool to room temperature.

4 Prepare a medium-hot fire in your grill.

5 Place the turkey directly over the coals, cover, and grill, turning and basting every 15 minutes, until an instant-read thermometer meat inserted into the breast and thigh, away from the bone, registers 165 degrees F, about 1 1/2 hours total. Let rest for 10 minutes before carving.

BARBECUED BABY TURKEY WITH SWEET GARLIC RUB AND CHILI APPLE BASTE
Prepare an indirect fire, then place the turkey on the pit, cover, and cook at 230 to 250 degrees F for 3 hours, basting every 30 minutes. Turn the turkey and continue to cook, basting, until cooked through, about 4 hours total.

Bob Lyon's Patio Classic Smoked Turkey

This is one of Bob's specialties, which he makes for the holidays on his Patio Classic. He recommends that you smoke one turkey the day before Thanksgiving to give away to friends and relations—and to use as an insurance policy in case your other turkey doesn't turn out as planned. This turkey takes about 8 hours to smoke, so plan ahead. SERVES 8 TO 10

One 12- to 14-pound turkey, thawed if
    necessary

THANKSGIVING TURKEY RUB

1/4 cup granulated cane sugar

2 tablespoons firmly packed light brown sugar

2 tablespoons seasoned salt, homemade (page
    108) or store-bought

1 tablespoon onion salt

1 tablespoon celery salt

2 tablespoons sweet Hungarian paprika

1 tablespoon rubbed sage

1 teaspoon freshly ground black pepper

1/2 cup safflower oil

2 Granny Smith apples, quartered and cored

2 medium-size onions, quartered

1 cup apple juice (optional)

1   Remove the giblets and neck from the turkey; rinse the turkey inside and out under cold running water, and pat dry with paper towels.

2   To make the rub, combine the rub ingredients in a small bowl and blend well. Rub half the oil inside the turkey and season evenly with half the rub. Place the apples and onions in the cavity,

then rub the outside of the turkey with the remaining oil and sprinkle evenly with the remaining rub. Fix the wings under the turkey so that it will sit level on your smoker grill.

3   Prepare an indirect fire.

4   Place the turkey on the pit breast side down, cover, and cook at 230 to 250 degrees F for 3 hours. Turn the turkey so the breast side is up and the side that was farthest from the coals is now closer to them. Baste at least once with the apple juice, if desired, until cooked through. Add hot coals and a wood chunk every 1 to 1½ hours, depending on the rate at which the charcoal is burning. Insert an instant-read meat thermometer into each thigh after 6 hours. The internal temperature should be approaching 160 degrees F. Reverse the turkey's position again. The turkey is done when it reaches an internal temperature of 165 degrees F, 7 to 8 hours total cooking time. Let rest for 15 minutes before carving.

Not-at-All-Boring Barbecued Turkey

For the holidays, this recipe is a nice change from boring roast turkey. Just make sure you allow at least 8 hours to smoke the turkey. It could take longer on a cold, rainy, or wet day. SERVES 8 TO 10

One 10- to 12-pound turkey or one 7- to
    9-pound turkey breast, thawed if necessary

1/2 cup (1 stick) chilled unsalted butter, split in
    half lengthwise and softened a bit

1¼ cups Creole Seasoning (page 118)

1 large onion, quartered

¼ cup canola oil

Oil-based baste of your choice
(pages 58–85)

1 Remove the giblets and neck from the turkey; rinse it inside and out under cold running water and pat dry with paper towels. Place the butter under the breast skin on both sides of the turkey from the back cavity to the wing, taking care not to tear the skin. Season the cavity with 2 to 4 teaspoons of the Creole Seasoning and insert the onion. Fix the wings under the turkey so that it will sit level on your smoker grill. Rub the outside of the turkey with the canola oil and season evenly with the remaining Creole Seasoning. (It's hot, so use with caution and season as desired.)

2 Prepare an indirect fire.

3 Place the turkey on the pit breast side down, cover, and cook at 230 to 250 degrees F for 3 hours. Turn the turkey so the breast side is up and the side that was farthest from the coals is now closer to them. Start to baste every 30 minutes until cooked through. Add hot coals and a wood chunk every 1 to 1½ hours, depending on the rate at which the charcoal is burning. After 6 hours, insert an instant-read meat thermometer into each thigh, or into the thickest part of the breast, if smoking a breast. The internal temperature should be approaching 160 degrees F. Reverse the turkey's position again and continue basting. The turkey is done when it reaches an internal temperature of 165 degrees F, 7 to 8 hours total cooking time. Let rest for 15 minutes before carving.

Sweet Crab-Apple-Glazed Barbecued Turkey

This glaze is also good on a regular roasted turkey.
SERVES 10 TO 12

2 cups (4 sticks) unsalted butter

¼ cup fresh lemon juice (about 2 lemons)

1 tablespoon kosher salt

2 teaspoons freshly ground black pepper

One 10- to 12-pound turkey, thawed if necessary

SWEET CRAB-APPLE GLAZE

One 16-ounce jar crab-apple jelly

½ cup Rhine white wine, such as Liebfraumilch or Riesling

½ cup pineapple juice

½ cup dark corn syrup

2 tablespoons fresh lemon juice

2 tablespoons cornstarch

3 tablespoons cold water

1 Place the butter and lemon juice in a medium-size nonreactive saucepan over medium heat and stir until the butter has melted. Remove from the heat and let cool to room temperature. Stir in the salt and pepper.

2 Meanwhile, remove the giblets and neck from the turkey and reserve for another use. Rinse the turkey inside and out under cold running water and pat dry with paper towels. Paint the turkey inside and out with the lemon-butter mixture. Reserve the remaining lemon butter.

3 To make the glaze, combine the jelly, wine, pineapple juice, corn syrup, and lemon juice in a

medium-size nonreactive saucepan over medium heat, stirring until heated through. Combine the cornstarch and cold water in a small bowl and add to the hot jelly mixture, stirring with a wire whisk until the mixture is thick and shiny. Remove from the heat.

4 Prepare an indirect fire.

5 Place the turkey on the pit breast side down, cover, and cook at 230 to 250 degrees F for 3 hours. Turn the turkey so the breast side is up and the side that was farthest from the coals is now closer to them. Cook for 3 hours, then reverse the turkey's position again, baste with the remaining lemon butter, close the lid, and cook 1½ hours longer. Turn the turkey and baste again. Continue to baste and turn about every 45 minutes. Add hot coals and a wood chunk every 1 to 1½ hours, depending on the rate at which the charcoal is burning. After 6 hours, insert an instant-read meat thermometer into each thigh, away from the bone. The turkey is done when it reaches an internal temperature of 165 degrees F, 10 to 12 hours total cooking time.

6 During the last hour of cooking, paint the turkey with the glaze every 15 minutes. Let rest for 15 minutes before carving.

Barbecued Wild Turkey with Sweet Black Pepper Rub

If you ever get a chance, try some wild turkey; it has a far better flavor than the domesticated variety. However, it does not have as much fat as a domestic bird, so slow smoking is the way to go, though this recipe works equally well with a domesticated bird. Powdered spices, such as marjoram, are available from better spice companies, including Penzeys and Zach's (see Sources). SERVES 10 TO 12

One 10- to 12-pound turkey, thawed if necessary

½ cup (1 stick) unsalted butter, split in half lengthwise and frozen

SWEET BLACK PEPPER RUB

2 tablespoons granulated cane sugar

1 tablespoon seasoned salt, homemade (page 108) or store-bought

1 tablespoon onion salt

1 tablespoon celery salt

2 teaspoons freshly ground black pepper

1 teaspoon ground marjoram

½ teaspoon ground thyme

4 cups apple juice, as needed

1 Remove the giblets and neck from the turkey and reserve for another use. Rinse the turkey inside and out under cold running water and pat dry with paper towels. Place the butter under the breast skin, preferably at the top, on both sides of the breastbone, being careful not to tear the skin.

2 To make the rub, combine the rub ingredients and blend well. Season the turkey evenly inside and out with the rub mixture.

3 Prepare an indirect fire.

4 Place the turkey on the pit, breast side up, cover, and cook at 230 to 250 degrees F for 3 hours. Turn the turkey so the breast side is down and the side that was farthest from the coals is now closer to them, baste with the apple juice, and close the lid. Baste every hour with the apple

juice. After another 1½ hours, turn the turkey over again and close the lid. After 6 hours, insert an instant-read meat thermometer into each thigh, away from the bone. The turkey is done when it reaches an internal temperature of 165 degrees F, 6 to 8 hours total cooking time. Let rest for 15 minutes before carving.

Hawaiian Smoked Turkey with Sherried Soy Marinade

I got this recipe from the chef at the Out Rigger Club in Hawaii. This larger-size turkey takes about 10 to 12 hours to slow smoke. SERVES 8 TO 12

One 12- to 14-pound turkey, thawed if
necessary

SHERRIED SOY MARINADE

1 cup light soy sauce

½ cup safflower oil

¼ cup sweet sherry

¼ cup grated onions

¼ cup firmly packed light brown sugar

2 cloves garlic, pressed

1 teaspoon kosher salt

½ teaspoon freshly ground black pepper

1 Remove the giblets and neck from the turkey and reserve for another use. Rinse the turkey inside and out under cold running water and pat dry with paper towels. Place the turkey in a heavy-duty extra-large zippered-top plastic bag or double up the bags.

2 To make the marinade, combine all the marinade ingredients in a medium-size nonreactive bowl, blend well, and pour into the cavity of the turkey. Seal the bag and let marinate in the refrigerator for at least 4 hours.

3 Prepare an indirect fire.

4 Remove the turkey from the marinade and pat dry with paper towels. Transfer the marinade to a medium-size nonreactive saucepan and bring to a boil over medium-high heat; let simmer for 5 minutes, then set aside.

5 Place the turkey on the pit breast side down, cover, and cook at 230 to 250 degrees F for 3 hours. Turn the turkey so the breast side is up and the side that was farthest from the coals is now closer to them. Baste every 30 minutes with the reserved marinade. Add hot coals and a wood chunk every 1 to 1½ hours, depending on the rate at which the charcoal is burning. After 6 hours, insert an instant-read meat thermometer into each thigh, away from the bone. The internal temperature should be approaching 160 degrees F. Reverse the turkey's position again and continue basting. The turkey is done when it reaches an internal temperature of 165 degrees F, 10 to 12 hours total cooking time. Let rest for 15 minutes before carving.

Smoked Turkey Sandwich with Barbecue Thousand Island Dressing

This is a real Dagwood sandwich, if ever there was one, with an outstanding flavor that is all the better when made with your own barbecued turkey leftovers. Do note that the dressing contains raw eggs—make sure yours are really fresh to avoid the possibility of salmonella. SERVES 4

BARBECUE THOUSAND ISLAND DRESSING

2 very fresh large eggs

1 tablespoon granulated cane sugar

1 teaspoon dry mustard (I use Colman's)

1/2 teaspoon non-iodized salt

2 tablespoons distilled white vinegar

1/2 teaspoon sweet Hungarian paprika

1/4 teaspoon cayenne pepper

2 cups canola oil

1 1/2 cups barbecue sauce of your choice (pages 136–161)

1/2 cup sweet pickle relish

1/4 cup finely grated onion

2 tablespoons minced pimento olives

OPEN-FACED SANDWICH

4 slices rye bread

4 to 8 slices Swiss cheese

8 slices ripe red tomatoes

8 lettuce leaves

8 strips bacon, fried until crisp and drained on paper towels

8 slices smoked turkey, (1 1/2 to 2 pounds), breast or thigh meat

1 To make the dressing, beat the eggs with a whisk in a medium-size bowl until thick. Add the sugar, mustard, salt, vinegar, paprika, and cayenne and whisk to combine. Add the canola oil drop by drop, beating constantly until all the oil is incorporated and the dressing is thick. (This step, with these ingredients, can be eliminated by using a good mayonnaise, but it is better to make it yourself.) Add the barbecue sauce gradually, then stir in the pickle relish, onion, and pimento. Store, covered, in the refrigerator for 2 to 4 hours before using to let the flavors develop.

2 To assemble the sandwich, place 1 slice of bread for each sandwich on 4 luncheon plates. Top with 1 to 2 slices of Swiss cheese, 2 tomato slices, 2 lettuce leaves, 2 strips of bacon, and 2 slices of smoked turkey. Top each sandwich with a generous portion of dressing. Cut in half on the diagonal. Serve with fresh fruit and the remaining dressing on the side.

Grilled Wild Duck with Red Currant Sauce

Whether you use wild mallard or teal, domestic Long Island, or the huge moulard or Muscovy duck breasts for this recipe, you're in for some good eatin'. Wild duck breasts do not have much fat, so slather on some melted butter before grilling. Go easier with the butter on domestic duck. There are two keys to great grilled duck breasts— a medium fire and a spray bottle of water to douse any flare-ups; the fatter the duck breast, the more flare-ups you'll get, so watch carefully as you grill. SERVES 4

Eight 4-ounce wild mallard or teal duck breasts or four 8-ounce or larger Muscovy duck breasts

1/4 cup (1/2 stick) unsalted butter, melted

1 tablespoon garlic salt

2 teaspoons coarsely ground black pepper

RED CURRANT SAUCE

1/2 cup red currant jelly

1/2 cup seedless raspberry preserves

1/4 cup orange juice

1 tablespoon Triple Sec or other orange-flavored liqueur

1 tablespoon Worcestershire sauce, homemade (page 50) or store-bought

1 tablespoon dry mustard (I use Colman's)

1 teaspoon ground ginger

1 teaspoon fine sea salt

1 Rinse the duck under cold running water and pat dry with paper towels. Brush the duck breasts all over with the melted butter and season with the salt and pepper.

2 To make the sauce, in a medium-size nonreactive saucepan, stir together the sauce ingredients over medium-low heat until the jelly has melted. Simmer, covered, for about 10 minutes. Set aside.

3 Prepare a medium fire in your grill.

4 Place the duck directly over the coals, cover, and grill for 3 to 5 minutes per side for medium rare to medium or to your desired degree of doneness. Serve with the sauce drizzled over the duck breasts.

Smoked Fermented Black Bean Duck

I got this recipe from a Chinese cooking course I took in Wainnai, Hawaii. Fermented black beans are available at Asian markets and contribute an aromatic flavor to the duck. SERVES 2 TO 4

FERMENTED BLACK BEAN MARINADE

1 cup water

1/4 cup dried fermented black beans, cracked

1/2 cup soy sauce

1/4 cup clover honey

3 tablespoons hoisin sauce

2 tablespoons sweet sherry

2 tablespoons peeled and grated fresh ginger

4 green onions, cut into 1/2-inch-thick slices

2 teaspoons ground cinnamon

1 teaspoon freshly ground black pepper

1/2 teaspoon Chinese 5-spice powder, homemade (page 112) or store-bought

One 4- to 5-pound duck, trimmed of extra fat and skin

1 To make the marinade, in a medium-size nonreactive saucepan, bring the water and black beans to a boil over medium-high heat. Reduce the heat to medium-low and simmer for 5 minutes. Add the remaining marinade ingredients, stirring until everything is blended and dissolved. Let cool to room temperature.

2 Rinse the duck inside and out under cold running water, remove the giblets and neck, and pat dry with paper towels. Place the duck in a large nonreactive bowl or large, heavy-duty zippered-top plastic bag. Pour the marinade over

the duck, turning the duck so it is covered inside and out, then cover with plastic wrap or seal. Let marinate at least 4 to 6 hours or overnight in the refrigerator.

3 Prepare an indirect fire.

4 Remove the duck from the marinade. Transfer the remaining marinade to a medium-size nonreactive saucepan and bring to a boil over medium-high heat; let simmer for 5 minutes, then set aside to cool. Refrigerate until ready to baste.

5 Place the duck on the pit breast side down, cover, and cook at 230 to 250 degrees F for 3½ to 4 hours, turning once about halfway through the cooking time and basting with the reserved marinade every 30 minutes thereafter, until an instant-read meat thermometer inserted into the breast and thigh, away from the bone, registers 165 degrees F. Let rest for 15 minutes before carving.

Szechuan Smoked Duck

This duck has a little heat, but it is fantastic. I think it's better than Peking duck. SERVES 2 TO 4

SZECHUAN RUB

¼ cup firmly packed dark brown sugar

2 tablespoons Szechuan Peppercorn Salt (page 110)

1 tablespoon garlic salt

1 tablespoon onion salt

2 tablespoons sweet Hungarian paprika

1 teaspoons ground ginger

1 teaspoon Chinese dry mustard

1 teaspoon cayenne pepper

½ teaspoon ground star anise

One 4- to 5-pound duck, trimmed of extra fat and skin

½ cup toasted sesame oil

1 recipe Picante Beer Marinade (page 68)

1 To make the rub, combine the rub ingredients in a small bowl and blend well.

2 Rinse the duck inside and out under cold running water, remove the giblets and neck, and pat dry with paper towels. Rub the duck inside and out with the sesame oil, then season evenly with the rub inside and out to taste; remember, this dish is spicy.

3 Prepare an indirect fire.

4 Place the duck on the pit breast side down, cover, and cook at 230 to 250 degrees F for 2 hours. Turn the duck, baste with the marinade, and continue to cook, basting every 30 minutes, until an instant-read meat thermometer inserted into the breast and thigh, away from the bone, registers 165 degrees F, about 4 hours total. Let rest for 15 minutes before carving.

Barbecued Duck in White Wine Marinade

I like this marinated duck because the wine doesn't overpower the delicate flavor of the meat. SERVES 2 TO 4

1 cup White Wine Marinade with Peppercorns, Bay Leaf, and Juniper (page 63)

½ cup sweet vermouth

½ cup soy sauce

One 4- to 5-pound duck, trimmed of extra fat and skin

1 Combine the marinade, vermouth, and soy sauce in a medium-size nonreactive bowl and blend well.

2 Rinse the duck inside and out under cold running water, remove the giblets and neck, and pat dry with paper towels. Place the duck in a large nonreactive bowl or large, heavy-duty zippered-top plastic bag. Pour the marinade over the duck, turning the duck so it is covered inside and out, and cover with plastic wrap or seal. Let marinate for at least 4 to 6 hours or overnight in the refrigerator.

3 Prepare an indirect fire.

4 Remove the duck from the marinade. Transfer the remaining marinade to a medium-size nonreactive saucepan and bring to a boil over medium-high heat; let simmer for 5 minutes, then set aside to cool. Refrigerate until ready to baste.

5 Place the duck on the pit breast side down, cover, and cook at 230 to 250 degrees F, turning once about halfway through the cooking time, until an instant-read meat thermometer inserted into the breast and thigh, away from the bone, registers 165 degrees F, 3½ to 4 hours. Glaze the duck with the marinade every 10 to 15 minutes during the last 30 to 45 minutes of cooking time. Let rest for 15 minutes before carving.

Honey-Glazed Barbecued Duck

This duck is more like Peking duck, except it is crisp, sweet, and tasty. When done, the skin will be a dark mahogany. SERVES 2 TO 4

HONEY GLAZE

2 cups orange juice or juice of your choice

¼ cup cider vinegar

¼ cup clover honey

3 tablespoons vanilla extract

1 tablespoon fresh rosemary leaves, minced

1 tablespoon fresh thyme leaves

1 teaspoon fine sea salt

½ teaspoon white pepper

¼ teaspoon ground cinnamon

¼ teaspoon ground cloves

One 4- to 5-pound duck, trimmed of extra fat and skin

1 tablespoon garlic salt

2 teaspoons freshly ground black pepper

½ teaspoon ground cloves

8 cloves

1 orange

2 sprigs fresh thyme

1 cup apple juice

1 To make the glaze, combine the glaze ingredients in a medium-size nonreactive saucepan over medium-high heat and bring to a boil. Reduce the heat to medium-low and simmer until reduced to about 1½ cups, 25 to 30 minutes. Strain through a fine-mesh strainer into a bowl. Set aside.

2 Prepare an indirect fire.

3   Rinse the duck inside and out under cold running water, remove the giblets and neck, and pat dry with paper towels. Combine the garlic salt, pepper, and ground cloves in a small bowl and blend well; set aside. Stick the whole cloves into the orange, then quarter the orange. Rub the salt-and-pepper seasoning all over the duck inside and out and place the orange sections and thyme sprigs in the cavity of the duck.

4   Place the duck on the pit breast side down, cover, and cook at 230 to 250 degrees F for 3½ to 4 hours, basting once with the apple juice, until an instant-read meat thermometer inserted into the breast and thigh, away from the bone, registers 165 degrees F. Glaze the duck every 10 to 15 minutes during the last 30 to 45 minutes of cooking time. Let rest for 15 minutes before carving.

Smoked Hawaiian Honeyed Wild Duck

Rub a whole wild duck with fragrant spices, stuff it with fresh pineapple and orange, smoke it over a sweet wood such as apple or cherry, and baste it with a honeyed pineapple and orange sauce with just a hint of ginger. That's eatin'! In this recipe, you smoke the duck at a higher temperature than usual—250 to 300 degrees F—to give it a crisp skin and a tender texture. Fried rice or rice pilaf goes well with the sweet-sour flavor of this dish. Grilled sweet Maui onions are also a great accompaniment.

SERVES 2 TO 4

One 2½-pound wild duck

2 tablespoons fine sea salt

1 tablespoon dark brown sugar

1 teaspoon ground ginger

1 teaspoon ground basil

1 teaspoon freshly ground black pepper

1 orange, left unpeeled and cut into ½-inch-thick slices

3 cored and peeled fresh pineapple slices

HAWAIIAN HONEY SAUCE

¾ cup clover or other light honey

¼ cup (½ stick) unsalted butter, melted

¼ cup pineapple juice

¼ cup orange juice

2 tablespoons fresh lemon juice

2 teaspoons peeled and grated fresh ginger

1 teaspoon dry mustard (I use Colman's)

1 teaspoon grated orange zest

2 tablespoons cornstarch

2 tablespoons cold water

1   Rinse the duck inside and out under cold running water, remove the giblets and neck, and pat dry with paper towels. Combine the salt, brown sugar, ginger, basil, and pepper in a small bowl. Rub the duck all over with the seasoning mixture. Stuff the cavity of the duck with the orange and pineapple slices.

2   To make the sauce, combine the sauce ingredients, except the cornstarch and cold water, in a medium-size nonreactive saucepan and simmer over medium heat for 10 minutes. Combine the cornstarch and water in a small bowl to make a paste. Whisk the paste, 1 teaspoon at a time, into the hot sauce until it thickens. Remove from the heat and set aside.

3   Prepare an indirect fire.

4   Place the duck on the pit, cover, and cook at 250 to 300 degrees F for 1½ hours. Baste the duck with the sauce and continue to baste every

15 minutes. Cook until an instant-read meat thermometer inserted into the breast and thigh, away from the bone, registers 135 to 140 degrees F, about 1½ hours longer. Let the duck rest for 15 minutes before carving.

Grilled Pheasant Breast with Port Wine Sauce

I usually get my wild pheasant already skinned—and the breasts already boned—from my hunter friends. The cook removes the skin and feathers from wild pheasant because hunters don't want to take all that time to pluck it in the field and because wild pheasant skin gets as tough as leather when you cook it. If you buy pheasant that has been raised domestically—what you usually find in grocery stores—the skin will probably still be on; leave it on. Pheasant, either wild or domestic, is a lean bird and is best when grilled medium rare or medium so it's not too dry. I like to throw on a chunk or two of apple wood for a more aromatic flavor. SERVES 4

4 pheasant breast halves

¼ cup (½ stick) unsalted butter, softened

Salt and freshly ground black pepper to taste

PORT WINE SAUCE

½ cup chicken broth or game stock

¼ cup port wine

2 tablespoons unsalted butter, frozen and cut into small pieces

1 Rinse the pheasant breasts under cold running water and pat dry with paper towels. Rub each breast half with 1 tablespoon of the butter and season with the salt and pepper.

2 Prepare a medium-hot fire in your grill.

3 Combine the broth and port in a small nonreactive saucepan over medium-high heat, bring to a boil, and cook until reduced by half, about 5 minutes. Whisk in the frozen butter, one piece at a time, until the sauce has thickened and become shiny. Remove from the heat.

4 Place the pheasant directly over the coals, cover, and grill for 5 to 7 minutes per side for medium rare to medium or to your desired degree of doneness.

5 To serve, place a tablespoonful of sauce on each serving plate, slice the breast at an angle, and fan over the sauce.

Bacon-Wrapped Dove Breasts on the Grill

Another way to keep game birds moist and succulent is to wrap them in bacon, as is done in this recipe. Traditionally, dove is a Southern breakfast dish, but I have friends in the Midwest who hunt and eat dove as well. Doves are difficult birds to hunt because they're fast and change direction quickly. It has a mild flavor like that of quail. In fact, you could grill quail exactly the same way. SERVES 4

8 to 12 boneless dove breasts

2 tablespoons firmly packed dark brown sugar

1 tablespoon seasoned salt, homemade (page 108) or store-bought

2 teaspoons onion salt

1 teaspoon celery salt

1 teaspoon freshly ground black pepper

8 to 12 strips bacon

1 Rinse the dove breasts under cold running water and pat dry with paper towels. Combine the brown sugar, seasoned salt, onion salt, celery salt, and pepper in a small bowl. Sprinkle the seasoning mixture all over the dove breasts. Wrap each breast in a bacon strip, securing the bacon with toothpicks.

2 Prepare a medium-hot fire in your grill.

3 Place the dove breasts directly over the coals, cover, and grill for 5 to 7 minutes per side for medium rare to medium or to your desired degree of doneness. Discard the bacon before eating, if you wish.

Simple Grilled Quail

Whether wild or domestic, quail is delicious on the grill, especially basted with this easy sauce. I like to throw a chunk or two of apple wood on the fire for a more aromatic flavor. SERVES 4

    4 quail
    Salt and freshly ground black pepper to taste
    $1/2$ cup (1 stick) unsalted butter, melted
    1 cup of your favorite barbecue sauce (pages 136–161)

1 Rinse the quail under cold running water and pat dry with paper towels. Season all over with the salt and pepper. In a small bowl, combine the melted butter and barbecue sauce and set aside.

2 Prepare a medium-hot fire in your grill.

3 Brush the quail with the sauce, set directly over the coals, cover, and grill, basting frequently, for 4 to 5 minutes per side for medium rare to medium or to your desired degree of doneness.

Grilled Quail with Brandied Apple Sauce

Serve this grilled quail dish with the delicious sauce spooned over it and topped with crumbled bacon. A spoonful of homemade applesauce is mighty good with this, too. A few chunks of apple wood on the fire give a pretty tasty result. SERVES 4

    4 quail
    8 strips bacon, fried until crisp, drained, and crumbled, bacon fat reserved
    $1/4$ cup firmly packed light brown sugar
    2 large tart apples, such as Granny Smith, left unpeeled, cored and sliced
    1 cup golden raisins
    1 cup salted cashews
    $1/4$ cup brandy

1 Rinse the quail under cold running water and pat dry with paper towels. Brush them all over with the reserved melted bacon fat.

2 In a medium-size nonreactive saucepan, combine the brown sugar, apples, raisins, cashews, and brandy. Simmer over medium-low heat, covered, until the apples are tender, about 10 minutes. Set aside.

3 Prepare a medium-hot fire in your grill.

4 Place the quail directly over the coals, cover, and grill for 4 to 5 minutes per side for medium rare to medium or to your desired degree of doneness.

5 To serve, place each quail on a serving plate, spoon the sauce over the top, and sprinkle with the crumbled bacon.

Smokin' with

BAR-E
BARBEQUE & SAUSAGE
CITY MARKET
LULING, TEXAS

the Fishes

When I was growing up in the Midwest, most people did not associate fish and shellfish with barbecuing or grilling. I was lucky because my father was a pilot and when he got the Boston run, he would return home with fresh lobster, clams, and oysters. So, unlike other families in my neighborhood, I grew up with fresh seafood. As a chef, I have also cooked with fresh seafood shipped to the restaurants I've worked at in the Midwest. Still, my knowledge is relatively limited, so I asked my foodie friends for help.

The first to offer advice is Gunner Roe, a fish and shellfish guru from Galena, Maryland, who is also known as the Grill Meister. I've also turned to my Kansas City friends Karen Adler and Judith Fertig, also known as the Barbecue Queens (they wear tiaras sometimes, go figure), who have written *Fish and Shellfish, Grilled and Smoked* (The Harvard Common Press, 2002).

Grilling versus Smoking

For grilling, you prepare a medium-hot or hot fire in a grill and cook the fish or shellfish directly over the coals. For smoking, you prepare an indirect fire (see Setting Up the Pit, pages 18–22) using the wood of your choice and cook the fish away from the coals. Grilled fish will have grill marks and a slightly carbonized flavor. Smoked fish will not have grill marks, may have a burnished appearance, and will have a slightly smoky flavor. The two recipes that follow illustrate the difference in techniques.

Simple Grilled Fish Fillets

It doesn't get any simpler than this. SERVES 6 TO 8

> Eight 4- to 6-ounce fish fillets, such as rockfish (striped bass), Atlantic croaker (hardhead), sea trout, or drum
>
> ½ cup olive oil
>
> 2 teaspoons freshly ground black pepper
>
> 1 teaspoon Old Bay seasoning, homemade (page 119) or store-bought

1 Prepare a medium-hot fire in your grill.

2 Rinse the fillets, pat dry with paper towels, and brush both sides with the olive oil. Season evenly with the pepper and Old Bay.

3 Place the fillets in a grilling basket and set directly over the coals. Grill for 10 minutes per inch of thickness, turning once. The fish should flake and be firm to the touch when done.

Simple Smoked Fish Fillets

Pecan, grapevine, or apple wood give fish a nice flavor. Smoking times will vary depending on the size and thickness of the fillets. SERVES 6 TO 8

> Eight 4- to 6-ounce fish fillets, such as rockfish (striped bass), Atlantic croaker (hardhead), sea trout, or drum
>
> ½ cup olive oil
>
> 1 teaspoon fine sea salt

The GRILL MEISTER'S TIPS on
Preparing Fish and Shellfish for Grilling

According to my barbecue buddy Gunner Roe, you should always keep fish and shellfish refrigerated until you are ready to prep it. Keep prepped shellfish in the refrigerator until you are ready to cook it.

Grilling Tips:

* Marinating the fish first helps keep it moist during grilling, but don't marinate fish for longer than 30 to 60 minutes or the flesh can start to get mushy.

* Use a hinged grill basket when working with more delicate white-fleshed fish. It allows for easier turning and control when putting the fillets on and pulling them off the grill, and it allows you to adjust the cooking height. You can also use a perforated grill rack.

* Preheat the grill basket or perforated grill rack over the grill first, then coat it with nonstick cooking spray or oil, then add the fish.

* Use a medium-hot to hot fire when grilling.

* Fish fillets are best grilled with the skin left on.

* Start grilling fish skin side down.

* Fish is done when it begins to flake when tested with a fork. Shellfish is done when it turns opaque.

* When grilling fish that has been brushed with or marinated in oil, be careful of flare-ups.

---

1 teaspoon freshly ground black pepper

1 teaspoon Old Bay seasoning, homemade (page 119) or store-bought

1 Prepare an indirect fire.

2 Rinse the fillets and pat them dry with paper towels. Brush both sides with the olive oil and season evenly with the salt, pepper, and Old Bay.

3 Place the fillets in a disposable aluminum pan, skin side down, place the pan on the pit, cover, and cook at 230 to 250 degrees F until the fillets flake easily and are firm to the touch, 1½ to 2 hours.

The BARBECUE QUEENS on Grilling and Smoking Fish and Shellfish

With whole fish, look for a clear eye and a shiny exterior. When you smell a whole fish, a fillet, or steak, the aroma should be briny like the sea, with no hint of ammonia. When you touch the fillet or steak in the thickest part, the flesh should not stay indented or shred. Just as you should develop a relationship with your butcher, you should also develop one with your fishmonger so you get the freshest, best product.

SUGGESTED WOODS FOR FISH AND SHELLFISH

The classic hardwoods for smoking fish include alder in the Northwest, hickory in the Midwest, and milder maple in the Northeast. Because fish doesn't take very long to smoke, as opposed to a pork shoulder or a beef brisket, for instance, you could even use mesquite for a short while, as some folks in Texas like to do. For sweeter-tasting shellfish, I recommend fruit woods such as apple, cherry, and pear. But I'm always experimenting with woods and combinations of woods, and I encourage you to do the same. Any single selection or combination of woods you like is a winner.

Handy Utensils for Grilling or Smoking Fish and Shellfish

Several basic tools make grilling or smoking fish and shellfish easier. A local restaurant supply store or a barbecue and grill shop are good sources for finding the items listed.

* Grill toppers or perforated grill racks are grates placed on top of the grill to accommodate small or delicate items, such as fish fillets, scallops, shrimp, and vegetables. Always oil the grill topper before using so the fish won't stick.

* Hinged grill baskets or fish baskets hold foods in place and make turning an easy process.

* Grill woks, one of the newest additions to grilling gadgetry, make "stir-grilling" possible. The wok has holes to let in smoky flavor and it sits directly on top of the grill. Stir-grill marinated fish and vegetables by tossing with wooden paddles. The grill wok enables totally oil-free cooking and is sure to become a staple with health-conscious grill chefs.

* Long-handled, spring-loaded tongs are easier to use than the scissors type. They are great for turning shrimp, scallops, sliced vegetables, and skewers.

* Skewers—wood or metal—allow smaller items to be threaded loosely together and then placed on the grill to cook. Wooden or bamboo skewers should be soaked for 20 to 30 minutes before using so the ends won't char during grilling and so they won't absorb moisture from the food and cause sticking. Flat metal skewers are preferred, so that cubed food doesn't spin while turning.

* A long, wooden-handled offset spatula with a 5- to 6-inch blade is essential for turning fish fillets. Oil it well to avoid sticking.

* Disposable aluminum pans are the easiest utensils to use on a grill or smoker and are available at the grocery store. Always oil pans before using so the fish won't stick.

Fish and Shellfish for Grilling

For the novice fish griller, firm-fleshed fish steaks (salmon, tuna, swordfish, shark) and firmer-fleshed fillets of farm-raised catfish are the easiest to grill. They require the least amount of special equipment because their firmness allows cooking directly on a regular grill rack. They're also easier to turn.

Shellfish such as shrimp, oysters, and scallops are also great on the grill.

Grilling Time

The general rule of thumb is to cook fish for 10 minutes per inch of thickness over a hot fire. For example, if a fish fillet is 1 inch thick, grill it for 5 minutes on each side. Grilling fish over a medium fire takes a little longer. Try to turn fish only once, as it is delicate and can fall apart, even in a grill basket.

When Are Grilled Fish and Shellfish Done?

Use the suggested cooking times given in each recipe but also watch your fish while it's grilling—when the color turns opaque and the flesh just begins to flake when tested with a fork, grilled fish is done. When grilled shellfish turns opaque and is firm to the touch, it is done.

Fish and Shellfish for Smoking

There are basically two kinds of smoking for fish and shellfish: cold smoking and hot smoking. Cold smoking involves curing or brining the fish for several hours, washing off some of the cure or brine, and letting the rest dry on the surface of the fish to form a sort of burnished glaze or pellicle. Then the fish or seafood is smoked over indirect heat at a temperature below 200 degrees F. Cold smoking requires very specialized equipment, as the food must be very far away from the heat source. Because the fish is smoked at lower temperatures, it is preserved, but it doesn't really cook. This is the process that yields translucent, moist thin fillets of smoked salmon available in flat packages.

Hot smoking involves marinating or seasoning the fish, which may also be lightly brined ahead of time. Then the fish or shellfish is smoked over indirect heat at a temperature between 230 and 250 degrees F. With the hot-smoking process, the fish is cooked, not preserved, although it will keep for several days in the refrigerator and for months in the freezer. The end result is a moist, tender opaque fish with a smoky flavor. Alder, fruit woods, pecan, oak, and even hickory are good for smoking fish and shellfish.

Almost any fish or shellfish can be smoked or barbecued.

Preparing Fish and Shellfish for Smoking

Prepare fish and shellfish for smoking or indirect cooking the same as you do for grilling. Always rinse fish in cold water to remove any bacteria and pat it dry before marinating, seasoning, or cooking. Fish that will be smoked needs a liquid as a baste or cooking medium. The longer smoking process can dry out fish that is not properly moistened.

For the novice fish smoker, whole fish (trout, char, or catfish) and thick fillets are the easiest to smoke. Just place the fish in a disposable aluminum pan, cover, and smoke. There is no turning, but maybe a little basting.

Smoking Time

With smoking, it is less crucial to be exact than it is with grilling, as smoking is a gentler cooking process. But smoking food too long will give it a bitter, acrid flavor.

When Are Smoked Fish and Shellfish Done?

Watch your fish while it's smoking—when the color turns opaque and the flesh just begins to flake when tested with a fork, smoked fish is done. When smoked shellfish turns opaque and is firm to the touch, it is done.

Honey Mustard Grilled Bluefish

Just thinking about this recipe makes my mouth water. Bluefish is a firmer fleshed variety from the Atlantic Coast, with an oil content like that of salmon. The key to good bluefish is that it be fresh, fresh, fresh. SERVES 6

GARLIC-SOY MARINADE

1/2 cup soy sauce

2 tablespoons olive oil

1 tablespoon granulated cane sugar

1 teaspoon ground ginger

1 teaspoon granulated garlic

1 teaspoon freshly ground black pepper

Six 6-ounce bluefish fillets

HONEY MUSTARD GLAZE

1/4 cup clover honey

2 tablespoons Dijon mustard

2 teaspoons Worcestershire sauce, homemade (page 50) or store-bought

1 teaspoon dried parsley flakes

1 teaspoon coarse sea salt

1 teaspoon freshly ground black pepper

1/2 teaspoon cayenne pepper

Nonstick cooking spray

1 To make the marinade, combine the marinade ingredients in a small nonreactive bowl, blending with a wire whisk. Rinse the fish under cold running water and pat dry with paper towels. Place the fish in a nonreactive baking dish or a zippered-top plastic bag, pour the marinade over the fillets, coating them completely, cover with plastic wrap or seal the bag, and let marinate for 30 minutes to 1 hour in the refrigerator.

2 To make the glaze, in another small bowl, combine the glaze ingredients with a wire whisk until well blended.

3 When ready to cook, prepare a medium-hot fire in your grill.

4 Remove the fillets from the marinade, discarding the marinade. Coat the inside of the grill basket with the cooking spray. Place the fillets in the basket and set directly over the coals. Cover and grill for 7 to 9 minutes. Turn, brush with the glaze about every 3 minutes, and cook, covered, until the fish flakes, 7 to 9 minutes longer.

Lemon-Soy Marinated Catfish

Farm-raised catfish has a lot of things going for it, namely great taste and texture. It can take almost any flavoring or seasoning. Although catfish fillets are firm enough to grill without a basket or rack, I always use a grill basket if I'm cooking it in competition. SERVES 4

LEMON-SOY MARINADE

1/4 cup soy sauce

1 tablespoon granulated cane sugar

1 tablespoon fresh lemon juice

1 teaspoon granulated garlic

1 teaspoon freshly ground black pepper

1/2 teaspoon fine sea salt

Four 6- to 8-ounce catfish fillets

Nonstick cooking spray

1 Prepare a medium-hot fire in your grill.

2 Meanwhile, make the marinade. Combine the marinade ingredients in a small nonreactive bowl, blending well. Rinse the fish under cold running water and pat dry with paper towels. Place the fillets in a nonreactive baking dish or zippered-top plastic bag, pour the marinade over the fish, and let marinate at room temperature for about 5 minutes.

3 Remove the fish from the marinade. Transfer the remaining marinade to a small saucepan and bring to a boil over medium-high heat. Let boil for 5 minutes, then set aside. Coat the inside of the grill basket with the cooking spray.

4 Place the fillets in the grill basket and set on the grill directly over the coals. Cover and cook until the fish flakes easily, 4 to 5 minutes per side, basting with the reserved marinade every 2 to 3 minutes.

Cajun Catfish with Spicy Strawberry Sauce

This recipe may seem to be a strange combination, but the sweet tanginess of the sauce complements the bite of the farm-raised catfish. SERVES 8

Eight 6- to 8-ounce catfish fillets

1/4 cup Cajun or Creole Seasoning (page 117 or 118)

SPICY STRAWBERRY SAUCE

1 1/2 cups strawberry preserves

1/2 cup red wine vinegar

1/4 cup cocktail sauce

1 tablespoon soy sauce

2 cloves garlic, pressed

2 teaspoons prepared horseradish

1 teaspoon Tabasco sauce

1/2 cup olive oil

8 ripe strawberries, hulled

8 sprigs fresh mint

1 Rinse the fish under cold running water and pat dry with paper towels. Sprinkle the fillets all over with the seasoning. Place in a nonreactive baking dish or on a plate, cover with plastic wrap, and let marinate for 1 hour in the refrigerator.

2 Meanwhile, make the sauce. Combine the sauce ingredients in a medium-size nonreactive saucepan. Simmer over medium heat, stirring, until the sauce is well blended and heated through. Keep warm.

3 When ready to cook, prepare a medium-hot fire in your grill.

4 Remove the fillets from the refrigerator and dip each one into the olive oil, letting the excess oil drain back into the bowl. Place the fillets in a grill basket and set directly over the coals, being careful with the flare-ups from the oil. Cover and grill until the flesh flakes, 5 to 7 minutes per side.

5 To serve, place 2 tablespoons of the sauce on each plate and place a fillet on top. Garnish with a

fresh strawberry and a sprig of fresh mint and serve immediately.

Chef Dan's Barbecued Caribbean Stuffed Catfish

This recipe is from Chef Dan Morley of Chef Dan's BBQ Sauce, a.k.a. Blackberry Dan. I told you that catfish was pretty versatile. I like to use fruit woods (apple, cherry, grapevine) to smoke this fish. SERVES 6

CARIBBEAN STUFFING

2 tablespoons (1/4 stick) unsalted butter

1/4 cup minced onion

2 tablespoons seeded and minced green bell pepper

2 teaspoons seeded and minced jalapeño chiles

1/2 cup fresh bread crumbs

1/4 cup almonds, toasted (see page 322) and finely chopped

2 tablespoons fresh lime juice (about 2 limes)

1 tablespoon minced fresh oregano leaves

1 tablespoon minced fresh cilantro leaves

1 tablespoon minced fresh parsley leaves

1 teaspoon fine sea salt

1 teaspoon freshly ground black pepper

1/4 teaspoon ground nutmeg

1 to 2 tablespoons water or chicken broth, as needed

LIME BUTTER BASTE

1/2 cup (1 stick) unsalted butter

2 tablespoons fresh lime juice (about 2 limes)

Six GREAT FISH for Grilling

Okay, I live in the land-locked Midwest, but we can still get fresh fish flown in from the coast. We can also get freshwater farm-raised catfish and walleye. And I know plenty of people who go fishing for trout and don't forget their old friend Paul. Here is a short list of my favorite fish for grilling, along with their substitutes. You never know what's going to be available or not when you go to the fish counter, after all.

FARM-RAISED CATFISH: Fillets or whole fish. If you've never grilled fish before, start with this one. It has a mild flavor and holds together on the grill grates when you turn it. Substitute tilapia, orange roughy, or ocean perch, which are similar in flavor and texture.

GROUPER: Fillets or steaks. Firm enough to grill and use for kabobs, grouper has a mild flavor and is great with citrus-style marinades and sauces. Substitute snapper, mahi-mahi, or lingcod, which are similar in flavor and texture.

SALMON: Fillets or steaks. It's hard to go wrong with salmon. Wild varieties are available summer through fall, farm-raised in winter and spring. Substitute char, halibut, or tuna.

TROUT: Fillets or whole fish. Trout is delicious grilled. Substitute char, walleye, or whitefish, which are similar in flavor and texture.

TUNA: Steaks. I love tuna grilled like a steak—medium rare. Substitute salmon, shark, or swordfish, which are similar in flavor and texture.

WHITEFISH: Whole fish. Apple or hickory smoke is good with whitefish. Substitute Northern pike, trout, or walleye, which are similar in flavor and texture.

Six 6- to 8-ounce catfish fillets

3 tablespoons garlic salt

2 teaspoons finely ground black pepper

1 teaspoon ground allspice

1/4 teaspoon powdered bay leaf

Nonstick cooking spray

1 teaspoon crushed red pepper

1 teaspoon minced lime zest

1 To make the stuffing, in a medium-size skillet over medium-high heat, melt the butter, then add the onion, bell pepper, and jalapeño and cook, stirring, until soft but not browned. Add the bread crumbs, almonds, lime juice, oregano, cilantro, parsley, salt, pepper, and nutmeg and cook until well blended but still moist, about 2 minutes. Add water, as needed, if the mixture is too dry.

2 To make the baste, in a small nonreactive saucepan, melt the butter, then stir in the lime juice. Remove from the heat and use a pastry brush to baste the fillets with some of the mixture. Reserve the rest.

3 Prepare an indirect fire.

4 Meanwhile, combine the garlic salt, black pepper, allspice, and bay leaf in a small bowl and blend well. Rinse the fish under cold running water and pat dry with paper towels. Season the fillets evenly all over with the mixture. Spoon some of the filling down the center of each catfish fillet. Roll up and secure with toothpicks.

5 Coat the rolled-up fillets with the cooking spray, place on the pit, cover, and cook at 230 to 250 degrees F until the fish flakes easily, 40 to 50 minutes, brushing with the remaining baste every 10 to 15 minutes, but do not turn.

6 Season the roll-ups with the crushed red pepper and lime zest just before serving.

Rib Doctor's Grilled Whole Catfish with Lemon Butter Baste

This recipe is from the files of the Kansas Rib Doctor, Guy Simpson, not the California Rib Doctor, Hayward Harris. Use farm-raised catfish for the best flavor and texture.
SERVES 6

Six 10- to 12-ounce whole catfish, cleaned

LEMON BUTTER BASTE

1/2 cup (1 stick) unsalted butter, melted

Juice of 6 lemons

2 tablespoons Worcestershire sauce, homemade (page 50) or store-bought

2 teaspoons prepared yellow mustard

1 teaspoon sweet Hungarian paprika

1 teaspoon fine sea salt

1/2 teaspoon freshly ground white pepper

Tabasco sauce (optional)

Nonstick cooking spray

1 Prepare a medium-hot fire in your grill.

2 Rinse the catfish under cool running water and pat dry with paper towels.

3 To make the baste, combine the melted butter, lemon juice, Worcestershire sauce, mustard, paprika, salt, and pepper in a small nonreactive bowl, blending well with a wire whisk, and season to taste with Tabasco, if desired.

4 Coat the fish with the cooking spray, place directly over the coals, cover, and grill for 8 to 10 minutes. Turn, baste, cover, and cook 8 to 10 minutes longer, then turn, baste, cover, and cook 10 minutes longer, basting and turning as often as you feel is necessary. Cook until the fish flakes easily, 30 to 40 minutes total.

Jessica Kirk's Championship Smoked Catfish

This simple recipe helped my wife win the First Kansas State Barbecue Championship in Lenexa, Kansas, in 1984.

Besides being simple, it was delicious. Use farm-raised catfish. SERVES 10 TO 12

One 4- to 6-pound catfish, cleaned

1 cup canola oil

2 tablespoons fine sea salt

2 cups apple juice, as needed

1 Prepare an indirect fire.

2 Rinse the catfish inside and out under cool running water. Pat dry with paper towels. Brush the catfish inside and out with the oil and season lightly with the salt. Place on the pit, cover, and cook for 2 hours, then turn and begin basting with apple juice every 30 minutes without turning it. The fish is done when it begins to flake easily, about 4 hours total.

Hot Smoked Eel

Eel is a whole new adventure, but its rich taste is well worth the effort. You can buy live eels at Asian markets with a fresh seafood department, or have your fishmonger order one for you. You smoke eel at a slightly higher temperature, 275 to 325 degrees F, so make sure your fire is stoked. SERVES 4 TO 6

2 live eels

1/2 cup mirin

1/4 cup soy sauce

2 cloves garlic, pressed

1 Kill the eels by cutting off their heads. With a sharp knife, make a lengthwise cut up the center of the underside of each eel from the tail to about 3 inches from the neck. Gut and clean the inside, using a spoon to scrape the insides to remove all the viscera, then remove the backbone with a sharp knife. Rinse the fish under cold running water and pat dry with paper towels. Cut each eel into 2- to 3-inch sections and put the pieces in a fish basket.

2 Combine the mirin, soy sauce, and garlic.

3 Prepare an indirect fire.

4 Place the eels in the smoker, cover, and smoke at 275 to 325 degrees F, basting with the mirin mixture every 15 minutes, until the eel flakes when tested with a fork, 30 to 45 minutes.

Grilled Grouper with Cool Vegetable Salsa

If you have never tasted grouper, you are in for a treat. Grouper are caught off the Florida coast and are delicious served with this salsa. SERVES 6 TO 8

COOL VEGETABLE SALSA

1 cup peeled, seeded, and diced fresh tomatoes

1/2 cup peeled, seeded, and diced cucumber

1/2 red bell pepper, seeded and diced (roasted red pepper is also good)

1/4 cup diced onion

1 tablespoon minced fresh cilantro leaves

1 tablespoon minced fresh parsley leaves

1 clove garlic, pressed

1 teaspoon fine sea salt

1 teaspoon freshly ground black pepper

1 green jalapeño chile, seeded and minced

1/4 cup V-8 juice or tomato juice

2 tablespoons fresh lime juice (about 2 limes)

2 tablespoons red wine vinegar

2 tablespoons olive oil

Eight 6- to 8-ounce grouper fillets

$^1/_4$ cup ($^1/_2$ stick) unsalted butter, melted

1 tablespoon seasoned salt, homemade (page 108) or store-bought

1 tablespoon freshly ground black pepper

1 To make the salsa, in a large nonreactive bowl, combine the tomatoes, cucumber, bell pepper, onion, cilantro, parsley, and garlic. In a small nonreactive bowl or a jar with a tight-fitting lid, combine the salt, black pepper, jalapeño, V-8 juice, lime juice, vinegar, and olive oil, blending with a wire whisk or shaking the sealed jar vigorously. Pour the liquid over the vegetables and toss gently. Cover with plastic wrap and chill in the refrigerator for at least 1 hour to develop the flavors.

2 Prepare a medium-hot fire in your grill.

3 Meanwhile, rinse the fish under cold running water and pat dry with paper towels. Place the grouper fillets on a tray or large plate and, with a clean pastry brush, coat one side of each fillet with the melted butter and sprinkle evenly with the seasoned salt and pepper. Turn over and repeat the process.

4 Place the fillets directly over the coals, cover, and grill until the fish flakes easily, 4 to 5 minutes per side.

5 To serve, place the fillets on serving plates and top with a heaping scoop of salsa.

Grilled Spanish Mackerel

Another Atlantic fish, mackerel has a high oil content and is best eaten the day it's caught. Grilling the whole fish makes for a great show at your backyard party. SERVES 6 TO 8

GARLIC LEMON BASTE

$^1/_2$ cup fresh lemon juice (4 to 5 lemons)

$^1/_4$ cup olive oil

2 teaspoons garlic salt

1 teaspoon dried oregano leaves

1 teaspoon freshly ground black pepper

One 3-pound mackerel, cleaned

Nonstick cooking spray

1 To make the baste, in a small nonreactive bowl, combine the baste ingredients, blending with a wire whisk.

2 Prepare a medium-hot fire in your grill.

3 Rinse the fish under cold running water and pat dry with paper towels. Cut 4 to 5 slits on both sides of the fish; brush it inside and out with the baste. Coat the fish with the cooking spray. Place the fish on the grill directly over the coals, cover, and grill for 6 to 8 minutes. Brush with the baste, turn, and cook until the skin is crisp and the flesh flakes, 6 to 8 minutes longer.

Simple Smoked Mackerel with Mustard Barbecue Sauce

If you can get really fresh mackerel, try smoking it this way. Mackerel is an oilier fish, like salmon and tuna, and it has a somewhat assertive flavor that, to me, stands up to a mustard-based sauce, such as Mustard Barbecue Sauce (page 149), Golden Gourmet Mustard Barbecue Sauce (page 149), or Spicy Honey Mustard Barbecue Sauce (page 152). SERVES 6

One 3- to 3½-pound mackerel, cleaned

2 tablespoons olive oil

2 teaspoons coarse sea salt

2 teaspoons lemon pepper seasoning

1 recipe mustard barbecue sauce of your choice (pages 149–152)

1 Prepare an indirect fire.

2 Rinse the mackerel under cold running water inside and out and pat dry with paper towels. Rub the fish all over with the olive oil, then sprinkle with the salt and lemon pepper.

3 Place the fish on the pit, cover, and cook at 230 to 250 degrees F until the flesh flakes easily, 60 to 75 minutes. Serve with the sauce on the side.

Grilled Monkfish in Gingered Soy Sauce

Sometimes called poor man's lobster because the fillets can look and have a texture somewhat like that of lobster tails, monkfish holds up well on the grill. SERVES 4

GINGERED SOY MARINADE

½ cup light soy sauce

1 tablespoon peeled and grated fresh ginger

1 tablespoon granulated cane sugar

2 cloves garlic, pressed

1 teaspoon freshly ground white pepper

Four 6- to 8-ounce monkfish fillets

Nonstick cooking spray

1 To make the marinade, combine the marinade ingredients in a small nonreactive bowl and blend well with a wire whisk. Rinse the fish under cold running water and pat dry with paper towels. Place the fish in a nonreactive baking dish or zippered-top plastic bag, pour the marinade over them, seal or cover with plastic wrap, and let marinate in the refrigerator for 30 minutes, turning once.

2 When ready to cook, prepare a medium-hot fire in your grill.

3 Remove the fish from the marinade. Transfer the remaining marinade to a small saucepan and bring to a boil over medium-high heat; let simmer for 5 minutes, then set aside.

4 Coat the fillets with the cooking spray, place directly over the coals, cover, and cook, basting the cooked sides with the reserved marinade, until the fish turns opaque and begins to flake when tested with a fork, 5 to 6 minutes per side.

Orange Roughy with Sun-Dried Tomato, Caper, and Anchovy Sauce

Orange roughy is not an oily fish, so make sure you coat the fillets and the grill with nonstick cooking spray or use a wire grill rack or basket. SERVES 4

SUN-DRIED TOMATO, CAPER, AND ANCHOVY SAUCE

1/4 cup dry vermouth

1/2 teaspoon fennel seeds, coarsely chopped

Two 8-ounce bottles clam juice

1/2 cup oil-packed sun-dried tomatoes, drained and thinly sliced

2 tablespoons capers, drained

1 1/2 tablespoons chopped anchovies

1 tablespoon minced fresh Italian parsley leaves

1 teaspoon freshly ground black pepper

1 1/2 to 2 pounds orange roughy fillets

1/4 cup olive oil

2 tablespoons garlic salt

2 teaspoons freshly ground black pepper

2 tablespoons basil-flavored olive oil (optional)

1 To make the sauce, combine the vermouth and fennel seeds in a medium-size nonreactive saucepan. Bring to a boil over medium-high heat and let boil until reduced by half, 3 to 4 minutes. Add the clam juice and reduce by half, 6 to 8 minutes. Stir in the tomatoes, capers, and anchovies, reduce the heat to medium-low, and simmer for 2 minutes to blend the flavors. Stir in the parsley and season with the pepper. Keep warm.

2 Prepare a medium-hot fire in your grill.

3 Rinse the fish under cold running water and pat dry with paper towels. Brush the fillets with the olive oil, then season evenly with the garlic salt and pepper.

4 Place the fish on the grill directly over the coals, cover, and grill until the center is opaque, about 3 minutes per side.

5 Transfer the fish to serving plates and top with some of the warm sauce, serving the remainder on the side. Drizzle the basil oil around the fish on the plate, if desired. Serve immediately.

Grilled Northern Pike

Because this is a very delicate freshwater fish, you're better off grilling it in a fish basket so you don't tear up the fillets. SERVES 4 TO 6

SAVORY BUTTER MARINADE

1/4 cup (1/2 stick) unsalted butter, melted

1/4 cup Worcestershire sauce, homemade (page 50) or store-bought

GARLIC SEAFOOD SEASONING

1 tablespoon Old Bay seasoning, homemade (page 119) or store-bought

2 teaspoons garlic salt

1 teaspoon granulated cane sugar

1 teaspoon freshly ground black pepper

1 1/2 pounds northern pike fillets

Nonstick cooking spray

1 To make the marinade, combine the marinade ingredients in a small bowl and set aside.

2 To make the seasoning, combine the seasoning ingredients in a small bowl or place in a shaker and set aside.

3 Rinse the fish under cold running water and pat dry with paper towels. Place the fillets in a nonreactive baking dish and pour the marinade over them, coating all sides. Let marinate at room temperature for 10 to 15 minutes.

4 Prepare a medium-hot fire in your grill.

5 Remove the fillets from the marinade and sprinkle evenly on both sides with the seasoning mixture. Coat the fillets with the cooking spray. Place the fillets directly over the coals, cover, and grill until the fish flakes easily, 2 to 3 minutes per side.

Fresh Basil-Basted Walleye

The biggest problem with this freshwater fish from the Great Lakes area is finding a supply of it. I have an abundance of friends who fish for walleye and perch, so I know whom to call when I need some. SERVES 4 TO 6

BASIL PASTE

¼ cup canola oil

2 tablespoons white wine

2 tablespoons minced fresh basil leaves

1 tablespoon Dijon mustard

1 tablespoon fresh lemon juice

3 cloves garlic, pressed

1 teaspoon fine sea salt

1 teaspoon finely ground black pepper

1½ pounds walleye fillets, skin left on

Nonstick cooking spray

1 To make the paste, combine the basil paste ingredients in a blender and process for about 2 minutes, but don't emulsify the mixture. Rinse the fish under cold running water and pat dry with paper towels. With a pastry brush, paint the paste on the meat side of the fish fillets. Place on a plate or baking dish, cover with plastic wrap, and let marinate for 30 minutes in the refrigerator.

2 Prepare a medium-hot fire in your grill.

3 Coat the fish with the cooking spray. Place the fish directly over the coals, flesh side down, cover, and cook until the flesh flakes easily, 7 to 9 minutes per side. Baste the flesh side with any remaining paste after you turn the fish.

Mason Steinberg's Honey Barbecue Salmon Satay

Mason Steinberg is one of the finest cooks Omaha, Nebraska, has to offer. We've worked on many recipes together, and this is one of his favorites. This satay can be served as an appetizer without the rice. You'll need thirty-six 4-inch wooden skewers for this; remember to soak them in water for 30 minutes before using them. SERVES 6

HONEY BARBECUE MARINADE

$\frac{1}{2}$ cup tomato ketchup, homemade (page 43) or store-bought

$\frac{1}{2}$ cup clover honey

2 tablespoons Dijon mustard

$\frac{1}{2}$ cup rice vinegar

$\frac{1}{4}$ cup firmly packed light brown sugar

1 tablespoon seeded and minced jalapeño chiles

1 tablespoon pressed garlic

1 tablespoon Worcestershire sauce, homemade (page 50) or store-bought

1 tablespoon soy sauce

1 tablespoon canola oil

1 tablespoon minced shallot

1 tablespoon fresh lemon juice

2 teaspoons sweet Hungarian paprika

2 teaspoons curry powder

1 teaspoon white pepper

1 teaspoon Louisiana hot sauce

$2\frac{1}{4}$ pounds fresh salmon fillets, skin removed and cut into 2-inch cubes

2 large yellow onions, cut the same size as the salmon and steamed for 15 minutes

Nonstick cooking spray

2 cups cooked rice

1 recipe Spicy Peanut Sauce (page 160)

1 To make the marinade, combine all the marinade ingredients in a medium-size nonreactive bowl and blend with a wire whisk. Rinse the fish under cold running water and pat dry with paper towels.

2 Alternately thread the onions with the salmon (2 pieces of salmon per skewer) onto the skewers. Place the skewers in a large nonreactive baking dish and pour the marinade over them, coating everything. Let marinate, covered with plastic wrap, in the refrigerator for about 1 hour.

3 Prepare a medium-hot fire in your grill.

4 Remove the salmon skewers from the dish, pat dry with paper towels, transfer the remaining marinade to a medium-size nonreactive saucepan and bring to a boil; let simmer for 5 minutes. Coat the salmon with the cooking spray.

5 Place the skewers directly over the coals and grill until the salmon just flakes, about 2 minutes per side, brushing several times with the reserved marinade. Serve over rice with the peanut sauce on the side for dipping.

Garlic-Lemon Marinated Salmon with Lemon-Tarragon Sauce

This is a very light and delicate entrée to serve to family and friends. SERVES 4 TO 6

GARLIC-LEMON MARINADE

$\frac{1}{4}$ cup fresh lemon juice (about 2 lemons)

$\frac{1}{4}$ cup olive oil

4 cloves garlic, pressed

1 teaspoon fine sea salt

1 teaspoon freshly ground black pepper

$1\frac{1}{2}$ pounds salmon fillets, skin left on

LEMON-TARRAGON SAUCE

$\frac{1}{2}$ cup sour cream

2 tablespoons buttermilk

1 tablespoon fresh lemon juice

1 tablespoon granulated cane sugar

2 teaspoons minced lemon zest

2 teaspoons minced fresh tarragon leaves or
   1/2 teaspoon dried tarragon leaves

1/2 teaspoon fine sea salt

1 To make the marinade, combine the marinade ingredients in a small nonreactive bowl, blending with a wire whisk. Rinse the fish under cold running water and pat dry with paper towels. Place the fillets in a nonreactive baking dish or zippered-top plastic bag, pour the marinade over them, making sure they are completely coated, cover with plastic wrap or seal, and let marinate for 1 hour in the refrigerator.

2 To make the sauce, in a small bowl, combine the sauce ingredients, blending well with a wire whisk. Cover with plastic wrap and chill in the refrigerator until ready to serve.

3 When ready to cook, prepare a medium-hot fire in your grill.

4 Remove the salmon from the marinade, discarding the marinade, and cut each fillet into 4 to 6 pieces. Place the salmon flesh side down directly over the coals, cover, and grill until it flakes, about 5 minutes per side.

5 Serve the salmon hot with a dollop of the chilled sauce on top of each piece.

Grill Meister's Herb-Crusted Salmon with Mustard Slather

Gunner Roe, the Grill Meister, cooked this salmon for us at the World Barbecue Championship in Lebanon, Tennessee.
SERVES 6 TO 8

Eight 6- to 8-ounce salmon fillets

1/2 cup hot mustard or mustard slather of your choice (pages 86–101)

1 1/2 cups finely chopped fresh herbs of your choice (tarragon, basil, chives, cilantro, oregano, chervil, or your favorites)

1/4 cup olive oil

1 Prepare a medium-hot fire in your grill. Rinse the fish under cold running water and pat dry with paper towels.

2 Spread the mustard on both sides of the salmon and cover evenly with the herbs. Coat a grill basket with the olive oil. Place the fillets in the basket, set directly over the coals, cover, and grill until the fish flakes easily, 3 to 5 minutes per side.

Turkish-Style Salmon Steaks

This is another superbly simple grilled salmon recipe. All you need are the seasonings and olive oil. SERVES 6

2 tablespoons Turkish Mixed Spices (page 122)

1 tablespoon garlic salt

1 tablespoon sweet Hungarian paprika

6 salmon steaks, 1 to 1½ inches thick

¼ cup olive oil

1 Prepare a medium-hot fire in your grill.

2 Combine the Turkish spice mix, garlic salt, and paprika in a small bowl and blend well.

3 Rinse the fish under cold running water and pat dry with paper towels. Rub the salmon steaks all over with the olive oil, then sprinkle evenly with the seasoning.

4 Throw a chunk of apple wood on the hot coals, place the steaks directly over the coals, cover, and grill until the fish begins to flake, 4 to 5 minutes per side.

Jack Daniel's Marinated Grilled Salmon

This is a recipe to get excited about! Of course, I think Jack Daniel's Sour Mash in anything is great! SERVES 8 TO 10

One 3-pound salmon fillet, skin removed

1 cup olive oil

JACK DANIEL'S MARINADE

1 cup Jack Daniel's Sour Mash Whiskey

1 cup soy sauce

¼ cup firmly packed light brown sugar

⅓ cup peeled and shredded fresh ginger

2 tablespoons cracked black peppercorns

1 tablespoon minced garlic

1 teaspoon chili powder, homemade (page 111) or store-bought

½ teaspoon coarse sea salt

¼ cup toasted sesame oil

1 Rinse the fish under cold running water and pat dry with paper towels. Brush the salmon generously all over with the olive oil. Place in a large nonreactive baking dish or zippered-top plastic bag, cover with plastic wrap or seal, and chill for 1 hour in the refrigerator. Reserve any unused oil.

2 To make the marinade, combine the whiskey, soy sauce, brown sugar, ginger, pepper, garlic, chili powder, and salt in a medium-size nonreactive bowl and blend with a wire whisk. Whisking, blend in the sesame oil and the reserved olive oil until well combined. After the salmon has chilled, pour the marinade over it, turning several times to coat, cover or seal again, and let marinate 30 to 60 minutes longer in the refrigerator.

3 When ready to cook, prepare a medium-hot fire in your grill.

4 Remove the salmon from the marinade. Throw some mesquite wood chunks on the coals, then place the salmon directly over the coals, cover, and grill until the fish flakes, 5 to 7 minutes per side.

Amarillo Salmon

I didn't think Texans knew much about salmon, but this recipe proves that theory wrong. This is how some folks grill it in Amarillo. SERVES 4

> 1/2 cup Spicy, Hot, and Chunky Barbecue Sauce (page 145)
>
> 1/4 cup prepared horseradish
>
> 1/4 cup (1/2 stick) unsalted butter
>
> Four 6- to 8-ounce salmon steaks or fillets
>
> 1/4 cup soybean or other vegetable oil
>
> 2 tablespoons lemon pepper seasoning

1 Prepare a medium-hot fire in your grill.

2 Meanwhile, combine the barbecue sauce, horseradish, and butter in a small nonreactive saucepan over medium heat, whisking until the butter has melted and blended in.

3 Rinse the fish under cold running water and pat dry with paper towels. Coat the salmon with the oil and season with the lemon pepper on both sides. Place the salmon directly over the coals, cover, and grill for 5 to 6 minutes. Turn, baste the cooked side with the sauce mixture, cover, and cook 5 to 6 minutes longer. Flip again, baste the other side with the sauce mixture, and cook until the fish is flaky, 4 to 5 minutes longer. Serve any extra sauce on the side.

Pecan-Smoked Salmon

I prefer to use pecan chips with lump charcoal when smoking salmon. Apple and grapevine also add a nice subtle flavor. SERVES 6 TO 8

> 1 1/2 to 2 pounds salmon fillets, skin left on
>
> 1/2 cup olive oil
>
> 2 tablespoons Old Bay seasoning, homemade (page 119) or store-bought
>
> 1 tablespoon coarse sea salt
>
> 1 tablespoon freshly ground black pepper

1 Prepare an indirect fire. When it's ready, place 1 1/2 cups of pecan chips on the coals.

2 Rinse the fish under cold running water and pat dry with paper towels. Brush the salmon on both sides with the olive oil, then season evenly on both sides with the Old Bay, salt, and pepper.

3 Place the fillets on the pit, cover, and cook at 230 to 250 degrees F until the salmon flakes easily, about 2 hours.

New Century Catering Smoked Salmon

I developed this recipe for New Century Catering; it was a standard on our catering menu. It makes a great appetizer. SERVES 8 TO 10

> One 5- to 6-pound salmon fillet, skin left on
>
> 1/2 cup Dijon mustard
>
> 1/4 cup New Century Catering Barbeque Seasoning and Rub (page 132)

1 Prepare an indirect fire.

2 Rinse the fish under cold running water and pat dry with paper towels. Paint the salmon (flesh side only) with the mustard and sprinkle evenly (flesh side only) with the rub.

3 Place the salmon on the pit, cover, and cook at 230 to 250 degrees F until the flesh flakes easily, 1 1/2 to 2 hours.

Smoked Mustard-Lime Marinated Salmon with Sesame Seeds

When I cook this salmon, I want some heat, so I add a little crushed red pepper to the marinade. Again, I like pecan chips for smoking salmon, but use whatever wood you prefer. SERVES 4

MUSTARD-LIME MARINADE

1/4 cup fresh lime juice (about 4 limes)

2 tablespoons olive oil

1 tablespoon Dijon mustard

1 teaspoon grated lime zest

1 teaspoon non-iodized salt

1 teaspoon finely ground black pepper

4 salmon steaks, 1 inch thick (about 1 1/2 pounds)

1/3 cup sesame seeds, toasted in a dry skillet over medium heat until fragrant

1 To make the marinade, in a shallow nonreactive baking dish, combine the marinade ingredients, blending with a wire whisk. Rinse the fish under cold running water and pat dry with paper towels. Add the fish to the marinade, turning to coat. Cover with plastic wrap and let marinate at room temperature for 30 minutes.

2 Prepare an indirect fire.

3 Remove the fish from the marinade. Transfer the remaining marinade to a nonreactive saucepan and bring to a boil over medium-high heat; simmer for 5 minutes, let cool, then refrigerate until ready to use. Sprinkle the salmon (flesh side only) evenly with the toasted sesame seeds.

4 Place the salmon on the pit, cover, and cook at 230 to 250 degrees F for 20 minutes. Baste with the reserved marinade, turn, cover, and cook until the salmon flakes easily with a fork, 20 to 40 minutes longer.

Smoky Hickory and Brown Sugar Cured Salmon

This salmon is quick cured first to draw out extra moisture, then hot smoked over hickory wood for a firmer texture. Morton's Tender Quick is a curing mixture available in the spice section of the grocery store. SERVES 6 TO 8

1/2 cup firmly packed dark brown sugar

1 tablespoon Old Bay seasoning, homemade (page 119) or store-bought

1 tablespoon Morton's Tender Quick

1 teaspoon freshly ground black pepper

Six 6- to 8-ounce salmon fillets, skin left on

1 Combine the brown sugar, Old Bay, Tender Quick, and pepper in a small bowl and blend well.

2 Rinse the salmon under cold running water and pat dry with paper towels. Cover the fillets evenly on both sides with the brown sugar mixture and pack them in a large nonreactive baking dish, covering them with any remaining sugar mixture. Cover with plastic wrap and let cure, or

marinate, in the refrigerator for at least 2 hours or overnight.

3 Prepare an indirect fire. When it's ready, throw on 1½ cups of hickory chips.

4 Place the fillets on the pit, cover, and cook until the fish flakes easily, 40 to 60 minutes.

Barbecued Turkish Sea Bass

Sea bass is a moderately oily fish with a firm texture. It is delicious barbecued or grilled. **SERVES 6 TO 8**

DRIED HERB MARINADE
½ cup dry white wine
1 tablespoon granulated cane sugar
2 teaspoons dried parsley flakes
2 teaspoons garlic salt
2 teaspoons freshly ground black pepper
1 teaspoon dried basil leaves
½ teaspoon dried oregano leaves
¼ cup olive oil

2 pounds sea bass fillets
1 cup pitted black olives, drained and chopped

1 To make the marinade, combine the marinade ingredients in a small bowl, blending well with a wire whisk. Rinse the fish under cold running water and pat dry with paper towels. Place the fillets in a nonreactive baking dish or zippered-top plastic bag and pour the marinade over them, making sure all sides are coated. Cover with plastic wrap or seal and let marinate in the refrigerator for 30 minutes to 1 hour.

2 When ready to cook, prepare an indirect fire.

3 Remove the fillets from the marinade, discarding the marinade. Place the fish on the pit, cover, and cook at 230 to 250 degrees F until the flesh flakes easily, about 40 minutes.

4 Serve garnished with the olives.

Shark Bites with Lemony Fresh Herb Marinade

This shark recipe has a little bite, pun intended, but to add even more, increase the amount of red pepper and add 1 teaspoon of cayenne pepper. **SERVES 4**

LEMONY FRESH HERB MARINADE
¼ cup fresh lemon juice (about 2 lemons)
2 tablespoons minced fresh parsley leaves
2 tablespoons minced fresh cilantro leaves
2 tablespoons minced fresh basil leaves
2 tablespoons cocktail sauce
2 tablespoons soy sauce
1 tablespoon granulated cane sugar
4 cloves garlic, pressed
1 teaspoon finely ground black pepper
1 teaspoon crushed red pepper

Four 6- to 8-ounce shark steaks

1 To make the marinade, combine the marinade ingredients in a small nonreactive bowl and blend well. Rinse the fish under cold running water and pat dry with paper towels. Place the shark steaks in a zippered-top plastic bag, pour the marinade over them, seal, shake to coat the steaks, and let

marinate for 30 minutes at room temperature or for 1 hour in the refrigerator.

2 When ready to cook, prepare a medium-hot fire in your grill.

3 Remove the fish from the marinade. Transfer the marinade to a small nonreactive saucepan, bring to a boil, reduce the heat to medium-low, and simmer until the marinade is reduced by half, about 10 minutes. Keep warm.

4 Place the fish directly over the coals, cover, and grill until the flesh flakes easily, 7 to 9 minutes per side.

5 Serve with the reserved marinade on the side or spooned over the top of the fish.

Mako Shark Steak au Poivre with Creamy Cognac Sauce

Mako shark is the most popular and best-known shark in the United States. It is great on the grill, especially in this take on the classic French recipe. SERVES 4

1/4 cup cracked black peppercorns

2 tablespoons kosher salt

Four 8-ounce mako shark steaks, skin removed

CREAMY COGNAC SAUCE

2 tablespoons unsalted butter

1/4 cup minced shallots

1 large clove garlic, pressed

1/3 cup Cognac or brandy

2 cups heavy cream

1/4 cup beef broth or bouillon

1 teaspoon fine sea salt

1/2 teaspoon finely ground black pepper

1/2 cup drawn butter (see page 341)

1 Combine the cracked pepper and kosher salt in a small bowl and blend well. Rinse the shark steaks under cold running water and pat dry with paper towels. Pour the pepper-and-salt mixture onto a plate and press the steaks into the mixture, coating them evenly on both sides. Place the encrusted steaks on a tray or another plate, cover with plastic wrap, and set aside at room temperature for 30 minutes or in the refrigerator for 1 hour.

2 To make the sauce, in a medium-size saucepan, melt the butter over medium heat, then add the shallots and garlic and cook, stirring, until softened, 2 to 3 minutes. Carefully add the Cognac, then stir in the cream and broth. Bring to a boil and cook at a boil until the sauce lightly coats the back of a spoon, about 10 minutes. Add the salt and pepper. Keep warm.

3 Prepare a medium-hot fire in your grill.

4 Remove the plastic wrap from the fish, brush both sides of each steak with the drawn butter, place directly over the coals, cover, and grill until the flesh flakes, 7 to 9 minutes per side.

5 Serve with a spoonful of the warm sauce over each steak.

Swordfish Mirabeau

I first encountered the inspiration for this recipe at a restaurant in Tampa Bay, Florida. I was on the Sprint PCS/NFL Tailgate Tour and, because I like anchovies, this dish caught my eye. Here is my version. Anchovy butter is good on almost all grilled or smoked fish. **SERVES 4**

- ¼ cup (½ stick) unsalted butter, at room temperature
- 1 to 2 tablespoons anchovy paste, to your taste
- 1 tablespoon fine sea salt
- 1 tablespoon freshly ground black pepper
- ½ cup olive oil
- 4 swordfish steaks, 1¼ inches thick
- 4 lemon slices
- 4 oil-cured Niçoise or Kalamata olives
- 4 anchovy fillets

1 Prepare a medium-hot fire in your grill.

2 In a small bowl, combine the butter and anchovy paste and blend well with a wire whisk. Cover and set aside.

3 Combine the salt and pepper in a small bowl and blend well.

4 Pour the olive oil into a medium-size nonreactive bowl or baking dish. Rinse the fish under cold running water and pat dry with paper towels. Dip the steaks into the oil, coating them on both sides; sprinkle evenly with the salt-and-pepper mixture. Place the steaks directly over the coals, cover, and grill until the fish flakes easily, 7 to 8 minutes per side, being careful not to overcook.

5 Remove the steaks from the grill and spread them with the anchovy butter. Garnish each steak with a lemon slice, an olive, and an anchovy fillet, secured with a toothpick.

Margarita Swordfish

Viva la swordfish flavored with tequila! This marinade is also good on other kinds of grilled fish or chicken. **SERVES 4**

TEQUILA MARINADE
- ½ cup fish stock or chicken broth
- ¼ cup fresh lime juice (about 4 limes)
- 2 tablespoons tequila
- 2 tablespoons granulated cane sugar
- 1 tablespoon Triple Sec
- 1 teaspoon grated lime zest
- 1 teaspoon fine sea salt
- 1 teaspoon freshly ground black pepper
- ½ teaspoon ground coriander

- 4 swordfish steaks, at least 1 inch thick
- 2 tablespoons margarita salt or other coarse salt
- 1 tablespoon freshly ground black pepper
- Nonstick cooking spray
- 1 lime, cut into wedges
- 1 lemon, cut into wedges
- 4 orange slices

1 To make the marinade, in a small nonreactive bowl, combine the marinade ingredients and blend well. Rinse the fish under cold running water and pat dry with paper towels. Place the steaks in a nonreactive baking dish or zippered-top plastic bag, pour the marinade over the fish, coating all over, cover with plastic wrap or seal, and let marinate for 30 minutes at room temperature or for 1 hour in the refrigerator.

2 Prepare a medium-hot fire in your grill.

3 Combine the margarita salt and pepper in a small bowl and blend well. Remove the fish from the marinade, discarding the marinade. Season all over with the salt-and-pepper mixture. Coat the steaks with the cooking spray and place directly over the coals. Cover and grill until the fish flakes easily, 7 to 8 minutes per side.

4 Serve the steaks garnished with the lime and lemon wedges and orange slices.

Grilled Swordfish with Charmoula

Grilled swordfish is extremely popular all over the globe and is a great addition to your backyard grill. Charmoula is a Moroccan fresh herb, vegetable, and spice paste that is also delicious on salmon. SERVES 4

CHARMOULA

1 cup peeled, seeded, and diced Roma
    tomatoes

1/4 cup olive oil

1 tablespoon fresh lemon juice

2 tablespoons tomato paste

2 tablespoons minced fresh Italian parsley
    leaves

2 tablespoons minced fresh curly parsley leaves

1 tablespoon granulated cane sugar

1 tablespoon sweet Hungarian paprika

2 teaspoons Barbecue Seasoning (page 114)

1 teaspoon ground cumin

1 teaspoon ground ginger

1 teaspoon fine sea salt

1/2 teaspoon freshly ground black pepper

1/2 teaspoon dried oregano leaves

2 tablespoons garlic salt

1 tablespoon lemon pepper seasoning

4 swordfish steaks, 1 inch thick (about 2
    pounds)

1/2 cup olive oil

1 To make the charmoula, combine the charmoula ingredients in a food processor and process just until the mixture becomes a coarse purée.

2 Prepare a medium-hot fire in your grill.

3 Combine the garlic salt and lemon pepper in a small bowl and blend well. Rinse the fish under cold running water and pat dry with paper towels. Coat the swordfish with the olive oil and sprinkle evenly all over with the seasoning mixture.

4 Place the steaks directly over the coals, cover, and cook until the fish flakes easily, 7 to 8 minutes per side.

5 Serve the swordfish with the charmoula on the side.

Citrus Swordfish

This swordfish recipe is popular in the Cuban section of Miami, except they use sour orange or blood orange juice. Those juices can be hard to find, so I substitute orange juice blended with lime juice, a mixture that approximates the taste of sour orange. SERVES 4

CITRUS BARBECUE SAUCE

2 tablespoons soybean oil or other vegetable oil

1 tablespoon unsalted butter

1 cup minced onion

1 tablespoon pure ground red chile of your
    choice

1 dried ancho chile, seeded, soaked in hot water
    until softened, drained, and minced

$\frac{1}{2}$ teaspoon pure ground chipotle chile

1 cup fresh orange juice (about 4 oranges)

$\frac{1}{2}$ cup fresh lime juice (about 8 limes)

2 tablespoons fresh lemon juice

$\frac{1}{4}$ cup granulated cane sugar

1 tablespoon minced fresh cilantro leaves

1 teaspoon fine sea salt

$\frac{1}{2}$ teaspoon freshly ground white pepper

4 swordfish steaks, at least 1 inch thick (about 2 pounds)

1 tablespoon coarse sea salt

1 tablespoon freshly ground black pepper

Nonstick cooking spray

1 To make the barbecue sauce, combine the oil and butter in a medium-size nonreactive saucepan over medium heat. Add the onion, ground red chile, ancho chile, and chipotle chile and cook, stirring frequently, until the onion is tender but not browned. Stir in the citrus juices, sugar, cilantro, fine sea salt, and white pepper and bring to a boil. Reduce the heat to medium-low and simmer for 15 to 20 minutes, stirring occasionally.

2 Rinse the fish under cold running water and pat dry with paper towels. Place the swordfish in a nonreactive baking dish or zippered-top plastic bag and pour 1 cup of the barbecue sauce over the fish, making sure the steaks are coated all over. Cover with plastic wrap or seal and let marinate for 30 minutes at room temperature or for 1 hour in the refrigerator. Reserve the remaining marinade.

3 Prepare a medium-hot fire in your grill.

4 Combine the coarse sea salt and black pepper in a small bowl and blend well. Remove the steaks from the marinade, shaking off any excess. Discard the marinade. Sprinkle the steaks with the seasoning mixture and coat with the cooking spray. Place the steaks directly over the coals, cover, and grill until the fish flakes easily, 7 to 8 minutes per side.

5 Serve the swordfish with the remaining barbecue sauce on the side.

Grilled Swordfish with Thai Banana Salsa

Normally I don't like doing recipes in which a lot of bottled products are used, but this recipe is an exception. You can find the oyster sauce, fish sauce, and chili sauce in the international products section of your supermarket.
SERVES 4

THAI MARINADE

$\frac{1}{4}$ cup light soy sauce

2 tablespoons dry sherry

2 tablespoons canola oil

2 tablespoons oyster sauce

1 tablespoon clover honey

1 tablespoon firmly packed dark brown sugar

$\frac{1}{2}$ teaspoon coarse sea salt

$\frac{1}{2}$ teaspoon freshly ground white pepper

4 swordfish steaks, 1 inch thick (about 2 pounds)

THAI BANANA SALSA

2 cups peeled and diced ripe bananas

1 serrano chile, seeded and minced

2 tablespoons minced fresh cilantro leaves

2 tablespoons minced fresh parsley leaves (see Note)

2 tablespoons peeled and minced fresh ginger

2 tablespoons fresh orange juice

2 tablespoons fresh lime juice (about 2 limes)

2 tablespoons firmly packed light brown sugar

2 tablespoons Asian fish sauce

2 tablespoons Thai chili sauce

1 To make the marinade, combine the marinade ingredients in a small nonreactive bowl and blend well with a wire whisk. Rinse the fish under cold running water and pat dry with paper towels. Place the swordfish steaks in a nonreactive baking dish or zippered-top plastic bag and pour the marinade over them, being sure to coat them well. Cover with plastic wrap or seal and let marinate for 30 minutes at room temperature or for 1 hour in the refrigerator.

2 To make the salsa, combine the salsa ingredients in a medium-size nonreactive bowl and gently mix, being careful not to mash the bananas. Cover with plastic wrap and refrigerate until ready to serve.

3 When ready to cook, prepare a medium-hot fire in your grill.

4 Remove the fish from the marinade, discarding the marinade. Place the fish directly over the coals, cover, and grill until the fish feels firm to the touch or flakes easily, 7 to 8 minutes per side.

5 Serve the swordfish with the salsa on the side.

NOTE I don't like the overpowering flavor of cilantro, so I add parsley to cut its bite.

Grilled Sesame Trout

This recipe is quick, easy, and tasty. SERVES 6

1 cup (2 sticks) unsalted butter

1/2 cup fresh lemon juice (4 to 5 lemons)

Six 8-ounce trout, cleaned, with the head and tail left on

2 tablespoons seasoned salt, homemade (page 108) or store-bought

2 teaspoons freshly ground black pepper

1/4 cup sesame seeds, toasted in a dry skillet over medium heat until fragrant

1 Combine the butter and lemon juice in a medium-size nonreactive saucepan over medium heat until the butter melts, blending with a whisk. Set aside.

2 Rinse the fish under cold running water and pat dry with paper towels. With a sharp knife, make 3 light cuts in each side of the trout; don't cut too deeply into the flesh. Place the trout in a large nonreactive baking dish and pour the lemon-butter mixture over them, turning to coat all over. Cover with plastic wrap and let marinate for 30 minutes at room temperature or for 1 hour in the refrigerator.

3 Combine the seasoned salt and pepper in a small bowl and blend well.

4 When ready to cook, prepare a medium-hot fire in your grill.

5 Remove the trout from the marinade. Transfer the remaining marinade to a saucepan and bring to a boil over medium-high heat; let simmer for 5 minutes, then set aside. Sprinkle the trout evenly

with the salt-and-pepper mixture on all sides. Add the sesame seeds to the cooked marinade.

6 Place the trout directly over the coals, cover, and grill until the fish begins to flake in the thickest part, 5 to 7 minutes per side, turn, baste with the reserved marinade every 2 to 3 minutes, and grill 5 to 7 minutes longer.

Campfire Grilled Rainbow Trout

This recipe comes from a southern Missouri experience of many years ago. SERVES 4

2 tablespoons garlic salt

1 tablespoon lemon pepper seasoning

Four 8-ounce rainbow trout, cleaned, with the head and tail left on

1/2 cup olive oil

1 lemon, quartered

1 Prepare a medium-hot fire in your grill or prepare a campfire.

2 Combine the garlic salt and lemon pepper and blend well. Rinse the fish under cold running water and pat dry with paper towels. Rub the trout down with the olive oil. Season inside and out with the salt-and-pepper mixture.

3 Place the trout directly over the coals, being careful of any flare-ups from the oil. Cook until the fish flakes easily, 5 to 7 minutes per side. The skin will be charred, but the flesh will be moist and tender.

4 Serve each trout with a lemon wedge.

Smoked Trout with Gribiche Horseradish Sauce

This horseradish sauce is good with any fish; you can also give it a shot of Tabasco sauce for some added punch. Just remember the sauce contains a raw egg, so use only the freshest eggs to avoid the possibility of salmonella and keep the sauce refrigerated until you are ready to serve it. And, of course, the smoked trout is wonderful with or without the sauce. SERVES 4 TO 8

GRIBICHE HORSERADISH SAUCE

2 tablespoons Dijon mustard

2 tablespoons minced shallot

2 tablespoons minced onion

1 very fresh large egg yolk

1 hard-cooked large egg, peeled and mashed

1 teaspoon fine sea salt

1/2 teaspoon freshly ground white pepper

2 tablespoons red wine vinegar

1 tablespoon fresh lemon juice

1 cup sunflower oil

1/4 cup prepared horseradish

2 tablespoons minced fresh parsley leaves

2 teaspoons minced fresh tarragon leaves

Eight 4- to 6-ounce trout fillets

1/2 cup olive oil

2 tablespoons Hotsy Totsy Seafood Seasoning (page 120)

2 lemons, quartered

1 To make the sauce, combine the mustard, shallot, onion, egg yolk, hard-cooked egg, salt, pepper, vinegar, and lemon juice in a blender. Turn on the blender and add the oil through the

top in a thin, steady stream until the mixture thickens. Transfer to a medium-size nonreactive bowl, add the horseradish, parsley, and tarragon, and whip with a wire whisk until well blended. Cover with plastic wrap and refrigerate until ready to use.

2   Prepare an indirect fire.

3   Rinse the trout fillets under cold running water and pat dry with paper towels. Brush the fillets on both sides with the oil and sprinkle evenly with the seasoning.

4   Place the fillets on the pit, cover, and cook at 230 to 250 degrees F until they flake easily, 20 to 30 minutes.

5   To serve, plate the fillets and serve with the sauce on the side and a wedge of lemon.

GRILLED TROUT WITH GRIBICHE HORSERADISH SAUCE

To grill the trout, prepare a medium-hot fire in your grill. Place the oiled and seasoned trout directly over the coals, cover, and cook until they begin to flake in the thickest part, 5 to 7 minutes per side. Serve as directed above.

Smoked Trout with Watercress Sauce

Watercress sauce is good on any grilled or smoked fish. I first served it on a poached salmon at a chef's dinner for 600 people. SERVES 4 TO 8

WATERCRESS SAUCE

1½ cups packed watercress sprigs

1 cup full-fat sour cream

2 tablespoons fresh lemon juice

1 teaspoon Louisiana hot sauce

1 teaspoon fine sea salt

1 teaspoon freshly ground black pepper

Eight 4- to 6-ounce trout fillets

2 tablespoons Old Bay seasoning, homemade (page 119) or store-bought

1 tablespoon firmly packed light brown sugar

½ cup canola oil

2 lemons, quartered

8 sprigs watercress

1   To make the sauce, place the sauce ingredients in a blender and process on high until very smooth, about 30 seconds.

2   Prepare an indirect fire.

3   Rinse the trout fillets under cold running water and pat dry with paper towels. Combine the Old Bay seasoning and brown sugar in a small bowl and blend well. Rub the fillets with the oil and season evenly all over with the brown sugar mixture.

4   Place the fish on the pit, cover, and cook at 230 to 250 degrees F until the flesh flakes easily, 30 to 40 minutes.

5   Serve the fillets with the sauce drizzled crosswise over the center and garnish with a lemon wedge and a sprig of watercress.

Barbecued or Grilled Green Onion Trout

This recipe has two titles because it can be grilled or cooked indirectly. Try it smoked with some apple wood. It's simple and delicious. SERVES 8

GREEN ONION SAUCE

1/2 cup (1 stick) unsalted butter

1 cup thinly sliced green onions (white and green parts)

4 cloves garlic, pressed

1 tablespoon fresh lemon juice

1 teaspoon fine sea salt

1 teaspoon freshly ground black pepper

Eight 12- to 16-ounce trout, cleaned, with head and tail left on

1 tablespoon coarse sea salt

1 tablespoon freshly ground black pepper

2 tablespoons minced fresh parsley leaves

1 To make the sauce, melt the butter in a medium-size saucepan over medium heat. Add the green onions and garlic and cook, stirring, until softened but not browned. Add the remaining sauce ingredients, stir, remove from the heat, and keep warm.

2 Prepare an indirect fire.

3 Rinse the trout under cold running water inside and out and pat dry with paper towels. Sprinkle them evenly with the salt and pepper.

4 Place the fish on the pit, cover, and cook at 230 to 250 degrees F until the fish flakes easily, about 1 hour.

5 To serve, place a trout on a serving plate, top with the green onion sauce, and garnish with the parsley.

VARIATION

To grill the trout, prepare a medium-hot fire in your grill. Place the seasoned trout directly over the coals and cook until the flesh begins to flake in the thickest part, 5 to 7 minutes per side. Serve as directed above.

Smoked Trout with Garlic and Rosemary

One night when I was serving rack of lamb, I remarked how rosemary and garlic brought out the flavor of lamb and how my guest ought to also try it on trout. I was told in so many words that the combination would not work, because rosemary was for beef and lamb. But trout is delicious this way—just not too much rosemary, please. SERVES 4

4 trout, cleaned, with head and tail left on

1/4 cup olive oil

4 cloves garlic, pressed

1 tablespoon minced fresh rosemary leaves

1 lemon, quartered

1 Prepare an indirect fire.

2 Rinse the trout under cold running water and pat dry with paper towels. Combine the olive oil and garlic and blend well. Rub the olive oil mixture over the inside and outside surfaces of each fish. Season the fish inside and out evenly with the rosemary.

3   Place the fish on the pit, cover, and cook at 230 to 250 degrees F until it flakes easily, 1½ to 2 hours.

4   Serve each trout garnished with a lemon wedge.

Apple and Cherry Smoked Trout

Fruit woods combine to give this trout a sweet, aromatic wood smoke flavor. This is just as tasty served hot as an entrée or chilled as an appetizer.   SERVES 4

Four 12- to 16-ounce rainbow trout, cleaned, with head and tail left on

2 tablespoons New Century Catering Barbeque Seasoning and Rub (page 132)

1 tablespoon firmly packed light brown sugar

½ cup canola oil

2 limes, sliced

2 lemons, sliced

1   Prepare an indirect fire. When it's ready, add 3 apple and wild cherry wood chunks to the coals.

2   Rinse the trout under cold running water and pat dry with paper towels. Combine the rub and brown sugar and blend well. Rub the inside of the trout with the oil. Sprinkle the inside of the trout with some of the rub mixture. In the cavity of each fish, place the lime and lemon slices, alternating the citrus slices. Rub the outside of the fish with the remaining oil and season with the rub mixture.

3   Place the fish on the pit, cover, and cook at 230 to 250 degrees F until they flake easily, 40 to 60 minutes.

Brithyll a Cig Moch (Smoked Welsh Trout and Bacon)

The first time I had catfish fixed this way, we were on a canoe trip in the Ozarks in southern Missouri. My father cooked them in mud or, as he called it, clay, right in the fire, and it was outstanding. You can also wrap the fish in aluminum foil and grill it, but it's much tastier done in the smoker.   SERVES 4

12 strips bacon, diced

¼ cup fresh sage leaves

¼ cup fresh parsley leaves

1 tablespoon fresh rosemary leaves

1 tablespoon fresh thyme leaves

1 teaspoon fine sea salt

1 teaspoon finely ground black pepper

Four 8-ounce trout, cleaned, with head and tail left on

1   In a medium-size skillet over medium heat, fry the bacon until cooked but not crisp. Add the herbs, cook about 1 minute, and remove from the heat. Add the salt and pepper and blend well. Remove the bacon mixture from the skillet with a slotted spoon and let cool slightly, reserving any excess bacon grease. Divide the bacon mixture into 4 equal parts and stuff each trout with it. Close the trout belly flaps and secure them with toothpicks.

2   Prepare an indirect fire.

3   Rinse the fish under cold running water and pat dry with paper towels. With a pastry brush, coat the outside of the trout with the reserved

bacon grease. Place the trout on the pit, cover, and cook at 230 to 250 degrees F until the fish flakes easily, 30 to 35 minutes, basting every 15 minutes with the bacon grease.

Smoky River Valley Trout

This dish makes a great summer night supper. SERVES 4

>   1 cup chopped onion
>   1/4 cup peeled, seeded, and chopped ripe tomato
>   4 cloves garlic, chopped
>   1 teaspoon fine sea salt
>   1 teaspoon freshly ground black pepper
>   1/4 cup olive oil
>   Four 8-ounce trout, cleaned, with head and tail left on

1 In a blender, combine the onion, tomato, garlic, salt, and pepper and process until smooth. While the machine is running, slowly add the olive oil through the top in a thin stream until it is well incorporated. Rinse the fish under cold running water and pat dry with paper towels. Rub the onion paste all over the edible parts of the trout, place in a large nonreactive baking dish, and cover with plastic wrap. Let marinate for 30 minutes at room temperature or for 1 hour in the refrigerator.

2 Prepare an indirect fire. When it's ready, throw 3 chunks of apple wood on the coals.

3 Place the trout on the pit, cover, and cook at 230 to 250 degrees F until the flesh flakes easily, 30 to 45 minutes.

Cayenne and Garlic Marinated Tuna

One thing you need to be aware of if you haven't worked with fresh tuna before is that you prepare and eat it as you would fresh beef. Fresh tuna resembles raw steak; it is a nice dark red. It can be eaten raw or cooked and anywhere from rare to well done but, in my opinion, well-done tuna is as repulsive as well-done beef. I prefer both to be on the medium-rare side. But check with your guests before you cook it. I suggest that you cook tuna to a medium rare, but only if it is really fresh. If you can't get good fresh tuna, then substitute sea bass or salmon. SERVES 4

>   CAYENNE AND GARLIC MARINADE
>   1/4 cup olive oil
>   1/4 cup fresh lemon juice
>   2 tablespoons minced fresh parsley leaves
>   2 tablespoons minced fresh cilantro leaves
>   2 tablespoons grated shallot
>   4 cloves garlic, pressed
>   1 teaspoon ground cumin
>   1 teaspoon crushed red pepper
>   1 teaspoon cayenne pepper
>   1 teaspoon coarse sea salt
>   1 teaspoon freshly ground black pepper
>
>   Four 6- to 8-ounce tuna steaks
>   1 lemon, quartered
>   Sprigs fresh parsley and cilantro for garnish

1 To make the marinade, combine the marinade ingredients in a small nonreactive bowl and blend with a wire whisk. Rinse the fish under cold running water and pat dry with paper towels. Place the tuna steaks in a zippered-top plastic bag or nonreactive baking dish and pour the marinade over them, turning to coat evenly. Seal or cover with

plastic wrap and let marinate for 30 minutes at room temperature or for 1 hour in the refrigerator.

2 Prepare a hot fire in your grill. When it's ready, throw 3 chunks of mesquite wood on the coals.

3 Remove the tuna from the marinade, discarding the marinade. Place the steaks directly over the coals, cover, and grill to your desired degree of doneness, 5 to 7 minutes per side for medium rare.

4 Serve with a lemon wedge and garnished with a sprig of parsley.

Grill Meister's Pepper-Crusted Grilled Tuna

This is another recipe from my barbecue buddy Gunner Roe, the Grill Meister. This also works great with wahoo, shark, or dolphin fish (mahi-mahi). SERVES 6

> Six 8-ounce tuna steaks
>
> ¹/₂ cup hot mustard or mustard slather of your choice (pages 86–101)
>
> 1 to 2 tablespoons cracked black peppercorns, to your taste
>
> 1 tablespoon fine sea salt

1 Prepare a medium-hot fire in your grill.

2 Rinse the fish under cold running water and pat dry with paper towels. Spread both sides of the tuna steaks with the mustard, then sprinkle evenly all over with the pepper and salt, patting it down a bit so it adheres to the mustard.

3 Place the tuna in a grill basket and set directly over the coals. Cover and grill to your desired degree of doneness, 5 to 7 minutes per side for medium rare.

Rainbow Tuna Steaks au Poivre

Rainbow peppercorns give this tuna an outstanding flavor—simply delicious. SERVES 8

> ¹/₄ cup freshly ground rainbow peppercorns (green, pink, black, two kinds of white, and a bit of Szechuan)
>
> Eight 8-ounce tuna steaks
>
> 1 cup (2 sticks) unsalted butter, at room temperature

1 Prepare a hot fire in your grill.

2 Spread the ground pepper on a plate. Rinse the fish under cold running water and pat dry with paper towels. Smear the steaks all over with the butter, then press the steaks into the pepper, covering them completely and evenly.

3 Place the steaks directly over the coals, cover, and cook to your desired degree of doneness, 5 to 7 minutes per side for medium rare.

Szechuan Ginger Tuna with Creamy Hot Szechuan Sauce

This is a meal fit for an emperor and a king. I always like to have my girlfriend ginger in a recipe. SERVES 4

SZECHUAN GINGER MARINADE

1/4 cup soy sauce

1/4 cup clover honey

1/4 cup water

2 tablespoons granulated cane sugar

1 tablespoon freshly coarse-ground Szechuan peppercorns

1 tablespoon peeled and grated fresh ginger

Four 6- to 8-ounce tuna steaks

CREAMY HOT SZECHUAN SAUCE

1/4 cup mayonnaise

1 tablespoon clover honey

2 teaspoons finely ground Szechuan peppercorns

1 teaspoon Louisiana hot sauce

1/2 teaspoon fine sea salt

1 To make the marinade, combine the marinade ingredients in a small nonreactive saucepan over low heat. Heat, stirring, until everything has blended. Remove from the heat and let cool. Rinse the fish under cold running water and pat dry with paper towels. Place the tuna steaks in a nonreactive baking dish or a zippered-top plastic bag and pour the marinade over them, making sure all sides are coated. Cover with plastic wrap or seal and let marinate for 30 minutes at room temperature or for 1 hour in the refrigerator.

2 To make the sauce, combine the sauce ingredients in a small bowl and blend well with a wire whisk. Cover with plastic wrap and refrigerate until needed.

3 Prepare a hot fire in your grill.

4 Remove the tuna from the marinade, discarding the marinade. Place the steaks directly over the coals, cover, and cook to your desired degree of doneness, 5 to 7 minutes per side for medium rare.

5 Serve the steaks with the sauce on the side.

Grilled Tuna Steaks with Anchovy and Black Olive Sauce

When I make this recipe in my Kansas City back yard on a hot summer day, I can take an instant lawn-chair trip to the Mediterranean with just one bite. SERVES 4

ANCHOVY AND BLACK OLIVE SAUCE

One 2-ounce can oil-packed anchovies, rinsed and drained

8 oil-cured Mediterranean-style black olives, pitted and crushed

2 cloves garlic, pressed

1/4 cup chicken broth

2 tablespoons fresh lemon juice

2 tablespoons minced fresh parsley leaves

2 tablespoons capers, drained

1/2 teaspoon fine sea salt

1/2 teaspoon freshly ground white pepper

Four 6- to 8-ounce tuna steaks

1/4 cup olive oil

1 tablespoon coarse sea salt

1 tablespoon freshly ground black pepper

1 To make the sauce, combine the sauce ingredients in a blender and process until smooth. Transfer to a bowl, cover with plastic wrap, and refrigerate until needed.

2 Prepare a hot fire in your grill.

3 Rinse the fish under cold running water and pat dry with paper towels. Brush the steaks with the olive oil, then sprinkle evenly with the salt and pepper. Place the steaks directly over the coals, cover, and grill to your desired degree of doneness, 5 to 7 minutes per side for medium rare.

4 To serve, spread 1 tablespoon of the sauce over each grilled tuna steak. Serve immediately, with additional sauce on the side.

Herbed Lemon Grilled Tuna

Simple, easy, delicious, and impressive, this recipe has it all. SERVES 4

HERBED LEMON BUTTER BASTE
1/4 cup (1/2 stick) unsalted butter

1 tablespoon olive oil

1 tablespoon fresh lemon juice

1/4 cup minced shallots

2 tablespoons minced fresh parsley leaves

1 tablespoon minced fresh cilantro leaves

1 tablespoon coarse sea salt

1 tablespoon lemon pepper seasoning

Four 8-ounce tuna steaks

1 To make the baste, combine the butter, olive oil, and lemon juice in a small nonreactive saucepan over medium heat and heat until the butter melts. Add the shallots, parsley, and cilantro and cook for 2 minutes, stirring. Remove from the heat.

2 Prepare a medium-hot fire in your grill.

3 Combine the salt and lemon pepper in a small bowl and blend well. Rinse the fish under cold running water and pat dry with paper towels. Sprinkle the steaks all over with the seasoning, then press them into the butter mixture, coating them completely.

4 Place the steaks directly over the coals, cover, and grill to your desired degree of doneness, 5 to 7 minutes per side for medium rare, basting with the remaining butter mixture when you turn the steaks.

Sweet and Hot Balsamic Tuna Steaks

This tuna is for the big tuna—your boss. SERVES 8

SWEET AND HOT BALSAMIC MARINADE
1 cup (2 sticks) unsalted butter, melted

2 tablespoons balsamic vinegar

2 tablespoons fresh lemon juice

2 tablespoons Worcestershire sauce, homemade (page 50) or store-bought

2 tablespoons firmly packed light brown sugar

1 tablespoon Louisiana hot sauce

4 large cloves garlic, pressed

1 teaspoon Old Bay seasoning, homemade (page 119) or store-bought

1 teaspoon kosher salt

1 teaspoon cracked black peppercorns

Eight 8-ounce tuna steaks

1   To make the marinade, combine the marinade ingredients in a medium-size nonreactive bowl and blend well. Rinse the fish under cold running water and pat dry with paper towels. Place the tuna steaks in a zippered-top plastic bag or nonreactive baking dish and pour the marinade over the fish, coating them well. Seal or cover with plastic wrap and let marinate for 30 minutes at room temperature or for 1 hour in the refrigerator.

2   Prepare a hot fire in your grill.

3   Remove the steaks from the marinade. Transfer the remaining marinade to a saucepan and bring to a boil over medium-high heat; let simmer for 5 minutes, then set aside.

4   Place the steaks directly over the coals, cover, and grill to your desired degree of doneness, 5 to 7 minutes per side for medium rare, basting with the reserved marinade when you turn the steaks.

Honey-Lime-Ginger Glazed Tuna Steaks

This tuna has a nice, light Asian flavor. You can also serve the marinade as a dipping sauce for the tuna; if you'd like to do this, make a double batch of the marinade and set half of it aside for dipping at the table. SERVES 4

HONEY-LIME-GINGER MARINADE

1/4 cup light soy sauce

1/4 cup clover honey

2 tablespoons firmly packed light brown sugar

2 tablespoons peeled and grated fresh ginger

2 tablespoons fresh lime juice (about 2 limes)

2 tablespoons toasted sesame oil

4 cloves garlic, pressed

2 teaspoons seeded and minced jalapeño chiles

1 teaspoon minced lime zest

4 tuna steaks, 1 inch thick

1   To make the marinade, combine the marinade ingredients in a small nonreactive bowl and blend well with a wire whisk. Rinse the fish under cold running water and pat dry with paper towels. Place the tuna steaks in a nonreactive baking dish or a zippered-top plastic bag. Pour the marinade over the steaks, coating them well, cover with plastic wrap or seal, and let marinate for 30 minutes at room temperature or for 1 hour in the refrigerator.

2   Prepare a medium-hot fire in your grill.

3   Remove the tuna from the marinade. Transfer the remaining marinade to a saucepan and bring to a boil over medium-high heat; let simmer for 5 minutes, then set aside.

4   Place the steaks directly over the coals, cover, and grill to your desired degree of doneness, 5 to 7 minutes for medium rare, basting with the reserved marinade when you turn the steaks.

Tequila Tuna

Remember that the marinade is for the fish, not the fisherman or the cook. SERVES 4

TEQUILA MARINADE

1/4 cup water

2 tablespoons unsalted butter

2 tablespoons tequila

2 tablespoons fresh lime juice (about 2 limes)

1 tablespoon granulated cane sugar

1 teaspoon instant chicken bouillon granules

1 teaspoon ground coriander

1 teaspoon crushed red pepper

1 teaspoon kosher salt

1/2 teaspoon freshly ground black pepper

Four 6- to 8-ounce tuna steaks

1 lime, cut into wedges

Kosher salt, as needed

1 To make the marinade, combine the marinade ingredients in a small nonreactive skillet and heat over medium heat until the butter has melted. Remove from the heat and let cool to below 100 degrees F. Rinse the fish under cold running water and pat dry with paper towels. Place the tuna in a nonreactive baking dish or a zippered-top plastic bag, pour the cooled marinade over the steaks, coating them well, cover with plastic wrap or seal, and let marinate for 30 minutes at room temperature.

2 Prepare a medium-hot fire in your grill.

3 Remove the steaks from the marinade, place directly over the coals, cover, and grill to your desired degree of doneness, 5 to 7 minutes per side for medium rare.

4 Serve the steaks garnished with lime wedges dipped in kosher salt.

Tuna on the Grill Orientale with Lobster Sauce

Yes, it's okay to pick this recipe because of the sauce, but be warned that it contains no lobster. Its name comes from traditionally being served over lobster. The tuna steaks are coated with cornstarch to give a light crust. SERVES 4

1/4 cup peeled and finely grated fresh ginger

1 tablespoon coarse sea salt

1 tablespoon freshly ground black pepper

Four 6- to 8-ounce tuna steaks

2 tablespoons cornstarch

LOBSTER SAUCE

1 tablespoon fermented black beans (available in the Asian section of the supermarket)

2 cloves garlic, pressed

4 scallions (white and green parts), sliced 1/4 inch thick

2 tablespoons light soy sauce

1 tablespoon dry sherry

1 tablespoon granulated cane sugar

1/2 cup chicken broth or fish stock

2 tablespoons sunflower oil

1/4 pound lean ground pork

2 tablespoons cornstarch

1/4 cup cold water

Nonstick cooking spray

1 Combine the ginger, salt, and pepper in a small bowl and blend well. Rinse the fish under

cold running water and pat dry with paper towels. Coat both sides of the tuna with the mixture. Sprinkle both sides of the fish evenly with the cornstarch. Cover with plastic wrap and refrigerate for 30 minutes.

2   To make the sauce, place the black beans in a small bowl; cover with hot water and let set for 5 minutes. Stir for about 2 minutes. Drain, then mash the beans with the garlic. In another small bowl, combine the scallions, soy sauce, sherry, sugar, and broth. Heat the sunflower oil in a medium-size skillet over medium-high heat, add the black bean mixture, and cook, stirring, until pungent, about 1 minute. Add the ground pork and cook, stirring, until no longer pink, about 2 minutes. Add the scallion mixture, bring to a boil, reduce the heat to medium-low, and simmer for about 5 minutes. In a small bowl, blend the cornstarch and cold water into a paste, then stir into the skillet until the mixture thickens. Simmer until the sauce is shiny, about 2 minutes. Cover and remove from the heat, keeping it warm.

3   Prepare a medium-hot fire in your grill.

4   Coat the tuna all over with the cooking spray. Place directly over the coals, cover, and grill to your desired degree of doneness, 5 to 7 minutes per side for medium rare.

5   To serve, put a tablespoon of sauce on a plate and top with a tuna steak. Pass the rest of the sauce at the table.

Fennel-Pepper Tuna Steaks with Smoked Garlic and Basil Sauce

I normally make this sauce with yogurt rather than sour cream because I think it more effectively brings out the flavor of the basil. SERVES 4

SMOKED GARLIC AND BASIL SAUCE
1 cup plain yogurt or sour cream
1/3 cup fresh basil leaves
1/4 cup smoked garlic paste (page 98)
1 teaspoon fine sea salt
1/2 teaspoon freshly ground white pepper

FENNEL-PEPPER SEASONING
1 tablespoon kosher salt
1 tablespoon cracked black peppercorns
2 teaspoons fennel seeds, pulverized
1 teaspoon cayenne pepper

4 tuna steaks, 1 inch thick
Nonstick cooking spray

1   If you are using yogurt in the sauce, spoon it into a strainer lined with a paper coffee filter or several layers of cheesecloth. Set the strainer in a bowl and refrigerate until most of the liquid has drained off the yogurt, 2 to 3 hours.

2   To make the seasoning, combine the fennel-pepper seasoning ingredients in a small bowl and blend well. Sprinkle the tuna steaks all over with the mixture, cover with plastic wrap, and let marinate for 30 minutes at room temperature or for 1 hour in the refrigerator.

3   To make the sauce, place the basil and garlic paste in a blender and process until smooth. Combine the drained yogurt (if using), basil purée, salt, and pepper in a medium-size bowl and blend well with a wire whisk. Cover with plastic wrap and refrigerate until needed.

4   Build a medium-hot fire in your grill.

5   Rinse the fish under cold running water and pat dry with paper towels. Coat the steaks all over with the cooking spray. Place them directly over the coals, cover, and grill to your desired degree of doneness, 5 to 7 minutes per side for medium rare.

6   To serve, put a tablespoon of sauce on a plate and top with a tuna steak. Pass the rest of the sauce at the table.

Simple Smoked Whitefish

Smoked whitefish is a great delicacy in the Great Lakes region, where it's usually cold smoked. Some inventive guys even tinker with old refrigerators to get the perfect distance and the perfect flue for cold smoking whitefish below 230 degrees F. My version is hot smoked between 230 and 250 degrees F, and I use my standard wood mixture of oak, apple, and hickory. Smoked whitefish is good on its own or made into a smoked whitefish salad—just like you'd make a tuna fish salad, only better. SERVES 4

> One 3- to 3¹/₂-pound whitefish, cleaned and dressed
>
> 2 tablespoons olive oil
>
> 2 tablespoons Italian Seafood Seasoning (page 120)

1   Prepare an indirect fire.

2   Rinse the whitefish under cold running water inside and out and pat dry with paper towels. Rub the fish all over with the olive oil, then sprinkle evenly with the seasoning.

3   Place the fish on the pit, cover, and cook at 230 to 250 degrees F until the flesh flakes easily, 60 to 75 minutes.

Smoked Thyme- Garlic Marinated Whitefish

Whitefish are best in the spring and fall on the East Coast and in the Great Lakes region. When they're smoked, they are tender, succulent, and aromatic. SERVES 6 TO 8

> **THYME-GARLIC MARINADE**
>
> ¹/₄ cup olive oil
>
> 3 to 4 cloves garlic, to your taste, pressed
>
> 1 tablespoon minced fresh thyme leaves
>
> One 3- to 4-pound whitefish, cleaned and dressed

1   To make the marinade, combine the marinade ingredients in a small bowl and blend well. Put the fish in a zippered-top plastic bag or nonreactive baking dish and pour the marinade over it. Seal or cover with plastic wrap and let marinate in the refrigerator for about 2 hours.

2   Prepare an indirect fire.

3   Remove the fish from the marinade, discarding the marinade. Place the fish on the pit, cover, and cook at 230 to 250 degrees F until the flesh flakes easily, about 2¹/₂ hours.

Grill Meister's Grilled Crab Cakes

This recipe from fish maven Gunner Roe is one that I have feasted on and always look forward to. And yes, you can grill crab cakes, but be sure to use a grill basket. SERVES 2 TO 4; MAKES 6 TO 8 CRAB CAKES

- 1 pound lump crabmeat, picked over for shells and cartilage
- 1 large egg
- 1/4 cup fresh bread crumbs
- 2 tablespoons hot mustard
- 1 tablespoon mayonnaise
- 1 teaspoon Worcestershire sauce, homemade (page 50) or store-bought
- 1 teaspoon Old Bay seasoning, homemade (page 119) or store-bought
- 1/2 teaspoon freshly ground white pepper
- Nonstick cooking spray

1 Combine all the ingredients in a medium-size bowl and blend well. Form crab cakes 3 to 4 inches in diameter and 1 inch thick. Cover with plastic wrap and refrigerate for 1 hour to firm up.

2 When ready to cook, prepare a medium-hot fire in your grill.

3 Coat a grill basket with the cooking spray, place the crab cakes in the basket, set directly over the coals, cover, and cook until both sides are golden brown, about 10 minutes.

Gunner's Grilled Soft-Shell Crabs

This is another example of Gunner's love for seafood. Soft-shell crabs are available in late May and early June when blue crabs have shed their old shells and are just beginning to form new ones. I buy mine already cleaned. If yours aren't, have your fishmonger clean them for you. Be sure to cook crabs the day you buy them. SERVES 6 TO 8

- 12 to 16 soft-shell crabs, cleaned
- 1/2 cup olive oil
- 1 tablespoon freshly ground black pepper
- 1 tablespoon Old Bay seasoning, homemade (page 119) or store-bought
- 1 teaspoon fine sea salt
- 1 recipe Barbecue Cocktail Sauce (page 52)
- Nonstick cooking spray

1 Prepare a medium-hot fire in your grill.

2 Rinse the crabs under cold running water and pat dry with paper towels. Brush them lightly with the olive oil and sprinkle evenly on both sides with the pepper, Old Bay, and salt.

3 Coat a grill basket with the cooking spray, place the crabs, in batches, in the grill basket, set it directly over the coals, cover, and cook until they turn reddish brown, 3 to 5 minutes per side.

4 Serve the crabs hot with the sauce on the side.

Crabmeat-Stuffed Soft-Shell Crabs

If you can get soft-shell crabs, this is a real treat. I buy my soft-shells already cleaned. If yours aren't, ask you fishmonger to do it for you. SERVES 6 TO 8

12 soft-shell crabs, cleaned

CRABMEAT STUFFING

1 pound lump crabmeat, picked over for shells and cartilage

2 large egg whites

2 tablespoons mayonnaise

2 tablespoons hot mustard

Juice of 1 lemon

1 teaspoon freshly ground black pepper

$1/2$ teaspoon Old Bay seasoning, homemade (page 119) or store-bought

$1/2$ teaspoon fine sea salt

SEASONING

1 teaspoon garlic salt

1 teaspoon freshly ground black pepper

1 teaspoon Old Bay seasoning, homemade (page 119) or store-bought

$1/2$ cup olive oil

Nonstick cooking spray

1 Rinse the crabs under cold running water and pat dry with paper towels.

2 To make the stuffing, place the crabmeat, egg whites, mayonnaise, mustard, and lemon juice in a medium-size nonreactive bowl. Add the pepper, Old Bay, and salt and gently fold the mixture together, trying not to break up the crab lumps too much. Stuff the crabs with the mixture in the small opening between the top shell and the body of the crab using your fingers or a spoon. The amount of crabmeat mixture used will vary according to the size of the soft-shell crab.

3 Prepare a hot fire in your grill.

4 To make the seasoning, in a small bowl, combine the seasoning ingredients and blend well.

5 Brush the outside of the stuffed crabs with the olive oil and sprinkle evenly with the seasoning. Coat a grill basket with the cooking spray, place the crabs in the basket, set directly over the coals, cover, and cook until they turn reddish brown, 3 to 5 minutes per side. Serve immediately.

Grilled Soft-Shell Crab Sandwich with Paprika Aioli

Soft-shell crab is available only for a short time each year, and the people who have been introduced to them wait in line to get them. I buy mine already cleaned. If yours aren't, ask your fishmonger to do it for you. SERVES 8

PAPRIKA AIOLI

1 cup mayonnaise

8 cloves smoked garlic (see page 98), mashed

1 tablespoon fresh lemon juice

2 teaspoons sweet Hungarian paprika

$1/4$ teaspoon cayenne pepper or pure ground chipotle chile

$1/2$ teaspoon fine sea salt

$1/4$ teaspoon freshly ground white pepper

8 soft-shell crabs, cleaned

$1/4$ cup olive oil

Salt and freshly ground black pepper to taste

Nonstick cooking spray

8 large crusty buns or 16 slices fresh Italian bread

2 cups watercress or arugula

1 To make the aioli, combine all the aioli ingredients in a medium-size bowl and blend well.

2 Prepare a medium-hot fire in your grill.

3 Rinse the crabs under cold running water and pat dry with paper towels. Brush the crabs with the olive oil and season with the salt and pepper. Coat a grill basket with the cooking spray, place the crabs in the basket, set it directly over the coals, cover, and grill until they turn reddish brown, 3 to 5 minutes per side.

4 To serve, place a crab on a bun, spread with the aioli, and top with watercress and the other half of the bun.

Grilled Rock Lobster

This recipe is livin' high on the hog. SERVES 2

LOBSTER MARINADE

2 teaspoons garlic salt

1 teaspoon sweet Hungarian paprika

1/2 teaspoon Old Bay seasoning, homemade (page 119) or store-bought

1/2 teaspoon freshly ground white pepper

Juice of 1 lemon

1/2 cup olive oil

Two 10-ounce rock lobster tails

Drawn butter (see page 341) or Drawn Roasted Garlic Butter (page 341)

Lemon wedges

1 Prepare a medium-hot fire in your grill.

2 To make the marinade, combine the garlic salt, paprika, Old Bay, pepper, and lemon juice in

a small bowl. Blend in the olive oil with a wire whisk, mixing well.

3 Split the lobster tails lengthwise with a large knife. Using a pastry brush, brush the meat side of the tails with the marinade.

4 Place the lobster tails, meat side down, directly over the coals, cover, and cook until well seared. Turn over, cover, and cook 5 to 6 minutes longer, basting with the remaining marinade. The lobster is done when it is opaque and firm to the touch.

5 Serve with the drawn butter and lemon wedges.

Smoke-Roasted Mussels with Garlic Butter and Hot Mustard Sauce

Mussels are a family favorite—we figure at least 1¼ to 1½ pounds per person at our house. Smoke-roasting makes them even more wonderful than just plain steaming. Use this technique instead of smoking (which is done at a lower temperature) because mussels and other shellfish need a higher cooking temperature to open their shells. SERVES 3 OR 4

HOT MUSTARD SAUCE

1/4 cup rice vinegar

1/4 cup dry mustard (I use Colman's)

2 tablespoons dark soy sauce

1 tablespoon granulated cane sugar

GARLIC BUTTER

1 cup (2 sticks) unsalted butter

6 to 8 large cloves garlic, to your taste, pressed

5 pounds small cultivated mussels

Nonstick cooking spray

1 To make the sauce, in a small nonreactive bowl, stir the vinegar into the mustard to form a thick paste. Cover and let rest for 30 minutes. Stir in the soy sauce and sugar until the sugar dissolves. Cover and let rest for 2 hours or, better yet, overnight. If you want a thinner sauce, add a little water.

2 To make the garlic butter, place the butter and garlic in a medium-size saucepan over medium heat and cook, stirring, until the butter has melted and the garlic is fragrant, 3 to 4 minutes. Set aside and keep warm.

3 Scrub the mussels, removing their beards. Discard any that will not close.

4 When ready to cook, prepare a medium-hot fire in your grill. Coat a perforated grill rack with the cooking spray and place on the grill. Throw a chunk of apple wood on the fire, then place the mussels evenly over the grill rack, cover, and cook until they open, 10 to 15 minutes. Discard any that will not open.

5 Serve the hot mussels in their shells with the mustard sauce and garlic butter in separate bowls for dipping.

Grilled Mussels, Clams, and Oysters

Whichever one you choose, you can't go wrong. SERVES 1 TO 500, DEPENDING ON HOW MANY YOU WANT TO COOK, OR FEED, OR HOW HUNGRY YOU ARE

Mussels, littleneck clams, and oysters

Nonstick cooking spray

Melted butter

Lemon wedges

1 Prepare a hot fire in your grill.

2 Rinse and scrub the mussels (also removing their beards), clams, and oysters, discarding any that will not close.

3 Coat a perforated grill rack with the cooking spray and place on the grill. Throw some wood chunks (pecan, grapevine, or apple) on the fire, then place the mollusks evenly over the grill rack. Cover and cook until they open, 10 to 15 minutes, checking every 5 minutes and removing those that have opened from the grill. Discard any that will not open. Mussels and clams should open first. The oysters will take a little longer, depending on their size.

4 Serve the hot mollusks in their shells with the melted butter and lemon wedges.

NOTE For added smoky flavor, try melting the butter in a small pan on the grill while cooking.

Martini Oysters

Have your drink and eat it too! SERVES 2 TO 4

1 cup vodka

1 whisper of vermouth

2 tablespoons seeded and minced jalapeño or serrano chiles

2 tablespoons thinly sliced green onions (white and green parts)

1 teaspoon finely minced lemon zest

2 dozen oysters on the half shell

1 Combine the vodka, chiles, green onions, and lemon zest in a jar with a tight-fitting lid and shake, don't stir.

2 Prepare a hot fire in your grill.

3 Spoon a little of the martini mixture over each oyster. Place the jar with the remaining martini mixture in the freezer.

4 Place the oysters directly over the coals, cover, and cook until the edges curl, 3 to 5 minutes.

5 Remove from the grill and serve with the remaining martini mixture for dipping.

Grilled Oysters with Chipotle Mignonette, Ginger-Lime Relish, and Barbecue Horseradish Dipping Sauce

If you enjoy oysters like I do, this is a serving for one. It's also a good appetizer for a party. Have your guests grill their own oysters, if they desire; it makes for a lot of fun. They can also choose their own sauce. SERVES 4 TO 8

CHIPOTLE MIGNONETTE

1 cup mayonnaise

¼ cup red wine vinegar

¼ cup minced shallots

One 7-ounce can chipotle chiles in adobo sauce, or to taste, puréed

1 tablespoon clover honey

1 tablespoon coarsely ground black pepper

1 teaspoon fine sea salt

½ teaspoon freshly ground white pepper

GINGER-LIME RELISH

2 cups fresh lime juice (about 32 limes)

1 cup fresh orange juice (about 4 oranges)

2 tablespoons peeled and grated fresh ginger

1 tablespoon pressed garlic

1 tablespoon clover honey

4 limes, peeled, segmented, seeded, and chopped

1 orange, peeled, segmented, seeded if necessary, and chopped

½ cup minced shallots

2 tablespoons minced fresh cilantro leaves

1 tablespoon minced fresh parsley leaves

1 tablespoon grated lime zest

1 teaspoon fine sea salt

1 teaspoon freshly ground black pepper

BARBECUE HORSERADISH SAUCE

1 cup barbecue sauce of your choice (pages 136–161) or flavored ketchup (see Sources)

2 tablespoons peeled and grated fresh horseradish

2 teaspoons Worcestershire sauce, homemade (page 50) or store-bought

1 teaspoon fresh lime juice

1 teaspoon Louisiana hot sauce, or to taste

½ teaspoon fine sea salt

½ teaspoon freshly ground black pepper

24 to 48 Blue Point oysters, scrubbed, any that will not close discarded

1 To make the mignonette, combine the mignonette ingredients in a medium-size bowl

and blend well with a wire whisk. Cover with plastic wrap and chill.

2 To make the relish, combine the lime juice, orange juice, ginger, garlic, and honey in a medium-size nonreactive saucepan over medium-high heat and bring to a boil. Reduce the heat to medium-low and simmer until the liquid has reduced by half, 30 minutes. Set aside to cool. Combine the chopped citrus, shallots, cilantro, parsley, lime zest, salt, and pepper in a medium-size nonreactive bowl. Pour the cooled liquid over the citrus mixture and gently toss. Cover with plastic wrap and chill.

3 To make the sauce, combine all the barbecue sauce ingredients in a small nonreactive bowl and blend well with a wire whisk. Cover and chill.

4 Prepare a hot fire in your grill.

5 Place the oysters directly over the coals, cover, and grill until they open, about 5 minutes. Discard any that will not open.

6 Remove the top shells and serve the oysters with the dipping sauces.

Grill Meister's Pecan-Smoked Oysters Stuffed with Crabmeat

Use pecan or a mixture of pecan and grapevine on the fire; it really sets this dish off from the ordinary. SERVES 6 TO 8

1 pound lump crabmeat, picked over for shells and cartilage

2 tablespoons mayonnaise

2 tablespoons hot mustard

2 large egg whites, lightly beaten

Juice of 1 lemon

1/2 teaspoon fine sea salt

1/2 teaspoon freshly ground white pepper

24 oysters on the half shell

1 Prepare an indirect fire. When it's ready, throw 3 chunks of pecan wood and/or grapevine on the coals.

2 Place the crabmeat, mayonnaise, mustard, egg whites, lemon juice, salt, and pepper in a medium-size nonreactive bowl and blend gently. Top the oysters evenly with the crabmeat mixture.

3 Place the oysters in disposable aluminum pans or on a perforated grill rack, set on the pit, cover, and cook at 230 to 250 degrees F until the crabmeat is golden brown, 45 to 60 minutes.

Grilled Scallops with Radicchio and Pancetta

This recipe requires a bit of work, but it's delicious! You'll need 24 short wooden skewers for this; remember to soak them in water for at least 30 minutes first to keep the ends from scorching. SERVES 12

1/4 cup (1/2 stick) unsalted butter, at room temperature

2 to 4 cloves garlic, to your taste, pressed

24 large sea scallops

24 radicchio leaves, rinsed and dried

¹/₂ teaspoon fine sea salt

¹/₂ teaspoon freshly ground black pepper

24 thin slices pancetta or bacon

1 Combine the butter and garlic in a small bowl and blend well. Rinse the scallops under cold running water and pat dry with paper towels. Spread the butter mixture all over the scallops and place each in the center of a radicchio leaf. Season the scallops evenly with the salt and pepper. Wrap each scallop in the radicchio. Fold a slice of pancetta around each packet, securing it with a skewer.

2 Prepare a medium-hot fire in your grill.

3 Place the scallop packets directly over the coals, turning them constantly until the pancetta is crisp, 4 to 5 minutes. Serve immediately.

Mediterranean Octopus in Garlic-Oregano Marinade

This recipe is for the adventurous! You'll need to special order a whole octopus from your local fishmonger.
SERVES 6 TO 8

1 cleaned octopus (3 to 4 pounds), thawed if
   necessary

GARLIC-OREGANO MARINADE

³/₄ cup olive oil

¹/₂ cup red wine vinegar

¹/₂ cup fresh lemon juice (4 to 5 lemons)

2 tablespoons fresh oregano leaves, minced

6 to 8 large cloves garlic, to your taste, pressed

1 teaspoon fine sea salt

¹/₂ teaspoon coarsely ground black pepper

1 Cover the octopus with a clean cloth towel and beat it with a wooden mallet or rolling pin to soften it. This could take 15 to 20 minutes. Cut the octopus into pieces twice the size you want to serve because it will shrink when cooked.

2 To make the marinade, combine the marinade ingredients in a medium-size nonreactive bowl and blend well. Divide in half. Place the octopus in a nonreactive baking dish or a zippered-top plastic bag. Pour one-half of the marinade over the octopus, stirring to coat all of it. Cover with plastic wrap or seal the bag and let marinate overnight in the refrigerator.

3 When you're ready to cook, prepare a medium fire in your grill.

4 Remove the octopus from the marinade. Transfer the remaining marinade to a saucepan and bring to a boil over medium-high heat; let simmer for 5 minutes, then set aside. If your grill doesn't have small grates, cover it with expanded metal mesh or a perforated grill rack. Place the octopus directly over the coals and grill until opaque, 4 to 5 minutes per side, basting with the reserved marinade. Serve immediately.

Grilled Octopus Salad

This is a tasty luncheon or light dinner party entrée.
SERVES 4

OCTOPUS MARINADE

1/2 cup extra virgin olive oil

1/4 cup balsamic vinegar

1/4 cup fresh lemon juice (about 2 lemons)

2 to 4 cloves garlic, to your taste, pressed

1 teaspoon fine sea salt

1/2 teaspoon freshly ground black pepper

SALAD DRESSING

1/2 cup olive oil

1/4 cup red wine vinegar

1/4 cup fresh lemon juice

1 tablespoon granulated cane sugar

2 teaspoons Dijon mustard

1 teaspoon fine sea salt

1 teaspoon freshly ground black pepper

SALAD

1 1/2 pounds octopus tentacles, cleaned, thawed if necessary, and tenderized (see step 1 on page 417)

2 ripe avocados

2 tablespoons fresh lemon or lime juice

12 ounces mixed salad greens

1 cup cherry tomatoes, rinsed and cut in half

1 cup black olives, drained, for garnish

1 To make the marinade, combine the marinade ingredients in a small nonreactive bowl, blend well, and set aside.

2 To make the dressing, in another small non-reactive bowl, combine the dressing ingredients and blend well with a wire whisk. Cover and set aside.

3 To make the salad, blanch the larger octopus tentacles in boiling lightly salted water for 1 minute to further tenderize. Drain, then place the octopus in a zippered-top plastic bag, pour in the marinade, seal, and let marinate for 1 to 3 hours in the refrigerator.

4 Prepare a medium-hot fire in your grill.

5 Remove the octopus from the marinade. Transfer the remaining marinade to a saucepan and bring to a boil over medium-high heat; let simmer for 5 minutes, then set aside.

6 If your grill doesn't have small grates, cover it with expanded metal mesh or a perforated grill rack. Place the octopus directly over the coals and grill until opaque, 4 to 5 minutes per side, basting with the reserved marinade. Remove from the grill, let cool, and slice into 1- to 2-inch chunks.

7 Peel and remove the stones from the avocados, cut into chunks, and toss with the lemon juice. Place the mixed greens and tomatoes in a large salad bowl, add the avocados and octopus, and toss. Blend the salad dressing again and add, to taste, to the salad. Toss again with the dressing to coat everything evenly. Divide the salad among 4 large plates or salad bowls and garnish with the olives.

Sesame Scallops with Grilled Vegetables

This is big platter of food at its finest. Grill the vegetables first, top with the grilled scallops, and garnish with sesame seeds. Then dig in! SERVES 6 TO 8

TOASTED SESAME MARINADE

1/4 cup soy sauce

1/4 cup water

2 tablespoons rice vinegar

1 to 2 tablespoons peeled and grated fresh
    ginger, to your taste

1 tablespoon toasted sesame oil

1 tablespoon canola oil

1 to 2 pounds sea scallops

GRILLED VEGETABLES

1 red bell pepper, seeded and cut into strips

1 yellow bell pepper, seeded and cut into strips

1 cup snow peas, strings trimmed

3 tablespoons canola oil

Nonstick cooking spray

2 tablespoons sesame seeds, toasted in a dry
    skillet over medium heat until fragrant

1 To make the marinade, combine the marinade ingredients in a small nonreactive bowl and blend well. Rinse the scallops under cold running water and pat dry with paper towels. Place the scallops in a zippered-top plastic bag and pour in the marinade, turning to coat the scallops. Seal the bag and let marinate for 30 to 40 minutes in the refrigerator.

2 To make the grilled vegetables, place the bell peppers and snow peas in a large bowl or zippered-top plastic bag, pour the oil over them and seal, tossing to coat everything.

3 Prepare a medium-hot fire in your grill.

4 Using a grill wok or a sheet of small-mesh metal, grill the vegetables for 5 to 7 minutes, until they're how you like them. Set aside and keep warm.

5 Remove the scallops from the marinade, discarding the marinade. Coat a grill basket with the cooking spray, place the scallops in the basket, place the basket grill directly over the coals, and grill the scallops until opaque, 3 to 5 minutes per side.

6 Place the grilled vegetables on a platter, top with the grilled scallops, and garnish with the toasted sesame seeds.

Black Pepper Shrimp

If you like shrimp, this recipe doesn't get any easier. SERVES 6 TO 8

2 pounds large shrimp (21 to 25 count per
    pound)

1 cup olive oil

1 tablespoon freshly ground black pepper

1 tablespoon Old Bay seasoning, homemade
    (page 119) or store-bought

Nonstick cooking spray

1 Peel the shrimp, leaving the tail shell on. Brush the shrimp with the olive oil and season with the pepper and Old Bay.

2 Prepare a medium-hot fire in your grill.

3 Coat a grill basket with the cooking spray, place the shrimp in the basket, set directly over the coals, and cook until pink on both sides, 2 to 3 minutes per side. You can also prepare these in a grill wok or on skewers, if desired.

Bacon-Wrapped Shrimp Stuffed with Jalapeño and Monterey Jack Cheese

This is a David Klose (of Klose Pits fame, see Sources) special—everyone thinks he builds the world's best barbecue pits. He has several variations of this recipe that he'll cook up for you. You'll need 42 to 50 wooden skewers for this; don't forget to soak them in water first. **SERVES 6 TO 8**

2 pounds large shrimp (21 to 25 count per pound)

1/2 pound jalapeño pepper cheese

1/2 pound Monterey jack cheese

1 teaspoon freshly ground black pepper

1 teaspoon Old Bay seasoning, homemade (page 119) or store-bought

42 to 50 strips bacon, cut in half

Nonstick cooking spray

1 Peel the shrimp, leaving on the shell on the tail. Devein the shrimp and cut a slit down the back deep enough to add a sliver of both cheeses. Season the shrimp with the pepper and Old Bay. Wrap each shrimp in a piece of bacon and secure

with a wooden skewer. Coat a grill basket with the cooking spray.

2 Prepare a medium-hot fire in your grill.

3 Place the shrimp in the grill basket, place the basket directly over the coals, and cook until the bacon is crispy on both sides, 5 to 7 minutes per side. Serve immediately.

Barbecue Butter-Grilled Shrimp

Shrimp are delicious and easy to grill if you use either a wire mesh grill cover or a perforated grill rack so the shrimp don't fall through the grates, as they will on most grills. You can also use wooden or metal skewers. Some people use grill woks, which also work well. You just use a wooden paddle or metal grill spatula to keep turning the shrimp. **SERVES 6 TO 8**

5 pounds large shrimp (21 to 25 count per pound), peeled and deveined

BARBECUE BUTTER MARINADE

2 cups (4 sticks) unsalted butter, melted

1/4 cup dry white wine

2 tablespoons fresh lemon juice

2 tablespoons Worcestershire sauce, homemade (page 50) or store-bought

2 cloves garlic, pressed

2 teaspoons The Baron's Barbecue Spice (page 115)

2 teaspoons liquid crab boil or Old Bay seasoning, homemade (page 119) or store-bought

2 teaspoons freshly ground black pepper

1 teaspoon crushed red pepper

1 teaspoon fine sea salt

Tabasco sauce to taste

Nonstick cooking spray, if needed

1 Rinse the shrimp under cold running water and drain.

2 To make the marinade, combine the marinade ingredients in a medium-size nonreactive bowl and blend well. Place the shrimp in a large zippered-top plastic bag; the 2-gallon size should work. Pour the marinade over the shrimp, seal the bag, shake to coat all the shrimp, and let marinate for 20 minutes at room temperature.

3 Prepare a medium-hot fire in your grill.

4 Remove the shrimp from the marinade. Transfer the remaining marinade to a saucepan and bring to a boil over medium-high heat; let simmer for 5 minutes, then set aside.

5 Coat a perforated grill rack with the cooking spray and place it or a grill wok on the grill. Place the shrimp on the grill rack or in the wok and cook, basting with the reserved marinade and turning, until pink on both sides, 2 to 3 minutes per side,. Be careful not to overcook the shrimp. Serve immediately.

Marinated Shrimp and Tortellini Brochettes

You will need 40 cocktail-size wooden skewers, soaked in water for 30 minutes and drained. If you would like, you can use longer skewers; the small ones are for party time.

MAKES 40 APPETIZER BROCHETTES; SERVES 8 TO 10

40 spinach-cheese tortellini

SHRIMP MARINADE

1 cup dry white wine

$1/2$ cup canola oil

2 tablespoons fresh lemon juice

1 tablespoon minced lemon zest

1 tablespoon granulated cane sugar

$1/2$ teaspoon dried tarragon leaves

$1/2$ teaspoon fine sea salt

$1/2$ teaspoon freshly ground black pepper

$1/4$ teaspoon jalapeño Tabasco sauce, or to taste

$2^{1}/2$ pounds medium-size (31 to 32 count per pound) shrimp (about 80), peeled and deveined

40 pearl onions, parboiled for 2 minutes, drained, and peeled

40 bottled mushroom caps

1 Cook the tortellini according to the package directions or however you prefer them. Drain and rinse under cold running water to stop the cooking process.

2 To make the marinade, combine the marinade ingredients in a large nonreactive bowl and blend well with a wire whisk. Add the shrimp, tortellini, onions, and mushrooms to the bowl and toss gently to coat everything. Cover with plastic wrap and let marinate for 2 to 4 hours in the refrigerator.

3 Thread the skewers with 1 onion, 1 shrimp (back side first), 1 tortellini, 1 shrimp (belly side first), then 1 mushroom. The two shrimp should circle the tortellini.

4 Prepare a medium hot fire in your grill.

5 Place the skewers directly over the coals, cover, and cook until the shrimp are pink on both sides, 1 to 2 minutes per side. Serve immediately.

Salt and Pepper Prawns with Blue Cheese Dipping Sauce and Garlic Shrimp Sauce

When is a shrimp a prawn or a prawn a shrimp? I don't know. I just know they're great to grill and eat. SERVES 10 TO 12 AS A FIRST COURSE OR 6 TO 8 AS AN ENTRÉE

BLUE CHEESE DIPPING SAUCE

1 cup crumbled blue cheese (I like Maytag, made in Iowa)

1/3 cup olive oil

1 tablespoon fresh lemon juice

1/2 teaspoon freshly ground white pepper

1/4 teaspoon Tabasco sauce

3/4 cup whipping cream

GARLIC SHRIMP SAUCE

1/2 cup minced fresh parsley leaves

1/3 cup sunflower oil

1/4 cup medium dry sherry

3 tablespoons pressed garlic

2 tablespoons Louisiana hot sauce

2 tablespoons fresh lime juice (about 2 limes)

1 teaspoon fine sea salt

1 teaspoon freshly ground black pepper

3 pounds large shrimp (21 to 25 count per pound), peeled and deveined

1/2 cup olive oil

2 tablespoons fine sea salt

2 tablespoons coarsely ground black pepper

Nonstick cooking spray

1 bunch celery, trimmed and cut into thin sticks

1 To make the dipping sauce, combine the blue cheese dipping sauce ingredients, except the cream, in a blender and process until smooth. Pour into a medium-size nonreactive bowl and blend in the cream with a wire whisk. Cover with plastic wrap and chill.

2 To make the shrimp sauce, combine the garlic shrimp sauce ingredients in a small bowl and blend well. Cover with plastic wrap and set aside until ready to use or place in the refrigerator.

3 Prepare a medium-hot fire in your grill.

4 Place the shrimp in a large bowl, pour the olive oil over them, and toss to coat. Mix the salt and pepper together in a small bowl. Season the shrimp evenly with the mixture, tossing to blend.

5 Coat a grill rack or a grill wok with the cooking spray and place on the grill. Place the shrimp on the rack or in the wok directly over the coals and cook, turning, until the shrimp are pink on both sides, 2 to 3 minutes per side.

6 Transfer the cooked shrimp to a clean large bowl, pour the shrimp sauce over them, and toss to coat. Place the shrimp on a tray or serving plate and serve hot or cold with the dipping sauce and celery sticks.

Garlic-Basil Shrimp on Skewers

This recipe is easy shrimp on a stick, or make it shrimp on a sword! The potent marinade is also delicious on fish, shellfish, and chicken. You'll need 30 to 75 wooden

skewers; be sure to soak them first. Serve with Peach Chipotle Salsa (page 156) or Watermelon Fire and Ice Salsa (page 156). SERVES 4 TO 8

GARLIC BASIL MARINADE

1 cup olive oil

1/4 cup pressed garlic

1/4 cup red wine vinegar

2 tablespoons minced fresh basil leaves

1 tablespoon tomato paste

1 tablespoon granulated cane sugar

1 teaspoon fine sea salt

1 teaspoon freshly ground black pepper

1 1/2 to 3 pounds large shrimp (21 to 25 count per pound), peeled and deveined

1 To make the marinade, combine the marinade ingredients in a large nonreactive bowl and blend well with a wire whisk. Add the shrimp and toss to coat. Cover with plastic wrap and refrigerate for 1 to 2 hours, tossing the shrimp occasionally.

2 Prepare a medium-hot fire in your grill.

3 Remove the shrimp from the marinade. Transfer the remaining marinade to a saucepan and bring to a boil over medium-high heat; let simmer for 5 minutes, then set aside. Skewer the shrimp by bending each one almost in half, so the large end nearly touches the tail end. Insert the skewer above the tail and skewer it through the top so it passes through the shrimp twice.

4 Place the skewers directly over the coals and grill until pink on both sides, 2 to 3 minutes per side, basting frequently with the reserved marinade.

5 Serve hot.

Grilled Shrimp Scampi

This shrimp will ward off vampires! You'll need 6 wooden skewers; don't forget to soak them first. SERVES 4 TO 6

SCAMPI MARINADE

1/2 cup olive oil

1/4 cup fresh lemon juice (about 2 lemons)

2 tablespoons minced garlic

1 tablespoon minced fresh parsley leaves

1 tablespoon grated lemon zest

1 teaspoon fine sea salt

1 teaspoon freshly ground black pepper

1 1/2 pounds large shrimp (21 to 25 count per pound), peeled with tail shell left on and deveined

1 To make the marinade, combine the marinade ingredients in a small nonreactive bowl and blend well with a wire whisk until almost emulsified.

2 Rinse the shrimp under cold running water and drain on paper towels. Thread them onto 6 skewers. Place the skewers in a large nonreactive baking dish and pour the marinade over them, turning so all the shrimp are coated. Cover with plastic wrap and let marinate for 10 to 15 minutes at room temperature.

3 Prepare a medium-hot fire in your grill.

4 Remove the skewers from the marinade. Transfer the remaining marinade to a saucepan and bring to a boil over medium-high heat; let simmer for 2 minutes, then set aside. Place the skewers directly over the coals and cook until pink on both sides, 2 to 3 minutes per side, being

careful not to overcook. Baste with the reserved marinade while cooking.

Shrimp and Calamari Salad with Anchovy Balsamic Dressing

This is a very good dinner salad and, yes, ranch or Caesar dressing can be substituted. SERVES 6 TO 8

SWEET AND SOUR GARLIC MARINADE

1/2 cup olive oil

3 tablespoons fresh lemon juice

1 tablespoon granulated cane sugar

8 large cloves garlic, pressed

1 teaspoon fine sea salt

1 teaspoon freshly ground black pepper

1 pound large shrimp (21 to 25 count per pound), peeled and deveined

1/2 pound cleaned squid bodies, cut crosswise into rings 1/4 inch wide

ANCHOVY BALSAMIC DRESSING

2 to 4 oil-packed flat anchovies, to your taste, rinsed and patted dry

2 tablespoons balsamic vinegar

1 tablespoon fresh lemon juice

1 clove garlic, pressed

1/2 teaspoon freshly ground black pepper

1/4 teaspoon fine sea salt

1/4 cup olive oil

1/2 cup oil-packed sun-dried tomatoes, drained and slivered

1/2 cup packed fresh basil leaves, chopped

1 To make the marinade, combine the marinade ingredients in a large nonreactive bowl and blend well with a wire whisk.

2 Butterfly each shrimp; use a paring knife to cut a slit, starting at the head, halfway through the length of the shrimp, almost to the tail. Add the butterflied shrimp and squid to the marinade and toss to coat. Cover with plastic wrap and let marinate for about 1 hour in the refrigerator.

3 To make the dressing, combine the anchovies, vinegar, lemon juice, garlic, pepper, and salt in a blender or food processor and process until smooth. With the motor running, slowly pour the olive oil through the feed tube in a thin, steady stream, processing until the dressing thickens, about 2 minutes.

4 Prepare a medium-hot fire in your grill.

5 If your grill doesn't have small grates, cover it with expanded metal mesh or a perforated grill rack so the shrimp and squid won't fall through. Remove the shrimp and squid from the marinade and place directly over the coals until lightly charred and cooked through, 3 to 5 minutes per side.

6 Transfer the shrimp and squid to a large nonreactive bowl and toss with the sun-dried tomatoes and basil. Pour the anchovy dressing over the mixture and toss to coat. Serve immediately.

Grilled Squid Brochettes with Anchovy Butter

There you go again, judging a recipe by its sauce. I had planned to enter this recipe in the Miscellaneous category of a barbecue contest, but we decided to go with golden trout instead, so we ate the squid and I do believe it would have come in first! The trout took second. You'll need 12 wooden skewers for this; don't forget to soak them in water first. SERVES 4 TO 6

1 pound cleaned small squid, no more than 4 inches long, thawed if necessary

8 oil-packed anchovy fillets

$1/4$ cup ($1/2$ stick) unsalted butter, softened

1 large clove garlic, pressed

2 teaspoons fresh lemon juice

$1/4$ teaspoon fine sea salt

$1/4$ teaspoon freshly ground black pepper

$1/4$ to $1/2$ cup olive oil, as needed

1 Prepare the squid by cutting off the tentacles in one piece. Cut the bodies crosswise into 1-inch-thick rings. Thread 3 to 4 squid rings onto each skewer and finish with 1 or 2 tentacles.

2 In a small nonreactive bowl, combine the anchovies, butter, and garlic and blend thoroughly, using a fork. Add the lemon juice, salt, and pepper and blend well. Set aside.

3 Prepare a hot fire in your grill.

4 Brush the squid brochettes with the olive oil and place directly over the coals. Grill just until opaque, 1 to 2 minutes per side, lightly charring them.

5 Transfer the brochettes to a serving platter and dab generously with the anchovy butter. Serve at once.

SMOKIN JOE

On the Side—and

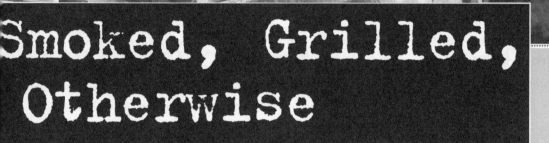

Smoked, Grilled, Otherwise

Potato salads, cole slaws, and baked or barbecued beans are the classic side dishes that go with great barbecue. You'd think that every cole slaw there ever was has already been created and tasted, but not so. At the 2002 American Royal, a cole slaw that was just that little bit different won in the Side Dish category.

Doing something a little bit different is what you want to do with your side dishes. Have a familiar dish, but with your own unique touch. You don't want to go into a long explanation about your dish to your guests or barbecue contest judges. They should just be able to see what it is, taste it, and then grin.

Take beans, for instance. If you imagine baked beans made with canned beans, that's fine. But why not smoke your bean dish along with your ribs and brisket (and add some of those smoked meat trimmings to the beans) for Barbecued Beans (pages 445–447)? Or use pinto beans instead of Great Northern, as I do in Yee-Haw Texas Pinto Beans (page 447)?

For an extra hit of smoky flavor, hot smoke your bacon before you add it to a potato salad, as in Smoky Bacon Potato Salad (page 430), or add a smoke-roasted red pepper (see page 431).

As with barbecue rubs, sauces, and slathers, your side dishes need to have well-balanced flavor. Experiment with a variety of seasonings and condiments to accentuate but not overpower the flavor of even the most basic potato salad, baked beans, or slaw. Add seasonings a little at a time when you're experimenting with a new dish. And always think color—in the form of chopped vegetables, sauces, and fresh herbs.

Mustard Potato Salad

Because of its homemade mayonnaise-type dressing, this colorful and tasty dish needs to be refrigerated. To minimize the possibility of salmonella, use very fresh eggs and keep the salad refrigerated. SERVES 6 TO 8

SALAD

1 1/2 to 2 pounds new red potatoes

1 cup frozen green peas, thawed

1/2 cup minced celery

1/4 cup seeded and diced red bell pepper

1/4 cup diced red onion

2 tablespoons minced fresh parsley leaves

1/2 teaspoon fine sea salt

1/2 teaspoon freshly ground black pepper

DRESSING

1 very fresh large egg

2 tablespoons cider vinegar

2 tablespoons Dijon mustard

1/2 teaspoon dried tarragon leaves

1/2 teaspoon fine sea salt

1/4 teaspoon white pepper

1/4 teaspoon cayenne pepper

3/4 cup soy oil

1 To make the salad, place the potatoes in a large saucepan and cover with cold water. Bring to a boil. Reduce the heat to medium and simmer until fork-tender, 10 to 12 minutes. Drain. When the potatoes have cooled enough to handle, cut into wedges. Combine the potatoes, peas, celery,

Vegetables ON THE GRILL and in the Smoker

At a barbecue competition in which you're up all night in any kind of weather, you usually want a traditional side dish, such as slaw, potato casserole, or beans of some kind, to go with your slow-smoked food. Something substantial. You might even enter a traditional side dish in the Side Dish category, as that seems to be what judges like best.

At home or in the Miscellaneous or Anything But category, it's a different story.

ON THE GRILL Those are the times when I like to do grilled vegetables, and the simpler, the better. You can't go wrong with a mixture of melted butter or olive oil, garlic, and a little salt and pepper brushed on mushrooms of all kinds, asparagus, or slices of skin-on eggplant that are then grilled on both sides. I like to marinate onion slices and strips of zucchini or bell peppers in an Italian vinaigrette, then grill them on a perforated grill rack.

I also like to take fresh shucked corn, place each ear on a piece of aluminum foil, then tuck a folded paper towel under the corn. I drizzle the corn with 1 tablespoon of balsamic vinegar or dry red wine, place a pat of butter on top, then wrap it up in the foil. I grill the corn for 5 to 10 minutes over medium heat. And it's good! The paper towel soaks up the vinegar or wine and steams the corn.

For sweet potatoes, I like to slow smoke or bake them whole until almost done. Then I slice them into circles, dip them into drawn butter (see page 341) and a little brown sugar, and grill them over medium heat on both sides, about 8 minutes total.

IN THE SMOKER Vegetables on the smoker get very soft and moist with a burnished appearance and smoky flavor, but they do not caramelize like they do on the grill.

Soft vegetables, such as tomatoes and bell peppers, are delicious smoked, but their appearance is soft and squishy. They look better as additions to a vegetable relish or a pasta sauce than served alone. Corn on the cob tastes better grilled than smoked, as do zucchini, summer squash, asparagus, and eggplant. You don't want the smoke flavor to overpower the natural flavor of the vegetable.

Hard vegetables, such as potatoes, sweet potatoes, and onions, do very well in the smoker, but they take a long time to cook. Figure you're cooking them at 225 degrees F as opposed to 350 or 400 degrees F, so it takes about 2 to 3 hours for them to cook all the way through. A smoked potato or sweet potato is delicious served just like you would a baked potato, or cut up into chunks for a casserole. A smoked whole large onion, especially a sweet variety such as Vidalia, is very easy to prepare. Trim the ends off the onion, peel it, then cut out a section 2 to 3 inches from the top or stem end of the onion. In this cavity, drizzle some heavy cream or melted butter and crumbled fried bacon, dried herbs such as thyme, and salt and pepper. Then smoke the onion until it has softened, about 2 to 3 hours.

bell pepper, onion, parsley, salt, and black pepper in a large bowl.

2   To make the dressing, combine the egg, vinegar, mustard, tarragon, salt, white pepper, and cayenne in a blender and process for 1 to 2 minutes to combine. With the machine running, pour in the oil in a thin, steady stream until emulsified. Pour over potato mixture and gently toss to coat and blend well. Refrigerate until ready to serve. You can make this up to a day ahead.

Smoky Bacon Potato Salad

For this German-style potato salad with a smoky twist, if you smoke the bacon first, then fry it, you get a great flavor addition and that extra edge in competition. Most barbecuers would put the bacon on to smoke when they're already smoking something else. To smoke the bacon (you're really double smoking it, since it's already been smoked once), set up your covered grill for indirect cooking. Soak mesquite or hickory wood chunks or chips in water for at least 20 minutes, then place on the hot coals. Place the bacon strips in a disposable aluminum pan and set the pan away from the coals. Close the lid and smoke for 1 to 2 hours. Remove the bacon, fry it in a skillet, then proceed with the rest of the recipe. **SERVES 10 TO 12**

    4 cups peeled and cubed cooked potatoes

    8 to 10 slices bacon, smoked (optional; see headnote), fried until crisp, drained on paper towels, and crumbled

    1 cup finely diced celery

    6 green onions (green and white parts), thinly sliced

    1 cup mayonnaise

    1/4 cup cider vinegar

    1/4 cup granulated cane sugar

    1 tablespoon Dijon mustard

    1 teaspoon fine sea salt

    1 teaspoon freshly ground black pepper

1   Combine the potatoes, bacon, celery, and green onions in a large bowl, tossing gently to blend.

2   In a medium-size nonreactive bowl, combine the mayonnaise, vinegar, sugar, mustard, salt, and pepper, blending with a wire whisk. Pour over the potato mixture and gently toss to coat. Cover and chill for several hours before serving.

Grilled Potato Salad

I entered this potato salad recipe in the 2000 American Royal Barbecue Side Dish Contest and tied for tenth place out of 353 contestants! **SERVES 10 TO 12**

    1/2 cup olive oil

    6 green onions

    2 pounds new red potatoes, cut in half

    1 tablespoon minced fresh parsley leaves

    2 tablespoons white wine vinegar

    1 tablespoon spicy brown mustard

    1 teaspoon fine sea salt

    1 teaspoon freshly ground black pepper

    2 large red bell peppers, smoke roasted (see page 431), peeled, seeded, and chopped

    1/4 cup minced onion

1   Prepare a medium-hot fire in your grill.

2   In a medium-size bowl, combine the olive oil and green onions, turning to coat them. Remove the green onions, reserving the olive oil. Grill the

SMOKE ROASTING Red Bell Peppers

Smoke roasting instead of just roasting red bell peppers gives them that extra flavor from wood smoke. Smoke-roasted red bell peppers are great in salads, side dishes, barbecue sauces, salsas, and relishes. Here's how to smoke roast them:

1. Set up your covered grill for indirect cooking. Soak mesquite or hickory wood chunks or chips in water for at least 20 minutes, then place on the hot coals.

2. Cut red bell peppers in half, remove the seeds, and place cut side down on the grill, farthest away from the coals. Close the lid and smoke for about 3 hours.

3. Remove from the smoker and, when cool enough to handle, remove the skin with a paring knife, if you wish, and chop coarsely. Smoke-roasted peppers will keep in the refrigerator for up to 1 week or in the freezer for up to 3 months.

green onions for 1 to 2 minutes, turning so they don't burn. Remove from the grill and set aside.

3 Add the potatoes and parsley to the olive oil and toss to coat. Thread the parsley-covered potatoes on skewers and place directly over the coals. Reserve the remaining olive oil. Cover and cook for 7 to 8 minutes. Turn and cook 7 to 8 minutes longer. Continue to cook until the potatoes are just fork-tender and lightly browned.

4 In a small nonreactive bowl, mix together the vinegar, mustard, salt, and pepper. Blend in the reserved olive oil-and-parsley mixture with a wire whisk.

5 Slice or chop the grilled green onions. Remove the potatoes from the skewers. Combine the potatoes, roasted peppers, onion, and green onions in a large nonreactive bowl, pour the

dressing over the mixture, and toss gently. Serve warm or at room temperature.

Not-Entered-Yet Grilled Potato Salad

This recipe is as good as the other grilled potato salad recipe. I just haven't entered it in a contest yet. Now, don't you go and beat me to it! SERVES 10 TO 12

SALAD

3 pounds small new red potatoes, halved

1/2 cup olive oil

1 cup thin green beans, ends trimmed, blanched in boiling water for 2 minutes, drained, and cut into 3-inch pieces

DRESSING

$1/3$ cup cider vinegar

$1/4$ cup chopped shallots

1 tablespoon Dijon mustard

1 tablespoon minced fresh flatleaf parsley leaves

2 cloves garlic, pressed

2 teaspoons minced lemon zest

$1/2$ teaspoon fine sea salt

$1/2$ teaspoon freshly ground black pepper

$2/3$ cup olive oil

GARNISH

$1/2$ cup crumbled feta cheese

$1/4$ cup chopped fresh dill

$1/2$ teaspoon fine sea salt

$1/2$ teaspoon freshly ground black pepper

1 Prepare a medium-hot fire in your grill.

2 To make the salad, place the potatoes in a large saucepan and cover with cold water. Bring to a boil, then reduce the heat to medium and simmer until the potatoes are just tender, 10 to 12 minutes. Drain and cool under cold running water. Drain again and pat dry. Place potatoes in a large bowl and pour the $1/2$ cup of olive oil over; toss to coat.

3 Place the potatoes in a vegetable basket or on a perforated grill rack directly over the coals, cover, and grill, turning often, until tender and light brown, 4 to 5 minutes. Transfer to a large bowl and add the green beans.

4 To make the dressing, combine the vinegar, shallots, mustard, parsley, garlic, lemon zest, salt, and pepper in a blender or food processor and process for about 2 minutes. Add the $2/3$ cup oil in a thin, steady stream and process until it is incorporated and the dressing has emulsified.

5 To make the garnish, sprinkle the cheese and dill over the potatoes and beans. Pour the dressing over and toss to coat. Add the salt and pepper and toss again. Serve warm or at room temperature.

Acadian Potato Salad

The term "Cajun" is used to refer to people of Acadian descent—French immigrants who first came to the Acadian region of Nova Scotia, then were forced out by the British—who settled in the bayous of Louisiana in the eighteenth century. They sure brought some good eatin' with them, and not every dish is hot and spicy, as you'll find out with this slightly sweet potato salad.

SERVES 16 TO 20

5 pounds medium-size red potatoes

DRESSING

3 cups mayonnaise

$1^1/2$ cups diced onions

$1^1/2$ cups peeled, seeded, and chopped cucumbers

1 cup chopped celery

1 cup seeded and chopped green bell peppers

1 cup sweet gherkins, diced

$1/2$ cup seeded and diced red bell peppers

$1/3$ cup pickle juice

3 tablespoons cider vinegar

2 tablespoons kosher salt

Celery leaves

Cherry tomatoes, cut in half

Black ripe olives

1 Place the potatoes in a large saucepan and cover with salted water. Bring to a boil, cover, reduce the heat to medium, and simmer just until tender, 30 to 40 minutes. Drain and refrigerate until chilled.

2 To make the dressing, in a large nonreactive bowl, combine all the dressing ingredients and mix well.

3 Peel the chilled potatoes and cut into the desired size. Add to the dressing; toss gently until the potatoes are well coated. Cover and refrigerate again until well chilled, several hours or overnight.

4 To serve, garnish with the celery leaves, cherry tomatoes, and black olives.

Potato, Cucumber, and Dill Salad

This recipe requires a little more work, because you need to toast the coriander seeds, but it's worth the effort.

SERVES 6 TO 8

SALAD

1 pound small new potatoes, quartered

2 cups seeded and cubed ($\frac{1}{2}$ inch) cucumbers

6 green onions (white and green parts), thinly sliced

DRESSING

1 cup plain yogurt or sour cream

1 tablespoon chopped fresh dill or 1$\frac{1}{2}$ teaspoons dillweed

1 tablespoon fresh lemon juice

2 cloves garlic, pressed, or 1 teaspoon granulated garlic

1 teaspoon fine sea salt

1 teaspoon freshly ground black pepper

$\frac{1}{2}$ teaspoon coriander seeds, toasted in a dry skillet over medium heat until fragrant, then ground

1 To make the salad, place the potatoes in a large saucepan and cover with salted water. Bring to a boil, then reduce the heat to medium and simmer briskly until the potatoes are fork-tender, 5 to 7 minutes. Drain the potatoes in a colander and rinse with cold running water to cool. Combine the potatoes, cucumbers, and green onions in a large nonreactive bowl.

2 To make the dressing, in a small bowl, combine the dressing ingredients and blend well with a wire whisk. Pour over the potato mixture and toss to coat well. Serve cold or at room temperature.

Creamy, Crunchy Potato Casserole

You never know what kind of weather you're going to face at the American Royal Invitational, held every year on the first weekend in October. Some years, it's blazing hot; others, it's durn cold. When you're barbecuing outdoors in cold, rainy weather, this is just the easy-to-put-together side dish you want to warm you up. SERVES 16 TO 20

Three 15-ounce packages frozen shredded hash brown potatoes, thawed and drained

One 6-ounce jar processed jalapeño cheese (I use Kraft Jalapeño Cheese Whiz)

1 cup sour cream

$1/2$ cup minced onion

One 10-ounce package shredded cheddar cheese

Two 10.75-ounce cans condensed cream of chicken soup

One 10.75-ounce can condensed cream of celery soup

One 8-ounce package frozen corn with green/red peppers, thawed and drained

1 teaspoon fine sea salt

1 teaspoon finely ground black pepper

2 cups cornflake cereal

$1/2$ cup (1 stick) unsalted butter, melted

1 Preheat the oven to 350 degrees F.

2 Combine the hash browns, processed cheese, sour cream, onion, cheddar cheese, chicken soup, celery soup, corn, salt, and pepper in a large bowl and mix well.

3 Spread the mixture in a 9 x 13-inch baking dish. Top with the corn flakes and drizzle with the butter. Bake until browned and bubbling, 45 to 60 minutes. Serve hot.

Cheesy Garlic Potatoes

This recipe is a lot less work than most potato recipes, because you use the barbecuer's side dish secret—packages of frozen hash brown potatoes. The smoked garlic adds a mellow smokiness that puts this casserole in the blue ribbon realm. SERVES 10 TO 12

2 pounds frozen hash browns, thawed and drained

1 cup diced onion

One 14.75-ounce can condensed cream of roasted garlic soup

1 cup sour cream

$1/2$ pound mozzarella cheese, shredded

4 cloves smoked garlic (see page 98), mashed (1 tablespoon)

1 teaspoon fine sea salt

1 teaspoon freshly ground black pepper

$1/4$ cup ($1/2$ stick) unsalted butter, melted

1 Preheat the oven to 350 degrees F. Grease a 9 x 13-inch baking dish.

2 Combine the hash browns and onion in a large bowl. In a medium-size bowl, combine the soup, sour cream, cheese, garlic, salt, and pepper and blend well. Pour over the potato mixture and blend well.

3 Pour the mixture into the prepared pan and spread out evenly. Drizzle the melted butter evenly over the top. Cover with aluminum foil and bake for 45 minutes.

4 Remove the foil and bake until the top is golden brown, about 15 minutes longer.

Getting Your PH. B.

The Ph.B., or Doctor of Barbecue Philosophy degree, was first conceived in 1984. Ardie Davis, a Kansas City barbecue expert, was getting the Diddy-Wa-Diddy National Barbecue Sauce Contest going at the American Royal. He wanted to give his barbecue name—Remus Powers—a "barbecue accent," so he became Remus Powers, Ph.B. And the idea caught on.

Ardie has probably done the most to promote the Ph. B. degree and the general idea that barbecue is fun, but the degree is also about gaining arcane knowledge. If anybody should hand out the Ph.B., it's Ardie. Not only is he a real barbecuer, but he has also written several cookbooks on the topic and is an expert on barbecue sauces. He likes to pair barbecue with wine and stretch the boundaries of slow-smoked foods by picking up recipes on his travels around the world.

So, Ardie assembled the distinguished faculty of the fictitious Greasehouse University—the Baron of Barbecue himself among the notables—and started looking for degree candidates.

If a dedicated barbecuer is interested in pursuing a Ph.B., the first step is to talk to Ardie. The barbecuer summarizes his or her career in barbecue, namely outstanding accomplishments at contests and contributions to the promotion of barbecue. If the barbecuer passes the credentials test, then Ardie assigns a dissertation topic, which is usually something fun such as "The History of the Flying Pig." The dissertation is closer to an essay than a real dissertation, but then, this is barbecue, not academia.

The dissertation is then submitted to the other faculty members for review and comment. If approved unanimously by the faculty, the candidate moves to the next stage, the oral exam.

The faculty agrees to meet as a group—and with the barbecue grad student—at an upcoming barbecue contest. As you might guess, I'm the antagonizer of the bunch, so I get to give the students a hard time. I like to keep things stirred up.

Oral exam questions range from how to tell the difference between real and fake barbecue to explaining the differences among the sanctioning requirements and judging standards of the IBCA, KCBS, and MIM. (You could probably read this book and be ready for the oral exam, not to give you any ideas, of course.)

If all goes well, we award each new Ph.B. with a frame-it-yourself certificate as the graduate walks across the stage at a major barbecue contest. In 2002, we awarded five Ph.B.s at the Jack Daniel's contest.

Grilled Potatoes with Lemon and Olive Oil

This recipe is from John Raven, Ph.B., known as The Commissioner of Barbecue. John is the founder of the *Goat Gap Gazette* tabloid, which calls itself the "Clarion of the Chili World" and also contains information for the dedicated barbecuer. He writes for the Texas Cooking Online Email Newsletter at www.texascooking.com as well. John is a true Legend of Barbecue, and this inspired potato dish could be a legend at your own gatherings, in the back yard or at a barbecue contest. **SERVES 4**

4 large red potatoes, each cut into 8 wedges

1/4 cup olive oil

1 tablespoon grated lemon zest

1 teaspoon non-iodized salt

1/2 teaspoon freshly ground black pepper

1 Prepare a medium-hot fire in your grill.

2 Place the potatoes in a large bowl. Pour the oil over them, sprinkle with the lemon zest, salt, and pepper, and toss gently to coat.

3 Place the potatoes in a vegetable basket or on a perforated grill rack directly over the coals, reserving any remaining oil. Cover and grill until light brown, about 15 minutes. Turn, basting with the reserved oil, and cook until brown and tender, 15 minutes longer. Serve hot.

Creamy Cole Slaw

This traditional creamy slaw will feed a crowd. **SERVES 12 TO 16**

DRESSING

1/2 cup mayonnaise

1/2 cup sour cream

2 tablespoons Dijon mustard

2 tablespoons granulated cane sugar

1 tablespoon fresh lemon juice

1 teaspoon celery seeds

1 teaspoon non-iodized salt

1 teaspoon freshly ground black pepper

SLAW

8 cups cored, shredded, and chopped green cabbage (about 1 head)

2 cups chopped celery

1 cup seeded and diced red bell pepper

1 large carrot, grated

1 medium-size onion, diced

1 To make the dressing, combine the dressing ingredients in a small nonreactive bowl and blend well with a wire whisk.

2 To make the slaw, combine the slaw ingredients in a large nonreactive bowl and blend well. Pour the dressing over the slaw and toss to blend. Serve cold.

Technicolor Cole Slaw with Buttermilk Dressing

This recipe is simple and colorful. The buttermilk dressing gives it a bit of a tang. SERVES 12 TO 16

SLAW

8 cups cored and finely chopped or shredded green cabbage (about 1 head)

1 cup diced celery

$1/2$ cup diced onion

1 large carrot, grated

$1/4$ cup seeded and diced green bell pepper

$1/4$ cup seeded and diced red bell pepper

DRESSING

1 cup mayonnaise

$1/2$ cup granulated cane sugar

$1/2$ cup buttermilk

2 tablespoons fresh lemon juice

2 tablespoons distilled white vinegar

1 teaspoon fine sea salt

1 teaspoon finely ground black pepper

1 To make the slaw, combine the slaw ingredients in a large nonreactive bowl. Toss gently to blend.

2 To make the dressing, in a medium-size nonreactive bowl, combine the dressing ingredients and blend with a wire whisk. Pour over the slaw and blend gently until well coated. Cover and chill for several hours before serving.

Tangy Vinegar Cole Slaw

I like to put this Carolina-style slaw on my pulled pork sandwiches. It's also good served alongside smoked chicken. SERVES 10 TO 12

SLAW

8 cups cored and shredded or chopped green cabbage (about 1 head)

$1/2$ cup diced red onion

$1/4$ cup shredded carrot

DRESSING

1 cup granulated cane sugar

2 tablespoons garlic salt

1 teaspoon freshly ground black pepper

1 teaspoon celery seeds

1 cup cider vinegar

Juice of 1 lemon

1 To make the slaw, combine the slaw ingredients in a large nonreactive bowl and blend gently.

2 To make the dressing, in a medium-size nonreactive bowl, combine the sugar, garlic salt, pepper, and celery seeds. Pour the vinegar and lemon juice over the seasonings and blend with a wire whisk to dissolve the spices. Pour the dressing over the cabbage mixture and gently blend well. Cover and chill for several hours before serving.

Toasted Sesame Oriental Cabbage Slaw

I get a lot of catering calls for this recipe, which goes well with any Asian-style barbecued pork, chicken, or beef. SERVES 6 TO 8

SLAW

3 cups cored and shredded green cabbage

1 cup snow peas, strings trimmed, blanched in boiling water for 2 minutes, drained, chilled, and cut in half

1/4 cup sliced water chestnuts, drained and cut in half

6 green onions (white and green parts), thinly sliced

1 large carrot, grated

DRESSING

1/4 cup red wine vinegar

2 tablespoons granulated cane sugar

2 tablespoons soy sauce

1 tablespoon soybean oil or other vegetable oil

2 cloves garlic, pressed

1/2 teaspoon fine sea salt

1/2 teaspoon freshly ground black pepper

One 3-ounce package ramen noodles, broken up and toasted (see Note below)

1/2 cup sliced almonds, toasted (see Note below)

2 tablespoons sesame seeds, toasted in a dry skillet over medium heat until fragrant

1 To make the slaw, combine the slaw ingredients in a large serving bowl.

2 To make the dressing, in a small nonreactive bowl, combine the dressing ingredients and blend well. Pour over the slaw mixture. Top with the toasted ramen noodles, almonds, and sesame seeds, toss, and serve immediately.

NOTE To toast the noodles and almonds, place on a baking sheet and bake in a preheated 350 degree F oven until golden brown, 7 to 10 minutes.

Sweet Honey Mustard Slaw

This is a good change-of-pace slaw, with the mellow heat of poblano chile, the fresh taste of cilantro, the kick of lime juice, and the sweetness of honey. SERVES 6 TO 8

DRESSING

1/2 cup mayonnaise

1/4 cup Dijon mustard

1/4 cup fresh lime juice (about 4 limes)

2 tablespoons clover honey

1 teaspoon fine sea salt

1/2 teaspoon freshly ground black pepper

SLAW

1/2 head green cabbage, cored, shredded, and chopped

1/2 head red cabbage, cored, shredded, and chopped

1 small onion, diced

1 poblano chile, seeded and diced

1/2 cup chopped fresh cilantro leaves

1/2 cup chopped fresh parsley leaves

1 To make the dressing, combine the dressing ingredients in a small nonreactive bowl and blend well with a wire whisk.

2 To make the slaw, combine the slaw ingredients in a large nonreactive bowl. Pour the dressing

over the slaw and toss to coat well. Cover and refrigerate for at least 1 hour to let the flavors develop. Serve cold.

Braggin' Rights Slaw

This is an entirely different slaw from the others in this book. Basically, you make an uncooked tomato-based barbecue sauce dressing and toss it with the slaw. And it's gooooood! SERVES 8 TO 10

SLAW

1 large head green cabbage, cored, shredded, and chopped

2 cups peeled, seeded, and chopped Roma tomatoes

1 medium-size onion, diced

1 large green bell pepper, seeded and diced

1 tablespoon yellow mustard seeds or 1 teaspoon celery seeds

DRESSING

1/2 cup tomato ketchup, homemade (page 43) or store-bought

1/2 cup firmly packed dark brown sugar

1/2 cup distilled white vinegar

1/4 cup fresh lemon juice (about 2 lemons)

1/4 cup prepared yellow mustard

2 teaspoons fine sea salt

1 teaspoon freshly ground black pepper

1/2 teaspoon cayenne pepper

1 To make the slaw, combine the slaw ingredients in a large nonreactive bowl.

2 To make the dressing, combine the dressing ingredients in a medium-size nonreactive bowl and blend well with a wire whisk. Pour the dress-

ing over the slaw and toss to coat evenly. Cover and refrigerate for at least 1 hour. Serve cold.

Fresh Apple Slaw

This salad is light and complements any good barbecue. Use a green such as Granny Smith and a red apple such as Red Delicious for color contrast. SERVES 8 TO 10

SLAW

2 tablespoons fresh lemon juice

2 cups water

2 cups cored and thinly sliced apples

3 cups cored and thinly shredded green cabbage

1 cup thinly sliced celery

1/2 cup diced red onion

1/4 cup shredded carrot

DRESSING

1/2 cup sour cream

1/4 cup mayonnaise

1 teaspoon celery seeds

1/2 teaspoon freshly ground black pepper

1/2 teaspoon celery salt

1 To make the slaw, combine the lemon juice and water in a large nonreactive bowl, add the apples, and let acidulate for 1 minute (that will keep them from browning). In another large nonreactive bowl, combine the cabbage, celery, onion, and carrot. Drain the apples and add to the cabbage.

2 To make the dressing, combine the dressing ingredients in a small bowl, blending well with a wire whisk or fork. Pour the dressing over the slaw mixture, blending well. Cover and chill for at least 2 hours. Serve cold.

Summer Macaroni Salad

Cool, creamy, and colorful, this macaroni salad goes well with barbecued ribs or brisket. This is so much better than what you can buy in the grocery store. SERVES 8 TO 10

- 1 cup elbow macaroni
- 1 cup frozen peas, thawed
- 1/2 cup diced sharp cheddar cheese
- 1/4 cup diced sweet pickles
- 1/4 cup diced onion
- 2 tablespoons seeded and diced red bell pepper
- 1 tablespoon seeded and diced green bell pepper
- 1/2 cup mayonnaise
- 1/4 cup heavy cream or half-and-half
- 1 tablespoon Dijon mustard
- 2 teaspoons granulated cane sugar
- 1 teaspoon fine sea salt
- 1 teaspoon freshly ground black pepper

1 Bring a pot of water to a boil, add the pasta, and cook until just tender, about 12 minutes. Drain and rinse the macaroni, then cover and chill for 1 hour.

2 In a medium-size bowl, combine the chilled macaroni, peas, cheese, pickles, onion, and bell peppers.

3 In a small bowl, combine the mayonnaise, cream, mustard, sugar, salt and pepper, blending with a wire whisk. Pour the mayonnaise mixture over the macaroni mixture and toss until coated. Cover and refrigerate until ready to serve. Serve cold.

Creole Macaroni Salad with Garlic Buttermilk Dressing

Just say BAM!, and throw this salad together. What makes this salad Creole is the addition of sliced, stuffed green olives in the style of the famous New Orleans muffaletta sandwich. SERVES 12 TO 16

SALAD
- 1 pound elbow macaroni, cooked according to package instructions, drained, and rinsed
- 2 cups peeled, seeded, and diced fresh tomatoes
- 1 cup diced sharp cheddar cheese
- 1/2 cup diced celery
- 1/2 cup diced onion
- 1/2 cup seeded and diced green bell pepper
- 1/4 cup sliced stuffed green olives

DRESSING
- 1 cup mayonnaise
- 1/4 cup buttermilk
- 2 cloves garlic, pressed
- 1 teaspoon fine sea salt
- 1/2 teaspoon white pepper
- 1/2 teaspoon cayenne pepper

1 To make the salad, in a large serving bowl, combine the salad ingredients and toss gently to blend.

2 To make the dressing, in a medium-size nonreactive bowl, combine the dressing ingredients, blending with a wire whisk. Pour the dressing over the macaroni mixture and toss gently to coat

everything well. Cover and chill for several hours before serving. Serve cold.

Barbecue-Style Shell Pasta Salad

This recipe is another take on pasta salad, with an attractive pink tinge from the tomato. It's a colorful and flavorful addition to the salad table at a barbecue event. **SERVES 12 TO 16**

> 1 pound shell pasta
>
> One 10.75-ounce can condensed tomato soup
>
> 1 cup cider vinegar
>
> $1/2$ cup granulated cane sugar
>
> $1/2$ cup soybean oil or other vegetable oil
>
> 1 cup peeled, seeded, and diced cucumber
>
> 1 cup seeded and diced green bell pepper
>
> $1/2$ cup seeded and diced red bell pepper
>
> $1/2$ cup diced onion
>
> 6 green onions (white and green parts), thinly sliced
>
> 4 cloves garlic, pressed
>
> 1 teaspoon fine sea salt
>
> 1 teaspoon freshly ground black pepper

1 Bring a pot of water to a boil, add the pasta, and cook until just tender, about 12 minutes. Drain and rinse the pasta under cold running water. Drain thoroughly and place in a large serving bowl.

2 Combine the soup, vinegar, sugar, and oil in a medium-size nonreactive bowl, blending well. Pour the soup mixture over the pasta and gently toss to coat. Cover and refrigerate for several hours or overnight.

3 When ready to serve, stir in the cucumber, green and red peppers, onion, green onions, garlic, salt, and black pepper and toss gently again. Serve cold.

Curried Rice Salad

This recipe was given to me by Bill Felsing, a friend from Winthrop, Washington, who got it from his mother's cookbook. It's a great accompaniment to grilled or smoked fish and chicken. **SERVES 6 TO 8**

SALAD

> 4 cups cooked white rice
>
> $3/4$ cup thinly sliced celery
>
> $3/4$ cup peas, cooked and drained
>
> $1/4$ cup sliced almonds, lightly toasted (see page 322)

DRESSING

> $1/2$ cup sour cream
>
> $1/2$ cup mayonnaise
>
> 2 to 4 teaspoons curry powder, homemade (page 112) or store-bought, to your taste
>
> $1/2$ teaspoon fine sea salt
>
> $1/2$ teaspoon freshly ground black pepper

1 To make the salad, combine the salad ingredients in a large serving bowl and blend carefully.

2 To make the dressing, combine the sour cream, mayonnaise, curry powder, salt, and pepper in a small bowl and blend well. Pour the dressing over the salad and toss gently to coat. Chill overnight for best results. Serve cold.

Cub Scout Mom's Best Broccoli and Bacon Salad

I got this recipe from a Cub Scout mother at a banquet that I cater every year. Make sure you cut the broccoli into very small florets, as this salad is served raw. **SERVES 10 TO 12**

SALAD

3 bunches broccoli

1 cup minced red onion

1 pound bacon, fried until crisp, drained, and crumbled

1 cup roasted sunflower seed kernels

1 cup raisins, plumped in hot water to cover and drained if necesary

DRESSING

1½ cups mayonnaise

½ cup granulated cane sugar

2 tablespoons distilled white vinegar

1 To make the salad, cut the broccoli into very small florets and discard the stalks. Combine the broccoli, onion, bacon, sunflower seeds, and raisins in a large serving bowl, tossing gently to combine.

2 To make the dressing, in a medium-size non-reactive bowl, combine the dressing ingredients, blending with a wire whisk. Pour over the broccoli mixture and toss gently until coated. Chill before serving. Served chilled or at room temperature.

A Friend of a Friend of a Friend's Fresh Broccoli Salad

This recipe is from my friend Sandra Lyon's daughter, Lisa Faehnrich, who got it from a friend, who got it from a friend. With such a lineage, you know it must be good! **SERVES 6 TO 8**

SALAD

4 cups small broccoli florets and coins

10 strips bacon, cut into ¼-inch slices, cooked until crisp, and drained on paper towels

6 green onions (white and green parts), thinly sliced

½ cup golden raisins

½ cup slivered almonds, lightly toasted (see page 322), or ½ cup smoked almonds, slivered

DRESSING

½ cup mayonnaise

2 tablespoons granulated cane sugar

1 tablespoon cider vinegar

1 To make the salad, steam or blanch the broccoli in boiling salted water until crisp-tender, 3 to 4 minutes. Immerse in ice water to stop the cooking process, then drain well. Combine the broccoli, bacon, green onions, raisins, and almonds in a large serving bowl and toss gently.

2 To make the dressing, combine the dressing ingredients in a small nonreactive bowl and blend well. Pour over the salad and blend gently to coat well. Chill and serve.

Summer and Winter Corn and Pea Salad with Sweet and Sour Dressing

This salad tastes great, no matter what the season. In summer, use fresh vegetables. In winter, use frozen or canned vegetables. SERVES 6 TO 8

SALAD

2 cups white corn kernels, fresh or frozen and cooked, or canned and drained

1 cup yellow corn kernels, fresh or frozen and cooked, or canned and drained

1 cup small green peas, fresh or frozen and cooked

1 medium-size red bell pepper, seeded and diced

1 medium-size green bell pepper, seeded and diced

1 cup diced celery

6 green onions (green and white parts), thinly sliced

2 cloves garlic, pressed

1 jalapeño chile (optional), seeded and minced

1 teaspoon fine sea salt

1 teaspoon freshly ground black pepper

SWEET-AND-SOUR DRESSING

1 cup granulated cane sugar

3/4 cup cider vinegar

1/2 cup canola oil

1 To make the salad, combine the salad ingredients in a large serving bowl.

2 To make the dressing, combine the dressing ingredients in a medium-size nonreactive sauce-pan and bring to a boil, stirring to dissolve the sugar. Simmer for 1 minute. Remove from the heat and let cool. Pour over the salad and toss to coat. Cover and refrigerate overnight or longer. Serve cold or at room temperature.

Fresh Green Bean Salad with Tarragon Cream Cheese Dressing

Make this salad in early summer when green beans are in season. Cook and chill the green beans ahead of time, then assemble the salad. SERVES 6 TO 8

1/2 pound fresh green beans, ends trimmed

1 small onion, cut into thin strips (about 1 cup)

1 medium-size cucumber, peeled, seeded, and cut into thin strips (about 1 cup)

1/2 cup seeded red bell pepper cut into thin strips

4 cloves garlic, pressed

4 ounces (half an 8-ounce package) cream cheese, softened

2 tablespoons tarragon vinegar

1 tablespoon granulated cane sugar

1 teaspoon fine sea salt

1 teaspoon freshly ground black pepper

2 tablespoons whole milk

1 Cook the beans in boiling water until crisp-tender, 5 to 6 minutes. Drain, then plunge into ice water to stop the cooking process. Drain again and chill for 1 hour.

2 Combine the chilled green beans, onion, cucumber, bell pepper, and garlic in a large bowl.

3 In a small bowl, combine the cream cheese, vinegar, sugar, salt, and pepper and blend with an electric mixer until smooth. Blend in the milk, then pour over the green bean mixture and toss gently to coat thoroughly. Chill before serving.

Southern Kidney Bean Salad

How easy can it get? This marinated bean salad is both slightly sweet and savory. SERVES 6 TO 8

- 1/2 cup Hidden Valley Ranch salad dressing prepared according to package directions
- One 15-ounce can red kidney beans, drained and rinsed
- 1/2 cup sweet pickle relish
- 1/2 cup diced celery
- 1/2 cup diced onion
- 1/2 cup seeded and diced red bell pepper
- 2 hard-cooked eggs, peeled and chopped
- 1 tablespoon prepared yellow mustard
- 1 teaspoon fine sea salt
- 1 teaspoon freshly ground black pepper

Combine all the ingredients in a large serving bowl and mix well. Cover and refrigerate for at least 2 hours or overnight before serving. Serve cold.

Black and White Bean Salad

This recipe is adapted from one in *The New Basics Cookbook* by Julee Rosso and Sheila Lukins (New York: Workman Publishing, 1989). I serve this salad often at home with barbecue meals. It's especially good for warm weather meals in lieu of baked beans. SERVES 6 TO 8

- One 15-ounce can black beans, drained and rinsed
- One 15-ounce can white beans, drained and rinsed
- 1 cup diced red onion
- 1 cup seeded and diced red bell pepper
- 1 cup fresh corn kernels, cooked and cooled, or canned, drained and rinsed
- 1/4 cup chopped fresh cilantro leaves
- 1 cup bottled vinaigrette of your choice
- 1 to 2 teaspoons ground cumin, to your taste

Combine all the ingredients in a large serving bowl, folding gently. Chill before serving.

Corn and Red Bean Salad with Balsamic Vinaigrette

Corn and beans make a delightful base for a salad, and balsamic vinaigrette adds a finishing touch. When fresh corn is in season, cook and use the kernels from 8 ears instead of the canned corn. This is also good as a salsa served with tortilla chips. SERVES 10 TO 12

SALAD

- Two 11-ounce cans corn kernels, drained
- One 15-ounce can small red beans, drained and rinsed
- 1 red bell pepper, seeded and diced
- 6 green onions (green and white parts), thinly sliced

1 tablespoon minced fresh cilantro leaves

1 tablespoon minced fresh parsley leaves

2 cloves garlic, pressed

DRESSING

¼ cup balsamic vinegar

2 tablespoons olive oil

1 teaspoon seasoned salt, homemade (page 108) or store-bought

1 teaspoon freshly ground black pepper

1 teaspoon crushed red pepper

1 To make the salad, combine the salad ingredients in a medium-size serving bowl and toss gently to blend.

2 To make the dressing, combine the dressing ingredients in a small nonreactive bowl and blend well with a fork. Pour over the corn mixture and toss to coat. Cover and refrigerate for 2 hours or overnight before serving. Serve as a salad or as a salsa with chips.

Barbecued Brisket Baked Beans for a Crowd

This dish is an absolute must at any barbecue. If you've never tasted baked beans that have added flavor from barbecued beef brisket, then you're in for a treat. For a truly outstanding flavor, use a disposable aluminum pan for the beans, set it on your smoker, and let the beans smoke for several hours instead of baking them in the oven. I use a food service–size can of pork and beans, which I buy at a wholesale club; a 104-ounce can equals about 13 cups. If you like soupier beans, add the greater quantity of brown sugar and sauce. **SERVES 12 TO 16**

¼ cup bacon drippings (bacon grease) or salad oil of your choice

1 medium-size onion, diced

1 medium green bell pepper, seeded and diced

One 104-ounce can pork and beans, drained and rinsed

1 to 2 cups firmly packed light brown sugar, to your taste

1 to 2 cups barbecue sauce of your choice, homemade (pages 136–161) or store-bought, to your taste

1 tablespoon seasoned salt or barbecue rub, homemade (page 108 or 114) or store-bought

1 tablespoon liquid smoke flavoring (optional)

½ to 1 pound barbecued brisket trimmings, chopped

1 Preheat the oven to 350 degrees F or prepare an indirect fire.

2 Heat the bacon drippings in a large skillet over medium heat and cook the onion and bell pepper, stirring, until soft but not browned. In a large, nonreactive bowl, combine the sautéed vegetables with the beans, brown sugar, barbecue sauce, salt, liquid smoke (if using), and chopped meat and mix well.

3 Pour into a large baking dish and bake, uncovered, until browned and bubbling, 45 minutes. Or place the beans in the pit, cover, and cook until smoky and bubbling, about 3 hours.

Burnt Ends, Brisket, and Pork Butt Beans

Traditionally, baked beans have been flavored with smoked bacon, but barbecuers have other options. After you've sliced up your barbecued meats for judging, save those bits and pieces—burnt ends from a brisket, chopped-up brisket slices, barbecued pork butt shreds, or whatever you have—for a baked bean recipe like this one. You can smoke these beans, too, instead of baking them. SERVES 6 TO 8

> 2 tablespoons bacon drippings (bacon grease)
>
> 1/2 cup diced onion
>
> Two 16-ounce cans pork and beans, drained and rinsed
>
> 1/2 cup firmly packed light brown sugar
>
> 1/2 cup barbecue sauce of your choice, homemade (pages 136–161) or store-bought
>
> 1 teaspoon Worcestershire sauce, homemade (page 50) or store-bought
>
> 1 tablespoon prepared yellow mustard
>
> 2 teaspoons liquid smoke flavoring (optional)
>
> 1 cup burnt ends, chopped barbecued brisket, or barbecued pork butt shreds, or 4 slices bacon, cooked until crisp, drained, and crumbled

1 Preheat the oven to 350 degrees F or prepare an indirect fire.

2 Heat the bacon drippings in a small skillet over medium heat and cook the onion, stirring, until soft but not browned. In a large, nonreactive bowl, combine the onion with the remaining ingredients and mix well.

3 Pour into a large baking dish and bake, uncovered, until browned and bubbling, about 45 minutes. Or place the beans in the pit, cover, and cook until smoky and bubbling, about 3 hours.

Burnt End and Bark Beans

Burnt ends from brisket or the bark from a barbecued pork butt along with a little hot sauce make this baked bean dish a winner. You can bake or smoke these beans. SERVES 6 TO 8

> 2 tablespoons bacon drippings (bacon grease) or vegetable oil
>
> 1 cup diced onion
>
> Two 16-ounce cans pork and beans, drained and rinsed
>
> 2 cups burnt ends, chopped barbecued beef brisket, or barbecued pork butt shreds
>
> 2 cups barbecue sauce of your choice, homemade (pages 136–161) or store-bought
>
> 1 cup firmly packed light brown sugar
>
> 2 tablespoons Worcestershire sauce, homemade (page 50) or store-bought
>
> 2 tablespoons prepared yellow mustard
>
> 2 teaspoons rub of your choice, homemade (pages 115–132) or store-bought
>
> 2 teaspoons liquid smoke flavoring (optional)
>
> 1 teaspoon Louisiana hot sauce

1 Preheat the oven to 350 degrees F or prepare an indirect fire.

2 Heat the bacon drippings in a small skillet over medium heat and cook the onions, stirring, until soft but not browned. In a large, nonreactive bowl, combine the onions with the remaining ingredients and mix well.

3 Pour into a large baking dish and bake, uncovered, until browned and bubbling, about 45 minutes. Or place the beans in the pit, cover, and cook until smoky and bubbling, about 3 hours.

Barbecued Beer Beans for a Big Crowd

Use a beer with full-bodied flavor. Please don't use lite beer! The better the beer, the better the beans. Use the greater amount of brown sugar if you like sweeter beans.
SERVES 25 TO 30

- ½ cup dehydrated onion
- 1 tablespoon dehydrated garlic
- Two 104-ounce cans pork and beans, drained and rinsed
- 1 to 2 cups firmly packed light brown sugar
- 2 cups barbecue sauce of your choice, homemade (pages 136–161) or store-bought
- 2 cups burnt ends, chopped barbecued beef brisket, barbecued pork butt shreds, or chopped smoked sausage
- One 12-ounce can beer (I use Red Hook Ale)
- 1 tablespoon rub of your choice, homemade (pages 115–132) or store-bought
- 1 teaspoon freshly ground black pepper

1 Preheat the oven to 325 degrees F.

2 Hydrate the onions and garlic by combining them in a bowl and covering with boiling water. Cover with plastic wrap and set aside for 15 to 20 minutes.

3 Combine the hydrated onions and garlic with the remaining ingredients in a large bowl and blend well. Pour into a large baking dish and bake, uncovered, for at least 1 hour, until the liquid is cooked away and the beans are firm.

Yee-Haw Texas Pinto Beans

If you are ever in a barbecue contest in Texas, don't make the mistake of doing baked or barbecued Great Northern or white beans. They want pinto beans. Rinse and soak the beans overnight in cold water so you'll be ready to roll the next day. If you've never cooked pinto beans before, they're a little different than white beans. Pintos cook to a pinkish brown in a milky, creamy liquid. **SERVES 10 TO 12**

- 1 pound dried pinto beans, picked over
- 2 cups chopped onions
- ½ cup seeded and chopped red bell pepper
- 4 to 6 cloves garlic, to your taste, minced
- 1 jalapeño chile, seeded and minced
- 2 cups chopped barbecue burnt ends or barbecued pork butt shreds
- 2 to 3 tablespoons chili powder, to your taste, homemade (page 111) or store-bought
- 2 tablespoons Worcestershire sauce, homemade (page 50) or store-bought
- 1 tablespoon dry mustard (I use Colman's)
- One 15.5-ounce can chopped tomatoes with jalapeño chiles (I use Rotel)
- 1 teaspoon non-iodized salt
- 1 teaspoon freshly ground black pepper

1 Rinse and soak the beans in cold water to cover for 8 hours or overnight.

2 Drain the beans and combine with the onions, bell pepper, garlic, and jalapeño in a large saucepan. Cover with cold water to reach 2 inches above the beans, bring to a boil, reduce the heat to medium-low, and simmer until the beans begin to get soft, 45 to 60 minutes.

3 Stir in the remaining ingredients and simmer until the beans are soft and milky or creamy, like a thickened sauce, 15 to 30 minutes. Serve hot.

Caribbean Pinto Beans

I developed this recipe for the Barbecue Company of Aruba. If you're ever in Aruba, check out their great barbecue. SERVES 10 TO 12

- 1 pound dried pinto beans, picked over
- 1 large red onion, diced
- 1 red bell pepper, seeded and diced
- 2 tablespoons minced garlic
- 1 tablespoon seasoned salt, homemade (page 108) or store-bought, or rub of your choice (pages 115–132)
- 2 teaspoons ground allspice
- 2 cups chopped barbecue burnt ends or barbecued pork butt shreds
- 1 cup barbecue sauce of your choice, homemade (pages 136–161) or store-bought

1 Rinse and soak the beans in cold water to cover for 8 hours or overnight.

2 Drain the beans, place in a large saucepan, and cover with cold water to 2 inches over the beans. Add the onion, bell pepper, and garlic, bring to a boil, reduce the heat to a steady simmer, stirring occasionally, and cook until the beans are soft, 45 to 60 minutes.

3 Stir in the remaining ingredients and simmer until the beans are soft and milky, 15 to 30 minutes. Serve hot.

Southern Cornbread

Cornbread is a standard side dish for barbecue, in the South or anywhere else. SERVES 8

- ¼ cup bacon drippings (bacon grease)
- 1½ cups cornmeal
- ½ cup self-rising flour
- 1 large egg
- 1 cup whole milk

1 Preheat the oven to 500 degrees F. Pour the bacon drippings into a 9-inch cast-iron skillet or a 9-inch square baking pan and heat in the oven for 3 to 4 minutes.

2 Combine the cornmeal, flour, egg, and milk in a medium-size bowl and blend with a wire whisk or a fork.

3 Remove the skillet from the oven and blend half of the melted bacon drippings into the cornmeal mixture. Pour the batter into the hot pan containing the remaining bacon drippings. Bake until risen and golden and a toothpick inserted into the center comes out clean, 15 minutes. Cut into wedges or squares. Serve warm with butter and sorghum and your barbecue.

Yankee Cornbread

"Yankee" in the title of this cornbread means it has sugar in it. Southern cornbread is never sweet. SERVES 6 TO 8

- 1 cup yellow, white, or blue cornmeal
- 1 cup all-purpose flour
- ¼ cup granulated cane sugar
- 2 teaspoons baking powder
- 1 teaspoon non-iodized salt

1 large egg

1 cup sour cream

1/3 cup milk

1/4 cup (1/2 stick) unsalted butter, melted

1 Preheat the oven to 400 degrees F. Grease an 8-inch square baking pan.

2 In a large bowl, combine the cornmeal, flour, sugar, baking powder, and salt. In a medium-size bowl, combine the egg, sour cream, milk, and melted butter; stir into the dry ingredients just until moistened.

3 Pour the batter into the prepared pan and bake until risen and golden and a toothpick inserted into the center comes out clean, 20 to 25 minutes. Cut into wedges or squares. Serve warm with butter and sorghum and your barbecue.

Creamed Corn Cornbread

I don't call this one Yankee or Southern, I just call it good.
SERVES 6 TO 8

1 cup yellow cornmeal

3/4 cup all-purpose flour

1 tablespoon granulated cane sugar

1 tablespoon baking powder

1 teaspoon non-iodized salt

3/4 cup milk

1 large egg

2 tablespoons canola oil

One 8.75-ounce can cream-style corn

Nonstick cooking spray

1 Preheat the oven to 450 degrees F. Place a 9-inch cast-iron skillet in the hot oven for 5 minutes.

2 Combine the cornmeal, flour, sugar, baking powder, and salt in a large bowl and blend. Make a well in the center. In a medium-size bowl, combine the milk, egg, oil, and creamed corn and blend well. Pour the liquid ingredients into the well of the dry ingredients, stirring just until moistened.

3 Remove the skillet from the oven and coat it heavily with the nonstick cooking spray. Immediately spoon the batter into the hot skillet. Bake until risen and golden and a toothpick inserted into the center comes out clean, 25 to 30 minutes. Cut into wedges. Serve warm with butter and molasses and your barbecue.

Hoe Cakes

If you prefer Yankee-style hoe cakes, just add 1 or 2 tablespoons of granulated cane sugar. Serve these as part of a pulled pork or whole hog barbecue feast. SERVES 6

Vegetable shortening

1 cup yellow cornmeal

1 teaspoon fine sea salt

1 cup boiling water

1 Heat enough vegetable shortening so it melts to a depth of about 1/4 inch in a heavy 9- or 10-inch cast-iron skillet over high heat until it is almost smoking.

2 While the shortening is heating, combine the cornmeal and salt in a medium-size bowl. Beat in the boiling water with a spoon until you achieve a soupy consistency. Drop the batter from the

spoon into the hot shortening and fry until golden on the bottom. Turn and fry on the other side. Drain on paper towels.

The Baron's Famous Garlic Bread

At all my family get-togethers, I make the garlic bread because none of my sisters likes garlic as much as I do. They just said, "You make it from now on, Paul." And I am such a mellow guy that I always do what my sisters tell me to do. You can wrap the loaf in foil and bake it in the oven or throw it on the grill. When it's hot to the touch, it's garlic bread! Sometimes I also add about 1/4 teaspoon of white pepper to the butter if I'm in the mood. SERVES 6 TO 8 OR JUST ME

    1 cup (2 sticks) unsalted butter, softened

    4 to 6 large cloves garlic, to your taste, pressed

    1 tablespoon minced fresh basil leaves

    1 tablespoon minced fresh parsley leaves

    1 loaf French or Italian bread

1 Preheat the oven to 225 degrees F or prepare an indirect fire.

2 Combine the butter, garlic, basil, and parsley in a small bowl and blend well. Cover and set aside.

3 Cut the bread diagonally into 1-inch-thick slices, but don't cut all the way through (leave the slices still hanging together at the bottom). Spread the butter mixture evenly on both sides of each slice. Wrap and seal in aluminum foil. Bake or place in the pit, cover, and cook for about 1 hour, until hot and crispy.

The Baron's Favorite Bruschetta

One of my fetishes (that's what other people call it) is my love for the Stinking Rose—garlic. As I travel around the country teaching barbecue, I get to eat in some fine restaurants. One thing I try to order with dinner is garlic butter to put on my bread or rolls, but I can't always get it. I find this amazing, and not in a good way. I first had this wonderful bruschetta at Bob and Sandra Lyon's home in the Pacific Northwest several years ago. It is truly outstanding. SERVES 6 TO 8 OR JUST ME

    1 loaf Italian or French bread, cut on the diagonal into 1-inch-thick slices

    6 to 10 cloves garlic, to your taste, peeled with the tip trimmed off

    1/4 to 1/2 cup olive oil, as needed

1 Prepare a medium-hot fire in your grill.

2 Toast the bread slices for about 2 minutes on each side, being careful not to get them too brown (as in burnt). Rub one side of the bread all over with a clove of garlic. Drizzle olive oil over the garlic side and serve.

Grill and Smoker Manufacturers

BARBEQUES GALORE
10 Orchard Road, Suite 200
Lake Forest, CA 92630
(800) 752-3085
www.bbqgalore.com
Grill manufacturer with a retail division of more than 60 stores nationwide, which also carry barbecue utensils, accessories, books, woods, charcoal, and more.

BIG GREEN EGG
3414 Clairmont Road
Atlanta, GA 30319
(800) 939-3447
www.biggreenegg.com
Large producer of an egg-shaped, ceramic Kamado-style combination smoker/grill that cooks at a higher temperature than traditional cookers.

BRINKMANN CORPORATION
4821 Simonton Road
Dallas, TX 75244
(800) 527-0717
www.thebrinkmanncorp.com
Manufacturer of bullet-shaped charcoal and electric smokers and grills.

GRILLS TO GO
5659 W. San Madele Way
Fresno, CA 93722
(877) 869-2253
www.grillstogo.com
Manufacturer of towable commercial charcoal, wood, and gas barbecue grills.

KINGFISHER KOOKERS
1107 South Main
Kingfisher, OK 73750
(866) 542-5665
www.kingfisherkookers.com
Manufacturer of Kingfisher Kookers, grills and smokers in all shapes and sizes.

BBQ PITS BY KLOSE
2216 West 34th Street
Houston, TX 77018
(800) 487-PITS
www.bbqpits.com
When I needed my own custom rig made—my pig cooker—I called David Klose, and he fixed me right up. Klose carries ready-made smokers in just about every size—from 24-inch long models to huge commercial rigs. Or they'll make one for you.

NEW BRAUNFELS SMOKER COMPANY

146 Highway 46 East

New Braunfels, TX 78130

(830) 625-9138

www.nbsmoker.com

Manufacturer of heavy-gauge steel smokers and grills.

PITT'S & SPITT'S

14221 Eastex Freeway

Houston, TX 77032

(800) 521-2947

www.pittsandspitts.com

Manufacturer of grills and smokers, especially cookers for competition. Plus stainless-steel utensils, thermometers, cookbooks, and their own line of barbecue seasonings, spices, and sauces.

TRAEGER INDUSTRIES

P.O. Box 829

1385 East College Street

Mt. Angel, OR 97362

(800) 872-3437

www.traegerindustries.com

Manufacturer of the original electric-powered wood pellet grill/smokers. Wood pellets are augered into the firebox and provide both fuel and flavor.

WEBER-STEPHEN PRODUCTS CO.

200 East Daniels Rd.

Palatine, IL 60067-6266

(800) 446-1071

www.weber.com/bbq

Manufacturer of the original Weber grill since 1951. Grills, smokers, and all of their accessories, as well as Weber Smokey Mountain Cooker, charcoal chimney starter, Weber Rib Rack, and more. Weber is a nationally recognized name in barbecuing and grilling products, which are available at hardware stores, barbecue and grill shops, and discount houses.

Books, Videos, and Classes

Paul Kirk's Championship Barbecue Sauces: 175 Make-Your-Own Sauces, Marinades, Dry Rubs, Wet Rubs, Mops, and Salsas

by Paul Kirk (The Harvard Common Press, 1998). Spice theory, rubs, and sauces that you'd get at one of Paul Kirk's Pitmaster classes. Lots of interesting recipes, as well as a primer on the basics of equipment, fuels, barbecue technique, and barbecue meats. An important addition to your barbecue library.

Smoke & Spice: Cooking with Smoke, the Real Way to Barbecue, Revised Edition

by Cheryl Alters Jamison, Bill Jamison (The Harvard Common Press, 2003). This book is practically a legend in barbecue circles. Lots of good information about the art of barbecue, many delicious recipes, and some interesting tips and trivia thrown in for good measure.

PAUL KIRK BARBECUE VIDEOS

(800) 963-5227

(816) 765-5891

e-mail: bbqbaron@hotmail.com

A series of three informative videos from the Baron of Barbecue, seven-time barbecue world champion. Volume 1 covers ribs, chicken, and basic rubs. Volume 2 covers brisket, pork butt, and basic barbecue sauces. Volume 3 covers whole hog, salmon, lamb, turkey, sauces, and rubs.

PAUL KIRK PITMASTER CLASSES

(800) 963-5227

(816) 765-5891

e-mail: bbqbaron@hotmail.com

Paul Kirk, the Baron of Barbecue, presents a one-day class in which students spend 12 grueling hours cooking and presenting the four competition barbecue meats—brisket, pork butt, pork ribs, and chicken. He also covers sauces and rubs, with students creating their own signature rub under the Baron's watchful eye. The day ends with a mock competition in which students present their four entries and participate in the judging process. Classes are usually organized by state or local barbecue associations.

Cooking Supplies

ALLIED KENCO SALES

26 Lyerly Street

Houston, TX 77022

(800) 356-5189

www.alliedkenco.com

"Supplying everything but the meat," Allied Kenco focuses on supplies for sausage making, jerky making, and outdoor cooking. This is your source for sausage casings, spices, seasoning kits, sausage-making starter kits, Morton Tender Quick curing salts, and tons of other interesting items you never knew you needed.

PENZEYS SPICES

19300 West Janacek Court

Brookfield, WI 53008

(800) 741-7787

www.penzeys.com

One of the best online sources for spices, herbs, and seasonings, such as horseradish powder. Penzeys has every spice imaginable—and some you've never heard of. These products are much fresher than the ones you buy in the grocery store, and most are available in larger quantities. Their catalog is very informative.

ZACH'S SPICE COMPANY

1001 Georgia Avenue

Deer Park, TX 77536

(800) 460-0521

www.zachsspice.com

Check out their online catalog for unusual seasonings, such as Worcestershire powder. The company specializes in ingredients you need for barbecuing and grilling in general as well as those for making sausage, dry rubs, and barbecue sauces.

Woods for Smoking, Hardwood Charcoal, etc.

I suggest that you buy smoke wood locally whenever possible because it is less expensive that way. However, hickory and mesquite chunks are readily available at most hardware stores and home centers. Check Home Depot, Lowes, Wal-Mart, Orchard Supply Hardware, Ace Hardware, True Value Hardware, and other such stores for bags of hardwood lump charcoal and different woods. Better grocery stores often have these products, too.

Alder, apple, cherry, oak, and pecan chunks can be purchased at specialty stores such as Barbeques Galore and from suppliers such as Peoples Woods (800-729-5800, www.peopleswoods.com).

AMERICAN WOOD PRODUCTS

9540 Riggs Street
Overland Park, KS 66212
(800) 223-9046

This company sells bags of mesquite lump charcoal as well as a variety of woods: mesquite, pecan, hickory, grape, oak, apple, cherry, sassafras, peach, and alder in logs, slabs, chunks, and chips.

BBQR'S DELIGHT

P.O. Box 8727
6109 Celia Road
Pine Bluff, Arkansas 71611
(877) 275-9591
www.bbqrsdelight.com

Wood pellets for fuel and smoke in hickory, mesquite, pecan, apple, cherry, oak, black walnut, and sugar maple.

CHIGGER CREEK PRODUCTS

4200 Highway D
Syracuse, MO 65354
(660) 298-3188
www.bbqads.com/chigger/chigger.htm

Hardwood lump charcoal as well as a variety of woods—hickory, apple, cherry, pecan, grape, sugar maple, alder, oak, mesquite, peach, sassafras, persimmon, pear, and their apple/hickory and cherry/oak blends—in chips, chunks, and logs.

FAIRLANE BAR-BQ WOOD

12520 Third Street
Grandview, MO 64030
(816) 761-1350

A company that specializes in mesquite, pecan, hickory, oak, apple, cherry, and sassafras woods sold in bags of chunks.

Index